ADOLESCENCE AND YOUTH

ADOLESCENCE AND YOUTH

Psychological Development in a Changing World

JOHN JANEWAY CONGER

University of Colorado School of Medicine

FOURTH EDITION

HarperCollins*Publishers*

Sponsoring Editor: Anne Harvey
Project Editor: Steven Pisano
Art Direction: Claudia DePolo
Text and Cover Design: Circa 86, Inc.
Cover Photo: © Joel Gordon, 1988
Photo Research: Elsa Peterson
Production Manager: Willie Lane
Compositor: York Graphic Services, Inc.
Printer and Binder: R. R. Donnelley & Sons Company
Cover Printer: Lehigh Press

For permission to use copyrighted material, grateful acknowledgment is made to the copyright holders on pp. 645–646, which are hereby made part of this copyright page.

Adolescence and Youth: Psychological Development in a Changing World, Fourth Edition

Library of Congress Cataloging-in-Publication Data

Conger, John Janeway.
    Adolescence and youth : psychological development in a changing
world / John Janeway Conger.—4th ed.
        p. cm.
    Includes bibliographical references.
    Includes index.
    ISBN 0-06-041343-3
    1. Adolescence.   I. Title
    [DNLM: 1. Adolescence.   2. Adolescent Behavior.   3. Adolescent
Psychology.   WS 462 C749a]
    HQ796.C76   1991
    305.23′5—dc20
    DLC
    for Library of Congress   90-5099
                                                                      CIP

    91 92 93 9 8 7 6 5 4 3 2

I have sent forth my prayers.
Our children,
Even those who have erected their shelters
At the edge of the wilderness,
May their roads come in safely,
May the forests
And the brush
Stretch out their water-filled arms
To shield their hearts;
May their roads come in safely;
May their roads all be fulfilled,
May it not somehow become difficult for them
When they have gone but a little way.

May all the young boys,
All the young girls,
And those whose roads are ahead,
May they have powerful hearts,
Strong spirits;
On roads reaching to Dawn Lake
May they grow old.

—Zuñi Indian Prayer

For Chloë and Eleanor

CONTENTS

PREFACE

In the twenty years since I began work on the first edition of this book, the world in which young people are coming to maturity has changed dramatically. In 1970, America had just emerged from the "youth revolution" and societal discord of the turbulent sixties, and the future directions of a rapidly changing society appeared shrouded in uncertainty. In 1990, "people's revolutions" are spreading like a prairie fire across the face of Europe and much of the rest of the world—again with unpredictable long-term consequences, socially, economically, and politically. Like the "youth revolution"—indeed, like all revolutions—these newer revolutions appear likely to have their own share of victories and victims, of clarity and confusion, of new hope and opportunity for some and disappointment or despair for others. But one thing seems certain: The world that today's adolescents and youth are entering will be very different from the world in which they were born and raised, and at least as complex and demanding.

If young people are going to be ready to meet the challenges of new realities—in work, in their personal lives, and as citizens—they will need to be emotionally mature, well-educated, socially responsible, and sure of their own goals and values. This will require the enlightened support and encouragement of families, schools, the business community, and government.

Success will not come easily. The challenges confronting the family as a social institution have increased and become still more complex. If young people are to be able to function successfully in a rapidly changing global economy, many will need to raise their vocational sights and to shift away from traditional occupations to newly emerging ones. Our educational institutions will have to play a major role in helping them to do so. American youth cannot continue to be so poorly informed about their own history and culture, and to rank near the bottom among industrialized nations in mathematical and scientific skills. Yet reduced budgets, ideological differences regarding the fundamental purposes of education, and social disintegration of previously stable families and neighborhoods in the face of poverty, crime, and drugs, have created increasingly critical problems for our schools. Changing sex roles, particularly for women, are leading to changes in educational and vocational opportunities, and, in many instances, to reappraisals of personal and social goals.

All these changes, and others, have affected the individual adolescent's development and the challenges he or she faces in the search for a stable, workable sense of identity. Much of the new material in this edition reflects the influence of these changes. This is particularly the case in the chapters on the family, parent–adolescent relationships, the schools, vocational choice, drug use, alienation and delinquency, and psychological problems. New data have led to new or expanded coverage of many topics of current social concern. Examples include: adolescent pregnancy and parenting, school dropouts, adolescent runaways, teenage employment, changing values, sexual attitudes and behavior, trends in adolescent drug use, effects of "crack" cocaine and other drugs, youth gangs, AIDS, health and behavior, adolescent depression and suicide, and eating disorders.

More broadly, the book as a whole reflects the remarkable progress in the caliber of research on adolescent development that has taken place in the past decade—in areas as diverse as hormonal influences on behavior, cognitive processes, moral development, sex roles, and patterns of family interaction. After years of lagging behind the explosion of productive research in infancy and early childhood, research on adolescence, and especially early adolescence, has finally come into its own. Inasmuch as the biological, psychological, cognitive, and social changes taking place in the years surrounding puberty are greater than at any other age since the second year of life, recent progress seems overdue—though no less welcome.

In an effort to make the book maximally useful to undergraduate students in developmental psychology and other behavioral sciences and to interested parents and adolescents, as well as to advanced students and established professionals, I have tried to combine thorough, current coverage of the research literature and detailed bibliographic references with a straightforward and, I hope, well-organized and integrated presentation of the text. If desired, most chapters can be read or assigned separately as a coherent, self-contained presentation of the topic under consideration.

New Pedagogical Features. A number of features have been added to help students organize and learn the material, to start to think about issues, and to encourage students to pursue some topics in depth. Each chapter has a **detailed outline** in the table of contents and at the beginning of the chapter. Chapter **summaries** are comprehensive and written to help students integrate the contents. **Key terms** in each chapter are printed in bold face type, and a **glossary** of terms that may be unfamiliar is included at the back of the book. A number of **boxes** have been inserted throughout the text dealing with important social issues, case studies, or particularly interesting and important research. **Review questions** at the end of each chapter are designed to help students think actively about the major topics covered. At the end of each chapter a short list of **recommended readings** is added for those wishing to pursue chapter topics in greater depth. Over 1800 **references** are cited at the back of the book. This bibliography should prove useful to students in preparing term papers and to investigators in gaining a broad overview of particular areas of research.

Acknowledgments. Many people have made important contributions to the preparation of this book. I especially want to thank Dorothy R. Townsend, who played an indispensable role in putting together the manuscript, correcting errors, tracking down references, and making helpful editorial suggestions. I am also grateful to Carolyn Smith for her skillful and perceptive editing of the entire manuscript.

For reading various chapters and making helpful suggestions, I would like to express my deep appreciation to the following colleagues and friends: Donald Bechtold, Jeanne Brooks-Gunn, Thomas J. Crowley, Lois W. Hoffman, Jerome

Kagan, Paul H. Mussen, and Anne C. Petersen.

For reviewing the manuscript as a whole and making valuable comments, I would like to thank the following: Lisa Crockett, Pennsylvania State University; William Gray, University of Toledo; William Hall, University of Maryland; William E. Hauck, Bucknell University; D. Lamar Jacks, Santa Fe Community College; Natividad Macaranas, Eastern New Mexico University; Robyn Rogers, Southwest Texas State University, and Eduard H. Schludermann, The University of Manitoba.

Finally, a book such as this inevitably reflects not only the current status of an area of scientific investigation, but, at least to some extent, the outlook of the author—his own values, hopes and fears, perceptions and blind spots. To the extent that the hopes outweigh the fears and that, despite the blind spots, there is some understanding, my greatest single debt is to my family. For they have provided not only pleasure and love, but equally important, a meaningful link between the best of the past, present, and future.

John Janeway Conger

1

INTRODUCTION

H umankind has long been preoccupied with its youth. In the collective life of societies, each new generation has been perceived as a fragile vessel by which the best of the past is transmitted into the present. And in the faces of each new generation we see written the future of nations and cultures— indeed, the future of humanity itself. Despite the decline in concern with the problems of children and adolescents in our society during the past decade (Conger, 1981, 1988), we still recognize that much of human history is the story of successive generations of young men and women.

There is also a personal and subjective side to our fascination with youth. Over the centuries—from the time of the ancient Egyptians to the present— people have tended to conceptualize their own lives largely in terms of their adolescent years. Most of us perceive our childhood as a period of becoming, whereas adolescence is remembered as the time when our identities were established, when our potential for accomplishment—though not the accomplishments themselves—was at its height. For many, like Joseph Conrad, adolescence is remembered as the time when one was most alive: "a flick of sunshine upon a strange shore, the time to remember, the time for a sigh..." (Conrad, 1902, p. 843). The friendships we formed in these years, as well as our first loves, have a special permanence in our minds.

When we think about whether we have changed over the years, whether we have been true to our hopes and dreams, whether we have realized our potential, the inevitable comparison is not with the years of childhood or intervening adulthood but, rather, with the brief period of our youth. We may no longer wish to be young, but despite the frequent heartaches of adolescence we treasure its memory, and indeed we cannot conceive of not having been young.

Consequently, when we look at adolescents we see not merely a necessary generational link between the past and the future but also ourselves. In many ways, we react to adolescents in much the same way that we react to projective personality tests, like the vaguely defined Rorschach inkblots. We see in youth not merely what is actually there but the mirror of our own desires, hopes, satisfactions, frustrations, fears, and disappointments.

A NEW GENERATION

Some observers believe that today's young people are more rootless, more emotionally troubled, and more self-centered and materialistic than their counterparts of earlier generations. In support of this view they cite high rates of delinquency, drug use, and adolescent suicide; high rates of adolescent pregnancy; and young people's apparent preoccupation with self-fulfillment at the expense of societal concerns (Conger, 1981, 1988; Wolfe, 1976). Other observers are convinced that adolescents today are better informed about the world than their predecessors were; that they are no less idealistic, though more pragmatic and less sentimental; and that they are more open, honest, and tolerant, and less given to viewing others in terms of simplistic stereotypes. We are informed that these young people have, if anything, a clearer sense of their own identity and are less emotionally conflicted than their parents were at the same age. Still another group of observers feel that presumed differences—good or bad—between today's adolescents and those of earlier generations are largely illusory and more a matter of form than of substance, or that they stem from unwarranted generalizations based on the behavior of a small number of atypical young people.

One of the aims of this book is to examine the evidence for or against such contrasting views and to attempt to arrive at a balanced judgment about the problems confronting today's adolescents and their responses to those problems. In the process, we may also learn a little more about ourselves.

HISTORICAL ROOTS OF THE CONCEPT OF ADOLESCENCE

Although concern with adolescence and youth became especially intense during the "youth revolution" of the 1960's, the years surrounding puberty have long been viewed as a distinct and noteworthy period in the life span. Comments on the distinctive characteristics of youth occurred in the writings of the ancient Egyptians many centuries before the emergence of Christianity. Then as now, such comments often served as a basis for dire predictions regarding the likely behavior of adolescents.

Reflecting the early Greek philosophers' interest in human nature, Plato offered advice on the socialization of children from their earliest years through adolescence and young adulthood. He pointed out that during the developmental years "more than at any other time the character is engrained by habit" (Plato, 1953, p. 359). However, he also acknowledged that "the characters of young men are subject to many changes in the course of their lives." He ad-

"Adolescence is remembered by many as a time when they were most alive."

vised that boys not be allowed to drink until they were 18 because of their excitable nature: "Fire must not be poured on fire." And he warned that adolescents were prone to argument for its own sake. In their enthusiasm they would, he commented, "leave no stone unturned, and in their delight at the first taste of wisdom, they would annoy everyone with their arguments" (quoted in Muus, 1988, pp. 5–6).

Perhaps the best early characterizations of the period that we now recognize as adolescence is contained in the words of another perceptive observer:

> The young are in character prone to desire and ready to carry any desire they may have formed into action. Of bodily desires it is the sexual to which they are most disposed to give way, and in regard to sexual desire they exercise no self-restraint. They are changeful too, and fickle in their desires, which are as transitory as they are vehement; for their wishes are keen without being permanent, like a sick man's fits of hunger and thirst.
>
> They are passionate, irascible, and apt to be carried away by their impulses. They are the slaves, too, of their passion, as their ambition prevents their ever brooking a slight and renders them indignant at the mere idea of enduring an injury . . . They are fonder both of honor and of victory than of money, the reason why they care so little for money being that they have never yet had experience of want.
>
> They are charitable rather than the reverse, as they have never yet been witnesses of many villainies; and they are trustful, as they have not yet been often deceived. . . . They have high aspirations; for they have never yet been humiliated by the experience of life, but are unacquainted with the limiting force of circumstances. . . .
>
> If the young commit a fault, it is always on the side of excess and exaggeration for they carry everything too far, whether it be their love or hatred or anything else. They regard themselves as omniscient and are positive in their assertions; this is, in fact, the reason of their carrying everything too far (quoted in Kiell, 1967, pp. 18–19).

These words sound as though they might have been written by a contemporary social critic, but in fact they were written by Aristotle 2300 years ago. In Aristotle's view, children and animals alike were under the control of what today would be called Freud's pleasure principle ("children and brutes pursue pleasures"), and although they had the capacity for voluntary action, they did not have the capacity for choice ("acts done on the spur of the moment we describe as voluntary, but not as chosen") (Aristotle, 1941, pp. 967–968).

An important characteristic of adolescence was the development of the ability to choose. Aristotle's emphasis on voluntary and deliberate choice as necessary for the attainment of maturity is not unlike that of some contemporary social critics, who believe that "with prolonged education and prolonged dependency we have reduced choices for adolescents to the extent that we interfere with their attainment of maturity" (Muus, 1988, p. 8).

Much of the astute reasoning and empirically based observation that characterized Aristotle and other Greek philosophers was obscured by the impact of early Christian theology. However, preoccupation with the "ages of life" reappeared in the pseudoscientific treatises of the Middle Ages (Ariès, 1962).

Consider the following passage from *Le grand proprietaire de toutes choses,* a kind of encyclopedia of "scientific" knowledge published in 1556:

> Afterward [i.e., after infancy and childhood] follows the third age, which is called adolescence, which ends according to Constantine in his viaticum in the twenty-first year, but according to Isidore it lasts until twenty-eight . . . and it can go on until thirty or thirty-five. This age is called adolescence because the person is big enough to beget children, says Isidore. In this age the limbs are soft and able to grow and receive strength and vigour from natural heat. And because the person grows in this age to the size allotted to him by Nature (quoted in Ariès, 1962, p. 21).

In reading such pseudoscientific (and rather pretentious) speculations, one is reminded of current discussions about the "proper" duration of adolescence and the effects of an extended "psychosocial moratorium"—a period of prolonged freedom from adult responsibilities (Erickson, 1950, 1968).

In a seventeenth-century volume entitled *The Office of Christian Parents* (1616), the life span was divided into six stages: infancy (birth to age 7), childhood (ages 7–14), youth (14–28), manhood (28–50), gravity (50–70), and old age (over 70). It is interesting to note that "youth" was viewed as extending from 14 to 28, the period we currently call young adulthood. This designation probably reflected the social and economic circumstances of the time. Typically, an older male youth who had completed a period of apprenticeship was likely to be an unmarried journeyman living in the home of his master. For seventeenth-century males, marriage and the setting up of a separate household typically occurred at about age 27 (Smith, 1975).

It appears that the clergy were greatly concerned about the need to provide guidance to these unsettled youth, and groups of young journeymen were often subjected to prolonged sermons. (In one recorded instance a sermon was presented by a "relay team" of six successive ministers and extended over many hours.) That their self-assigned task was not viewed as an easy one and frequently missed the mark was drily noted by John Bunyan (1686; quoted in Smith, 1975, p. 495):

> Our ministers, long time by word and pen,
> Dealt with them, counting them not boys but men:
> Thunderbolts they shot at them, and their toys:
> But hurt them not, 'cause they were girls and boys.

It was commonly agreed that young people were fickle, vain, unsettled, susceptible to peer pressure, unreasonable, and "unconcerned about the big questions of life." One clergyman compared youth to "a new ship launching out into the main ocean without a helm and ballast or pilot to steer her." Another observed that human beings are sinful at all ages, but that youth "is carried with more headlong force into vice, lust, and vain pleasures of the flesh" (quoted in Smith, 1975, pp. 497–498).

Other observers, however, were impressed with the positive side of youth: "Now your parts are lively, senses fresh, memory strong, and nature vigorous."

In *Words to Give to the Young Man Knowledge and Discretion* (Fuller, 1685), we learn that youth is the best time in life "for action, both as to the natural and moral frame of the body and mind," because it is a period of "strength and vigor, of purer conscience, and a softer heart than an old man" (quoted in Smith, 1975, p. 498). The principal danger for youth in the seventeenth century was thought to be sinfulness, and religious conversion (usually after age 20) was seen as the antidote. Steven Smith notes that "the early modern conception of youth seems to have some similarity [despite important differences] with the modern conception in that both recognize some sort of 'identity crisis.' Furthermore, there is in the early modern conception some foreshadowing of the modern romanticization of youth" (Smith, 1975, p. 513).

Nevertheless, the dominant theme of seventeenth-century writings by clergymen and others was the need to help undependable youth master their unruly impulses (Spacks, 1981). The romantic preoccupation with the psychological complexities and special needs of adolescence that we see today was still largely absent. Young people were not yet important enough to be taken as seriously as older and wiser adults.

Not until the late nineteenth century do we encounter precursors of the modern concern with adolescence as a socially significant and psychologically complex period. The reasons are both demographic and cultural. The perception of adolescence as a truly distinctive stage of development depends at least in part on the existence of communities of young people who share similar experiences at about the same age and are isolated to some extent from the adult world. It is not surprising, therefore, that much of the so-called youth culture of the late 1960s and early 1970s centered on schools and colleges, where large numbers of young people congregate in age-segregated groups.

Such conditions did not exist before about 1890. The idea of a large city school with 500 or more tenth-grade students living, studying, and interacting in relative isolation from younger children and older adults would have seemed incomprehensible. For one thing, in the United States and other Western countries most of the population lived in rural areas or in small towns and cities. Moreover, there was far less separation between adults and young people. In the 1700s and 1800s most young people became involved in the world of work sometime between the age of 7 and the onset of puberty, whether on the family farm, as "boys (girls) of all work" in other households, as helpers or apprentices to skilled craftsmen and shopowners, or as workers in mills and small factories. In many instances, it was necessary to send children away from home at an early age because there were too many mouths to feed or because of the death of one or both parents. (In the first half of the nineteenth century only 20 percent of mothers survived their youngest child's maturity.) Even among the upper classes, however, the practice of sending young children away from home was not uncommon; wealthy merchants, for example, "often sent their sons out as cabin boys at 8 or 9 or as supercargo at 15 or 16 as part of a process of growing that was to lead to a junior partnership at 21" (Kett, 1977, p. 23).

Few children continued their education into the adolescent years. Even for those who did, however, the experience was far different from that of a junior high or high school student today. School attendance was generally sporadic; for example, at Pinkerton Academy in Massachusetts, of thirty students enrolled for the winter term in 1950 only ten were in attendance for the spring term. Moreover, there was little of the age grading that is typical of modern schools. In 1812 the age range at Exeter Academy was 10–28; the age range of students in public district schools was equally broad (Kett, 1977). Many students wandered casually back and forth between school and work throughout childhood and adolescence.

Such circumstances of work and education obviously did little to encourage the development of a youth culture or a perception of adolescence as a distinct stage of development. As historian Joseph Kett comments, "If adolescence is defined as the period after puberty during which a young person is institutionally segregated from casual contacts with a broad range of adults, then it can scarcely be said to have existed at all, even for those young people who attended school beyond age 14" (1977, p. 36).

The Impact of Industrialization

In the late nineteenth century the situation began to change, largely as a result of industrialization and migration to the cities. Although the majority of young people continued to work, the nature of work was changing. The difference was partly one of scale. The relationship between an individual craftsman, shopkeeper, or mill owner and a young helper or apprentice was qualitatively different from that between a factory owner and the scores of "bobbin boys" (or girls) working in the factory. In addition, with the mechanization of many tasks the division between dead-end jobs and those offering the possibility of advancement became more sharply defined. Young people—both boys and girls—soon learned that the least skilled jobs carried little hope of advancement. Even worse, they frequently discovered that when they reached the usual "adult" age of 17 or 18 and began asking for adult wages they would be replaced by younger children. In contrast, fewer young people were available to fill the growing number of more complex, higher-level jobs, and those who did qualify were more richly rewarded. The better jobs, however, required greater maturity and more education.

Consequently, increased education and delayed entrance into the work force became more highly valued. But for the mass of families these goals were unattainable. Many needed the earnings of their young to survive, and thus the generational cycle of poverty and despair that was one of the bitter fruits of the industrial revolution gained momentum. For the upper classes and the emerging middle classes, however, the story was different. Greater wealth and a marked decrease in average family size allowed them to make what they perceived as an investment in the future by providing more education for their children. Parental attitudes toward children were altered in the process.

Increasingly, each individual child was treated (according to sex) without prejudice to his or her place in the birth order. "Give the boys a good education and a start

The relation of an individual craftsman or shopkeeper to a younger helper or apprentice was much more personal and direct than that of a factory owner employing scores of "bobbin boys."

in life," wrote J. E. Panton in 1889, "and provide the girls with £150 a year, either when they marry or at your own death, and you have done your duty by your children. The girls cannot starve on that income, and neither would they be prey of any fortune hunter; but no one has a right to bring children into the world in the ranks of the upper middle class and do less" (quoted in Gillis, 1974, p. 99).

The result was a rapid increase in the number of schools, academies, and colleges. These institutions quickly became less casual, more tightly organized, and more academically demanding, with a sharp narrowing of the age ranges included at each educational level. Thus, the preconditions were set for the delineation of adolescence as a distinct stage of development: age segregation, a specific set of expectations for—and demands on—youth, and increased isolation from adults and the world of work. As we have noted, this phenomenon was initially restricted to young people from economically advantaged backgrounds. But it established a model that would eventually be democratized and considered normal for young people generally.

The "Era of Adolescence"

Once broad economic and social conditions had begun to create a visible category of segregated youth, the time was ripe for speculations about the psychological nature of youth, for concerns about how it should be controlled, and prognoses for its future. Each of these areas of speculation would vary over time as society itself changed. The important fact, however, is that by 1900 the "era of adolescence" in the modern sense of the term had begun.

Although middle- and upper-class youth were the initial beneficiaries of the new concept of adolescence (which included the idea that adolescents are still developing and require special nurturance), gradually poorer youth began to benefit as well. Incredible as it may seem, in America in 1904 only 17 states had any age limits on employment in coal mining, and in those that did, the highest minimum age was 14. Even in those states, however, desperate 12-year-olds lied about their age in order to work 10 to 12 hours a day in the mines for 35 cents a day. The 1900 U.S. census found over three-quarters of a million children aged 10 to 13 employed in sweatshops, factories, mines, and other work settings. In England around the same time, only 9 percent of young people were still in school at age 14. The child labor laws and later school-leaving ages of subsequent decades were an outgrowth of a new view of the nature of childhood and adolescence, as well as social and religious pressures and a more enlightened view of the value of human life generally.

Widespread popular awareness of youth really came into its own, however, only after World War I, when young people became conscious of themselves as a group. A foreshadowing of the generational conflict of the 1960s could be seen in the solid opposition of young veterans to the older generations who had been spared the fighting. From that point on, popular notions of, and preoccupation with, adolescence occupied an increasingly important place in social thought. As Philippe Ariès commented, "It is as if, to every period of history, there corresponded a privileged age and a particular division of human life: 'youth' is the privileged age of the seventeenth century, childhood of the nineteenth, adolescence of the twentieth" (1962, p. 32).

THE SCIENTIFIC STUDY OF ADOLESCENCE

Although serious literary concern with the phenomenon of adolescence had already developed, the scientific study of adolescence as a separate and distinct phase of human development really began with the work of G. Stanley Hall, who published his two-volume work *Adolescence* in 1904. Hall was a remarkable man: He obtained America's first Ph.D. in psychology, was the founder of the American Psychological Association, initiated the child study movement in this country, and served as president of Clark University from its inception in 1887 until his retirement. It was he who invited Sigmund Freud to Clark, in the only journey that the founder of psychoanalysis made to this country. Although Hall and his students did much to introduce scientific techniques into the study of adolescence and to delineate it as a separate field of study, Hall's interests were far more global—some would say grandiose.

Enchanted by Darwin's concept of evolution and by the related notion that ontogeny recapitulates phylogeny (i.e., individual development parallels the evolutionary development of the race), Hall developed a psychological theory of **recapitulation** (Grinder & Strickland, 1969; Hall, 1904, 1923; Muus, 1988). According to this theory, during its development the individual organism passes through stages comparable to those that occurred during the history of humankind—"from early animal-like primitivism, through periods of savagery [i.e., later childhood and prepubescence], to the more recent civilized ways of life which characterize maturity" (Muus, 1988, p. 21).

Partly owing to his Germanically inspired romanticism (he was influenced by the works of Schiller and Goethe) and partly because of his lofty expectations for adolescents, Hall formulated what was probably his most controversial concept regarding adolescent development, namely, that adolescence is a period of extreme "storm and stress" (Sturm und Drang).

Contrary to popular perceptions, Hall believed that cultural influences play at least as large a role as maturational factors in the oscillations of behavior that, in his view, are characteristic of adolescence: energy alternating with lethargy; exaltation with depressive gloom; childish selfishness with altruistic selflessness; conceit with humility; tenderness with cruelty; curiosity with apathy. As we shall see in some detail in this book, not only the presumed bases for adolescent storm and stress but the extent of the phenomenon itself have generated considerable controversy.

G. Stanley Hall began the modern, scientific investigation of adolescence with the publication of his two-volume work Adolescence *in 1904.*

ISSUES IN ADOLESCENT DEVELOPMENT

However anachronistic some of Hall's notions may seem today, they set the stage for the development of a scientific psychology of adolescence. They also led to a clearer delineation of the most important theoretical and empirical issues to be addressed by researchers in the field of adolescent development. Among those issues are the following:

1. What is the relative importance of biological and cultural influences on adolescent development, and what is the nature of their interaction?
2. Is adolescence a relatively placid time characterized by essentially benign "normative crises" or is it characterized by a clinically demonstrable psychological disturbance similar to the emotional disorders of adulthood?
3. What is the nature of physical and physiological development in adolescence, and how does it unfold?
4. Should adolescent development be viewed as basically continuous with earlier and later development, or is adolescence a separate, distinct **stage** or **critical period** in development (in terms of physiological and psychological processes, culturally defined "developmental tasks," or both)?

In the remainder of this section we will take a closer look at each of these issues.

Biological Versus Cultural Determinants of Adolescent Behavior

Although the weight of empirical evidence fails to support Hall's concept of adolescence as a time of storm and stress (at least for the average adolescent), most behavioral scientists agree that in our society adolescence generally represents a more difficult developmental period than middle childhood. They are far from unanimous, however, about the principal sources of this difficulty. Those who are biologically oriented view adolescent behavior primarily as reflecting the unfolding of a biologically programmed process of **maturation.** According to some of these theorists, individual differences in adolescent adjustment are due largely to biologically determined, usually genetic, differences in basic temperament (Muus, 1988). Others emphasize the psychological changes required to adjust to the physiological changes of puberty, including increases in sex hormones and changes in both body structure and function.

In contrast, other theorists view adolescent adjustment problems as primarily cultural in origin. They emphasize the many demands society makes on youth during this period—for independence, for peer and heterosexual adjustments, for educational and vocational preparation, and for the development of a workable set of personal and social values. They assert that in cultures in which these demands are less complex and are not limited to a specific age range, adolescence is not viewed as a particularly difficult period.

Arnold Gesell, a pioneer in the systematic study of infant and child development, favored a biological orientation, although he did not deny the role of culture. "The culture inflects and channelizes," he wrote, "but it does not generate the progressions and trends of development" (Gesell, Ilg, & Ames, 1956, p. 19). For Gesell, development involved maturationally determined, recurring cycles of "innovation, integration, and equilibrium." In other words, each major advance in development disturbs a previously existing equilibrium and requires a period of integration—often characterized by awkwardness and partial regression—until a new equilibrium is established.

Gesell's descriptions of modal or "normal" behaviors at various ages—descriptions that served as a kind of bible for middle-class parents before the publication of Benjamin Spock's (1946) *Pocket Book of Baby and Child Care*—reflect this rather reassuring view of development. Whether a particular age promises to be a difficult or placid experience for parent and child depends on the child's position in one or another of these recurring cycles of equilibrium and disequilibrium. In periods of innovation and incomplete integration, greater difficulty can be expected; in periods of equilibrium, on the other hand, both parent and child experience a respite from the maturational struggle.

Thus, in Gesell's view, "Ten [is a year of] consummation as well as of transition—an amiable, relatively relaxed interlude in which the organism assimilates, consolidates, and balances its attained resources. Only mildly does he foreshadow the tensions of later youth. In a frank, unself-conscious manner he tends to accept life and the world as they are with free and easy give-and-take. It is a golden age of developmental equipoise" (1956, p. 37). In contrast, "Eleven, like Five-and-a-half to Six, is 'loosening up,' 'snapping old bonds.'" The child is restive, investigative, talkative, argumentative; his moods are likely to be intense and to fluctuate rapidly—gay and enthusiastic at one moment, gloomy or angry the next. But peace gradually returns, and "Twelve [becomes] more positive in mood, smoother in relationships." And so it goes: "Thirteen pulls inward; Fourteen thrusts out; Fifteen specifies and organizes; Sixteen again achieves a more golden mean" (p. 19).

Gesell made valuable contributions to developmental psychology by insisting on careful and detailed observations of behavior (as opposed to reliance on anecdotal or clinical impressions) and by developing some ingenious techniques for studying infant and child development. His theoretical model appears somewhat simplistic, however, especially when applied to older age groups. Although his observations were often perceptive, his generalizations appear overly broad and inclusive, and they fail to account adequately for deviations from established norms. More important, his model does not provide a means for conceptualizing the processes through which biological, psychological, and cultural factors may interact to produce deviant as well as normative behavior.

It seems likely that a more fruitful biological approach to development is represented by current research into the complex interactive effects of hormones and other influences on physical and psychological development, both prenatally and throughout the life span (Petersen, 1988; Petersen & Taylor,

1980). We need to know much more, for example, about the possible effects of rapidly changing levels of sex hormones on affective (i.e., emotional) states during puberty, as well as on sexual, aggressive, and other behaviors (see pages 98–101). There is evidence, for example, that levels of pubertal hormones are related in boys (but not girls) to acting-out behavior and to "emotional dispositions" like sadness and anxiety (Susman et al., 1987). Among girls, patterns of intense exercise, together with restricted food intake, can alter growth patterns and body shape (Brooks-Gunn & Warren, 1985). Pubertal timing also appears to be related to intellectual functioning, with early maturers having a small but consistent advantage on intelligence tests (Newcombe & Dubas, 1987; Petersen, 1988).

Cultural and Social Influences. Some theorists—including cultural anthropologists and social psychologists—emphasize the importance of cultural influences on adolescent behavior. Utilizing comparative studies of preliterate cultures, historical accounts of social change, and clinical observations of adolescents in our own society, these theorists have demonstrated that human personality and behavior may vary over an extremely wide range. Often these variations are a function of the social structure of a culture, especially its child-rearing practices.

Many different behavior patterns may be considered normal and adaptive within the context of a particular culture. Sometimes, however, the social structure of a culture may produce neurotic or destructive personalities. For example, culturally oriented psychoanalysts like Erich Fromm, author of *Escape to Freedom,* and Karen Horney, author of *The Neurotic Personality of Our Time,* emphasized the maladaptive consequences of societal and family structures in which love is lacking; in which a sense of community is absent; in which individuals are emotionally isolated, deprived of roots, and treated impersonally; and in which competition is stressed at the expense of cooperation. Such conditions, they believed, violate humanity's "essential nature" and are likely to lead to neurotic distortions in relations with the self and others (Fromm, 1941, 1955; Horney, 1937, 1950).

According to Horney, in our own society individuals may develop "overdetermined" and exaggerated needs for affection and approval, for dependence, for power, for exploiting others, or for personal admiration. They may develop a false kind of defensive independence that leads them to become "lone wolves" or causes them to live narrow, restricted lives. Long before the youth revolution of the 1960s, both Horney and Fromm called attention to the internal contradictions inherent in much of contemporary society: the contradiction between rewards for "competition and success on the one hand and brotherly love and humility on the other"; the conflict between the stimulation of desires through marketing and the frustration often encountered in trying to satisfy those desires; the contradiction between the concepts of individual freedom and equal opportunity, on the one hand, and the fact that for the majority of people opportunities are quite limited, on the other.

As we shall see in later chapters, many aspects of development—from the growth of independence and the development of sexual attitudes and behavior to the formation of moral values and cognitive styles—are dependent at least partially on cultural influences. We shall also see that the question of the relative influence of nature and nurture has not one but many answers, depending on the characteristics under consideration, the individual involved, and his or her biological and cultural heritage.

Historical Versus Situational Determinants of Adolescent Behavior

Another important theoretical dimension of adolescent personality and behavior is the extent to which an individual's behavior is elicited by his or her biological and experiential past as opposed to the particular situation in which he or she is functioning at any given time. Although most behavioral scientists are unlikely to take either an exclusively historical or an exclusively situational approach, they are likely to differ in the degree to which they look toward the individual's past or to influences in the current situation for an understanding of behavior and personality characteristics. To what extent, for example, is a violent attack by a student on a member of another ethnic group in a racially troubled high school, or by a young gang member on another youth in an urban ghetto, a consequence of the kind of person he has become—the personality traits, motives, psychological defenses, and world view that he has acquired in the course of his development? To what extent are they a result, instead, of influences that are unique to the particular situation in which he finds himself?

One observer might look primarily (though not exclusively) to a youth's developmental history for experiences that may have predisposed him to violence—hostility toward parents, peers, or a society that has denigrated and abused him—or that may have deprived him of love and of opportunities to develop rewarding relationships with others. Another observer might say that although each of us reflects the effects of our individual developmental history, we all have a capacity for violence toward others; consequently, we must look primarily to the unique aspects of the individual's current situation for an understanding of his behavior. Such an observer might argue, for example, that a soldier who has killed children and raped women in a remote jungle village was perceived as a kind and considerate person in his own family and community, and that therefore the explanation for his violent behavior must be sought primarily in specific aspects of his present situation.

Classical psychoanalytic theory emphasized genetic programming and the enduring effects of early-childhood experiences. There was *relatively little* emphasis on social and cultural influences. Thus, it may be viewed as a theoretical system that is primarily historical in orientation. However, later analytic theorists such as Erik Erikson and some psychoanalytically oriented "ego psychologists"—and even Freud himself to some extent in his later years—gave increasing importance to cultural and situational determinants of behavior and noted that personality could be modified in important ways well beyond childhood. Anna Freud (1968) made an important contribution by emphasiz-

Anna Freud at age 16 and at age 85 with her puppy, Jo-Fi.

ing the opportunities adolescence may sometimes provide for undoing the effects of prior adverse experiences. And in his discussions of the development of **ego identity** in adolescence (see pages 54–59) Erikson points out that the adolescent's chances of establishing a stable identity and finding meaning in life depend on the ethical soundness, credibility, and rational consistency of his or her social environment as well as on the psychological assets and liabilities that the young person brings to the adolescent experience (Erikson, 1968, 1983).

In contrast to classical psychoanalytic theory, a theoretical system that has given rise to a more thoughtful and sophisticated exploration of situational determinants of behavior is the **field theory** of Kurt Lewin (1935, 1946, 1951). Lewin, one of the most innovative psychologists of this century, came to the United States from Germany, where he had studied at the University of Berlin (Morrow, 1969; Muus, 1988). Undoubtedly he was influenced by the Gestalt school of psychology, with its assertion, derived largely from studies of perception, that the dynamic unity of the whole is greater than the sum of its parts. He probably was also affected by his observation of the rise of Hitlerism in Europe—which revealed how easily, often tragically, human behavior can be swayed by the social climate of the times.

As a core concept of his theory, Lewin proposed the following formula: Behavior (B) is a function (f) of the person (P) and his or her environment (E), or $B = f(PE)$. In this formula P and E are viewed as interdependent variables— "An unstable psychological environment during adolescence brings about instability in an individual" (Lewin, 1951, p. 8). Therefore, to understand the behavior of a child or adolescent one must consider both the individual and his or her environment as a constellation of dynamically interacting, interdependent factors.

Lewin's concepts, along with his breadth of vision, curiosity, charm, and infectious enthusiasm, had a significant impact on the development of social psychology. They moved social-psychological research toward "real-life experiments" in the field—from studies of racial prejudice to the effects of authoritarian, democratic, and laissez-faire leadership on individual and group behavior in boys' clubs (Lewin, 1951; Lewin, Lippitt, & White, 1939; Morrow, 1969; Muus, 1988). Less well known, however, is the extent to which Lewin proposed a relatively integrated and specific theory of adolescent development. In Lewin's view, many American adolescents know that it is important for them to get somewhere in a hurry, but they know only roughly where they need to go and have an even poorer idea of how to proceed. Moreover, they have no real status in our society during this period. The adolescent has renounced childhood but has not yet been fully accepted as an adult. Partly accepted and partly rejected by the privileged group (i.e., adults), the adolescent is in a position somewhat similar to that of what sociologists call the "marginal man." Lewin noted that behavior that is characteristic of the marginal man can often be found in the adolescent as well: "He too is oversensitive, easily shifted from one extreme to the other, and particularly sensitive to the shortcomings of his younger fellows. Indeed, his position is sociologically the same as that of the marginal man; he does not wish to belong any longer to a group which is, after all, less privileged than the group of adults; but at the same time he knows that he is not fully accepted by the adult" (1939, pp. 882–883).

Lewin's emphasis on the importance of understanding the "dynamic" interaction between the growing person and his or her environment laid the theoretical groundwork for what is now known as **ecological psychology.** This term was first used by Roger Barker and H. F. Wright (1971) to describe the study of how children's surroundings affect their behavior and development. Barker and his colleagues have shown, for example, how behavior is influenced by the social setting, such as a school, in which it occurs (Barker & Gump, 1964; Barker & Wright, 1971) (see pages 335–337). More broadly, the work of ecological psychologists "focuses on the progressive accommodation, throughout the life span, between the growing human organism and the changing environments in which it actually lives and grows" (Bronfenbrenner, 1977, p. 513). Those environments include not only smaller settings like the home, family, or peer group but also larger social and economic systems (Bronfenbrenner, 1977; Bronfenbrenner, Moen, & Garbarino, 1984; Bronfenbrenner & Weiss, 1983; Garbarino, 1985). Urie Bronfenbrenner, for example, is interested in the effects of urban living, poverty, current welfare policies, and employment procedures on family life and parent-child relationships. He and other ecological psychologists are also interested in the question of whether society can find better alternatives to current policies in these areas.

Adolescence as a Stage of Development

Still another important theoretical and empirical question is whether adolescence should be viewed as a distinct **stage** or **critical period** in development. To the extent to which the development is viewed as steady, continuous, and gradual, a concept of adolescence as a stage of development would appear redundant and misleading. Such a view was expressed by Leta Hollingsworth (1928), who took sharp exception to Hall's concept of adolescence as a period involving dramatic storm and stress: "A child grows by imperceptible degrees into an adolescent, and the adolescent turns by gradual degrees into the adult. . . . The widespread myth that every child is a changeling, who at puberty comes forth as a different personality, is doubtless a survival in folklore of the ceremonial rebirth, which constituted the formal initiation of our savage ancestors into manhood and womanhood" (pp. 16–17).

Among contemporary psychologists, social-learning theorists like Albert Bandura also tend to view development as a continuous process without abrupt changes at any one age level (Bandura, 1977; Bandura & McDonald, 1963; Bandura & Walters, 1959; Muus, 1988). In Bandura's view, much of the "storm and stress, tension, rebellion, dependency conflicts, [and] peer-group conformity" commonly associated with the adolescent transition are not widespread (Bandura, 1964, p. 224). When they do occur, they are more likely to result from external social experiences than from age-related maturational forces (Bandura, 1967; Bandura & McDonald, 1963).

To the degree that such views emphasize that there are important continuities in development that might otherwise be ignored, they may perform a useful function. For example, longitudinal research on personality development has shown that there are some basic psychological characteristics (e.g., passive withdrawal from stressful situations, dependency, involvement in intellectual mastery) that show a remarkable degree of stability and consistency from the early school years through adolescence (Brim & Kagan, 1980; Kagan, Reznick, & Snidman, 1988; Plomin, 1986).

Although most theorists do not deny the existence of significant continuities in development, they have been impressed with what they perceive as crucial changes during puberty and the years immediately thereafter. These changes can be viewed quantitatively, in terms of an accelerated rate of change. They can also be viewed qualitatively, in terms of personality organization and defense mechanisms; the emergence of new needs, motives, capabilities, and concerns; and new developmental tasks. For such theorists, the concept of adolescence as a distinct developmental stage is considered useful because it serves to focus attention on the importance of these perceived changes. However, the nature of adolescence as a stage of development varies from one theorist to another, depending on what each considers to be the essential aspects of this developmental period.

Thus, for Sigmund Freud adolescence was a stage of development characterized by a breakthrough of the sexual impulses, which occurred largely as a result of the physiological changes accompanying puberty (Freud, 1953). This phase of development (which was preceded by "oral," "anal," and "phallic" stages) was referred to as the "genital" stage. Among other things, it involved a revival of earlier oedipal attachments and rivalries within the family, along with the need to resolve them in the direction of greater independence from parents and a shifting of the adolescent's attachments to new "love objects."

Erik Erikson, while acknowledging his debt to Freud's biologically oriented ("historical") views, has stressed what he considers to be the unique psychological tasks of the adolescent. Strongly influenced by the findings of cultural anthropology and by his own background as an artist, writer, and educator of young people as well as a psychoanalyst, Erikson believes that the quintessential task of adolescence is to establish a sense of **identity** as a unique person ("ego identity") while avoiding role or **identity confusion** (see pages 61–62).

For Peter Blos—who, like Erikson, is both a psychologist and a psychoanalyst—the onset of puberty, accompanied by an increased sexual drive, disturbs the relative equilibrium of middle childhood. The resulting "instinctual tensions" lead to **regression**—a reactivation of infantile needs and behavior, such as messiness, bathroom humor, restless activity, impulsiveness, and sudden episodes of childish dependency. This occurs most conspicuously in boys, but it can also be observed in girls. According to Blos, this regression, far from being negative in its effects, is not only positive but necessary: "Adolescent development progresses via the detour of regression" (1979, p. 58). By revisiting, as it were, earlier experiences and conflicts (e.g., a distorted perception of the parents) with a more mature ego and greater cognitive ability, the adolescent reworks and resolves long-standing, inappropriate ways of responding that may be impeding his or her further development. This opens the way to what Blos calls a "second individuation," an effort to define who and what one is and is not, frequently through such "adolescent" means as opposition to parental dictates, trying out different roles, or developing sudden and transitory loves and hates. The process of individuation—which may be accompanied by feelings of isolation, loneliness, and confusion—is consistent with Erikson's concept of the development of a stable sense of identity (Blos, 1971, 1979; Conger, 1981).

The distinguished Swiss psychologist Jean Piaget focused on cognitive development in children and adolescents (see Chapter 4). In his view, adolescence is characterized by development of the capacity to think abstractly and to generate alternative hypotheses and test them against evidence; this is the stage of "formal operations," which replace the "concrete operations" of middle childhood. Lawrence Kohlberg, a distinguished psychologist at Harvard, was strongly influenced by Piaget's thought. He conducted extensive studies of moral development in childhood and adolescence. In his view, adolescence involves reaching what he called *postconventional* stages of moral development, which are characterized by "a major thrust toward autonomous moral principles which have validity and application apart from authority of the groups or persons who hold them and apart from the individual's identification with those persons or groups" (Kohlberg & Gilligan, 1971, pp. 1066–1067). (See Chapter 13.)

Carol Gilligan (1977, 1981), a former colleague of Kohlberg, believes that Kohlberg's emphasis on morality as a sense of justice based on abstract moral principles is one-sided and reflects a masculine view (see pages 479–481). She has called attention to the importance of another moral imperative—"a different voice"—that she believes is more characteristic of women and involves "an injunction to care, a responsibility to discern and alleviate the real and recognizable trouble of the world" (Gilligan, 1977, p. 50).

All such descriptions of adolescence as a stage of development have a certain arbitrary quality (Kagan, 1971). Although some theorists tend to view their formulations as having a kind of independent existence, in reality each represents only the theorist's judgment (often astute) of what is *most* important about a particular developmental period. It is also important to recognize that some characteristics that may appear to be an inevitable accompaniment of an adolescent stage of development may in fact be reflecting to an important degree the effects of social change. The proverbial man from Mars, if asked to bring back a report of what earthly adolescents were like, would probably have brought back somewhat different reports in 1950, 1968 (at the height of the youth revolution), and 1990.

"Normal" Adolescent Turmoil Versus Psychological Disorder

One of the problems that has long plagued clinicians in their efforts to classify and diagnose psychological disorders in adolescents stems from the fact that adolescence is a period of transition and rapid change. In contrast to more stable periods in the life cycle, such as middle childhood and adulthood, adolescence is characterized by accelerated physical, physiological, and cognitive development as well as by new and changing social demands. As a consequence, many normal adolescents, in their efforts to deal with them, may display alterations of mood; distressing, turbulent, and unpredictable thoughts; manifestations of anxiety and exaggerated defenses against anxiety; and impulsive, inappropriate, or inconsistent behaviors that would be viewed as symptoms of psychological disorders if they occurred in adults. This raises two important questions: (1) Should adolescent turmoil be viewed as a disturbed state? (2) How widespread, in fact, is adolescent turmoil?

Adolescence as a Disturbed State. Although they can be traced to G. Stanley Hall and his conceptions of adolescent storm and stress, current formulations of adolescence as a disturbed, maladjusted (but temporary) state stem primarily from psychoanalytic conceptualizations like those of Anna Freud and others. In the words of one theorist,

> The fluidity of the adolescent's self-image, his changing aims and aspirations, his sex drives, his unstable powers of repression, his struggle to readapt his childhood standards of right and wrong to the needs of maturity bring into sharp focus every conflict, past and present, that he has failed to solve. The protective coloring of the personality is stripped off, and the deeper emotional currents are laid bare (Ackerman, 1958, pp. 227–228).

Similarly, Irene Josselyn (1968), a prominent psychoanalyst who was experienced in the treatment of adolescents, stated that although adolescents have a greater "ego capacity" than they had at an earlier age, this new-found resource is likely to be exhausted by the difficulty of integrating stronger sexual, aggressive, and other impulses, the demands of conscience, and the demands of reality: "Adolescence, as is equally true of the neuroses and psychoses, is characterized by the relative failure of the ego" (1954, p. 225). Despite the apparent severity of this description, Josselyn differentiates this state of relative "ego failure" from psychopathology: "The normal adolescent is inevitably a mixed-up person, but not at all in the sense of being a psychologically sick person." Most adolescents, she maintains, actually have "sufficient inherent personality strengths to emerge from their confusion as relatively healthy adults" (1959, p. 43).

Equating adolescent disturbance with normal adolescent development has some interesting implications. A number of analytic theorists have presented the view that adolescent disturbance is sufficiently normal that its *absence* may be a greater source of concern than its presence (Weiner, 1970). Anna Freud, in discussing the normality (and desirability) of "adolescent upheaval," remarks:

> We all know individual children who as late as the ages of 14, 15, or 16 show no such outer evidence of inner unrest. They remain as they have been during the latency [i.e., middle childhood] period, "good" children, wrapped up in their family relationships, considerate sons of their mothers, submissive to their fathers, in accord with the atmosphere, ideas, and ideals of their childhood background. Convenient as this may be, it signifies a delay of normal development and, as such, is a sign to be taken seriously. The first impression conveyed by these cases may be that of a quantitative deficiency of drive endowment, a suspicion which will usually prove unfounded. . . . These are children who have built up excessive defenses against their drive activities and are now crippled by the results, which act as barriers against a normal maturational process of phase development. They are perhaps, more than any others, in need of therapeutic help to remove the inner restrictions and clear the path for normal development, however "upsetting" the latter may prove to be (1968, p. 14).

Whether it is useful to label *normative* adolescent upheavals as a *disturbed state* is debatable. To the extent that transient variations in mood, thought, and action do occur in the "normal" course of adolescence, and to the extent that they resemble more serious psychiatric symptoms in adults, it may be valuable to identify those similarities and then to note explicitly the differences in their significance for adolescents and adults.

On the other hand, there is the inherent danger that, in identifying normative adolescent phenomena as disturbed, we may be tempted to view *nonnormative, nontransient* disturbances as normal when in fact they may indicate the presence of serious disorders that require prompt attention. Less skilled clinicians than Anna Freud or Irene Josselyn may be tempted to ignore or dismiss signs of psychopathology on the assumption that they represent normal adolescent turmoil and will pass. The findings of a number of investigators who followed up samples of adolescents who had been initially diagnosed as suffering from "transient situational personality disorder" or "situational adjustment reaction of adolescence" attest to this potential danger. In a signifi-cant number of cases (approximately 50 percent in one study), these young people either ended up in psychiatric treatment or showed continued, and in some instances more serious, problems several years later (Graham & Rutter, 1985; Masterson 1967, 1968; Parry-Jones, 1985; Rutter, 1980).

The Extent of Adolescent Turmoil

A more crucial empirical question than the proper labeling of adolescent turmoil, however, is determining how much adolescent turmoil the average young person actually undergoes. Available data suggest that the extent of adolescent turmoil is, in fact, exaggerated (Ebata, Petersen, & Conger, in press; Offer & Offer, 1975; Parry-Jones, 1985; Petersen, 1988). This is not to say that some normal adolescents may not undergo considerable turmoil dur-ing this period; indeed, this is clearly the case. What is questioned is the pre-sumed universality of these phenomena.

A large body of data is accumulating to suggest that "the modal teenager is a reasonably well-adjusted individual whose daily functioning is minimally marred by psychological incapacity" (Weiner, 1970, p. 48; Larson & Lampman-Petraitis, 1989; Parry-Jones, 1985; Petersen, 1988). A longitudinal investigation of middle-class midwestern adolescent boys revealed little evi-dence of a high degree of turmoil or chaos in the life of the average boy (Offer, Marcus, & Offer, 1970; Offer & Offer, 1974, 1975). Among the sample selected to be in the modal (most frequent) range of psychological functioning, only about one subject in five displayed the extent of adolescent turmoil (anxiety, depression, distrust, extreme mood swings, lack of self-confidence) that some clinicians consider typical. Many of these subjects were sensitive and intro-spective individuals who took great interest in exploring their inner world. About one-third of them had received some form of therapy or counseling. For the parents of this group, separation from their sons (e.g., when they went away to school or college) tended to be painful, and many of those parents appeared unsure of their own values and, hence, unable to present well-defined values to their children.

Most of the remaining subjects fell into one of two groups: a *continuous-growth* group and a *surgent-growth* group. Members of the continuous-growth group (about 25 percent) had strong egos, "were able to cope well with internal and external stimuli, and had mastered previous developmental stages without serious setbacks. They had accepted general cultural and societal norms, and felt comfortable within their context" (Offer & Offer, 1974, p. 212). Although they had reasonably active fantasy lives, subjects in this group tended to be oriented toward reality and action. "The balance between the intensity of the drives and the ego capacity to tolerate new impulses was good. They had a realistic self-image, a sense of humor, and were relatively happy human be-ings" (Offer & Offer, 1974, p. 212). Parents of these subjects were generally able to tolerate their children's growth and gradual assumption of indepen-dence, and there was mutual respect, trust, and affection between the genera-tions.

Box 1.1 STUDYING THE DAILY EMOTIONAL STATES OF CHILDREN AND ADOLESCENTS

Reed Larson and Claudia Lampman-Petraitis (1989) studied the daily emotional states of a large number of midwestern children and adolescents ages 9–15. They used electronic pagers or "beepers" to signal the participants to report on their subjective emotional experiences at random times during the day and evening. At the sound of the beeper, the participant was asked to stop and rate his or her present emotional state or mood, using six 7-part scales (e.g., happy–unhappy, cheerful–irritable, excited–bored). The possible scores ranged from −3 (most negative) to +3 (most positive). The frequency of self-reported states by grade is presented in Figure B1.1.

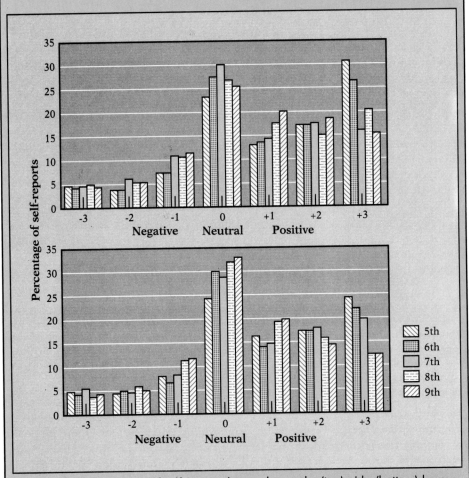

Figure B1.1 Frequency of self-reported states by grade: (top) girls; (bottom) boys. (From R. Larson & C. Lampman-Petraitis, Daily emotional states as reported by children and adolescents. *Child Development*, 1989, 60, 1250–1260. By permission.)

The investigators found few age differences in the variability of moods throughout the day (although the moods of adolescent girls were somewhat more variable than those of younger girls). However, significant age trends in *average* daily emotional states were found (see Table B1.1). The average state, or "emotional baseline," was lower among older subjects than among younger ones. For example, among both boys and girls, fifth-graders used the most positive score (+3) to describe their emotional states twice as often as ninth-graders. In a similarly designed earlier study comparing high school students and adults, average mood levels were similar for the two groups, but adolescents reported more occasions of both positive and negative extremes (Larson, Csikszentmihalyi, & Graef, 1980).

What accounts for the fact that adolescents had more negative moods than younger children and a higher frequency of extreme emotions—both positive and negative—than adults? Possibilities include increasingly stressful events during adolescence (Brooks-Gunn & Warren, 1989), hormonal changes (Nottleman et al., 1987; Petersen, 1988), and a higher degree of conflicts over independence and dependence (Larson & Lampman-Petraitis, 1989). Clearly, further research is needed to determine the relative importance of these and other factors.

T A B L E B1.1 AGE TRENDS IN THE MEANS OF REPORTED DAILY EMOTIONAL STATES

	\multicolumn{5}{c	}{Grade}	t for Linear Trend	p	Correlation with Grade
	5	6	7	8	9			
Girls:								
Happy	5.61	5.43	5.10	5.14	4.98	−4.22	.001	−.28
Cheerful	5.34	5.25	4.92	5.11	4.83	−2.64	.009	−.17
Friendly	5.60	5.41	4.98	5.12	5.11	−3.19	.002	−.21
Alert	4.45	4.58	4.24	4.31	4.48	−.42	.68	−.04
Strong	4.46	4.68	4.28	4.34	4.42	−2.07	.04	−.14
Excited	4.77	4.64	4.25	4.44	4.42	−2.07	.04	−.14
Boys:								
Happy	5.27	5.18	4.96	4.86	4.90	−2.81	.005	−.19
Cheerful	4.94	4.90	5.01	4.60	4.46	−3.03	.003	−.19
Friendly	5.26	4.93	4.88	4.78	4.75	−3.04	.003	−.20
Alert	4.67	4.77	4.47	4.26	4.12	−3.30	.001	−.21
Strong	4.92	4.99	4.89	4.52	4.58	−2.62	.009	−.17
Excited	4.53	4.40	4.38	4.26	4.44	−1.08	.48	−.06

NOTE: Table shows the mean frequency with which students used each of the gradations on the scales to identify their daily emotional states.

Source: R. Larson and C. Lampman-Petraitis, Daily emotional states as reported by children and adolescents. *Child Development,* 1989, 60, 1250–1260. By permission.

Members of the surgent-growth group (about 35 percent), although reasonably well adjusted and capable of meeting the developmental demands of adolescence, tended to have somewhat greater difficulty dealing with unexpected stresses. They tended to use projection, anger, and regression at such times (see pages 48–53). Among parents of this group, there were more likely to be value conflicts between mother and father and maternal difficulty in separating from children.

A similar (and continuing) study has found that about 11 percent of young adolescents have serious chronic difficulties; 32 percent have more intermittent, probably largely situational difficulties; and 57 percent show basically positive, healthy development during adolescence (Ebata, 1987; Petersen, 1988; Petersen & Ebata, 1987).

In an earlier study of 3000 adolescents, the investigators concluded that the traditional psychoanalytic view of adolescence as a period in which the adolescent "responds to the instinctual and psychosocial upheaval of puberty by disorder, by failures of ego-synthesis, and by a tendency to abandon earlier values and object attachments" is primarily a description of the sensitive, articulate, upper-middle-class adolescent. Indeed, the researchers express some dismay at the relative absence of turmoil in many adolescents, attributing much of it to "premature identity consolidation, ego and ideological construction, and a general unwillingness to take psychic risks" (Douvan & Adelson, 1966, p. 351).

It appears from these and other studies that the stresses that adolescence imposes on the individual do not, in the majority of cases, lead to the high degree of emotional turmoil, violent mood swings, and threatened loss of control suggested by some theorists. All of these consequences may be seen in some adolescents, but the evidence suggests that some clinicians have been too quick to generalize to the "average" adolescent findings that were obtained from a limited segment of the population (Block, 1971; Grinker & Werble, 1974; Holzman & Grinker, 1977; Larson & Lampman-Petraitis, 1989; Parry-Jones, 1985; Rutter, 1979). While many adolescents face occasional periods of uncertainty and self-doubt, loneliness and sadness, and anxiety and concern for the future, they are also likely to experience joy, excitement, curiosity, a sense of adventure, and a feeling of competence as they master new challenges.

As will be apparent throughout this book, many of the issues discussed in this chapter are still subjects of active research and debate. In many instances, however, the recent expansion of research on adolescence has succeeded in reducing the areas of uncertainty and in better defining some of the questions that remain to be answered.

SUMMARY

Some observers believe that today's young people are more rootless, more emotionally troubled, and more self-centered and materialistic than their counterparts of earlier generations; as evidence, they cite high rates of drug use, delinquency, and adolescent pregnancy. Others maintain that today's youth are better informed, more pragmatic, and more open and honest. Still others believe that presumed differences between present and past generations of adolescents are largely illusory. One aim of this book is to arrive at a balanced view of adolescents today.

Concern with adolescence and youth is not new; it dates back at least as far as Plato and Aristotle, whose views about adolescents seem remarkably contemporary. A preoccupation with the "ages of life," including adolescence, was evident in the pseudoscientific treatises of the Middle Ages. Seventeenth-century writings focused on helping "undependable" youth to master their "unruly" impulses. But not until the end of the nineteenth century do we encounter the precursors of the modern concern with adolescence as a socially significant and psychologically complex period. By the turn of the century, urban migration and industrialization had led to the creation of large numbers of more complex, better-paying jobs requiring greater maturity and more education. While these goals were beyond the reach of most families, those in the upper and middle classes came to regard education—and the time it requires—as an investment in the future.

Once economic and social conditions had begun to create a visible group of segregated youth, the time was ripe for speculations about the psychological nature of adolescents. By 1900 the "era of adolescence" had begun, although in the absence of child labor laws a majority of adolescents were still working full time, often under deplorable conditions. Only after World War I did concern with adolescence as a privileged age become widespread.

The scientific study of adolescence began with the work of G. Stanley Hall, who developed the theory of *recapitulation* and viewed adolescence as a period of storm and stress. However anachronistic some of his views may seem today, Hall set the stage for the development of a scientific psychology of adolescence and a clearer definition of many of the most important theoretical and empirical issues to be addressed by researchers in the field. Those issues include the relative importance of biological (maturational) versus cultural determinants of adolescent behavior. The maturational emphasis is exemplified by the work of Arnold Gesell, who described modal behavior for each age period; in contrast, cultural anthropologists, social psychologists, and others (including Erik Fromm and Karen Horney) emphasized the maladaptive consequences of disturbed societal and family structures.

Another important issue is the extent to which an individual's behavior is determined by his or her biological and psychological past, as opposed to the specific situation at any given time. Sigmund Freud's classical psychoanalytic theory emphasized the importance of genetic programming and early-childhood experiences; later psychoanalytic theorists like Erik Erikson and Anna Freud placed more stress on cultural and even situational influences. However, Kurt Lewin initiated the most sophisticated explanation of situational determinants of behavior with his field theory, which can be represented by the formula $B = f(PE)$. Lewin's emphasis on the importance of understanding the "dynamic" interaction between a young person and his or her environment laid the theoretical groundwork for contemporary ecological psychology as exemplified by the works of Roger Barker, Urie Bronfenbrenner, and others.

Still another major issue is whether adolescence should be viewed as a separate, distinct stage of development or as a continuous process without abrupt changes at any age level. The former approach may be seen in Freud's psychosexual stages, Erikson's eight stages of development, Blos' "second individuation," Piaget's stages of cognitive development, and Kohlberg's and Gilligan's stages of moral development.

Finally, there is the issue of whether adolescence should be viewed as at least a transiently disturbed (though temporary) state characterized by a high degree of turmoil, as Hall and other theorists and clinicians have asserted, or whether the actual extent of adolescent turmoil has been exaggerated, as recent research indicates.

As will become apparent, many of the issues raised in this chapter are still with us, although recent research on adolescence has greatly increased our knowledge and succeeded in reducing the areas of uncertainty.

REVIEW QUESTIONS

1. Discuss Aristotle's views about the nature of adolescence.
2. What was the principal theme of seventeenth-century writings about youth? How was that theme related to the social and economic circumstances of the time?
3. What role did industrialization play in the delineation of adolescence as a distinct stage of development?
4. Discuss G. Stanley Hall's theory of recapitulation and his concept of storm and stress.
5. Name four basic issues in adolescent development that arose out of Hall's work, and discuss each briefly.
6. How did Sigmund Freud's view of adolescence differ from that of Kurt Lewin's?
7. Discuss arguments for and against viewing adolescence as a distinct stage of development.
8. Name several stage theorists. How do they differ in their views regarding the key characteristics of adolescence as a stage of development?
9. What do recent research findings tell us about the extent of adolescent turmoil? Has the idea of adolescent turmoil been exaggerated in the past?

RECOMMENDED READINGS

Conger, John J. (1981). Freedom and commitment: Families, youth and social change. *American Psychologist*, **36**, 1475–1484.

Kett, Joseph F. (1977). *Rites of passage: Adolescence in America, 1790 to the present.* New York: Basic Books.

Muus, Rolf E. (1988). *Theories of adolescence* (5th ed.). New York: Random House.

Spacks, Patricia M. (1981). *The adolescent idea: Myths of youth and the adult imagination.* New York: Basic Books.

VIEWING DEVELOPMENT: CHANGE AND CHALLENGE

Standing in front of the mirror,
I'm wondering what that person is all about.

Tony Hall, age 16

Adolescence can be many things: a time of irrepressible joy and inconsolable sadness; gregariousness and loneliness; altruism and self-centeredness; insatiable curiosity and boredom; confidence and self-doubt. It can be an exciting and hopeful time, filled with promise and opportunity, a time when, in Matthew Arnold's words, the world stands before us "so beautiful, so various, so new." But it can also be a time of apathy, anger, or despair—especially for those who have felt the sting of parental neglect and abuse, rejection by peers, or societal discrimination.

More than anything else, however, adolescence is a period of rapid change—physical, sexual, and cognitive changes within the young person, and changes in the adolescent's world and in the demands placed on him or her by society. Indeed, at no time between the age of 2 and the onset of puberty does a person undergo as many, and as rapid, changes as occur during adolescence. It should hardly seem surprising, then, that many adolescents, faced with a changing physical image and conscious of new, sometimes strange feelings and thoughts, may ask themselves "what that person is all about" (Conger, 1979).

As we shall see in subsequent chapters, the maturational changes of puberty—the growth spurt in height and weight, changing physical proportions, hormonal changes, the development of primary and secondary sexual characteristics, accelerated cognitive development—all provide adolescence what universality it has as a separate developmental stage.

DEVELOPMENTAL TASKS OF ADOLESCENCE

Although these maturational changes are universal, the demands placed on the young person during adolescence—the "developmental tasks" that must be mastered if he or she is to function successfully in adult society—vary considerably from one society to another. Among the Mountain Arapesh of New Guinea, for example, there is a very gradual transition from a high degree of dependence in infancy and early childhood to increasing independence as the child grows older. In that culture, unlike much of the industrialized world, there is no discernible "spurt" during puberty or adolescence.

Developmental tasks also vary from one era to another. The sexual, social, and vocational roles of men and women that contemporary American adolescents are expected to master are very different, and in some ways much more complex, than was the case in the 1940s and 1950s.

Despite such variations in developmental tasks, there are some important commonalities. If an adolescent is to become truly adult, and not just physically mature, he or she must gradually achieve independence from parents, adjust to sexual maturation, establish cooperative and workable relationships with peers without being dominated by them, and decide on and prepare for a meaningful vocation (Conger, 1979, 1981; Havighurst, 1953). In the process of meeting these challenges, young people must also gradually develop a philosophy of life and a set of guiding moral beliefs and standards that, however simple, are "nonnegotiable." A basic philosophy gives order and consistency to the many decisions and actions the individual must carry out in a diverse and changing world. As we shall see, the young person must also develop a sense of **identity.** Before adolescents can successfully abandon the security of childhood dependence on others, they must have some idea of who they are, where they are going, and what the possibilities are of getting there (Erikson, 1956, 1968).

If we are to understand the nature of these factors, and the ways in which they interact in the course of development, we need to set forth briefly some of the basic principles and concepts of development that relate not only to adolescence but to the entire life span.

INTERACTION BETWEEN INDIVIDUAL AND ENVIRONMENT

A fundamental assumption underlying our conception not only of adolescent development but of development in general is that an individual becomes the kind of person he or she is as a result of the continuing and continuous interaction between a growing, changing biological organism and its physical, psychological, and social environment.

Even in the earliest stages of prenatal development, when the future poet, executive, or scientist is represented by only a few, seemingly simple and identical cells, the individual's genetic inheritance is already interacting with a physical environment that can have a variety of nurturant or harmful effects. Future development may also be affected by the adequacy or inadequacy of the mother's nutritional status; by the effects of any drugs she may take; by certain diseases that she may contract (e.g., rubella, or German measles); and even by her emotions, which can liberate soothing or irritating chemicals into her bloodstream (Guttmacher & Kaiser, 1986; Illingworth, 1987; Moore, 1982; Plomin, 1986). To take just one example, recent lawsuits have drawn attention to the fact that a significant number of the daughters of women who took the drug stilbestrol (an estrogenic compound) during pregnancy to prevent miscarriage developed cancer of the vagina during adolescence (Illingworth, 1987).

As growth and development proceed, the biological organism becomes increasingly complex as a function both of maturation and of prior interactions between organism and environment. The environment also becomes more complex, first within the womb and later in the ever-expanding world outside it. Initial encounters with the mother and father and a relatively simple world of sight, sound, and touch are soon augmented by interactions with family, peers, and community. Eventually, of course, the individual exists within, and interacts with, a far wider world. These days, in fact, he or she may be affected immediately, through satellites and television, by events occurring on distant continents. In later chapters we will examine in some detail the importance of environmental influences like peers, parents, school, and the world of work in an adolescent's development.

Antecedent–Consequent Relationships

Implicit in this view of development is the concept of **antecedent–consequent relationships**—the idea that the effects of events occurring at any one stage of development depend on and proceed from earlier developmental events and will, in turn, influence the individual's responses to future events. In this respect, development may be viewed much like a growing tree: The possibilities of present and future growth, flexible and varied though they may be, are still dependent on and limited by the nature of the tree and by patterns of prior growth.

For example, a study of all children born on the Hawaiian island of Kaui over a period of more than a decade focused on the longer-term consequences of **perinatal stress** (problems occurring around the time of birth). Except in instances of severe central nervous system impairment, "perinatal complications were consistently related to later impaired physical and psychological development *only* when combined with persistently poor environmental circumstances (e.g., chronic poverty, family instability, or maternal health problem). Children who were raised in more affluent homes, with an intact family and a well-educated mother, showed few, if any, negative effects from [perinatal] stress" (Werner & Smith, 1982, p. 31). Similarly, adolescents who were sexually abused as children can often be helped a great deal by appropriate treatment, although they may carry the psychological scars of their experiences throughout their lives (see pages 201–202).

The readiness of adolescents to cope with the increased demands of the adolescent years depends to a large extent on the whole array of intellectual, physical, and social competencies and the feelings of security, confidence, and self-esteem that they have acquired since infancy. In turn, the amount of success they have in mastering the tasks of the adolescent period and developing a stable, clearly defined sense of their own identity strongly affects their chances of leading a rewarding, fulfilling adult life—whether as worker, lover, spouse, parent, or citizen.

In this connection it is important to stress that, although the chances of achieving these goals are strongly influenced by the young person's inherent resources and by the facilitating or inhibiting effects of prior experience, these factors do not constitute insurmountable barriers. Despite the popular notion that the early-childhood years are all-important in determining future adjustment—that, as one worried mother remarked, "the game is over by the age of 6"—the adolescent years present important opportunities for continued growth and development and for repairing the damaging effects of adverse prior experiences (Blos, 1971, 1979; A. Freud, 1958; Hartup, 1970, 1983). For example, a supportive, understanding, nonexploitive friend may play an important, sometimes crucial, role in helping a boy or girl gain a clearer concept of self, a feeling of personal worth, and renewed hope for the future (see pages 280–281).

In many respects, what Erik Erikson calls a **psychosocial moratorium**—a period in which the adolescent has an opportunity to develop an identity of his or her own, relatively free of adult responsibilities—may represent for some young people the last sustained opportunity for significant psychological change and restructuring before the onset of adulthood and entrance into the world of work, marriage, and social and personal responsibility.

BIOLOGICAL INFLUENCES ON DEVELOPMENT

As we have already noted, a young person's behavior and development at any one time are a product of the continuing interaction between nature and nurture. Even the effect of a single gene depends on the constellation of other genes present in the same cell. Nevertheless, genetic and other biological influences may play a stronger role in determining some characteristics or sets of behavior, while environmental factors may play a greater role in determining other characteristics. In later chapters we will examine the relative roles of biological and environmental factors in physical maturation, in the development of intelligence, and in the etiology (causation) of major mental disorders such as schizophrenia and severe depression.

A supportive friend can often help an adolescent to gain a clearer self-concept and a better understanding of his or her problems and goals.

Biology and Personality

Although investigation of the role of genetic influences in the development of personality characteristics presents special problems, progress is being made. This is especially evident in comparative studies of **monozygotic twins,** who are genetically identical, and **dizygotic** or "fraternal" **twins,** who are no more closely related genetically than other brothers and sisters (Plomin, 1986; Scarr & Kidd, 1983). In general, it appears that genetic influences are strongest for basic temperamental characteristics (e.g., calm–easily distressed, active–passive, impulsive–reflective, gregarious–shy), which tend to be relatively stable during development. They appear to be weakest for characteristics that are highly dependent on learning and social experience, such as ethical and social values (Buss & Plomin, 1984; Goldsmith & Campos, 1982; Kagan, Reznick, & Snidman, 1988; Matheny, 1983).

From infancy to adolescence, monozygotic (MZ) twins resemble each other significantly more than dizygotic (DZ) twins do in many temperamental traits, including activity, attention, task persistence, irritability, emotionality, sociability, and impulsiveness (Buss & Plomin, 1984; Cohen, Dibble, & Grawe, 1977; Goldsmith, 1983, 1984; Matheny, 1983; Torgersen & Kringlen, 1978). In addition, at later ages MZ twins resemble each other more than DZ twins do in

Studies of genetic influences on personality characteristics often compare identical twins with fraternal twins and nontwin siblings.

such characteristics as introversion–extroversion and neuroticism (Floderus-Myrhed, Pederson, & Rasmuson, 1980; Matheny, 1983; Plomin, 1986; Scarr & Kidd, 1983).

Although these studies suggest that genetic factors have a significant influence on **temperament,** it should be kept in mind that virtually all personality characteristics are influenced by both genes and environment. Moreover, genetic predispositions can frequently be "overridden" by environmental influences. Naturally shy individuals can often be helped to become more assertive, and punitive experiences can cause exuberant extraverts to become hesitant or withdrawn.

LEARNING

The continuing interaction that takes place between the growing individual and his or her environment is not a random one. It is governed by specific principles and conditions that are commonly referred to as principles, or laws, of **learning.** To the average person, learning means something done in school or while acquiring a vocational skill (e.g., "learning" to be a mechanic or an airline pilot). As the term is employed by psychologists, however, its connotations are far broader. Stated in its simplest form, *learning is the process by which behavior or the potentiality for behavior is modified as a result of experience.* Behaviors that are subject to learning may be as varied as thoughts and images, motor acts (e.g., driving a car), and physiological responses—even so-called "involuntary" responses like changes in heart rate, blood pressure, or electrical activity of the brain.

Learning and Innate Responses

Not all of the behaviors—even complex behaviors—that seem to require learning are in fact learned. Ethologists have demonstrated that in animals, highly specific external stimuli may "release" complex patterns of behavioral response in the absence of any opportunity for prior learning (Hess, 1970; Lorenz, 1981). In a male stickleback, for example, the sight of the red underbelly of another fish will provoke complex fighting behavior. Even dummies that look very little like sticklebacks will provoke the response as long as the essential elements of the key stimulus are present (Lorenz, 1966, 1981). In many instances, maternal behavior appears to be unlearned. Thus, animals ranging from rats to birds will build nests in preparation for their young, even though they may never have witnessed such activities themselves.

It is far more difficult to isolate and study complex human behaviors that may have been innately programmed and not learned. It appears that complex behavior in humans is generally much more dependent on learning and much less dependent on innate response tendencies. It is possible, however, that some types of human behavior that were previously assumed to be learned may turn out to depend at least in part on such tendencies (Lorenz, 1965; Tanner, 1970). For example, some investigators have suggested that some of the complex psychological and physiological responses of females to a "baby-ness" appearance in children or animals may be innately programmed (Bowlby, 1969; Hess, 1970). Such a response could serve an important evolutionary purpose: helping to insure the infant's survival by attracting caretakers and maintaining their interest in feeding, caring for, and sheltering their young (Clarke-Stewart & Friedman, 1987; Corter et al., 1978; Klaus & Kennell, 1976).

Kinds of Learning

Classical Conditioning. Probably the most basic category of learning is **classical conditioning,** in which a reflexive response (i.e., one that is automatically elicited by a specific, or "unconditioned," stimulus) becomes associated with a previously neutral stimulus. The response can be an overt action (e.g., withdrawing one's hand from a hot stove) or a physiological reaction (e.g., a change in heart rate in response to an electric shock). In either case the response is a naturally occurring reaction to an existing stimulus.

In a pioneering experiment, the great Russian physiologist Ivan Pavlov demonstrated that a dog can be taught to salivate in response to the stimulus (cue) of a buzzer through repeated pairings of the sound of the buzzer with the presentation of food (an *unconditioned stimulus*). Eventually, the buzzer alone becomes capable of eliciting the salivation response. The buzzer thus is a *conditioned stimulus.*

Similar conditioning takes place in humans. For example, within a few weeks after birth the infant's sucking reflex, an innate (unconditioned) response to a nipple in the mouth, is readily conditioned to previous neutral stimuli such as the sight, smell, and sound of the mother as she prepares to feed the infant. Through association with the unconditioned stimulus of the nipple, these stimuli become capable of eliciting sucking.

Operant or Instrumental Conditioning. Many instances of learning in older children and adolescents cannot be explained by simple classical conditioning. A more complex kind of learning is involved, called **operant** or **instrumental conditioning.** Here the response to be learned is not automatically elicited by a known stimulus but must be developed gradually. A familiar example is teaching a dog to play dead, roll over, or shake hands. In essence, this technique involves rewarding appropriate responses whenever they happen to occur.

In operant conditioning, the subject's own response is *instrumental* in producing the reward—it *operates* to bring about the reward; hence the term *instrumental* or *operant conditioning.* Through operant or "shaping" procedures animals can often be taught surprisingly complex sequences of behaviors. For example, operant-conditioning procedures have been used to teach dolphins to deliver equipment to divers in undersea explorations.

Behavior Modification. Similar techniques are being applied to humans in what is known as *behavior modification* or *behavior therapy* (Chesney, 1984; Ross, 1978; Yule, 1985). Gerald Patterson and his associates at the Oregon Social Learning Center have had remarkable success in helping parents learn to deal with excessive aggression in children and adolescents through identification and consistent reinforcement of appropriate responses (Patterson, 1976, 1979; Snyder & Patterson, 1987). Their approach is described in Box 2.1.

In other studies, behavior modification procedures have been employed to overcome social withdrawal and increase social interaction in children. Such procedures have also been used to decrease stammering, to treat disorders such as enuresis and insomnia, to discourage smoking or drug use, and to increase the incidence of appropriate behaviors among adolescent delinquents (see Chapter 13) (Burns & Brady, 1980; Kazdin, 1978; Lichtenstein & Mermelstein, 1984; Rutter & Giller, 1984; Snyder & Patterson, 1987).

Biofeedback. The use of operant-conditioning techniques is not restricted to behavioral responses; it may include a variety of so-called involuntary physiological responses involving the autonomic nervous system (Miller, 1980, 1984; Miller & Dworkin, 1977, 1980; Shapiro & Surwit, 1979; Stoyva et al., 1979). Operant-conditioning techniques have been employed in the treatment of physiological disorders in which psychological factors play a role, such as tension (frontal) headaches, hypertension (high blood pressure), gastric ulcers, and migraines. For example, psychologists have shown that it is possible to teach patients to control tension headaches by using a biofeedback technique.

Tension headaches are produced by sustained contraction of the neck and scalp muscles. In the biofeedback treatment, electrodes are applied to the frontalis (forehead) muscle and the patient wears a set of earphones. Minute variations in the amount of electrical energy resulting from contraction or relaxation of this muscle (electromyographic activity) are converted into auditory stimuli that can be "fed back" to the patient. When muscle tension is high, the patient hears a high-pitched tone; when tension decreases, the frequency of the tone also decreases. The patient is instructed to keep the pitch of the tone low.

After several weeks of biofeedback training, most people are able both to recognize the onset of tension and to reduce it without feedback from the machine (Budzynski, Stoyva, & Peffer, 1980; Miller, 1980; Phillips, 1979; Tarler-Benlolo, 1978). Other promising applications of biofeedback training include controlling blood pressure and cardiac arrhythmia (irregular heartbeat), physical rehabilitation following injury, and treatment of sexual dysfunctions (LoPiccolo & Hogan, 1979; Miller, 1984; Miller & Dworkin, 1980; Patel, 1984).

Observational or Vicarious Learning. Not all learning depends on conditioning. Many human activities, especially complex responses, are acquired by observing the behavior of others. Thus, a teacher may interrupt a

Box 2.1 DEALING WITH HIGHLY AGGRESSIVE CHILDREN AND ADOLESCENTS

Gerald Patterson and his colleagues compared families of children who were highly aggressive and unruly, both at home and at school, with a control group of families that were similar in age, socioeconomic status, and number of children, but whose children were not excessively aggressive. They identified some significant differences: Unlike the families in the control group, the families of highly aggressive children were found to be unwittingly rewarding aggressive behavior. For example, members of those families were five times as likely to respond to the child's actions in ways that tended to maintain aggression. Thus, a sister who teased her brother after he yelled increased the likelihood that the brother would respond in a hostile manner, such as hitting, often setting in motion an escalating exchange.

The parents of the problem children tended to be inconsistent in their handling of aggressive responses. At times they reinforced those actions by approving, paying attention, or complying with the child's wishes; at other times they threatened the child with punishment, although they often failed to back up their threats (Patterson, 1976; Patterson, DeBaryshe, & Ramsey, 1989; Snyder & Patterson, 1987). In contrast, the parents in the control group tended to be evenhanded and consistent in their use of punishment.

On the basis of such findings, Patterson and his colleagues concluded that parents can control a child's aggressive behavior if they apply certain specific techniques when interacting with the child. They explained the basic principles of learning to the parents and showed them how to identify undesirable aggressive behaviors and keep accurate records of their occurrence and the conditions surrounding them. Modeling and role procedures were used to teach the parents how to reinforce appropriate behavior with warmth and affection, and to reduce deviant behavior by not giving in to the child's aggression and not allowing their own coercion to escalate. Techniques of control using rewards for desirable responses and calm forms of punishment such as "time-out" (removing the child from an activity until he or she stops using coercive tactics) were substituted for more severe forms of punishment.

The effectiveness of this approach was tested systematically over a twelve-month period in twenty-seven families with boys between the ages of 5 and 15 who were considered to show excessive aggression. The program was highly successful. After the treatment approximately three-fourths of the boys showed significant reductions in amount of aggression expressed and in number of "bursts" of aggressive behaviors. Moreover, when the program was completed, *all* members of the family showed less aggression and provided fewer of the kinds of stimuli that had originally provoked the problem child's aggressive behavior.

Through modeling and role playing, parents of aggressive children can learn more effective ways of responding to aggressive behavior.

student's unsuccessful attempt to solve a problem in order to demonstrate the correct approach. Adolescents in particular are likely to observe the behavior of their peers carefully in order to learn which ways of dressing, talking, and acting lead to approval and which ones have the opposite effect. Social-learning theorists like Albert Bandura emphasize the importance of **observational learning** and the factors that influence the likelihood that a person will repeat responses acquired through observation (Bandura, 1977a, 1977b, 1982; Muus, 1988).

Social-learning theorists have found that subjects are more likely to imitate the behavior of prestigious models than that of nonprestigious models. In addition, models who are similar to the subject have a greater effect on behavior than models who do not resemble the subject. Thus, an adolescent boy is more likely to imitate the behavior of a male peer whom he views as having similar interests and abilities, and who belongs to the same social clique or group, than to imitate that of a younger girl with different interests and talents.

Cognition and Learning. Social-learning theorists tend to place greater emphasis on **cognitive processes** than learning theorists, whose primary interest is in basic conditioning. They point out that because humans can think and represent situations symbolically, they can foresee the probable consequences of their actions and alter their behavior accordingly: "Anticipated consequences, represented symbolically in one's thoughts, can motivate behavior in much the same way that actual consequences can" (Hilgard, Atkinson, & Atkinson, 1979, p. 318). Children and adolescents therefore are more likely to imitate the behavior of models who are rewarded for their actions than that of models who are punished or not rewarded.

Cognitive psychologists view the individual as "an active seeker of knowledge and processor of information" (Klatzky, 1980). They view learning as "the step in which we acquire information that we then modify, manipulate, store, and use in various ways" (Kagan & Segal, 1988, p. 181; Klatzky, 1980). Because of the complexity of human mental processes, much human learning cannot be adequately understood without an understanding of cognitive development, including the ways in which individuals at different stages of development acquire and process information, use problem-solving strategies, store information and solutions in short-term ("working") and long-term memory, and retrieve stored information for later use (Siegler & Richards, 1988; Sternberg, 1985; Sternberg & Powell, 1983). In Chapter 4 we will discuss current theories of cognitive development and information processing in some detail.

The Role of Reinforcement

You have probably noted that in several of the examples presented earlier the subject was given a reward or reinforcement whenever he or she made the desired response. How important is reinforcement or reward in facilitating learning? Psychologists differ in their answers to this question. Some argue that reinforcement is not a necessary condition for learning and that its apparent importance in some cases is really only incidental—it helps motivate the individual and ensures that the appropriate response will occur in the presence of the stimulus and not under other conditions (Atkinson et al., 1987; Bower & Hilgard, 1981).

In contrast, other psychologists assert that reinforcement is always necessary for learning and that instances in which learning appears to take place without reinforcement are deceptive. In their view, reinforcement was actually present in such cases but the psychologist was not aware of it. Although these *reinforcement theorists* may differ regarding the specific ways in which reinforcement or reward operates, they agree that some sort of reinforcement is necessary for learning.

Still other psychologists—perhaps a majority—maintain that although reinforcement may not be a necessary condition for all learning (e.g., some conditioned responses that involve the autonomic nervous system) it is important for many and perhaps most forms of learning, particularly social learning (Atkinson et al., 1987; Bower & Hilgard, 1981). They note, for example, that a child or adolescent who finally makes the correct response in a complicated learning problem is more likely to repeat it the next time it is presented if he or she is rewarded for it and is not rewarded for incorrect responses. The reward may be a piece of candy, a grade of A, or simply a congratulatory statement like "very good"—as long as the "reward" actually is rewarding for that particular child.

On the basis of the evidence available to date, these questions regarding the role of reinforcement cannot be answered definitively. However, we believe that reward or reinforcement plays an important role in most of the kinds of social learning that we shall be concerned with throughout this book.

MOTIVATION

In general, the term **motivation** refers to the needs, goals, and desires that provoke an individual to action. More specifically, there are basic biological needs, commonly called *primary needs*, that must be met if the individual is to survive; these include the needs for food, water, warmth, and oxygen as well as other needs (e.g., sex).

There are, of course, many other sources of motivation besides primary needs. There is nothing innate about the need for social status, for security, for love from one's parents, for money, or for acceptance by one's friends. These needs are learned (Bower & Hilgard, 1981; Miller, 1951, 1984). In common with primary needs, however, learned needs, or *motives*, may serve to motivate future learning. Moreover, as with primary needs, the individual has to learn a set of behaviors to gratify the learned needs. One of the common sources of tension and anxiety in human beings is the chronic presence of a learned need without a means of gratifying it.

Learned needs or motives may play an important role in the acquisition of additional, more complex motives. For example, if a mother gives love to her son only if he is orderly and conscientious, the child may develop needs for orderliness and conscientiousness that will be manifested even when the mother is not around. He may even learn to perform numerous behaviors, such as always putting his toys away, never getting his clothes dirty, washing his hands frequently, and always doing what he is told, in order to satisfy those needs.

One of the important characteristics of needs or motives (both primary and learned) is that they *energize* behavior. When an individual is hungry or thirsty, or anxious or in need of nurturance, he or she tends to become active and to engage in a variety of behaviors, some of which may be reinforced and lead to further learning.

The Principle of Generalization

If an individual could profit from past learning only when he or she encountered *exactly* the same situation again, opportunities for continued development would be severely limited. Fortunately, this is not the case. When a young boy has been trained to avoid a particular hot radiator or stove, he will tend to avoid similar radiators or stoves in other locations. But how does this happen? If the stimuli (cues) presented are not identical, why doesn't the child have to learn all over again to make the appropriate response in the new situation?

The answer to this question requires an additional learning principle: **stimulus generalization.** This principle states that when a response has been learned to one stimulus, it is likely to occur to similar stimuli. The greater the degree of similarity between the original stimulus and the new one, the greater the likelihood that the response will occur, and the stronger it will be. This is called the *gradient of generalization* (Miller, 1984).

Generalization may play a crucial role in adjustment to the developmental demands of adolescence. A girl who has learned to fear a father who was harsh and punitive or who continually criticized and ridiculed her is likely to have difficulty relating to male peers during adolescence. Her deeply ingrained, or "overlearned," responses to her father are likely to generalize to her male contemporaries, so that (consciously or unconsciously) she anticipates similar treatment from them—even though they may in fact be kindly, considerate, and admiring. She may know intellectually that such responses are inappropriate and unrealistic, but that knowledge will do little to help her overcome her reluctance to relate to male peers. Similarly, a boy who has learned to fear a dominating father may later find himself reacting with fear and submissiveness to his male employer, even though the employer may actually wish to encourage initiative and independence.

Discrimination. Initially, generalization is likely to be extensive. A young boy who has learned to attach the label "dog" to the family pet is likely to extend that label to all four-footed animals he meets, including sheep, cows, and horses. Gradually, however, through a process called **discrimination** he will learn to limit the label to dogs. Similarly, the adolescent girl who initially generalizes her negative responses to her father to all males may learn through discrimination to limit such responses to the father alone. A primary aim of much psychotherapy is to undo the effects of inappropriate generalizations based on unfortunate learning experiences earlier in life.

Whereas generalization involves "reaction to similarities," discrimination is "reaction to differences" (Atkinson et al., 1987, p. 219). Discrimination is brought about by selective reinforcement of responses that have been appropriately generalized and by the elimination, or *extinction,* of incorrectly generalized responses.

Extinction. The fact that a response is learned does not mean that it will always remain strong. Consider the problem of getting a baby boy to sleep. The baby may have learned that if he cries after he has gone to bed his mother will come in, pick him up, and give him additional attention. As a result, he is rewarded for crying and is likely to cry rather than go to sleep, even though he may be tired. However, if the mother stopped responding to the baby's cries— that is, stopped reinforcing the undesired behavior—the crying response probably would eventually cease; it would undergo extinction. Likewise, an adolescent who is loud and aggressive in order to attract attention is likely to abandon those behaviors if they are ignored by others.

The Complexity of Adolescent Needs and Motives

The newborn's repertory of needs is largely restricted to primary needs, such as the needs for food, sleep, physical contact, environmental stimulation, and protection from extremes of heat or cold. In contrast, the adolescent has had many years in which to develop an elaborate set of learned needs or motives— for social approval, friendship, love from parents and others (including opposite-sex peers), independence (or dependence), nurturance of others, achievement, self-esteem, and a sense of identity. Even the adolescent's biologically based needs are likely to be more numerous and more inextricably intertwined with socially learned motives (e.g., tastes for special foods rather than simply food per se).

It should be emphasized that the individual need not be, and probably never is, fully aware of all his or her motives. Many motives remain at least partially unconscious. For example, the adolescent girl who astounds both herself and her parents by suddenly "blowing up" at her mother and is unable to provide any reason for her behavior may be motivated by unconscious aggressive needs. Many adolescents are puzzled or alarmed by such evidences of unconsciously motivated behaviors. Some may be led to wonder if they are "losing their minds" because of what may appear, even to themselves, to be irrational, unmotivated thoughts or acts.

Motives are most likely to remain unconscious when they involve thoughts or feelings that are inconsistent with the individual's self-concept or unacceptable to his or her conscience (superego). As we shall see in the following section, awareness of such motives would probably lead to painful feelings of anxiety, guilt, or self-blame.

ANXIETY

Anxiety is a major determinant of human behavior, for it arouses internal responses (thoughts, feelings, psychophysiological reactions) and behaviors that conflict with the satisfaction of other needs or motives. A young child wants to jump off a diving board with her friends, but she is afraid. An adolescent boy would like to ask a girl for a date, but he fears being rebuffed. A college student wants to do well on an examination, but the anxiety aroused by her fear of failure makes her unable to order her thoughts and concentrate on the task at hand.

At a more complex level, a dutiful adolescent son may resent the "unreasonable" demands of his parents but fear retribution or loss of their love if he acknowledges his resentment, even to himself. A father may feel hostile toward, and critical of, his daughter's boyfriends because he unconsciously views them as rivals for her affection; a mother may have similar feelings toward her daughter-in-law. In each of these instances life would be easier and psychological tensions would be reduced if the individual admitted these secret feelings to himself or herself; but even thinking such "unacceptable" thoughts would produce too much anxiety. Therefore, the individual learns to avoid these thoughts and acts because avoidance is rewarding (i.e., it is reinforced by a reduction in the anxiety aroused by the thoughts). As we shall see, this avoidance may involve use of a variety of techniques that are commonly referred to as **defense mechanisms.**

How does anxiety begin? What produces the feelings of discomfort, the perspiration, the trembling, the exaggerated startle response, the dryness of the throat and mouth, and other indicators of anxiety? Anxiety involves both a physiological component and a cognitive component (Barlow, 1988). The physiological component of anxiety is not learned but is part of the constitutional make-up of the individual. What is learned is an association between a person, object, or situation and the combined feelings, images, and physiological reactions that characterize anxiety. In other words, it is the *arousal* of anxiety that is learned (Miller, 1951, 1984).

Moreover, because anxiety is a learned response, it follows the same principles of learning (e.g., extinction and generalization) that apply to other behaviors. For example, if an adolescent has had humiliating experiences with the first few girls that he has attempted to date, and has learned to fear such experiences, he may generalize this reaction to girls in general, even though these other girls might be far less likely to humiliate him. At a more profound level, an adolescent girl who as a child learned to fear a sexually abusive father may generalize this fear to all males and be unable to relate to boys her own age with pleasure.

Sources of Anxiety in Adolescents

Although the physiological potential to become anxious exists in any individual, many of the situations or events to which anxiety may become attached are a function of learning. This is an important point; use of the term *anxiety* without stipulating the source of the anxiety is not helpful in understanding or predicting behavior.

Many of the sources of anxiety in adolescents are carried over from earlier years. Both children and adolescents may be anxious about potential physical harm; loss of parental love; inability to master the environment or meet personal, parental, or cultural standards; or aggressive or sexual impulses. Guilt, a special form of anxiety that may occur as early as 3 or 4 years of age, may arise from anticipation of violating a rule or standard, or may be experienced after the violation of an internal standard or value. It is characterized by feelings of self-derogation and unworthiness.

There may also be differences between childhood and adolescent anxiety either in the level of anxiety experienced or in its source. Anna Freud (1969) and others (e.g., Blos, 1979) emphasize that the physiological changes of adolescence, together with their psychological manifestations, bring about a psychological disequilibrium—a disruption of whatever balance may previously have been achieved between the individual's basic needs and impulses, on the one hand, and the demands of conscience, on the other. In this new situation the ego (the aspect of the self that is responsible for arbitrating such conflicts) may be hard pressed to restore equilibrium and prevent disorganization.

Thus, among the potential sources of adolescent anxiety is *fear of loss of control* and breakdown in the organization of the self. Most adults can recall some time in their adolescence when they experienced such ego anxiety, which is often expressed as fear of "going crazy." This broader source of anxiety may be accompanied by, and related to, more specific anxieties. Although all normal children are socialized to feel anxiety about the expression of aggression, that anxiety is likely to be heightened in adolescence as the strength (and hence the potential danger) of aggressive impulses or feelings increases following puberty. In fact, a longitudinal study of normal middle-class adolescent boys found that aggressive and angry feelings and problems with coping with them were most strongly manifested around the ages of 12 and 13, although they extended beyond those ages in somewhat attenuated form (Offer, 1969).

Sexuality is another prominent source of potential anxiety for adolescents. Sometimes anxiety is aroused by sexual impulses themselves (which may be viewed as evil, bad, or dirty); sometimes the anxiety is a function not so much of the impulses themselves as of the objects toward which they are directed. Thus, the girl who has been "daddy's little darling," and has always had a close and affectionate relationship with her father, may become extremely anxious if, as a consequence of sexual maturation, she finds erotic elements intruding into the relationship. Usually such unacceptable feelings remain unconscious, although they may continue to influence behavior.

Sometimes sexual impulses arouse anxiety because in their intensity they threaten to overwhelm the adolescent's sense of self-control, posing the danger of ego disorganization or giving rise to the fear that the individual will engage in sexual behavior that violates self-imposed internal standards or conscience.

Anxiety over *dependence–independence* is also likely to be intensified during adolescence. As we shall see in Chapter 7, demands (and rewards) for achieving independence increase during the adolescent years. Young people may truly desire these rewards, but they may also be anxious about their ability to achieve independence, to "stand on their own two feet" and take responsibility for their actions, including the consequences of ill-considered ventures.

Anxiety over *rationality*, though often unrecognized, can be a significant problem for adolescents. In our society it is assumed (despite considerable evidence to the contrary) that the normal person is rational and can give clear reasons and justifications for his or her motives, moods, and behaviors (Mussen, Conger, Kagan, & Huston, 1990). Consequently, any indication of an inability to provide a logical accounting to oneself or others threatens the adolescent's self-image and generates anxiety. For the adolescent who oscillates from euphoria to depression, from lethargy to frantic anxiety, or from careful planning to impulsive action, the lack of an explanation for such fluctuations can generate considerable anxiety.

Anxiety over *acceptance by peers* is, of course, not confined to adolescents. But with the loosening of parental ties and emancipation of the adolescent from the comfort and protection of the family, acceptance by peers becomes

Anxiety about acceptance by peers become more urgent during adolescence, as family ties loosen.

more urgent. This is so not only because in emotional terms the adolescent is placing "more eggs in one basket" but also because, from an objective standpoint, the peer group has the power to affect the adolescent's future opportunities, status, and well-being. This point will be discussed further in Chapter 8.

The increased demands on the adolescent for achievement and mastery of varied, often complex, developmental tasks may give rise to anxiety over *competence.* For boys, such anxiety has traditionally centered on mastery of objective tasks or skills; for girls, it has tended to involve competence in interpersonal relationships, although at present such sex-related distinctions are decreasing somewhat.

The adolescent's rapid physical maturation is likely to precipitate *anxiety over one's body image* as well as concern about real or fancied deficiencies in one's physical self (see Chapter 3).

In addition, demands for a clearly defined **sexual identity** increase during adolescence. This developmental change has been labeled "gender intensification": The changes of puberty, which result in a more differentiated male or female appearance, are accompanied by changes in degree of sex-role orientation as masculine or feminine (Hill & Lynch, 1983). The individual needs to feel secure in, and comfortable about, his or her status as a male or female. Especially in adolescence, the need for conformity, together with heightened awareness of body image and sex, can generate anxiety over the extent to which one is "male enough" or "female enough." The adolescent whose prior developmental experiences have failed to create a secure, stable sexual identity may encounter increased *anxiety over sexual identity*.

Obviously, there are many other potential sources of anxiety in adolescence. Some of them will become evident in later chapters. But the examples just presented should serve to emphasize our initial point: that anxiety is an important determinant of adolescent (indeed, human) behavior.

Coping with Stress

Because anxiety represents a painful state of heightened tension that markedly disturbs psychological equilibrium, responses that lead to a reduction in anxiety tend to be learned. In the course of the individual's development, he or she acquires a variety of techniques for coping with, or defending against, the anxiety generated by stressful situations. Coping takes two primary forms: **problem-focused coping** and **emotion-focused coping** (Lazarus & Folkman, 1984).

Problem-Focused Coping. In problem-focused coping, the individual confronts and evaluates the stressful situation and then takes steps to deal with it. This may involve efforts to change the situation, to change one's own behavior, or a mixture of the two (Kagan & Segal, 1988). A young woman who discovers that she is in danger of failing a course may evaluate the reasons for her difficulty and then take remedial actions such as cutting back on extracurricular activities, developing a regular work schedule, or finding a tutor (Atkinson et al., 1987; Cohen, 1984). Or, after seeking counseling, a premedical student may realize that he is having difficulty with the required coursework, not because of lack of ability but because his heart is not in the work. He may discover that he has been attempting, albeit unconsciously, to satisfy the hopes of his physician father rather than his own artistic talents and interests. He may then change his major to fine arts. In a third example, a young couple experiencing marital problems may go to see a marriage counselor in an effort to resolve their difficulties. They may discover that both partners must make changes in their attitudes and behavior if the marriage is to succeed. In each of these examples, the individuals involved confronted and evaluated the stressful problem situation and then took action to resolve it. The emphasis is on objectivity, flexibility, logical analysis, and active problem solving (Haan, 1977; Horowitz, 1988; Lazarus & Folkman, 1984; Swanson, 1988).

Emotion-Focused Coping. In contrast, emotion-focused coping centers on emotional responses to the problem; "the individual tries to reduce anxiety without dealing directly with the anxiety-producing situation" (Atkinson et al., 1987, p. 475). Although emotion-focused coping techniques may be employed in a wide variety of situations, they are most likely to occur in stressful problem situations that are, or appear to be, insoluble. These techniques can be relatively straightforward and adaptive, or they can be maladaptive. Engaging in physical exercise to reduce tension, seeking support from friends, or temporarily putting a problem aside may be adaptive (Horowitz, 1988). At a more complex level, one may cope with an overwhelming loss, such as the death of a loved one, by only gradually coming to accept the full impact of the tragedy. In contrast, an individual may resort to coping techniques that, while they may reduce anxiety at the time, are ultimately maladaptive and self-defeating. Consider a woman who ignores the early warning signs of possible cancer by telling herself that they mean nothing or a young man who denies that he is in serious trouble in his academic work or in his job, despite every sign to the contrary; both are courting disaster (Horowitz, 1988).

Anxiety and Defenses

One of the principal contributions of psychoanalytic theory to our knowledge of personality development is the elucidation of a variety of a largely unconscious, emotion-focused techniques, termed **defense mechanisms,** that help defend an individual against anxiety, often by distorting reality in some way (Atkinson et al., 1988; A. Freud, 1966; Haan, 1977; Horowitz, 1988; Swanson, 1988). Many of these defenses were originally conceptualized in an effort to make sense of otherwise inexplicable psychological phenomena such as amnesia, phobias, severe obsessions and compulsions, and apparent physical disabilities for which no organic impairment could be found. In many instances the source of these symptoms seemed to lie in unconscious thoughts, feelings, or impulses that the individual could not admit without experiencing painful increases in anxiety or sometimes even panic. The seemingly senseless symptoms served to protect or defend the individual from such awareness. Thus, a painful episode may not be remembered precisely *because* it was so painful.

Frequently anxiety also includes guilt because it involves impulses, thoughts, or fears that are unacceptable to the conscience or superego—that is, the person's internal standards regarding what is right and wrong. A young combat infantryman may become extremely fearful of getting killed. But admitting this feeling to himself would produce acute anxiety, since such "cowardice" would violate his internal standards of acceptable behavior. Consequently, he may keep any awareness of this fear out of his consciousness (i.e., repress it) and solve the dilemma by developing paralysis in one leg. This physical symptom enables him to continue repressing his unacceptable fear while still avoiding the original anxiety-producing situation (see p. 49).

As this illustration implies, the basic function of defense mechanisms is to help the individual avoid painful feelings of anxiety without being consciously aware of doing so; however, some defense mechanisms have the additional advantage of allowing the gratification of unconscious needs or impulses. In effect, such defense mechanisms are doubly reinforcing. A classic example is the censor of pornographic literature or films who is able to reassure herself that she has no unacceptable sexual impulses. Simultaneously, however, she gains secret satisfaction from reading the suspect books or viewing the films in order to "protect" others.

Although many of the symptoms of psychological disorders reflect the presence (or the failure) of defense mechanisms, most of these mechanisms also play a role in the development and functioning of normal individuals (Haan, 1977; Horowitz, 1988; Swanson, 1988; Vaillant, 1971, 1987). The kinds of defense mechanisms employed by any given individual will vary, depending on personality, learning experiences, age, and level of cognitive development. Some defense mechanisms are most easily seen in children because of their relative lack of sophistication and the immaturity of their egos. Others, as we shall see later, depend on the attainment of a fairly advanced level of intellectual and cognitive functioning, and for that reason they are most likely to become evident during adolescence.

Repression. Repression, which serves as a basis for many other defenses, is apparent at all ages from early childhood on. In repression, anxiety-producing thoughts, impulses, and memories are kept from conscious awareness. If these painful thoughts and feelings threaten to become conscious, anxiety increases and the person's thoughts veer off in another, safer direction—with the consequence that anxiety decreases. Repression thus is reinforced by a reduction in anxiety and tends to be learned and employed unconsciously (Dollard & Miller, 1950; Horowitz, 1988). Repression may be limited or pervasive, temporary or persistent. One may experience a temporary failure to remember the name of a familiar person whom one dislikes. In contrast, an entire period of childhood may be repressed in order to avoid the discomfort of remembering painful instances of maltreatment or unacceptable desires or behaviors (e.g., sexual or aggressive impulses or encounters) associated with that period (Horowitz, 1988).

Repression is neither a refusal to remember an event nor a denial of its reality. Rather, the thought or event has been removed from consciousness by forces beyond the individual's control. For example, a girl may repress her memory of a violent argument between her parents or of resentful thoughts toward one of them. Although she once was clearly aware of those thoughts, after they have been repressed, she is unaware of them, and questioning her will not bring them to light.

Suppression. Repression must be distinguished from suppression. Whereas repression is an involuntary process, **suppression** involves a voluntary effort to exclude thoughts from conscious awareness. Suppression was originally conceived of as a pathological defense mechanism that might result in a "bottling up of the emotions" and psychophysiological symptoms (Horowitz, 1988, p. 191). However, longitudinal studies of men from their college years through middle age have shown that the ability to consciously and deliberately put unpleasant and unsolvable stressors out of one's mind can be adaptive and can actually improve coping skills (Haan, 1977; Vaillant, 1977).

Denial. In **denial,** obvious realities are treated as if they did not exist. An amusing, if touching, example, is the little girl who, while sobbing her heart out, keeps insisting, "I am not unhappy!" Denial involves insisting that an anxiety-arousing event or situation is not true—and believing it. For example, a boy who has been openly rejected or even abused by his mother may deny that she is hostile and insist that she is a kind and loving person. Some children who have experienced parental rejection claim that they were adopted and that their "real" parents love them. Because denial is "at once so simple and so supremely efficacious" in eliminating anxiety and pain, it is used extensively, particularly by children (A. Freud, 1946, p. 85).

Within limits, denial can be considered a normal process. As noted earlier, denial can help delay full recognition of bad news, such as the death of a loved one or a diagnosis of cancer, until we are better prepared to deal with it. However, denial is maladaptive if it interferes with rational action. It is clearly maladaptive to convince oneself that all the classic signs of a heart attack are only indigestion or to insist that a person truly loves you when in fact he or she is being hostile and destructive.

Projection and Displacement. In both projection and displacement, an unacceptable feeling or impulse is acknowledged but is attributed to other sources. **Projection** is ascribing an undesirable thought or action of one's own to another person. The plea, "He started the fight, not me," is a common example of projection in young children. At a more serious level, the troubled adolescent who ascribes overwhelming hostility, blatant self-serving, or sexual license to peers or adults when there is no evidence to support these claims is likely to be projecting his or her own unacceptable impulses onto others. To the extent that the individual employs projection as a defense, "his ability to see the world truly, accurately, is in some degree diminished" (A. Freud, 1946, p. 90). When carried to a pathological extreme, projection can result in paranoid delusional thinking.

In **displacement,** the individual has the appropriate emotional response, but it is not attributed to its true source. A boy's fear of his father, for example, may be too painful for him to acknowledge consciously, but he is fearful and needs to account for his condition. As a result, he may attribute the fear to an acceptable symbolic substitute for the father (e.g., lions or robbers). As we shall see in Chapter 14, displacement plays an important part in school phobias.

Rationalization. **Rationalization** is a comforting defense that all of us—children, adolescents, and adults—engage in. It involves giving oneself socially acceptable reasons for one's behavior or attitudes when the real reason would not be acceptable to one's conscience and, if admitted, would give rise to painful anxiety and guilt. A father who harshly punishes his son out of intense anger toward him, but says that he is doing it for the child's own good, is engaging in rationalization. An adolescent who is bored with his long-time girlfriend and wants to pursue other girls, but who would feel guilty if he were to "dump" the girl, may tell himself—and the girl—that he isn't a good influence on her, that she would be better off without him, or that she needs the experience of dating other boys while she is still young. Such assertions might or might not be true; true or not, they do not reflect the boy's actual motivation and are rationalizations.

Reaction Formation. In **reaction formation,** a "warded-off [repressed] idea or feeling is replaced by an unconsciously denied but consciously felt emphasis on its opposite" (Horowitz, 1988, p. 194). Reaction formation was illustrated earlier in the example of the censor of pornographic films and books. Another example is the child who is preoccupied with being clean and tidy but may actually be defending himself against an unacceptable desire to be dirty either literally or symbolically (e.g., sexually). It is as though he were saying, "I can't have any desire to be messy or dirty; look how preoccupied I am with being clean."

Withdrawal. **Withdrawal** is a defense that may be used both by young children and by adolescents or adults; it involves direct avoidance of, or flight from, threatening situations or people. A young girl may hide her eyes or run to her room when a stranger enters the house, or refuse to approach a group of strange children despite her desire to play with them. An adolescent boy who fears being rebuffed by girls or doubts his ability to gain recognition from male peers may withdraw into a world of his own. Withdrawal may temporarily remove the individual from feared situations, but there is the danger that through reinforcement (i.e., reduced anxiety) the response may become stronger each time it is employed. "The young person who refuses to cope with stressful situations may eventually become fearful of all problems and stresses, and may never learn to handle adequately the crises that are inevitable in the course of development" (Mussen, Conger, & Kagan, 1979, p. 349).

Regression. **Regression** involves the adoption—or, more accurately, readoption—of a response that was characteristic of an earlier phase of development. The school-age child who resorts to bedwetting or thumbsucking upon the arrival of a new baby is engaging in regressive behavior. Finding that more mature responses are no longer effective in getting the desired amount of parental attention, the child resorts to the earlier, less mature means that were successful in the past.

Some of the infantile or childish behaviors that may occur in early adolescence may be due to regression. Faced on the one hand by the problem of coping with rapid physical and sexual changes and the anxiety that they create, and on the other hand by greatly increased social demands, including the demand for greater independence, the adolescent may temporarily abandon more mature ways of responding and retreat to more "primitive" responses that were successful in an earlier, simpler period.

Within limits, regression can be adaptive. Indeed, Peter Blos (see page 18) comments that "adolescent development progresses via the detour of regression," or what he calls "regression in the service of development" (Blos, 1971, p. 58; 1979). Not all regression serves positive functions, however. For the young person who enters adolescence unprepared to meet its demands, regression may be purely defensive and may lead to "developmental arrest and symptom formation" (Blos, 1979, p. 484).

Asceticism and Intellectualization. More than 30 years ago, Anna Freud called attention to two additional defense mechanisms that, in contrast to those of younger children, seem to be characteristic of adolescents; they are **asceticism** and **intellectualization.** Asceticism involves an attempt to deny one's bodily needs and desires. The young person may—perhaps outwardly in the name of religious dedication or self-discipline—seek to avoid any semblance of giving in to sexual desires, tastes in food or drink, sometimes even such basic bodily needs as sleep or protection from cold. Unlike individuals with specific neurotic problems, who may feel a need to repress specific (e.g., sexual or aggressive) impulses but feel free to express others, adolescent ascetics feel a need to repress all "instinctual" impulses. "They mistrust enjoyment in general and so their safest policy appears to be simply to counter more urgent desires with more stringent prohibitions" (A. Freud, 1946, p. 168). It is as though the disruption of psychological equilibrium and control that accompanies puberty creates conflicts and anxieties that the young person attempts to counteract by simply avoiding all basic impulses.

Up to a point, in Anna Freud's view, ascetic responses to adolescent anxiety and confusion can be considered normal. However, when carried to extremes asceticism may go beyond normal limits—as in the case of one adolescent girl who not only gave up "frivolous entertainment," sexual pleasures, and indulgence in favorite foods, but also tried to deprive herself of sleep, reduced all food intake to a minimum, and constantly tested her capacity to withstand pain or cold "on the grounds that one ought not to be 'driven by' one's physical needs" (A. Freud, 1946, p. 169). The aim of this defense appears to be to control an outer and especially, inner world that the adolescent perceives as out of control. Extreme forms of this defense are likely to be involved in disorders like anorexia nervosa (see Chapter 15).

In **intellectualization,** an individual avoids the emotional implications of a topic by dealing with it on a purely ideational level (A. Freud, 1946; Horowitz, 1988). This defense may be employed by some adolescents to deal with anxieties that may be too painful to deal with directly. Thus, apparently impersonal, highly intellectual and philosophical discussions of committed versus "open" sexual relationships, of the role of aggression in human affairs, of responsibility versus freedom, of the nature of friendship, of the existence of God—the possibilities are almost limitless—may in fact reflect deep-seated personal concerns. They may indicate strong concern with how to handle the unfamiliar and insistent stirring of sexual or aggressive feelings; they may indicate conflicts between childlike gratification of desires, on the one hand, and an increasingly demanding conscience, on the other. Or they may reflect concern for acceptance by others despite doubts of one's own worth, or a feeling of existential abandonment generated by the loss of the protection and nurturance not only of one's parents but even of a "Heavenly Father."

None of these statements should be interpreted as implying that the content of the abstract intellectual discussions of some adolescents may not be valuable, or that the motivations involved are necessarily restricted to concern with personal needs, doubts, and conflicts. Discussions of this sort may give adolescents practice in exercising their capacity for abstract thought and in formulating and testing hypotheses (see Chapter 4), and at times they may lead to conclusions that are valid and useful in their own right. Moreover, a significant part of the motivation (and reinforcement) for such discussions may come simply from the pleasure of finding that one is able to engage in higher-level cognitive tasks.

Dramatic examples of both asceticism and intellectualization are frequently found in the writings of gifted adolescents—in poems and diaries, for example—and in the behavior of some intelligent, well-educated young people. There is reason to believe, however, that the extent to which both of these defenses are employed by adolescents in general has been exaggerated (Douvan & Adelson, 1966; Offer, 1969; Swanson, 1988; Vaillant, 1987).

Any of the defenses summarized here, as well as others, may be resorted to by adolescents. In fact, as a result of the constant shifting of internal forces and external pressures that occurs during adolescence, and the resulting disruption of equilibrium, it appears that a greater variety of defenses is employed during adolescence than during more placid periods of development. Moreover, flexibility and variety in the use of defenses at this stage appear to provide greater insurance against the development of psychopathology than rigid and inflexible reliance on particular defenses.

IDENTIFICATION

The concept of **identification** was introduced by Freud and refers to the process by which one is led to think, feel, and behave as though the characteristics of another person (or "model") belonged to oneself (Freud, 1953; Kagan, 1964; Mussen et al., 1990). Although identification may involve imitation of a model (e.g., a boy who identifies with his father may imitate his father's verbal expressions or his habit of reading the sports page), the two terms are not synonymous. Simple imitation may involve nothing more than the emulation of a specific behavior carried out by a model (e.g., operating a lawnmower or baking a cake)—a behavior that may persist if it is reinforced. Identification is a more complex process. It involves responding as though one *were* the other person. Thus, a young girl who identifies with her mother is likely to feel sad when her mother receives bad news; a young boy who identifies with his father will respond with pleasure and pride when his father defeats a rival on the tennis court. Whereas simple imitative responses are likely to involve conscious awareness, identification responses frequently occur unconsciously and may have an emotional intensity that is lacking in simple imitation (Bronfenbrenner, 1960; Horowitz, 1988).

Identification appears to be a far more complex process than simple imitation. It involves responding as though one were the other person.

Identification is not an all-or-none phenomenon. Children and adolescents identify to varying degrees with both parents, and they identify with adults and peers outside the family as their social contacts and cultural awareness expand. As Erik Erikson has observed, the successive and interrelated identifications of childhood can provide a child with "a set of expectations as to what he is going to be when he grows older" (Erikson, 1968, p. 159). But as will become apparent in the next section, patterns of childhood identifications, though essential, are not by themselves capable of providing adolescents with a coherent, reasonably stable and consistent image of the self—that is, a sense of identity.

IDENTITY

A central task of adolescence is to find a workable answer to the question, "Who am I?" Although this question has preoccupied humankind for many centuries and has been the subject of innumerable poems, novels, and autobiographies, only in recent decades has it become an important concern of psychologists, beginning with the writings of Erik Erikson (Erikson, 1968).

Adolescents and adults with a strong sense of their own identity see themselves as separate, distinct individuals. The very word *individual,* as a synonym for *person,* implies a need to perceive oneself as somehow separate from others, no matter how much one may share with them. Closely related is the need for self-consistency, a feeling of wholeness. When we speak of the integrity of the self, we imply both separateness from others and unity of the self—a workable integration of the person's needs, motives, and patterns of responding.

In order to have a clear sense of identity, an adolescent or adult also needs a sense of continuity of the self over time. In Erikson's words, "the younger person, in order to experience wholeness, must feel a progressive continuity between that which he has come to be during the long years of childhood and that which he promises to become in the anticipated future" (Erikson, 1956, p. 91). In addition, according to Erikson, a sense of identity requires **psychosocial reciprocity**—consistency "between that which he conceives himself to be and that which he perceives others to see in him and expect of him" (Erikson, 1956, p. 94). Erikson's assertion that one's sense of identity is tied at least partly to social reality is important; it emphasizes the fact that rejection can seriously impair the individual's chances of establishing a strong, secure sense of identity.

Any developmental influences that contribute to one's perception of oneself as separate and distinct from others, as reasonably consistent and integrated, as having continuity over time, and as being similar to the way others perceive one to be will foster an overall sense of identity. By the same token, influences

In Erik Erikson's view, a central task of adolescence is the development of a clear sense of identity.

that interfere with these self-perceptions will foster identity confusion (or identity diffusion), "a failure to achieve the integration and continuity of self-images" (Erikson, 1968, p. 212).

Developing a Sense of Identity

The development of a sense of identity does not begin or end in adolescence. The elements of an individual's identity are already being shaped during early childhood, beginning, in Erikson's view, with the infant's basic trust or mistrust of the people and the world around it (see Box 2.2) Under favorable conditions, identity development does not end during adolescence. Unfortunately, some men and women, once they have grown up, gone to work, and gotten married, seem almost to become caricatures of their former selves; instead of finding themselves, they become more like everybody else. However, others—including Eleanor Roosevelt, Winston Churchill, dancer and choreographer Martha Graham, Mahatma Gandhi, and Erikson himself, as well as many less public figures—become more genuinely individual as they grow older (Conger, 1979; Lynd, 1966).

The search for a sense of identity becomes especially relevant during adolescence. As we have already noted, during adolescence the young person is confronted with a host of psychological, physiological, sexual, and cognitive changes, as well as new and varied intellectual, social, and cognitive demands. Like the young poet quoted at the beginning of the chapter, adolescents may at times feel like spectators observing their changing selves. They need time to integrate the rapid changes of body and mind into a gradually emerging sense of identity.

Identification and Identity

For Erikson, earlier and continuing identifications play an important part in determining an individual's sense of identity, but they alone do not "result in a functioning personality" (1968, p. 158). Also needed is *the capacity to synthesize successive identifications into a coherent, consistent, and unique whole.*

Consider the following example: When one adolescent girl was asked why she had three distinctly different handwriting styles, she replied, "How can I only write one way till I know who I am?" (Conger, 1979, p. 495). Although she had a number of identifications, as indicated by her varied handwriting styles, she had not yet synthesized them into a coherent whole that was uniquely her own. Many adolescents have similar feelings. Not only do they find themselves playing roles that shift from one situation, or one time, to another, and worry about "which, if any, is the real me," but they also self-consciously try out different roles in the hope of finding one that seems to fit.

Achieving a clear sense of identity depends partly on cognitive skills. The young person must be able to conceptualize herself or himself in abstract terms. As we shall see in Chapter 4, an increased capacity for abstract and hypothetical thinking, along with the ability to take a future time perspective, aids the adolescent in the search for an individual identity but at the same time makes the search more difficult. As Erikson puts it, "From among all possible

Box 2.2 ERIKSON'S EIGHT STAGES OF DEVELOPMENT

Erik Erikson, a psychoanalytic theorist, proposed major revisions in Freud's ideas about stages of development. Erikson thought that Freud had overemphasized the biological and sexual determinants of developmental change while underemphasizing the importance of childhood experiences, social relationships, and cultural influences on the development of ego or self. He also believed that major developmental changes occur after childhood. He proposed a series of eight stages of development stretching over the entire life span. Erikson's theory has stimulated little research on young children, but it has been influential in generating research on adolescent and adult development.

The eight stages proposed by Erikson are presented in the accompanying chart. Each stage is defined by a developmental task or crisis that needs to be resolved if the individual is to continue a healthy pattern of development.

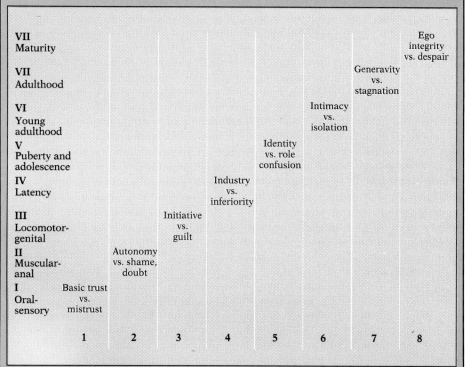

Figure B2.1 The eight stages of development in Erikson's theory. On the left side the approximate ages or Freudian psychosexual stages corresponding to each stage are listed. The conflicts central to each stage in Erikson's theory are shown on the diagonal. (From E. Erikson. *Childhood and society* (2nd ed.). New York: Norton, 1963, p. 273.

The major concern of the first stage is establishment of trust. Erikson believed that infants develop trust when their world is consistent and predictable—when they are fed, warmed, and comforted in a consistent manner.

The second stage is described as a conflict between autonomy and shame and doubt. In the toddler period children begin to assert independence—they say no, and they can walk and run where they choose. Toilet training, often begun during this period, can become a battlefield where the child refuses to do what the parent wishes. Erikson believed that it is important to give children a sense of autonomy and not to be harsh or punitive during this period. Parents who shame their children for misbehavior could create basic doubt about being independent.

The third stage entails a conflict between initiative and guilt. The child in this stage begins to be task oriented and to plan new activities. It is a period when masturbation and sexual curiosity are often noticed by parents. The danger in this period, according to Erikson, is that the child may develop excessive guilt about his or her actions.

During middle childhood children need to solve the conflict between industry and inferiority. Children enter school, begin to perform tasks, and acquire important skills. Achievement and a sense of competence become important; a child who has no particular competences or experiences repeated failure may develop strong feelings of inferiority.

The major conflict in adolescence is between identity formation and role confusion. The young person solidifies many elements of his or her childhood identity and forms a clear vocational and personal identity. Failure to solve this conflict can result in role confusion or diffusion of identity. In young adulthood the major conflict is between intimacy and isolation. Deep, enduring personal relationships need to be formed. A person who does not form such relationships may be psychologically isolated from others and have only superficial social relationships. The most important intimate relationship, according to Erikson, is a committed sexual relationship with a partner of the other sex. This view has been challenged as unnecessarily narrow; some people have argued that many kinds of intimate relationships are important and rewarding.

In middle adulthood the conflict is between generativity and stagnation. Generativity involves satisfactions gained from contributing to the development of others—particularly the young—or from dedication to other forms of altruism or creativity that transcend the self. Without generativity, Erikson argued, an adult stagnates and ceases to grow.

The final conflict is between ego integrity and despair. People with ego integrity have a sense of order and meaning in life and a feeling of satisfaction with what they have accomplished. There is a sense of being part of a larger culture or world. Despair can occur when people become afraid of death or do not accept the life they have led as satisfying or worthy (Erikson, 1963, 1968, 1985; Mussen, Conger, Kagan, & Huston, 1990).

and imaginable relations, [the adolescent] must make a series of ever-narrowing selections of personal, occupational, sexual, and ideological commitments" (1968, p. 245).

Self-Concept and Identity. Adolescents have a much more sophisticated view of what is involved in a sense of self than younger children have. Whereas the self-descriptions of younger children tend to center on concrete characteristics, those of adolescents are likely to be more abstract and to include psychological characteristics, interpersonal relationships, self-evaluations, and conflicting feelings (Harter, 1983; Hill & Palmquist, 1978; Montemayor & Eisen, 1977; Selman, 1980). Self-conceptions also become more differentiated and better organized during adolescence (Chandler et al., 1985).

For example, note the concrete flavor of this 9-year-old boy's self-description, emphasizing his age, sex, physical characteristics, and likes and dislikes:

> My name is Bruce C. I have brown eyes. I have brown hair. I have brown eyebrows. I'm nine years old. I LOVE! Sports. I have seven people in my family. I have great! eye site. I have lots! of friends. I live on 1923 Pinecrest Dr. I'm going on 10 in September. I'm a boy. I have a uncle that is almost 7 feet tall. My school is Pinecrest. My teacher is Mrs. V. I play Hockey! I'am almost the smartest boy in the class. I LOVE! food. I love fresh air. I LOVE School.

Now consider the self-description of this 11½-year-old girl. Although she, too, speaks of her likes, she stresses psychological characteristics and interpersonal relationships:

> My name is A. I'm a human being. I'm a girl. I'm a truthful person. I'm not pretty. I do so-so in my studies. I'm a very good cellist. I'm a very good pianist. I'm a swimmer. I try to be helpful. I'm always ready to be friends with anybody. Mostly I'm good, but I lose my temper. I'm not well-liked by some girls and boys. I don't know if I'm liked by boys or not.

Finally, note how this 17-year-old twelfth-grader is preoccupied with describing her identity in terms of her psychological characteristics, moods, and ideological concerns:

> I am a human being. I am a girl. I am an individual. I don't know who I am. I am a Pisces. I am a moody person. I am an ambitious person. I am a very curious person. I am not an individual. I am a loner. I am an American (God help me). I am a Democrat. I am a liberal person. I am a radical. I am a conservative. I am a pseudoliberal. I am an atheist. I am not a classifiable person [i.e., I don't want to be].

The authors of the study from which these descriptions are taken add the following comment:

> Children describe where they live, what they look like, and what they do. Their self-concept seems somewhat shallow and undifferentiated, both from other people

and from their environment. Adolescents, however, describe themselves in terms of their beliefs and personality characteristics, qualities which are more essential and intrinsic to the self and which produce a picture of the self that is sharp and unique. (Montemayor & Eisen, 1977, p. 318).

The Role of the Family in Identity Development

An adolescent's freedom to explore a variety of possibilities in forming an individual identity is significantly influenced by relationships within the family (Cooper & Grotevant, 1989; Cooper, Grotevant, & Condon, 1983; Grotevant & Cooper, 1983, 1985; Kamptner, 1988; Marcia, 1980; Youniss & Smollar, 1985) (see Chapter 6). One study of family interactions found that adolescents who scored high on a measure of identity exploration were more likely to come from families in which self-assertion and freedom to disagree ("separateness") were encouraged *along with* "connectedness" to the family, including openness or responsiveness to the views of others ("plurality") and sensitivity to and respect for the ideas of others ("mutuality"). In the words of one high-scoring participant, "I have a say but not a deciding vote in family decisions" (Cooper, Grotevant, & Condon, 1983, p. 54).

Adolescents who scored lower in identity exploration were more likely to come from families in which individuality was not encouraged and mutual support and agreement were emphasized. One low-scoring young woman, referring to her efforts to choose a career, said, "I'm having a hard time deciding

Adolescents who are involved actively in pursuit of an individual identity are more likely to come from families that encourage self-assertion and the freedom to disagree, as well as respect for the ideas of others.

what to do. It would be easier if they would tell me what to do, but of course I don't want that" (Cooper et al., 1983, p. 55).

The findings of studies like this one (see pages 223–225) are consistent with Erikson's view that people with a strong sense of identity perceive themselves as separate, distinct individuals. They also support the idea that openness and responsiveness to the views of others are important "because identity function requires the consideration, selection, and interpretation of possible sources of information about the self and others" (Cooper, Grotevant, & Condon, 1983, p. 53). These characteristics of family interaction facilitate access to such information.

Identity Foreclosure and Identity Confusion

Erikson (1968) pointed out two important ways in which the search for identity can go wrong: It may be prematurely foreclosed (i.e., crystallized too early), or it may be indefinitely extended. These two pitfalls are referred to as identity foreclosure and identity confusion (Archer & Waterman, 1990).

Identity Foreclosure. **Identity foreclosure** is an interruption in the process of identity formation, a premature fixing of the adolescent's self-image that interferes with the development of other possibilities for self-definition. Young people whose identities have been prematurely foreclosed are likely to be highly approval oriented. They base their self-esteem largely on recognition by others, usually have high respect for authority, and tend to be more conforming and less autonomous than other youth (Bourne, 1978a, 1978b; Marcia, 1980; Waterman & Waterman, 1974). Compared to adolescents who have not experienced identity foreclosure, they are more interested in traditional religious values, less thoughtful and reflective, less anxious, and more stereotyped and superficial, as well as less intimate in their personal relationships (Orlofsky, 1978; Orlofsky, Marcia, & Lesser, 1973; St. Clair & Day, 1979).

Although they do not differ from their peers in overall intelligence, identity-foreclosed youth have difficulty being flexible and responding appropriately when confronted with stressful cognitive tasks; they seem to have a greater need for structure and order in their lives. They tend to have close relationships with their parents (especially in the case of sons and their fathers) and to adopt their parents' values. Their parents, in turn, generally appear to be accepting and encouraging while at the same time exerting considerable pressure for conformity to family values (Bourne, 1978a, 1978b; Donovan, 1975; Marcia, 1980; St. Clair & Day, 1979).

Identity Confusion. Other adolescents may go through a prolonged period of **identity confusion.** Some never develop a strong, clear sense of identity; these are adolescents who "cannot 'find themselves,' who keep themselves loose and unattached, committed to a bachelorhood of pre-identity" (Douvan & Adelson, 1966, p. 16). Such a person may exhibit a pathologically prolonged identity crisis, never achieving any consistent loyalties or commitments.

Young people who experience identity confusion often have low underlying self-esteem and immature moral reasoning. They are impulsive, are disorganized in their thinking, and have difficulty taking responsibility for their own lives. They tend to be focused on themselves, and their relationships are often superficial and sporadic. Although they are generally dissatisfied with their parents' way of life, they have difficulty fashioning a life of their own (Adams, Abraham, & Markstrom, 1987; Donovan, 1975; Marcia, 1980; Orlofsky, 1978; Waterman & Waterman, 1974).

Achieved Ego Identity

Individuals who have achieved a strong sense of identity, especially after a period of active searching, are likely to be more autonomous, creative, and complex in their thinking; more open, less self-conscious, and less self-absorbed; and more resistant to pressure for conformity than adolescents who experience either identity foreclosure or identity confusion. (Adams, Abraham, & Markstram, 1987; Bourne, 1978a, 1978b; Marcia, 1980; Toder & Marcia, 1973). They also exhibit greater capacity for intimacy, a more confident sexual identity, a more positive self-concept, and more mature moral reasoning. Although their relationships with their parents are generally positive, they have typically achieved considerable independence from their families (Cooper & Grotevant, 1987; Hodgson & Fischer, 1978; Orlofsky, 1978; Rowe & Marcia, 1980; St. Clair & Day, 1979).

Young women who have achieved a clear sense of identity usually have weighed a variety of occupational and ideological options and arrived at conclusions to which they are committed. They also have yielded less to pressures for conformity and experience less discomfort under pressure than adolescents who lack a well-defined identity (Toder & Marcia, 1973). In addition, they tend to choose relatively difficult college majors and manifest fewer negative feelings, such as anxiety, hostility, or depression, than women without a firm identity status (Marcia, 1980).

Variations in Identity Formation

Thus far we have discussed identity formation as though it were a single task at which a young person either succeeds or fails. In reality the matter is more complex. Patterns of identity formation may vary widely as a result of influences that range from parent–child relationships to cultural pressures and the rate of social change (Archer & Waterman, 1990; Mussen et al., 1990). In a simpler society, where there are only a limited number of adult roles and little social change, identity formation may be a relatively simple task that is quickly accomplished. But in a rapidly changing, complex society like our own, where there is so much choice, the search for identity can be difficult and prolonged (Conger, 1979; Erikson, 1968; Marcia, 1980; Mussen et al., 1990; Waterman, 1982, 1984).

Within a particular society, identities may be typical or deviant: Individuals may seek personal, social, and vocational roles that are expected and approved by society, or they may adopt more idiosyncratic roles. Some unusual roles are positive and constructive, as in the case of the artist or poet who "marches to a different drummer"; others, however, are negative, as in the case of the long-term drug addict or career criminal (Conger & Petersen, 1984; Erikson, 1968).

It is important to keep in mind that the process of identity formation varies from one person to another. The popular stereotype of an acute and prolonged "identity crisis" is probably exaggerated. Indeed, Erikson himself was moved to ask, "Would so many of our youth act so openly confused and confusing if they did not *know* they were supposed to have an identity crisis?" (1968, p. 18–19). The belief that the absence of a period of intense turmoil during adolescence portends later emotional disturbance is not supported by research findings; many adolescents achieve a strong sense of ego identity without serious "storm and stress" (see pages 19–22).

Gender Identity and Sex-Role Identity

An important aspect of identity is **gender identity,** an awareness and acceptance of one's basic biological nature as a male or a female. Most people acquire gender identity early in life (Huston, 1983; Mussen et al., 1990). With the notable exception of transsexuals (who typically report having felt, even as children, that they were trapped in a body of the wrong sex), the great majority of people, including most homosexuals, appear to be content with being male or female and have no desire to change (Green, 1974, 1987; Spence, 1984; Stoller, 1980).

But for those who resent their gender—who are uncomfortable about their sexual nature and procreative capabilities or are hostile toward members of their own or the other sex—adolescence can be a particularly stressful and confusing period. Rapid sexual maturation calls dramatic attention to the fact that one's gender is a biological fact. Conflicts about gender identity are difficult to deal with and are likely to create significant problems in the development of a confident, secure overall identity.

Another sex-related aspect of identity, **sex role identity** enables one to perceive oneself as masculine or feminine according to one's own definition of these terms. This does not require rigid conformity to sex-role stereotypes. In the words of Jeanne Block, a pioneer in sex-role research, "sexual identity means, or will mean, the earning of a sense of self that includes a recognition of gender secure enough to permit the individual to manifest human qualities that our society, until now, has labeled unmanly or unwomanly" (Block, 1984, p. 1). For example, two young women may both have clear and confident sex role identities but may define them quite differently. One may feel that being employed as an independent, competitive corporate executive in a traditionally male business is entirely consistent with a feminine sex role identity, while the other may feel that her feminine identity is best expressed by devoting herself primarily to the roles of wife, mother, and homemaker.

A pattern that has been labeled *androgyny*—the combination of socially valued "masculine" and "feminine" characteristics in the same individual—has recently come to be viewed as socially adaptive (Bem, 1981; Block, 1984; Huston, 1983; Spence, 1984; Spence & Helmreich, 1978; Spence, Helmreich, & Holahan, 1979). In one study, four groups of adolescents and youth were compared: (1) those who scored high on both socially positive masculine characteristics (e.g., independence, assertiveness) and socially positive feminine characteristics (e.g., nurturance, understanding)—the androgyny group; (2) those who scored high only on masculine items; (3) those who scored high only on feminine items; and (4) those who scored low on both, who were referred to as "undifferentiated." As may be seen in Table 2.1, relatively few males or females were "cross-typed"; that is, few males scored highest on feminine items and few females scored highest on masculine items.

Androgynous individuals of both sexes scored highest on measures of self-esteem, followed by the masculine, feminine, and undifferentiated groups. Androgynous individuals also reported receiving more academic and extracurricular honors than undifferentiated individuals. Female athletes and scientists are more likely to score high on androgyny or masculinity rather than solely on femininity. Masculine and androgynous self-perceptions characterize young people of both sexes who value and expect to do well in mathematics, formal logic, and spatial skills (Huston, 1983; Mullis & McKinley, 1989; Nash, 1979; Spence & Helmreich, 1978).

Androgyny is defined by socially valued attributes of both sexes. Negatively valued masculine attributes (e.g., arrogance, greed, hostility) and negatively valued feminine attributes (e.g., being gullible, servile, whiny, nagging) have also been measured. Neither males nor females with such characteristics fare well. They generally have low self-esteem and experience problems of adjustment because they are vulnerable, insecure, and hypersensitive. Individuals of

T A B L E 2.1 PERCENTAGE OF STUDENTS FALLING INTO EACH OF THE FOUR PERSONAL-ATTRIBUTES CATEGORIES FOR COLLEGE AND HIGH SCHOOL SAMPLES

	College Sample			
	Undifferentiated	Feminine	Masculine	Androgynous
Males	25	8	34	32
Females	28	32	14	27

	High School Sample			
	Undifferentiated	Feminine	Masculine	Androgynous
Males	23	8	44	25
Females	18	35	14	35

Source: J. T. Spence. *Traits, roles, and the concept of androgyny.* Paper presented at the Conference on Perspectives on the Psychology of Women, Michigan State University, May 13–14, 1977. By permission.

both sexes with negative masculine attributes tend to be overly aggressive and critical of others (Block, 1973, 1984; Spence, Helmreich, & Holahan, 1979).

Thus, it appears to be desirable to permit individuals of both sexes to be "both independent and tender, assertive and yielding, masculine and feminine, allowing people to cope more effectively with diverse situations" (Bem, 1975, p. 62). Indeed, many people do vary from one situation, task, or setting to another in the extent to which they exhibit one or another gender-related psychological characteristic (Spence, 1984). A young executive may act quite differently in the office than at home with his or her spouse and children. It should be noted, however, that positive masculine attributes, such as independence and self-confidence, are the most important and adaptive components of androgyny, especially for females (Huston, 1983; Mullis & McKinley, 1989).

SUMMARY

Adolescence is a period of rapid change—physical, sexual, and cognitive changes within the young person and changes in the adolescent's world and the demands of society. The physical and sexual maturational changes of puberty are universal. In contrast, the "developmental tasks" that adolescents must master vary in form and difficulty from one society or era to another. Despite these variations, there are some commonalities: In one way or another the young person must achieve independence from parents, adjust to sexual maturation, establish workable relations with peers and adults, prepare for a vocation, and develop a philosophy of life and a set of guiding values.

A fundamental principle of development is that a person evolves as a result of continuing and continuous interaction between a growing, changing biological organism and its physical, psychological, and social environment; that interaction begins in the earliest stages of prenatal development. Implicit in this principle is the concept of antecedent–consequent relationships—the idea that events occurring at one stage of development depend on prior developmental events and, in turn, influence responses to future events.

Biological factors play a role in physical maturation, the development of intelligence, and some mental disorders. They also appear to influence some personality characteristics, particularly basic temperamental characteristics.

The continuing interaction between the growing, changing individual and his or her environment is not random. It is governed by specific principles known as principles, or laws, of learning. *Learning* is the process by which behavior or the potentiality for behavior is modified as a result of experience. Not all behaviors are learned, however; even some complex behaviors, such as nest building, are innately programmed.

Two basic kinds of learning are *classical conditioning* and *operant* or *instrumental conditioning.* Among the more complex human applications of the latter are *behavior modification, behavior therapy,* and *biofeedback.* Not all learning depends on conditioning; many human activities are acquired vicariously through observation of the behavior of others (*observational learning*), a fact that is stressed by *social-learning theorists.* In addition, cognitive psychologists stress the importance of *cognitive processes* in learning; these include processing information, using problem-solving strategies, and storing information in memory and retrieving it.

Important issues in learning theory include the roles of *reinforcement* (reward) and *motivation* (which may include both *primary* and *learned* needs). Other important learning principles are the principle of (stimulus) generalization, the gradient of generalization, discrimination, and extinction.

Adolescents' needs and motives are far more complex than the basic biological needs of the infant, and in some instances they may be unconscious or only partially conscious, particularly when conscious awareness would lead to anxiety or guilt. Sources of anxiety in adolescents may include: fear of loss of control; anxiety about expressing aggression; anxiety over sexuality; anxiety over conflicting dependence and independence needs; anxiety over rationality; anxiety over acceptance by peers; anxiety over competence; anxiety over one's body image; and anxiety over sexual identity.

Because anxiety represents a painful state of tension, individuals are motivated to develop techniques for coping with or defending against anxiety. Coping takes two main forms: *problem-focused coping* and *emotion-focused coping*. An important contribution of psychoanalytic theory is the elucidation of a variety of largely unconscious emotion-focused coping techniques called *defense mechanisms*. These include repression, suppression, denial, projection and displacement, rationalization, reaction formation, withdrawal, regression, and asceticism and intellectualization.

Identification, a concept that was introduced by Freud, refers to the process by which one is led to think, feel, and behave as though the characteristics of another person (or *model*) belong to oneself. Identification goes beyond simple imitation, although it may include imitation of the model's behavior. Identifications with parents and other important figures play an important part in an individual's development, but they cannot by themselves give adolescents a stable, clear sense of identity.

Adolescents must develop a sense of *identity*—an answer to the age-old question, "Who am I?" Individuals with a strong sense of identity perceive themselves as separate from others. They possess self-consistency or a feeling of wholeness, and they have a sense of continuity of the self over time. The development of identity is aided by *psychosocial reciprocity*, or consistency between one's self-perceptions and the way one is perceived by others.

The search for a sense of identity becomes especially relevant during adolescence because the young person is confronted with so many psychological, physiological, sexual, and cognitive changes, as well as so many new demands and expectations. Although earlier identifications play an important role in identity development, something more is needed: *the capacity to synthesize successive identifications into a coherent, consistent, and unique whole*—a capacity aided by the adolescent's more advanced cognitive skills. Self-conceptions become more differentiated and better organized during adolescence.

Identity formation is significantly influenced by relationships within the family. Adolescents who score high on measures of *identity exploration* are likely to come from families in which self-assertion and freedom to disagree ("separateness") are encouraged along with "connectedness" to the family. Two important ways in which identity development can go wrong are *identity foreclosure,* in which identity development is prematurely cut short, and *identity confusion,* in which the development of a clear sense of identity is delayed, in some cases permanently. Individuals who have achieved a strong sense of identity are likely to be more autonomous, creative, resistant to pressure for conformity, and capable of intimacy than those who experience identity foreclosure or identity confusion.

An important aspect of identity is *gender identity,* awareness and acceptance of one's basic biological nature as a male or a female. A confident, secure *sex role identity* entails the perception of oneself as masculine or feminine according to one's own definition of the term; it does not require conformity to sexrole stereotypes. A pattern called *androgyny*—the combination of positive "masculine" and "feminine" characteristics in the same individual—has come to be viewed as socially adaptive.

REVIEW QUESTIONS

1. What roles do reinforcement and motivation play in learning? What is meant by the terms *generalization, discrimination,* and *extinction*?
2. Discuss the more frequent sources of anxiety among adolescents.
3. Describe the two main types of coping techniques. Which category includes psychoanalytic defense mechanisms?
4. What is meant by the terms *identification* and *identity*? How are they related?
5. What are the three main characteristics of a fully developed sense of identity?
6. How do the personality characteristics and parent–child relationships of adolescents and youth with an achieved sense of identity differ from those of young people who have experienced identity foreclosure or identity confusion?
7. Distinguish between gender identity and sex role identity. How is sex role identity related to overall identity?

RECOMMENDED READINGS

Block, J. H. (1984). *Sex role identity and ego development.* San Francisco: Jossey-Bass.

Bower, G. H., & Hilgard, E. R. (1981). *Theories of learning* (5th ed.). Englewood Cliffs, NJ: Prentice-Hall.

Erikson, E. H. (1968). *Identity: Youth and crisis.* New York: Norton.

Frank, A. (1972). *Diary of a young girl* (B. M. Mooyart, trans.). New York: Pocket Books.

Miller, N. E. (1984). Learning: Some facts and needed research relevant to maintaining health. In J. Matarazzo, S. W. Weiss, J. A. Herd, N. Miller, & S. M. Weiss (Eds.), *Behavioral health: A handbook of health enhancement and disease prevention* (pp. 199–208). New York: Wiley.

BIOLOGICAL CHANGES IN ADOLESCENCE

Adolescence, it has been said, begins in biology and ends in culture. The biological changes that accompany adolescence are inevitable and dramatic. They include rapid increases in height and weight, changes in body proportions, the development of secondary sex characteristics, the maturation of reproductive capacity, and further growth and differentiation of cognitive abilities. These biological changes and the young person's need to adjust to them differentiate adolescence from earlier periods of development. In contrast, culture determines whether adolescence is long or short and whether its social demands represent an abrupt change or only a gradual transition from earlier periods of development.

The culture of a society may facilitate or hinder the young person's adjustment to the biological changes of puberty. It also influences whether these changes are a source of pride or of anxiety and confusion. But culture cannot change the fact that these changes will occur and must be coped with somehow. Moreover, were it not for the biological maturation that occurs during adolescence, young people would not be able to meet many of the demands made upon them in most cultures—whether the demands are for academic competence; for physical or vocational skills; or for heterosexual relationships, marriage, and parenthood.

For all of these reasons, as well as the fact that development results from the interaction between a biological organism and its environment, it is important to consider in some detail the nature of the biological changes that accompany adolescence and their effects on the individual. In this chapter we are concerned primarily with physical and physiological development—the external and internal aspects of biological development. Later we will consider intellectual and cognitive development and the psychological and behavioral consequences of sexual maturation.

PUBERTY

The term **puberty** refers to the first phase of adolescence, when sexual maturation becomes evident. Strictly speaking, puberty begins with hormonal increases and their manifestations, such as gradual enlargement of the ovaries in females and testicular cell growth in males. But because these changes are not outwardly observable, the onset of puberty is often measured by such events as the emergence of pubic hair in boys and girls, the beginning of elevation of the breasts in girls, and growth of the penis and testicles in boys. Another major aspect of puberty is an accelerated increase in height and weight that usually lasts about four years.

Hormonal Factors in Development

As we shall see, the timing and course of the various developmental phenomena that surround puberty—such as the so-called "growth spurt" and sexual maturation—are closely related. This should not be surprising in view of the fact that hormones from the endocrine glands are among the principal agents "for translating the instructions of the genes into the reality of the adult form" (Tanner, 1970, p. 112). And the actions of these hormones in stimulating physical growth, sexual maturation, and other physiological aspects of development are themselves interrelated.

The **pituitary gland,** located immediately below the brain, is critical to the orderly regulation of growth . When the cells of the hypothalamus, a central regulating nerve center in the brain, mature, signals are sent to the pituitary gland to begin releasing certain hormones (Higham, 1980; Petersen, 1988; Petersen & Taylor, 1980). Those hormones, in turn, stimulate other endocrine glands, including the thyroid and adrenal glands and the testes and ovaries, to release specific growth and sex-related hormones. The latter include **androgens** (masculinizing hormones), **estrogens** (feminizing hormones), and **progestins** (pregnancy hormones). These and other hormones interact in complex ways to stimulate the orderly progression of physical and physiological development during puberty and adolescence. For example, the development of pubic and other body hair is linked to the production of adrenal androgens, while the development of fluctuating levels of estrogen and progesterone are involved in **menarche** (the onset of menstruation) (Bell, 1987; Money & Ehrhardt, 1972).

The Timing of Puberty

Exactly when puberty begins depends on a variety of factors, not all of which are understood. Genetic influences obviously play a role; for example, the onset of puberty and subsequent events, such as menarche, occur closer together among identical (monozygotic) twins than among nonidentical (dizygotic) twins (Marshall, 1978; Tanner, 1970). Within the limits set by heredity, environmental influences—especially nutrition and health—are also important. Puberty occurs earlier among young people who have been well nourished throughout their development; chronic illness and hazardous living conditions are also associated with delayed puberty (Marshall, 1978).

There are also some racial and ethnic differences in the timing of puberty; for example, African girls experience menarche earlier than European girls (Eveleth & Tanner, 1978). However, when variations in general health and nutrition between and within countries are taken into account, such differences are significantly reduced or eliminated (see Figure 3.1).

Hormonal Dimorphism

In the early days of sex hormone research, when sex differences were thought to be absolute, it was assumed that females produce only female sex hormones and males only male sex hormones. In reality, however, the hormones of both sexes are present in both men and women (Gupta, Attanasio, & Raaf, 1975; Money & Erhardt, 1972; Petersen & Taylor, 1980). All three kinds of sex hormones are similar in chemical structure, and each may be produced in the ovary or testis, the cortex of the adrenal gland, or other glands or tissues. The hormonal differences between the sexes, and corresponding differences in

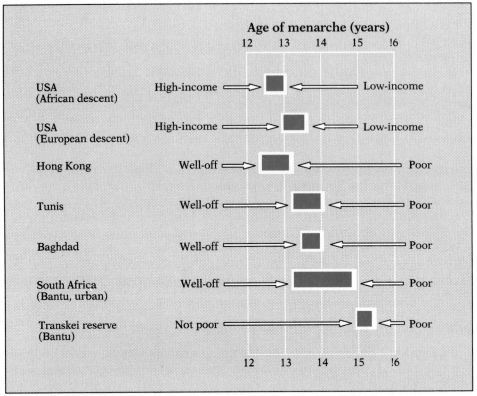

Figure 3.1 Median ages of menarche in well-off and poor population samples. Shaded areas show difference between median ages in each geographic area. (From P. B. Eveleth & J. M. Tanner (1978), *Worldwide variation in human growth*. Cambridge: Cambridge University Press. By permission.)

sexual characteristics, are actually differences in the proportions of masculinizing and feminizing hormones present in males and females. As may be seen in Figure 3.2, as puberty proceeds, the ratio of estrogen to testosterone increases in girls and decreases in boys.

THE ADOLESCENT GROWTH SPURT

The term *growth spurt* refers to the accelerated rate of increase in height and weight that accompanies the onset of adolescence. This increase varies widely in intensity, duration, and timing from one child to another, even among entirely normal children—a fact that is often poorly understood by adolescents and their parents and, hence, too often a source of needless concern.

In both boys and girls, the **adolescent growth spurt** takes about $4\frac{1}{2}$ years (Faust, 1977; Tanner, 1970; Thissen, Bock, Wainer, & Roche, 1976). For the

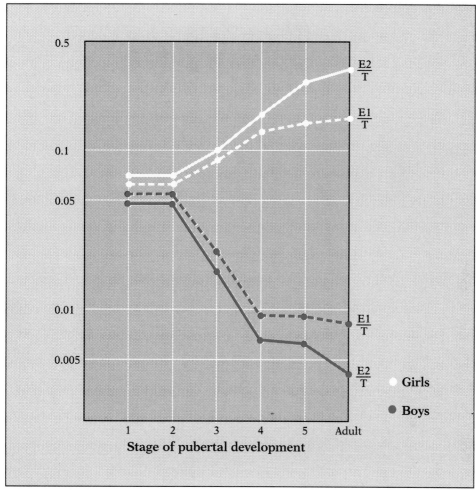

Figure 3.2 Mean trends in estrogen/testosterone ratios during pubertal development for girls and boys. Two measures of estrogen levels are shown: estrone (E1) and the more potent estradiol (E2). (From D. Gupta, A. Attanasio, & S. Raaf. Plasma estrogen and androgen concentrations in children during adolescence. *Journal of Clinical Endrochrinology and Metabolism*, 1975, 40, 636–643. By permission.)

average boy in the United States, peak growth occurs at age 13; in girls it occurs about two years earlier, at age 11. Whereas in the average boy the adolescent growth spurt begins a few months before his eleventh birthday, it may begin as early as age 9; the spurt usually ends shortly after age 15, but it may continue until age 17. In girls the entire process begins, and ends, about two years earlier. Further slow growth may continue for several years after the spurt has ended (see Figure 3.3).

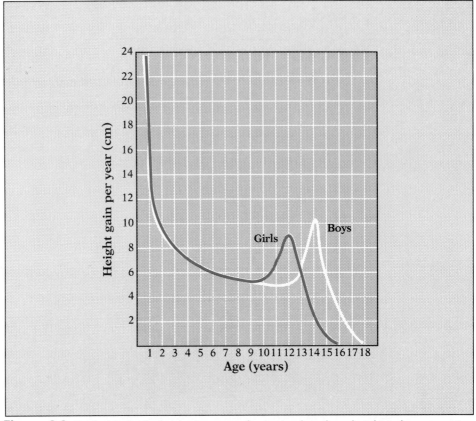

Figure 3.3 Typical individual velocity curves for supine length or height in boys or girls. These curves represent the velocity of the typical boy or girl at any given instant. (From J. M. Tanner, R. H. Whitehouse, & M. Takaishi. Standards from birth to maturing for height velocity, and weight velocity: British children, 1965. *Archives of Disease in Childhood,* 1966, 41, 455–471. By permission.)

Because the timing of the growth spurt is so variable, some young people will complete the spurt before others have begun. Figure 3.4 illustrates how widely the onset, pattern, and end of the growth spurt can vary among normal adolescent girls; as can be seen, girl A's growth spurt was completed a year before girl B's began. Clearly, *normal* does not mean average.

Events occurring within the normal growth spurt are not independent of one another. For example, girls with an early growth spurt tend to reach menarche earlier than those with a later growth spurt (Faust, 1977; Onat & Ertem, 1974; Petersen, 1979; Tanner, 1970). Similarly, in boys the period of most rapid growth tends to be closely related to the development of secondary sex characteristics like axillary (body) hair and pubic hair.

One of the matters that are likely to generate concern in adolescents and their parents is ultimate height (Conger, 1979). In view of current masculine and feminine stereotypes, this is especially true of boys who are short and girls who are afraid of growing too tall. Much of this concern is exaggerated, however. Height before the growth spurt is correlated with ultimate height, which means, for example, that a young person who is in the twenty-fifth percentile in height prior to the growth spurt is likely to be in the twenty-fifth percentile after puberty (Faust, 1977; Tanner, 1970). Girls who are early maturers do tend to be somewhat shorter at the onset of puberty than late maturers, but they also grow more rapidly during the growth spurt and their growth spurt tends to be longer. Conversely, late maturers tend to be somewhat taller at the beginning of the growth spurt, but they also tend to have shorter, less intense periods of growth. The net result is that early maturers as a group do not end up any taller or shorter than girls who mature later (Faust, 1977). Once an

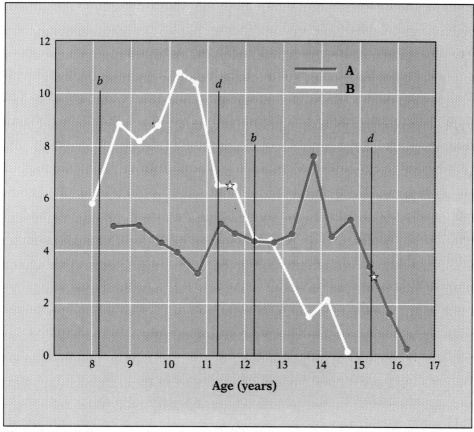

Figure 3.4 Differences in timing of the pubertal growth period in height. The early developing girl reached the end (d) of the pubertal period before the late-developing girl reached onset (b). Stars indicate onset of menarche. (From M. S. Faust. Somatic development of adolescent girls. *Monographs of the Society for Research in Child Development,* 1977, 42, 1, Serial No. 169. By permission.)

Because the timing of the growth spurt is so variable, some adolescents will complete the growth spurt before others have begun.

early-maturing girl and her late-maturing peers have passed the period of rapid growth, their comparative heights are most likely to resemble those of the period before adolescence. Similar developmental phenomena occur in boys.

Although increases in weight tend to follow the general curve for height in both males and females, there are some differences. While increased weight obviously reflects skeletal growth, it also reflects increases in muscle and fat tissue and in the size of various internal organs. As we shall see, several of these systems, though not unrelated to skeletal development, have their own timetables. Because weight reflects a combination of developmental events, it is not a very informative statistic. For example, an increase in weight may reflect increased bone or muscle development or simply an increase in fat. Thus, an adolescent's weight curve may suggest continued normal development when this is not in fact the case. Similarly, failure to gain weight or even actual loss of weight in an adolescent may merely reflect increased attention to diet and exercise. In contrast, failure to gain greater height and more muscle may be a sign of an endocrinological or other disorder.

Environmental conditions such as malnutrition, disease, and severe psychological stress may affect growth rate, final height, and (to a lesser extent) body shape (Eveleth & Tanner, 1978; Tanner, 1970). Under optimal conditions, however, genetic factors appear to play a major role. Nancy Bayley has shown that there is an increasingly significant correlation between midparent height (average height of the two parents) and the heights of their children at increasing ages from 6 to 18. Interestingly, correlations appear to be highest for fathers and daughters, followed by fathers and sons, mothers and daughters, and mothers and sons (Bayley, 1954; Eichorn, 1970, 1975).

The Shape of Things to Come

Rapid acceleration in height and weight is accompanied by changes in body proportions in both males and females. Although virtually all parts of the skeletal and muscular systems take part in the growth spurt, they do so to differing extents and according to different timetables. The parts of the body that reach adult size and form earliest are the head, hands, and feet. Increases in the length of arms and legs reach their peak before increases in body width (including shoulder width). Adult trunk length is achieved last, although it accounts for the greatest proportion of the total increase in height during the growth spurt. The effect is that "a boy stops growing out of his trousers (at least in length) a year before he stops growing out of his jackets" (Tanner, 1970, p. 94).

The disparate rates of growth in the various parts of the skeletal structure (which are even more varied in some atypical young people) often produce feelings of awkwardness. Adolescents may feel at times that their hands and feet are too big or that they are "all legs."

More subtle changes in physique also occur during this period. The last traces of the baby face of childhood disappear. The forehead becomes higher and wider; the mouth widens, and the relatively flat lips of childhood become fuller; the slightly receding chin of earlier years begins to jut out (Mussen, Conger, & Kagan, 1979). And of course, as head growth diminishes while other parts of the skeletal system continue to grow, the large head that is characteristic of childhood becomes smaller in relation to total body size (see Figure 3.5).

Changes like those just described reflect the fact that as skeletal structures increase in length they also change in width, proportions, and composition.

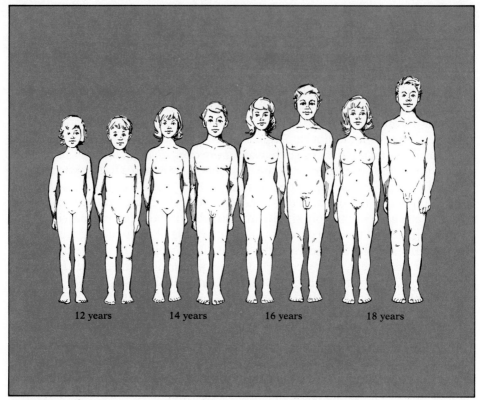

Figure 3.5 Body growth and development from age 12 to age 18.

Thus, bone width, as well as length, increases during this period. Interestingly, differences in bone width between boys and girls are minimal during childhood, although from birth onward girls are slightly ahead of boys in bone age (Marshall & Tanner, 1970; Neinstein, 1984; Tanner, 1968, 1970, 1971). However, bone growth is clearly greater in males during adolescence. The composition of the skeletal structure also changes. During early childhood the bones have relatively more cartilage and fibrous tissues and less mineral matter than is the case later. This makes the bones somewhat spongy and soft as well as more flexible. But as the skeletal structures increase in size, the cartilage begins to calcify, making the bones harder, denser, and more brittle.

Although before puberty the ratio of shoulder width to hip width is higher for girls than for boys, the picture reverses dramatically soon after the beginning of the growth spurt. The extent of this difference continues to increase until adult height is reached. However, variability in hip width is significantly greater among girls than among boys at all stages of development (Faust, 1977; Tanner, 1970, 1971).

Differential Development of Muscle and Fat. Changes in adolescent physique reflect changes in the development of muscle and body fat as well as changes in skeletal structure. In both boys and girls muscular development proceeds rapidly as height increases, reaching a peak rate of growth slightly after the peak in the rate of increase in height. Boys, however, experience a more rapid rate of increase than girls do, with the result that their overall gain in muscle tissue during this period is greater than that for girls—an advantage they retain throughout the adult years (Marino & King, 1980; Neinstein, 1984; Tanner, 1968, 1970).

Conversely, in both boys and girls there is a decline in the rate of development of fat during the growth spurt—a decline that reaches its maximum velocity at the point of maximum increase in height. In girls the decline is not enough to offset a modest absolute gain in fat during this period (as many girls are only too aware). In boys, however, the rate of decline is so great that it produces an actual (though temporary) loss of fat in the months preceding and following the point of peak increase in height.

Although both muscle and fat are influenced by the sex hormones, they are also influenced by exercise, an activity that also differs in boys and girls. Studies that control for amount of exercise still find male-female differences in the percentage of body weight due to fat, but the differences are much smaller than those found in the population as a whole (Woods, Haskell, Stern, & Perry, 1977).

Changes in Strength and Tolerance for Exercise. The acceleration of muscular development that takes place during adolescence is, not surprisingly, accompanied by increases in strength, as measured by such indices as hand grip and pulling and pushing strength in the arms (Carron & Bailey, 1974; Faust, 1977; Malina, 1974). On the average, the greatest overall increment in strength occurs about one year after the peak increase in height and weight. The relative increases are much greater for boys than for girls, although the distribution of overall strength scores (arm pull, arm thrust, hand grip) of boys and girls overlaps at every point in development (see Figure 3.6). For the most part, prepubescent boys and girls are similar in strength, but after adolescence boys are much stronger. This greater strength is primarily a function of greater muscular development; however, it is probably due partly to certain related factors as well. Thus, relative to their size, boys develop larger lungs and heart, higher systolic blood pressure, greater capacity for carrying oxygen in the blood, lower heart rate while at rest, and greater ability to neutralize the chemical products of muscular exercise, such as lactic acid, which is felt as fatigue (Tanner, 1970). It seems likely that some of the greater increase in strength and tolerance for exercise among boys has been due—at least until recently—to more physical exercise, since there was a cultural pressure on girls to decrease such "masculine" activity at adolescence (Petersen & Taylor, 1980).

Increases in strength during adolescence are probably reflected in the greater emphasis on athletic activities that is likely to occur at this time, partic-

The acceleration of muscular development that takes place in adolescence is accompanied by marked increases in strength and exercise tolerance.

ularly in boys. In this connection, Tanner lays to rest the popular notion of a boy outgrowing his strength during these years. He comments:

> A short period may exist when the adolescent, having completed his skeletal and probably also muscular growth, still does not have the strength of a young adult of the same body size and shape. But this is a temporary phase; considered absolutely, power, athletic skill, and physical endurance all increase progressively and rapidly throughout adolescence. It is certainly not true that the changes accompanying adolescence enfeeble, even temporarily. If the adolescent becomes weak and easily exhausted, it is for psychological reasons and not physiological ones (1970, pp. 96–97).

Other Aspects of Adolescent Growth

While the visible aspects of the growth spurt, such as increased height and weight and changes in muscle and fat, are taking place, other less readily apparent but equally important changes are also occurring. As already noted, a number of these changes, though related to the onset and course of the rapid increase in height, have their own timetables within the overall developmental sequence.

Growth of the Heart. During the adolescent years, the heart's transverse diameter increases by about half and its weight almost doubles. In the earlier years of childhood, boys' hearts are slightly larger than girls'. Although acceleration in the growth rate of the heart occurs earlier in girls (in accordance with their earlier overall growth spurt), the total growth is not as great for girls as it is for boys. The result is that by late adolescence boys have significantly larger hearts than girls do (Litt & Vaughn, 1987). Whereas heart rate in both boys and girls falls gradually during the entire period of growth, the decline during adolescence is slightly faster for boys, so that by age 17 the average boy's heart rate is about 5 beats per minute slower than the average girl's (Eichorn, 1970; Neinstein, 1984).

Conversely, systolic blood pressure rises steadily throughout childhood, accelerating rapidly during the years immediately prior to puberty and for about six months thereafter. It then tends to settle at a somewhat lower level; sexual maturity apparently stabilizes the upward trend of blood pressure. The pulse rate also increases during the prepubescent years, reaching a maximum prior to puberty and declining thereafter (Behrman, Vaughn, & Nelson, 1987).

Growth of the Lungs. Lung growth is similar to heart growth. The steady gradual increase of the childhood years gives way to a rapid acceleration dur-

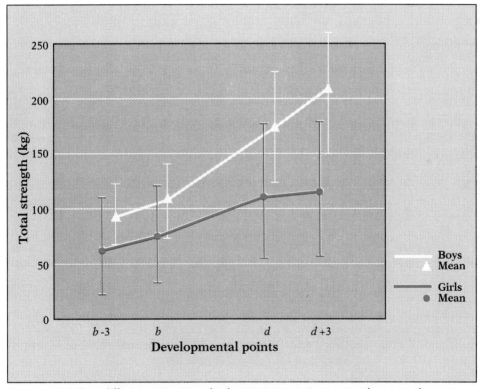

Figure 3.6 Sex differences in strength, showing extreme scores and mean values at four developmental points: beginning of prepuberty (b−3), onset (b) and end (d) of pubertal period, and end of postpubertal period (d+3). (From M. S. Faust. Somatic development of adolescent girls. *Monographs of the Society for Research in Child Development,* 1977, 42, 1, Serial No. 169. By permission.)

ing the years of maximum growth in both boys and girls; the greatest growth occurs in boys. On measures of vital capacity (the amount of air that can be exhaled after a deep breath), boys exceed girls up until about 10 years of age, at which point there is no significant difference between the two. However, beginning at about 11½, boys again exceed girls, and the difference continues to increase throughout the growth years as a function both of boys' larger hearts and of their typically greater amount of exercise (Ferris, Whittenberger, & Gallagher, 1952; Litt & Vaughn, 1987).

Development of the Brain. In contrast to the marked increases in the heart and lungs that accompany adolescence, there is little further growth in the size of the brain during this period. Whereas the average child has acquired only about 50 percent of total adult weight by the age of 10, he or she has acquired 95 percent of adult brain weight (Litt & Vaughn, 1987; Neinstein, 1984; Tanner, 1970, 1971).

Although the size of the brain changes little after age 5, neural changes continue to occur (Graber & Petersen, in press). **Myelination** (the development of a fatty sheath around certain nerve fibers) facilitates rapid transmission of neural impulses. This process continues at least to puberty and may be lifelong (Yakoler & Lecours, 1967). Recent evidence suggests that overproduction of neural pathways occurs from age 5 to age 10, with a significant decline from age 10 to age 15; this decline is thought to reflect fine-tuning of the neurological system (Feinberg, 1987).

Basal Metabolism. Another change occurring during this period is a rather sudden decline in basal metabolism (the energy turnover of the body at a standard low level of activity). Although both boys and girls show a continuous decrease in metabolic rate following puberty, boys retain a higher rate than girls do, probably partly as a function of greater muscular development, which requires greater consumption of oxygen, and perhaps also because of hormonal differences between boys and girls (Tanner, 1962, 1970, 1971).

Nutritional Needs. The nutritional needs of the young person during the years of accelerated growth increase considerably. although there is a wide variation from one individual to another, depending on both body size and activity level. On the average, young people gain 50 percent of their adult weight, 20 percent of their adult height, and 50 percent of their adult skeletal mass during adolescence (Litt & Vaughn, 1987; Neinstein, 1984). For this reason, and because dietary habits formed in adolescence are likely to continue into adulthood, it is important for adolescents to learn sound nutritional practices (see pages 108–109). As can be seen in Table 3.1, the nutritional needs of the average boy consistently exceed those of the average girl, although sex differences are far greater following the growth spurt owing primarily to size differences. Nevertheless, at any age a large, extremely active girl will obviously have greater nutritional needs than a small, relatively inactive boy (Alton, 1982; Dwyer, 1980; Marino & King, 1980; Neinstein, 1984). The needs

T A B L E 3.1 RECOMMENDED DAILY DIETARY ALLOWANCES (CALORIES)

	Age	Weight (lb.)	Height (in.)	Calories
Boys	11–14	99	61	2700
	15–18	145	69	2800
	19–22	154	69	2800
Girls	11–14	101	61	2200
	15–18	121	64	2200
	19–22	121	64	2200

Sources: National Academy of Sciences, National Research Council. *Recommended dietary allowances.* Washington, D.C.: National Academy of Sciences, National Research Council, 1980 (9th ed.); Alton, I. R., 1982; Neinstein, 1984.

of early and late maturers will also differ. Both persistent overeating and chronic loss of appetite (anorexia nervosa) may result from emotional problems during the adolescent years (see Chapter 15).

Severe undernutrition in infancy has been found to have long-term effects on development that continue through adolescence (Galler, 1984). Interestingly, effects on physical growth can be corrected, but behavioral and cognitive effects persist even after adequate nutrition has been restored (Lozoff, 1989; Petersen, Beard, & Susman, 1989).

SEXUAL MATURATION

The adolescent growth spurt is accompanied by sexual maturation in both boys and girls. The rapidity of all these changes—most of which take place within a period of only about four years—may give young people a feeling of being spectators of their own growth and development. Many adolescents seem to be waiting, sometimes self-consciously, to find out what will happen next.

Sexual Maturation in Boys

Although testicular cell growth and secretion of male sex hormones begin earlier—typically about 11½ (Litt & Vaughn, 1987; Neinstein, 1984; Tanner, 1962, 1970)—the first outward sign of impending sexual maturity in boys is usually an increase in the rate of growth of the testes and scrotum (the baglike structure enclosing the testes) (see Table 3.2). Growth of pubic hair may also begin at about the same time or shortly thereafter. Approximately a year later an acceleration in the rate of growth of the penis accompanies the beginning of the growth spurt in height. Axillary (body) and facial hair usually make their first appearance about two years after the beginning of pubic-hair growth, although the relationship between the two is variable and in a few boys axillary

The rapidity of physical growth and sexual maturation sometimes gives young people a feeling of being spectators of their own growth and development.

hair actually appears first (Harlan, Grillo, Cornoni-Huntley, & Leaverton, 1979; Neinstein, 1984; Tanner, 1970, 1971). The ultimate amount of body hair developed by both males and females appears to depend largely on genetic factors.

Although the process begins earlier, a definite lowering of the voice usually occurs fairly late in puberty. In some boys this voice change is rather abrupt and dramatic, whereas in others it occurs so gradually that it is hardly perceptible. During this process the larynx (Adam's apple) enlarges significantly and the vocal cords (which it contains) approximately double in length, with a consequent drop in pitch of about an octave. It may take two or more years for a boy to achieve control of his voice in the lower register, and during that time the instability of his vocal tones may become a source of embarrassment.

The insensitivity of adults who tease boys about these changes, even in a friendly manner, is obvious. The first shave may be a welcome sign of adulthood or an embarrassing experience for a boy, depending on whether his parents treat it as a matter of course or poke fun at him (Conger, 1979).

During adolescence the male breast also undergoes changes. The diameter of the areola (the area surrounding the nipple) increases considerably (although not as much as in girls) and is accompanied by elevation of the nipple. In some boys (perhaps 20–30 percent) there may also be a distinct enlargement of the breast about midway through adolescence (Bell, 1987; Tanner, 1970); this usually disappears within a year or so. Although this enlargement is

---

T A B L E 3.2 MATURATION IN BOYS AND IN GIRLS

Although there may be some individual—and perfectly normal—variations in the sequence of events leading to physical and sexual maturity in boys, the following sequence is typical:

1. Testes and scrotum begin to increase in size.
2. Pubic hair begins to appear.
3. Adolescent growth spurt starts; the penis begins to enlarge.
4. Voice deepens as the larynx grows.
5. Hair begins to appear under the arms and on the upper lip.
6. Sperm production increases, and nocturnal emission (ejaculation of semen during sleep) may occur.
7. Growth spurt reaches peak rate; pubic hair becomes pigmented.
8. Prostate gland enlarges.
9. Sperm production becomes sufficient for fertility; growth rate decreases.
10. Physical strength reaches a peak.

Although, as in the case of boys, there may be normal variations in the sequence of physical and sexual maturation in girls, a typical sequence of events is as follows:

1. Adolescent growth spurt begins.
2. Downy (nonpigmented) pubic hair makes its initial appearance.
3. Elevation of the breast (the so-called bud stage of development) and rounding of the hips begin, accompanied by the appearance of downy axillary (armpit) hair.
4. The uterus and vagina, as well as the labia and clitoris, increase in size.
5. Pubic hair grows rapidly and becomes slightly pigmented.
6. Breasts develop further; nipple pigmentation begins; areola increases in size; axillary hair becomes slightly pigmented.
7. Growth spurt reaches peak rate and then declines.
8. Menarche (onset of menstruation) occurs.
9. Pubic hair development is completed, followed by mature breast development and completion of axillary hair development.
10. Period of "adolescent sterility" ends; girl becomes capable of conception (up to a year or so after menarche).

---

usually temporary and is quite normal, its superficial resemblance to female breast development can be a source of needless anxiety to the boy and his parents.

Prepubescent boys may also show a tendency toward adiposity in the lower torso, which, again, may suggest feminine body contours to the apprehensive adolescent or adult. Although this body configuration typically disappears with the growth spurt in height, it also may generate unnecessary concern. There is no evidence that in the absence of specific pathology either of these conditions is related to any deficiency in sexual functioning. As in so many other areas of adolescent development, more accurate knowledge could eliminate a great deal of unnecessary anxiety and even misery.

Sexual Maturation in Girls

Although hormonal stimulation of the sex glands begins earlier, at about age 9 or 10 the appearance of unpigmented, downy pubic hair is usually the first outward sign of sexual maturity in girls (Faiman & Winter, 1974; Harlan, Harlan, & Grillo, 1980). However, in about 17 percent of girls the beginning of elevation of the breasts (the so-called bud stage of breast development) may precede the appearance of pubic hair (Faust, 1977). Budding of the breasts is accompanied by the emergence of downy, unpigmented axillary (body) hair and by increases in estrogen secretion. In the following year the uterus and vagina show accelerated growth; the labia and clitoris also enlarge (Petersen & Taylor, 1980). Pubic hair becomes moderately well developed, and vaginal secretion begins. By age 12 the nipples show pigmentation and the breasts show further development toward their mature form. At about 12½ (i.e., fairly late in the developmental sequence) the first menstruation occurs. By this time, most girls are in the final stages of pubic-hair development and are approaching the final stages of breast and axillary-hair development.

Frequently there is a period which may last up to a year and a half following the beginning of menstruation, during which the adolescent girl is not yet physiologically capable of conception. Similarly, boys are able to have intercourse long before the emergence of live spermatozoa. However, because of significant individual differences sexually active adolescents cannot assume that they are "safe" from conception because of their age. Some girls are capable of conception within the first year after menarche, a period that was formerly thought to be "safe" (Zabin, Kantner, & Zelnick, 1979).

Normal Variations in Development

It should be emphasized that the average developmental sequences for boys and girls discussed here are just that—*average*. Among normal boys and girls there are wide variations in the age of onset of the developmental sequence, as well as significant, though generally much smaller, variations in the interrelationships among events within the sequence (Eichorn, 1975). For example, whereas maturation of the penis may be complete in some boys by age 13½, for others it may not be complete until 17 or even later. Pubic-hair development may vary even more. The bud stage of breast development may occur as early as age 8 in some girls and as late as 13 in others (Faust, 1960; Harlan et al., 1980; Tanner, 1969, 1970). Age of menarche may vary from about 9 to 16½. The great differences in rates of development that occur among normal boys and girls are illustrated in Figure 3.7, which shows the differing degrees of pubertal maturity among three normal boys, all aged 14¾, and three normal girls, all age 12¾.

As we have noted, although the age of onset of the developmental sequence may vary widely, there is much less variation within individual sequences, that is, the order in which various developmental changes occur. For example, in a longitudinal study of forty-nine normal girls at the Fels Research Institute, the correlation between age at appearance of breast buds and age at subsequent

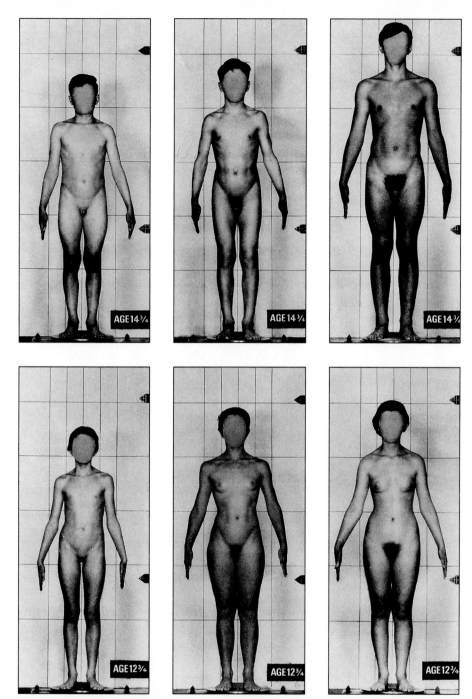

Figure 3.7 Different degrees of pubertal development at the same chronological age. Upper row: three boys, all age 14¾. Lower row: three girls all age 12¾. (From J. M. Tanner. Growth and endocrinology of the adolescent. In J. J. Gardner [Ed.], *Endocrine and genetic diseases of childhood* (2nd ed.). Philadelphia: Saunders, 1975. By permission.)

Box 3.1 CHILDREN AS MOTHERS?

During the past century there has been a trend toward earlier physical and sexual maturation among both boys and girls, including a slower rate of change among U.S. adolescents (see figure B3.1). Does this mean, as a number of social scientists have concluded, that a relentless evolutionary trend is at work and that we can expect the average girl in the next century to begin menstruation at 9 or 10?

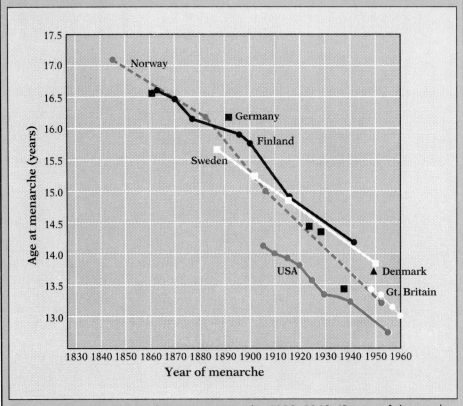

Figure B3.1 Secular trend in age at menarche, 1830–1960. (Source of data and method of plotting detailed in J. M. Tanner, *Growth at Adolescence*.)

Fortunately, the answer is no. When age of menarche is compared across generations reared under nearly identical conditions, no dramatic downward trend in menarcheal age is found. Rather than being due to a continuing evolutionary trend, earlier maturation appears to be a result of general health and nutrition throughout the entire developmental period. For example, during World War II age of menarche was significantly retarded in a number of European countries with temporarily inadequate diets.

Moreover, although good nutrition and health care and an optimal physical environment may accelerate maturation, it appears that they can do so only within the ultimate, genetically determined limits for a particular population. Current estimates of the biological limit for age of menarche for the *average* girl are around 12¼ years. While we can and should be concerned about the recent "epidemic" of adolescent pregnancies, we are not likely to have to set up prenatal classes for 9-year-olds.

Sources: (1) *A history of the study of human growth.* Cambridge, England: Cambridge University Press, 1981. (2) A. F. Roche (Ed.). Secular trends in human growth, maturation, and development. *Monographs of the Society for Research in Child Development,* 1979. Serial No. 179. (3) V. L. Bullough. Age at menarche: A misunderstanding. *Science,* 1981, **213,** 365–366.

menarche was .86, a very high correlation for biological events. Similar relationships were found among various developmental measures for boys (Reynolds & Wines, 1948, 1951). Even such high correlations allow room for a fair amount of individual variation, however (Eichorn, 1975). For example, in the Fels study, genital maturation began before the appearance of pubic hair in 70 percent of the boys; the two events occurred at approximately the same age in 16 percent; and in 14 percent the order of appearance was reversed.

PSYCHOLOGICAL ASPECTS OF ADOLESCENT GROWTH AND DEVELOPMENT

Many adults have managed to repress anxiety-producing memories of the needs, desires, and fears associated with their own adolescence. Even college students are better at remembering events that occurred in earlier years than events occurring around puberty. Consequently, adults are likely to have only a vague recollection of how acutely aware they were of the adolescent growth process.

The intensity of the adolescent's awareness of his or her own development stems largely from the rapid changes occurring during this period. As discussed earlier, a central problem of the adolescent period is the development of a sense of identity. This requires, among other things, a feeling of *consistency over time*—of being similar to, and having consistent links with, the person one was yesterday and will be tomorrow (see pages 54–56). The adolescent is faced with rapid increases in height, changing body proportions, and the objective and subjective changes related to sexual maturation. All of these changes threaten the feeling of self-consistency, and the adolescent needs time to integrate them into a positive, self-confident personal identity.

Developmental changes and the need to adjust to them cause adolescents to focus on physical aspects of the self. However, the nature of that concern is influenced by a number of other factors. With the onset of adolescence and the shift from the family to the peer group as a major source of security and status, conformity to the behavior, appearance, and physical skills of peers becomes increasingly important (see pages 52–54). Like any group that is concerned about where it stands and where it is going, the adolescent peer group tends to be more harshly critical of deviation than groups that are more secure and confident in their social identity. Although there are signs of somewhat greater tolerance for diversity among some groups of youth today, deviance in rate of development and physical appearance can still be an agonizing experience for many adolescents, particularly younger ones (Conger, 1979).

In addition to feeling that they must conform to the norms of their peer group, adolescents tend to have idealized norms of physical appearance and skills that are based on cultural stereotypes of masculinity and femininity. Advertisements in popular magazines, for example, reflect stereotypes that bear little relationship to real people (Faust, 1983)—yet adolescents yearn to resemble the athletic men or the trim, slim women portrayed in them. This is a difficult enough ideal for boys to obtain, but it is an impossible one for girls (Brooks-Gunn, 1988; Striegel-Moore, Silberstein, & Rodin, 1986). As we have seen, among boys adolescent weight gain occurs primarily in muscle and lean tissue; in girls, however, the gain is mainly in fat tissue. Before puberty girls have 10–15 percent more fat than boys, but after puberty they have nearly twice as much (Marino & King, 1980). Thus, "whereas physical maturation brings boys closer to the masculine ideal, for most girls it means a development away from what is currently considered beautiful" (Striegel-Moore et al., 1986, p. 250).

Not surprisingly, although both boys and girls are sensitive to, and often critical of, their changing physical selves (Blyth et al., 1981; Blyth, Simmons, & Zakin, 1985; Clausen, 1975; Lerner & Karabenick, 1974; Petersen, 1988), girls are more likely than boys to be dissatisfied with their appearance and body image—particularly in the early adolescent years (Brooks-Gunn, 1988; Crockett & Petersen, 1987; Simmons & Rosenberg, 1975; Striegel-Moore et al., 1986). Moreover, for girls outward appearance and inner self-image are more closely linked than for boys. Girls are more likely than boys to interpret objective remarks about appearance, such as "You look awful," to mean "You are awful." Despite recent changes in sex role concepts, which have resulted in more flexibility and greater allowance for individual differences, the average girl's self-esteem is still more anchored to interpersonal relationships than is the case for boys (Lerner & Karabenick, 1974; Marshall & Karabenick, 1975; Petersen, 1988). These findings may help explain why girls are somewhat more likely than boys to go through a period of lower self-esteem and more depressed feelings during early to middle adolescence, when maturational changes are greatest (Brooks-Gunn, 1988; Petersen, 1988; Simmons, Blyth, & McKinney, 1983).

It is important to note that self-perceptions are not always a result of objective realities. Adolescents' body image may be influenced by prior experiences that have led them to view themselves as attractive or unattractive, strong or weak, masculine or feminine—regardless of their actual appearance and capabilities. Thus, a boy with low self-esteem who is of average overall size and strength may view himself as smaller and weaker than he really is. Not infrequently, a boy or girl who feels guilty about masturbation may find "evidence" of resulting physical abnormalities ranging from acne, circles under the eyes, or fatigue to supposed deformities in the appearance of the sexual organs—none of which has any objective basis. Or a girl who is quite beautiful in terms of cultural stereotypes may view herself as unattractive because she has been told for years that she looks like a parent or other relative whom she resents or whom others have denigrated.

Whereas adolescents' perceptions of their physical appearance can be influenced by their general image of themselves as people—that is, their overall self-esteem or lack of it—the reverse can also occur. Unfair as it may seem, a young person who meets cultural standards of physical appearance and ability, and receives approval from peers and adults for these characteristics, may gain a better self-image in other respects as well (Lerner & Karabenick, 1974; Lerner, Karabenick, & Stuart, 1973; Lerner & Korn, 1972).

Finally, while conformity to cultural stereotypes regarding appearance may be a social asset, it may also present problems (Conger, 1979; Lerner & Karabenick, 1974; Zakin, Blyth, & Simmons, 1984). Extremely attractive adolescents may receive special treatment that they have not earned; as a result, they may fail to recognize the need to establish competence in other areas of life. Being a high school beauty queen, for instance, may be a very pleasant experience, but it does little to prepare one for the demands and stresses of adult life.

Psychological Aspects of Menstruation

To the adolescent girl, menstruation is much more than a physiological readjustment. It is a symbol of sexual maturity—of her future status as a woman. Because a girl's reaction to menstruation may generalize so broadly, it is vital that her initial experiences be positive (Brooks-Gunn & Ruble, 1983).

Increasing numbers of girls view the onset of menstruation calmly, and some look forward to it as a symbol of increased status (Brooks-Gunn & Ruble, 1983; Ruble & Brooks-Gunn, 1982). In the words of one adolescent girl, "It seemed that all my friends had gotten their period already, or were just having it. I felt left out. I began to think of it as a symbol. When I got my period, I would be a *woman*." Unfortunately, however, many other girls react negatively to this normal—and inevitable—development. One study found that a majority of preadolescent and adolescent American girls view the effects of menstruation as either negative or at best neutral; only 39 percent of those surveyed expressed the view that it was something to be happy about. Most felt that menstruation "is something women just have to put up with" (Ruble & Brooks, 1977).

Why do many adolescent girls react negatively to the onset of menstruation? One reason is the negative attitude of others. If a girl's parents and friends act as though she requires sympathy for her "plight"—an attitude that is reflected in euphemisms like "the curse"—the girl is likely to react in a similar fashion. Another reason is lack of adequate preparation for menarche (Brooks-Gunn & Ruble, 1983; Konopka, 1976). If a mother or other caretaker waits until menstruation has actually begun before explaining its functions, the girl may be surprised and shocked by the sudden appearance of menstrual blood, believing that she has injured herself. Some girls have actually thought that they were dying:

> I didn't know what was happening. I had these cramps and a headache, so I went to the bathroom, but it wasn't like I had the flu or anything. I didn't know what I had. When I got up from the toilet I noticed this blood in there and then I saw some blood on my thigh, so I started to scream. I thought I was bleeding to death. Nobody told me about periods, nobody told me about anything (Bell, 1987, p. 32).

Fortunately, such events are much rarer today as a result of greater openness regarding sexual matters. However, researchers have found that premenarcheal girls still expect more menstrual difficulties than postmenarcheal girls of the same age actually report (Brooks-Gunn & Ruble, 1983; Petersen, 1983). Moreover, such expectations are related to later experiences of premenstrual pain.

Attitudes toward menstruation are also likely to be influenced by the time at which menarche occurs relative to peers (Brooks-Gunn, 1988; Petersen, 1983; Rierdan & Koff, 1985). In one study, college women were asked to recall their age at menarche, estimate the percentage of their peers who reached menarche before them, and describe their initial experience of menstruation (Rierdan & Koff, 1985). Those who perceived themselves as reaching menarche early relative to their peers had more negative memories of menarche than those who perceived themselves as either "on time" or late.

In view of the concern of adolescents (especially younger ones) with conformity and belonging (see pages 280–281), these findings should not be surprising. Girls who perceive themselves as maturing early may have a sense of being "off time." In contrast, girls who see themselves as "on time" can feel assured of their normality (Koff, Rierdan & Sheingold, 1982; Petersen, 1983; Whisnant & Zegans, 1975). The girl who experiences menarche late is, like the early maturer, also "off time." In her case, however, the onset of menstruation ends her status as socially deviant. Menarche, again, provides reassurance of normality. Thus, "the late-maturing girl, like the on-time girl, can respond to menarche with relatively positive feelings" (Rierdan & Koff, 1985, p. 242).

Some reactions to menstruation are, of course, related to the actual experience of negative side effects. These may include headaches, backaches, skin problems, cramps, nausea, and water retention (Bell, 1987). Some young women experience none or only some of these effects. Gini, a 16-year-old swimmer and lacrosse player, reports:

> My period is no problem and it never really was. When I first got it, I got it when I woke up one morning, and even now, four years later, it still usually comes in the morning, so I almost always know I have it before I go to school. I also had no trouble learning how to use tampons—I used them right from the beginning. And I hardly ever get cramps. I mean, I feel so lucky about that. Some of my friends really get pretty bad cramps, they even have to miss classes sometimes, but for me my period doesn't affect my life at all (Bell, 1987, p. 35).

Ruth, also 16, reports quite a different experience:

I hate my period. I almost always get really bad cramps, and for about a week before it comes I am the biggest bitch and I cry at the drop of a hat. I hate it. I never know when it's coming, and even now, after I've had it for three years, it's so irregular that sometimes I skip a whole month. I know a lot of people who don't have any problems with their period at all, but for me it's the biggest problem of my life (Bell, 1987, p. 36).

In a National Health Examination survey conducted in the early 1980s, approximately 60 percent of a sample of American female adolescents reported having experienced some dysmenorrhea, that is, cramps before or during menses (Klein & Litt, 1983). Contrary to the popular belief that cramps and other menstrual symptoms are worse during the early postmenarcheal years, reports of at least mild pain increase from 31 percent to 78 percent over the first five years after menarche and then level off at about 70 percent. Only 14 percent of those who experience pain describe it as severe.

Relief from menstrual pain may be provided by several drugs, including aspirin, that inhibit the primary substance (prostaglandins) that produces cramps. Improved nutrition, exercise, and other health practices may also be helpful (Bell, 1987; McCoy & Wibbelsman, 1984).

In addition to experiencing physical symptoms, some adolescent girls report mood changes and negative or depressed feelings that appear to be linked to monthly variations in levels of estrogen and progesterone (see Figure 3.8). Other adolescents report no such effects or even experience an increase in positive feelings (Bell, 1987; Brooks-Gunn & Ruble, 1983; Dan, 1980; Ivey & Bardwick, 1968; Parlee, 1980). Although some of the individual variation in mood or affect is linked to variations in biological factors, psychological and social influences may also play a significant part. For example, girls who felt adequately prepared for menarche and girls whose fathers were aware of their daughter's first menstruation without being told by her report less premenstrual and menstrual negative affect, as well as fewer physical problems such as dysmenorrhea (Brooks-Gunn & Ruble, 1978, 1983).

An experiment in which some girls were led to believe that they were premenstrual while others were told that their period was two weeks away revealed that beliefs about menstrual-cycle effects may be stronger than changes that are actually experienced (Ruble, 1977). Other studies of adolescents have found that boys and premenarcheal girls describe the stereotypical patterns of mood changes, assuming stronger negative effects than are reported by girls who are actually menstruating (Brooks-Gunn & Ruble, 1983). In sum, while there is no doubt that some girls and women do experience physiologically based psychological effects of menstruation, traditional beliefs about such effects have tended to exaggerate the prevalence and perhaps the intensity of those effects.

The effects of hormonal variations in females (and, in a less clearly understood fashion, in males) are of considerable interest, but they provide no scien-

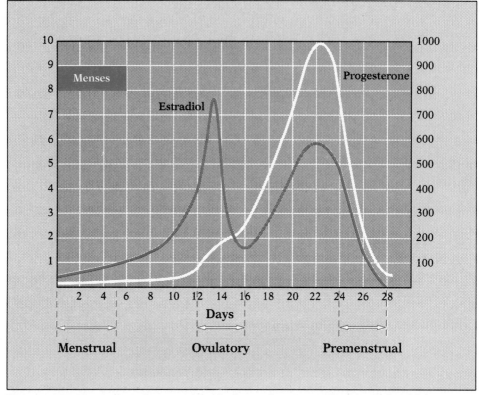

Figure 3.8 Variations in hormonal levels during the menstrual cycle. (Adapted from L. Speroff & R. L. Van de Wiele. *American Journal of Obstetrics and Gynecology,* 1971, *109,* 234–247. By permission.)

tific basis for what Karen Paige refers to as the "raging-hormone" theory (Bell, 1987; Paige, 1973; Ramey, 1973). In earlier generations, many girls were brought up expecting to feel weak, sick, or depressed before and during their periods, and to be unable to engage in normal activities, including vigorous physical exercise. Not surprisingly, many girls responded as expected. In reality, the danger is not that the girl will exercise too vigorously but that she will use menstruation as an excuse for retreating from normal activities, gaining attention or avoiding other problems. A healthy girl can exercise, go to classes, work, go to parties, or do anything else she likes while menstruating (Conger, 1975).

There are, of course, other reasons why an adolescent girl may react negatively to menstruation. If she resents or fears growing up, or if she has been unable to establish a satisfactory feminine identity, she may be disturbed by the unmistakable message that she is a developing woman and there is nothing she can do to change the fact.

Recent educational materials for boys and girls, such as *Changing Bodies, Changing Lives* (Bell, 1987), describe the changes accompanying menarche and menstruation more accurately than earlier publications did. But accurate educational materials cannot do the job alone; parents play an essential role. Many negative reactions to menstruation could be avoided or alleviated if parents employed a wise and understanding approach. By explaining to the girl the naturalness of the phenomenon, by seeing that she receives adequate medical care in case of any physical difficulties, and by showing pride and pleasure in her maturity, parents can help make the onset of menstruation a rewarding, rather than a feared or hated, event. Although the mother usually plays the major part in this process, the father can be very helpful too. Wardell Pomeroy, a clinical psychologist and one of the authors of the Kinsey Report, describes one father "who observed the occasion of his daughter's first menstruation by bringing her flowers and making a little ceremony of the fact that she had now become a young lady. That daughter could not help feeling proud and good about becoming an adolescent" (1969, p. 47).

Erection, Ejaculation, and Nocturnal Emission

Just as the onset of menstruation may cause concern in a pubescent girl, so may uncontrolled erection and initial ejaculation cause surprise and worry in a pubescent boy. The penis is capable of erection from birth on, and erection is frequently seen in male infants during bathing or prior to elimination. Most often it results from local stimulation or related physical events (such as a full bladder). Although genital stimulation (as well as other forms of bodily stimulation) is clearly pleasurable for male (and female) infants and children, neither erection nor genital stimulation usually carries with it the sense of sexual urgency that arises during puberty; moreover, erection is much less frequent in earlier years.

Prior to puberty boys may produce an erection and are capable of penetration, though without ejaculation. During puberty, however, the penis begins to tumesce very readily, either spontaneously or in response to a variety of stimuli: "provocative sights, sounds, smells, language, or whatever—the [younger] male adolescent inhabits a libidinized life-space where almost anything can take on a sexual meaning" (Stone & Church, 1973, p. 424). Although boys may be proud of their capacity for erection, they may also be worried or embarrassed by an apparent inability to control this response. They may become apprehensive about dancing with a girl or even about having to stand up in class to give a report. They may wonder whether other boys experience a similar apparent lack of control.

The adolescent boy's first ejaculation is likely to occur within a year of the beginning of the growth spurt (around age 13 or 14, although it may occur as early as 11 or as late as 16) (McCoy & Wibbelsman, 1984). First ejaculation may occur as a result of masturbation or nocturnal emission (ejaculation of seminal fluid during sleep)—or even as a result of spontaneous waking orgasm. A boy who has previously masturbated, with accompanying pleasant sensations but without ejaculation, may wonder whether the ejaculation of seminal fluid is harmful or an indication that something is physically wrong with him.

Today the first ejaculation is far less likely to be a source of concern and more likely to be a source of positive feelings than was the case in earlier times (Bell, 1980, 1987; Gaddis & Brooks-Gunn, 1985). In one limited survey, 73 percent of early adolescents reported being excited by this event; 55 percent felt more grown up, and 36 percent felt happy and proud (Gaddis & Brooks-Gunn, 1985). However, a minority felt somewhat embarrassed, and nearly half reported feeling "a little scared."

According to Kinsey, approximately 83 percent of males report experiencing nocturnal emissions, or "wet dreams" at some time in their lives, usually beginning a year or two after the onset of puberty (Kinsey, Pomeroy, & Martin, 1948). Frequently, these emissions are accompanied by erotic dreams. Nocturnal emissions occur more frequently among youth without other sexual outlets such as masturbation, petting to orgasm, or intercourse. The female equivalent of nocturnal emissions, nocturnal dreams with orgasm, is far less frequent (probably under 10 percent of females) and tends not to occur at all until after adolescence (Kinsey, Pomeroy, & Martin, 1953; Money & Ehrhardt, 1972).

Contemporary adolescents are generally better informed and less likely to be concerned about developmental events like menstruation or nocturnal emission than those of earlier generations (Bell, 1987; Gaddis & Brooks-Gunn, 1985). Nevertheless, many boys and girls, especially in the early years of adolescence, do not receive proper instruction from parents, schools, or peers and may torture themselves with unnecessary fears.

Hormonal Influences on Sexual Interest and Behavior

The hormonal changes accompanying puberty play an important but by no means exclusive role in fostering increased sexual interest and activity during this period, most clearly for males (Udry, Billy, Morris, Groff, & Raj, 1985; Udry, Talbert, & Morris, 1986). In males, increased sex drive (manifested in nocturnal emissions and masturbation) and such behaviors as dating and falling in love correspond with the rapid rise in testosterone levels between the ages of 12 and 14 (Higham, 1980). A decline in the frequency of sexual activity with age during the adult years also tends to parallel decreasing testosterone levels (Money & Ehrhardt, 1972). Antiandrogen drugs can reduce the sex drive in males.

In females, the relationships between hormonal levels and psychosexual functioning are more complex and are not completely understood (Higham, 1980; Petersen & Taylor, 1980; Susman et al., 1985). Androgen (testosterone) levels increase in girls during puberty, but much less than in boys (see Figure 3.9). Nevertheless, androgens appear to play some role in the female sex drive; administration of testosterone can result in increased sexual interest and activity, as can androgen-producing tumors of the ovary.

Although hormones play a role in sexual interest and arousal, environmental factors (particularly sex of rearing) appear to have the greatest influence on

The hormonal changes accompanying puberty play an important, but by no means exclusive, role in fostering increased sexual interest and activity during this period.

gender identity and the direction of sexual preference. These factors will be discussed more fully in Chapter 7.

Psychoanalytic theory emphasizes an upsurge in both sexual and aggressive impulses at the onset of adolescence, particularly in males (A. Freud, 1958). Social and clinical observers also call attention to the restlessness of younger adolescent boys, as well as to their greater preoccupation with sexual activity. The magnitude of the sex difference in **testosterone** levels following puberty, along with the fact that testosterone level is related to activity levels and aggressive (including sexual) behavior, may help account not only for relatively greater aggressiveness of adolescent males but also for the more imperious and less easily suppressed quality of the male sexual drive during adolescence (Ehrhardt & Baker, 1975; Hamburg & Trudeau, 1981; Inoff-Germain et al., 1988; Petersen, 1988; Susman et al., 1985). However, in discussing the greater aggressiveness of adolescent males it is important to note that this does not mean that females are either angelic or weak. As Eleanor Maccoby and Carol Jacklin point out,

Women share with men the human capacity to heap all sorts of injuries upon their fellows. And in almost every group that has been observed, there are some women who are fully as aggressive as the men. Furthermore, an individual's aggressive behavior is strengthened, weakened, redirected, or altered in form by his or her unique pattern of experiences. All we mean to argue is that there is a sex-linked differential readiness to respond in aggressive ways to the relevant experiences (1974, p. 247).

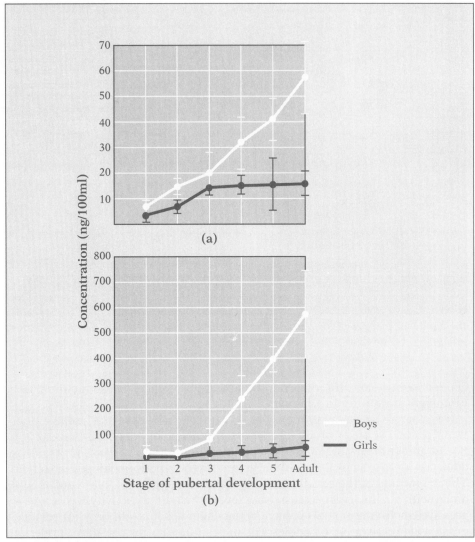

Figure 3.9 Androgens during pubertal development. Mean trends in plasma concentrations of (a) dihydrotestosterone and (b) testosterone related to pubertal developmental stages. (From D. Gupta, A. Attanasio, & S. Raaf. Plasma estrogen and androgen concentrations in children during adolescence. *Journal of Clinical Endrocrinology and Metabolism,* 1975, 40, 636–643. By permission.)

In addition to influencing adolescent sexuality, hormonal changes during pubertal development may have some direct temporary relationship to depressed feelings and other adjustment problems. However, any such effects appear slight compared with the effects of social and psychological factors, including negative life events (Brooks-Gunn, 1988; Nottelman et al., 1987a, 1987b; Susman et al., 1985).

Early and Late Maturation

As we have already seen, young people vary widely in the age at which they reach puberty. At age 15 one boy may be small, with no pubertal development of the reproductive organs or pubic hair. Another boy of the same age may look like a grown man, with broad shoulders, strong muscles, adult genitalia, and a bass voice (Tanner, 1970, 1971). Even though such variations are normal and do not either promote or hinder the eventual achievement of full physical and sexual maturity, they can affect the way adolescents view themselves—and the way they are viewed by others.

Early Versus Late Maturation in Males. In general, the psychological effects of early or late maturation appear to be more direct and easier to understand among boys than among girls. Adults and other adolescents tend to think of the 14- or 15-year-old boy who looks 17 or 18 as older than he actually is. They are likely to expect more mature behavior from him than they would from a physically less developed boy of the same age (Conger, 1979; Steinberg & Hill, 1978). Because there is less difference in height between an early-maturing boy and most girls his own age (owing to the earlier growth spurt in females), he may become involved in boy-girl relationships sooner and with more self-confidence. Moreover, a physically more developed male has an advantage in many activities, especially athletics. Although a boy who matures much faster than most of his peers may feel somewhat different, he is not likely to feel insecure about the difference. After all, with his more rugged physique, increased strength, and greater sexual maturity, he can assure himself that he is simply changing in the direction society expects and approves of (Blyth et al., 1981; Mussen, Conger, Kagan, & Huston, 1990; Simmons, et al., 1979, 1983; Tobin-Richards, Boxer, & Petersen, 1983).

In contrast, the late-maturing boy is more likely to be treated like a child. He is likely to have a harder time excelling in athletic and other activities and establishing relationships with girls. He may wonder when, if ever, he will reach full physical and sexual maturity.

These differences tend to produce certain differences between the personalities of early and late maturers. Extensive long-term studies at the University of California found that males who matured late tended to be less poised, more tense and talkative, and more self-conscious and affected in their manner. They were also likely to be more restless, "overeager," impulsive, bossy, and "attention seeking." Although there were exceptions, late maturers tended to be less popular with peers and less likely to be leaders. Early maturers, on the other hand, appeared more reserved, self-assured, and matter-of-fact, and were more likely to engage easily in socially appropriate behavior. They were also better able to laugh at themselves (Blyth et al., 1981; Clausen, 1975; Jones, 1954, 1957; Mussen & Jones, 1957; Simmons et al., 1979, 1983).

Recent research has found an essentially linear relationship (for boys) between timing of puberty and positive feelings about oneself (Crockett & Petersen, 1982; Tobin-Richards et al., 1983). Adolescent boys who perceived themselves as early maturers had a more positive body image and mood, and a greater sense of their own attractiveness. In contrast, those who perceived themselves as late maturers had a more negative body image and a decreased sense of attractiveness, while those who perceived themselves as maturing at the expected time fell between the two extremes. In another study, early pubertal development in boys was related to more positive body image and higher self-esteem (Blyth et al., 1981).

Although early-maturing boys generally have an advantage over those who mature late, the picture is not entirely one-sided. When early- and late-maturing groups were compared at or after (but *not* before) the beginning of puberty, late-maturing boys were found to be more intellectually curious and more likely to engage in exploratory behavior and social initiatives (Livson & Peskin, 1980; Peskin, 1967, 1973). In contrast, early maturers tended to avoid problem solving or new situations unless urged. "The early maturers appeared to approach cognitive tasks cautiously and timidly, with a preference for rules, routines, and imitative action" (Livson & Peskin, 1980, p. 73).

On psychological tests late maturers were found to have more feelings of inadequacy, a poorer self-concept, and more feelings of being rejected or dominated by others. Somewhat paradoxically, they were more likely to combine persisting dependency needs with a seemingly rebellious search for independence and freedom from parental and social restraints (Mussen & Jones, 1957). In other words, late maturers appeared more likely to prolong the typical adolescent independence-dependence conflict than early maturers (Weatherley, 1964).

A far-ranging follow-up study of the participants in the California studies makes clear that differences between early and late maturers—both positive and negative—can persist into adulthood (Clausen, 1975; Jones, 1965; Livson & Peskin, 1980). As adults (age 38) the early-maturing males were found to be more responsible, cooperative, sociable, and self-contained, but also more conventional, conforming, moralistic, humorless, and concerned with making a good impression. On the other hand, the late maturers remained less controlled, less responsible, and more impulsive and assertive, but also "more insightful, perceptive, creatively playful, and able to cope with the ambiguity of new situations" (Livson & Peskin, 1980, p. 71).

Much can be done by parents, teachers, and others to minimize the anxiety and other negative psychological effects of late maturation. Adults can make a conscious effort to avoid treating a late maturer as younger than he actually is (Mussen et al., 1990). They can help him realize that his slower maturation is normal—that he will indeed "grow up" and be as physically and sexually masculine as his peers. And they can help him achieve success in activities in which his lesser size and strength are not a handicap. For example, whereas immaturity and smaller size can be a handicap for a football player, they may be assets for a diver or a tumbler.

Conversely, parents and others can assist early maturers by not having unrealistic expectations of maturity based on physical appearance. They can also encourage early-maturing boys—and, as we shall see, girls—to take the time to catch up psychologically and socially with their physical development instead of rushing headlong into adult activities.

Early Versus Late Maturation in Females. Although early or average maturation is generally advantageous to boys, among girls the differences between early and late maturers are less extensive and more variable (Faust, 1960, 1977, 1983; Jones & Mussen, 1958; Livson & Peskin, 1980; Petersen, 1988; Simmons et al., 1979, 1983). Initially, early-maturing girls tend to be less satisfied with their body image; more easily disorganized under stress; more restless, listless, moody, and complaining; and less popular with same-sex peers (Blyth et al., 1981; Crockett & Petersen, 1987; Faust, 1960, 1977; Peskin, 1973; Tobin-Richards, Boxer, & Petersen, 1983). They are more likely to perform poorly in school, score lower in achievement tests, exhibit problem behaviors in school, and have lower academic aspirations (Simmons et al., 1979, 1983). However, they also emerge as more independent, more popular with opposite-sex peers, and more interested in dating.

Of particular interest is the clear difference in body image between early-maturing boys and girls. While the early-maturing boy is steadily developing in the direction of favored adult norms, the same is not the case for early-maturing girls, who tend initially to be bigger, heavier, and fatter than their more "petite" late-maturing peers (Crockett & Petersen, 1987; Petersen, 1988; Simmons et al., 1983; Tobin-Richards et al., 1983). Our society's emphasis on being tall and slim may help explain the finding that the heavier a girl is—or thinks she is—the more dissatisfied she is with her weight and body shape (Faust, 1983). In contrast, late-maturing girls initially are more gregarious, poised, assertive, and active; more popular with peers; and less concerned about and more satisfied with their body image. They also do better academically and exhibit fewer behavior problems in school, and have higher academic aspirations (Faust, 1960, 1983; Peskin, 1973; Petersen, 1988; Petersen & Crockett, 1985; Simmons et al., 1983).

By late adolescence and adulthood the picture changes significantly. Earlier studies indicated that the formerly stress-ridden early-maturing girl became more popular with peers of both sexes than the late-maturing girl, as well as more self-possessed, coping, and self-directed cognitively, socially, and emotionally (Faust, 1960; Livson & Peskin, 1980; Peskin,1973). In one recent study, however, early-maturing girls were found to have a poorer self-image, especially body image, during late adolescence (Petersen, 1989). Whether these findings are specific to the sample of adolescents studied or are a reflection of changing times is a subject for further research.

How can we explain this change, as well as the fact that early maturation is clearly a more favorable event for boys? First, early-maturing adolescents are in a minority among their peers, which is no longer the case when all of their peers have also matured (Simmons et al., 1983). Second, society favors early

Box 3.2 THE CONTEXT OF PUBERTAL TIMING

The effects of maturational timing depend, at least in part, on the social context in which it occurs (Brooks-Gunn, 1988; Brooks-Gunn & Warren, 1985; Petersen, 1988; Simmons, Blyth, & Kenney, 1983). In activities and occupations like gymnastics or ballet, in which there is a professional emphasis on leanness and a more "prepubertal" figure, late maturation may be more adaptive (and normative) than early or even average maturation. Dancers with delayed menarche are different physically: They weigh much less than dancers for whom menarche is "on time," and they appear to have

In activities and occupations like gymnastics or ballet, late maturation may be more adaptive than early or even average maturation.

greater control over their eating habits. They also tend to have longer limbs (Brooks-Gunn & Warren, 1985; Frisch et al., 1980, 1981; Warren, 1980).

In a comparative study of private-school students and students in a ballet school, girls between the ages of 14 and 18 were classified as early, on-time, or late maturers on the basis of age at menarche (Brooks-Gunn & Warren, 1985). The dancers were far more likely to be late maturers than the private-school students (155 percent vs. 29 percent). Among dancers, those who were "on time" in their development had significantly higher scores than late maturers on measures of psychopathology, perfectionism, and bulimic tendencies, and lower scores on measures of body image, family relationships, and education. (There were too few early-maturing dancers to provide useful comparisons.) In contrast, and in accordance with other studies, being on time presented no such problems among private-school students. Indeed, on-time maturers in this group had a more positive body image than either early or late maturers.

The importance of social context was also demonstrated in a pioneering study of students in Milwaukee schools (Simmons et al., 1979; Simmons et al., 1983). The investigators found that the effects of maturational timing varied as a function of school context and of transition from one kind of school to another. Among seventh-graders, those who had moved into junior high school had more difficulty adjusting and demonstrated lower self-esteem and more negative changes than girls who remained in a K–8 system (Simmons et al., 1979). However, changing schools was harder on early-maturing than on late-maturing girls: "In seventh grade, girls were more likely to exhibit lower self-esteem if they incurred these life changes simultaneously—change in school type, early pubertal change, and early assumption of dating behavior" (Simmons et al., 1983, p. 265). The same finding was obtained for both boys and girls in a second study (Petersen, Kennedy, & Sullivan, in press).

maturity in adolescent males more clearly and less ambiguously than early maturity in females. In young men, early maturity means greater strength and physical prowess and, eventually, active sexual behavior. Among girls, early maturity may mean being temporarily bigger and heavier than female peers and taller than boys of the same age; in our society it may also mean being subjected to more conflicting sexual messages than is the case for males.

Is beginning sexual activity at an earlier age than one's peers good or bad? Society gives adolescent girls mixed messages on this matter, as do their peers. Parents worry that a girl who is sexually attractive at an early age will attract the attention of older boys. If she dates boys who are considerably older than she is, she may not form strong relationships with girls and boys her own age or develop as an independent individual in her own right. She may also come to feel that she is gaining attention merely as a sex object rather than as a complete person (Mussen et al., 1990). On the other hand, her attractiveness can add to her prestige in her peer group, thereby making her social relationships more positive.

In the case of an early-maturing female, parents and other adults should be careful to avoid pressing her into heterosexual relationships, such as dating, too early. They can help her develop her own interests and maintain her friendships with peers her own age, assuring her that the other girls will soon catch up.

Adults need to assure a late-maturing girl that she will ultimately attain physical and sexual maturity. If they can help her realize that there is no need to rush things, that in fact gradual maturation can be useful in that it allows her to devote her energies to other developmental tasks, much unnecessary concern can be avoided (Conger, 1979).

HEALTH CARE FOR ADOLESCENTS

Because adolescence is a unique developmental period involving rapid physical, psychological, and social change, adolescents have special health care needs (Bell, 1987; McCoy & Wibbelsman, 1984; Neinstein, 1984; Riggs & Cheng, 1988). Adolescents seek professional care and treatment for a wide range of problems, including acne or allergies, concerns about diet and exercise; headaches or fatigue; delayed puberty or very rapid growth; sexual activity, contraception, or pregnancy; menstrual difficulties or worries about sexually transmitted diseases; problems with parents, peers, or teachers; and feelings of acute self-consciousness, anxiety, or depression (Earls et al., 1989; Dryfoos & Klerman, 1988; Riggs & Cheng, 1988). Adolescents may be concerned about several such problems at any one time; not infrequently, too, they seek treatment for a set of complaints that are really of secondary concern as a way of "testing the water" (whether consciously or unconsciously) to see whether it is safe to explore more pressing and painful psychological or physical problems.

All of this requires that the physician or other health care professional be sensitive not only to the unique physical and medical needs of adolescents but to their psychological and social needs as well. Consequently, it is desirable that physicians and others involved in caring for and treating adolescents receive special training in adolescent medicine. Although the number of adolescent health care specialists is still relatively small, it is increasing.

It is also desirable for adolescents to have easy access to a health care facility where they are treated with understanding and respect, their privacy is protected, and a variety of services are readily available. A promising development in the past decade has been the growth of hospital-based comprehensive-care clinics in the United States and Canada; there are now about 100 such clinics (Earls et al., 1989; McCoy & Wibbelsman, 1984). These clinics are staffed by physicians, nurses, and other health care professionals, including psychologists and social workers, who have special training in the physiology and psy-

John D., a student at Taft High School in the Bronx, first came to the Taft Teen Health Center when, as he describes it, "Someone punched me in the jaw for no reason." Now John, a recent immigrant from Surinam, is on the Center's student advisory committee. "Sometimes I come by without an appointment, and I can be sure someone will talk with me, even for just a few minutes. It gives you a feeling of security, because you know they'll be here for you." (From Making connections: A summary of Robert Wood Johnson Foundation programs for adolescents. Princeton, NJ: Robert Wood Johnson Foundation. By permission.)

chology of adolescents. They offer a wide variety of services at low cost, usually based on ability to pay.

Another important development is the growth of school-based clinics (Dryfoos & Klerman, 1988; Hayes, 1987; Kirby, 1985; Robert Wood Johnson Foundation, 1990; Schorr, 1988). Mounting concern among youth advocacy groups, health professionals, and educators has led to the creation of 43 such clinics in junior and senior high schools in 24 communities, and more than 50 others are being developed. School-based clinics are intended to capitalize on many of the features to which adolescents are likely to respond, including convenience, comfort, confidentiality, and low cost.

Located within the school building or on school grounds, such clinics are accessible. Students don't have to take a bus or drive to another part of town or request their parents' assistance in getting them to the services. Most clinics operate during school hours and do not require appointments. Because they are visible entities in the school, clinic staff become familiar to students and vice versa. In addition, because the programs are geared to the needs of adolescents and students are aware that their friends use the services, school-based clinics seem more approachable to many young people than doctors' offices, hospitals, or freestanding adult clinics (Hayes, 1987, p. 169–170).

School-based clinics vary in the range of family-planning services they provide (Dryfoos & Klerman, 1988). At a minimum, most provide counseling and referrals to family-planning clinics, such as Planned Parenthood, or private physicians, and follow-up after referrals (Hayes, 1987; Kirby, 1985). Although less than one-third dispense contraceptives, those that do have had considerable success in reducing rates of teenage pregnancy (see pages 260–261).

Other clinics that provide comprehensive health care to adolescents are community based. One such clinic is located on the Lower East Side of New York City (Kyman, Berger, & Perez, 1987). Its services include routine medical care; management of acute and chronic illnesses; assistance in coping with social, psychological, family, peer, or school problems; counseling related to health care and nutrition; and family-planning services. A one-year study found that family-planning education significantly increased contraceptive use among the 35 percent of adolescents who were sexually active when they entered the clinic (Kyman, Berger, & Perez, 1987). Among active females, contraceptive use increased during the course of the year from 22 percent to 70 percent; among males, the increase was from 33 percent to 83 percent. Among adolescents who were not sexually active when they first visited the clinic, only 3 percent became active during this period—far fewer than would generally be expected. In addition, possibly because the clinic provides continuous and comprehensive services in an atmosphere of trust and caring, most adolescent clients have been responsible about keeping appointments and complying with treatment procedures.

HEALTH AND BEHAVIOR

Advances in medicine and public-health practices during the last fifty years have led to a dramatic decline in mortality from infectious diseases. As a consequence, most health problems are now related to "aspects of individual behavior, especially long-term patterns of behavior referred to as 'lifestyle'" (Hamburg et al., 1982, p. 3). Indeed, as much as 50 percent of current mortality from the ten leading causes of death in America today (e.g., cardiovascular disease, cancer, accidents) can be traced to aspects of lifestyle (Hamburg, Elliott, & Parron, 1982; *Healthy people*, 1979; Matarazzo, 1984).

Many of the values, interests, behavior patterns, and ways of coping that will characterize an individual's adult life-style are formed during adolescence (Conger, 1987; Hamburg et al., 1982; Jessor, 1984). If a young person can develop adaptive ways of responding to the challenges and stresses of life, while avoiding health-damaging behaviors, he or she is likely to continue to respond in these ways in the adult years. For example, if a young person can avoid smoking, excessive alcohol or drug use, sexual acting out, or disturbed eating patterns during this transitional period, he or she is markedly less likely to engage in these behaviors in subsequent years (Coates, Petersen, & Perry, 1982; Evans, 1984; Jessor, 1984). This is one of the principal reasons that smoking and other prevention programs have focused on the preadolescent and early adolescent years (Hamburg et al., 1982; Jessor, 1984). Similarly, the establishment of healthful patterns of exercise and nutrition, a positive attitude toward health, and adaptive mechanisms for coping with stress is also likely to yield continued future benefits (Conger, 1987; Elliott & Einsdorfer, 1982; Matarazzo et al., 1984).

At the same time, however, adolescents are more vulnerable than adults to the adoption of health-damaging behaviors. In part, this reflects their openness to change, their uncertain sense of self, their need to define themselves as separate from parents, their greater dependence on peers, the greater risks to which they are exposed, and their relatively limited time perspective (Conger, 1987). But it also reflects the effects of social changes that have increased adolescents' vulnerability to maladaptive behaviors. For one thing, opportunities for becoming involved in drug use, unplanned pregnancy, and other problem behaviors abound. For another, contemporary adult society, lacking a strong, coherent, unified set of moral and social values of its own, provides at best a fragmented, inadequate model for young people (Conger, 1987, 1988). In the final analysis, success in creating a growth-enhancing, health-promoting climate, both for young people and for society itself, will require far greater commitment to meeting the needs of children and youth than our society has shown up to now.

SUMMARY

Adolescence is a period of rapid physical, sexual, psychological, cognitive, and social changes. *Puberty* refers to the biological changes of adolescence, including sexual maturation and the *adolescent growth spurt*. It is initiated by the release of certain activating hormones by the pituitary gland. Those hormones, stimulate other endocrine glands to begin releasing growth- and sex-related hormones, including *androgens, estrogens,* and *progestins*. The hormonal differences between the sexes are actually differences in the proportions of masculinizing and feminizing hormones present in each sex.

The age of onset and the duration of the adolescent growth spurt—an accelerated rate of increase in height and weight—vary widely among normal young people. However, the average age at which the growth spurt begins is about 11 in girls and 13 in boys; the period of rapid growth lasts about $4\frac{1}{2}$ years, with the peak rate of growth occurring about a year after onset.

Changes in height and weight are accompanied by changes in body proportions. Sex differences in body shape also are magnified during early adolescence. Changes in physique reflect changes in the development of muscle, body fat, and skeletal structure and help account for differences in strength and tolerance for exercise. The nutritional needs of the average adolescent boy consistently exceed those of the average girl. Dietary habits formed in adolescence are likely to continue into adulthood.

In males, sexual maturation begins with an increase in the growth of the testes and scrotum, followed by an acceleration in growth of the penis, the appearance of axillary hair, and lowering of the voice. In females, the first sign of sexual maturity is the appearance of pubic hair and "budding" of the breasts. These changes are followed by accelerated growth of the reproductive organs and finally by *menarche* (onset of menstruation).

For adolescent girls, the onset of menstruation is a symbol of womanhood. However, a majority of American girls react negatively—or at best neutrally—to menarche, partly because of the negative attitudes of others and partly because of associated physical discomfort. For adolescent boys, uncontrolled erection and initial ejaculation may be sources of worry and embarrassment.

Early-maturing males face higher expectations for mature behavior and have an advantage in many activities, especially athletics. Late-maturing males are more likely to be treated like children and are likely to have more difficulty excelling in athletics and other activities. These differences result in personality differences that tend to favor early-maturing boys, who tend to be more self-assured and able to engage easily in socially appropriate behavior, although in the long run, late maturers emerge as more intellectually and socially curious.

The effects of early versus late maturation are generally less extensive and more variable for girls than for boys. Initially, early-maturing girls tend to be less satisfied with their body image, more restless and moody, and less popular with same-sex peers than late-maturing girls; however, these differences diminish with age.

Because adolescence is a unique developmental period, adolescents have special health care needs ranging from concerns about diet or problems with parents or peers to concerns about sexual activity, anxiety, or depressed feelings. This requires that health care professionals be sensitive, not only to the unique physical and medical needs of adolescents, but also to their psychological and social needs. The health care needs of young people can best be met in adolescent clinics that provide comprehensive health care, whether they are located in schools, hospitals, or the community.

As much as half of current mortality can be traced to lifestyle patterns, and many of those patterns are established during adolescence. If a young person can develop adaptive ways of responding to the stresses of life, while avoiding health-damaging behaviors, he or she is likely to continue to respond in these ways in adulthood.

REVIEW QUESTIONS

1. Briefly describe the role of hormonal factors in pubertal development.
2. Briefly discuss the age of onset and duration of the adolescent growth spurt in boys and girls, and describe the resulting changes in height, weight, and other physical characteristics.
3. How does sexual maturation progress in adolescent males and females?
4. What are the effects of maturation, especially early or late maturation, on the psychological adjustment of adolescent boys and girls?
5. What factors influence whether the onset of menstruation will be a positive, neutral, or negative experience for girls?
6. Discuss briefly the effects of pubertal hormones on sexual interest and behavior.
7. Why do adolescents have special health care needs? How can those needs best be met?
8. Why is it especially important to learn adaptive ways of responding to stress and avoiding health-damaging behaviors during the early adolescent years?

RECOMMENDED READINGS

Bell, R., & others (1987). *Changing bodies, changing lives* (revised ed.). New York: Vintage Books.

Brooks-Gunn, J., & Petersen, A. C. (1983). *Girls at puberty: Biological, psychological, and social perspectives.* New York: Plenum.

Jessor, R. (1984). Adolescent development and behavioral health. In J. D. Matarazzo, S. M. Weiss, J. A. Herd, N. E. Miller, & S. M. Weiss (Eds.), *Behavioral health: A handbook of health enhancement and disease prevention* (pp. 69–90). New York: Wiley.

Litt, I. F., & Vaughn, V. C. III (1987).

Growth and development during adolescence. In R. E. Behrman, V. C. Vaughn, & W. E. Nelson (Eds.), *Textbook of pediatrics* (13th ed.) (pp. 20–24). Philadelphia: W. B. Saunders.

Neinstein, L. S. (1985). *Adolescent health care: A practical guide.* Baltimore: Urban & Schwarzenberg.

Tanner, J. M. (1971). Sequence, tempo, and individual variation in the growth and development of boys and girls aged twelve to sixteen. *Daedalus, 100,* No. 4, 907–930. Also in J. Kagan and R. Coles (Eds.) (1972), *12 to 16: Early adolescence.* New York: Norton.

INTELLIGENCE AND COGNITIVE DEVELOPMENT

The impressive gains in physical and physiological development that are made during adolescence are accompanied by equally impressive gains in intellectual and cognitive development. For example, if asked why we should keep away from bad company, a 15-year-old might say, "They will lead you into temptation," or, "To keep from being influenced by them." A younger child might say, "'Cause they're bad," or, "My mother wouldn't like it." When asked to listen to a series of numbers and then repeat them, the average 15-year-old will be able to remember more numbers in the correct order. Similar results are found on a variety of indexes of mental ability, ranging from measures of general information, abstract verbal reasoning, and commonsense understanding of everyday events to tests of arithmetic skill and mechanical ability. Although parents may express consternation about the apparent inability of adolescent children to follow instructions for such simple tasks as straightening up a bedroom, taking out the garbage, or putting the cap back on the toothpaste tube, the fact is that adolescents are much more advanced cognitively than their younger brothers and sisters.

David Elkind, an authority on adolescent **cognitive development,** has observed that the gains made during this period can be viewed both quantitatively and qualitatively. The cognitive gains of adolescence are *quantitative* in the sense that the adolescent becomes capable of accomplishing more easily, more quickly, and more efficiently intellectual tasks that he or she previously was able to accomplish only slowly, inefficiently, and with great difficulty, if at all. They are *qualitative* in the sense that significant changes occur in the nature of the adolescent's mental processes—in the ways in which he or she can define problems and reason about them.

For many years the primary focus of psychologists was on the quantitative aspects of cognitive development as exemplified by traditional intelligence testing with its emphasis on individual and age-related differences in ability to perform a variety of verbal and performance tasks. Only in recent decades has there been a comparable emphasis on the qualitative aspects—on the underlying processes involved in cognitive development, as exemplified by the developmental psychology of Jean Piaget and others (Flavell, 1985; Keating, 1980; Neimark, 1975a, 1975b). Of course, distinctions between quantitative and qualitative aspects of cognitive development are somewhat arbitrary and primarily reflect differences in emphasis. The quantitative approach does not deny that modes of thought differ with age. Similarly, the qualitative approach "does not deny that individual differences in brightness exist, and such differences are used to account for the finding that some children attain particular mental abilities before or after the majority of their age mates" (Elkind, 1968, p. 129). In brief, the quantitative and qualitative approaches to cognitive development represent two sides of the same coin, which complement, rather than contradict, each other.

Without these quantitative and qualitative gains in their cognitive capability, young people would be unable to confront and deal successfully with many of the important demands made on them during adolescence. This may appear obvious in the case of demands for educational achievement and the development of vocational skills, but as we shall see, it is equally true in the case of nonacademic tasks like the development of personal, social, and political values and a sense of ego identity.

DEFINING AND MEASURING INTELLIGENCE

The quantitative approach to intellectual development dates from the pioneering work of Alfred Binet, a French psychologist who originated the modern intelligence test. In 1904 the French government, concerned about the many nonlearners in the schools of Paris, asked Binet to develop a test to determine which children were too dull to profit from ordinary schooling. In collaboration with another French psychologist, Theodore Simon, Binet set about devising a test that would "separate the generally dull from those who had adequate educability" (Cronbach, 1949, p. 103). Their responsibility was not to devise a measure of intellectual achievement but to create a way of measuring **intelligence,** or intellectual ability. That is, they were to assess not what students had accomplished but what they *might be able to* accomplish. This is not a simple task, and it requires the adoption of a number of assumptions about the nature of intelligence and how it develops. To understand what Binet and Simon faced, it is necessary to explore somewhat further what is actually meant by the term intelligence and to distinguish tests of intelligence from tests of achievement.

The Meaning of Intelligence

What do we actually mean by intelligence? To the ordinary person the answer may seem obvious. We believe that we understand the term when we say, "He is not very bright," "As any normally intelligent person can see . . . ," and so on. However, the matter is more complex than it may appear. In attempting to clarify the issue, it is probably best to begin by stating what intelligence is not.

People tend to think that because many words stand for things, all words do. This idea is false. Many words are simply useful scientific fictions (i.e., hypothetical constructs like the concepts of time and force) that help us explain observable events. But they do not stand for objects, or classes of objects, in the way that words like *tree* and *chair* do. In the same way, no one has ever seen, heard, or touched intelligence. It too is a hypothetical construct; it was invented to help explain and predict behavior. And because intelligence is hypothetical, there is no single correct definition of the term, although one definition may be more useful for some purposes than another. Over the years a number of psychologists have defined intelligence, and although the terminology used differs, most experts agree that intelligence involves the ability to benefit from experience and to learn new ideas or new sets of behaviors easily. For example, David Wechsler (1981), who developed the widely used Wechsler Intelligence Scales for children, adolescents, and adults, defines intelligence as the aggregate or global capacity of the individual to comprehend the world and to deal effectively with its challenges. Another expert, Robert Sternberg, refers to intelligence as "goal-directed adaptive behavior" (Sternberg, 1985).

It is generally assumed that every individual has a "ceiling," a point above which he or she will not be able to profit from experience in a particular activity, and that the ceiling is set by hereditary factors. How nearly any individual approaches the ceiling, and the rate at which he or she does so, is determined by a variety of factors, including his or her rate of physiological maturation and the richness of the environment to which he or she is exposed.

A person's potential ceiling may be lowered in the course of development by a variety of external and internal events. Examples include physiological events such as brain injury or disease. Less obviously, it is possible that if the developing biological organism does not receive a certain amount of psychological and physical stimulation from its environment during certain critical periods, it will be handicapped in its ability to profit from subsequent learning opportunities.

Is Intelligence Multidimensional?

At first, intelligence was considered to be a general competence—an ability that is developed across a wide variety of tasks (Mussen et al., 1990; Sternberg, 1982a, 1985; Sternberg & Powell, 1982). Over time, however, psychologists began to challenge this view. Some argued that what is called general intelligence actually consists of a variety of intellectual skills that do not necessarily vary together. Others argued that individuals possess not only a general intelligence factor but also a variety of special factors, or abilities, that may vary independently of one another (Atkinson et al., 1987; Cronbach, 1984; Ekstrom, French, & Harman, 1976; Spearman, 1927).

Although disputes about the relative importance of general and specific factors in intellectual functioning have not been fully resolved (Caroll, 1988; Sternberg & Powell, 1983), most psychologists agree that patterns of ability differ among different children, adolescents, and adults. For example, some adolescents have outstanding verbal skills but have difficulty in mathematics or in visualizing spatial relationships; for others the reverse may be true.

Dimensions of Intelligence

Scientists are more likely to agree that intelligence is multidimensional, involving a variety of abilities, than they are to agree on the nature of these abilities (Atkinson et al., 1987; Guilford, 1967, 1982; Mussen et al., 1990; Sternberg, 1982a, 1985). L. L. Thurstone, a pioneer in the study of intelligence, concluded that in addition to a general intelligence factor, intelligence involves seven *primary mental abilities:* verbal comprehension, word fluency, ability to manipulate numbers, ability to visualize spatial relationships, associative memory (ability to memorize quickly and correctly), perceptual speed, and general reasoning ability (Thurstone, 1938). A majority of currently used intelligence tests measure performance in most of these abilities (Kagan & Segal, 1988).

More recently, psychologist Howard Gardner has proposed six distinct kinds of intelligence: linguistic ability; logical mathematical reasoning; spatial ability; musical ability; bodily-kinesthetic skills, which are involved in controlling bodily movements (as in dance, playing the piano, or performing surgery); and personal intelligence (Gardner, 1983). Personal intelligence, in turn, has two components that can be viewed as distinct: *intrapersonal* intelligence, which includes the ability to monitor one's own feelings and emotions; and *interpersonal* intelligence, which includes the ability to notice and understand the feelings, needs, and intentions of others.

Gardner's first three abilities are familiar aspects of intelligence and are typically included in intelligence tests; the latter three are more novel and more difficult to measure. Nevertheless, it would be hard to argue that they are unimportant or that they necessarily co-vary with more traditional measures of intelligence.

Robert Sternberg (1985), a prominent cognitive psychologist at Yale University, also takes a broader view of the nature of intelligence. He has developed a "triarchic" (three-part) theory of intelligence in which intelligence has three major components: (1) *cognitive processes* (e.g., planning and problem solving)

Howard Gardner has proposed six distinct kinds of intelligence, including musical ability and bodily-kinesthetic skills.

and *knowledge acquisition;* (2) the ease with which one deals with new experiences (i.e., how rapidly one learns); and (3) the ability to adapt to and influence one's social and cultural environment. While most traditional intelligence tests are reasonably effective in measuring problem-solving skills and the acquisition of knowledge, they are generally not very helpful in assessing these broader aspects of intellectual functioning. New methods will have to be devised to accurately assess the broader, more novel aspects of intelligence proposed by Gardner and Sternberg (Atkinson et al., 1987).

Is an Intelligence Test a "Pure" Measure of Intelligence?

In any consideration of intelligence, and particularly of intelligence testing (i.e., the determination of IQ), it is important to stress that there is no way to measure directly an individual's intellectual potential (i.e., his or her ultimate "ceiling"). We can only measure what a person can do (whether the task is verbal or psychomotor). This means that we can measure only the results of an interaction between the individual (and his or her potential) and the environment. To take an extreme example, a child who was raised in silence in a dark room from birth would obviously be unable to perform any of the tasks on a standard intelligence test. But this does not mean that his or her intellectual potential is zero. We may use indirect means to estimate a child's or adolescent's intellectual potential, and indeed this is one of the purposes of an intelligence test (as distinguished from an achievement test).

Intelligence tests try to control for environmental influences, on the assumption that differences in performance will then reflect differences in intellectual potential. But because we can never be certain that we have succeeded in controlling for the effects of all environmental influences or other relevant factors, such as motivation or transient physical or psychological states, we can never be sure that an IQ represents a person's full intellectual potential. A practical rule of thumb is that people are unlikely to be *less* capable than their IQ score indicates but that, depending on circumstances, they may well be *more* capable.

Constructing Intelligence Tests

The manner in which the creators of intelligence tests attempt to control for the potentially distorting effects of environmental influences can be illustrated by considering an example of intelligence-test construction. Here we return to the task confronting Alfred Binet at the turn of the century. Binet assumed that a dull child was like a normal one only retarded in mental growth; he reasoned that the dull child would perform on tests like a normal child of younger age. He therefore decided to scale intelligence as the kind of change that occurs in the course of a child's maturation.

Accordingly, Binet set about constructing a scale of units of *mental age* (MA). Average mental-age scores would correspond to *chronological age* (CA) (i.e., age determined from date of birth). A bright girl's MA would be above her CA; a retarded child would have an MA below his CA. The mental-age scale could easily be interpreted by teachers and others who deal with children whose mental ability differs.

Item Selection. Because Binet conceived of intelligence as an individual's global capacity to profit from experience, he attempted to sample a wide range of mental abilities. Included were measures of verbal ability, perceptual-motor coordination, memory, perception, logical reasoning, and the like. Scores on these individual measures could be combined to form an estimate of overall ability.

Because he was attempting, albeit indirectly, to measure intellectual ability or potential rather than achievement, Binet tried to select tasks that would not unduly favor individuals with specific training or unduly penalize those without it. His assumption was that if the kind of task selected did not favor a child with specific training, then differences in children's levels of performance would be more likely to reflect differences in their basic potential. There are two basic ways to find items on which success is not influenced by special training. One is to choose *novel items* on which an untaught child has just as much chance to succeed as one who has been taught at home or in school (Atkinson et al., 1987). Figure 4.1 illustrates such items. In this example the child is directed to select figures that are alike; it is assumed that the designs are unfamiliar to all children.

The second way is to select *familiar items,* on the assumption that those for whom the test is designed have the necessary experience to deal with them. To illustrate, the Wechsler Adult Intelligence Scale-Revised (WAIS-R), which is widely used in assessing adolescents and adults, contains an *information* subtest that includes the following item: "How many weeks are there in a year?" It is assumed that virtually all children in our society (for whom the test was designed) have been exposed to this information. Whether they have incorporated it into their store of knowledge is assumed to depend on their underlying level of mental ability. A similar rationale applies to the following item involving "commonsense" reasoning, from another Wechsler subtest *(comprehen-*

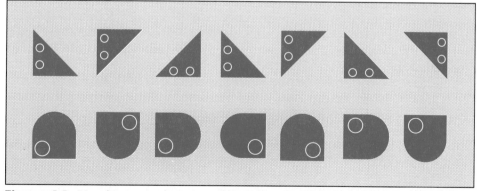

Figure 4.1 Novel items used in an intelligence test. The following instructions accompany the test: "Here are some cards for you to mark. In each row mark every card that is like the first card in the row." (From L. L. Thurstone & T. G. Thurstone. Factorial studies of intelligence. *Psychometric Monographs* [No. 2]. Chicago: University of Chicago Press, 1941. By permission.)

sion): "If you were lost in the forest in the daytime, how would you go about finding your way out?" (Wechsler, 1981).

Unfortunately, in attempting to measure differences in underlying potential, an intelligence test cannot provide for differences among individual experiences. Thus, in this example environmental exposure may indeed be more or less equal for most children. However, even a relatively dull child or adolescent who had just spent a summer at a camp that taught camping and mountaineering skills would be likely to come up with the correct answer, if only because he or she had been specifically and repeatedly told what to do in such a situation. On the other hand, the experience of a disadvantaged ghetto child or one who was raised in relative isolation in a rural area may be such that he or she will be penalized to some extent by questions designed for, and standardized on, a representative sample of children or adolescents.

In some respects the intelligence test is a crude instrument, since its assumptions can never be strictly met. "The language spoken in one home is never exactly the same as that spoken in another; available reading matter and the stress on cognitive abilities also vary. Even the novel items depend upon perceptual discriminations that may be acquired in one culture and not in another" (Atkinson et al., 1987, p. 390). For example, Kpelle rice farmers in Nigeria perform better than American adults when asked to estimate the amounts of rice in bowls of different sizes, but more poorly when asked to estimate the lengths of objects, because Kpelle culture has a standardized system for measuring volume (used in buying and selling rice) but not for measuring length (Laboratory of Comparative Human Cognition, 1983; Mussen, Conger, Kagan, & Huston, 1990). Despite these difficulties, test items can be chosen that work reasonably well for many purposes.

Once a large number of items have been selected for possible use, construction of the test can begin. Binet and his immediate successors did this by noting the changes in the proportions of children of different ages who answered a particular item correctly. They reasoned that unless older children were more successful than younger ones in answering the item, the item was unsatisfactory for a test based on the concept of mental development. On other tests, such as the Wechsler scales for children and adults, difficulty is determined by the percentage of subjects in a given population who can answer a particular item correctly. Thus, within each of the subtests included in the Wechsler test (see Table 4.1), the items answered correctly by almost all subjects are listed first and those answered correctly by almost none are listed last. Items that everybody passed or failed would, of course, be of no help and would be thrown out, as would ambiguous or poorly worded questions. The assumption is that the more items a person answers correctly, the greater his or her ability.

Determining IQ. The test items originally developed by Binet were adapted by Lewis Terman of Stanford University and subsequently revised to create what is now known as the *Stanford-Binet Intelligence Scale* (Terman &

T A B L E 4.1 TESTS COMPRISING THE WECHSLER ADULT INTELLIGENCE SCALE AND THE WECHSLER
INTELLIGENCE SCALE FOR CHILDREN

Verbal	Performance
Information	Digit symbol[a]
Comprehension	Picture completion
Arithmetic	Block design
Similarities	Picture arrangement
Digit span[b]	Object assembly
Vocabulary	Coding[c]
	Mazes[d]

Source: Data from D. Wechsler. *Manual for the Wechsler Intelligence Scale for Children—Revised;* and D. Wechsler. *Manual for the Wechsler Adult Intelligence Scale—Revised.* New York: Psychological Corporation, 1974, 1981.

[a]Adult scale only.
[b]Adult scale; alternate test for children.
[c]Scale for children only.
[d]Alternate test for children.

Merrill, 1960; Thorndike, Hagen, & Sattler, 1986). To standardize the test for American schoolchildren, items were administered to a representative sample of children of different ages. Each was assigned to an age level on the basis of the youngest age at which a majority of children answered it correctly. A child's mental age could be determined by adding up the number of items answered correctly at each age level. An intelligence quotient, or IQ, could then be computed by dividing the child's mental age by his or her actual age:

$$IQ = 100 \times \frac{\text{Mental age (MA)}}{\text{Chronological age (CA)}}$$

The most recent version of the Stanford-Binet differs from earlier versions in two important ways:

1. In accordance with current views of intelligence as multidimensional, scores on the 1986 revision are determined for four broad categories of intellectual functioning: *verbal reasoning, quantitative reasoning, abstract/visual reasoning,* and *short-term memory* (Thorndike, Hagen, & Sattler, 1986).

2. Like other recently developed tests of intelligence, such as the WAIS-R, the revised Stanford-Binet determines IQ on the basis of the percentage of subjects in the standardization group falling above or below a certain score. The higher an individual's IQ, the smaller the percentage of his or her contemporaries who perform at or about this level (see Table 4.2). As can be seen in Figure 4.2, the distribution of IQs takes the form of a curve that is typical of many differences among individuals (e.g., differences in height). This is known as the *bell-shaped normal-distribution* curve, in which most individuals cluster around the midpoint and only a few score at either extreme.

T A B L E 4.2 INTELLIGENCE CLASSIFICATIONS

IQ	Classification	Percent Included
130 and above	Very superior	2.2
120–129	Superior	6.7
110–119	High average	16.1
90–109	Average	50.0
80–89	Low average	16.1
70–79	Borderline	6.7
69 and below	Mentally retarded	2.2

Source: D. Wechsler. *WAIS-R Manual: Wechsler Adult Intelligence Scale—Revised.* New York: Psychological Corporation, 1981. By permission.

IQ Constancy

The practical utility of an intelligence test score depends partly on its stability or constancy—that is, its capacity to predict scores on future tests. How confidently can we predict that a child or adolescent who obtains a superior score at one age will obtain a comparable score at a later age? Whereas tests given to infants under 2 years of age have little value for the prediction of future intelligence scores, tests given to older children and adolescents are more highly predictive (Sternberg & Powell, 1983).

Table 4.3 shows the correlations between intelligence test scores during the middle-childhood years and at ages 10 and 18. During the middle-childhood years the correlation between Stanford-Binet test scores given one or two years apart is very high (around .90). Moreover, tests given during this period are fairly good predictors of intellectual status in later adolescence (age 18).

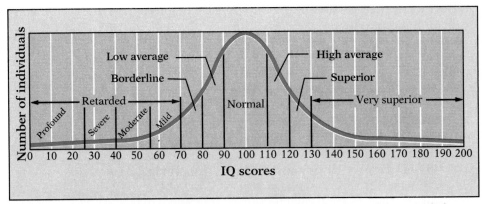

Figure 4.2 The distribution of IQ test categories. Subclassifications of the retarded group are based on criteria adopted by the American Association on Mental Deficiency.

T A B L E 4.3 CORRELATIONS AMONG INTELLIGENCE TEST SCORES AT DIFFERENT AGES

Test age (years)	Retest Age (years)			
	7	10	14	18
2	.46	.37	.28	.31
7		.77	.75	.71
10			.86	.73
14				.76

Source: A. R. Jensen, *Educability and group differences.* New York: Harper & Row: 1973. By permission.

Note: Table entries show correlation between IQs obtained from the same individuals at different ages.

Nevertheless, despite the fact that the IQ becomes more stable in later ages, we must be cautious in using test scores for predicting the future status of individual children because the correlations are not high enough to preclude the possibility of marked changes in individual IQs. Repeated testing of large groups of children between the ages of 6 and 18 found that the IQs of over half the children varied by 15 points or more at some time during the school years, and one-third varied by as much as 20 points. Variations of as much as 50 IQ points were obtained for 0.5 percent of the subjects (Honzik, 1973; Honzik, Macfarlane, & Allen, 1948; Sontag, Baker, & Nelson, 1958).

In general, children and adolescents whose IQ scores increase with age are likely to come from socioeconomically favored environments, whereas those whose scores decrease are likely to come from culturally isolated environments (e.g., remote rural mountain villages) or disadvantaged settings (e.g., inner-city slums) (Bayley, 1968; McCall, Applebaum, & Hogarty, 1973; Roberts, 1971). A wide range of more specific factors have also been found to be related to changes in IQ during the course of development. For example, parents who display interest in their child's educational achievement during the preschool years are more likely to have children who show gains in IQ. One study, however, strongly suggests that parental encouragement is less effective if it is combined with either very harsh or very weak and ineffective discipline. In contrast, "parents of children who show gains in IQ provide their children with acceleration and encouragement for intellectual tasks and take a moderate, rationally structured approach to discipline" (McCall, Applebaum, & Hogarty, 1973, p. 71).

Earlier studies found that children whose IQ scores increase are more independent, competitive, and verbally aggressive than those whose scores decrease (Kagan, Sontag, Baker, & Nelson, 1958; Sontag et al., 1958). Although no relationship was found between pattern of IQ changes and degree of friendliness with age-mates, children whose IQs increased worked harder in school, showed a strong desire to master intellectual problems, and were unlikely to

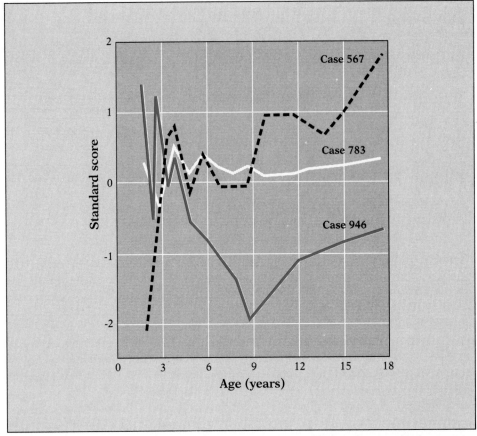

Figure 4.3 IQ scores of three children on successive tests (plotted in standard scores with the mean for children in the overall study taken as 0). (From M. P. Honzik, J. W. McFarlane, and L. Allen (1948). The stability of mental test performance between 2 and 18 years. *Journal of Experimental Education,* **17,** 309–324. Adapted by P. H. Mussen & M. R. Rozensweig et al. in *Psychology: An Introduction.* Lexington, Mass.: Heath, 1973. By permission.)

withdraw from difficult problem situations. Apparently, children and adolescents who attempt to master challenging problems are more likely to show increases in IQ than those who withdraw from such situations.

More individual, idiosyncratic influences, which can be detected only through detailed case histories, may also result in IQ changes upward or downward. Figure 4.3 shows the results of repeated tests of three subjects from the longitudinal Guidance Study at the Institute of Human Development at the University of California, Berkeley (Honzik, 1957). As can be seen, these subjects showed markedly different patterns of change between the ages of 3 and 18. Their individual histories suggest some of the factors that may have been involved:

Case 783 changed very little in IQ through the years, although he had poor health, was insecure, did poorly in school, and had a number of symptoms of emotional disturbance. Case 946 scored as low as 87 and as high as 142. She was the daughter of unhappily married immigrant parents who were divorced when the girl was seven. When she was nine her mother remarried but the girl was very insecure and unhappy at home. When she became better adjusted in her family, her IQ scores rose. Case 567 showed consistent improvement. In her early years she was sickly and shy, but after age 10 her social life expanded and she became very much involved in music and sports. These changes were reflected in her improved test scores (Mussen & Rosenzweig, 1973, p. 365).

Despite such variations, prediction of adult intelligence is more reliable at adolescence than at any earlier age (Siegler & Richards, 1988). In one study, 111 boys and girls were tested as preschoolers, adolescents, and adults (Bayley, 1949). Preschool and adult IQs showed a correlation of .65 (Stanford-Binet), while adolescent and adult IQs showed correlations of .85 (Stanford-Binet) and .80 (Stanford-Binet and WAIS). In general, adolescent measures of IQ appear to be fairly good predictors of adult IQs.

How Useful Are IQs?

What do we actually know when a child or adolescent obtains an IQ of, for example, 119 on the Wechsler Adult Intelligence Scale? At the very least, we know that he or she can complete the items on that test better than approximately nine-tenths of people the same age on whom the test was standardized. And we know that those items are probably representative of a large variety of tasks that are commonly performed by people in their daily lives.

In this sense, the author of the test feels justified in calling it a measure of *general intelligence.* But how useful is such knowledge? Few teachers or potential employers are interested in whether an adolescent can put a manikin together, assemble blocks, or tell you how many weeks there are in a year. They want to know whether he or she will be able to do satisfactory academic work or perform a particular kind of job. In the former case, the only way of settling the question is by examining the actual relationship between IQ and school success. In general, IQ scores have been found to be fairly good predictors of academic performance (Atkinson et al., 1987; Carroll, 1982; Siegler & Richards, 1982). Of course, the fairly high correlation between school success and IQ scores may be attributed partly to the fact that similar kinds of behavior are measured in both cases. Indeed, when it comes to predicting success in less related fields, such as mechanical trades, music, and art, the intelligence test does a far less adequate job, although *on the average* there are IQ differences between people who hold different kinds of jobs (Harrell & Harrell, 1945). For example, accountants, lawyers, and physicians have average IQ scores in the superior range (over 120), while farm hands, laborers, and truck drivers all score in the average range.

Interestingly, in both academic and vocational performance the spread in IQs is greater at lower levels than at higher levels (Bodmer & Cavalli-Sforza, 1970). Thus, although the mean IQ of unskilled workers is below 90, individual workers may score in the very-superior range. On the other hand, among physicians and other professionals whose mean scores are in the superior or very-superior range, one does not find individuals scoring in the 80s. The obvious implication is that although certain tasks—academic or vocational—require a certain minimum level of intellectual capability, intelligence alone does not guarantee success; other factors, ranging from motivation and personality characteristics to environmental stimulation and opportunity, may be necessary as well.

COGNITIVE DEVELOPMENT IN ADOLESCENCE

Although the average individual's IQ remains fairly stable as he or she grows older, mental ability does not. This is a frequent source of confusion. The explanation is that a mental-ability score is an *absolute* measure (i.e., an average 15-year-old can pass more and harder items than an average 5-year-old). IQ, on the other hand, is a *relative* measure; it is based on the individual's ability *in relation to that of his or her contemporaries.* Thus, both the 5-year-old and the 15-year-old may have the same IQ, but the 15-year-old can do many tasks that the 5-year-old cannot; the older child's mental ability is greater.

It is clear from any number of investigations that mental ability, as distinguished from IQ, increases rapidly from birth through adolescence (see Figure 4.4) (Bayley, 1970; Honzik, 1973; Siegler & Richards, 1982). Moreover, certain components of overall mental ability appear to mature more rapidly than oth-

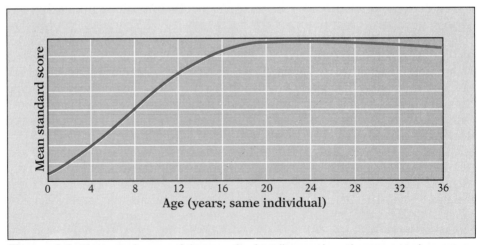

Figure 4.4 Theoretical curve of the growth of intelligence based on repeated examination of the same individuals in the Berkeley Growth Study with infant and preschool intelligence tests, the S-B, W-B, and WAIS. N = 61 cases; the number of cases tested at each of 42 ages averaged 54 per age. (Adapted from N. Bayley. Development of mental abilities. In P. H. Mussen [Ed.], *Carmichael's manual of child psychology* [Vol. 1]. New York: Wiley, 1970. p. 1176, Fig. 3 [3rd ed.]. By permission.)

ers. Thus, so-called *fluid* measures, which appear to depend most heavily on flexibility, adaptability, and speed of information processing (e.g., perceptual speed, conceptualizing the relationships among objects in space, and psychomotor speed and coordination) tend to develop more rapidly than so-called *crystallized* measures, which are influenced more by experience and acquired knowledge (e.g., word fluency, general information, and verbal comprehension) and less by immediate adaptability (Carroll & Maxwell, 1979; Cattell, 1963; Horn, 1976; Snow & Yalow, 1982). Thus, the average young person's score on perceptual speed reaches 80 percent of his or her ultimate peak score by age 12; in contrast, the 80 percent level for verbal comprehension is not reached until age 18; in the case of word fluency that level is reached after age 20.

On measures of *overall* intelligence there appears to be a leveling off during young adulthood, with a slight decline in middle age and a more rapid decline in old age (Baltes, Reese, & Lipsitt, 1978; Bayley, 1970, 1971; Carroll & Maxwell, 1979; Horn & Donaldson, 1980). However, these overall results can be deceptive. They mask the fact that some abilities improve well into the middle years while others reach a peak in the early adult years and then decline. For example, in the Berkeley Growth Study, which involved repeated measurement of the same subjects over the years, scores on **crystallized** measures from the Wechsler intelligence test scales, such as vocabulary and verbal comprehension, were still improving at age 36 (Bayley, 1971). In contrast, scales that appear to depend more on **fluid** abilities, such as object assembly and block design (jigsaw-type tasks), which involve speed of perception and response and the ability to conceptualize objects in space, and digit symbol, a coding task in which response speed is important, peaked in early adulthood and then began to decline (see Figure 4.5).

In the light of such findings, it is not surprising that people in fields like mathematics and physics tend to make their most significant contributions relatively early in life (in their twenties in the case of mathematicians). Those fields require "pure ability," flexibility, and intellectual adaptability. In contrast, the great historians and social philosophers tend to reach their intellectual peak in middle age; in those fields experience, distilled knowledge, and judgment play a relatively greater role.

The course of mental development in later life is less clear, although longitudinal studies suggest that more abilities hold up reasonably well into the sixties and beyond than was previously thought (Baltes et al., 1980; Datan, Rodeheaver, & Hughes, 1987; Schaie & Herzog, 1983). This is particularly true of abilities in which experience, knowledge, and judgment play a major role. Elderly people do less well on tasks that depend heavily on perceptual and response speed, speed of information processing, and the necessity for encoding information, storing it in memory for moderate lengths of time, and then retrieving it. Even here, however, there is some evidence that performance can be improved through training and practice (Baltes et al., 1980; Schaie & Willis, 1986).

In sum, further research is needed to determine the exact rates of develop-

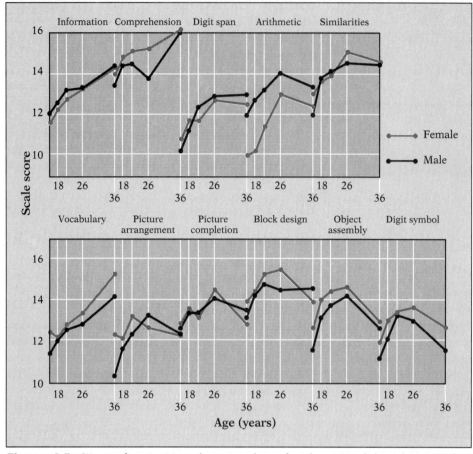

Figure 4.5 Curves of mean scores by sex and age for eleven Wechsler subtests, Berkeley Growth Study. (From N. Bayley. Learning in adulthood: *The role of intelligence.* In H. J. Klausmeier & C. W. Harris [Eds.], *Analysis of conceptual learning.* New York: Academic Press, 1966. By permission.)

ment and decline of various mental functions. Nevertheless, it seems clear that the level of intellectual functioning achieved by late adolescence or early adulthood, and the extent to which that capacity is exploited during this period, largely determine the course of cognitive development in adulthood. As Alfred North Whitehead once remarked, "the imagination is most active between the ages of 19 and 35 and we must keep going thereafter on whatever fizz we have experienced then" (quoted in Elkind, 1968, p. 132).

Sex Differences

There are consistent differences in intellectual functioning between male and female children and adolescents (Deaux, 1985; Linn & Petersen, 1985).

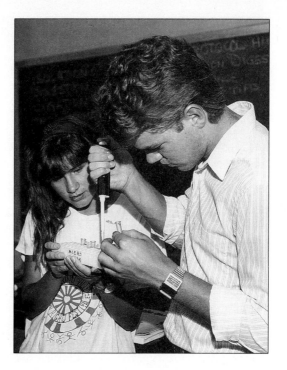

The Livermore Berkeley Laboratory at the University of California, Berkeley, conducts a summer research workshop for selected high school honors students to study basic and applied biology. Here, students are learning techniques for working with DNA (deoxyribonucleic acid), the basic hereditary material of all organisms.

Beginning at about age 10 or 11, girls outperform boys on numerous measures of verbal ability, including language production, creative writing, comprehension of difficult written material, and verbal fluency (Applebee, Langer, & Mullis, 1986; Maccoby & Jacklin, 1974; National Assessment, 1986). At about the same time boys overtake girls on measures of spatial ability and mathematics (Benbow & Stanley, 1980; McGee 1979a; Scarr & Carter-Saltzman, 1982). Spatial ability requires skill in visual transformations. This ability has been studied a great deal, using many different measures (McGee, 1979a, 1979b; Sanders, Soares, & D'Aquila, 1982; Scarr & Carter-Saltzman, 1982). All of the measures are interrelated, but most investigators conceive of at least two distinct types of spatial ability: (1) *spatial visualization,* or the ability to conceptualize a transformed visual arrangement, such as imagining how an object in space would look from a different angle, or deducing from a drawing of a set of gears how movement in one gear would affect the direction and speed of movement in another gear (see Figure 4.6); and (2) *spatial relations* or *spatial orientation*—comprehension of the arrangement of elements within a visual stimulus pattern (e.g., looking at complex designs and seeing if they are the same or, if not, how they differ). Visual-spatial tasks, such as those involved in architecture, engineering, geometry, or graphic arts, use these two abilities to varying degrees.

The strongest sex differences in spatial ability have been found on tasks that have a visualization component (Scarr & Carter-Saltzman, 1982; Vandenberg & Kuse, 1979). Perhaps because the most discriminating measures of this ability are too difficult for younger children, the largest sex differences in spatial

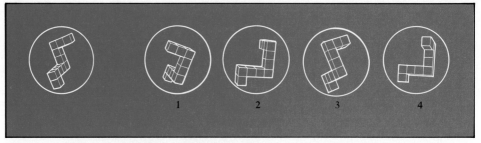

Figure 4.6 Sample item from Vandenberg and Kuse's Mental Rotation Test (From "Mental rotations: A group test of three-dimensional spatial visualization," by S. G. Vandenberg & A. R. Kuse. *Perceptual and Motor Skills,* 1978, **47,** 599–604. Reproduced with permission of authors and publisher.

visualization emerge in adolescence, "when males move well ahead of their female peers, most of whom never catch up" (Scarr & Carter-Saltzman, 1982, p. 870).

During adolescence, boys begin to perform better, on the average, than girls on mathematics tests (Becker, 1983; Dossey, Mullis, & Lindquist, 1977). Much recent research has focused on sex differences in mathematics ability in an effort to determine why such differences exist (Board on Mathematical Sciences, 1989; Dossey, Mullis, Lindquist, & Chambers, 1988). Some studies have found that sex differences disappear when the number of mathematics courses the adolescent has taken is considered (Board, 1989). However, more boys than girls are identified as mathematically precocious *prior* to the time that mathematics courses become elective (Benbow & Stanley, 1980).

It should be stressed that average sex differences in these various abilities, while consistent, are not large; moreover, there is much overlap. Many boys are highly proficient in verbal skills, and many girls do very well at spatial reasoning and mathematics. Nevertheless, the reasons for these differences have been vigorously debated. Because sex differences tend to increase during adolescence, some investigators have concluded that these differences are due primarily to differences in training and social expectations (Board, 1989). Indeed, boys are more often expected to be interested in, and to do well in mathematics and in mechanical tasks, and girls are more often encouraged to pursue and excel in the arts, languages, and literature—although in recent years such gender-oriented expectations have diminished. But it is also possible that biological factors play a significant role in determining some of the sex differences that become more apparent during adolescence (Scarr & Carter-Saltzman, 1982). For example, late maturers of both sexes tend to outperform early maturers on visual-spatial tasks (McGee, 1979a, 1979b; Petersen, 1981; Sanders & Soares, 1986; Scarr & Carter-Saltzman, 1982). Late maturers are also more likely to have higher spatial than verbal scores, whereas among early maturers the reverse is true (Atkinson et al., 1987; Newcombe & Bandura, 1983; Waber, 1977, 1979; Waber et al., 1985). In one extensive study, late-maturing girls outperformed male peers of the same age on tests of mathematical ability, whereas early-maturing boys had better verbal skills than late maturers (Carlsmith, Dornbusch, & Gross, 1983).

In brief, early maturation appears to favor verbal ability, while late maturation appears to favor visual-spatial and mathematical skills. Because females generally mature about two years earlier than males, rates of physical maturation may be one determinant of sex differences in ability (Atkinson et al., 1987). In addition, a number of studies of sex differences in spatial abilities, particularly spatial visualization, have attempted to link these differences to specific genetic factors—possibly a recessive gene located on the X chromosome (Bouchard & McGee, 1977; Scarr & Carter-Saltzman, 1988; Vandenberg & Kuse, 1978). However, much additional research must be done before any firm conclusions can be reached on this question.

It seems likely that both environmental and biological influences may play a part in determining sex differences in some cognitive abilities. Even so, sex differences in these abilities are generally small, and there is much overlap. Moreover, in many other cognitive abilities—such as concept mastery and reasoning—there are no consistent differences between adolescent boys and girls.

It is also clear that sex differences in intellectual functioning do not explain the different numbers of men and women found in certain occupations. For example, even if we assume that a very high level of spatial ability (ninety-fifth percentile) is required for engineering—and this is true in only a few areas of engineering—the ratio of men to women in that occupation on the basis of spatial ability would be 2:1 rather than 15:1, as it is at present (Hyde, 1981; U.S. Bureau of the Census, 1990).

GENETIC DETERMINANTS OF MENTAL ABILITY

If the measures employed on intelligence tests reflect underlying ability and not merely the results of specific learning opportunities (at least for the average individual in the population on which the test was standardized), and if the potential ceiling on an individual's ability is, as assumed, set by heredity, then we might expect to find evidence of genetic influences on intelligence test performance. To what extent are the kinds of abilities measured by intelligence tests in fact influenced by heredity? This is a controversial topic, and discussions of it frequently generate much more heat than light. Some authorities assert that genetic influences play a dominant role in determining intellectual abilities; others claim that the evidence to support such an assertion is slight at best. How can these conflicting views be resolved?

If genetic factors do play a significant role in determining an individual's intellectual abilities, we would expect to find that a child's or adolescent's IQ is more highly correlated with the IQs of his or her parents and other immediate relatives than with those of randomly selected nonrelatives. This is indeed the case. However, the matter is not so simple. Parents who may have provided their children with a superior genetic endowment may also be providing them with other advantages that may be related to intellectual ability—good health, a stimulating home environment, superior educational opportunities, and the like. Thus, if we are to isolate the potential contributions of heredity, a way must be found to control for the potential effects of such environmental variables.

Twin Studies

The investigation of the effects of heredity on intellectual ability is greatly aided by comparing **monozygotic** (MZ) twins with ordinary brothers and sisters and with **dizygotic** (DZ) twins. (The latter are no more alike genetically than ordinary siblings.) If genetic influences play an important role in the determination of intellectual ability, we would expect the IQs of monozygotic twins to be more highly correlated than those of dizygotic twins or nontwin siblings.

This turns out to be true. A review of thirty studies comparing the intelligence and abilities of monzygotic and dizygotic twins of the same sex found average correlations of .85 for monozygotic twins and .58 for dyzygotic twins (Bouchard & McGee, 1981). The correlation for dizygotic twins is approximately the same as that for nontwin siblings raised in the same family. Both of these, in turn, are substantially higher than the correlation for unrelated individuals raised in the same family (Loehlin, Willerman, & Horn, 1988; Plomin, 1986; Scarr & Kidd, 1983; Segal, 1985).

One fascinating investigation has found that even the patterns of developmental change at early ages may have a genetic component (Wilson, 1972, 1975, 1983; Wilson & Harpring, 1972). Repeated measurements of mental and motor development were conducted during the first two years of life. When the scores of 261 pairs of monozygotic and dizygotic twins were analyzed, the profiles of their developmental spurts and lags were very similar, especially for MZ twins (see Figure 4.7). Apparently "the developmental sequence is an expression of timed gene action which may produce spurts or lags between ages" (Wilson & Harpring, 1972, p. 280). In a follow-up study of the same subjects during the preschool and school years, similar results were found; indeed, the mental-developmental correlations between MZ twins rose slightly with age, while those for DZ twins showed a significant decrease (Wilson, 1975, 1977, 1983).

Although twin studies comparing monozygotic and dizygotic twins can be extremely valuable in the search for genetic influences, some qualifications should be kept in mind. For one thing, it is frequently assumed that because they have the same genetic makeup, monozygotic twins are biologically identical at birth. This is not necessarily so. For example, one twin usually weighs slightly more than the other, perhaps because the two fetuses shared unequally in intrauterine blood circulation. It has been shown that even small differences between identical twins at birth can interact with the environment to produce larger differences in behavior (Smith, 1976).

Another inaccurate assumption is that the environmental influences to which DZ twins are exposed are as similar as those to which MZ twins are exposed (Plomin, 1986). It is true that both DZ and MZ twins grow up in the

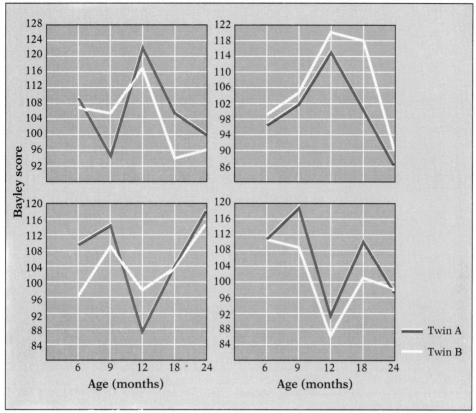

Figure 4.7 Bayley score profiles for four pairs of twins illustrating concordance in developmental status at each age and congruence for the pattern of changes over age. (From R. S. Wilson & E. B. Harpring. Mental and motor development in infant twins. *Developmental Psychology,* 1972, **7,** 277–287. Copyright 1972, American Psychological Association. By permission.)

same family and share many experiences. However, several studies have found that compared with fraternal twins, identical twins spend more time together, have more similar reputations, and are more likely to be in the same classrooms, have similar health records, and in many other respects share a nearly identical physical and social environment (Jones, 1946, 1954). MZ twins may also be treated in more similar ways by parents, siblings, peers, and others than DZ twins, partly because they look alike and partly because their behavior is more similar to begin with (Lytton, 1977; Plomin, Willerman, & Loehlin, 1976; Scarr & Carter-Saltzman, 1979; Willerman, 1979). Even in twin studies, then, environmental influences cannot be fully controlled.

Adoption Studies

Another useful way to investigate genetic influences on intelligence is to study children and adolescents who have been raised by adoptive parents from

Studies have found that the IQs of adopted children tend to be closer to the IQs of their natural parents than of their adopted parents, although environmental influences are also important.

a very early age and to compare their IQs with those of their biological and adoptive parents (Loehlin et al., 1988; Plomin, 1986; Plomin & DeFries, 1985). Because these children have had little or no contact with their biological parents, any similarity to those parents is assumed to reflect genetic influences. The correlation between the IQs of children and their adopted parents is assumed to indicate environmental influences.

A comprehensive analysis of the best-controlled investigations that had been carried out as of 1975 found that when all subjects from these studies were combined, there was a correlation of .19 between adoptive parents' intelligence test scores (obtained by averaging mother's and father's scores) and those of their adopted children (Munsinger, 1975). In contrast, the correlation between those children's scores and those of their biological parents was .48. However, the correlation between parents' and children's scores for children raised by their biological parents was .58, suggesting that both heredity *and* environment made important contributions.

In a French adoption study, children who had been born to unskilled parents and raised in upper-income professional families were studied (Schiff, Duyme, Dumaret, & Tomkiewicz, 1982). The investigators found that the IQs

Box 4.1 MINORITY GROUP MEMBERSHIP AND INTELLIGENCE

A number of investigations have indicated that the *average* IQ scores of members of some minority groups tend to be lower than the average scores of socioeconomically advantaged whites and of the U.S. population as a whole (Baughman, 1971; Dreger & Miller, 1960, 1966; Roberts, 1971). These findings have led some people to conclude that members of certain groups, on the average, are genetically limited in intellectual capacities compared with advantaged whites and that their IQ scores are lower at least partly because they have less potential ability (Eysenck, 1981; Jensen, 1969). Others have argued that any differences in average IQ scores are due to environmental factors such as poor prenatal nutrition, poor health, less stimulating early environments, inferior schools, and discrimination (Botwinick, 1977; Bradley, Caldwell, & Elardo, 1977; Nichols, 1984). When efforts are made to equalize some of these factors, the IQ differences are consistently reduced (Bodmer & Cavalli-Sforza, 1970; Frazer & Nora, 1966; Kamin, 1981; Layzer, 1974; Lazar & Darlington, 1982).

Whether proper control of all relevant environmental factors would eliminate all differences in intellectual functioning cannot be conclusively demonstrated at present. The question can ultimately be answered only by making certain that all potentially relevant environmental differences between racial or ethnic groups have been equalized or adequately controlled for—a goal that is still a long way off.

But even if a definitive study could be conducted, it is hard to see how the results could affect the way members of either majority or minority groups *should* reasonably act (although they might affect how they *would* act). It should not be forgotten that even under present social conditions, variations in IQ within any racial or ethnic group are far larger than any differences that might exist between groups, and there is a wide overlap in their distribution curves. Therefore, it is impossible to predict an individual's IQ from the color of his or her skin (Baughman, 1971; Nora & Fraser, 1986). And this will always be the case, regardless of the findings of any future genetic research. There will always be many black adolescents who are brighter than many white (or brown or red) adolescents, as well as the reverse.

The only possible conclusion, in our view, is that each individual must be judged on his or her own merits—which is, after all, the presumed aim of any truly democratic society. But as long as racial or ethnic discrimination persists, attempts to apply comparative IQ data inappropriately must be resisted while we seek to create social conditions that will provide every individual "with equal opportunities to develop all his potential qualities, both intellective and nonintellective" (Baughman, 1971, p. 13).

of the adopted children were similar to those of natural children from the same socioeconomically advantage group, and 14 points higher than those of children of unskilled workers in general. Similar results were found in a study of black and interracial children who had been adopted in infancy by middle-class white families (Scarr & Weinberg, 1976).

In sum, similarities in IQ are highest between people who are closely related genetically (i.e., monozygotic twins) and lowest between people who are unrelated. It seems clear that an individual's genetic inheritance is an important determinant of IQ. However, there are also similarities between the IQs of adoptive parents and their adopted children. Although some of these similarities could be due to selective placement by adoption agencies, they also reflect the importance of the home environment (Scarr & Kidd, 1983; Munsinger, 1975; Willerman, 1979). Environmental as well as genetic factors are important in raising or lowering a child's level of intellectual performance. However, environmental forces are effective only within the ultimate limits set by heredity.

CREATIVITY

Although it is difficult to define objectively, *creativity* impresses us as an important concept (Hocevar, 1981; Kogan, 1983; Wallach, 1985). We all know people, including adolescents, whom we acknowledge to be intelligent but who appear to lack creativity. Similarly, we know people who appear to be highly creative even though they may not obtain particularly high scores on an intelligence test. But what exactly do we mean by creativity?

Perhaps the best way to approach the definition of creativity is to consider the intellectual experiences of successful artists and scientists. When we do this, a significant focus emerges:

> The majority of the available introspective accounts have in common a concern with associative freedom and uniqueness. These accounts consistently stressed the ability to give birth to associative content that is abundant and original, yet relevant to the task at hand rather than bizarre. The writer's classical fear of "drying up" and of never being able to produce another word, the composer's worry over not having another piece of music within him, the scientist's concern that he won't be able to think of another experiment to perform—these are but indications of how preoccupied creative individuals can become with the question of associative flow. Introspections about times of creative insight also seem to reflect a kind of task-centered, permissive, or playful set on the part of the person doing the associating. Einstein refers to the "associative play" or "combinatory play." The person stands aside a bit as associative material is given freedom to reach the surface (Wallach & Kogan, 1971, p. 88).

This kind of "playful," uninhibited associative freedom is similar to what psychoanalysts have in mind when they speak of "regression in the service of the ego"—the ability to relinquish conscious controls and allow free expression of previously subconscious associations—as an essential element of creativity (Kris, 1952). Investigators have used a variety of techniques to measure

Creativity requires more than intelligence alone. We all know people, including adolescents, whom we acknowledge to be intelligent, but who appear singularly lacking in creativity.

associative freedom, or divergent thinking, in studies of the relationship between creativity and personality characteristics, familial influences, and the like (Amabile, 1983; Guilford, 1975; Kogan, 1983; Wallach, 1985).

One such study sought to determine whether creativity could be differentiated from intelligence per se, and also investigated the relationship of personality characteristics and social behavior to creativity (Wallach & Kogan, 1971). The subjects, fifth-grade boys and girls, were given standard intelligence tests as well as tests of creativity. The creativity measures required subjects to gen-

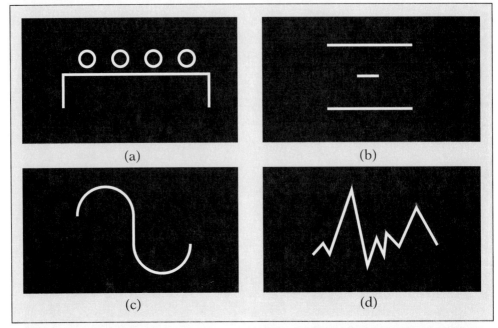

Figure 4.8 Drawings used to test creativity. (From *Modes of thinking in young children: A study of the creativity-intelligence distinction*, by M. A. Wallach & N. Kogan. Copyright 1965 by Holt, Rinehart and Winston, Inc. Reprinted by permission of Holt, Rinehart and Winston, Inc.)

erate many unusual hypotheses. For example, in one test the subjects were told a characteristic and then asked to name as many objects as they could that had that characteristic (e.g., "Name all the things you know that are *sharp*"). Subjects were also asked to think up various uses for objects (e.g., "Tell me all the different ways that you would use a *newspaper*"). In a third test the young people were shown line drawings (see Figure 4.8 *a* and *b*) and asked to think of all the things the drawings might be. They were also shown nonsense line designs (see Figure 4.8 *c* and *d*) and asked to enumerate all the things the designs made them think of. Subjects were classified as creative if they gave many answers, some of which were unusual or unique compared with those given by other children. These measures of creativity correlated highly with one another, but they showed little correlation with the various measures of intelligence employed in the study. These findings suggest that creativity and intelligence can indeed be meaningfully differentiated from each other.[1]

[1]The results of other investigations indicate that a moderately high level of intellectual ability is essential for creativity but that beyond a basic "floor" that varies in different fields, there is little relationship between intellectual abilities and creativity. For example, in several investigations of creative writing, modest correlations between creativity and intelligence test scores were obtained over the total range of intelligence, but beyond an IQ level of 120 intelligence was a negligible factor in creativity (Barron, 1963; MacKinnon, 1983; Walberg, 1971; Wallach, 1985).

Subjects were then grouped into four categories: high creativity–high intelligence, high creativity–low intelligence, low creativity–high intelligence, and low creativity–low intelligence. Using observations of the subjects' classroom behavior over a two-week period, as well as other information, such as the results of tests of emotional sensitivity and anxiety, the investigators found a number of significant differences among the four groups of subjects. Those who were high in both creativity and intelligence appeared self-confident, independent, and able to "exercise within themselves both control and freedom, both adult-like and child-like kinds of behavior" (Wallach & Kogan, 1971, p. 98). Those who were high in creativity but low in intelligence appeared to be in angry conflict with themselves and with their school environment. They were "beset by feelings of unworthiness and inadequacy. In a stress-free context, however, they can blossom forth cognitively" (Wallach & Kogan, 1971, p. 98). In contrast, subjects who were low in creativity but high in intelligence were loath to "stick their necks out" or try anything that was "far out" or unconventional. Their social behavior, academic efforts, emotional responses, and thinking all tended to be cautious, conventional, and concerned primarily with "correctness." Finally, subjects who were low in both creativity and intelligence seemed bewildered. They engaged in "various defensive maneuvers ranging from useful adaptations such as intensive social activity to regressions such as passivity or psychosomatic symptoms" (Wallach & Kogan, 1971, p. 98).

Of special interest were the findings on anxiety in the four groups. The level of anxiety was highest in the low-creativity–low-intelligence group and lowest in the low-creativity–high-intelligence group, with the two high-creativity groups scoring in the middle range. These findings agree with those of other investigations, which indicate that creativity tends to be greatest in the presence of an intermediate level of anxiety. If anxiety is either too low or too high, creativity is reduced. It appears that "creativity need not be all sweetness and light . . . but may well involve a tolerance for and understanding of sadness and pain. To think otherwise is to fall prey to the rather widespread American stereotype that suffering is always a bad thing and is to be avoided at all cost" (Wallach & Kogan, 1971, p. 97). By "playing it safe," members of the high-intelligence–low-creativity group were better able to avoid anxiety, but at the cost of seriously limiting their creative potential and inner freedom (Leith, 1972; Wallach & Kogan, 1971).

Other studies have found that even among gifted adolescents there are differences between those who score higher on originality than on intellectual mastery and those who score higher on intellectual mastery than on originality (Hogan, 1980; Horowitz & O'Brian, 1985; Welsh, 1975, 1977). The former tend to be more sociable, impulsive, and nonconforming; their thinking is generally less precise and more fantasy based. In contrast, the latter tend to be more shy and guarded and more conventional; their thinking is more deliberate, logical, and narrowly analytical—it focuses more on individual trees than on the forest as a whole (Hogan, 1980).

In another approach, the attitude patterns of high school seniors who scored high on measures of creativity were compared with those of *unselected* adolescents who were similar in age, socioeconomic status, and parental occupation. As can be seen in Table 4.4, the creative seniors emerged as far more intuitive, independent, and willing to experiment, as well as more resistant to social pressures. In contrast, seniors in the unselected comparison group were oriented much more toward rules and tradition, structure, and passive compliance.

Other studies have yielded similar results. Depending somewhat on area of talent, creative adolescents have been found to be more independent, unconventional, self-reliant, and imaginative, and more spontaneous and energetic. They appear to be better able to tolerate the tension that comes from holding strongly opposed values, as well as more capable of reconciling them; they are more flexible, intuitive, and capable of tolerating ambiguity; more open to feelings; and generally more socially poised and self-confident than their less creative peers (Albert & Runco, 1989; Barron & Harrington, 1981; Dellas & Gaier, 1970; Janos & Robinson, 1985).

Promoting Creativity in Adolescents

Whether creative thinking can be promoted among adolescents appears to depend on a variety of external as well as internal factors, including family influences and the attitudes and behaviors of teachers and school administrators. Creativity appears to be fostered in direct proportion to the extent that

T A B L E 4.4 COMPARISON OF HIGH PATTERNS OF HIGHLY CREATIVE HIGH SCHOOL SENIORS AND A SIMILAR UNSELECTED GROUP ON THE RUNNER STUDIES OF ATTITUDE PATTERNS

Attitude or orientation	Creative seniors (N = 115)		Unselected (N = 100)	
	Number	Percent	Number	Percent
Experimental	94	82	23	23[a]
Intuitive	105	91	56	56[a]
Rules and tradition	22	19	40	40[a]
Planfulness (structure)	17	15	44	44[a]
Power and authority	18	17	18	18
Passive compliance	38	33	56	56[a]
Extraversiveness	51	44	44	44
Hostility and blame	47	41	59	59[b]
Resistance to social pressure	76	66	35	35[a]
Social anxiety	91	79	70	70
Pleasure in tool-implemented hand skills	66	57	78	78
Performance anxiety	88	76	70	70

Source: E. P. Torrance and D. C. Dauw. Attitude patterns of creatively gifted high school seniors. *Gifted Child Quarterly,* Summer 1966, 53–57. By permission.

[a]Difference in percentages is significant at better than .01 level.
[b]Difference in percentages is significant at better than .05 level.

parents and the schools value creative thinking, curiosity, and unusual questions and interests; recognize and reward unusual skills and talents; and try to provide a rich and varied cultural and educational atmosphere, one that includes opportunities for self-initiated learning (Bloom, 1985; Hogan, 1980; Lytton, 1972; Walberg, 1971). One investigation found that parents of high-intelligence–low-creativity adolescents tend to emphasize grades, conformity, cleanliness, and manners (Wallach & Kogan, 1971). In contrast, parents of high-intelligence–high creativity adolescents are less critical of their children and encourage openness, enthusiasm, and interest in new experiences.

Adolescence is the stage in development when the individual, with greatly expanded cognitive skills, is most open to curiosity, exploration, and a sense of adventure—intellectually as well as in other areas. For this reason, failure to take advantage of the adolescent's creative potential (or, worse, actively discouraging it) is not only disheartening but wasteful.

QUALITATIVE ASPECTS OF COGNITIVE DEVELOPMENT

As noted earlier, the changes in cognitive functioning that take place during adolescence are both qualitative and quantitative. Although for many years quantitative aspects received the greatest emphasis, in recent years interest in the qualitative aspects of mental development—maturational changes in the processes underlying intellectual performance—has grown rapidly. Inherent in the idea of qualitative changes with age is the concept of *stages* in the development of mental functioning, together with the assumption of a progression,

The emphasis on stages of cognitive development owes more to the Swiss psychologist Jean Piaget than to any other theorist or investigator.

or sequence, from one stage to another (Fischer & Silvern, 1985). In other words, regardless of the age at which a given child or adolescent reaches a particular stage, he or she cannot reach that stage without having first completed earlier stages.

The recent emphasis on stages of cognitive development owes more to the Swiss psychologist Jean Piaget than to any other theorist or investigator (Flavell, 1963, 1985). Piaget viewed human cognition as "a specific form of biological adaptation of a complex organism in a complex environment" (Flavell, 1985, p. 4). The focus of Piaget's concern was not on individual differences (as in the case of standard intelligence tests) but, rather, on the sequence of cognitive stages that children pass through on their way to mature logical reasoning.

According to Piaget, there are four major stages in cognitive development: (1) the **sensorimotor stage** (birth to 18 months), (2) the **preoperational stage** (18 months to 7 years), (3) the stage of **concrete** operations (7 to 12 years), and (4) the stage of **formal operations** (from about age 12 on) (Piaget, 1954, 1970). In this theoretical system, thought is viewed as developing through the gradual internalization of action (Inhelder & Piaget, 1958). During the sensorimotor stage (the period prior to the acquisition of language), the child is developing rather simple generalized responses, or schemas of action, to objects and persons in the world around him or her. He or she may discover that already acquired responses may be applied to new objects (i.e., shaking or banging an unfamiliar toy), a process called *assimilation*. However, in addition to incorporating new objects into existing schemas or response systems, the young child is also learning to modify existing responses to adjust to the unique characteristics of new objects; this process is called *accommodation*.

> The 2-year-old child who has never been exposed to a magnet may initially assimilate it to prior schemata and act toward the magnet as he or she does toward a familiar toy. The child may bang it, bounce it, throw it, or try to make it produce a noise. But once the child discovers the unique quality of the magnet, that it attracts metal, he or she will now accommodate to that quality and begin to apply the magnet to a variety of objects to see if they will adhere to it (Mussen, Conger, & Kagan, 1979, p. 17).

Obviously, unless the young child is capable of accommodation as well as assimilation, progress in mental development would not be possible. Assimilation provides for continuity in development and enables the child to profit from his or her past experiences; accommodation provides for meaningful growth and change. Much of a child's mental development, in Piaget's view, involves the resolution of tensions between the opposing processes of assimilation and accommodation.

During the preoperational stage, children's mental growth advances significantly, for they now have the tool of language and can manipulate meanings as well as objects. They can deal with objects as symbols for other objects (e.g., pretend that a block of wood is a toy car, or that a doll is a baby girl). But their conceptual ability is still relatively rudimentary, although recent research indicates that when dealing with relatively simple and familiar events and objects preschool children are likely to display greater cognitive ability than Piagetian theory would predict (Gelman, 1978; Keating, 1975, 1980; Mussen et al., 1990).

The Stage of Concrete Operations

In middle and late childhood (about ages 7–11) the child's thought shows impressive advances from the preoperational period. The preoperational child functions largely in terms of "the phenomenal, before-the-eye reality" (Flavell, 1963, p. 203). Even when the child is treating an object symbolically (e.g., pretending that a block of wood is a toy car), he or she is still dealing with it primarily in terms of actual, unsystematic (Piaget calls it "intuitive") physical manipulation in the here and now. For example, the child does not mentally explore the various situations in which the "car" might logically become involved. In contrast, in the period of concrete operations the child begins to extend thought from the *actual* toward the *potential* (Elkind, 1970; Flavell, 1963, 1985). This extension is aided by the development of concrete-operational cognitive structures. Unlike preoperational children, who are basically limited to responding directly to the properties of objects themselves, 7- to 11-year-olds become increasingly capable of dealing not only with the properties of objects but also with the relationships among them.

The concrete-operational child begins to utilize a new set of rules, called *groupings*, for dealing with these relationships. Those rules greatly increase the flexibility and power of the child's thinking. One such rule is the rule of equivalence: If A is equal to B in some way (e.g., length) and if B is equal to C, then it must be true that A is equal to C. Given this information, the child does not have to measure A and C to know that this is the case.

Another rule that the child recognizes is that there are certain fixed relationships among objects or properties of objects. For example, the concrete-operational child can appreciate that if A is longer than B and B is longer than C, then A must be longer than C. The child at this stage also realizes that objects (or their qualities) can belong to more than one category or *class* (e.g., a chocolate bar can belong both to a class of objects that are sweet and to a class of objects that are brown. In addition, he or she begins to recognize that classes can be *hierarchical.* For example, the concrete-operational child can accept the idea that an orange belongs to the class *fruit,* which, in turn, belongs in the larger class *food.*

An important point is that the concrete-operational child is able to engage in intellectual operations that are *reversible.* For example, the child recognizes that if four poker chips are removed from a pile of six chips and those four chips are further subdivided into two piles of two each, after which the whole procedure is reversed, the final pile must contain the original number of chips. Concrete-operational children can also *decenter;* that is, "they can focus their attention on several attributes of an object or event simultaneously and understand the relations among dimensions or attributes" (Mussen et al., 1990, p. 276). For example, a pebble is both small and light; a bowling ball, on the other hand, is both large and heavy.

The development of this system of concrete operations makes possible a kind of reasoning that does not appear in the preschool years: Children become increasingly able to think in *relational* terms. Where previously they might have been able to describe an object in absolute terms as dark, they now become able to think *relatively* as well, so that they can also describe the object as darker than or lighter than another object. Because they are less limited by the absolute properties of objects, concrete-operational children can also deal with *class inclusion:* They can reason simultaneously about part of the whole and the whole. For example, if younger children are shown ten red blocks and five yellow blocks and asked whether there are more red blocks or more blocks, they are likely to reply that there are more red blocks. As soon as they deal with subclasses, the larger class is destroyed, since they cannot conceive that a particular object can belong to two classes at the same time. A 6- or 7-year-old child, on the other hand, can view red blocks as included in the more general class *blocks,* and will give the correct answer.

Another important operation that is mastered by the school-age child is *conservation.* The idea that liquids and solids can change in shape without changing in volume or mass is a result of concrete-operational thinking. For example, it is not until about age 6 or 7 that the child is able to grasp the fact that an amount of liquid poured from a large glass into two smaller glasses remains the same. A 4- or 5-year-old believes that if one changes the shape of an object one also changes it quantity; the child does not realize that its quantity is *conserved.*

> The concrete-operational child solves the problem by taking account of both the width of the container and the levels of the liquids at the same time. He thus comes to realize that for every change in the level of the liquids there is a corresponding change in the widths of the containers which exactly compensates for change in level. The awareness of reversibility, thanks to the concrete-operational system, allows the child to discover the conservation of quantities (Elkind, 1968, p. 141).

Similarly, having gained the ability to depart from the absolute properties of objects, the concrete-operational child becomes capable of *serialization* (or serial ordering)—the ability to arrange objects along some abstract dimension such as size, weight, or brightness (e.g., to arrange dolls in order of height from shortest to tallest). The child is able to do this because he or she can comprehend that doll B must be viewed *both* as taller than doll A *and* as shorter than doll C if it is to fit into its proper place. Younger children fail at such tasks because they cannot recognize that an element can simultaneously stand in two different relations with other elements.

Piaget notes that the concrete-operational child's ability to move from the actual to the potential is a logical consequence of just such processes as these. For example, once a child can view doll A as shorter than doll B, which, in turn, is shorter than doll C, it is "a simple potential prolongation of the actions or operations applied to the given content" to extend thought to the *possibility* of a doll D that would be taller than doll C (Inhelder & Piaget, 1958). In John Flavell's words, "The structures of concrete operations are, to use a homely analogy, rather like parking lots whose individual parking spaces are now occupied and now empty; the squares themselves endure, however, and lead their owner to look beyond the cars actually present towards potential, future occupants of the vacant and to-be-vacant spaces" (1963, p. 203).

The child's thought clearly makes many significant advances during the concrete-operational period, and those advances continue to play an important role throughout life. However, the child's thinking is still limited when contrasted with that of the adolescent. As Piaget and his collaborator, Barbel Inhelder, noted, "concrete thought remains essentially attached to empirical reality. . . . Therefore, it attains no more than a concept of 'what is possible,' which is a simple (and not very great) extension of the empirical situation" (1958, p. 250).

In other words, the starting point for concrete-operational children is always the real rather than the potential, and they can reason only about things with which they have had direct personal experience. Moreover, they have difficulty as soon as they have to deal with a hypothetical or contrary-to-fact proposition. And while they can deal simultaneously with two classes, relations, or quantitative dimensions, such as size and color, that is about the limit of their capabilities. As soon as more than two variables have to be taken into account, they run into trouble (Elkind, 1968).

The Stage of Formal Operations

During the stage of formal operations—usually beginning around age 12 but with marked individual variations—the adolescent gains a number of important capabilities that were not present in the middle-childhood years. In Piaget's view, the most basic of those capabilities is a shift of emphasis from the *real* to the *possible*, from *what is* to *what might be*. The concrete-operational child mentally manipulates objects and events; the formal-operational child can manipulate ideas about *hypothetical* situations. For example, if a 7-year-old is asked, "If all creatures from outer space have yellow feet, and this creature has yellow feet, is it from outer space?" he or she is likely to say, "I never saw a creature from outer space," or, "Things don't have yellow feet" (Mussen, Conger, Kagan, & Huston, 1990). The 7-year-old has trouble reasoning about unreal or improbable events. When asked the same question, an adolescent can reach a conclusion based solely on logic. "The child usually begins with reality and moves reluctantly, if at all, to possibility; in contrast, the adolescent or adult is more apt to begin with possibility and only subsequently proceed to reality" (Flavell, 1985, p. 98).

Hypothetico-Deductive Reasoning. The subordination of the real to the possible is reflected in the way adolescents approach problems (Flavell, 1985). Unlike the concrete-operational child, the adolescent is able to approach a problem by trying to imagine all the possible relationships among items in a given body of data. Then, through a process that combines logical analysis and experimental verification, he or she can determine which of the possible relationships actually holds true. In short, the adolescent becomes more capable of *hypothetico-deductive* thinking, which is much like the reasoning of the scientist. The process of deduction is no longer confined to perceived realities but extends to hypothetical statements.

The development of hypothetico-deductive thinking and related aspects of formal operations makes adolescent thought much richer, broader, and more flexible than that of the concrete-operational child. Although the latter is capable of a rudimentary form of hypothesis formation closely linked to concrete experience, the limits of this capability are readily apparent. For example, once they have thought of one possible explanation for a problem situation, younger children are likely to immediately accept it as true. In contrast, adolescents are likely to recognize the arbitrary nature of hypotheses. Consequently, they tend to consider all possible explanations, even those that may be rather fanciful, and to examine the evidence for or against each, before adopting one of them. Even then, as we shall see, they may hesitate to commit themselves.

This fundamental difference in approach between the younger child and the average adolescent was clearly demonstrated in an experiment by David Elkind. Two groups of subjects, children 8–9 years old and adolescents 13–14 years old, were given a concept formation problem involving pictures of wheeled and nonwheeled tools and wheeled and nonwheeled vehicles. The pictures were presented in pairs, with each pair including both a wheeled object and a nonwheeled object. In each case the subject was asked to choose one member of the pair. Choosing a wheeled object always made a light go on whereas choosing a nonwheeled object did not. The subject was asked to determine the kind of picture that would make the signal light go on every time.

Adolescents and younger children handled the task in very different ways:

> Only half of the children were able to arrive at the notion that it was the choice of wheeled objects which made the light go on. Furthermore, it took those children who did succeed almost all of the allotted 72 trials to arrive at a correct solution. On the other hand, *all* of the adolescents solved the problem and many did so in as few as 10 trials (Elkind, 1966, p. 145).

The tendency of adolescents to consider a series of alternative hypotheses, testing each against the facts and discarding those that prove to be wrong, was apparent in their spontaneous verbalizations during the experiment ("Maybe it's transportation. . . . No, it must be something else, I'll try . . ."). In this fashion adolescents quickly solved the problem. The children, on the other hand, appeared to become fixated on an initial hypothesis that was strongly suggested by the data (e.g., tool versus nontool or vehicle versus nonvehicle). They clung to that hypothesis even though they continued to fail on most tests. Although the adolescents also might have considered such hypotheses initially, they quickly discarded them when they were not verified by experience. It appears that an important part of the child's lack of flexibility is an inability to clearly differentiate hypotheses from reality. Once a hypothesis had been adopted, it became "true" and the child felt no need to test it further. "Indeed,

Adolescents who have attained the stage of formal operations can reason about hypothetical problems and explore alternative possibilities in a systematic search for solutions to problems.

[the child] seems unaware of the hypothetical quality of his strategy and seems to feel that it is imposed from without rather than constructed from within" (Elkind, 1966, p. 146). In Piaget's view, it is the adolescent's awareness of *possibility* that enables him or her to distinguish thought from reality (Inhelder & Piaget, 1958).

Other related differences distinguish the thought of an adolescent from that of a concrete-operational child. Unlike the child, the adolescent can take his or her own thought as an object and reason about it. Formal thinking is, above all, *propositional thinking* (Flavell, 1985). As Piaget commented, "When verbal statements are substituted for objects, a new type of thinking—propositional logic—is imposed on the logic of classes and relations relevant to these objects" (Inhelder & Piaget, 1958, p. 253). This capability may lead adolescents to search for inconsistencies or fallacies in their own thought. Thus, a 14-year-old girl may become preoccupied with the following propositions:

1. God loves humanity.
2. There are many suffering human beings (Mussen et al., 1990, p. 281).

The apparent incompatibility of these propositions may lead her to try to resolve the tension, either by finding a way to reconcile the propositions or by questioning the validity of one or the other.

At times adolescents may feel almost like spectators at the creation of their own thoughts. One adolescent remarked, "I found myself thinking about my future, and then I began to think about why I was thinking about my future, and then I began to think about why I was thinking about why I was thinking about my future." This preoccupation with thought itself is characteristic of the emergence of the stage of formal operations.

Other Characteristics of Adolescent Thought

In addition to the aspects of adolescent thought that were emphasized by Piaget, there are a number of other changes to which psychologists have recently called attention. Compared with younger children, adolescents are more likely to be aware of the distinction between simply perceiving something and storing it in memory; they are also more likely to be aware of their own memory capacities and limitations, and to use sophisticated techniques (mnemonic devices) to help them remember, such as dividing a long number into "chunks." "The common thread is the individual's awareness and knowledge about cognitive activity itself and about the mechanisms that can make it more or less efficient" (Keating, 1980, p. 215).

Adolescents are also more likely to use efficient problem-solving strategies in approaching a wide variety of tasks. A good example is the game of "Twenty Questions," in which one player has to determine what the other player is thinking of, using as few questions as possible. An adolescent or adult is far more likely than a younger child to adopt an overall strategy that involves asking a series of increasingly narrow categorical questions (e.g., "Is it alive?" "Is it an animal?" etc.). In contrast, the younger child is more likely to adopt the more concrete and considerably less efficient procedure of asking specific questions from the outset (e.g., "Is it a dog?") (Flavell, 1985).

The future time perspective of adolescents is greater than that of younger children (Keating, 1980). Adolescents begin to think about what they will be doing with their lives—whether they will go to college, what kind of work they may be doing, whether they will marry, what the world will be like in five or ten years. To the younger child, the prospect of three months of summer vacation may seem like an eternity; his or her attention is likely to be focused on an upcoming birthday party or a trip to the zoo.

In general, adolescents and adults are more likely than younger children to have what John Flavell calls "a sense of the game"—an awareness that much of life consists of anticipating, formulating, and developing strategies for dealing with problems, whether they involve developing a household budget to avoid financial crisis or estimating the interactions and probable behavior of other people (Flavell, 1985; Flavell & Ross, 1981; Ford, 1982).

The Generality of Formal Operations

Many experts agree that there is a level of cognitive development beyond that of the concrete-operational child, and that it conforms generally to the description of formal-operational thinking provided here (Flavell, 1985; Keating, 1988; Neimark, 1975a, 1975b). However, there is less agreement about how universal and age-specific that level of development may be. Doubts have also been raised about the extent to which the specific competencies that reflect the development of formal-operational thinking develop together and represent a distinct departure from earlier modes of thinking, as the theory would suggest (Flavell, 1985; Ginsberg & Opper, 1979; Mussen et al., 1990).

Investigators have found some aspects of formal thinking in highly intelligent younger children (Keating, 1975, 1980). Conversely, some adolescents and adults never attain true formal-operational thought because of limited ability or cultural limitations, both in our own society and in others (Flavell, 1985; Keating, 1980; Neimark, 1975a; Ross, 1973). Even very bright adolescents and adults do not always employ their capacity for formal-operational thinking. This may occur, for example, when a problem seems too far removed from reality, or when they are bored, tired, frustrated, or overly involved emotionally (Mussen et al., 1990; Neimark, 1975a, 1975b). Take the familiar example of an intelligent young woman searching for a missing earring when she is already late for a date. Frustrated by her failure to find it, she is likely to end up looking in the same place repeatedly, despite the certain knowledge that it is not there. Even supposedly objective scientists may be inclined to look for evidence that will confirm their hypotheses while ignoring equally solid evidence that appears to contradict them (Neimark, 1975a).

Finally, it should be realized that formal-operational thought is not an all-or-nothing affair, although for the sake of simplicity we may have appeared to suggest otherwise. The really gifted adolescent girl or boy is likely to display more imagination, flexibility, and precision in the exercise of formal-operational thinking than less gifted peers, although the basic processes involved may be similar (Kohlberg & Gilligan, 1971).

Social Cognition

If deviations from formal-operational thinking often occur in dealing with intellectual problems, what may we expect when the far more elusive and emotion-laden problems of human affairs are involved? The scientific investigation of this kind of problem solving is called **social cognition.** It implies attempts to understand in what manner, to what extent, and how accurately people of different ages and differing levels of ability are able to infer what others are thinking or feeling, what they are like psychologically, how they view the world, what their intentions are, and the nature of their relationships with others (e.g., friendship, love, power, fear, admiration) (Flavell, 1985; Higgins & Bargh, 1987; Higgins, Ruble, & Hartup, 1983; Selman, 1980; Shantz, 1983).

Research has shown that children tend to improve in all of these capabilities as they grow older. Preschoolers can identify certain simple emotions in others through facial and other cues, but they appear to be unable to anticipate another person's thoughts, and they tend to describe others in terms of their physical appearance, their behavior, where they live, their family, their possessions, or shared activities rather than in terms of their psychological or social characteristics (Livesley & Bromley, 1973; Shantz, 1975, 1983; Selman, 1980).

During middle childhood dramatic advances occur in the child's social understanding. As one observer has written,

> Social inferences now progress to the level of the child's understanding that his own thoughts, feelings, and intentions can be the object of another's thinking. He can view simple social episodes from the position of each participant and maintain a consistency among viewpoints on the episode . . . In addition, the child shows an ability to infer the feelings of others when others are in situations largely unfamiliar to him (Shantz, 1975, p. 312).

Moreover, beginning in early middle childhood, children describe others less in terms of outward characteristics like appearance, possessions, and behavior and more in terms of inner attributes—attitudes, abilities, and interests. And they begin to attend less to the physical aspects of interpersonal interactions and more to the inferred inner experiences and social relations of the participants.

Social cognition continues to develop during adolescence. Adolescents extend their perspective to include the self, the other person, the inner experiences of each, and the relationship between the self and the other as an observer might understand it (Shantz, 1983; Shultz, 1980). "In social episodes, the adolescent is much more oriented toward and accurate in making inferences about the thoughts, intentions, and feelings of each participant in the episode" (Shantz, 1975, pp. 312–313).

Adolescents are also likely to go beyond merely describing thoughts and feelings, both of the self and others, and try to explain them. They also become increasingly likely to extend their efforts to understand thoughts, feelings, and motives beyond those of individuals to those of social groups and people in general (Collins, 1980; Flavell, 1985; Shantz, 1975, 1983).

Despite these remarkable advances in cognitive capacity, both adolescents and adults can, and often do, fail to perceive accurately the thoughts, feelings, and intentions of others and the nature of their interactions with them (Higgins & Bargh, 1987). This may occur for a variety of reasons, including lack of relevant information on which to base inferences. Most often, however, it is likely to result from *egocentrism*—failure to distinguish sufficiently clearly between one's own point of view and that of others (Shantz, 1975).

EFFECTS OF ADOLESCENT MENTAL GROWTH ON PERSONALITY AND SOCIAL DEVELOPMENT

It would be difficult to overestimate the importance of the quantitative and qualitative changes in cognitive development (particularly the shift to formal operations) that take place during adolescence. It is not difficult to appreciate the critical role that these changes play in helping the adolescent deal with increasingly complex educational and vocational demands; it would be virtually impossible to master such subjects as calculus or the use of metaphor in poetry without a high level of abstract thinking. Further reflection should make it clear that many other aspects of adolescent development also depend on the cognitive advances occurring during this period. Changes in the nature of parent–child relationships; emerging personality characteristics and psychological defense mechanisms; establishment of educational and vocational goals; mounting concern with social, political, and personal values; even a developing sense of ego identity—all are strongly influenced by these cognitive changes.

As we have noted, one of the most important aspects of the emergence of formal-operational thought is the ability to entertain hypotheses or theoretical propositions that depart from immediately observable events. In contrast to the child, who for the most part is preoccupied with learning how to function in the here and now, the adolescent is able not only to grasp the immediate state of things but also the state they might or could assume (Elkind, 1968). The implications of this change are vast.

For example, many adolescents exhibit a newfound talent for discovering their previously idealized parents' feet of clay—questioning their values; comparing them with other, "more understanding" parents; and accusing them of hypocritical inconsistencies between professed values and behavior. All of these changes appear to depend on changes in the adolescent's cognitive ability: "The awareness of the discrepancy between the actual and the possible also helps to make the adolescent a rebel. He is always comparing the possible with the actual and discovering that the actual is frequently wanting" (Elkind, 1968, p. 152).

The tendency of some adolescents to criticize existing social, political, and religious systems and attempt to construct alternative systems depends on their emerging capacity for formal-operational thought. The fact that much of an adolescent's concern with the deficiencies of parents and the social order turns out to be more a matter of word than of deed may reflect the fact that this kind of formal operational thinking is still relatively new and not yet fully integrated into the adolescent's adaptation to life.

At the same time, however, it is important to recognize the positive aspects of the adolescent's newly acquired ability to conceptualize and reason abstractly about hypothetical possibilities (Conger, 1979; Elkind, 1984). Although younger adolescents may seem to be playing a game of ideas, this is nonetheless an important and productive exercise. What may appear to an adult to be "vain rehashing or sterile questioning of old worn-out problems" is, for the young person, "youthful explorations and true discoveries" (Osterrieth, 1969, p. 15).

As already noted, preoccupation with thought itself, particularly with one's own thoughts about oneself, is characteristic of formal operations. An adolescent girl or boy is likely to become more introspective and analytical. Many adolescents are concerned about such issues as whether the world that they perceive actually exists, and indeed whether they themselves are real or a product of consciousness.

In addition, adolescents' thought and behavior may appear egocentric (Elkind, 1968, 1984; Enright, Lapsley & Shukla, 1979). Because during this period of rapid change adolescents are likely to focus on themselves, they often conclude that other people are equally obsessed with their behavior and appearance. One of the consequences of this egocentrism is a feeling of constantly being onstage, and as a result much of the adolescent's time is spent constructing, or reacting to, an **imaginary audience** (Elkind, 1966). It is an audience because the adolescent feels that all eyes are focused on him or her, and it is imaginary because in reality this is seldom the case. In David Elkind's view, the construction of imaginary audiences helps account for a variety of adolescent behaviors and experiences, including the adolescent's sometimes excruciating self-consciousness. When the adolescent is feeling self-critical, he or she is likely to anticipate that the audience will be similarly critical.

By the same token, when the adolescent is in an ebullient, self-admiring mood, he or she may project these feelings onto peers or adults. The younger adolescent boy who stands before the mirror flexing his muscles and admiring his profile, or the girl who spends hours applying makeup or trying one hairstyle or dress after another, may be dreaming of the impression he or she will make on a date or at a party. It is a minor tragedy of adolescent life that when these young people actually meet, each is likely to be more preoccupied with himself or herself than with observing the other. "Gatherings of young adolescents are unique in the sense that each young person is simultaneously an actor to himself and an audience to others" (Elkind, 1966, p. 1030). Researchers have found, as Elkind's concept of imaginary audience would predict, that self-consciousness tends to be greatest in early adolescence (around age 12) and declines in later years (Simmons, Rosenberg, & Rosenberg, 1973).

Elkind also postulates a mental construction that is complementary to the imaginary audience. He calls it the **personal fable.**

> While the adolescent fails to differentiate the concerns of his own thought from those of others, he at the same time overdifferentiates his feelings. Perhaps because he believes he is of importance to so many people, the imaginary audience, he comes to regard himself, and particularly his feelings, as something special and unique. Only he can suffer with such agonized intensity, or experience such exquisite rapture. How many parents have been confronted with the typically adolescent phrase, "But you don't know how it feels" . . . (1966, p. 1031) (see Box 4.2).

A number of other characteristics of adolescents appear to be related at least in part to their level of cognitive development. Thus, the adolescent's frequent use of irony—of the "put-on" or the "put-down"—while clearly serving other motivations as well, can be understood partly as an exercise of his or her newfound talents for thinking at the symbolic level of metaphor, the "as if," and the manifestly absurd (Elkind, 1970, 1984). The defense mechanisms employed by adolescents may also reflect their level of cognitive development. Indeed, awareness of the role of cognitive factors in the adolescent's use of defenses may help explain an apparent inconsistency in the findings of various clinical investigations. A number of psychoanalysts have stressed the importance of characteristically adolescent defenses such as intellectualization and asceticism, which they have encountered both in the literature of youth and in their analyses of intelligent, sensitive adolescent patients (see Chapter 3). However, on the basis of studies of more representative samples of young

---

Box 4.2 ADOLESCENT EGOCENTRISM: IMAGINARY AUDIENCE, PERSONAL FABLE, AND SELF-FOCUS

Several studies have provided empirical support for Elkind's constructs regarding adolescent egocentrism. In one such effort, scales were developed for *personal fable, imaginary audience,* and *focus on the self* (e.g., one item on the imaginary-audience scale asked how important the individual considered "being able to daydream about great successes and thinking of other people's reactions"). The researchers predicted that these three aspects of adolescent egocentrism would be correlated with one another, and that all three would decline with age (Enright, Lapsley, & Shukla, 1979; Enright, Shukla, & Lapsley, 1980).

As predicted, both imaginary audience and personal fable declined from early to late adolescence. The findings regarding self-focus were more complex. Instead of a steady decline, a curvilinear relationship was found; that is, self-focus was highest at the sixth-grade and college levels and lower during the eighth, tenth, and twelfth grades. The investigators' interpretation is that, instead of an overall decline in self-focus from early to late adolescence, there is a change in the nature of the self-focus: "It should be noted that this late adolescent focus on the self appears to be without a self-conscious expectation of others' reactions or an insistence on considering oneself totally unique and special. Most likely it is an un-self-conscious stirring for betterment of the self in the college years which tends to overshadow other concerns" (Enright, Lapsley, & Shukla, 1979, p. 694). Moreover, in early adolescence self-focus appears to take place at the expense of societal concerns, while in late adolescence concern with society increases (Enright, Shukla, & Lapsley, 1980).

---

people, other investigators believe that estimates of the frequency with which adolescents use such defenses are exaggerated. These discrepancies may reflect differences in the severity of the emotional conflicts encountered in different samples of adolescents, but they may also reflect differences in cognitive level. At any rate, it appears that the use of such "primitive" defenses as denial, so frequently found in younger children, requires a far lower level of cognitive development than the use of more sophisticated defenses like intellectualization.

The adolescent's cognitive development also plays an important role in the emergence of a well-defined sense of identity. It seems likely that the degree of differentiation and definiteness that an individual is able to achieve in the course of identity development depends on his or her cognitive capability. As Paul Osterrieth eloquently observes,

By getting away from the concrete, by reasoning, by "concentrating," by trying out hypotheses, he meets up with himself. Who is he, this person who thinks, who adopts an attitude, who speaks his opinion? What is he? What is it in him, what is this center where his ideas are shaped, where his thoughts are produced, where his assumptions are formulated? Is it not himself? . . .

It is apparent that intellectual transformations bring the youngster to ask himself questions about himself, to wonder, to acknowledge himself, just as much as do the physical transformations and just about at the same time. The values that the adolescent is "trying out," not without paradoxes and sophisms, the opinions that he defends sometimes with as much fire as thoughtlessness, are these not just so many ways of looking for himself, of defining himself, so many attempts to be and to become himself? (1969, pp. 15–16).

As we shall see later, the level and complexity of the adolescent's political thinking, value systems, and conceptions of morality also depend to a significant extent on his or her degree of cognitive development.

INFORMATION PROCESSING AND COGNITIVE DEVELOPMENT

Although the Piagetian approach is more concerned with the mental processes underlying cognitive development than the quantitative, psychometric approach, neither says much about the specific mechanisms involved in intellectual performance (Siegler & Richards, 1982; Sternberg, 1985). The **information-processing** approach attempts to do just that. It views intelligence as derived from the ways in which people mentally represent and process information (Sternberg & Powell, 1983). Researchers and theorists who favor this approach often use computer simulation techniques to create models of human intellectual functioning. Both computers and humans are involved in attending to, and gaining information from, their environment; processing that information; using problem-solving strategies; storing information and solutions in short-term ("working") and long-term memory; and retrieving stored information for subsequent use (Atkinson & Shifrin, 1977; Siegler & Richards, 1988; Sternberg & Powell, 1983).

Because the steps carried out by computers in dealing with information and solving problems are highly specific and detailed, they may help us understand the steps that humans go through in performing similar tasks. For example, an information-processing analysis may show that an adolescent who is having difficulty solving a problem is using inappropriate *strategies* to attack the problem, is unable to *retrieve* information from memory, or is unable to transfer what was learned in a previous situation to the current problem (Atkinson et al., 1987; Campione, Brown, & Ferrara, 1982; Sternberg, 1985).

At the same time, it is important to recognize that computers and the human mind do not always function in the same ways. Table 4.5 presents some similarities and differences between human and computer memory, each of which has both advantages and disadvantages. For many tasks the computer's storage capacity and speed of processing, storage, and retrieval can be highly advantageous. For other tasks, however, the human mind functions in far more complex, flexible, and creative ways than even the most advanced computers

T A B L E 4.5 A COMPARISON OF HUMAN AND COMPUTER MEMORY[a]

	Human memory	Computer memory
Preferred method of storage	Time-oriented	List-oriented
Retention of information	Graded	All-or-none
Efficiency (bits of information per second)	Low	High
Capacity	Dependent on experience	Independent of experience
Retrieval		
Relative to context	Strongly dependent	Independent
Relative to previous retrievals	Dependent	Independent
Purpose	General purpose: open set of functions	Special or general purpose: closed set of functions

Source: From W. K. Estes. Is human memory obsolete? *American Scientist,* 1980, **68,** 62–69. By permission.

[a]The flexibility and adaptability to new problems and situations of human memory offset the greater precision and speed of computer memory.

(Miller, 1983). It is also important to emphasize that information-processing approaches to development, with their emphasis on the cognitive processes and strategies that children and adolescents actually employ, extend well beyond the use of computer modeling (Sternberg & Powell, 1983).

Developmental Changes in Information-Processing Abilities

The application of the information-processing approach to the study of cognitive development is still relatively new. To date, most efforts have been concentrated in two areas: memory and problem solving (Siegler & Richards, 1982). For example, the fact that adolescents are much better able than younger children to repeat a series of numbers has been attributed to an increase in short-term memory capacity with age (Pascual-Leone, 1970). However, other investigators maintain that these results could also be explained by developmental differences in attention span, speed in processing information, or the ability to use a variety of information-processing strategies like increased knowledge, rehearsal, and mnemonic devices (aids to remembering) (Brown, 1975; Brown et al., 1983; Flavell, 1985; Siegler & Richards, 1988).

Robert Sternberg and his colleagues have used an information-processing approach to study age differences in problem solving (Sternberg, 1982b; Sternberg & Nigro, 1980; Sternberg & Rifkin, 1979). In a study of analogical reasoning, they presented a number of different analogies to third-, sixth-, and ninth-graders and to college students. The type of problem used is illustrated in Figure 4.9. Elements A, B, and C are given; the task of the subject is to select

Figure 4.9 A representative analogy item. (From "The development of analogical reasoning processes," by R. J. Sternberg & B. Rifkin. *Journal of Experimental Child Psychology*, 1979, **27**, 195–232. Copyright © 1979 by Academic Press. Reprinted by permission.)

element D so that C has the same relationship to D that A has to B (A:B::C:?). As can be seen, A and B have the same similarities (jersey, umbrella, and shoes) and the same difference (hat color) as C and figure 1. Therefore, figure 1 is the correct choice. Arriving at the correct choice involves at least three mental processes: *encoding* (noting the attributes of each figure); *inference* (finding similarities and differences between A and B on each attribute); and *application* (finding a relationship between C and D that parallels the relationship between A and B). Although both children and adults generally used all of these operations, adults carried out each step exhaustively whereas younger children tended to cut the process short, presumably owing to inability to memorize all the attributes of each figure.

As these examples suggest, the information-processing approach to developmental changes holds promise, but considerably more research will be needed before firm conclusions can be reached (Siegler & Richards, 1982; Sternberg, 1982a).

SUMMARY

The impressive gains in physical and physiological development that take place in adolescence are accompanied by equally impressive gains in intellectual and cognitive development. These gains are both quantitative and qualitative: They are quantitative in the sense that the young person can accomplish intellectual tasks more easily, quickly, and efficiently than was possible during childhood or preadolescence. They are qualitative in the sense that significant changes also occur in the nature of the adolescent's mental processes. The quantitative approach dates back at least to Alfred Binet's development of the intelligence test. The qualitative approach has its roots in Jean Piaget's theory of cognitive development.

Intelligence is a hypothetical construct; it has been defined as the aggregate or global capacity of the individual to comprehend the world and deal effectively with its challenges. It is generally assumed that every individual has an intelligence "ceiling" that is set by heredity, but that how closely one approaches one's ceiling is determined by a variety of factors, including *physiological maturation* and the richness of one's environment. Most psychologists believe that intelligence is multidimensional—that it involves a variety of abilities—but they are less likely to agree on the nature of those abilities.

Intellectual potential cannot be measured directly. We can only measure what a person can do as a result of the interactions between organism and environment. Intelligence tests try to control for environmental influences, on the assumption that differences in performance will then reflect differences in intellectual potential. They do this by trying to select items to which most children will have been exposed (i.e., familiar items) or items that will be new to most children (i.e., novel items). Because one can never be sure that these assumptions have been met for any given individual, one can never be sure that an IQ score represents a person's full intellectual potential. Thus, IQ tests should be used with caution.

The practical utility of an intelligence test score depends partly on its stability over time. Although the prediction of adult intelligence is more reliable during adolescence than at earlier ages, some individuals show increases in IQ scores over time while others show declines.

Mental ability (as distinguished from IQ) increases rapidly from birth through adolescence. On measures of overall intelligence there appears to be a leveling off during young adulthood, with a slight decline in middle age and a more rapid decline in old age. However, some abilities (e.g., verbal comprehension) improve well into the middle years while others (e.g., speed of perception) reach a peak in the early adult years and then decline.

There are consistent differences in intellectual functioning between male and female children and adolescents; by age 10 or 11 girls begin to outperform boys on verbal ability while boys overtake girls on measures of mathematics and spatial ability (particularly spatial visualization). Studies comparing *monozygotic* (identical) and *dizygotic* (fraternal) twins, as well as studies of children who were adopted at an early age, make it clear that an individual's genetic inheritance is an important determinant of IQ, although the home environment also plays a significant role.

Although a moderately high level of intellectual ability is essential for creativity, beyond a basic "floor," which varies in different fields, there is little relationship between intellectual ability and creativity. Creative adolescents tend to be more independent, unconventional, self-reliant, perceptive, and rebellious than other young people.

In recent years there has been growing interest in qualitative aspects of mental development; this approach is exemplified by the pioneering work of Jean Piaget. Piaget assumed that the goal of intellectual development is adaptation. According to Piaget, there are four major stages in cognitive development: the *sensorimotor* stage (birth to 18 months), the *preoperational* stage (18 months to 7 years), the stage of *concrete operations* (ages 7–12), and the stage of *formal operations* (from about age 12 on).

With the advent of the capacity for formal operations, the young person is able to think more abstractly, to formulate and test hypotheses, and to consider what might be as well as what is. Psychologists have recently called attention to other changes in adolescent thinking, including more efficient problem-solving techniques, a longer time perspective, and what John Flavell calls "a sense of the game"—awareness of the complex strategies required in everyday life. Some aspects of formal thinking have been found in highly intelligent younger children; conversely, some adolescents and adults never attain true formal-operational thought.

Adolescents are also more advanced than younger children in *social cognition*—the ability to infer what others are thinking or feeling, what they are like psychologically, what their intentions are, and how they view the world.

Adolescent cognitive development can also be viewed in terms of greater capacity for *information processing,* including improved *strategies* for attacking problems, and greater speed and efficiency in *retrieving* information stored in memory and *transferring* what was learned in a previous situation to a current problem.

Many other aspects of adolescent development depend on the cognitive advances occurring during this period. Changes in the nature of parent–child relationships, emerging personality characteristics (including preoccupation with the self), psychological defense mechanisms, concern with social and personal values, and the development of a sense of ego identity—all are strongly influenced by these cognitive changes.

REVIEW QUESTIONS

1. In what ways do the quantitative and qualitative approaches to cognitive development differ?
2. What do we mean by the term *intelligence?* Is intelligence multidimensional? How have different theorists dealt with this question?
3. How do intelligence tests attempt to control for environmental influences?
4. How constant are IQ scores over time?
5. Distinguish between "fluid" and "crystallized" measures of intelligence. How does each change with age?
6. Discuss briefly the current stage of knowledge regarding sex differences in intellectual functioning.
7. What methods are used to investigate genetic influences on intelligence? What are the main findings of this research?

8. How do creative adolescents differ from adolescents in general? Can creativity be promoted in adolescents?

9. Name five cognitive capabilities that are likely to develop during adolescence. What are some of the effects of adolescent mental growth on personality and social development?

10. Discuss briefly the potential contributions of the information-processing approach to cognitive development.

RECOMMENDED READINGS

Elkind, D. (1978). Understanding the young adolescent, *Adolescence*, **13,** 127–134.

Flavell, J. H. (1985). *Cognitive development* (2nd ed.). Englewood Cliffs, NJ: Prentice-Hall.

Horowitz, F. D., & O'Brien, M. (1985). *The gifted and talented: Developmental perspectives*. Washington, DC: American Psychological Association.

Shantz, C. U. (1983). Social cognition. In P. H. Mussen (Series Ed.), J. H. Flavell & E. M. Markman (Eds.), *Handbook of child psychology, Vol. 3.*

Cognitive development (pp. 495–555, 4th ed.). New York: Wiley.

Sternberg, R. J. (1985). *Beyond IQ: A triarchic theory of intelligence*. San Diego, CA: Harcourt Brace Jovanovich.

Sternberg, R. J., & Powell, J. S. (1983). The development of intelligence. In P. H. Mussen (Series Ed.), J. H. Flavell, & E. M. Markman (Eds.), *Handbook of child psychology, Vol. 3: Cognitive development* (pp. 341–419, 4th ed.). New York: Wiley.

ADOLESCENTS, FAMILIES, AND SOCIAL CHANGE

In our culture, adolescence has traditionally been viewed as a more difficult period than either middle childhood or early adulthood. Although the *extent* of adolescent and parental turmoil during this period has frequently been exaggerated (see Chapter 1), there is broad agreement that adolescence, particularly early adolescence, can be a challenging and sometimes trying time both for young people and for their parents (Brooks-Gunn & Warren, 1989; Offer, Ostrov, & Howard, 1981; Steinberg & Silverberg, 1986). This should hardly be surprising in view of the many rapid changes that occur during adolescence. Both adolescents and their parents need time to adapt to these changes and their impact on the relations between them.

Moreover, the challenges of this period appear to have increased, partly as a consequence of changes in the nature of the family and in its relations to society and partly because of the accelerated rate at which such changes have occurred (Bronfenbrenner, 1985; Conger, 1971, 1981). In this chapter we will examine briefly the nature of some of these changes and consider their effects on contemporary adolescents and their parents.

THE CHANGING AMERICAN FAMILY

The nature of the American family, and its role in society and in the lives of its members, has changed significantly in the past fifty years. Moreover, in recent years the *rate* of change has been increasing rather than decreasing. Although the picture is complicated by socioeconomic, ethnic, religious, and other factors, certain general trends are apparent.

Increasing urbanization and geographic mobility have altered the face of the country and the nature of our social institutions (Bronfenbrenner, Moen, & Garbarino, 1984; Conger, 1981, 1988). In 1900 nearly two out of every three persons in the United States lived in rural areas; today that figure has declined to only about one person in four. Although the rate of migration to urban areas has slowed in recent years, almost three-fourths of the population is living in urban areas—on only 16 percent of the land (U.S. Bureau of the Census, 1974, 1989).

Even for those already living in urban areas, mobility continues; indeed, one-fifth of all Americans move every year, and approximately half of all families move every five years. The average American may expect to move thirteen or fourteen times in the course of a lifetime (U.S. Bureau of the Census, 1974, 1980, 1989).

A high degree of mobility tends to diminish personal, extended-family, and neighborhood ties and the social support they can provide (Bronfenbrenner, Moen, & Garbarino, 1984). A study of community attachment (Kasarda & Janowitz, 1974) revealed the importance of continuity of residence in the maintenance of social relationships. A clear link was found between length of residence and the number of acquaintances people had, the number of relatives who lived nearby, and the proportion of their friends and relatives who lived in the local community. Having roots in a community appears to be especially important for low-income families, which are more dependent on neighborhood sources of social support than those with higher incomes; "money enables people to reach beyond their own localities for their intimate ties, while the lack of money makes proximity important" (Fischer, 1977, p. 171).

Increased mobility, particularly between large metropolitan areas, has also reduced the number of opportunities for informal, direct communication between the family and other social institutions such as schools, churches, and agencies of local government; such communication is more likely to occur in small towns and cities with relatively stable populations (Bachman, O'Malley, & Johnston, 1978; Bronfenbrenner, 1975, 1985; Harevan, 1984). The significance of this loss is accentuated because it parallels the transfer of many functions that were formerly carried out by the family—educational, vocational, social, economic, and religious—to other social institutions, largely as a consequence of industrialization (Demos, 1970; Harevan, 1984).

These changes have weakened the stability and interdependence of communities as well as leaving the family more isolated from social support systems and more dependent on its own resources. We have become to a great extent, in Vance Packard's phrase, "a nation of strangers" (Packard, 1974).

Functions of the Family

Changes in the nature and functions of the family have placed additional demands on family members. Among those changes are a decrease in average family size and in the interdependence of family members. In the nineteenth century, marriage tended to occur later and families were larger. Between 1800 and 1930, for example, "the birth rate declined from an average of eight children per mother to slightly less than three" (Harevan, 1978, p. 60); it is now less than two children per mother (U.S. Bureau of the Census, 1989). Life expectancy, on the other hand, was far shorter than it is today. Consequently, marriages were frequently ended by the death of a spouse before the end of the child-rearing period, and few couples experienced the luxury (or the problems) of the "empty-nest stage," when most couples who remain married can look forward to many years together without children (Harevan, 1984). In addition, the likelihood that a grandparent would survive until the grandchild's adolescent years was remote.

On the other hand, because of higher mortality and fertility rates, "functions within the family were less specifically tied to age, and members of different age groups were consequently not so segregated by the tasks they were required to fulfill. . . . Children were accustomed to growing up with large numbers of siblings and were exposed to a greater variety of models from which to choose than they would have been in a small nuclear family" (Harevan, 1978, p. 62). Older children, particularly girls, often took care of younger siblings.

The family's functions differed also. In a world in which early parental death, illness, and economic insecurity were far more prevalent, members of both the nuclear family and the parents' families of origin, as well as relatives, were more dependent on one another for survival. This greater interdependence had both positive and negative effects.

Having the support of other family members tended to promote family solidarity. In addition, life transitions—the times when one is expected to be a dependent child, to go to school, to go to work, to leave home, to marry, and so on—were more flexible and less regularized than they are today. On the other hand, the freedom to take each of these steps was limited. If parents needed a child's help with work, he or she left school; if a younger daughter was needed to care for an aging parent, she might have to defer or abandon marriage plans. The time simply was not ripe for the contemporary idea that decisions about work and marriage and how to live one's life are individual, not family matters (Bellah et al., 1985; Harevan, 1984).

"Individualistic patterns of family behavior first appeared in the nineteenth century among the urban class, and with them came patterns of segregation in family roles" (Harevan, 1978, p. 67). Middle-class families were the first to initiate a regular, carefully timed progression for entering school, graduating, preparing for a vocation, leaving home, marrying, and forming a new family. In part, this was a consequence of greater affluence and increased parental longevity; in part, also, it was a result of the "discovery" of childhood and, later, of adolescence as distinct stages of development with their own special needs (Conger, 1981; Harevan, 1978, 1984).

As America entered the twentieth century, however, these middle-class patterns began to spread across the entire social spectrum. To some extent this was due to the migration of rural and small-town residents into increasingly homogeneous metropolitan areas, and to the gradual assimilation of second-generation immigrants into American cultural patterns. But other social changes also played a major role. In the words of historian Tamara Harevan, "As state institutions gradually took over the functions of welfare, education, and social control that had previously lodged in the family, there was greater conformity in timing of life transitions" (1978, p. 67). Compulsory school attendance, child labor legislation, age-segregated schools, social and recreational activities aimed at particular age groups, and mandatory retirement all combined to produce more rigid patterns of timing, both in the larger society and in family behavior.

The Emergence of the "Modern" Nuclear Family

All of the trends just described combined to foster the emergence of the "modern" nuclear family, which has played such a central role in society through much of the present century. As Edward Shorter observed in *The Making of the Modern Family*, today's nuclear family is as much a state of mind as it is a formal structure:

> What really distinguishes the nuclear family—father, mother, and children—from other patterns of family life in Western society is a special sense of solidarity that separates the domestic unit from the surrounding community. Its members feel they have much more in common with one another than they do with anyone else on the

outside—that they enjoy a privileged emotional climate they must protect from outside intrusion, through privacy and isolation (1975, p. 205).

In contrast to other family forms, the nuclear family tends to be child centered and to view the family as a focus of nurture and affection—"a warm shelter of domesticity from the cold, inhospitable night"—rather than as a means of assuring the economic survival of its members (Shorter, 1975, p. 205). As a consequence, the influence of extended kin, friends, and neighbors on family ties has weakened (Degler, 1980; Harevan, 1984). Moreover, as the need for women's and children's labor decreased, the roles of family members became more differentiated. "Wives were expected to be the custodians of the family and to protect the home as a refuge from the world of work, and children, although expected to help with household tasks, were freed from serious work responsibility until their late teens" (Harevan, 1978, p. 67).

The Nuclear Family in the 1950s

The stereotypical nuclear family reached its peak in terms of popular acclaim and social influence in the years following World War II. Returning veterans and their spouses longed for a period of normality. They felt an urgent need to resume their interrupted lives—to set about choosing a career, achieving financial security, getting married, buying a home, and raising a family. And in a period of rising prosperity such symbols of the American dream seemed attainable for the majority of the population (Conger, 1981).

This was also, however, the period of the cold war and heightened fear of nuclear destruction. Confronted by an inhospitable world, Americans began to develop a pervasive suspicion of "foreign subversives" and of nonconformity in general. The 1950s were the period portrayed in the movie *American Graffiti*—a decade characterized by drive-ins, "cruising," and the birth of rock-and-roll—but this was also the period of McCarthyism and that strangest of nondeclared wars, the Korean "episode" (Conger, 1981).

Not surprisingly, the family followed suit. In the pursuit of emotional security and "the good life" in the mushrooming suburbs—symbolized by what one social critic called "the split-level trap"—parents were willing to accept what in retrospect may appear to be excessive conformity in their social, political, sexual, and vocational roles. This was also the period of the "organization man" (Whyte, 1956).

Children went along with the spirit of the times. They were the "silent generation" of young people about whom philosopher-theologian Paul Tillich complained that they showed "an intensive desire for security both internal and external, the will to be accepted at any price and an unwillingness to show individual traits, acceptance of a limited happiness without serious risk" (quoted in Wolensky, 1977, p. 84). A study of college students in the late 1950s found them to be models of the status quo. They had few real commitments and valued a happy family life above everything else, with secure employment (preferably in a large corporation) running a close second. In the areas of politics and government, the dominant traits were apathy and conservatism

(Goldsen, Rosenberg, Williams, & Suchman, 1960). If there was intergenerational friction, as to some extent there always is, it was of a familiar and comfortable sort—a conviction on the part of youth that they could do a better job of running society than their "old-fashioned" parents, not the kind of frontal attacks on the basic values of the society and its institutions that characterized the 1960s.

In a way, the 1950s were an era of innocence, a time of fundamental faith in existing social institutions and prescribed social, sexual, and vocational roles. Even when the Korean conflict intruded, and even though it was the first unpopular war in this century, those who were unlucky enough to be called up were simply told (and told themselves) that "That's the way the ball bounces"; the rest of the nation continued its pursuit of "the good life" undisturbed (Conger, 1981).

In its more positive aspects, the period from World War II through the 1950s can be viewed as one of relative tranquility, of acceptance of the way things were, in which those who were psychologically capable of it could, and did, make personal commitments— to husbands, wives, children, and a way of life. Marriage vows still contained the words "for better or worse, for richer, for poorer, in sickness and in health, till death us do part"—instead of phrases like "as long as we continue to feel the way we do about each other." In other respects, however, the 1950s were an era of suppressed individuality, national paranoia, and largely unrecognized discrimination—against minorities, women, the poor, "foreigners," homosexuals, and indeed, most groups that dared to be different. In a number of respects, the era that came to an end with the onset of the 1960s was a time bomb waiting to explode. And explode it did.

The Turbulent 1960s

It is likely that no decade in our nation's history, with the possible exception of the Civil War era, contained as many shocks to the sense of cultural order, continuity, and national purpose as the period between the mid-1960s and the early 1970s. Consider for a moment what parents and their children went through in the few years after John Kennedy announced "the passing of the torch to a new generation": the beginning and abortive end of the much-heralded War on Poverty (a victim of the impossible goal of guns and butter too); the escalation of the nonviolent civil rights movement into inner-city riots stemming from frustration at the lack of progress; the assassinations of a president, a presidential candidate, and our most charismatic civil rights leader; the forced retirement of two presidents and a vice-president; and finally, the series of events that are summed up in the word *Watergate,* with its revelations of duplicity, deception, attempted corruption of federal agencies, and outright criminal behavior at the highest levels of the executive branch of government.

But of all the events of that turbulent decade none had a greater impact on the nation than the Vietnam War (Conger, 1975, 1976; Yankelovich, 1974). No other issue did so much to divide the nation, to set formerly respected national leaders—and even neighbors—at each other's throats, or to alienate some of

No other issue in the turbulent 1960s did so much to divide the nation as the war in Vietnam.

our brightest and most promising young people. Once the war had ended (at least for Americans), much of the feeling of urgency and outrage that it lent not only to antiwar protest but also to the struggle for civil rights and against poverty, discrimination, and deception and hypocrisy in politics and government declined significantly. This decline, it should be noted, occurred even though young people's perceptions of what they viewed as serious flaws in our society did not undergo a corresponding change (see Chapter 14). In short, what was to have been a new era turned into what Andrew Hacker has called the Age of Rubbish, a period characterized by violence, separatism, and a rudderless morality. To an unprecedented degree, young people were exposed to a deeply divided adult society.

The Decline in Adult Authority. An important consequence of these conditions was a decline in adult authority (Conger, 1971, 1981). In earlier periods adolescents were able to view adult society as relatively homogeneous. Although they may have felt that the adults were misguided, compromising, apathetic, or just plain wrong, adults constituted an identifiable, reasonably self-confident, confrontable "they." As such, parents were seen as having authority and wisdom and could serve as sympathetic guides to adult society and effective models for success in gaining entry into it.

In the 1960s and early 1970s, a majority of adolescents in this country were denied such coherent perceptions. From childhood on they were exposed to deep divisions among prestigious adults on almost every front, from the broadest social issues to questions of personal standards and morality. Even when adolescents could view adult society as speaking with one voice and planning a unified attack on the country's worsening problems, its apparent inability to achieve success was hardly reassuring. The authority of adult society thus was compromised in the eyes of many adolescents, and so was the authority of parents as family representatives of adult society, both in this country and in other industrialized nations (Conger, 1971; Yankelovich, 1969, 1974). The traditional assertion that "Father knows best" was likely to be met with the adolescent response of "Who's kidding whom?" As psychologist Diana Baumrind (1975) observed, it was not so much that the young were incapable of respecting authority as that they had so little reason to do so.

The Rise of the Youth Culture. At the same time that parental and societal authority were diminishing, the influence of the peer group increased. The rise of the "youth culture" of the 1960s and early 1970s (see pages 488–489) can be traced primarily to the disillusionment of young people with what they saw as the failures of adult society. However, its visibility and influence were heightened by rapid increases in the numbers of young people, their unprecedented concentration in age-segregated high schools and colleges, and the way they were viewed by the media—views that often bore little resemblance to the actual behavior, attitudes, and values of the average adolescent or youth (Conger, 1976).

Because of such stereotypes, some younger adolescents were led to see the so-called youth culture as more influential and homogeneous, and as promoting a wider variety of behaviors (e.g., sexual activities, use of drugs), than was actually the case. In an often mistaken effort to emulate older youth, some younger adolescents plunged into life-styles and behaviors that many older youth were not prepared to engage in.

Age Segregation. Accompanying the growth of a more visible adolescent peer culture was a further reduction in communication among age groups, both within the family and in the community. In part, this was a consequence of accelerated changes in residential patterns, a trend that had already received considerable impetus from the "flight to the suburbs" following World War II. Young married couples, particularly those in the middle class, tended to congregate in newer suburban areas, where the financing of subdivisions made it possible to buy a house with a minimal down payment and where they could find schools and same-age peers for their children. Single and older adults were left behind in older neighborhoods or "singles only" apartment complexes.

Educational patterns also contributed to age segregation, both of the young from adults and of young people of different ages from one another. At the turn of the century, only a small minority of youth in the high school age group could be found in school; the great majority were already at work. During the 1960s and 1970s, most adolescents were in school (between 1950 and 1976 alone, the percentage of young people completing high school rose from 52 percent to 82 percent); moreover, the schools they attended were growing ever larger and more age segregated. Even within a particular school it was not uncommon to find 1000 tenth-graders interacting "largely with others of the same level, much as any segregated social stratum with well-defined boundaries" (Clark, 1974, p. 82).

Clearly, the period from the early 1960s through the early 1970s was a difficult one both for parents and for their adolescent children. Although even at the height of the so-called youth revolution the "generation gap" between the

The flight of young couples to new suburbs following World War II resulted in a further reduction of interaction between age groups, both within the family and in the community. Pictured above: Levittown, Long Island.

average adolescent and his or her parents was much less than the media would have had us believe, there can be little doubt that these years took a toll on the integrity of the family. Like all revolutions, the "revolution" of the 1960s produced its share of casualties—shattered families, broken-hearted parents, and rootless, alienated, confused youth, some of whom are still trying to "find themselves." Although the majority of families survived intact, many had to struggle to keep open the lines of communication between generations. Many also were compelled to reexamine their own values and beliefs in the face of incredibly rapid social change (Conger, 1981).

The 1970s: "I Gotta Be Me"

Although some of the challenges faced by the family in the 1960s abated during the late 1970s, others remained. In addition, new, qualitatively different challenges arose. Political and social divisions between generations eased for a variety of reasons, including the end of the Vietnam War, a realization on the part of young people that social change was more complex and harder to achieve than they had thought, and a new and more sobering economic climate. Equally significant, a majority of adults who had earlier castigated youth for its suspicion and distrust of established social institutions came to share their skepticism.

Other challenges to the family continued, however. If anything, the relative isolation of the family from effective communication with, and influence over, other institutions increased. Age segregation—in education, housing, and social activities—showed little change. In addition, several significant social changes occurred that posed new challenges to traditional concepts of the nuclear family.

The Women's Movement. One of those changes was the rise of the women's movement, perhaps the single most significant event of the decade. A logical extension of earlier struggles for individual and group rights, beginning with the civil rights movement in the early 1960s, the women's movement has produced major changes in contemporary society. Not only has it fundamentally altered the way women, particularly younger women, view themselves, but it has also changed the way men view women—and themselves. Traditional stereotypes of the psychological, social, and emotional characteristics of men and women began to break down, as did notions of what could properly be considered "women's [or men's] work," or the appropriate roles of men and women in the larger society. Increasing numbers of women began insisting on being viewed as the equals of men and, just as important, as individuals, each with her own unique set of talents, interests, psychological and social needs, and personal idiosyncrasies.

These goals are still far from being attained, and there remain strong pockets of resistance, among women as much as among men. Nevertheless, an evolutionary process was set in motion in the 1970s that is unlikely to be reversed, despite slowdowns and occasional setbacks.

Women's Participation in the Labor Force. A closely related major change that accelerated in the 1970s was the increase in the number of women working outside the home. In 1950, only one-third of all women were employed outside the home; by 1970, the figure had increased to 43 percent; by 1980, it had reached 51 percent (U.S. Bureau of the Census, 1981). As we shall see, this trend continued unabated throughout the 1980s (see pages 509–511).

The reasons for these increases were varied. For some women, particularly those who were single parents or whose husbands were unemployed or underemployed, outside employment was an economic necessity. For others, it was

The women's movement throughout the 1970s helped break down traditional gender-related stereotypes.

a way of improving the family's living standards, coping with inflation, or remaining in contact with the world outside the home. For an increasing number of women, particularly those with interesting jobs or professions, it became a way of fulfilling vocational interests or career goals. Whatever the reasons for women's increased participation in the labor force, the implications for the family as a social institution, and for the lives of its members, are profound.

The "Me Decade." Still another major social force was at work during the 1970s. Although it was subtler and more difficult to define, its impact on the family was significant. In our characteristic predilection for finding simple terms to describe complex phenomena, we have sometimes labeled this force the "new narcissism" or the "me decade," but neither phrase seems adequate.

At the center of this new force was greater preoccupation with the self and diminished concern with the needs of others, particularly strangers. This preoccupation manifested itself in many ways, some positive, some negative. They ranged from jogging, health foods, and hot tubs to new religious cults, self-improvement programs, and so called psychological therapies (Conger, 1981, 1987). T-shirts and bumper stickers with individualistic slogans became a minor industry, leading Fran Lebowitz (1978) to ask, "If people don't want to talk to me, why would they want to talk to my T-shirt?"

So-called self-realization—whether physical, psychological, spiritual, or material—appeared to be Americans' chief preoccupation, along with a desire to be "free." But was this simply an expression of narcissism, as some have maintained, or was it, as others believe, a reaction to frustration—to a perceived inability to influence events or establish intimate and lasting relationships? It seems likely that all of these factors were involved and, further, that this development was not a cultural accident but a logical culmination of events that we have already described.

With the rise of the "modern" nuclear family, decreased economic interdependence, and greater emphasis on defining life stages came greater concern for people as individuals rather than primarily as members of a collective effort. Initially, however, the individual was expected to earn his or her share of the good life through conformity to societal expectations. The values of society, and the social institutions that supported them, were not basically in question, and part of the price of success in the late 1940s and the 1950s was "not rocking the boat."

All of this changed in the 1960s and early 1970s as Americans—first the young and then their elders—began to lose faith in government and other social institutions. The immediate results were increased political and social activism among some youth, and among others rejection of the social structure as a whole, along with a retreat (or escape) into "doing your own thing." This was the era of the hippie movement, which reached its height in 1967 during the "Summer of Love." (see pages 509–511).

By the middle of the 1970s, skepticism about government and other institutions had spread from the young to their elders, and generational conflicts had declined, at least in the political arena. The end of the Vietnam War had removed a major impetus to youthful revolt, and both young people and their elders began to doubt the capacity of either individuals or government to solve the nation's ever more complex social problems.

In addition, the nation entered a period of economic slowdown combined with inflation—a delayed legacy of the Johnson administration's policy of "guns and butter too." The days when young people could freely choose their jobs were ending, and economic well-being became a matter of growing concern for both young and old. There seems little doubt that a feeling of diminished ability to influence events played a significant part in the movement away from social concerns toward greater concern for the self.

At the same time, however, the greater "freedom to be me," to do one's own thing, that emerged from the 1960s was a genie that, though it might be restrained, was not going to be put back in its bottle. Newly established sexual and social life-styles were not about to be abandoned in favor of the more rigidly defined roles of family members and corporate employees that had characterized an earlier day.

New Challenges: The 1980s and Beyond

In many respects the 1980s witnessed a continuation of earlier trends. Women's participation in the work force continued to expand, both in terms of total numbers and in terms of the number of women entering nontraditional jobs (see Chapter 10). Age segregation and the relative isolation of the family from social institutions and community support systems accelerated, along with materialism and concern for the self; concern for others and the welfare of society as a whole continued to decrease (see Chapter 12). However, a number of additional forces were at work that had important implications for the American family.

A New Conservatism. Much of the emphasis on individual freedom in values and life-styles that characterized the 1970s carried over into the 1980s. At the same time, however, there was a significant shift toward greater conservatism in a number of areas, although not to the degree that some ideologues would have us believe. Attitudes toward unconstrained sexual freedom, homosexual behavior, and alcohol and drug use became more disapproving. Patterns of dress and manners became more traditional, to the delight of bridal consultants, dress designers, and renters of formal wear.

Politically, there was an overall shift to the right, although on many specific issues—ranging from birth control, abortion, and family planning to censorship, the rights of minorities and women, and constitutional safeguards against invasion of privacy—a majority of Americans remained more liberal than the Reagan and Bush administrations and the present Supreme Court. Toward the end of the decade political leaders of all stripes were expressing support for the family and policies designed to strengthen it.

On the face of it, a number of these trends would seem likely to support and strengthen the American family. Unfortunately, however, much of our proclaimed devotion to the welfare of the family is not supported by current economic trends and our social policy responses to them (Conger, 1988; Edelman, 1987; Schorr, 1988). This is an important issue that deserves a closer look.

The Changing Economy. Two major economic events of recent decades have had important consequences for families: the recession of the early 1980s, which was intentionally induced to combat inflation, and the accelerating shift from a goods-producing to a service-producing economy (see Chapter 11). For most Americans, recessions and the accompanying unemployment became things of the past as the economy expanded at an impressive rate in the late 1980s and unemployment rates reached historic lows. Nevertheless, many goods-producing jobs in industry, agriculture, and oil exploration and production were eliminated. As a result, hundreds of thousands of American workers who had viewed themselves as securely established members of the middle class found themselves unemployed. For many, especially older workers, the prospects of obtaining comparable jobs or of being successfully retrained for very different kinds of jobs in the "new economy" remain dim.

In some instances unemployment and economic dislocation and the resulting social, psychological, and economic stresses may bring families closer together and promote the development of autonomy and responsibility in children and adolescents (Elder, 1974, 1984). Far more often, however, the effects on family functioning are negative—sometimes disastrously so (Conger, 1984,

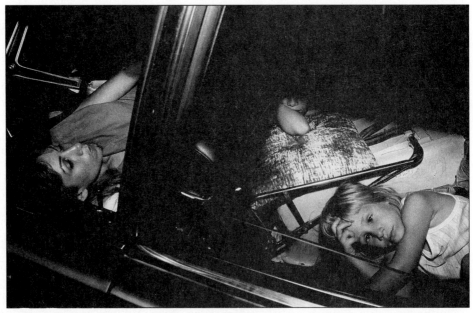

Many homeless families have been forced to live in their cars while searching for work. At present, one child in four and more than one adolescent in five, is living in poverty.

1987; Kahn, 1981; Pelletier, 1984). Studies of plant closings have documented many of the effects of prolonged job loss: distrust and pessimism, clinical depression, bitterness, anxiety, irritability, loss of self-esteem, and even suicide (Cobb & Kasl, 1977; Conger, 1987; Kahn, 1981). Not surprisingly, unemployment also leads to sharp increases in rates of child abuse, family violence, and divorce or separation. In the mid-1980s mental-health services in economically depressed areas of the midwestern farm and "rust" belts reported a dramatic upsurge in all of these problems (Conger, 1984).

Economic Change and Social Policy. How has society responded to the problems, not only of the "new poor" but also of the large number of families already living below the poverty line? For the most part, the response has been one of neglect (Conger, 1988; Moynihan, 1986; Schorr, 1988). During the past decade the gap between the wealthy and those living below the poverty line widened steadily: Between 1979 and 1987 the standard of living of the bottom one-fifth of American families declined by 9 percent, while among the top one-fifth it increased by 19 percent (Passell, 1989). In 1986 the top fifth of American families received 46 percent of all income, while the bottom fifth received only 4 percent (Wessel, 1986; U.S. Bureau of the Census, 1989) (see Box 5.1).

Governmental policies facilitated this process. Tax cuts favoring the wealthy coincided with marked reductions in programs aimed exclusively at the poor; for example, there was a 25 percent reduction in Aid to Families with Dependent Children but social programs that aid a broader group, such as Social Security, were not cut (Moynihan, 1986; Passell, 1989; Wessel, 1986). Many demonstrably successful and cost-effective services, ranging from prenatal and early postnatal nutritional and medical programs for low-income mothers and infants to health care, counseling, mental-health, and job-training programs for adolescents, were eliminated or severely cut back (Conger, 1988; Edelman, 1987; Hughes, Johnson, Rosenbaum, & Lin, 1989). At present, one child in four and more than one youth in five are living in poverty; indeed, currently "children are the only age group overrepresented in the poverty population" (Moynihan, 1986, p. 112).

Contrary to popular perceptions, over 60 percent of the 13.3 million poor children and adolescents in America are white; one-third are black, and one-fifth are Hispanic. The poverty rate for children in the expanding number of single-parent, female-headed households is much higher (54 percent) than the rate for children in all other families (12.5 percent) (Passell, 1989; U.S. Bureau of the Census, 1989).

CONSEQUENCES OF SOCIAL CHANGE

Changes in the nature of the family and its relation to society, and the rate at which those changes have occurred, clearly have increased the stresses experienced by the family. In a number of ways they have also altered the kinds of adaptations that family members must make if they are to survive and prosper.

Box 5.1 CHANGING THE NATIONAL CLIMATE FOR FAMILIES

Marian Wright Edelman, founder and president of the Children's Defense Fund, asserts that a major reason for the growing number of poor children and adolescents in the United States is that our nation has lost its moral bearings. The following passage is excerpted from her recent book *Families in Peril: An Agenda for Social Change:*

> We must work to change the national climate and focus attention on families and children. Recent federal government policy has spawned a new set of beatitudes which measure success not by how many needy pregnant women can be provided cost-effective prenatal care to prevent infant deaths and birth defects, but by how many families can be denied Medicaid and turned away from public health clinics. Not by how many hungry infants can be nourished, but by how many federal nutrition dollars can be held back as the waiting list of hungry babies grows. Not by how many poor homeless families are provided adequate shelter and minimum food, but by how many MX missiles we can find a hiding place for.
>
> The current national rhetoric tells us it is more blessed to judge than to help the poor; that private charity is an adequate substitute for public justice; that it is proper for government to subsidize three-martini corporate lunches but improper for government to subsidize child care to help millions of poor working mothers escape welfare; that spending millions of dollars on golf outings and sports tickets and barber shops for defense contractors is a more justifiable national security expenditure than teaching poor children to read, write, and compute; that more government support for rich families strengthens them; while more government help for poor families weakens them; that a child's right to life ends at birth and does not include the right to adequate prenatal and nutritional care before birth or survival health, housing, and family supports after birth.
>
> These perverse national values, hidden behind pro-family, "traditional values" rhetoric, are manifested in budget priorities that have cut billions each year since 1980 from survival programs for poor children and families. They are creating a new American apartheid between rich and poor, white and black, old and young, government and needy, corporation and individual, military and domestic needs—and have left millions of poor children to the wolves of hunger, homelessness, abuse, and even death.

Source: Marian Wright Edelman, *Families in Peril: An Agenda for Social Change.* © 1987 by the President and Fellows of Harvard College. Cambridge, MA: Harvard University Press.

Isolation of the Nuclear Family

For many modern parents, geographic isolation from the extended family—brothers and sisters, mothers and fathers, cousins, aunts and uncles—and from lifelong friends has significantly increased the stresses of child-rearing and other family responsibilities. Moreover, parents in relatively isolated nuclear families are more likely to find that they must learn appropriate techniques for raising their children with little help from others. In an earlier day, the puzzled parent could more readily turn to family members or close friends for help. In today's nuclear family, often living in a mobile community with transient acquaintances from diverse cultural and geographic backgrounds, parents frequently lack such support.

Of course, it is not only parents who gain a greater feeling of security and direction from living in a close-knit, relatively homogeneous community. Their children also are more likely to accept parental rules, standards, and beliefs when they see that these are supported by other adults (see Chapter 9). When the parents of adolescent peers communicate with one another, and when all of them expect adolescents to observe certain rules about such matters as drinking, smoking, marijuana use, or standards of social and sexual behavior, the adolescent is less likely to question those rules, and the parents' task is made easier. In this fashion, parents from different families can reinforce one another.

On the other hand, in communities where parents are unable to communicate closely with other parents, or where other parents follow widely varying practices, the opportunities for such adolescent "blackmail" techniques as "But all the other kids are allowed to do it," or, "Susie's parents don't act that way," are increased significantly. Moreover, the adolescents themselves may be genuinely confused or skeptical about the diversity they observe in the values, beliefs, and practices of their peers' parents.

Isolation of the nuclear family is likely to be stressful for all members of the family (Conger, 1975; Hamburg, Elliott, & Parron, 1982). However, it appears to have its greatest impact on wives and mothers during the child-rearing years. One study compared the incidence of psychiatric and psychosomatic symptoms (e.g., high blood pressure, peptic ulcer) in two rural areas, a relatively stable suburban county and a highly transient, socially mobile suburban county (both on the East Coast of the United States). The investigators found that the incidence of such disorders was highest for both sexes in the highly mobile suburb and lowest in the rural county, that the frequency of such symptoms increased rapidly in the highly mobile suburb during a decade in which the county grew rapidly, and that the greatest increase occurred among wives and mothers between the ages of 18 and 44 (Gordon & Gordon, 1960).

Isolation of the nuclear family may intensify other problems as well. The more the intimate emotional relationships of parents and children are confined to the nuclear family, and the smaller the family unit is, the more intense family relationships are likely to be and the more difficult and stressful to modify (Anthony & Benedek, 1970). Consequently, during periods like adolescence—when dependence must yield to independence, bonds to parents must be loosened and new ties established with peers, and intergenerational conflicts are likely to reach their peak—the isolated nuclear family is likely to experience considerable stress. In such a family it is more difficult for both parents and adolescents to adjust to changing circumstances than might be the case in an extended family in a close-knit community (Bronfenbrenner, 1985; Bronfenbrenner, Moen, & Garbarino, 1984).

The Rapidity of Social Change

The rapid rate of social change in the past several decades has also magnified the challenges of the adolescent period, both for parents and for their children. It means that adolescents have grown up in a markedly different world from that of their parents. When developmental experiences and social trends differ greatly between parents and their children, generational differences in values and outlook tend to be magnified (Conger, 1971, 1977; Keniston, 1960). Thus, to the extent that today's parents look only to their own experiences during adolescence for expectations about their children's behavior or guidance in understanding their needs and goals, they are bound to encounter frustration.

As we shall see, the psychological, social, and economic climate in which today's adolescents are coming to maturity, and the pressures they face, are significantly different from those encountered by their parents. Unless parents can understand the nature of these differences, their efforts to help their children fulfill their potential and avoid self-destructive behaviors are likely to fall wide of the mark. The task is not an easy one, and it is not made any easier by continued age segregation and the persistence of a youth culture with values and social pressures of its own.

Changes Within the Family

Even more important, however, are the changes that have been taking place within the family in recent years. Those changes have created new challenges for parents and have raised questions about the kinds of models parents can and should provide for their children.

As we have seen, in the homes in which the parents of today's adolescents grew up, the ideal stereotype portrayed a father who was the family's economic provider and protector and a mother who provided nurturance for the children and took care of the home. Unmarried couples did not state openly that they were living together; marriage was supposed to last forever; and divorce, when it occurred, was generally viewed as a sign of personal failure. Boys were supposed to be little men—outgoing and assertive—while girls were supposed to be dainty and conforming. The work ethic was strong, and instant gratification was not a socially approved goal.

Today the situation is far different. As a consequence of the women's movement and increasing female employment, previously accepted sex role standards and relations between spouses are being reevaluated, and many marriages have felt the strain. A husband may be unwilling to accept his wife's newfound need for more equal sharing of family decision making, household tasks, and child-rearing responsibilities, nor may he approve of her desire to have a career outside the home. In two-career families, fitting child care, household, and social responsibilities into busy work schedules can be a complicated and wearing process. In other instances parents may simply be confused; in a symposium on alternative family life-styles held at Tulane University, one young woman tentatively asked the panel, "I just want to get married and have children. Is that still OK?"

A majority of married women, including those with young children, are employed outside the home; however, the desirability of this arrangement is a subject of continuing debate. A national survey conducted in 1986 showed that although a majority of working mothers are employed full time with regular hours, only 13 percent favor this arrangement *(Newsweek,* 1986). Thirty-four percent would rather work part time; 24 percent would still like to work full time, but with regular hours; 12 percent wish they could work from their homes; and 16 percent would prefer not to be employed if financial circumstances permitted it.

In a *New York Times/CBS News* poll Americans were asked, "What kind of marriage do you think makes the more satisfying kind of life?" The choice was between a marriage in which the husband provides for the family and the wife takes care of the home and children and one in which both spouses have jobs, both do housework, and both take care of the children. In the youngest age group, 18–29-year-olds, only 27 percent preferred the traditional marriage. However, in the age groups whose members were most likely to be the parents of adolescents, 30–44-year-olds, 44 percent chose the traditional marriage; and among Americans age 45 and older this figure increased to 55 percent (Meislin, 1977).

Obviously, views of marriage and the family are in transition, and it is among the parents of today's adolescents that opinions regarding the merits of "traditional" versus "liberal" or "modern" arrangements are most likely to be divided and, hence, to be a source of stress. Opinions about whether working outside the home interferes with being a good mother are also divided. While 86 percent of all women believe that a mother who works part time can adequately fulfill her responsibilities to her children, only 50 percent think a mother who works full time can do so (65 percent of working mothers and 42 percent of nonworking mothers) *(Newsweek,* 1986). Younger people are more likely than older people to believe that working women are better mothers (Meislin, 1977).

Among high school seniors in the United States in 1989, only 10 percent of boys and 5 percent of girls considered it desirable for the husband to be employed while the wife remains at home if the couple has no children, although most considered this arrangement at least somewhat acceptable (Johnston, Bachman, & O'Malley, forthcoming). However, if the couple has one or more preschool children, the most preferred arrangement was for the husband to work full time while the wife remains at home or works part time. Less than 7 percent of seniors of both sexes considered it desirable for both spouses to work full time, and over one-third viewed such an arrangement as "not at all acceptable" (see Chapter 11).

Home and Family Life. From the standpoint of marriage and the family, what are the actual effects of increased participation of women in the labor force? The available evidence suggests that working women are more likely than nonworking women to postpone marriage, but they are only slightly less likely not to marry at all. They are, however, likely to have fewer children. An apparent exception is women executives in the higher ranks of the corporate world, who are less likely to be married than most women, both working and nonworking (U.S. Department of Labor, 1983; Taylor, 1986).

Although overall divorce rates have increased dramatically, there is no clear evidence indicating that employment of the wife leads to divorce or separation. It appears that in some cases (e.g., when the wife has a relatively high income, particularly when the husband earns less) divorce rates are somewhat higher. In cases in which the husband and wife are in agreement about the wife's employment, the wife finds satisfaction in her work, and the family's standard of living benefits, divorce rates are lower (Hoffman, 1984; Smith, 1979).

What about marital satisfaction? Again it is difficult to make generalizations. Overall, there is a tendency for working wives to be somewhat more satisfied than nonworking wives. Conversely, husbands of working wives report somewhat less satisfaction than those of nonworking wives, despite the fact that employment places heavier burdens on the typical wife's schedule, in terms of household tasks and child-rearing responsibilities, than on the husband's. (Although husbands of working wives participate slightly more in household and child-rearing tasks than husbands of nonworking wives, wives still typically have primary responsibility for these tasks.) However, this is not the whole story. Marital satisfaction for both partners appears to be enhanced when the wife works out of choice rather than out of necessity, has an interesting job, works part time, or works when the children are no longer of preschool age (Hoffman, 1984; Smith, 1979). On the other hand, satisfaction appears to suffer when the wife works out of necessity rather than preference, when her work is uninteresting or poorly paid, and when the burden of home responsibilities is great and little relief or outside help is possible.

Inasmuch as most wives and mothers will be working throughout the remainder of this century, it is important that efforts be made to ease the difficulties involved—through greater division of labor in the home, improved maternity benefits and leave allowances, increased availability of part-time jobs and more flexible work schedules, greater availability of high-quality day care, and more equal pay and benefits for both women and men.

Ultimately, however, the success of a majority of couples in creating an enduring, mutually rewarding, and growth enhancing family life will depend as much or more on the individuals themselves as on social policies like those just mentioned. Even under the best of circumstances, successful marriage and child rearing are not easy. They require maturity, the capacity for intimacy, the ability to change, patience, tolerance, and above all commitment—willingness to subordinate one's own desires to the welfare of another human being. As one social critic has observed, "Marriage presupposes a willingness to grow up." In the aftermath of the "me decade," with its emphasis on self-realization and reduced concern for others, it may be more difficult to attain this degree of maturity. As we have seen, achieving a sense of identity is an important developmental task. But maturity also requires the development of a capacity for intimacy and what Erikson calls "generativity"—the ability to gain satisfaction from contributing to the development of others, particularly the young (Erikson, 1963, 1983).

Divorce, Remarriage, and the Single-Parent Family.

As the functions of the family have changed and the stresses on it have increased, rates of separation, desertion, and divorce have also risen (Calhoun, Grotberg, & Rackey, 1980; Glick & Norton, 1979; U.S. Bureau of the Census, 1986, 1989). After a flurry of both marriages and divorces following World War II, the divorce rate declined throughout the 1950s. Since 1960, however, it has more than doubled (see Figure 5.1). Demographers predict that 40–50 percent of the children born during the 1970s will experience divorce or the death of a parent.

In addition, the percentage of births to unmarried women has increased more than fivefold since 1950 and more than doubled since 1970 (U.S. Bureau of the Census, 1978, 1989). As a result, in 1984 only about three out of every four children under 18 were living with two parents, and more than one in five were living in a single-parent family, more than double the number twenty five years ago. Moreover, among children who were living with two parents, at least one-sixth were living in households in which one or both spouses had remarried (Cherlin, 1981; Radish, Hofferth, & Evans, 1984). Only about one family in four now conforms to the traditional stereotype of the one-marriage, two-parent family, with the father as the breadwinner and the mother as the homemaker and primary caretaker of several dependent children.

For some, such trends are evidence of the decline of the family. Those who hold this view are likely to point to increases in rates of delinquency and adolescent pregnancy and to growing numbers of runaways, reported cases of child abuse and family violence, and children placed in foster care or institutions. In contrast, others see the increasing variety of family forms as a necessary, even positive, adaptation to social change (Rossi, 1978).

In our view, passionate advocates of both positions tend to ignore some important considerations. Those anticipating the imminent demise of the family overlook the fact that in one form or another the family has proved to be remarkably durable over many centuries. And the fact remains that despite increased rates of divorce, separation, and out-of-wedlock births, at any one time four out of every five children are living with two parents. Although divorce rates among women in their 30s continued to rise at a record high rate in the past decade, divorce rates among women in their 20s increased between 1975 and 1980 but have remained stable since then, suggesting that the current generation of young adults may find it easier to adjust to the new realities of marriage than members of the "baby boom" generation (Norton & Moorman, 1986).

Moreover, of those who do divorce, 75 percent of the women and over 80 percent of the men remarry, although the remarriage rate for single parents with children (95 percent of whom are women), particularly poor black

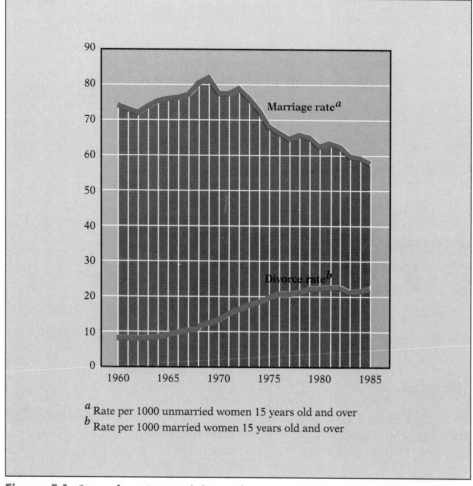

Figure 5.1 Rates of marriage and divorce for women 15 years old and over, 1960–1985. (From U.S. Department of Commerce, Bureau of the Census, *Statistical abstract of the United States, 1989*. Washington, D.C.: U.S. Government Printing Office, 1989 (109th ed.).)

women, is much lower (Cherlin, 1981; Glick & Norton, 1979; Radish, Hofferth, & Evans, 1984; U.S. Bureau of the Census, 1989). In short, despite all the difficulties, most people still prefer to live in families.

Those who see variations in family structure simply as creative responses to changing times may also be guilty of oversimplification. It is certainly true that some variations from traditional family structure, such as the small two-career family, can be rewarding for both parents and children. It also seems clear that children can be reared successfully in single-parent and "blended" families (those resulting from remarriage), particularly when the parents are psychologically mature and adequate social support is available. Indeed, children in such families may be better off than children in traditional families torn by dissent and frustration (Hetherington, 1979, 1989; Long & Forehand, 1987).

However, variations from traditional family structure can also be disruptive and painful. For example, many adolescent single mothers are emotionally immature, economically disadvantaged, and ill prepared to cope with the responsibilities of parenthood, and their children are at high risk for child abuse and problems of physical and mental health (see pages 256–258). Even mature and economically successful single parents—especially those who are divorced, abandoned, or widowed—are likely to suffer from loneliness and a sense of isolation.

Effects of Divorce. Although much can be done to minimize the adverse effects of divorce on both children and parents, few people emerge from the experience untroubled (Hetherington & Camara, 1984; Hetherington, Stanley-Hagan, & Andersen, 1989; Hodges & Bloom, 1984; Irion, Coon, & Blanchard-Fields, 1988; Wallerstein, Corbin, & Lewis 1988). As one family therapist states, "The child learns the rules of human relationships in the immediate household. When the child sees that world splitting up, he feels his world is shattered. His learned rules no longer make sense or are true" (Francke, 1980, p. 59). Consequently, in addition to experiencing a profound sense of loss, the child suddenly feels vulnerable to forces that are beyond his or her control.

With some variations, depending on age and sex, children may regress, withdraw, become aggressive or depressed, feel responsible for the divorce, blame one or both parents, or suffer from a conflict of loyalties (Guidubaldi & Perry, 1986; Hetherington et al., 1985; Wallerstein, Corbin, & Lewis, 1988). Most common among children of all ages is an obsessive desire to reunite the parents. For example, even though her parents had been separated for four years, one 13-year-old girl adamantly opposed their plan to divorce. "Once all the papers are signed, I wouldn't have a chance," she said. "Now I have hope" (Francke, 1980, p. 61).

The child's problems are often aggravated by the fact that the parents are preoccupied with their own problems, especially during the first year after the divorce, and have difficulty responding to the child's needs (Hetherington & Camara, 1984). Although the situation is likely to improve within a year or two (and although divorce no longer carries the social stigma it once did), a significant number of children continue to have difficulty adjusting (Guidubaldi & Perry, 1985; Hetherington & Camara, 1984; Hetherington, Cox, & Cox, 1985). One study found that five years after the parents' separation, one-third of the children appeared resilient, relaxed, and self-reliant; another third appeared to be coping fairly well; and the rest had significant psychological problems and still looked back with intense longing to life before the divorce (Wallerstein, 1985).

Studies have consistently found that boys, especially younger boys, are more vulnerable to the effects of divorce than girls are. Even six years after their parents' divorce, boys from divorced families performed more poorly than peers from intact families on a wide variety of academic and mental-health measures (Guidubaldi & Perry, 1985; Hetherington, 1989). They were also far more likely than girls from divorced families to manifest adverse effects of divorce, especially lack of social competence, noncompliance, and physical and verbal aggression. Girls who manifested problems after their parents' divorce were more likely to react with anxiety, sadness, passivity, isolation, and efforts to obtain reassurance (Hetherington et al., 1985).

As adolescents and young adults, many young people of both sexes—even though they may be getting on successfully with their own lives—still have strong memories of their parents' breakup, along with feelings of sadness, continuing resentment, and a sense of deprivation (Wallerstein, 1985; Wallerstein et al., 1988). And a significant number appear to have difficulty establishing intimate relationships. It is difficult to disagree with Albert Solnit, former director of the Yale Child Study Center, when he says, "Divorce is one of the most serious and complex mental health problems facing children [today]."

Remarriage. Remarriage can also be difficult for all concerned; this may account for the fact that 40 percent of such marriages fail, compared to about one in three first marriages. Children may resent a stepfather or stepmother because he or she has displaced the original parent or because the stepparent competes with the child for the other parent's love and attention. This is most likely to occur when a girl's mother remarries. As Mavis Hetherington and her colleagues observe, divorced mothers and sons are frequently involved in a mutual battle of wills and may "have much to gain from the addition of a responsive, authoritative stepfather, who offers support to both the mother and son" (Hetherington et al., 1985, p. 529). In contrast, after a divorce a mother and daughter are more likely to form a close alliance, and upon the mother's remarriage the daughter is more likely to view the stepfather as an intruder (Hetherington, 1989; Hetherington & Camara, 1984; Hetherington et al., 1985; Peterson & Zill, 1986; Zill & Peterson, 1983).

Stepparents themselves may feel insecure about interacting with newly acquired stepchildren (Spanier & Furstenberg, 1982). Where two sets of children live together in a "blended" family, there may be rivalries between them. Thus, although variations in family structure like those just described may be better for children's development than remaining in a crisis-ridden family with both original parents present, these variations should not be viewed simply as "creative alternatives."

Despite their differing perspectives, most observers of family life share a concern for the survival of the family as a social institution and view it as playing a vital and constructive role in the raising of children. They are in agreement on the need for a greater degree of societal and community support for families than currently exists. However, there is a group of social critics who assert that the nature and rate of recent social change have made parents largely irrelevant as models or guides for the development of their adolescent sons and daughters. The late Simone de Beauvoir, in her autobiography *All Said and Done* (1975), urged the abolition of the family and endorsed commu-

Living together in a "blended" family can be challenging for all concerned.

nal rearing of children. Somewhat ironically, however, in the same book she repeatedly stressed the importance of her own mother, father, and sister in her development as a woman and as a writer.

In a more moderate vein, Margaret Mead argued that today's parents of adolescents are pioneers, immigrants in an unexplored land, the "country of the young." In this new terrain the young person will have to chart his or her own path without significant assistance from either parents or peers. Under such circumstances about all that parents can provide are love and trust, although these are vital (Mead, 1970).

It appears clear that a climate of love and trust is, as Erik Erikson (1963, 1968) also asserts, fundamental. Without such a climate in the home, the child's chances of becoming a reasonably happy, effective, contributing adult, and of developing a positive self-image and a sense of identity, are seriously impaired (Conger, 1977; Maccoby & Martin, 1983). But there is little or no evidence to support the notion that the young have little to learn from parents. As will also become evident, the role of parental models in fostering or hindering their children's psychological development and preparing them to meet the challenges of adulthood extends far beyond these essential ingredients.

A Generation Gap?

The social trends that we have reviewed in this chapter have clearly increased the challenges of the adolescent period, both for parents and for young people. But have they also produced a largely unbridgeable generation gap between today's average parents and their adolescent young? On the basis of the available evidence, the best answer appears to be that there *is* a gap between parents and adolescents but that it is neither as wide nor as novel as many people have been led to believe. Even at the height of the so-called counterculture of the late 1960s, when generational conflicts were most apparent, approximately two out of three young people and seven out of ten parents expressed the view that a gap existed but that it had been exaggerated (Conger, 1971; Harris, 1971; Yankelovich, 1969). Only about one young person in four, and a similar percentage of parents, felt that there was a large gap; only a small minority of both groups (about one in twenty) felt that there was no gap at all.

When asked whether they thought that their values and ideals differed markedly from those of their parents, a majority of both younger and older adolescents of the late 1960s and early 1970s said that they did not. About three-fourths of adolescents stated that they accepted and generally agreed with their parents' values and ideals; most stated that whatever differences existed were either moderate (49 percent) or slight (35 percent) (Harris, 1971; Yankelovich, 1969). In view of popular stereotypes, it is interesting to note that parents were even less likely than their children to perceive significant differences in ideals and values. Thus, less than one parent in ten (9 percent) felt that the differences between themselves and their children were great; a majority (55 percent) felt that such differences were slight; and the remainder (36 percent) felt that they were moderate (Yankelovich, 1969).

Closing the Gap. Studies conducted in the 1980s indicate that in most areas the generation gap is narrower than it was in the late 1960s and even in the 1970s (*America's youth*, 1988; Bachman, Johnston, & O'Malley, 1981, 1987; National Association, 1984). In a nationwide survey of students in grades 7–12 conducted in 1984, three-fourths of the students reported that they had no serious problems getting along with their parents or other family members, compared to one-half a decade earlier. Indeed, only about 10 percent reported significant difficulties in relations with their mothers; a similar proportion reported problems with their fathers (National Association, 1984). And in a nationwide survey of American adolescents conducted in 1987 by the George H. Gallup International Institute (*America's youth*, 1988), 49 percent of males and 52 percent of females stated that they got along "very well" with their parents and 48 percent of males and 39 percent of females said that they got along "fairly well." Only about 5 percent of respondents of both sexes said that they did "not get along at all well" (see Table 5.1).

The conflicts that did arise were more likely to revolve around such issues as curfews, household chores, choice of friends, schoolwork, and hair or clothing styles than around basic values (*America's Youth*, 1988; National Association, 1984). Although in the 1980s many students—particularly older students— still voiced the age-old complaints that their parents were old-fashioned (40 percent) or treated them like children (30 percent), when it came to major substantive issues, such as educational values, use of drugs, or the work ethic,

T A B L E 5.1 PARENTAL RELATIONSHIPS OF AMERICAN ADOLESCENTS. QUESTION: *HOW WELL WOULD YOU SAY YOU GET ON WITH YOUR PARENTS: VERY WELL, FAIRLY WELL, OR NOT AT ALL WELL?*

	August 31–October 8, 1987		
	Very well	Fairly well	Not at all well
NATIONAL	52%	43%	5%
Sex			
Young men	49	46	5
Young women	56	39	5
Age			
13–15 years	48	47	5
16–17 years	58	37	5
Region			
East	51	45	4
Midwest	57	34	9
South	53	45	2
West	45	49	6
Academic Standing			
Above average	60	38	2
Average or below	43	48	9
Parent's occupation			
White collar	55	41	4
Blue collar	48	44	8
City size			
Metropolitan	55	43	2
Suburban	44	48	8
Nonmetropolitan	57	38	5
Religion			
Protestants	49	45	6
Catholics	57	41	2

Source: *America's youth 1977–1988.* Princeton, NJ: The George H. Gallup International Institute, 1988. By permission.

most junior and senior high school students (75–80 percent) appear to have adopted the views of their parents (National Association, 1984).

In 1989 students in a continuing national survey of high school seniors were asked how closely their ideas agreed with those of their parents on a wide range of topics (Johnston, Bachman, & O'Malley, forthcoming). Over 70 percent indicated that their ideas were "very similar" or "mostly similar" to those of their parents on use of drugs other than alcohol and marijuana, on what the young person should do with his or her life, on what values in life are important, on the value of education, on matters of religion, and on appropriate roles for women. In most instances the students perceived their views as more similar to those of their parents than was the case in 1980 or earlier—particularly regarding drug use and educational values.

There was somewhat less, though still substantial, agreement about politics, racial issues, conservation and pollution issues, and use of alcohol and marijuana. The least agreement was found on such topics as use of leisure time, how the young person spends money, and what things are OK to do on a date.

In still other areas, such as the need for reform of social institutions (ranging from government and the military to business, education, industry, and the communications media), there is considerable intergenerational agreement—primarily because adults themselves have become increasingly critical of these institutions (Conger, 1981; *New York Times*/CBS, 1986; Yankelovich, 1981). In sum, it appears that there is a generation gap but that for most adolescents it is not nearly as wide or as pervasive as many people have been led to believe.

How can we reconcile the discrepancies, not only between the apparent facts and popular stereotypes about the so-called generation gap but also between these facts and what we might expect theoretically, on the basis of the nature and rate of social change? A number of relevant factors are often overlooked. For one thing, there is a tendency to overgeneralize from the behavior of a minority of young people to adolescents and youth as a whole. This was particularly true during the late 1960s and early 1970s, when the mass media tended to portray young people (whether favorably or unfavorably) in terms of the attitudes and behavior of visible, controversial, sometimes highly articulate subgroups—whether white middle-class activists, minority-group militants, or hippies and teeny-boppers (Feigelson, 1970; Fort, 1969; Gerzon, 1970; Roszak, 1969). In contrast, adults of that period were commonly characterized as a "silent majority" of middle Americans ("Man and woman of the year," 1970).

Although there is currently less emphasis on such misleading stereotypes, we still frequently hear blanket statements about "today's youth." Simplistic comparisons between adolescents and adults ignore the fact that ours has long been a heterogeneous society. As we shall see in later chapters, variations among important subgroups of adolescents are at least as great as differences between the average adult and the average adolescent. This holds true in the areas of political and social values, sexual attitudes and behavior, patterns of drug use, and educational and vocational goals.

Popular stereotypes also confound comparisons between adults and adolescents in general with comparisons between individual parents and their adolescent sons and daughters, despite the fact that these may differ significantly. For example, in one national study two-thirds of adolescents age 15 and older replied positively to the question "Do your parents approve of your values and ideals?" but a majority answered negatively to the question "Do they approve of the way your generation expresses their ideals?" Adolescents also tend to be more critical of the older generation as a whole than of their own parents (Bachman et al., 1980, 1987; Conger, 1971; Harris, 1971; Norman & Harris, 1981). In some instances adolescents may come into conflict with the values of some adult authority figures in our society precisely because those values conflict with values the young person has acquired from, and shares with, his or her parents.

Finally, there is a widespread tendency to overlook the possibility that parents and adolescents may be able to differ in some of their values and modes of behavior and still maintain mutual understanding and respect. In a national survey of adolescent sexuality in the 1970s, 80 percent of adolescents stated that they had "a lot of respect" for their parents' ideas and opinions even though they disagreed with them on specific issues. For example, only 38 percent of this sample of young people (28 percent of boys and 49 percent of girls) agreed that "when it comes to sex, my attitudes and my parents' attitudes are pretty much the same" (Sorensen, 1973, p. 388).

Generational Differences and the Life Cycle.

> To everything there is a season
> And a time to every purpose under heaven
>> *Ecclesiastes 3:1*

The extent of generational differences may be expected to vary from one era to another, largely as a result of the speed and pervasiveness of social change. Nevertheless, there will always be some sort of generation gap—if only because successive generations occupy different positions in the life cycle (Conger, 1971, 1976). The adolescent who is just becoming aware of the insistent stirring of sexual impulses will inevitably differ from the middle-aged adult for whom the urgency of those impulses has declined. Adolescents need ways to consume their energy; adults look for ways to conserve it. Young people are concerned about where they are going, adults about where they have been. Having experienced the many partial victories and defeats and the inevitable compromises of living, adults tend to be moderate in their enthusiasms and cautious in their moral judgments. Young people, in contrast, tend to be impatient, impulsive, and given at times to imperious moral judgments that leave little room for shades of gray. They are more likely to move rapidly from profound joy to despair. Adults must worry about their children; adolescents must worry more about themselves. The psychological defense mechanisms of adolescents are in flux and only partially effective; those of adults tend, like arteries, to harden with age.

Despite such differences, adolescents and their elders can—indeed, need to—communicate with and learn from each other. How successfully they do so depends on many factors, including the social, economic, and political climate and the nature and rate of social change. But most of all, their success is likely to depend on the nature of parent–child relationships and the continued viability of the family as society's most basic and enduring social unit.

SUMMARY

The nature of the American family and its role in society are significantly different from what they were less than half a century ago. Increasing urbanization and geographic mobility have reduced the stability and interdependence of communities and left the modern family more isolated from personal, familial, and community support systems and more dependent on its own resources in an increasingly complex world. Moreover, the functions of the family have changed markedly, resulting in additional demands on its members. Up through the nineteenth century, families generally were larger and early parental death and economic insecurity were far more prevalent; as a result, families and relatives were more dependent on one another. This tended to promote family solidarity, but it left little room for individualism.

Individualistic patterns of family behavior and segregation of family roles first appeared in the urban middle class. Middle-class families were the first to initiate a regular, carefully timed progression for entering school, graduating, preparing for a vocation, leaving home, marrying, forming a new family. As America entered the twentieth century, these patterns began to spread across the social spectrum, leading to the transfer of many responsibilities from the family to other social institutions. This shift was manifested in child labor laws, compulsory school attendance, and age-segregated schools and social activities.

All of these forces combined to foster the emergence of the "modern" nuclear family, with its emphasis on privacy, solidarity, and child centeredness. The stereotypical nuclear family reached its peak in popular acclaim in the late 1940s and the 1950s. In pursuit of "the good life," both young people and their parents were willing to accept a high degree of conformity.

All this ended in the turbulent 1960s, beginning with the civil rights movement and followed by the divisive Vietnam War, the rise and fall of the War on Poverty, the assassinations of John and Robert Kennedy and Martin Luther King, Jr., and the Watergate Scandal. To an unprecedented degree young people were exposed to a deeply divided adult society. Among the consequences were a decline in adult authority and the rise of the "youth culture," both of which were accentuated by further increases in the age segregation of adolescents and youth.

In the 1970s some of the challenges faced by the family abated while others remained and new ones emerged. Generational differences in values diminished, but age segregation continued. The women's movement challenged gender-related stereotypes, as did the rapid increase in women's participation in the labor force. Still another social force affecting family values in the "me decade" was greater concern for the self, coupled with decreased concern with the needs of others. (The 1960s were also characterized by concern with self-realization and self-fulfillment—"doing your own thing"—but that concern was balanced by social activism and increased concern for others.)

Much of the emphasis on individual freedom that characterized the 1970s carried over into the 1980s; at the same time, however, there was a significant societal shift toward greater conservatism on social and political issues. Two major economic events of the 1980s had important consequences for families: the recession of the early 1980s and the accelerating shift from a goods-producing to a service economy. Together, these events placed enormous stress on many families, leading to sharp increases in rates of child abuse, family violence, and divorce or separation. The government's responses to the problems not only of the "new poor" but also of the larger number of families living below the poverty level was one of neglect; tax cuts favored the wealthy, while programs benefiting the poor were cut back. Today one child in four and one youth in five are living in poverty in the United States.

One of the consequences of these social changes has been increased isolation of the nuclear family. In addition, the rapidity of these changes has magnified the challenges of the adolescent period because it means that parents and adolescents have grown up in markedly different worlds. The stereotypical family of the 1950s, with its clearly defined sex role standards and work ethic, has been largely replaced by more egalitarian two-income families with fewer children. Only about one family in four now conforms to the traditional one-marriage, two-parent family, with the father as breadwinner and the mother as homemaker and primary caretaker of several dependent children. Combining work and child rearing—never an easy task—has become far more complex and calls for greater maturity. The difficulties are magnified for single-parent families, which are most likely to be poor.

Although much can be done to minimize the adverse effects of divorce, few children or adolescents emerge from the experience untroubled. Remarriage can also be difficult for all concerned. Some social critics have argued that the nature and rate of social change have made parents irrelevant as models for their adolescent sons and daughters. The fact is, however, that parental models play a major role in fostering or hindering children's development.

Although the generation gap between adolescents and their parents is much narrower than it was in the 1960s and early 1970s, a moderate gap remains, and probably always will—if only because parents and adolescents are at different stages in the life cycle. However, contrary to popular perceptions, most generational differences revolve around such issues as tastes in clothes and music, school work and household chores, and choice of friends, rather than around basic values and life goals. About 75 percent of all adolescents accept and generally agree with their parents' values and ideals, and most say that they get along well with their parents. Despite their differences, adolescents and their elders can and need to communicate with and learn from one another.

REVIEW QUESTIONS

1. Discuss the ways in which the nature of the American family and its functions in society have changed in the twentieth century.
2. Describe briefly the emergence of individualistic patterns of family behavior and segregation of family roles in urban middle-class families.
3. What attributes characterized the stereotypical nuclear family in the decade following World War II?
4. What effects did the events of the 1960s, including the Vietnam War, have on adolescents and youth? What roles did age segregation and the rise of the "youth culture" play?
5. What effects did the women's movement and women's increased partic-

ipation in the labor force have on the American family and on relations between men and women?

6. When we use the label "me-decade" to describe the 1970s, what are we referring to?

7. Discuss briefly the challenges faced by American families in the 1980s and 1990s.

8. How has the rapidity of recent social change, including changes within the family, affected communication between adolescents and their parents?

9. Discuss briefly the effects of the increased social isolation of the nuclear family on parent–child relationships.

10. How wide is the generation gap between adolescents and their parents? Is it greater or smaller than it was in the late 1960s and early 1970s? Why?

RECOMMENDED READINGS

Conger, J. J. (1981). Freedom and commitment: Families, youth, and social change. *American Psychologist, 36,* 1475–1484.

Harevan, T. K. (1984). Themes in the historical development of the family. In R. D. Parke (Ed.), *Review of child development research* (Vol. 7) (pp. 137–178). Chicago: University of Chicago Press.

Hetherington, E. M., Stanley-Hagan, M., & Anderson, E. R. (1989). Marital transitions: A child's perspective. *American Psychgologist,* **44,** 303–312.

Moynihan, D. P. (1986). *Family and nation.* New York: Harcourt Brace Jovanovich.

Ross, A. S., Kagan, J., & Harevan, T. K. (Eds.) (1984). *The family.* New York: Norton.

Shorter, E. (1975). *The making of the modern family.* New York: Basic Books.

PARENT–CHILD RELATIONS AND ADOLESCENT DEVELOPMENT

As we saw in the preceding chapter, recent social changes have had profound effects on the nature of the family and its relations with other social institutions. In the process, these changes have increased the stresses of adolescence, both for parents and for young people themselves. Despite the added difficulty, however, adolescents still must master the important developmental tasks of adolescence—adjusting to the physical and sexual changes of puberty, gaining **autonomy** from parents and other caretakers, establishing effective social and working relationships with same- and opposite-sex peers, preparing for a vocation, and developing a system of values and a sense of identity (Conger, 1971, 1979; Havighurst, 1953; Thomas, 1985).

The fact that in today's world these tasks are more complex, and that both parent and child have fewer blueprints to guide them, does not fundamentally alter the situation. The social roles of men and women may change, and the transition to adult roles may be more difficult; the responsibilities and privileges associated with independence may change; the difficulty of planning a career may increase; and the kind of personal and social identity that will be viable in tomorrow's world may change. But each of these tasks remains a critical and indispensable challenge for the adolescent. The question is, What factors will increase the likelihood that a young person can accomplish these tasks successfully and get through the adolescent period without excessive turmoil and with a reasonable degree of resilience to psychological difficulties and external pressures?

We clearly cannot look only to individual or familial factors for answers; as we have seen, social factors are also of major importance, particularly in a period of rapid social change (Bronfenbrenner, 1985; Conger, 1977). Even an adolescent growing up in a relatively isolated and homogeneous small town—where values are largely shared by the community as a whole and generally acceptable models of adult identity may be found—will face complex developmental demands. His or her task may be different from, and somewhat less difficult than, that of an adolescent growing up in a heterogeneous, frequently conflict-ridden, avant-garde urban area or in a socially disorganized ethnic ghetto. Nevertheless, the realities of the broader society, extensively communicated by the mass media, are the same everywhere and will inevitably affect the course of adolescent development.

Like all adolescents, those growing up in the 1990s must develop a personal and social identity, but for most this is a less confusing, less conflict-ridden task than it was in the 1960s (Conger, 1981). Even so, an increasing body of empirical data indicates that the single most important external influence on the average young person attempting to accomplish the developmental tasks of adolescence is his or her parents (Armsden & Greenberg, 1987; Baumrind, 1975, 1985; Garbarino, Schellenbach, & Sebes, 1986; Maccoby & Martin, 1984;). The real question is not, as some have argued, whether parental models are important; rather, it is what kinds of parental models are necessary and appropriate in preparing contemporary adolescents to cope with the largely unpredictable world of tomorrow.

MODELS OF PARENT–CHILD INTERACTION

In the case of adolescents, the question of what kinds of parental models are most helpful involves the effects not simply of current patterns of parent–child interaction but of a history of prior interactions extending back to early childhood. Parents may be loving or rejecting; calm or anxious; involved or uninvolved; rigid or flexible; controlling, guiding but encouraging autonomy, or very permissive. All of these qualities have been found to influence the child's subsequent behavior and adjustment. Particular attention has been focused on two major dimensions of parental behavior: *love–hostility* and *autonomy–control* (Elder, 1980; Baumrind, 1988, 1989; Benjamin, 1974, 1977; Humphrey & Benjamin, 1986; Maccoby & Martin, 1983; Schaefer, 1959, 1965; Wiggins, 1982).

Parental Love or Rejection

Although we refer to the first dimension as *love–hostility*, the exact labels employed vary from one investigator to another; examples include *warmth–hostility, acceptance–rejection,* and *responsive–unresponsive* (Maccoby & Martin, 1984; Martin, 1975; Parker, Tupling & Brown, 1979). At its positive end, this dimension refers to parents who are accepting, affectionate, understanding, responsive, child centered, and reassuring, and who use praise a great deal and punishment very little. At its negative end, it refers to the opposite set of these characteristics.

Erikson and Mead are referring to the positive end of this dimension when they speak of the child's need for love and trust. Indeed, numerous studies have shown that without strong and unambiguous manifestations of parental love, the child or adolescent has much more difficulty developing self-esteem, constructive and rewarding relationships with others, and a confident sense of his or her own identity (Bell et al., 1985; Kawash, Kerr, & Clews, 1985; Martin, 1975; Rosenberg, 1965; Rutter, 1979, 1980).

Parental hostility, rejection, or neglect occur more frequently than acceptance, love, and trust in the backgrounds of children with problems ranging from cognitive and academic difficulties and impaired social relationships with peers and adults, to neurotic disorders, psychophysiological disturbances, and character problems such as delinquency (Anthony & Benedek, 1970; Heilbrun, Orr & Harrell, 1966; Martin, 1975; Rutter & Garmezy, 1983; Rutter & Giller, 1985; Weiner, 1970). Most studies indicate that parental hostility or rejection tends to produce counterhostility on the part of their children, regardless of how it is expressed (Becker, 1964; Martin, 1975; Mussen et al., 1984).

Abusing Parents

In some cases parental hostility becomes extreme or gets out of control, and serious abuse of the child or adolescent occurs. Such abuse is widespread and appears to be increasing, although it is difficult to obtain accurate data on

Parents are the single most important influence on the average young person attempting to accomplish the developmental tasks of adolescence.

rates of incidence. Many cases are unreported or unrecognized by authorities, although the situation has clearly improved in recent years and all states now have laws requiring health care professionals to report cases of suspected child abuse. Over 1,300,000 cases of confirmed or suspected abuse are reported annually, and the actual incidence is probably much higher (U.S. Bureau of the Census, 1989).

In contrast to popular perceptions, a larger proportion of adolescents— particularly girls—are victims of abuse than children under 12 (Burgdorff, 1980; Garbarino, 1989; Olson & Holmes, 1983). Although child abuse occurs more often among parents, particularly mothers, who are poorly educated and economically deprived, it occurs with disturbing frequency among parents of both sexes at all socioeconomic levels (Garbarino et al., 1986; Helfer & Kempe, 1987). Moreover, parents who abuse adolescents are three times as likely to earn over $15,000 a year as those who abuse younger children (Garbarino & Kelly, 1986; National Center on Child Abuse & Neglect, 1981).

Box 6.1 SELF-DESTRUCTIVE BEHAVIOR IN AN ABUSED ADOLESCENT

Lana is an example of an older adolescent who developed a very different identity from that of her conservative, middle-class, upwardly mobile parents and her academically successful sisters and brother. A 17-year-old Chinese-American girl, Lana had been getting into trouble ever since high school—repeatedly running away, using drugs excessively, and associating with a pimp and his friends. She was not yet sexually involved with any of them, although she intended to become an expensive prostitute when she turned 18.

Lana had recently been kidnapped and raped by a man whom she had met at a shopping center. She was referred for psychotherapy by a probation officer who felt that she had self-destructive tendencies. Her therapist wondered why a streetwise girl would not have been suspicious of the man from the start. She pointed out that this and several other incidents in which she had exposed herself to danger had followed episodes in which she was berated by her parents:

Lana doubted that there were any connections between her parents berating her and her putting herself into positions of danger, but she did say that there were times when she wished she were dead—usually after one of her parents told her how awful she was.

Lana remembered that when she was a child her mother frequently beat her. Her mother apparently had attacks of uncontrollable rage, and Lana seemed to be the most frequent victim of those rages. Sometimes she was even beaten for her brother's or sisters' wrongdoings because she interceded to rescue them. These beatings, which had her father's tacit approval (he did not stop his wife), were the foundations for Lana's low self-esteem. If her mother did not like her, who could? The verbal beratings she was still receiving from both of her parents reinforced her negative self-image. Because Lana, as a child, put herself in a position to take punishment for her siblings, it might appear that she really liked to suffer. Actually, she was giving her mother one more chance to show if she really cared for her daughter. If she did not beat her, the mother would be sending Lana a message Lana really wanted to hear—that her mother did love her after all. Unfortunately, Lana never got the communication she wanted; she just received more beatings. There was a strong possibility that Lana, as a 17-year-old, put herself into potentially dangerous situations as a sort of test: Would she be harmed or wouldn't she? If she were not harmed, "mother nature" or "dame fate" would be telling her that she was a worthwhile person. Lana's lack of suspiciousness, which facilitated her being kidnapped and raped, was a test of this sort. Even though she never seemed to get the answer she wanted, Lana tried time and time again to somehow feel she was worthwhile; these attempts were the basis for her self-destructive tendencies.

Source: D. Lamb, *Psychotherapy with adolescent girls,* 2nd ed. New York: Plenum Press, 1986, p. 133

Much more needs to be learned about the factors that predispose a parent to child abuse. Nevertheless, certain characteristics stand out. The histories of abusive parents show a high incidence of early abuse, neglect, parental discord, harsh discipline, or parental loss or deprivation (Ciccheti & Carlson, 1989; Rutter, 1989). "In each generation we find, in one form or another, a distortion of the relationship between parents and children that deprives the children of the consistent nurturing of body and mind that would enable them to develop fully" (Kempe & Kempe, 1978, p. 13). Abuse confined to adolescence is less likely to be transmitted between generations than abuse beginning in childhood (Garbarino, 1989; Garbarino & Kelly, 1986; Pelcovitz et al, 1984).

It is important to note that although abusing parents were often victims of abuse themselves, this does not mean that a majority of abused children and adolescents will become abusing parents (Zigler & Hall, 1989). Many are able to break the cycle of abuse because of readily available support systems, fewer life stresses, healthier babies, better psychological understanding, or other favorable circumstances (Hunter & Kilstrom, 1979; Kaufman & Zigler, 1987; Zigler & Hall, 1989).

For the most part, abusing parents have not been exposed to models of successful parenting—models that they could apply in rearing their own children. Many abusing parents, including adolescent mothers, lack empathy, do not understand the complexity of social relationships, and have extremely unrealistic ideas about the behavior that can be expected of a child (Belsky & Vondra, 1989; Feshbach, 1980; Levine, Call, & Oh, 1984; Orlansky, 1990; Pianta, Egeland, & Erikson, 1989). Consequently, when an infant soils its diapers or cries continually, or when a child does not perform a task well, the parent views the child as willfully misbehaving and resorts to punishment, usually without success; this begins a downward spiral in which a deteriorating parent–child relationship is aggravated by further punishment

If lack of knowledge about child development were the only problem, however, it would be easier to help parents who abuse their children. Such help can often be useful, but the problem usually goes much deeper. Having been deprived of love and care themselves, many abusing parents are hungry for love and acceptance and find it difficult to subordinate their own needs to those of the child (Crittenden & Ainsworth, 1989; Pianta, Egeland, & Erickson, 1989; Steele, 1976, 1987). Moreover, they are often socially isolated, view themselves as bad or unlovable, and lack the ability to make friends or develop broader social support systems (Cicchetti & Carlson, 1989; Mueller & Silverman, 1989). Consequently, they may leap at the opportunity to marry and have a family as a way of satisfying their urgent need for love and approval. When it turns out that successful family life, especially in the case of young children, requires as much or more giving of love and care as the parent receives, frustration and a sense of betrayal are likely to result. If the problem is aggravated by other adverse conditions, such as developmental difficulties or chronic illness of the child, loss of a job, financial crises, lack of homemaking skills,

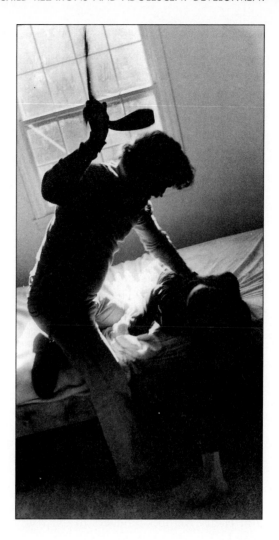

Many abusing parents have extremely unrealistic ideas about the behavior that can be expected of a child.

marital disputes, or inability to establish support systems outside the family, the stage is set for child abuse (Garbarino et al., 1986; Helfer & Kempe, 1987).

Brandt Steele, a pioneer in the study of the causes and treatment of child abuse, notes that physical abuse usually is not a constant or daily occurrence. Rather, he says, four conditions seem necessary for abuse to occur:

1. A caretaker who has the predisposition for abuse related to the psychological residues of neglect or abuse in his or her own early life.
2. A crisis of some sort placing extra stress on the caretaker.
3. Lack of lifelines or sources of help for the caretaker, either because he or she is unable to reach out or the facilities are not available.
4. A child who is perceived as being in some way unsatisfactory.

These four factors interact in a mutually reinforcing way:

> Abusive parents live in a state of precarious balance between emotional supply and demand. They are more needy because of their low self-esteem, but less able to reach out for pleasure and support, and so turn with the increased need to those who are least able to provide full satisfaction, their infants. Any crisis, even a small one such as a broken washing machine, becomes unmanageable because of the parent's poor coping techniques and inability or reluctance to seek help (Steele, 1980, pp. 89–90).

James Garbarino and his colleagues emphasize that family, parent, adolescents, and community support variables "are all interrelated and influence the dynamics and outcomes in high-risk families" (Garbarino & Guttman, 1986, p. 147). In high-risk families parents tend to lack coping skills and to be more punitive, less supportive, and more emotionally troubled, and family relationships tend to be more "chaotic," "enmeshed," and conflictful. If, in addition, adequate social, vocational, and community support systems are lacking, and the adolescent exhibits high levels of problem behavior and low levels of social competence, the stage is set for abuse. "All in all, high-risk families are best characterized as social systems with very high demand for adaptive behavior but low social and psychological resonance to sustain such desperately needed adaptive behavior" (Garbarino et al., 1986, p. 294).

Effects of Abuse. Many abused children, aided by the effects of beneficial experiences during development, "grow up to be essentially normal citizens and average parents" (Kempe & Kempe, 1978, p. 19; Zigler & Hall, 1989). However, many others show long-term adverse effects. They are likely to be easily distracted and lacking in persistence and ego control (Egeland, Sroufe & Erickson, 1983). Also, abused children and adolescents characteristically find it difficult to trust adults and often other children as well. Even in psychotherapy they tend to relapse into distrust at the slightest disappointment. As Ruth and Henry Kempe, pioneers in the study and treatment of child abuse, have noted,

> Abused children often continue to find relationships very difficult, even beyond the question of trust. They relate indiscriminately, quickly making superficial friendships but ready to discard them at the slightest sign of rejection. They come eagerly to treatment hours, but when the time is up they seem unable to deal with separation and quickly depart as if there were no next time. It seems to us that their early experiences have made it hard for them to acquire what is called object constancy—that is, the ability to see the people they love as always in existence and always basically the same no matter what. With these children it seems to be "out of sight, out of mind" (1978, p. 38).

Abused children and adolescents tend to have low self-esteem and to be lonely and friendless, already showing the same absence of joy and spontaneity that their parents exhibit (Cavaiola & Schiff, 1988; Oates, Forrest, & Peacock, 1985). "They may yearn for substitutes to love and often make great efforts to find a friend among youngsters of their own sex. But these attempts tend to fail because their demands are excessive and are not understood by the friend or his parents" (Kempe & Kempe, 1978, p. 10).

In addition, abused children all too often come to believe—at least consciously—that the "discipline" they received for "bad behavior" was justified and that such discipline is the right way to bring up recalcitrant children. At the same time, they are likely to develop strong underlying feelings of resentment and anger toward their parents—as much for their lack of care and understanding as for their physical abuse.

Not surprisingly, a history of child abuse and neglect is common among adolescent runaways and delinquents (Farber & Kinast, 1984; Garbarino et al., 1986; Janus, McCormack, Burgess, & Hartman, 1987; see Chapter 13). Many adolescents begin to express the anger that they have felt for so long in delinquent behavior outside the home. Membership in a peer group, which can provide a feeling of belonging and being wanted, can help the young person deal with feelings of emotional deprivation but at the same time it may provide a means of discharging pent-up aggression in group-approved delinquent activities.

In one study of 100 adolescent runaways and delinquents who were brought to a juvenile detention center for the first time, 84 had been neglected or abused before the age of 6, and 92 had been maltreated or sexually abused in the past eighteen months. "The great majority of families . . . were intact, and very few children came from an environment that in any way resembled the crowded inner city milieu of poverty and violence" (Steele, 1976, p. 20). Other studies of delinquent children and violent youthful criminals confirm that there is a strong link between the experience of being abused as a child and subsequent antisocial behavior (Kratcoski, 1982; Lewis, Mallouh, & Webb, 1989; Mouzakitis, 1981). These findings do not mean that most abused children become delinquent, but they do indicate that a history of prior abuse is common among those who later commit aggressive offenses.

Sexual Abuse. The effects of sexual abuse during childhood or adolescence are not uniform, either in kind or in severity. Much depends on the child's age at the time of abuse, the nature of the abusive act, the amount of aggression or physical abuse involved, the relationship between the abuser and the child, and the child's relationships with nonabusing caretakers before, during, and after the episodes of sexual abuse (Kempe & Kempe, 1984; Mrazek & Kempe, 1981; Mrazek & Mrazek, 1978). In general, sexual abuse by a parent, especially if it is accompanied by coercion, physical abuse, or general family disorganization, is likely to be more traumatic and to create more pervasive and lasting problems than abuse by a stranger when the child has the support of a loving family (Kempe & Kempe, 1984). Approximately 75 percent of incest and other family sexual involvement occurs between fathers and daughters, with the remaining 25 percent divided between mother–son, mother–daughter, father–son, and brother–sister involvement.

Among the longer-term effects that sexual abuse may have are feelings of having been exploited or abandoned; a sense of helplessness and inability to control one's own destiny; depression, anxiety, and insomnia or nightmares; substance abuse; and impaired ability to take pleasure in sexual activity, resulting in total withdrawal from sexual relationships or, in less severe instances, problems of sexual dysfunction. An adolescent girl who has been involved in father–daughter incest often eventually forgives her father, but rarely does she forgive the mother who failed to protect her (Kempe & Kempe, 1978, 1984; Lindberg & Distad, 1985; Mrazek & Kempe, 1978).

If it is begun soon enough and continued long enough, individual and group treatment of sexual abuse, including incest, can be successful and may even lead to the capacity to enjoy normal, trusting sexual relationships. Without intervention, however, serious long-term consequences may occur. Particularly in the case of sexually exploited adolescent girls, those effects may include severe loss of self-esteem ("I guess I'm a slut," "I guess I never was any good"), chronic depression, and social isolation or reckless promiscuity.

If begun soon enough and continued long enough, treatment of sexual abuse can be successful, even leading to the capacity in adulthood to enjoy normal, trusting sexual relationships.

Parental Control

Besides love–rejection, the other major dimension emerging from studies of parent–child relationships may be broadly termed *autonomy–control*. Here again, the precise label used varies from one investigator to another (e.g. permissiveness–restrictiveness, manage, control–endorse freedom, casual–demanding) (Baumrind, 1989, in press; Becker, 1964; Benjamin, 1974, 1977; Humphrey & Benjamin, 1986; Maccoby & Martin, 1983; Schaefer, 1959, 1971; Wiggins, 1982). At its controlling or restrictive end, this dimension refers to parental behaviors that involve many restrictions and strict enforcement of demands, including rigid insistence on neatness, orderliness, obedience, and inhibition of aggression (verbal or otherwise) toward parents, siblings, or peers. Extreme restrictiveness tends to foster inhibition not only in social behavior but also in creativity, initiative, and flexibility in approaching academic and practical problems (Baumrind 1975; Becker, 1964; Maccoby & Martin, 1983). It should be emphasized that a high level of restrictiveness, in the sense in which the term is used here, does not refer to clear parental expectations of socially appropriate behavior or achievement, which may restrict the child's freedom to some extent but which actually encourage him or her to develop capabilities and talents (see pages 206–207).

AN INTERACTIVE MODEL OF PARENTAL BEHAVIOR

Although it is possible to make meaningful generalizations about the probable effects of variations in parental behavior on each of these dimensions, more precise generalizations can be made when interactions between, or combinations of, these dimensions are considered. For example, a child who is subjected to covertly hostile, restrictive parental child-rearing practices is more likely to internalize angry feelings (as in the case of many neurotic children and adolescents); in contrast, a child who is reared under hostile but lax conditions is more likely to act out resentment (as in the case of many delinquents) (Baumrind, 1975, 1989, in press; Becker, 1964; Martin, 1975; Rutter & Giller, 1984). Similarly a recent longitudinal study found that in adolescent boys "ego control" (the capacity to modify impulses, feelings, and desires according to circumstances) is fostered by warm and interested mothers and by fathers who encourage high standards and rationality but also manifest genuine warmth in the father–son relationship. In contrast, "under control" was associated with paternal impatience and disappointment and maternal self-centeredness (Block, 1987).

In addition to considering combinations of dimensions, it is also important to consider where parental behavior falls *along* each dimension. Take the case of autonomy–control. Obviously, neither total control nor total autonomy is appropriate; moreover, the degree of autonomy that is appropriate varies with the age of the child (see page 208). Indeed, one of the adjustments that must be made by parents of adolescents is to realize that their 16-year-old is no longer a child and needs to be trusted with progressively greater autonomy if he or she is to be prepared for the independence and responsibilities of adulthood.

At all ages, however, children and adolescents require a judicious age-appropriate balance between autonomy and control, between freedom to develop as an individual and demands for disciplined, responsible behavior (Baumrind, 1968; Conger, 1971, 1979; Elder, 1980; Youniss & Smollar, 1985). Failure to appreciate this fact lies at the heart of much of the controversy and confusion surrounding emotion-laden terms like *permissiveness* and *authoritarianism* in relation to child rearing.

Authoritative Versus Authoritarian Parents

Does permissiveness mean indulgence, intimidation of parents by children, a laissez-faire parental attitude, or simply neglect? Or does this term, as it is

Independence, adaptability, and self-discipline are fostered best by parents who are authoritative without being authoritarian.

employed by some authoritarian adults, really refer to *any* encouragement of autonomy and participation in decision making by adolescents, even with parental guidance and ultimate authority? The presumed alternative to so-called permissiveness in the minds of some vociferous critics seems to be a "return" to an authoritarian or autocratic approach, one that might have prepared an adolescent for adulthood in a simpler era but cannot do so in today's unpredictable world (Conger, 1971, 1979). Many adults apparently would prefer to create a simpler society rather than face the task of preparing young people for the complex challenges of contemporary society.

Indeed, what some adults seem to fear is not so much the changing behavior of youth as the changing nature of society itself. Clearly, tomorrow's adults will need self-discipline, but they will also need independence, self-reliance, adaptability, creativity, a strong sense of their own values, and the ability to distinguish between assertiveness and hostility—in addition to a sense of humor. And these characteristics are not fostered by permissiveness or neglect, nor are they produced by autocratic or authoritarian child-rearing methods. Rather, research has shown that these qualities are best fostered by parents who show respect for their children, involve them in family affairs and decision making, and encourage the development of age-appropriate independence while retaining ultimate responsibility.

Such parents are, in the words of psychologist Diana Baumrind, *authoritative* without being *authoritarian* (Baumrind, 1968, 1989, in press). They value both autonomous self-will *and* disciplined behavior. They encourage verbal give and take, and when they exercise authority in the form of demands or prohibitions, they explain their reasons for doing so (Buri et al., 1988; Cohler & Boxer, 1984; Elder, 1963, 1980). The following description by a 16-year-old girl is typical of such parents:

> I guess the thing I think is great about my parents, compared to those of a lot of kids, is that they really listen. And they realize that eventually I'm going to have to live my own life—what I'm going to do with it. A lot of the time when I explain what I want to do, they'll go along with it. Sometimes, they'll warn me of the consequences I'll have to face if I'm wrong, or just give me advice. And sometimes, they just plain tell me no. But when they do, they explain why, and that makes it easier to take (Conger, 1979, p. 49).

"Because I Said So!" In contrast to the authoritative or democratic parent, the authoritarian (or, in a more extreme form, autocratic) parent simply tells the child what to do and feels no obligation to explain why. Such parents favor obedience as an absolute virtue and tend to deal with any attempts at protest with often forceful, punitive measures. Free discussion or two-way interaction between parent and child is discouraged out of the conviction that the young person should unquestioningly accept the parent's word about what is right (Baumrind, 1968, 1975, 1989, in press; Buri et al., 1988; Elder, 1980; Lesser & Kandel, 1969).

Some parents may take this stance out of a feeling of hostility or simply because they do not wish to be bothered. Others may be doing so because they think that this is the way to develop "respect for authority." However, while they may suppress dissent they do not usually eliminate it and at the same time they may generate resentment. In one extensive study, adolescents were asked whether they felt that their parents' ideas, rules, and principles about how they should behave were "good and reasonable or wrong and unreasonable"(Elder, 1980, p. 150). Children of democratic, authoritative parents were far more likely than those of authoritarian—especially autocratic—parents to consider their parents to be fair and reasonable. They were also far less likely to view their parents as unaffectionate or to feel rejected by them. Indeed, adolescents who were subjected to autocratic parental practices were almost four times as likely to feel rejected by their parents as those who were subjected to democratic practices.

The distinction between authoritarian and authoritative parental behaviors is important in the case of young children, but it takes on special significance in the case of adolescents. This is so because adolescents are capable of taking greater responsibility for their own behavior and because they will need to do so if they are to become mature, self-reliant adults. Because the adolescent can imagine viable alternatives to parental directives, the parent must be ready to defend his or her directives on rational grounds (Baumrind, 1975, in press; Pikas, 1961). Parental authority based on rational concern for the young person's welfare is generally accepted well, whereas authority based on the adult's desire to dominate or exploit is rejected.

Interestingly, one investigation found that parental discipline that the young person viewed as either very strict (authoritarian) or very permissive tended to be associated with lack of closeness between parent and child and rebellion against the parent's political and social views (Middleton & Snell, 1963). Similarly, junior and senior high school students were more likely to model themselves after their parents and to associate with peers whom their parents approved of if the parents explained their decisions and demands (Elder, 1963, 1980). These results are consistent with the hypothesis that communication between parents and children fosters identification, whereas unilateral exercise of power without communication is more likely to produce resentment (Block & Turula, 1963).

Laissez-Faire Parents

In sharp contrast to the authoritarian or autocratic parent, the **laissez-faire** parent allows the young person to disregard parental wishes (Elder, 1962, 1980). Parents who are laissez-faire or neglecting, or who promote an exaggerated egalitarianism in parent–child relations, also fail to provide the kind of support that adolescents need (Baumrind, in press; Conger, 1979; Jessor & Jessor, 1974). Among middle-class adolescents, high-risk drug use and other forms of socially deviant behavior have been found to occur most frequently among those whose parents, while outwardly expressing such values as individuality, self-understanding, readiness for change, and maximization of potential, and who stress egalitarianism within the family, are actually using those proclaimed values to avoid parental responsibility (Blum, 1977). The motivation to avoid responsibility stems variously from the parents' uncertainty about their own convictions, indecision about how to handle their children, the need to be liked or to feel youthful, or antagonism or ambivalence toward authority—whether parental or social.

Such parents "find it hard to make decisive value judgments that require the exercise of power over their children and prefer to escape from the obligation of being an authority figure—an untenable position if authority is distrusted in general or if there has been no identification in childhood with an admired authority" (Blum, 1972, p. 52). But by placing themselves on the same footing as peers, they end up leaving their children to drift essentially alone in an uncharted sea without any dependable models of responsible adult behavior (Conger, 1979). Ironically, despite their protestations of parent–child togetherness, the parents of high-risk drug users actually spend less time in activities with their children, enjoy their company less, and are less able to handle problems than the more traditional parents of adolescents who do not engage in high-risk drug use.

In another study, high school students who did not engage in problem behaviors (e.g., drug use, sexual activities, problem drinking) were found to have mothers who had firm, relatively traditional values; clearly stated their disapproval of deviant behaviors; and exerted reasonable controls (e.g., staying home at night, doing homework)—but also interacted frequently and affectionately with their children (Jessor & Jessor, 1974). No matter how much children and adolescents may protest at times, they do not really want their parents to be their equals. They want and need them to be parents—friendly, understanding parents, but parents nonetheless, dependable models of adult behavior (Conger, 1979; Youniss & Smollar, 1985).

Adolescent Transitions

The ease with which young people adjust to the changed roles and new demands of adolescence is clearly affected by the nature of prior parent–child relations. The overprotected child, who may have achieved a workable *modus vivendi* within the family during middle childhood, may find it extremely difficult to cope with the demands for independence and self-reliance during adolescence. Similarly, the overindulged child approaching adolescence may be frustrated by society's unwillingness to indulge him or her to the same extent. The child of hostile parents may have controlled his or her feelings of counter-hostility reasonably well until adolescence, only to lose that control under conditions of increased stress, conflict, and opportunities for acting-out behavior. Moreover, the appropriateness of current patterns of parental behavior may vary with the age of the child or adolescent. As we shall see in the next section, nowhere is this more apparent than in the development of adolescent autonomy.

PARENT–CHILD RELATIONS AND THE DEVELOPMENT OF AUTONOMY

The development of age-appropriate autonomy is a critically important task of adolescence, not only because autonomy itself is important but also because it is closely related to the performance of other tasks. Thus, if the adolescent does not resolve the conflict between continuing dependence on the family and the demands and privileges of independence, he or she will encounter difficulties in most other areas as well. Without the achievement of a reasonable degree of emotional separation and autonomy, the adolescent can hardly be expected to form mature heterosexual or peer relationships, confidently pursue a vocation, or gain a clear sense of identity—which requires a positive image of the self as separate, unified, and consistent over time (see pages 54–55).

As we have noted, American adolescents and their counterparts in other advanced nations are likely to encounter greater stress in developing autonomy than young people in societies in which social roles are simpler and more clearly defined and in which there is a very gradual transition from childhood dependence to adult independence. Nevertheless, most contemporary adolescents make this transition successfully, though not always easily.

Separation and Connectedness

What kinds of parent–child relationships facilitate this transition, and what kinds hinder it? In approaching this question, it is important to clarify what we mean by the development of age-appropriate autonomy. For some theorists, achieving autonomy involves freeing oneself from parental bonds in order to establish one's own identity: Adolescents "must find self-definition outside the parental bond and learn to think for themselves without relying on their parents for validation" (Youniss & Smollar, 1985, p. 91). In our view, such a position is both one-sided and exaggerated. It ignores the fact that in the development of age-appropriate autonomy dual processes, *separation* and *continued connectedness,* are involved (Cooper, Grotevant, & Condon, 1983; Grotevant & Cooper, 1983; Hartup, 1989; Hill & Holmbeck, 1986; Youniss & Smollar, 1985).

As adolescence progresses, young people need to be given sufficient freedom from parental authority and control to experience themselves as individuals with needs and feelings of their own, to make decisions about their own lives, and to take responsibility for the consequences of those decisions. At the same time, they continue to need their parents' guidance and support. "For parents to leave adolescents on their own would be irresponsible. For parents to seek to duplicate themselves in their sons and daughters would be equally dysfunctional" (Youniss & Smollar, 1985, p. 93). Recent research strongly supports this view (Baumrind, in press; Block, 1987; Grotevant & Cooper, 1983; Youniss & Smollar, 1985).

Before puberty the interactions between children and parents are dominated by parents (Steinberg, 1981; Steinberg & Hill, 1978; Youniss & Smollar, 1985). During adolescence, however, there is a gradual shift away from unilateral parental authority toward more cooperative parent–child interactions. This does not mean that parental authority is abandoned. Under favorable circumstances adolescents still view their parents as having the right to monitor and direct their behavior; to set rules and require that they be followed; and to expect that schoolwork, household chores, and other responsibilities will be carried out properly.

However, there are some important changes in the nature of parental authority during adolescence. First, parental authority is increasingly restricted to particular areas of adolescents' lives. Much of the average adolescent's social and personal life, particularly with peers, takes place outside the family circle. Whether because of lack of communication by the young person or because of parental respect for privacy, parents tend to be unaware of much of what their adolescent sons and daughters are doing or thinking. Consequently, adolescents are able to gain independence from parental authority in many more areas of their lives than is possible for younger children (Hill & Holmbeck, 1987; Wright & Keple, 1981; Youniss & Smollar, 1985).

Second, while parents can and do continue to assert unilateral authority at times, particularly with respect to basic social obligations like schoolwork, in other areas they are perceived by their children as more ready to discuss differences and seek compromise. Especially when dealing with personal problems or concerns, "if parents are involved at all, they act less as unilateral authorities and more as advisors willing to listen, seeking to understand" (Youniss & Smollar, 1985, p. 73). Moreover, even when they are asserting unilateral authority, authoritative (though not authoritarian or autocratic) parents are more likely to explain their actions.

Perceiving Parents as Individuals

As the relationship between adolescents and their parents shifts away from unilateral parental authority toward greater cooperation and mutuality, and as adolescents gain greater capacity for formal-operational thinking, adolescents' perceptions of their parents undergo a corresponding shift. As James Youniss (1980) notes, children's and preadolescents' descriptions of parent–child interactions lack any perception of parents as complex individuals, with likeable and unlikeable traits, emotional ups and downs, and varying competencies. Children are likely to perceive their parents as "*figures* who have knowledge and power to get things done, especially those things children need or want" (Youniss & Smollar, 1985, p. 75). In a sense, parents *are* what parents *do*.

In contrast, as they develop cognitively and experience more complex give and take interactions with their parents, adolescents begin to view their parents as unique individuals. They are better able to differentiate parents as *persons*, with their own unique needs and feelings, from the *roles* they play in carrying out their responsibilities as mothers or fathers. One older adolescent girl described her relationship with her mother as follows: "I'm more independent of her. Also, I am more free with my opinions even when I disagree. I realize she's not only my mother but an individual herself and I take her more on that level now. We still turn to each other when we have problems. We're still close" (Youniss & Smollar, 1985, p. 80). Similarly, a 15-year-old girl said of her mother, "She respects me more and lets me be on my own more. Treats me like a person, consults my opinion. I am a voice that is heard. Five years ago she was just a mother, now she's a person" (Youniss & Smollar, 1985, p. 80).

As these examples illustrate, granting adolescents greater freedom as they mature is not incompatible with maintaining elements of connectedness and control:

> Indeed, adolescents see freedom and connectedness as working together, insofar as parents are respected both as persons and in their role as parents. The result is that parents interact more cooperatively while they retain their authority status. The grounds for continuity may lie in the distribution of authority across areas so that cooperative discussion in one area is seen as fitting with unilateral assertion in a different area. The underlying theme to all of this is the adolescents' general belief that their parents act from a position of wanting to help their sons and daughters and, thus, operate at times from their roles as parents and at other times as persons (Youniss & Smollar, 1985, p. 80).

For parents to be perceived in this light, they must act accordingly. They need to recognize and encourage the adolescent's need for greater autonomy. Continuing to think of their adolescent child as "our darling little girl" or "our cute little boy" is a prescription for later disaster, whether it takes the form of explosive rebellion or increasingly inappropriate dependence (Conger, 1979). At the same time, parents need to recognize that true autonomy is not achieved in a day and that the need for dependence coexists—often in uneasy and fragile alliance—with the need for independence. Partly because so many things are changing in the adolescent's world, he or she urgently needs a base of security, support, guidance, and stability.

As we have noted, parents like those described here tend to be authoritative or democratic in exercising parental control. Research has shown that such parents are most likely to foster the development of responsibility or autonomy. Autocratic or authoritarian parents, on the other hand, tend to stifle the orderly acquisition of self-reliance and independence, while indifferent, laissez-faire, or completely permissive parents may fail to encourage the development of responsibility (Baumrind, 1975, 1989, in press; Buri et al., 1988; Elder, 1962, 1980; Lesser & Kandel, 1969; Santrock, 1987).

In a classic study, Glen Elder (1963, 1980) found that democratic (and permissive) parents who also provided frequent explanations for their rules of conduct and expectations were most likely to have adolescent sons and daughters who are confident in their own values and goals and are independent; that is, they wish to make up their own minds, although they may listen to other people's ideas. In contrast, autocratic nonexplaining parents were most likely to have adolescent children who are dependent and lacking in self confidence.

Similar results were obtained in an investigation of several thousand adolescents and their parents in the United States and Denmark (Kandel & Lesser,

1972; Lesser & Kandel, 1965). In both countries, democratic parents, who provided frequent explanations for their rules, were significantly more likely than either authoritarian or permissive parents to have adolescents who felt independent and viewed themselves as being treated in an adult manner by their parents. "In both countries, feelings of independence are enhanced when parents have few rules, when they provide explanations for their rules, and when they are democratic and engage the child actively in the decision-making process. Furthermore, feelings of independence from parents in both countries, far from leading to rebelliousness, are associated with closeness to parents and positive attitudes toward them" (Lesser & Kandel, 1969, p. 357).

Other studies have yielded similar results. Confidence and self-esteem appear to be highest among adolescents whose parents express strong interest in, and knowledge about, their opinions and activities and encourage them to behave autonomously and to participate actively in family affairs (Bachman, 1970; Baumrind, 1989, in press; Buri et al., 1988; Rosenberg, 1965). In an extensive study of children growing up in father-absent, mother-absent homes, and intact homes, it was found that the extent to which a single parent used authoritative parenting was strongly related to the development of social competence, whereas authoritarian or laissez-faire parental behaviors were either unrelated or negatively related to social competence (Santrock, 1987; Santrock & Warshak, 1979, 1986).

Sociocultural Influences and Parental Power Practice

The relationship of parental power practices to social class has also been investigated (Baumrind, 1975; Elder, 1980; Pearlin & Kohn, 1966). Overall, there is a slight tendency for middle-class parents to be viewed as more democratic, egalitarian, or permissive, and for lower-class parents to be viewed as more autocratic and authoritarian. Rural families have been shown to be more authoritarian and to delay independence in their children longer than urban families, both in the United States and in other Western countries.

In sum, it appears that democratic, authoritative practices, with frequent explanations of parental rules of conduct and expectations, foster responsible, autonomous behavior in several ways: (1) by providing opportunities for increasing autonomy, guided by interested parents who communicate with the child and exercise an appropriate degree of control; (2) by promoting positive identification with the parent, based on love and respect for the child, rather than rejection or indifference; and (3) by providing models of reasonable independence, that is, autonomy within a framework of democratic order. In contrast, a child of autocratic or indifferent parents is not exposed to models of responsible, cooperative independence; is less likely to be encouraged by parental acceptance to identify with adults; and is not given age-graded experiences in the orderly assumption of responsible autonomy (Baumrind, 1975, 1989, in press; Conger, 1971, 1977).

Although a number of these studies were conducted some years ago, they appear, if anything, to be even more relevant today. The democratic (authoritative) child-rearing structure, which provides for perceptions of parental fairness, feelings of personal security and being wanted, and the development of both responsibility and increasing autonomy, seems especially important in the current period of rapid social change. This is a time when the need for adult autonomy is at a premium, there are few clear-cut social guidelines for behavior, and opportunities for generational conflict, hostility, and alienation are legion.

Autocratic, or at least authoritarian, patterns of parental behavior may have been more workable in other times and other cultures in which the adolescent could expect to be reasonably successful in life simply by following in a parent's footsteps. Today, parents cannot provide detailed blueprints for mastering the demands of a constantly changing society. They can, however, provide models of autonomous, flexible, problem-solving behavior, and they can provide love and security. They can also teach their children how to think about and deal with challenging situations.

The laissez-faire or ignoring parent makes the task of achieving responsible independence or autonomy especially difficult. Other influences on adolescent behavior—peers, the adolescent culture, the adult world in general—seldom provide adequate or consistent guidelines for the kind of responsible behavior that is required in the contemporary world. Urie Bronfenbrenner argues that one of the reasons for the relatively higher rates of antisocial behavior in the United States and England is that to an increasing extent parents have become isolated from their children—and from child rearing—without providing adequate substitutes (e.g., through the schools, churches, peers or older adolescents, extended family and neighbors) (Bronfenbrenner, 1970; Bronfenbrenner & Crouter, 1982; Bronfenbrenner, Moen, & Garbarino, 1984).

THE ADOLESCENT IN THE FAMILY

Thus far, we have focused on the effects of parents on their adolescent daughters and sons. Indeed, this is the focus of most psychological research on parent–child relations. Clearly, however, the interaction between parent and child is not a one-way street (Bell, 1979; Bell & Harper, 1977; Hartup, 1989; Hill & Holmbeck, 1987; Mussen et al., 1984, 1990). Just as parental behavior affects the responses of children, the behavior of children and adolescents affects the responses of their parents. Moreover, both children and parents are members of a family system in which the behavior of individual members affects, and is affected by, the family as a dynamic whole—often in complex ways (Farley, 1979; Minuchin, 1974; Silverberg & Steinberg, 1987).

The Principle of Bidirectionality

The principle of *bidirectionality* states that parent–child influences go both ways—from parent to child and from child to parent. Consequently, the development of children and adolescents is "a product of their own characteristics and those of the people who socialize them" (Mussen et al., 1984, p. 143). This is apparent even in infancy. Parents are more likely to smile, talk to, and play with a baby who is cuddly, smiles readily, and is very socially responsive than one who is quieter, more sober, and more passive (Mussen et al., 1990).

Ironically, it is the bidirectional nature of parent–child relationships that puts adolescent mothers at greater risk of abusing their children. Adolescent mothers are likely to be poorly equipped socially and emotionally for the demanding task of being a parent. They are also more likely to have low-birth-weight infants who are more irritable, less healthy, and more difficult to care for (see pages 256–258). Frustrated in her efforts to quiet the baby or get it to smile and play, the inexperienced young mother may respond with anger and lash out at the child, thereby setting in motion a vicious cycle of potentially tragic events (Garbarino et al., 1986; Parke & Collmer, 1975; Steele, 1976, 1987). Among older children, Gerald Patterson has found that hyperaggressive boys tend to be unresponsive to punishment and that their unresponsiveness plays an important role in bringing about the continuation and escalation of parental efforts at coercion (Patterson, 1982).

The bidirectional nature of parent–child interactions is readily apparent in adolescence. Studies of adolescent boys show that parents respond to physical maturation in their children by treating early maturers as more mature, both cognitively and socially, than late maturers, regardless of the young person's chronological age or abstract reasoning ability (Mussen et al., 1984, 1990; Steinberg, 1981; Steinberg & Hill, 1978). Among pairs of adolescent siblings, the one who is psychologically better adjusted is likely to experience more maternal closeness and to be given a greater voice in family decision making; however, he or she is also subject to higher expectations in terms of responsibility for household chores (Daniels, Dunn, Furstenberg, & Plomin, 1985). Some parents who were very comfortable in their child-rearing role when their children were younger have difficult dealing with the fact that their adolescent son or daughter is no longer a child and that changes in their relationship are necessary and inevitable.

The Family as a System

Just as individuals differ in important ways, so too do families (Minuchin, S., 1985). Families may be organized or chaotic, close-knit or disengaged, communicative or uncommunicative, warm or cold, reserved or expressive, disturbed or essentially normal. All of these characteristics, and others, combine to create a unique family climate that can have profound effects on the development and functioning of each of the family's members, as well as on their interaction. And they can have equally profound effects on the interactions (or lack of them) between the family and people and institutions outside the family.

One of the most important dimensions of the family system is communication (Barnes & Olson, 1985; Cooper, Grotevant, & Condon, 1983; Grotevant & Cooper, 1983, 1985; Youniss, 1983). A recent large study of "normal" families found that those with better communication among parents and adolescents were higher in family cohesion, family adaptability, and family satisfaction (see Table 6.1). Families with good communication also tended to be satisfied

Good communication between parents and adolescents is associated with higher family cohesion, adaptability, and satisfaction.

with their overall quality of life. Their lower scores on "passive appraisal" indicated that "they tended not to be fatalistic about problems but would reframe problems and see them as a challenge to be overcome" (Barnes & Olson, 1985, p. 445).

Family communication appears to be particularly important during the adolescent years. The onset of puberty and subsequent physical, cognitive, and social development requires a reappraisal of earlier relationships by both parents and their adolescent children. Changing long-established patterns of parent–child interaction in order to adapt to new realities is seldom easy, either for parents or for their children. But the resolution of transitional difficulties and conflicts can be greatly facilitated by effective communication and openness in a family environment that provides both for "separateness," or individuality and self-exploration, and for continuing "connectedness," encouragement, and mutual support (Cooper, Grotevant & Condon, 1983; Youniss, 1983; Youniss & Smollar, 1985).

Indeed, effective communication plays a vital role in helping family mem-

T A B L E 6.1 VARIABLES DISTINGUISHING FAMILIES SCORING HIGH AND LOW ON PARENT–ADOLESCENT COMMUNICATION

Variable	Low-communication group mean	High-communication group mean	F^a
Family satisfaction	43.26	53.67	100.80
Passive appraisal (subscale of family coping)	52.78	46.86	38.08
Family cohesion	42.94	53.58	96.71
Satisfaction with quality of life	45.41	54.00	64.09
Family adaptability	44.79	54.53	87.29

Source: H. L. Barnes & D. H. Olson (1985). Parent–adolescent communication and the circumplex model. *Child Development,* **56,** 438–447. By permission.
[a]All are significant beyond .0001.

bers strike a balance between separateness from and connectedness to each other (Barnes & Olson, 1985; Grotevant & Cooper, 1983). Recent research indicates that effective family communication fosters adolescent identity formation and mature role-taking ability, both of which "require the adolescent to possess a viewpoint, to be aware of others' views, and both to integrate and to differentiate his or her own views from those of others" (Cooper et al., 1983, p. 48).

Communication Patterns in Troubled Families. Studies of parent–child interaction in troubled families, or in families with a mentally ill parent or child, have often found distortions in the capacity of parent and child to communicate with each other. For example, in one comprehensive study of adolescents on the Isle of Wight, altercations with parents, physical withdrawal (e.g., going to one's own room, or staying out of the house), and communication difficulties all occurred more frequently in the families of adolescents with psychological disorders (see Figure 6.1). In troubled families it often seems that family members are talking *past* each other (Goldstein, Baker, & Jamison, 1980; Rutter, 1980; Wynne, Singer, Bartko, & Toohey, 1976). The failure of parents to respond in a meaningful way in such situations is well illustrated in the following excerpt from a family therapy session:

Daughter (the patient): Nobody will listen to me. Everybody is trying to still me.
Mother: Nobody wants to kill you.
Father: If you're going to associate with intellectual people, you're going to have to remember that still is a noun and not a verb (Wynne et al., 1976, p. 195).

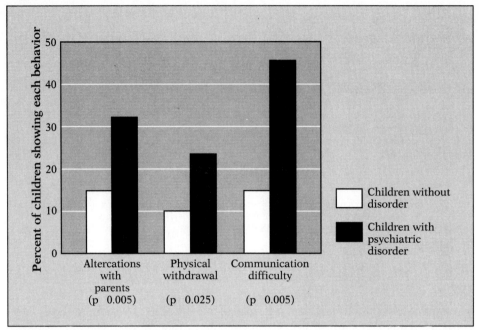

Figure 6.1 Parent–child alienation and psychiatric disorder at age 14. (From M. Rutter, O. F. D. Graham, W. Yule. Adolescent turmoil: Fact or fiction? *Journal of Child Psychology and Psychiatry,* 1976, **17,** 35–36. By permission.)

Adolescents whose problems become more severe, or who fail to get better, are more likely to have at least one parent who says confusing things, is overly critical or hostile, and is intrusive. These deviant communication patterns between adolescents and parents have been found in cases in which the adolescent was, or later became, schizophrenic (Goldstein & Jones, 1977; Jones, 1974; Jones, Rodnick, Goldstein, McPherson, & West, 1977). Of course, the presence of a schizophrenic child in a family could as easily precipitate communication difficulties as the reverse. However, there is some evidence that problems of communication occur more frequently in families in which an adolescent *later* becomes mentally ill or manifests less serious psychological problems (Goldstein et al., 1978).

Disordered communication patterns have also been observed in families of adolescents with other kinds of problems. Families of delinquent boys, for example, have higher rates of *defensive communications*—in which the purpose is to defend oneself—than families of normal boys (Alexander, 1973; Hetherington, Stouwie, & Redberg, 1971; Rutter & Giller, 1984). Defensive communications are more likely to be reciprocated between the delinquent and the parent, probably reflecting a higher level of anger and hostility in the families of delinquents. By contrast, in families of normal adolescents supportive, loving, and encouraging communications occur more often and are more often reciprocated.

Studies of families with disturbed adolescents have found a greater frequency of communications revealing negative feelings, particularly critical evaluations of the adolescent (Fischer, 1980; Goldstein, 1987; Jacob, 1975; Prinz, Rosenblum, & O'Leary, 1978; Tienari et al., 1987). For example, one study found that a negative emotional quality in verbal interactions between parent and child—such as harsh criticism, excessive intrusiveness, and guilt inducement—was related to lower self-esteem, a greater sense of isolation, and increased negative or contrary responses on the part of the adolescent (West, 1981).

Role Relations and Family Equilibrium

In addition to the overall characteristics that differentiate families from one another (e.g., communicative–noncommunicative, close-knit–disengaged), there are also differences in the roles played by individual family members and the way they relate to the overall functioning of the family system. For example, in studies of the parent–child relationships of normal middle-class adolescents, mothers have been found to be more open and communicative with their adolescent children and more involved in the details of their everyday lives (Cooper et al., 1983; Elder, 1980; Montemayor & Brownlee, 1987; Steinberg, 1981; Youniss & Ketterlinus, 1987; Youniss & Smollar, 1985). Fathers, on the other hand, tend "to administer authority indirectly and from a distance" (Youniss & Smollar, 1985, p. 78) and to focus on problem solving (Hauser et al., 1987; Power & Shanks, 1989). They are also more likely to make demands without modifying them in light of the adolescent's views. James Youniss and Jacqueline Smollar (1985) assert that fathers, by virtue of their lesser degree of involvement and more impersonal standards, tend to encourage separateness, whereas mothers, with their greater degree of involvement and more open communication, tend to encourage family cohesion and connectedness. In brief, in these families the roles played by the parents complement each other in fostering a balance between age-appropriate behavior and a continuing sense of security and belonging.

Such an outcome can be achieved in other family contexts as well. The important point here is that each family member functions as part of a complex, dynamic, interdependent whole.

Equilibrium and Disequilibrium in the Family.

Like other complex systems—from the human body to the ecology of the planet—families attempt to maintain an equilibrium in their relationships despite changes within the family and in the larger society (Farley, 1979; Minuchin, S., 1974). When that equilibrium is upset, efforts are often made, consciously or not, to restore the balance. For example, if the mother dies unexpectedly, the father may attempt to assume some of her functions as well as his own; an older adolescent may take greater responsibility for the care of younger children. Or if a formerly

---

Box 6.2 FAMILY THERAPY AND THE FAMILY SYSTEM

In some instances, disturbances in family equilibrium are not resolved satisfactorily. In other instances equilibrium may be achieved or restored, but in a destructive way (Dare, 1985; Farley, 1979; Minuchin, S., 1974). For example, a husband and wife may have been able to avoid facing up to serious problems in their relationship by attributing family discord to the disruptive or disturbed behavior of an adolescent son or daughter. In reality they needed the young person's disturbance in order to maintain equilibrium, albeit pathological, in the family as a whole.

Family therapists have found that in such situations treatment of the adolescent often fails if the larger problems of the family are not addressed. The parents may subtly sabotage the treatment process, or even withdraw the adolescent from treatment, while continuing to proclaim their desire to see the young person improve. In cases in which the adolescent is removed from the home for treatment at a residential center, another child in the family may exhibit symptoms of disturbance; or the absence of the adolescent as the focus of family discord may precipitate a marital crisis or breakup. The apparent recovery of the adolescent may have a similar effect.

Clearly, in such situations it is necessary to involve the entire family in the treatment process. Unfortunately, however, this can prove difficult or impossible when the family as a whole has a strong need to perceive the problem as resting exclusively with one family member (whom family therapists call the "i.p.," or *identified patient*).

---

passive, dependent husband or wife develops a new assertiveness and independence, disequilibrium will result and will require adjustments by the spouse and other family members. Serious illness or disability of one family member often requires major adjustments by the other members. And as children become adolescents and their parents approach middle age, successive changes are needed in the ways in which they relate to each other if a workable equilibrium is to be sustained (see pages 210–211).

PARENTAL STRESS AND ATTITUDES TOWARD ADOLESCENT AUTONOMY

As we have noted, there are likely to be contradictions in attitudes toward adolescent autonomy not only between different representatives of adult society but also within the individual parent. The latter type of contradiction is likely to be most difficult for the adolescent to cope with. When one voice of the adult world, such as the church, issues a particular set of directives for adolescent behavior, and another voice, such as the peer group, issues another, the adolescent may feel compelled to choose between them. But at least in such a situation the young person is choosing between two clearly defined alternatives. However, when a father proclaims that he wants his son to be independent but covertly does everything he can to prolong dependence, the result is likely to be confusing for the adolescent. The son's position becomes similar to that of Alice in her encounter with the Mad Hatter: Nothing is quite what it seems. Because of the difficulty of identifying and labeling parental attitudes, he may find it impossible to deal with them rationally.

Inconsistencies in parents' attitudes may simply reflect confusion about the roles society expects them to play. In a rapidly changing and deeply divided society, this is seldom a simple matter. (When should a parent permit a child to go out alone on dates, and with whom? Should a child be allowed to go to parties where adults are absent and alcohol and marijuana may be used? Should a child have his or her own spending money, and if so, how much? Where and when should a child be permitted to drive a car?) Such questions are easier to answer in communities that are characterized by extended-family and neighborhood ties. In such communities, fundamental values and social customs tend to be more firmly held and widely shared among both adults and adolescents.

Frequently, however, parents' inconsistencies stem from within—from contradictory needs that are deeply rooted and frequently unconscious. Many parents genuinely want their children to become able to handle their own affairs because they realize that ultimately this will be necessary. But at the same time they want to protect their children from the unpleasant realities of existence—an impossible task. There are, of course, many other possible sources of inconsistency in parental attitudes, including emotional problems and conflicts.

Sex Role Socialization and the Development of Autonomy

The past two decades have been marked by significant changes in women's roles and, more recently, in those of men. These changes can be seen in behavior, such as the increased participation of women in the labor force, as well as in attitudes, such as beliefs about whether specific tasks should be performed by men or by women. This major societal change has already had an impact on the development of autonomy and the resolution of conflicts over dependence and independence particularly in adolescent girls (Conger & Petersen, 1984).

Studies conducted in the 1960s and earlier indicated that girls experienced fewer and less stressful conflicts over the development of independence than boys (Blos, 1971; Coleman, 1961; Douvan & Adelson, 1966). In a national sample of adolescents surveyed in the early 1960s, boys emerged as significantly more likely than girls to be "actively involved in establishing independence from parental control" (Douvan & Adelson, 1966, p. 115). In contrast, girls were more likely than boys to consider their parents' rules to be fair, right, and lenient.

Since that time there have been important changes in the socialization and development of adolescent girls (Gilligan, 1979; Huston, 1983; Petersen, 1988). Autonomy and self-reliance are gaining greater approval among peers and in society generally, and this may be reflected in parent–child relations. In one recent study of fifth- to ninth-graders, girls scored higher than boys on all measures of emotional autonomy; they also described themselves as more self-reliant (Steinberg & Silverberg, 1986). Moreover, by the ninth grade girls were twice as likely as boys to score high in autonomy with respect to both parents *and* peers (see pages 285–287).

In contrast to earlier findings, another recent investigation found that adolescent girls were less likely than boys to consider their parents' rules lenient (Petersen & Gitelson, 1984). Still other studies have found fewer sex differences in attitudes related to autonomy and independence (Lerner, Sorrell, & Brackney, 1981; Offer, Ostrov & Howard, 1981; Steinberg, 1987). At this point, therefore, we should be cautious about concluding that contemporary adolescent girls are less concerned than boys with the development of autonomy and less likely to become involved in conflicts with parents over independence versus dependence.

As we have already noted, a consistent finding of both earlier and more recent studies is that female adolescents and young women who are more independent, self-reliant, and achievement oriented than their peers tend to have parents who, while fundamentally loving and caring, are not passively accepting of or overprotective toward their daughters. Indeed, the parents of such adolescents make strong demands for maturity, self-reliance, and a reasonable level of achievement (Baumrind, 1975, 1989, in press; Cooper & Grotevant, 1987; Elder, 1979; Hauser et al., 1987; Huston, 1983).

It seems likely that such parents promote these characteristics in their daughters by positively reinforcing evidence of such behavior while failing to reinforce, or negatively reinforcing, dependence and lack of instrumental competence. In addition, they provide models of independent, self-confident, achieving behavior. The fact that in many of these studies the correlations between parental behaviors and adolescent independence, achievement orientation, and self-reliance are stronger for girls than for boys suggests that models of parental independence are far more crucial for girls in our society, and also that a greater and more clearly defined effort to foster independence in girls is necessary in order to offset traditional societal and familial influences.

What seems most clear is that excessive sex role stereotyping tends to limit the development of individuals of both sexes. Neither the "supermale" (aggressive, but lacking nurturance and sensitivity) nor the supposedly fragile and delicate female (lacking instrumental independence and self-reliance) is well prepared for the demands of a changing society or able to sustain mature, mutually supportive heterosexual relationships (Bem, 1975, 1986; Huston, 1983). Moreover, among both males and females those who are most likely to be creative are those who combine positive traits that have traditionally been considered masculine (e.g., autonomy) or feminine (e.g., sensitivity) (Spence, 1985; Spence & Helmreich, 1978). They may also achieve more mature levels of moral development (Block, 1973). Such results suggest that rigid sex role stereotyping is dysfunctional in contemporary society. In our view, the ultimate aim of socialization should be to permit each adolescent to develop his or her unique potential as a human being, consistent with the rights of others.

PARENTAL STRESS IN THE ADOLESCENT YEARS

Much is made of adolescent identity problems. But adults, too, may have identity crises, and for a majority most such crises are likely to occur during the period when their children are coming to maturity (Small, Eastman, & Cornelius, 1988). Indeed, as one observer has noted, one reason that the adolescent years tend to be difficult ones for the family is that everyone concerned is likely to be in a "dangerous" stage of development (Chilman, 1968).

The average marriage is likely to be at midstage when the children are adolescents. At this juncture the wife is about 40 years old and her husband is about two years older. It is easy to see how this can be a difficult developmental stage for parents, entirely apart from the problems of raising children. For both husband and wife it is likely to be a time of reappraisal. In the case of the husband, whatever dreams he may have had of vocational or social glory either have been realized by age 42 (or shortly thereafter) or are unlikely ever to be realized. If he has not been successful in his own eyes or those of others, or if his job security is threatened, he will be only too aware of the difficulties encountered by people over 40 in obtaining or changing employment. This is likely to be a period of occupational restlessness, when a man may wonder whether he has chosen the wrong vocation in terms either of personal fulfillment or economic opportunity (Levinson et al., 1978; Vaillant, 1977).

Some parents have difficulty "letting go" when their adolescent children leave home.

Similarly, the wife, who may have suppressed other goals while raising children or may have viewed her relationship with her children as compensation for other disappointments, must face the fact her children will soon be gone. What will she do then? Indeed, who will she be then? A number of studies have indicated that bright, educated women who have chosen the homemaker lifestyle have greater difficulty adjusting to the departure of their children than those who have combined marriage and a career. This is especially true of noncareer women who have built their lives around "muting of self-assertion" and preoccupation with child rearing to the exclusion of outside interests and activities (Birnbaum, 1975; Gold & Andres, 1978; Hoffman, 1974, 1984).

Both parents are likely to become increasingly aware of the fact that they have passed their physical prime and that the rest of the road slopes downhill, however gently at first. In a society obsessed with youthfulness, in which old people may be ignored, condescended to, or treated as useless, and may be distant from their families and loved ones, the prospect can be chilling for many, especially the poor. Parents' growing awareness of aging is likely to be heightened by the obvious contrasts between themselves and their adolescent young, who are approaching the height of their physical, sexual, and mental capabilities.

For all of these reasons, there is often a temporary dip in marital satisfaction during the child-rearing years (Campbell, Converse, & Rodgers, 1976; Gove & Peterson, 1980; Rossi, 1978; Silverberg & Steinberg, 1987). In view of the stresses of this period, it is not surprising that parents may be more inconsistent in their attitudes toward their children's growing autonomy than might otherwise be the case. A father with a strong need to appear powerful and wise in the eyes of others may in reality have gained little recognition from the world at large. As a result, he may be unwilling to foster autonomy in his child because the corollary of autonomy is renunciation of the idea that anyone, including one's father, is always right.

Similarly, mothers and fathers who feel unloved by their marriage partners or their friends may be reluctant to see their children begin leading their own lives. Consciously or unconsciously, they know that another inevitable consequence of autonomy is a shift of affection to other important figures, even though a feeling of connectedness to parents may be retained. If the parent has satisfied his or her own needs by loving and controlling a child, or if the child is providing compensation for frustrations arising elsewhere, "letting go" can be very difficult.

So far, we seem to have painted a bleak picture of the situation of parents during their children's adolescence. But there is another side as well. For many parents who have lived full lives and have been reasonably successful vocationally, socially, in their marriage, and as parents, the disadvantages of this stage are outweighed by greater security, other interests, and continuing contact with their children. Erik Erikson observes that whereas the stage of young adulthood centrally involves "the search for intimacy," the proper concern of a mature middle-aged adult involves making the transition of what he calls generativity—satisfaction gained from contributing to the development and well-being of others, and particularly the young (Erikson, 1963, 1968).

Middle-aged adults who can gain satisfaction from using their experience, resources, security, and position in society and in the family in caring for others may have the best possible insurance against the disappointments and stresses of increasing age. However, even the fortunate parents who have achieved generativity and are able to meet their own needs through increasing concern for others, including their own adolescent children, are unlikely to be entirely free of conflict regarding their children's autonomy. Perhaps the most common source of parental ambivalence toward autonomy in adolescents is the realization that the child must some day stand on his or her own feet and in so doing could be deeply hurt. A great many of these fears, however, are unfounded. It is true that children will make mistakes, and they may even be hurt. But the chances of their being seriously harmed are smaller if they are allowed to gain autonomy gradually, while they are still able to turn to their parents for support, than if they are suddenly thrust into the world at the age of 21, totally unprepared to act independently.

PARENT–CHILD RELATIONS AND IDENTITY FORMATION

The ease with which adolescents are able to achieve a clear sense of identity depends on many factors, including the kinds of identifications they have developed and their ability to integrate those identifications with their newfound sexual maturity, the aptitudes and skills they have developed, and the opportunities provided by changing social roles. Perhaps most important, however, it depends on the kinds of relationships they have had and continue to have with their parents. The adolescent is more likely to establish a strong sense of identity if there is a rewarding, interactive relationship between the adolescent and *both* parents, and if both parents provide models of competent problem-solving behavior, a confident sense of their own identity (including gender identity), and a mutually supportive relationship with each other (Block, 1973, 1984; Hoffman, M. L., 1977; Huston, 1983; Maccoby & Martin, 1983). In addition, adolescents who are actively engaged in seeking an identity of their own are more likely to have parents who encourage self-assertion and freedom to disagree ("separateness") while at the same time encouraging "connectedness" to the family, including openness or responsiveness to the views of others ("plurality") and sensitivity to and respect for the ideas of others ("mutuality") (see pages 60–61) (Cooper, Grotevant, & Condon, 1983; Grotevant & Cooper, 1983; Youniss & Smollar, 1985). Within this general framework, the model provided by the same-sex parent, and the degree of approval and acceptance of this model by the opposite-sex parent, may play an important role.

Under such circumstances the adolescent is likely to have a favorable and clearly defined perception of himself or herself and is less likely to encounter conflicts between self-perceptions and the new demands arising during the adolescent years. Consistent with this reasoning, it has been shown that nurturance and warmth on the part of the same-sex parent facilitate the development of a clearer sense of personal identity—both as individuals and as members of their own sex—among adolescents. Moreover, it has been found that an adolescent boy's sense of identity is likely to be stronger when both parents behave similarly toward him: when the father is seen as strong but affectionate, spends a lot of time with his son, praises his efforts, and exercises moderate control over his activities; and when the mother supports the boy's identification with the father while herself avoiding an intrusive, demanding orientation toward the boy (Hetherington, 1967; LaVoie, 1976; Marcia, 1980; Matteson, 1974).

Similarly, among adolescent girls a strong sense of identity is facilitated by a mother who serves as a nurturant, effective role model and a father who is an effective person, who is affectionate, attentive, and supportive of his daughter's development as an individual and also shows approval of the mother as a marriage partner and as a role model for her daughter (Douvan & Adelson, 1966; Hetherington, 1967; Huston, 1983; Waterman, 1982). Moreover, mothers who encourage appropriate degrees of autonomy, achievement, and self-reliance while remaining supportive are more likely to have daughters who develop a clear sense of their own identity. Daughters in such families feel close to their mothers but are also very aware of differences between them (Baumrind, 1975, in press; Huston, 1983; Morse, 1973).

As both sets of findings suggest, the development of a sense of identity is influenced by the kinds of role models provided by both parents as well as by the relationship between the parents. When the parents' relationship is distorted or conflict-ridden, the young person has more difficulty forming an identity (Block, 1973). Domination of one parent by the other, mutual hostility, inadequacy in either parent, or parental role reversals that emphasize the most negative aspects or sex role stereotypes—all increase the difficulty of adolescent identity development (Block, 1973; Conger, 1977; Spence, 1985; Spence and Helmreich, 1978).

Sex-Typing and Sexual Identity

As already noted (see page 63), appropriate behavior as a man or woman need not involve rigid conformity to sex role stereotypes. Moreover, identification with the same-sex parent need not imply the adoption of traditional or exaggerated sex role stereotypes. From the point of view of the development of sexual identity the outward forms that role behavior takes are less important than the kind of parental identification on which it is at least in part based and whether, despite cultural variations, one's role behavior is consistent with one's basic biological nature.

For example, a girl who identifies with a very feminine mother (in the traditional sense) *and* a girl who identifies with a socially assertive, intellectual, highly independent mother may both achieve a relatively conflict-free adjustment and a strong sense of ego identity, even though the latter girl may score low on stereotyped measures of femininity. On the other hand, a girl whose sex role behavior is based on rejection of a nonnurturant mother (regardless of whether the mother is "traditional" or "modern") or on identification with a mother who rejects her basic biological identity (e.g., resents her sexual nature or her child-bearing capability) or who is hostile to her own or the opposite sex), will have difficulty establishing a stable, secure sense of identity (Block, 1973; Conger, 1977, 1979; Huston, 1983).

Fathers who are uninvolved, ineffective, or hostile can also make the development of a secure sense of identity, as well as the establishment of lasting heterosexual relationships, more difficult (Biller, 1971, 1974, 1981; Green, 1974, 1980; Marcia, 1980). In girls, sexual responsiveness and positive attitudes toward marriage and child rearing have been found to be related to having a warm, supportive father (Fischer, 1973). Among boys, having a passive, ineffective father and a dominant, intrusive mother is likely to hinder the development of identity, including sexual identity (Block, 1973).

ONE-PARENT FAMILIES

Thus far we have discussed the effects of parental influences in intact families. However, as we saw in the preceding chapter, one-parent families are becoming increasingly prevalent. Currently one out of every five children under the age of 18 is living in a one-parent family, and in 90 percent of those families the single parent is the mother. What, then, do we know about the effects of father absence?

Effects of Father Absence on Boys

Boys from homes in which the father is absent are somewhat more likely to encounter difficulties in social, emotional, and cognitive development and to perform below grade level in school (Adams, Milner, & Schrepf, 1984; Biller, 1974, 1981; Dornbusch, 1988; Dornbusch et al., 1985, 1987; Santrock, 1972, 1987). At a more subtle level, the quantitative skills of both boys and girls appear to be more adversely affected by the absence of the father than their verbal skills (Huston, 1983; Shinn, 1978). Boys from father-absent homes are also more likely to be impulsive and to have difficulty delaying gratification and assuming social responsibility (Biller & Bahm, 1971; Huston, 1984; Mischel, 1961a, 1961b). In one investigation children from father-present and father-absent homes were studied on a variety of measures at age 10 and followed up at age 15 (Fry & Scher, 1984). The investigators found that during the intervening years boys from father-absent homes showed declines in achievement motivation, desire for mastery, perseverance, and willingness to endure negative consequences.

Boys from father-absent homes are likely to be more immature, to have more difficulty forming peer relations, to be less popular with peers, and to have a poorer self-concept (Biller, 1971, 1981; Biller & Davids, 1973). Moreover, they are significantly more likely to drop out of school and to become involved in delinquent activities or exhibit conduct problems (Dornbusch et al., 1985).

The age at which the child is separated from the father appears to be important (Huston, 1983). Boys who are separated from their fathers early (i.e., before age 5) are likely to score lower than those who are separated later on measures of aggressiveness and *masculine* sex role preference. They also show more *feminine* patterns on tests of intellectual preference (e.g., higher scores in verbal ability than in mathematics, and a more global ["field-dependent"] and less analytical conceptual style) (Barclay & Cusumano, 1967; Biller & Bahm, 1971; Huston, 1983).

Overall, it appears that the presence in the home of a father who serves as a competent, effective role model and expresses interest in his son and interacts actively with him facilitates the boy's intellectual, psychological, and social development (Block, 1987). On the other hand, the absence of the father, or the presence of a father who is ineffective, distant, hostile, or rejecting, is likely to hinder the boy's development. Obviously, the presence or absence of an effective father is not the only factor affecting development; in either case the boy's development will depend partly on the qualities of the mother as well as on the availability of other male role models, such as a stepfather, older brother, uncle, "Big Brother" or Scout leader, or male family friend.

If the mother is psychologically strong, capable, and confident of her feminine identity, and if she is warm and caring without being clinging or overprotective, she can do much to guide her son's development. She can also promote her son's sex role development by showing a positive attitude toward the absent father and toward males in general, and by encouraging competency and independence in her son. Father-absent boys whose mothers accept and reinforce assertive, aggressive, and independent behavior are more confidently masculine (as measured by game preferences and peer interactions) than father-absent boys whose mothers disapprove of such behavior (Biller, 1969, 1971; Biller & Bahm, 1971; Huston, 1983).

Effects of Father Absence on Girls

The effects of father absence on girls have not been studied as extensively as the effects on boys. However, available evidence suggests that boys are somewhat more affected by father absence than girls (Dornbusch et al., 1985; Fry & Scher, 1984; Huston, 1983). This finding seems reasonable because of the importance of same-sex role models and also because adolescent boys in mother-only homes are more likely than girls to be in conflict with their mothers (Hetherington et al., 1985, 1989). Nevertheless, absence of the father can have important effects on a girl's development, especially when she reaches adolescence. As adolescents, girls from father-absent homes are more likely than those from intact families to show anxiety about and difficulty in relating to males. However, the kinds of problems, and the ways in which they are manifested, differ for girls who have lost their fathers through death and those whose parents are divorced.

E. Mavis Hetherington, a psychologist at the University of Virginia, studied

Much of a father-absent boy's ultimate success or failure will depend on the qualities of the mother as the remaining parent.

three groups of adolescent girls in a neighborhood recreation center: father-present girls, girls whose father had died, and girls whose fathers had left the home because of divorce (Hetherington, 1972; Hetherington & Parke, 1986). Using a variety of observational measures, psychological tests, and interviews, she found that daughters of widows tended to be shy and withdrawn, tense, and likely to avoid close proximity to male peers and adults. They also tended to begin dating later than other girls and to be sexually inhibited.

In contrast, daughters of divorced parents, while also anxious, tended to seek out male peers at the expense of interactions with other females. They were also likely to begin dating earlier than girls from father-present homes and to have sexual intercourse at earlier ages. Both groups of father-absent girls felt less secure around male peers and adults than did father-present girls. But although girls whose parents were divorced reported more conflict with their mothers than girls from father-present homes, those whose fathers had died reported less conflict. Girls whose fathers were absent as a result of death also had the most positive views about the father's warmth and competence and reported having had less conflict with him. Girls from father-present homes felt most confident about relations with other adult males and tended to have the highest levels of self-esteem.

As in the case of boys, the effects on girls of separation from fathers were more marked if the separation had occurred during early childhood. Apparently, "lack of opportunity for constructive interaction with a loving, attentive father has resulted in apprehension and inadequate skills in relating to males" (Hetherington, 1972, p. 324). In a related study of adolescent girls living in a lower-income environment, girls whose fathers were absent because of divorce were found to engage in more precocious dating behavior and to display greater sexual knowledge than otherwise similar girls from father-present homes (Nelson & Vangen, 1971).

In general, it appears that a girl's acquisition of feminine behavior and the skills involved in interacting with males is based at least partly on learning experiences and reinforcements received through interaction with her father. However, having a father present is not likely to be beneficial if the father is inadequate, passive, neglectful, or harsh and rejecting. Paternal rejection, for example, is associated with deficits in adolescent girls' cognitive and academic functioning. Even if a father is highly nurturant, he can inhibit his daughter's cognitive and psychological development if he reinforces such feminine stereotypes as dependence, timidity, and conformity (Biller, 1974; Chapman, 1977).

On the other hand, a father who is nurturant and caring and who praises and rewards his daughter's intellectual and creative efforts may facilitate both personal and cognitive development. Such a father clearly serves as an effective role model; equally important, however, he is demonstrating through his behavior and expectations that he (as a male) does not view independent-mindedness, creativity, and intellectual accomplishment as inconsistent with successful feminine development. High paternal expectations in the context of a warm father–daughter relationship "are conducive to the development of autonomy, independence, achievement, and creativity among girls" (Biller, 1974, p. 139).

Effects of Mother Absence

Relatively few systematic studies have focused on the effects of absence of the mother on either girls or boys, although it appears likely that more such studies will be conducted in the future as paternal custody becomes more common (Adams, Milner, & Schrepf, 1984). One extensive study of father-custody, mother-custody, and intact families suggests that girls' sex-typing and overall adjustment are affected more by absence of the mother than is the case for boys (Santrock & Warshak, 1979; Santrock, Warshak, Lindbergh, & Meadows, 1982). Girls in their father's custody were rated as less feminine, less independent, and more demanding than those in their mother's custody. In contrast, boys in their father's custody were rated as more mature and sociable than those in their mother's custody. Much depends, however, on whether a father who has custody of a son or daughter is active, caring, and involved, and—particularly in the case of girls—encourages autonomy, independence, and achievement (Biller, 1981; Fry & Scher, 1984; Huston, 1983).

These results suggest that absence of the same-sex parent can have pervasive effects on the emotional and social development of children and adolescents, not just on sex-typing (Huston, 1983; Mussen, Conger, Kagan, & Huston, 1990). In some instances absence of the same-sex parent may appear to encourage freedom from rigidly sex-typed attitudes and behavior based on cultural stereotypes. However, as Aletha Huston, an expert on sex-typing, notes, it would be a mistake simply to applaud such liberation from cultural strictures. Children whose same-sex parent is absent are also more likely "to lack self-esteem, social confidence, and other positive attributes associated with either masculinity or femininity." Huston points out that nonstereotyped socialization is more likely to be effective "when a child is living with a same-sex parent who departs from traditional roles than when the same-sex parent is absent altogether" (1983, p. 435).

SUMMARY

A variety of factors affect an individual's chances of successfully completing the developmental tasks of adolescence. However, an increasing body of research indicates that parents are the single most important external influence on the average adolescent attempting to deal with those tasks.

An important dimension of parental behavior is *love–hostility*. Parental hostility, rejection, or neglect occur more frequently than acceptance, love, and trust in the background of children with a wide range of problems. In some cases parental hostility results in serious physical or sexual abuse of a child or adolescent. Abusing parents generally have not been exposed to models of successful parenting themselves and may have extremely unrealistic ideas about the kind of behavior that can be expected of a child at a particular stage of development. Usually, however, the problem goes much deeper. Many abusing parents have themselves been deprived of love and care and find it difficult to subordinate their needs to those of the child. Often, too, they are socially isolated and lack the ability to make friends and develop broad social-support systems. Under such circumstances problems that place extra stress on the parent may precipitate abuse.

Abused children who are exposed to beneficial developmental experiences may grow up to be essentially normal; however, many exhibit lasting adverse effects of abuse, including distractibility, lack of ego control, and difficulty in trusting others. They often have low self-esteem, are lonely, and lack joy or spontaneity. A history of abuse and neglect, particularly sexual abuse, is common among adolescent runaways and delinquents.

The other major dimension of parental behavior is *autonomy–control.* Extreme restrictiveness tends to inhibit not only social development but also creativity, initiative, and flexibility.

It is important to consider where parental behavior falls along each of these major dimensions, as well as the age of the child or adolescent. *Authoritative* (or democratic) parents, who value both autonomous will and disciplined behavior, love and respect their children and involve them in family affairs, and encourage the development of age-appropriate independence, are most likely to foster the development of confidence, self-esteem, responsibility, and autonomy. Such parents provide explanations for their rules and expectations. *Authoritarian* (or autocratic) parents, in contrast, view obedience as an absolute virtue and discourage free discussion in the belief that the young person should unquestioningly accept the parent's word for what is right. In turn, their children are more likely to feel rejected and less likely to be self-reliant and able to think and act for themselves. Parents who are *laissez-faire, permissive,* or *neglecting* also fail to give adolescents the kind of support they need and allow their children to develop without providing dependable models of responsible adult behavior.

The development of age-appropriate autonomy requires not only increasing *separation* but also continued *connectedness.* As adolescence progresses, young people need sufficient freedom from parental control to experience themselves as individuals responsible for their own lives. At the same time, they continue to need their parents' love, guidance, and support. Democratic, authoritative practices foster responsible autonomous behavior by providing opportunities for autonomy guided by parents who communicate with the child and exercise appropriate control; by promoting positive identification with the parent; and by providing models of responsible autonomous behavior.

Parent–child interaction is not a one-way street; it is *bidirectional.* Just as parental behavior affects the responses of children, the behavior of children and adolescents affects the responses of their parents. Moreover, both children and their parents are members of a broader family system. Families may be organized or chaotic, close-knit or disengaged, disturbed or essentially normal. One of the most important dimensions of the family system is *communication,* particularly during the adolescent years. Effective communication helps family members strike a balance between separateness from and connectedness to one another. In troubled families, communication patterns tend to be distorted.

In addition to the overall characteristics that differentiate families from one another, there are differences in the roles played by individual family members. As adolescents mature, successive changes are needed in the roles of family members and the way they relate to one another if a workable equilibrium is to be preserved.

In the past two decades there have been marked changes in sex role socialization and the development of autonomy, particularly in girls. Female adolescents who are more independent, self-reliant, and achievement oriented tend to have parents who, while loving and caring, avoid being overprotective and demand self-reliance and a reasonable level of achievement.

The adolescent years can be difficult for parents as well as for adolescents themselves. The kinds of conflicts to which middle-aged parents are exposed during their children's adolescent years and the ways in which they cope with them can profoundly affect their children's chances of mastering the developmental tasks of adolescence.

The ease with which adolescents are able to achieve a clear sense of identity depends on the nature of their relationships with their parents. Active efforts to form an identity are fostered by parents who encourage self-assertion and freedom to disagree (i.e., separateness) while encouraging continued connectedness to the family, including openness to the views of others ("plurality") and sensitivity and respect for the views of others ("mutuality"). The kinds of models that parents provide also affect the development of sexual identity in both girls and boys.

In one-parent families the absence of either parent can make child rearing more difficult for the remaining parent and can affect the psychological development of both boys and girls. In general, boys appear to be somewhat more affected by absence of the father than girls, although absence of the father can have important effects on girls' development, particularly during adolescence. In addition, preliminary research findings suggest that girls' sex-typing and overall adjustment are affected more by absence of the mother than is the case for boys.

REVIEW QUESTIONS

1. What are the two primary dimensions of parental behavior? How do variations in these kinds of behaviors affect the development of adolescents?
2. Discuss the effects of physical or sexual abuse on the psychological development of children and adolescents.
3. How do authoritative child-rearing practices differ from authoritarian and laissez-faire practices? Which approach is most likely to foster the development of responsible, autonomous behavior? Which is most likely to lead to hostility or feelings of rejection? Why?
4. Discuss the dual processes of *separation* and *connectedness* in the development of age-appropriate autonomy during adolescence.
5. What is meant by the principle of bidirectionality?
6. What variables differentiate families scoring high and low on measures of parent–adolescent communication?
7. Discuss the effects of excessive sexual stereotyping on the development of male and female adolescents.
8. Why is stress on parents likely to reach a peak during their children's adolescent years?
9. What role do parents play in fostering a strong sense of identity, including sexual identity?
10. Discuss the effects of absence of the father on male and female children and adolescents.

RECOMMENDED READINGS

Baumrind, D. (1975). Early socialization and adolescent competence. In S. E. Dragastin & G. H. Elder, Jr. (Eds.). *Adolescence in the life cycle.* New York: Wiley.

Baumrind, D. (in press). Parenting styles and adolescent development. In J. Brooks-Gunn, R. Lerner & A.C. Petersen (Eds.). *The encyclopedia on adolescence.* New York: Garland.

Elder, G. H., Jr. (1980). *Family structure and socialization.* New York: Arno Press.

Garbarino, J., Schellenbach, C. J., & Sebes, J. M. (Eds.) (1986). *Troubled youth, troubled families: Understanding families at risk for adolescent maltreatment.* New York: Aldine de Gruyter.

Grotevant, H. D., & Cooper, C. R. (Eds.) (1983). *Adolescent development in the family.* San Francisco: Jossey-Bass.

Youniss, J., & Smollar, J. (1985). *Adolescent relations with mothers, fathers, and friends.* Chicago: University of Chicago Press.

ADOLESCENT SEXUALITY

Among the many developmental events that characterize puberty and the onset of adolescence, none is more dramatic than the physical and psychological changes associated with sexual maturation. The bodily proportions of boys and girls become increasingly differentiated: Boys develop broader shoulders and show a greater overall gain in muscle development, while girls undergo breast development and develop more rounded hips. Girls experience their first menstruation and boys their first ejaculation. In both sexes the genital organs—penis and scrotum in boys, clitoris, vagina, and labia in girls—increase in size, and the pubic hair develops. All of these physical changes require adjustments by the young person and lead to a changing self-image (see Chapter 4). As one 16-year-old girl expressed it, "When I was 14 my body started to go crazy" (Bell, 1987).

Although **sexuality**[1] in its broadest sense is a lifelong part of being human (even babies love to be held and may fondle their genitals), the hormonal changes that accompany puberty lead to stronger sexual feelings, although these feelings may be expressed in different ways by different individuals and by the same individual at different times. Adolescents may find themselves "thinking more about sex, getting sexually aroused more easily, even at times feeling preoccupied with sex" (Bell, 1987, p. 75). Or they may be involved in other interests and not particularly aware of sexual feelings. At the same age, one adolescent may be involved in sexual experimentation while another is not; one may be in love and going steady while another feels that it is much too early for such commitments (Conger, 1980; Luria, Freedman, & Rose, 1987).

Despite such individual variations, successfully integrating sexuality with other aspects of the young person's sense of self is a major developmental task for both boys and girls. How well this task is handled—the extent to which it becomes a source of joy or despair, challenge and success or failure and defeat—depends on many factors, ranging from the complexities of early parent–child relations to contemporary social standards and values.

SEX DIFFERENCES AND SIMILARITIES IN ADOLESCENT SEXUALITY

For most boys the rapid increase in sexual drive that accompanies puberty is difficult to deny and tends to be genitally oriented. The increased frequency of erection in response to a wide variety of stimuli (see page 97) calls attention to sexual arousal, sometimes under awkward circumstances. Self-perceived sex drive in males reaches a peak during adolescence, as does the frequency of total sexual outlet (primarily through masturbation) (Chilman, 1983; Conger, 1980; Kinsey, Pomeroy, & Martin, 1948).

---

[1]In contrast to the physical and physiological changes related to sexual maturation or to sexual behaviors, the term *sexuality* refers to the totality of our sexual thoughts, feelings, values, beliefs, actions, and relationships. "In human life, biological forces work in concert with cultural forces—and sex blossoms into sexuality" (Luria, Friedman, & Rose, 1987, p. 5).

Among adolescent girls there appears to be a much wider range of individual differences. Although some girls experience sexual desire in much the same way as the average boy, for a majority sexual feelings tend to be more diffuse, as well as more closely related to the fulfillment of other needs such as self-esteem, reassurance, affection, and love (Bell, 1987; Chilman, 1983; Katchadourian, 1989; Kinsey, Pomeroy, & Martin, 1953). For many girls the relationship with the boy she loves takes precedence over sexual release; consequently, control of sexual impulses may constitute a less urgent problem.

Although there is a significant increase in sexual interests and behavior among both boys and girls during adolescence, sexual activity in general—and masturbation in particular—is more prevalent among boys than among girls, although the extent of the difference has narrowed in recent years (see pages 247–250). Subjective awareness of specifically sexual pressure also appears to be greater among boys, particularly in early adolescence. The average adolescent boy experiences nocturnal emissions, whereas the average girl does not have orgasm dreams during adolescence (Katchadourian, 1985). Among sexually experienced American male and female adolescents ages 13–15 and 16–19, only in the case of 13- to 15-year-old adolescent boys did a majority reply affirmatively to the statement, "Sometimes I think I am addicted to sex, the way some people are addicted to drugs" (Sorensen, 1973).

In studies of sexual morality (e.g., attitudes toward premarital intercourse, the importance of love in a sexual relationship, avoidance of promiscuity, respect for parental or societal wishes), girls consistently display more conservative attitudes than boys do (see page 246). Obviously, we are speaking here only of *relative* differences. More girls than boys would agree with the girl who

In adolescence, sexual feelings may be expressed in different ways by different individuals and by the same individual at different times.

said, "I feel you have to be romantically involved because if you are not then the only motive behind the contact is sexual and has nothing to do with your emotional feelings" (Hass, 1979, p. 15). At the same time, many boys would agree with the boy who said, "I don't feel cheap sex accomplishes anything. If I am romantically involved, I feel it is somehow a statement of my affection" (Hass, 1979, p. 16). Conversely, a significant minority of girls would agree with the girl who stated that "if two people are physically attracted to each other, I don't see the necessity for a romantic relationship as long as both people understand the relationship is purely physical and there are no ties connected" (Hass, 1979, p. 17).

Findings indicating that sex differences in adolescents' attitudes, values, and behavior remain despite the so-called sexual revolution do not come as a surprise; however, the underlying reasons for such differences are still far from clear. A number of theories have been advanced, some primarily physiological and others primarily cultural. Recent changes in adolescent sexual interests, values, and behavior in our society, particularly among girls, as well as findings from other cultures (discussed later in the chapter), provide impressive evidence that cultural influences play a significant role in sexuality (Brooks-Gunn & Furstenberg, 1989; Conger, 1980).

The part played by physical, physiological, and hormonal factors is less evident. One hypothesis is that females are less likely than males to discover sexual responses spontaneously because the girl's sexual organs are less prominent (Bell, 1987; Chilman, 1983; Katchadourian, 1985). It has also been asserted that there may be basic physiological differences between males and females in sexual drive and responsiveness, in the capacity of various stimuli to arouse them, or both. Indeed, until the early decades of this century it was simply assumed that normal women did not have strong sexual drives or responses.

A majority of today's adolescent girls do not subscribe to such views. More than two-thirds of girls between the ages of 13 and 19 express the belief that women enjoy sex as much as men (Conger, 1980; Hunt, 1970, 1974). Only one out of every ten adolescent girls believes that women innately have less capacity for sexual pleasure than men. This view receives strong support from William Masters and Virginia Johnson, the first scientists to study human sexual responses comprehensively and objectively (Masters & Johnson, 1966, 1970; Masters, Johnson, & Koloday, 1988). They comment that the female's basic physiological capacity for sexual response surpasses that of males, in that women "have an unlimited orgasm potential, while men . . . are unable to have a rapid series of ejaculations" (Masters et al., 1988, p. 95). It has also been clearly documented that sexual behavior (e.g., frequency of orgasm) may vary over much wider ranges among girls than among boys (Kinsey, Pomeroy, & Martin, 1948, 1953).

An even more complex question involves the conditions under which sexual arousal is likely to occur. It has been argued that boys are more easily aroused by a wider variety of external "psychosexual stimuli," such as provocative behavior, erotic art, films, and literature (Chilman, 1983; Katchadourian, 1989; Kinsey et al., 1948, 1953; Wilson et al., 1971a, 1971b). Here, too, simplistic hypotheses appear inadequate. A wide-ranging series of experimental investigations showed that although males are more responsive, the differences between males and females are smaller than is generally supposed (Katchadourian, 1985). Moreover, in some situations some groups of females (those who are younger, more liberal, and more sexually experienced) report greater "sexual excitement" in response to various kinds of sexual stimuli than some groups of males (those who are older, more conservative, more inhibited, and less experienced) (Katchadourian, 1989; Schmidt, 1975; Wilson et al., 1971a, 1971b).

It is interesting to note that several studies have found that although males more frequently report subjective feelings of arousal, direct measurements of physiological-sexual response do not reveal substantial sex differences. This may suggest that conflicts between feelings of arousal and defenses against such feelings may occur more frequently among females. A study conducted in Germany found that "women have a stronger tendency to react with avoidance and an emotional defense reaction to pictorial and narrative stimuli than men" even when they are physiologically aroused (Schmidt & Sigusch, 1973, p. 126).

It is also possible that even in the absence of defensive reactions, physiological sexual arousal is more difficult for females to identify, whereas in males it can hardly fail to be noticed. Thus, in one study sexually experienced young women who had reported that they were strongly aroused by erotic stimuli nevertheless experienced greater difficulty than males in identifying physiological arousal when it was not accompanied by erotic or erotic-romantic stimuli (Heiman, 1977, 1980). Also, in the absence of socially ascribed meaning or personal learning experiences there may not be a clear link between bodily sensations and specific responses to them. A young adolescent girl who is attracted to a boy may experience bodily sensations that could be labeled as desire for sex or desire for a relationship, depending on the girl's values and attitudes (Petersen & Boxer, 1982).

The fact that significantly more females (particularly younger females) are reporting feelings of sexual arousal today than thirty years ago may be due in large measure to "cultural desensitization" regarding sexual expression by women (and perhaps also to more opportunities for specific learning of sexual responses). This, in turn, may have lowered women's psychological defenses against sexual arousal and awareness of it. In the past, sexual responsiveness in females was generally less accepted by society and less clearly acknowledged by girls themselves (Brooks-Gunn & Furstenberg, 1989). This situation has changed significantly. However, it should also be recognized that the current more permissive attitude toward female sexuality remains limited in certain respects. Information about what it means to be sexual and how sexuality is integrated with other aspects of life is lacking (Fine, 1988; Petersen & Boxer, 1982). Moreover, many girls are still brought up to be less accepting and proud of their sexuality than boys are. Although it is less rigid than in the past, the double standard persists:

A teenage boy finds that his sexual adventures are usually tolerated or even encouraged. (Of course, this is often hard for the boys who aren't interested!) A girl, however, is told she must be the one to say "No!" and to hold off a boy's sex drive. She rarely hears about her own sex drive. So it can be hard for her to let her sexual responses flow freely (Bell, 1987, p. 85).

It is also possible that sexuality is more closely tied to other aspects of personality in the case of girls, so that the conditions that must be satisfied for arousal to occur or be recognized may be more complex than is generally true for boys. Stimulation that cannot be related to the self as a total person because it is perceived as threatening, conflicts with existing value systems, is impersonal, or is aesthetically offensive may be more likely to "turn off" the average adolescent girl (Chilman, 1983; Conger, 1980; Meikle, Peitchnis, & Pearce, 1985; Miller & Simon, 1980, Sue, 1979). The fantasies described by both male and female college students during sexual arousal were most likely to involve petting or having intercourse with "someone you love or are fond of" (Miller & Simon, 1980). However, fantasies of sexual activity with strangers for whom they had no particular emotional attachment were almost as frequent for males (79 percent) but not for females (22 percent). Indeed, "doing nonsexual things with someone you are fond of or in love with" was second in frequency for females (74 percent) but not for males (48 percent).

As Patricia Miller and William Simon comment, for females

the investment of erotic meaning in both explicitly sexual and nonsexual symbols appears to be contingent on the emotional context. The two genders evaluate the meaning of potentially erotic symbols using distinctive sets of criteria. For males, the explicitly sexual is endowed with erotic meaning regardless of the emotional context. For females, the emotional context is endowed with erotic meaning without regard for the presence or absence of explicitly sexual symbols (1980, p. 403).

Finally, it is possible that the greater sexual assertiveness of adolescent males is related at least partly to the significant increases in testosterone levels that occur among males at puberty. It has been demonstrated that this hormone increases sexual and aggressive behavior in both sexes under experimental conditions (Hamburg & Trudeau, 1981; Katchadourian, 1985; Udry, 1988; Udry et al., 1985). Testosterone levels have been found to be associated with sexual activities in boys independent of secondary sexual development (which might itself influence sexual behavior) (Udry et al., 1985). Interestingly, in girls sexual *interests* but not *behavior* are associated with testosterone levels, "suggesting that social factors may play a greater role in their coital behavior" (Brooks-Gunn & Furstenberg, 1989, p. 251; Udry, Talbert, & Morris, 1986).

CULTURAL DIFFERENCES IN SEXUAL ATTITUDES AND BEHAVIOR

Learning appears to play a critical role in the development of sexual response patterns (Beach, 1977; Katchadourian, 1985). Hence, we would expect to find rather wide variations in sexual attitudes and behavior from one culture to another. Although there are some cultural generalities, even universals, that reflect commonalities in the human condition (e.g., some form of incest taboo), there are also marked differences between cultures. Such differences appear not only in the amount and type of sexual behavior that is socially accepted but also in the consistency of sexual standards as development proceeds (Barry & Schlegel, 1984, 1986; Ford, 1961; Ford & Beach, 1951.) Some cultures are restrictive with regard to sexual activity throughout childhood, adolescence, and even to some extent in adulthood. Others are thoroughly permissive at all ages. Still others are highly restrictive during childhood and adolescence and then suddenly become much more permissive about, and even demanding of, sexual activity in adulthood.

Among the Cuna of the coast of Panama, children remained largely ignorant of sexual matters until the last stages of the marriage ceremony. The Ashanti of the west central coast of Africa believed that sexual intercourse with a girl who had not undergone the puberty ceremony was so harmful to the community that the offense was punishable by death for both partners (Ford & Beach, 1951). In contrast, in some societies sexual experience is carefully nurtured from early childhood on. The Chewa of Africa believed that children must have sexual experiences early in life or they will never beget offspring. "Older children build little huts some distance from the village, and there, with the complete approval of their parents, boys and girls play at being husband and wife. Such child matings may extend well into adolescence, with periodic exchanges of partners until marriage occurs" (Ford & Beach, 1951, p. 190). Similarly, the Lepcha of India believed that girls "will not mature without benefit of sexual intercourse. Early sex play among boys and girls characteristically involves many forms of mutual masturbation and usually ends in attempted copulation. By the time they are 11 or 12 years old, most girls regularly engage in full intercourse" (Ford & Beach, 1951, p. 191). In Mangaia, a small Polynesian island in the South Pacific, the culture endorses sexual pleasure for everyone. Consequently, "less than one out of 100 girls, and even fewer boys—if, indeed, there are any exceptions in either sex—have *not* had substantial sexual experience prior to marriage" (Marshall, 1971, p. 117).

Until recently, Manus boys of the Admiralty Islands north of New Guinea were in much the same position in sexual matters as American middle-class adolescent boys at the turn of the century (Ausubel, 1954). Whereas the male physiological sex drive was recognized as natural, sexual behavior was strongly tabooed until marriage. Apparently, whatever relief of sexual tension was achieved was gained primarily through covert homosexual activity and solitary masturbation surrounded by shame. In turn, the Manus girl's position was highly reminiscent of that of a female of the Victorian era. She was taught that sex is not gratifying to women and, in fact, is loathsome, shameful, and repugnant. The difficulties experienced by women in both cultures in adjusting to intercourse after marriage can easily be imagined.

In our own society, despite the "sexual revolution," many children are still taught, consciously or unconsciously, to be anxious about sex and to inhibit and control sexual behavior. Then, when they marry, they are expected to be able to respond without inhibition or anxiety. In effect, children and adolescents are taught not sexual adaptation but rather sexual concern.

Sexual Attitudes and Cultural Values

The kind and timing of sexual training received by children and adolescents can be of major importance in determining the extent of their interest in sexual behavior. Sex training also determines whether they will view sex as pleasant and natural, as sinful and dangerous, as extremely exciting, or as a form of aggressive conquest. Socialization with respect to sex may also have broader effects on the adolescent's personality and perceptions of the larger society. In societies that begin inhibiting heterosexual behavior relatively late in childhood and avoid severe punishment or censure to achieve this aim, people are less likely to feel guilty about sex than is the case in societies characterized by early and relatively harsh training (Whiting & Child, 1953).

The relationship between sexual training and broader characteristics of the individual and his or her culture is not unidirectional. Sex training practices may be generalized to other aspects of social behavior, but they are also affected by broader cultural attitudes. Thus, among the Zuni, the relations—sexual and otherwise—between a husband and wife traditionally tended to be pleasant, cooperative, and untainted by feelings of guilt. Sexual intercourse was viewed as a cooperative rather than a competitive matter, not simply because of specific sex training but because cooperation was an integral part of the whole Zuni way of life (Benedict, 1954). A similar set of cultural values is found among the Mixtecan Indians of Mexico (Whiting, 1963). When a man takes a public office in the barrio, his wife shares both the honor and the responsibility. Exploitation of one sex by the other is rare, and children are not disciplined by physical or other severe punishment. One seldom encounters bickering and fighting among either adults or children. "From the barrio point of view, the use of sex for exploitative purposes is inconsistent with their attitudes, just as are all other forms of exploitation of human beings. Sexual power does not add to the luster of the individual within the barrio" (Whiting, 1963, pp. 565–566). In contrast, in societies such as the Mundugumor of New Guinea, aggression and competition play an important part in the individual's sexual relations largely because they pervade the entire Mundugumor way of life.

SEXUAL ATTITUDES AND VALUES OF CONTEMPORARY ADOLESCENTS

Today's adolescents are characterized by somewhat greater openness about sex than their counterparts of earlier generations. They also increasingly tend to base decisions about sexual behavior more on personal values and judgment and less on conformity to institutionalized social codes. This change has manifested itself in a variety of ways, ranging from greater freedom in sexual relations to a desire for more and better sex education, including access to information about birth control.

Sex Education

By age 19 approximately 60 percent of females and 52 percent of males have been exposed to a school program in sex education, although the quality of such programs varies widely (Dawson, 1986; Kenney, Marsiglio, & Mott, 1986; Muraskin, 1986; Paikoff & Brooks-Gunn, in press). In addition, the age at which formal contraceptive education (in school, clinic, or elsewhere) is first provided has been declining steadily. A recent study found that 47 percent of 15-year-olds have had such instruction by their fifteenth birthday, compared with 33 percent of 17-year-olds and only 26 percent of 19-year-olds (Dawson, 1986). School sex education programs enjoy widespread public support: 85 percent of parents favor sex education and think it fosters a healthy attitude toward sex (Harris, 1987). Nevertheless, the subject remains highly controversial among members of the militant right and some fundamentalist religious groups and their leaders—although more than two-thirds of all born-again Christians think sex education should be available (Harris, 1987).

Opponents of sex education tend to have traditional views regarding women's roles, the family, and sexuality, and many feel excluded from the social institutions, including school and government, that affect their lives (Mahoney, 1979; Richardson & Cranston, 1981). In their view, sex education, even at the high school level, is dangerous and premature for impressionable adolescents and is likely to lead to promiscuity and increased rates of adolescent pregnancy. Some believe that sex education should be carried out only by parents in the privacy of the home (Conger, 1987). Others appear to have

Adolescents who report they are able to discuss sex freely and openly with their parents are less, rather than more, likely to be involved in sexual intercourse.

reached the awesome conclusion that contemporary adolescents have nothing left to learn about sex—certainly nothing their parents could teach them!

In the light of current statistics on adolescent premarital intercourse, pregnancy, and abortion, as well as the general social climate, it is difficult to see how sex education for adolescents could be viewed as premature (Hofferth, Kahn, & Baldwin, 1987; Hofferth & Miller, 1989; Zelnik & Kantner, 1979). Indeed, a recent nationwide study found that among young women who first had sex at age 15, only 58 percent had already taken or were currently taking a sex education course; for young men the comparable figure was even lower—only 26 percent (Marsiglio & Mott, 1986).

Moreover, despite the greater openness about sex in contemporary society, many parents still do not provide the knowledge their children need (Bell, 1987; Conger, 1987; Harris, 1987; Meikle, Peitchnis, & Pearce, 1985). In one survey adolescents were asked whether they had ever tried to talk openly with either of their parents about sex; 44 percent of boys and 54 percent of girls reported that they had done so at one time or another. When asked how the parents responded, a minority reported positive responses like that described by a 16-year-old girl:

> Whenever I have sexual problems or questions I often consult my parents (usually my mother, but sometimes my father too). Our views aren't always the same. Sometimes we feel very different about some things. However, whether we agree or disagree, it's always nice to know that they will always be there and give their opinion if I have a question (Hass, 1979, p. 177).

Or this from a 15-year-old boy:

> I feel I can be very open to them about sex because I know they would always try to help me. I know that not many kids can tell their parents anything, but I can. I know that if I did anything wrong, like getting a girl pregnant, they would be upset, but in the end they would help (Hass, 1979, p. 176).

More often, however, parents responded with denial, avoidance, teasing, or disapproval. Frequently the young person felt lectured to instead of listened to; in the words of a 15-year-old boy, "She [his mother] began to preach about what is right and what is wrong. She just didn't understand" (Hass, 1979, p. 176).

Interestingly, however, adolescents who report that they are able to discuss sex freely and openly with their parents are less likely to be involved in sexual intercourse. Of this group, those who are sexually active are less likely to become pregnant (Conger, 1987; Sorensen, 1973). Moreover, recent research has shown that sex education programs are associated with *better* communication with parents about pregnancy and conception (Dawson, 1986; Sex education, 1986).

The notion of some adults that adolescents have nothing left to learn about sex also is not supported by the facts. Even today many adolescents think they cannot become pregnant if it is their first intercourse, or if they do not have an

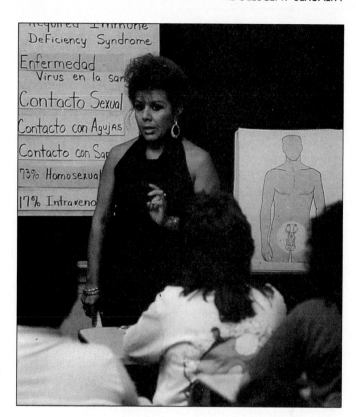

Despite the opposition of a vocal minority, school sex education programs enjoy widespread public support: 85 percent of parents favor sex education and think it fosters a healthy attitude toward sex.

orgasm, or do not want to become pregnant (Kantner & Zelnik, 1977; Meikle, Peitchnis, & Pearce, 1985; Morrison, 1985; Zelnik & Kantner, 1977, 1980). In one representative study, less than 40 percent of 15- to 19-year-old adolescent American girls clearly understood the relationship between pregnancy risk and the menstrual cycle; among those who had never had a sex education course, only 27 percent of 15- to 17-year-olds were correct (Hayes, 1987; Kantner & Zelnik, 1973).

There is also no consistent evidence that sex education, including contraceptive information, increases the likelihood that the adolescent will become sexually active (Kirby, 1988). On the other hand, there is considerable evidence that sexually active adolescents who have had *adequate* sex education (including instruction about contraception) are more likely to use effective birth control methods. In addition, teenagers who have had sex education courses are, if anything, less likely to become pregnant (Dawson, 1986; Marsiglio & Mott, 1986; Sex education, 1986).

Sexual Morality

In addition to greater openness and honesty, there is a growing tendency to view decisions about individual sexual behavior as a private rather than a public concern. In 1989 American high school seniors were asked how they felt about a man and woman living together without being married. About one in four said that the couple were experimenting with "a worthwhile alternate life style," and smaller minorities felt either that they were violating a basic principle of human morality or that they were living in a way that was destructive to society. In contrast, slightly over half expressed the view that the couple were "doing their own thing and not affecting anyone else" (Johnston, Bachman, & O'Malley, forthcoming). Among first-year college students surveyed in 1989, over half endorsed the proposition that people should live together before getting married, although as has been true in the past, there are significant differences between the sexes (57.3 percent of men versus 45.0 percent of women) (Astin et al., 1989).

In part, these trends appear to reflect a decline since the 1960s in the credibility and influence of established social, political, and religious institutions (Conger, 1981, 1988; Harris, 1987; Yankelovich, 1971, 1974, 1981). But it also appears to reflect greater emphasis on the quality of relationships. What many adolescents appear to be saying is that the morality of sexual behavior can often be judged not so much by the nature of the act itself as by its meaning to the individuals involved.

However, as we have already noted, adolescent girls continue to be more conservative than boys and to place greater emphasis on the nature of the relationship. For example, among American college freshmen in 1989, almost two-thirds of all males, but only a little over one-third of females, agreed with the statement, "Sex is okay if people like each other" (Astin et al., 1989). On the other hand, when there is deep involvement, as in living together prior to marriage, sex differences are smaller; only 32 percent of American adolescent girls and 21 percent of boys said that they would not do so (Norman & Harris, 1981).

When adolescents between the ages of 15 and 18 were asked, "Do you feel you have to be romantically involved with a girl (boy) before you have sexual contact with her (him)?" 68 percent of girls, but only 41 percent of boys, said yes (Hass, 1979). Most adolescents clearly oppose exploitation, pressure, or force in sex; sex solely for the sake of physical enjoyment; and sex between people who are too young to understand what they are getting into (Chilman, 1983; Conger, 1980; Darling et al., 1984; Dreyer, 1982).

Despite a growing emphasis among contemporary adolescents on openness, there is little evidence of an increased preoccupation with sex. Indeed, it may well be that the average adolescent is less preoccupied and concerned with sex than prior generations of young people. Greater acceptance of sex as a natural part of life may well lead to less preoccupation than did anxious concern in an atmosphere of secrecy and suppression. Nor has sex displaced or become synonymous with love in the eyes of most young people. Most adolescents (67–80 percent) disagree with the notion that the most important thing in a love relationship is sex, with older adolescents (both male and female) disagreeing more often than young adolescents (Hass, 1979; Norman & Harris, 1981; Sorensen, 1973). Interestingly, the percentage disagreeing is higher for nonvirgins than for virgins.

Finally, in ranking the relative importance of various goals, adolescents of both sexes stress such goals as having friends, being independent, doing well in school, preparing to accomplish things in life, getting along with parents, being romantically involved with someone, and athletics (Hass, 1979; Norman & Harris, 1981; Sorensen, 1973). In contrast, "having sex with someone" and "making out" consistently rank at or near the top among goals that are considered *least* important.

CHANGING VALUES AND SEXUAL BEHAVIOR

How are the continuing changes in sexual attitudes and values among contemporary adolescents reflected in behavior? The answer depends on what behaviors one is referring to, among which adolescents, and how recently.

Available information indicates that among boys the number who have engaged in masturbation by age 19 has remained fairly stable at around 85–90 percent since their parents' generation (Chilman, 1983; Conger, 1980; Masters et al., 1988). But it also appears that the number who have done so at younger ages is increasing significantly. In Kinsey's original sample, only 45 percent of males reported masturbating by age 13; in contrast, in more recent surveys that number had increased to between 52 and 65 percent (Hass, 1979; Hunt, 1974; Kinsey, Pomeroy, & Martin, 1948; Masters et al., 1988). Among girls, there has been an increase in masturbation at all age levels, with incidences in recent years of around 33 percent by age 13 (in contrast to 15 percent in Kinsey's original study) and between 60 and 75 percent by age 20 (compared to about 30 percent for their mothers at age 20) (Arafat & Cotton, 1974; Chilman, 1983; Hass, 1979; Kinsey et al., 1953; Masters et al., 1988).

Even with recent changes, however, girls appear to engage in masturbation during adolescence significantly less often than boys. Moreover, among adolescents who engage in masturbation, girls masturbate less frequently, on the average, though with wider interindividual variability (Chilman, 1983; Hass, 1979; Hunt, 1974; Sorensen, 1973). One might be tempted to conclude that masturbation would occur most commonly among adolescents who lack other sexual outlets. Interestingly, however, among contemporary adolescents masturbation occurs about three times as frequently among those engaged in sexual intercourse or petting to orgasm as among the sexually inexperienced.

Petting does appear to have increased somewhat in the past few decades, and it tends to occur at slightly earlier ages. The major change, however, has probably been in frequency of petting, intimacy of techniques involved, the frequency with which petting leads to erotic arousal or orgasm, and certainly, frankness about this activity (Conger, 1980; Luria et al., 1987; Vener & Stewart, 1974).

Premarital Sexual Intercourse

A topic of greater interest to adolescents and their parents, and a source of more controversy, is the extent of premarital sexual intercourse among contemporary adolescents. Until recently opinions on this subject were rife, but comprehensive data (except in the case of college students) were scarce. Consequently, as late as the mid-1970s some social observers were proclaiming a "sexual revolution" while others asserted that young people were actually no more sexually active than their parents, but simply more open and honest.

Recent national studies (both concurrent and retrospective) have made it clear that the youth revolution of the late 1960s did indeed lead to a transformation not only in sexual attitudes and values but in sexual behavior as well (Hofferth, 1987; Hofferth, Kahn, & Baldwin, 1987; London et al., 1989; Mott & Haurin, 1988; Sonenstein, Plack, & Ku, 1989; Zelnik & Kantner, 1980). For example, among American women who were teenagers in the late 1950s and early 1960s, slightly over 7 percent reported having had premarital sexual intercourse by age 16, and less than one-third had done so by age 19 (Hofferth, Kahn, & Baldwin, 1987). By 1971 the picture had changed significantly, with almost one in four 16-year-olds and about half of 19-year-olds reporting having had premarital intercourse (Brooks-Gunn & Furstenberg, 1989; Hofferth, Kahn, & Baldwin, 1987; Zelnik & Kantner, 1980).

In the intervening years, rates of intercourse among all unmarried 15–19-year-old female teenagers have continued to increase, so that by 1982, 30 percent of 16-year-olds and nearly three-fourths of 19-year-olds acknowledged having been sexually active (Hofferth, Kahn, & Baldwin, 1987; Moore, 1989). Although separate data for unmarried females are not yet available, preliminary findings from the 1988 *National Survey of Family Growth*, combining data on unmarried and married teenagers, appear to indicate that sexual activity increased between 1982 and 1988, particularly among white girls (London et al., 1989; see Table 7.1).

Overall changes are less dramatic for boys than for girls, and absolute incidence is higher, especially at younger ages. In a limited national survey conducted in the early 1970s, Robert Sorensen found that among teenage boys 44 percent reported having had intercourse by age 16 and 72 percent had done so by age 19 (Sorensen, 1973). By 1979, a majority (56 percent) of unmarried 17-year-olds and slightly over three-fourths (77 percent) of unmarried 19-year-olds reported having been sexually active (Zelnik & Kantner, 1980). By 1988, these percentages had increased to two-thirds of 17-year-olds and 86 percent of 19-year-olds (Sonenstein, Pleck, & Ku, 1989; see Table 7.2).

It is too early to predict the ultimate effects of the AIDS information campaign and programs to prevent adolescent pregnancy on the sexual attitudes and behavior of adolescents (Brooks-Gunn & Furstenberg, in press; Morgan, 1988; Task Force, 1989). However, the results of a 1988 national survey of adolescent males are interesting (Sonenstein et al., 1989). Although rates of sexual activity have continued to increase (see Table 7.2), condom use among sexually active 15–19-year-olds living in metropolitan areas increased from only 21 percent in 1979 to over 57 percent in 1988. Moreover, males whose first intercourse occurred in 1987–1988 were more than twice as likely to have used condoms in their most recent intercourse as those whose first intercourse occurred between 1975 and 1982. In brief, it appears that the widespread dissemination of information about AIDS since 1987 has begun to have a signifi-

T A B L E 7.1 PERCENT OF FEMALE TEENAGERS WHO HAVE EVER EXPERIENCED SEXUAL INTERCOURSE, BY RACE AND AGE, 1971–1988

	Whites						Blacks				
	Never-married teens			Never-married and married teens			Never-married teens			Never-married and married teens	
Age	1971	1976	1982	1982	1988	Age	1972	1976	1982	1982	1988
15	11%	14%	17%	18%	29%	15	31%	38%	28%	28%	26%
16	17%	23%	27%	29%	32%	16	46%	53%	41%	42%	46%
17	22%	36%	36%	40%	46%	17	59%	68%	55%	55%	69%
18	32%	44%	50%	55%	67%	18	63%	74%	76%	77%	69%
19	39%	49%	63%	69%	81%	19	76%	84%	81%	82%	81%

Source: Child Trends, Inc., 1989. M. Zelnik & J. F. Kantner, Sexual and contraceptive experience of young unmarried women in the United States, 1976 and 1971. *Family Planning Perspectives,* **9,** No. 2, March/April 1977, Table 1. National Center for Health Statistics, W. F. Pratt, W. D. Mosher, C. A. Bachrach, & M. C. Horn, Understanding U.S. fertility: Findings from the National Survey of Family Growth, Cycle III, *Population Bulletin,* **39,** No. 5, December 1984. Table 2. National Center for Health Statistics, K. A.London, W. D. Mosher, W. F. Pratt, & L. B. Williams, Preliminary findings from the National Survey of Family Growth, Cycle IV, March 1989.

Note: Data on never-married teens only are not yet available for 1988. Because of rapid changes in marriage patterns among teens during this time period, differences in sample definitions can affect conclusions about trends. Comparisons can safely be made only for never-married females between 1971 and 1982 and for females, both married and unmarried, between 1982 and 1988.

T A B L E 7.2 PERCENTAGES OF NEVER-MARRIED MALES AGED 15–19 WHO HAVE HAD SEXUAL INTERCOURSE, BY AGE, ACCORDING TO RACE/ETHNICITY, UNITED STATES, 1988

Age	All races (N = 1,880)	Black (N = 676)	White (N = 752)	Hispanic (N = 385)
15–19	**60.4**	**80.6**	**56.8**	**59.7**
15	32.6	68.6	25.6	32.8
16	49.9	70.1	46.7	47.2
17	65.6	89.6	59.1	87.6
18	71.6	82.5	71.4	52.8
19	85.7	95.9	84.5	82.2

Source: F. S. Sonenstein, J. H. Pleck, & L. C. Ku, Sexual activity, condom use and AIDS awareness among adolescent males. *Family Planning Perspectives,* 1989, **21,** 152–158, © 1989 The Alan Guttmacher Institute; based on data from K. Tanfer & L. Cope, *The national survey of adolescent males.* Philadelphia, PA: Institute for Survey Research, Temple University, 1989. By permission.

Notes: "All races" includes blacks, whites, Hispanics, and others. For each age except 19 years, racial differences were significant at $p < 0.001$; for the "All races" group, age differences were significant at $p < 0.001$ (chi-square).

cant effect (Brooks-Gunn & Furstenberg, in press; Sonenstein et al., 1989). Even in 1988, however, over 20 percent of males relied on female birth control methods without condoms, and another 20 percent used no contraceptive method at all (Sonenstein et al., 1989). Unfortunately, the lowest rates of use are reported by youth who engage in behaviors that put them at greater risk of contracting AIDS (Sonenstein et al., 1989; Tanfer & Cope, 1989).

Diversity of Sexual Attitudes and Behavior

Thus far we have focused on *overall* trends in sexual attitudes and behavior among contemporary adolescents and youth. Such trends have meaning and usefulness in their own right, but they should not deflect our attention from an equally important phenomenon: the diversity of sexual attitudes and behavior in different sectors of the adolescent and youth population. Such factors as age, sex, socioeconomic and educational level, race, religion, and even geographic area appear to be related to sexual attitudes, values, and behavior. For this reason, the results of almost any survey dealing with adolescent sexuality will inevitably seem exaggerated to some young people and adults, while others will view them as understated.

What do we know about some of these variations? First of all, we need to keep in mind that despite the "sexual revolution," many adolescents have not engaged in premarital sexual intercourse, including a majority of girls age 17 and under (Hofferth, Kahn, & Baldwin, 1987; London, 1989). Moreover, neither virgins nor nonvirgins constitute a homogeneous group. Thus, adolescents who have not had intercourse range from those with virtually no sexual experience to those with a variety of experiences short of intercourse, including petting to orgasm (Hass, 1979; Luria et al., 1987; Norman & Harris, 1981; Vener & Stewart, 1974).

Serial Monogamists and Sexual Adventurers. As we have already seen, female adolescents and youth continue to be more conservative than their male peers in attitudes, values, and behavior, although sex differences have narrowed. In a pioneering study of 13–19-year-olds, Robert Sorensen identified two major subgroups of nonvirgins: **serial monogamists** (the larger group), who generally had a relationship with only one partner over a period of time, and **sexual adventurers** (a much smaller group), who moved freely from one sexual partner to another and felt no obligation to be faithful to any one partner (Sorensen, 1973). Among the minority of adolescents who were sexual adventurers, 80 percent were male; in contrast, 64 percent of serial monogamists were female.

Not surprisingly, the two groups tended to vary significantly in attitudes as well as in behavior. Most monogamists believed that they loved and were loved by their partners, stressed openness and honesty between partners, and denied that sex was the most important thing in a love relationship—although they also expressed greater satisfaction with their sex lives than adventurers did. At the same time, their code emphasized personal freedom without commitment to marriage, although more than half believed that they would or might marry their partner eventually.

Sexual adventurers, in contrast, were primarily interested in variety of experience for its own sake, did not consider love to be a necessary part of sexual relationships, and felt no personal responsibility for their partners, although they did not believe in hurting others. For many adventurers, sex itself was viewed as an avenue to communication; as one young adventurer stated, "Having sex together is a good way for two people to become acquainted."

As a group, monogamists tended to be more satisfied with themselves and life in general, to get along better with their parents, and to be more conventional in their social, political, and religious beliefs. Despite their greater emphasis on sex as a goal in itself, female adventurers reported having orgasm during intercourse less frequently than monogamists.

Socioeconomic and Educational Status.

Economically privileged, more highly educated adolescents and youth are less conservative in their sexual attitudes and values (though not in their level of sexual activity) than less advantaged peers of the same age, although the differences appear to be decreasing (Chilman, 1983; Conger, 1980; Hayes, 1987) (see Chapter 13). Also, it is among economically favored college or college-bound adolescents and youth, especially females, that the greatest *changes* in sexual behavior have occurred. Prior to the mid-1960s the incidence of premarital experience among college seniors was about 55 percent for males and 25 percent for females. In contrast, several more recent investigations of American college and university students of comparable ages indicate a substantial upward shift for both sexes, but particularly among women (Chilman, 1983; Conger, 1980; Hayes, 1987; "Student survey," 1976). Thus, for males the incidence of premarital intercourse ranged up to a high of 82 percent; comparable percentages for females ranged up to a high of 76 percent. While the incidence for males appeared to reach a plateau in the early 1970s, the incidence for females continued to increase at least into the early 1980s.

Other factors are also related to sexual attitudes, values, and behavior. Younger adolescents are more conservative about sexual matters than older adolescents (Conger, 1980; Hass, 1979). Politically conservative and religiously oriented youth are more conservative in their sexual attitudes and behavior than liberal or religiously inactive young people (Chilman, 1983; Mussen, Conger, Kagan, & Huston, 1990).

Black adolescents, both male and female, are more active sexually than white adolescents (Hofferth, Kahn, & Baldwin, 1987; Kantner & Zelnik, 1972; Zelnik & Kantner, 1980). Interestingly, however, although the percentage of sexually active black females between the ages of 15 and 19 increased moderately between 1971 and 1979, it *declined* between 1979 and 1982, with the greatest decline occurring among younger adolescents (Hofferth, Kahn, & Baldwin, 1987). In contrast, among white females in the same age group the percentage who were sexually active rose steadily from 1971 to 1982 (Hofferth, Kahn, & Baldwin, 1987). Significant cultural differences also exist (Chilman, 1983; Christensen & Gregg, 1970; Jones et al., 1985). For both sexes, premarital intercourse is least common in Canada and most frequent in the Scandina-

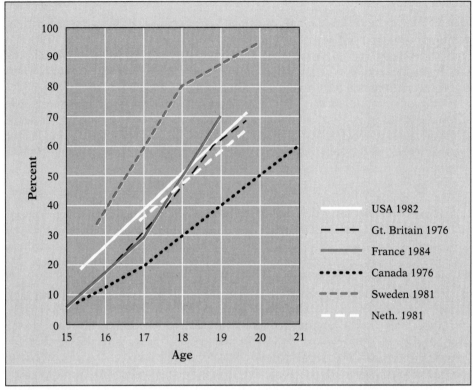

Figure 7.1 Percentage of women ever having had intercourse, by age. (from E. F. Jones, J. D. Forrest, N. Goldman, S. K. Henshaw, R. Lincoln, J. J. Rosoff, C. F. Wertoff, & D. Wulf. Teenage Pregnancy in developed countries: Determinants and policy implications. *Family planning perspectives*, 1985, **17**, 53–63. © 1985 The Alan Guttmacher Institute. By permission.)

vian countries, with the United States, Great Britain, and France falling in between (see Figure 7.1).

Influence of Parents and Peers

Farida Shah and Melvin Zelnik, population specialists at the Johns Hopkins University, used the data from a comprehensive survey of unmarried 15–19-year-old women in the United States to determine the influence of parents and peers on the views of the participants and to find out how that influence was related to premarital sexual behavior and other issues (Shah & Zelnik, 1981; Zelnik & Kantner, 1977, 1980). They found that on such issues as going to college and having a career, these young women were influenced more by parents than by friends. On the other hand, with respect to their attitudes toward premarital sex, their views resembled those of their friends much more than those of their parents. In sum, it appears that (1) while parents' views are more influential than those of peers on some issues (e.g., career plans), peer influence is clearly stronger for the average adolescent on attitudes toward premarital sex; (2) peer views are generally, but not always, more permissive than those of parents; and (3) black adolescents (and to a lesser extent their parents) are more permissive than whites. Other less comprehensive studies have yielded similar results.

In general, the attitudes of these adolescents were reflected in their sexual behavior. Thus, among those believing that premarital sex is acceptable whether one is engaged or not, 84 percent of blacks and 73.5 percent of whites had, in fact, had such experience. However, of those who viewed premarital sex as unacceptable under any circumstances, 24 percent of blacks and 7 percent of whites had nevertheless had some sexual experience. Rates of premarital sexual experience were lowest for young women whose views on sex before marriage were like their parents' views and highest for those with views like those of their friends (see Table 7.3). Moreover, particularly for whites, those with views like those of their parents were more likely to have had intercourse only once; they also were more likely to have had only one partner (Shah & Zelnik, 1981).

A "New Morality"

It seems clear that adolescent attitudes and values regarding sex, as well as their actual behavior, have changed dramatically since the early 1960s, although the extent of the change still varies widely among different segments of the youth population. There is a real danger in generalizing from specific subgroups (e.g., a particular college campus or small-town high school) to youth in general. Moreover, the greatest relative changes in both attitudes and behavior since their parents' generation have occurred among middle- and upper-class adolescents, particularly girls. Not surprisingly, it is among this more advantaged segment of the youth population that the "youth culture" of the 1960s initially took root.

T A B L E 7.3 PERCENTAGE OF 15- TO 19-YEAR-OLD WOMEN WITH PREMARITAL SEXUAL EXPERIENCE, BY SIMILARITY OF VIEWS ON SEX TO SIGNIFICANT OTHERS, BY RACE

Views on sex like:	Black		White	
	Percentage	N	Percentage	N
Parents	50.5	103	17.1	286
Friends	69.4	359	54.0	654
Both	63.1	65	28.4	225
Neither	63.0	154	34.6	301
All	64.5	681	38.9	1466

Source: F. Shah and M. Zelnik. Parent and peer influence on sexual behavior, contraceptive use, and pregnancy experience of young women. *Journal of Marriage and the Family,* 1981, **43,** 339–348. By permission.

Adolescent attitudes and values regarding sex have changed dramatically since the 1960s. Today adolescents are likely to base their decision about appropriate sexual behavior more on personal values than on institutionalized social codes.

Although the "new morality" of today's adolescents has many positive aspects—greater emphasis on openness, more mutual respect and less exploitation, and a more natural and somewhat better-informed approach to sex—it would be a mistake to conclude that the picture is unclouded. Many experienced adolescents, particularly older adolescents and youth, appear to be able to handle their sexual involvement and relationships without undue stress. However, significant minorities report feelings of conflict and guilt, feel exploited or rejected, or discover belatedly that they have gotten in over their heads emotionally (Bell, 1987; Goodchilds & Zellman, 1984; Morrison, 1985). Especially after the first experience of intercourse, girls are far more likely to experience negative feelings (Haas, 1979; Norman & Harris, 1981; Sorensen, 1973). Whereas boys are most likely to report being excited, satisfied, and happy, many girls report being afraid, guilty, worried, or embarrassed after their first intercourse.

There are obviously dangers in assuming that sexual involvement is "okay as long as you're in love." Encouraged by such a philosophy among peers, a young person may become more deeply involved emotionally than she or he can handle responsibly at his or her stage of maturity. An adolescent may also consciously think that his or her attitudes are more liberal than they actually are, and sexual involvement may lead to unanticipated feelings of guilt, anxiety, or depression.

PREGNANCY AND CONTRACEPTION

There are also some very practical problems associated with adolescent sexuality. Foremost of these are the possibility of pregnancy and the risk of contracting sexually transmitted diseases, including those for which there is currently no cure, such as genital herpes and—most tragically—AIDS (Furstenberg, Brooks-Gunn, & Chase-Landale, 1989; Task Force, 1989). Despite significant progress during the previous decade, among female adolescents who were sexually active in 1982 less than half consistently used some form of contraception—compared to approximately one-third in 1979 and a little over one-fourth in 1976 (Hayes, 1987; Zelnik & Kantner, 1980; see Table 7.4). Compared to younger adolescents (age 15), older adolescents (age 19) are twice as likely to have used contraceptives in their last intercourse (*Teenage pregnancy*, 1981; Zelnik & Kantner, 1977, 1980).

As a result of the widespread lack of proper contraceptive measures, together with current levels of premarital intercourse among adolescents, well over 1 million 15–19-year-old girls in the United States alone (about 11 percent of this age group) are becoming pregnant each year (Hayes, 1987; Hofferth, 1987). If contraceptive use had not increased in the past decade, these figures would have been even higher. (Two-thirds of these pregnancies are conceived out of wedlock.) In addition, 125,000 girls under the age of 15 are becoming pregnant each year, a rate far higher than in any other developed country (Edelman, 1987; Hayes, 1987) (see Box 7.1). More than one-third of sexually active adolescent girls become pregnant at some time during their adolescent years (Jones et al., 1987; Trussell, 1988; Zelnik & Kantner, 1980).

T A B L E 7.4 PERCENTAGE DISTRIBUTION OF SEXUALLY ACTIVE GIRLS AGES 15–19, BY CONTRACEPTIVE USE

	1982[a]			1979[b]			1976[b]		
Contraceptive use	Total (N = 945)	White (N = 579)	Black (N = 342)	Total (N = 937)	White (N = 478)	Black (N = 459)	Total (N = 724)	White (N = 349)	Black (N = 375)
Always used	48.2	52.1	36.0	34.2	35.0	31.2	28.7	28.9	28.0
Used at first intercourse but not always				14.7	16.1	9.7	9.5	10.1	8.1
Did not use at first intercourse but used at some time	37.2	34.9	43.7	24.5	24.9	23.3	26.3	28.6	20.2
Never used	14.6	13.0	20.3	26.6	24.0	35.9	35.5	32.4	43.7
Total	100.0	100.0	100.0	100.0	100.0	100.0	100.0	100.0	100.0

Source: D. Hayes (Ed.) (1987). *Risking the future: Adolescent sexuality, pregnancy, and childbearing,* Vol. 1. Based on unpublished tabulations from the 1982 National Survey of Family Growth: M. Zelnik & J. F. Kanter, 1980, "Sexual activity, contraceptive use, and pregnancy among metropolitan-area teenagers: 1971–1976," *Family Planning Perspectives,* **12,** September/October, © 1980 The Alan Guttmacher Institute. By permission.

[a]All women 15–19 sexually active, including married women.
[b]Premaritally sexually active women 15–19; contraceptive use refers to use prior to pregnancy, marriage, or time of survey, whichever event was earliest.

In the United States alone, over 1 million 15–19-year-old girls (about 11 percent of this age group) are becoming pregnant each year. If contraceptive use had not increased in the past decade, this figure would be even higher.

The consequences of this epidemic of adolescent pregnancies are serious indeed. In 1984, 47 percent of pregnant adolescents gave birth, while 40 percent had induced abortions; the remainder miscarried (Jones et al., 1987). Even when pregnancy occurs after marriage (i.e., in 27 percent of adolescent pregnancies), such problems are more frequent among adolescents than among older women.

Adolescent pregnancies are more likely to endanger the physical health of both mother and child, although the risks could be reduced substantially if more adequate prenatal and postnatal care, and better nutrition, were provided to all pregnant adolescents. In fact, several investigations have shown that older adolescents who bear children fare no worse (in terms of maternal and infant health outcomes) than other age groups, once social class and quality of care are controlled (Edelman, 1987; Gunter & LaBarba, 1980; Petersen & Boxer, 1982). At present, however, young teenage mothers are least likely to receive prenatal care, and their babies are most likely to have low birthweights (Hughes, Johnson, Rosenbaum, & Lin, 1989) (see Table 7.5). Low birthweight, in turn, is a major cause of infant mortality as well as neurological defects and

┌───┐
Box 7.1 TEENAGE PREGNANCY IN DEVELOPED COUNTRIES

A recent study by the Alan Guttmacher Institute has found that the United States leads nearly all developed countries in the incidence of adolescent pregnancy and childbearing (see Figures B7.1a and B7.1b). This holds true even for Western industrialized nations with comparable levels of sexual activity (Jones et al., 1985; Jones, Forrest, Henshaw, Silverman, & Torres, 1988). Pregnancy rates for white U.S. adolescents alone are higher than those in most other industrialized countries. Particularly troubling is the fact that the maximum difference in birthrates between the United States and other countries occurs among the most vulnerable adolescents, girls under 15; moreover, the United States is the only developed country in which rates of adolescent pregnancy have *increased* in recent years.

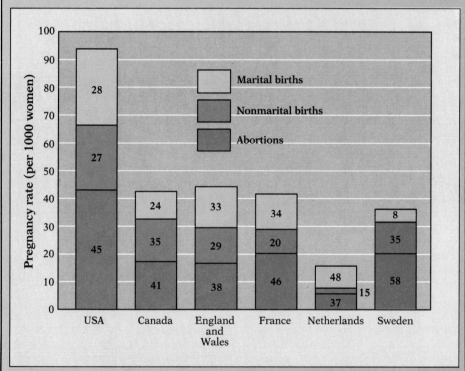

Figure B7.1a Pregnancy rates per 1,000 women by woman's age, 1981.

Opponents of preventive measures such as sex education and access to counseling and contraceptive services for sexually active adolescents have asserted that such measures would further increase already high rates of adolescent pregnancy, abortion, and childbearing. Ironically, the Guttmacher Institute study found just the opposite. The countries with the most

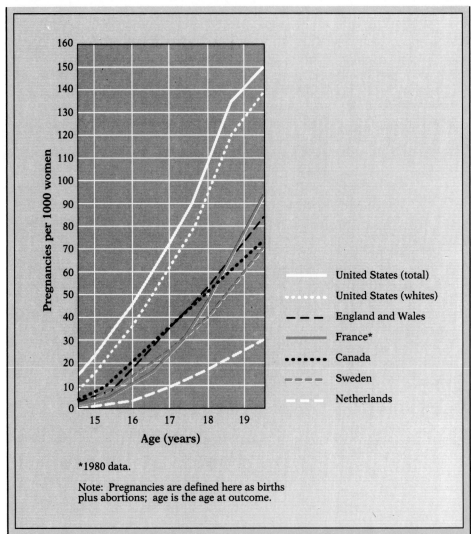

Figure B7.1b Percentage distribution of pregnancies, and pregnancy rates, by outcome, for women age 15–19, 1980–1981.

open and straightforward attitudes toward sex, the most effective formal and informal programs of sex education, and the most accessible counseling and contraceptive services for adolescents have the *lowest* rates of teenage pregnancy, abortion, and childbearing.

childhood illnesses. Adolescent mothers are also more likely to have complications of pregnancy such as toxemia and anemia. Among very young teenagers, pregnancy tends to deplete nutritional requirements needed for the girl's own growth, and this places her at higher risk for a variety of illnesses (Edelman, 1987; *Eleven million teenagers,* 1978; Hughes et al., 1989).

In addition, teenage mothers—90 percent of whom keep their babies—generally face significant problems in other areas. They are twice as likely as their peers to drop out of school, less likely to gain employment, and more likely to end up on welfare (Furstenberg, 1976; Furstenberg et al., 1989; Furstenberg, Brooks-Gunn, & Morgan, 1987; Hayes, 1987). Many still need mothering themselves and are ill prepared to take on the psychological, social, and economic responsibilities of motherhood (Osofsky, 1990). Their knowledge of an infant's needs and capabilities is often unrealistic, leading to expectations and demands that their infants cannot meet (see pages 200–201). Because of their immaturity and the greater stress to which they are subjected, adolescent mothers are more likely to abuse their children. Moreover, a single adolescent mother has less chance of getting married than her peers, and a much greater chance of divorce if she does marry (Furstenberg et al., 1986, 1989). Even adolescents who are already married when they become pregnant, or who marry prior to the birth of their child, have a far higher divorce rate than those who become mothers after age 20 (see pages 313–314).

This is not to say that all adolescent mothers are doomed to failure. In a seventeen-year study of young and poor black teenage mothers in Baltimore, one-quarter eventually were able, with appropriate health counseling and educational services, to make it into the middle class, though seldom without a struggle (Furstenberg et al., 1987, 1989). Those who stayed in school, who postponed second births, whose parents had a tenth-grade education or better, and who married were more likely to succeed economically and vocationally than other young mothers. "When asked how well they were doing at the 17-year follow-up, 48 percent of married women with fewer than 3 children who had completed high school replied 'very well'; only 2 percent said 'not so well' or 'not well at all.' In contrast, the percentage for unmarried dropouts with 3 or more children who were doing very well was 29 percent, and 11 percent indicated they were 'not so well or not well at all'" (Furstenberg et al., 1989, p. 316).

T A B L E 7.5 BIRTH OUTCOME AND PRENATAL CARE, BY AGE, UNITED STATES, 1986

	Under age 15	Ages 15–19	Ages 20–24	All women
Percentage of babies born at low birthweight (5.5 pounds or less)	13.8	9.3	7.0	6.8
Percentage of babies born to mothers who received early prenatal care	36.1	53.4	70.7	75.9
Percentage of babies born to mothers who received late or no prenatal care	20.8	12.5	7.4	6.9

Source: National Center for Health Statistics; Children's Defense Fund, 1989.

Reasons for Failure to Use Contraceptives. In several surveys, the main reasons given by adolescents for failure to use contraceptives were: (1) they (usually mistakenly) thought they could not become pregnant because of time of month, age, or infrequency of intercourse; or (2) contraceptives were not available when they needed them (Chilman, 1983; Morrison, 1985; Zelnick & Kantner, 1977). As we shall see, the former set of reasons could be remedied with better education, the latter with more adequate service programs (*Teenage pregnancy*, 1981).

Psychological studies comparing sexually active adolescent girls who do and do not use contraceptives (or use them rarely) have found that those who do not use contraceptives tend to hold fatalistic attitudes: They are more likely to feel unable to control their own lives, have a low sense of personal competence, and take a passive, dependent approach to male–female relationships. They are also more inclined to take risks and to cope with anxiety by attempting to deny possible dangers rather than facing up to them (Chilman, 1983).

Some adolescents avoid contraceptive use because they are afraid it will spoil the spontaneity of the relationship or because they think it would indicate that they expected to have intercourse. Since the frank pursuit of sexual relations is still considered to be more acceptable for boys than for girls (Goodchilds & Zellman, 1984; Santrock, 1987), for a significant number of adolescents it is more acceptable for a girl to be swept away by the passion of the moment than to use contraception (Morrison, 1985). Interestingly, girls who frankly accept their sexuality and girls who are able to discuss sexual matters easily with their parents are more likely to use contraceptives than those who deny their sexuality to themselves or others (Brooks-Gunn & Furstenberg, 1989; Chilman, 1983, 1986; Conger, 1987; Hayes, 1987; Hornick, Doran, & Crawford, 1979).

Consistent contraceptive use is more likely to occur among female adolescents who are older, are in love and involved in an ongoing relationship, have high self-esteem and self-confidence, are making normal progress in school, have positive attitudes toward their parents, and received sex education early and at home, rather than from an acquaintance (Chilman, 1983, 1986; Goldfarb et al., 1977; Hornick, Doran, & Crawford, 1979; Kelley, 1979; Zelnik & Kantner, 1977, 1978, 1980).

Among male adolescents, those who are most likely to employ contraceptive measures are older, more experienced in dating, and better organized and more responsible in their general approach to life; in addition, their parents are more likely to approve of their sexual activity. Males who are least likely to employ contraception tend to be either sexually naive or permissively reared and "exploitive," believing that contraception is the female's responsibility (Chilman, 1983; Goldfarb et al., 1977; Hornick, Doran, & Crawford, 1979; Kelley, 1979).

Desire for Pregnancy. Contrary to popular opinion, only one in fifteen pregnant adolescents fails to use contraceptives because she is trying to have a baby, and only one in eleven "didn't mind" getting pregnant (Chilman, 1983;

Eleven million teenagers, 1976; Hayes, 1987). However, among adolescents seeking or not objecting to pregnancy, a common theme is emotional deprivation. In the words of one pregnant 15-year-old, "I guess for once in my life, I wanted to have something I could call my own, that I could love and that would love me." Other related motivations include being accepted as an adult, getting back at one's parents, "holding" a boyfriend, gaining attention from peers, escaping from school, or just looking for a change in an unrewarding existence.

In discussing the results of a study of adolescent pregnancy in thirty-seven developed countries (see Box 7.1, page 257), the Alan Guttmacher Institute reported that "in every country, when respondents were pressed to describe the kind of young woman who would be most likely to bear a child, the answer was the same: economically and emotionally deprived adolescents who unrealistically seek gratification and fulfillment in a child of their own" (Guttmacher Institute, quoted in *Adolescent pregnancy*, 1986, p. 3).

Box 7.2 PREVENTING ADOLESCENT PREGNANCY

Much can be done to reduce the high rate of adolescent pregnancy, but only if the problem is approached realistically. Sloganeering, scapegoating, and self-righteous moralizing will not solve the problem, and there are no quick fixes or magic bullets waiting to be discovered (Edelman, 1987; Hayes, 1987). Nevertheless, collective action and willingness to be creative can make a major difference:

1. *Sex Education and Family Life Planning.* First, we need age-appropriate family life education, including sex education beginning in the early school years, for all children and adolescents. Adolescents in particular need to be told the facts about sexuality and parenthood; even more important, they need help "in integrating that information into their thinking about themselves and their futures" (Edelman, 1987, p. 58). And we need to encourage much greater participation by parents in these efforts.

2. *Access to Contraceptive Methods.* In addition to more comprehensive, integrated sex education and family life planning, sexually active adolescents need access to contraceptive methods. In many instances these needs can best be met by adolescent clinics, both within and outside the school setting, that provide comprehensive, high-quality, easily accessible health services for adolescents and preadolescents (*Adolescent pregnancy*, 1986; Dryfoos, 1988; Schorr, 1981; see pages 106–108). Although school-based clinics providing comprehensive health services constitute only a small percentage of all adolescent clinics, and although less than one-third of school clinics dispense contraceptives, some of those that do have produced some encouraging results.

At four of the oldest clinics, located in St. Paul, Minnesota, the overall annual rate of first-time pregnancies has been reduced from 80 to 35 per 1000, while repeat pregnancies have been reduced to only 1.4 percent, com-

Figure B7.2 One of the Children's Defense Fund's current activities is a five-year multimedia campaign to reduce the incidence of teenage pregnancy. (Reproduced with permission of the Children's Defense Fund, 1989.)

pared to 33 percent nationally (*Adolescent pregnancy*, 1986; Dryfoos, 1988; Kirby, 1985). One of the great advantages of adolescent clinics is that sexuality in all its aspects can be dealt with in the context of overall health care by a staff that is attuned to the special needs and concerns of this age group.

3. *The Life Options Approach.* Better sex education and family-planning services alone will not solve the problem of adolescent pregnancy, particularly for high-risk adolescents. Motivation to avoid pregnancy is also essential. Such motivation can come only when young people feel good about themselves and have a "clear vision of a successful and self-sufficient future" (Edelman, 1987, p. 58). This requires opportunities to build academic and work-related skills, job opportunities, life-planning assistance, and comprehensive health and mental-health services (*Adolescent pregnancy*, 1986; Edelman, 1987; Hayes, 1987).

An excellent example of the kind of approach that is needed is provided by the Children's Defense Fund's Agenda for Adolescent Pregnancy Prevention and Youth Self-Sufficiency (*Adolescent pregnancy*, 1986; Edelman, 1987). This program, which was developed in collaboration with other citizen groups across the nation, calls on federal, state, and local governments to provide more comprehensive sex education and life-planning programs in the schools. "But it further advocates establishing or strengthening vocational scholarships, community learning centers, job creation, school dropout prevention, adolescent health service, and after-school care for 10- to 15-year-olds" (*Adolescent pregnancy*, 1987). One of the CDF's current activities is a five-year multimedia campaign to increase public awareness of the problems created by teenage pregnancy (Edelman, 1987; see posters).

According to Marian Wright Edelman, president of CDF, "We need investments in young people that will enable them not only to make responsible decisions but to move along a steady path toward self-sufficiency" (*Adolescent pregnancy*, 1987, p. 4).

SEXUAL BEHAVIOR AND ADOLESCENT ADJUSTMENT

Masturbation

There are wide cultural differences in attitudes toward masturbation and in masturbatory behavior. Among the Apinaye of northeastern South Africa, for example, boys and girls "are warned from infancy not to masturbate and a severe thrashing awaits the child suspected of such behavior" (Ford & Beach, 1951, p. 180). In contrast, in some societies adults have actively participated in the sexual stimulation of infants and young children. In the United States and many other developed Western countries, masturbation has traditionally been condemned, often "as a perversion on a par with homosexual relations" (Ford, 1961, p. 308). Even at the turn of the century, many prominent physicians and teachers, as well as health publications of the United States government, warned that masturbation could weaken the individual or cause a variety of diseases, and that it might even result in insanity if practiced to excess (Kiell, 1964; Masters et al., 1988). Despite such warnings, most boys (and a much smaller number of girls) continued to engage in this activity, so it is not difficult to imagine the widespread anxiety, conflict, and depression that frequently ensued—in some cases even resulting in suicide.

Since that time public attitudes and the views of experts on sexual behavior have changed markedly. In a survey of 15- and 16-year-olds conducted in the late 1970s, 76 percent of boys and 70 percent of girls said that "it is okay for a boy (girl) my age to masturbate" (Haas, 1979). Among 17- and 18-year-olds, agreement increased to 85 percent for boys and 72 percent for girls. Nevertheless, many adolescents continue to have at least occasional feelings of guilt, anxiety, or depression about masturbation. In the words of one 15-year-old girl,

> When I was really little, my best girlfriend and I would sleep over at each other's house and we'd masturbate together in the same room. We even had our own name for it. We certainly didn't think there was anything wrong with what we were doing: It was just something we did that felt good. But in about fourth grade I found out more about sex and I realized that masturbating was *sexual*. Then, as far as I was concerned, it was definitely not OK to do anymore—especially not with somebody else in the same room. After that I used to feel guilty when I was doing it, like it was kind of humiliating, and I tried to stop myself. Then last year when I heard from a lot of my girlfriends that they do it too, I felt better about it (Bell, 1987, p. 83).

Investigators of sexual behavior among adolescents and adults still find that participants have more difficulty discussing masturbation than any other sexual topic (Luria et al., 1987). And there are still clinicians who, while avoiding the dire predictions of yesteryear, nevertheless assert that masturbation among children or adolescents is likely to make it difficult to engage in heterosexual sexual activities at a later stage of development.

What is the actual evidence? In boys, predictions that masturbation would seriously impair physical and psychological health have been clearly demonstrated to be erroneous, since the practice is virtually universal. Moreover, in the absence of previously acquired guilt or anxiety, masturbation may be enjoyable and may serve to reduce tension (Bell, 1987). It may also provide an opportunity to rehearse responses that will be required in heterosexual intercourse and to establish associations between appropriate cues (actual or fantasied) and sexual responses (Barbach, 1976; Comfort & Comfort, 1979; Masters et al., 1988; Sadock, 1985).

The opportunity to learn techniques of sexual arousal may be valuable for girls as well, since the relatively automatic arousal and subsequent orgasm that occurs among boys does not take place as readily among many girls. Experts on sexual response have found that orgasmic adequacy among females depends not only on the absence of culturally or parentally invoked patterns of anxiety and conflict but also on the learning and practicing of appropriate techniques—whether through masturbation or with a heterosexual partner, or both (Kaplan, 1979; Kinsey, Pomeroy, & Martin, 1948, 1953; Masters et al., 1988; Masters & Johnson, 1966, 1970). Sex therapists have been able to successfully treat orgasmic dysfunction in women, largely through training in methods of sexual arousal and anxiety reduction.

It is sometimes argued that masturbation, though not physically harmful, may be psychologically maladaptive because it may lead to a preoccupation with sex. However, preoccupation with sex is far more likely to result from constant, conflict-ridden attempts to avoid masturbation, particularly for males. At the same time, there can be little doubt that in some instances masturbation may be related to problems of adolescent adjustment. The adolescent whose masturbatory activities serve as a substitute for other activities in which he or she feels inadequate has a problem. So does the adolescent who engages in masturbation as a substitute for efforts to establish pleasant and meaningful social relations with opposite-sex peers. But in each of these instances the masturbatory activity is not primarily a *cause* of the individual's problems but, rather, a *response* to them.

Petting and Premarital Intercourse

Premarital experience in petting to orgasm may perform many of the functions that are ascribed to masturbation. Kinsey found that among females who had never engaged in petting to orgasm prior to marriage, slightly over one-third did not reach orgasm during the first year of marriage. In contrast, among those "who had reached orgasm in at least some of their premarital petting, only 10 percent had failed to achieve it in the first year of marriage. Similar differences were apparent for some 15 years after marriage" (Kinsey et al., 1953, p. 265).

Similarly, more than 50 percent of females in Kinsey's investigation who had had premarital intercourse that led to orgasm reached orgasm in virtually all their experiences of marital intercourse during the first year of marriage. Among those who had not had any premarital experience of intercourse and had not reached orgasm from any source before marriage, less than one-third "had approached a 100 percent response in the first year of marriage" (Kinsey et al., 1953, p. 329).

These correlations may have depended on selective factors, at least to some extent. Females who had abstained before marriage may have been physiologically less responsive to begin with. However, it also appears likely, in view of the therapeutic experiences of Masters and Johnson and others, that the experiences themselves promoted learning of sexual responsiveness to appropriate stimuli (Masters et al., 1988; Master & Johnson, 1966, 1970).

Petting to orgasm can give young people who are ready for an intimate relationship an opportunity to obtain mutual pleasure and release of tension without having to worry about pregnancy, if they are careful. On the other hand, premarital sexual experiences for which the individual is emotionally unprepared, that arouse guilt and anxiety, or that are traumatic in themselves or lead to unfortunate consequences may inhibit rather than facilitate the young person's capacity for successful response after marriage.

HOMOSEXUALITY AND HETEROSEXUALITY

Many young people fail to distinguish between homosexual *experience* and **homosexuality** (or, more accurately, a primarily homosexual *orientation*). Because they have had sexually tinged fantasies or dreams about a member of the same sex, have engaged in mutual sexual experimentation, or had a crush on a teacher or friend, they conclude that they are gay (Bell, 1987). And in a society in which many people still have a strong fear of homosexuality and gay males and lesbians are often viewed as immoral or "sick," this conclusion can lead to considerable anxiety, to the formation of defenses such as asceticism or masochistic self-denial, or even, on occasion, to suicide. Indeed, both male and female homosexual adolescents attempt suicide much more often than their heterosexual peers (*Report,* 1989b).

In reality, such concerns are usually groundless. Although many young people have had experiences like those just described, most of them go on to establish satisfying heterosexual adjustments. Among preadolescents, sex play with both same- and opposite-sex peers may involve pleasurable sexual stimulation, but it is usually motivated primarily by curiosity. Among adolescents, a significant number of boys and a much smaller percentage of girls have at least occasional active sexual contacts with others of the same sex (Bell, 1987; Chilman, 1983; Hunt, 1974; Kinsey et al., 1948). In one national study, 5 percent of boys age 13–15, and 17 percent of those age 16–19, reported having had some kind of homosexual experience (Sorensen, 1973). Among girls, 6 percent of those age 13–15, and a like percentage of those age 16–19, reported having had homosexual experiences (Sorensen, 1973).

An extensive study of homosexual and heterosexual adults by investigators at the Kinsey Institute for Sex Research suggests that having *predominantly or exclusively homosexual feelings* in childhood and adolescence is more closely related to the adoption of a homosexual orientation in adulthood than having had *homosexual experiences* during the developmental years (Bell & Weinberg, 1978; Bell, Weinberg, & Hammersmith, 1981). For example, among white males 21 percent of heterosexuals had engaged in mutual masturbation with other males prior to age 19, and a considerably larger number (51 percent) had been involved in some kind of sex play. Eighty-four percent of homosexuals had engaged in mutual masturbation; however, because there are so many fewer gay persons in the population, the total number of heterosexuals having such experience is far greater than the number of homosexuals.

In contrast, when both groups were asked whether their sexual feelings during childhood and adolescence were predominantly homosexual, 59 percent of homosexuals and only 1 percent of heterosexuals replied that they were. It is important to keep in mind the influence that an individual's current situation may have on a retrospective report. However, because these differences are so large, it seems unlikely that they would have resulted primarily from retrospective bias.

Similar results were obtained among white females, although the overall incidence of homosexual activity was far less. Four percent of heterosexuals reported having engaged in mutual masturbation prior to age 19, compared to 41 percent of homosexuals. As with males, however, the principal characteristic distinguishing those who became homosexual as adults from those who became heterosexual was whether their sexual feelings during childhood and adolescence had been predominantly homosexual (44 percent versus 1 percent). In brief, although homosexual adults are more likely than heterosexuals to have had homosexual experiences in childhood and adolescence, the predominance of homosexual over heterosexual feelings during this developmental period is a considerably better predictor of adult homosexuality.

While most young people (including many who have had some sort of sexual involvement with members of the same sex during childhood and adolescence) develop a heterosexual orientation as adults, a minority do not. Contemporary investigations suggest that about 2–3 percent of males and about 1–2 percent of females are more or less exclusively homosexual after adolescence, although perhaps 10–12 percent of males and about half that number of females have had at least one homosexual experience beyond age 19 (Chilman, 1983; Hunt, 1974).

In the 1970s a national sample of college students was asked to indicate sexual preferences. Ninety-three percent of the males and 91 percent of the females stated that they had an exclusive interest in the opposite sex; an additional 4 percent of the males and 5 percent of the females said that they were interested mostly in the opposite sex (Chilman, 1983; "Student survey," 1971, 1976). Only 1 percent of the males and 2 percent of the females indicated an exclusive interest in the same sex. The remainder reported equal interest in either sex or an interest mostly in the same sex. These figures are remarkably consistent with the results of a reanalysis of Kinsey's data on college males obtained more than thirty years ago, which indicated that only about 5 or 6 percent had any real homosexual experience after late adolescence.

In sum, contrary to the assertion of some social critics that greater freedom in discussing homosexuality and increased tolerance for homosexual preference is leading to an increase in the number of persons with a predominantly homosexual orientation, it appears clear that the incidence of homosexuality, if it has not diminished since Kinsey's time, has not demonstrably increased (Chilman, 1983; Hunt, 1974).

Nature Versus Nurture

How can homosexual orientations, either exclusive or partial, be understood? Are they primarily a result of nature (e.g., chromosomal or hormonal deviations) or of nurture (e.g., sex role or gender training, atypical parent–child relationships, unusual sociopsychological experiences), or some combination of the two?

Each of these positions has its advocates. In their book *Homosexuality in Perspective,* Masters and Johnson maintain that homosexuality is a result of learning—a view that is also endorsed by Kinsey and others (Beach, 1965; Kinsey, Pomeroy, & Martin, 1948; Masters & Johnson, 1979). In this view, sex drive, especially in humans, is not initially attached inflexibly to any particular object. Consequently, an individual's sexual potential can be channeled in either a homosexual or a heterosexual direction by various learning experiences.

In contrast, a number of other investigators assert that homosexuality has its roots in hormonal or other biological factors (Beach, 1977; Dorner, 1976; Gladue, Green, & Hellman, 1984; Katchadourian, 1987). Even among Kinsey's successors this view finds some support; in a recent Kinsey Institute study of the development of sexual preference in men and women the investigators conclude that "our findings are not inconsistent with what one would expect if, indeed, there were a biological basis for sexual preference" (Bell, Weinberg, & Hammersmith, 1981, p. 216). Still others find support for an "interactionist" view, in which biological predisposition, parental behaviors, and social experience interact to foster the development of a heterosexual orientation (Green, 1987).

We still have a great deal to learn about sexual preference, and it seems unlikely that definitive answers regarding the relative roles of nature and nurture in the development of homosexual (and, indeed, heterosexual) behavior will be found quickly. Nevertheless, recent research has provided some clarification of the issues.

Biological Influences on Sexual Orientation

A number of investigations suggest that prenatal hormonal influences may affect sexual and other behavior. In several species of lower animals, male and female sexual behavior is largely controlled by particular brain centers (in the area of the hypothalamus) that mature before or shortly after birth. If androgens (male hormones) are available during the maturation process (as in the case of normal male development), these brain centers become masculinized. However, if androgens "are not available during the maturing process, the hypothalamic centers which control sexual behavior mature in a feminine manner and the animal after puberty exhibits essentially female sexual behavior—even in the presence of male hormones" (Brecher, 1971, p. 250). On the other hand, when female guinea pigs were administered male hormones prenatally, they subsequently exhibited male copulatory behavior during adolescence and adulthood. Similarly, immature female rhesus monkeys that were exposed to androgens before birth adopted relatively masculine patterns of infant and youthful play (Harlow, 1965).

No such dramatic and clear-cut effects have been observed to date in humans (in whom learning presumably plays a relatively greater role than biologically predetermined behavior patterns). However, in several studies in which girls received excess androgens prenatally (either as a result of drugs administered to the mother or because of a genetic abnormality), the girls exhibited a higher incidence of "masculine" behaviors than their female peers (Ehrhardt & Baker, 1975; Ehrhardt & Money, 1967; Green, 1980; Money & Schwartz, 1977). Thus, in one study girls with adrenogenital syndrome (AGS), a genetic defect resulting in an excess of prenatal androgens, showed higher levels of rough-and-tumble play, initiation of fighting, and preference for boys as playmates than a control group of unaffected female siblings (Ehrhardt & Baker, 1975). They also appeared less interested in babies and more interested in jobs and careers. In another investigation adolescent girls with fetal hormonal androgenization were likely to begin dating later than their peers and reported difficulty in forming romantic attachments (Money & Schwartz, 1977). Such findings suggest that deviant hormonal or other biological factors may sometimes play a role in fostering personality characteristics and drive patterns that are more typical of one sex than of the other (Bermant & Davidson, 1974; Katchadourian, 1989; Money & Ehrhardt, 1972).

Hormonal Factors. Recently several investigators have explored the effects of estrogen (female hormone) on the production of luteinizing hormone (LH), a basic hormone produced by the anterior pituitary gland, which plays an important role in the reproductive cycle in females and in the stimulation of testosterone production in males, among other functions (Dorner et al., 1975; Gladue, Green, & Hellman, 1984; Green, 1980). Typically, when estrogen is administered to females, there is an initial drop in LH followed by a return *above the original level*. In males, the return is only to the original level.

In one study, estrogen was administered to homosexual and heterosexual males and to heterosexual females. The homosexual males' response was intermediate between that of the heterosexual females and that of the heterosexual males (see Figure 7.2). However, until such investigations are repeated and extended they cannot be considered conclusive.

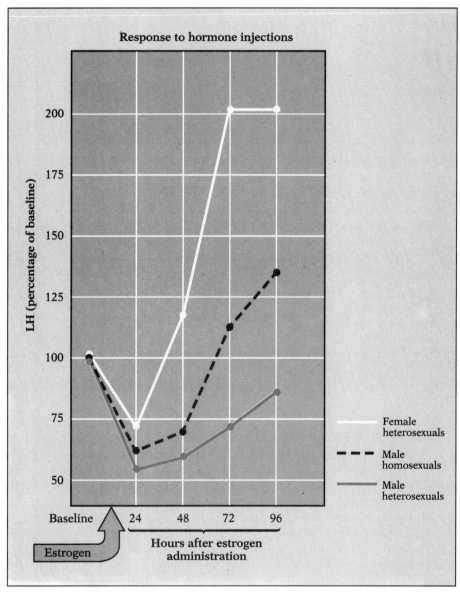

Figure 7.2 Luteinizing hormone (LH) responses to estrogen injections in female heterosexuals, male homosexuals, and male heterosexuals. The responses of male homosexuals were intermediate between those of female and male heterosexuals. (From B. A. Gladue, R. Green, & R. E. Hellman, Neuroendocrine response to estrogen and sexual orientation. *Science*, 1985, **225**, 1496–1499. By permission.)

Genetic Factors. A number of studies have examined the incidence of homosexuality among the twins of homosexual males (Green, 1980; Heston & Shields, 1968). In several studies, the likelihood that the twin would also be homosexual was found to be significantly greater for monozygotic (identical) twins than for dizygotic (nonidentical) twins. The results of some other studies are more ambiguous. Moreover, the studies conducted to date have been of twins reared together, and therefore they confound the possible effects of hereditary and environmental influences. In the absence of reared-together versus reared-apart monozygotic twins, or similarly controlled extended-family studies, no conclusive statements can be made about possible genetic influences on the development of a homosexual orientation.

Psychological and Social Influences on Gender Identity and Sexual Orientation

The research that has been conducted to date indicates that psychological and social factors can play an important role in the development of an individual's gender identity and sexual orientation. Perhaps the most dramatic evidence to support this statement comes from investigations by John Money, a psychologist at the Johns Hopkins University School of Medicine, and his associates. They studied individuals who were assigned to the chromosomally incorrect sex at birth because they exhibited deceptive developmental anomalies. In one series of nineteen cases, babies with a male chromosomal pattern were reared as girls and babies with a female chromosomal pattern were reared as boys. In all of these cases the young person developed a gender role and orientation consistent with assigned sex of rearing and inconsistent with chromosomal sex. Clearly, gender role and orientation as male or female developed independently of chromosomal sex but in close conformity with sex of rearing (Brecher, 1971; Money & Ehrhardt, 1972; Money, Hampson, & Hampson, 1955).

Psychological Factors in Homosexual Orientation. Although findings like those just described indicate that psychological factors can, under some circumstances, play a dominant role in the development of sexual orientation, they do not prove that such factors are responsible in most cases for the development of a primarily homosexual orientation. This can be done only through carefully controlled comparisons of representative groups of homosexuals and heterosexuals. Most such efforts have focused on possible differences in child rearing and parent–child relationships, although peer relationships and other psychological and social functions have also been studied (Bell & Weinberg, 1978; Bell, Weinberg, & Hammersmith, 1981; Bieber et al., 1962; Evans, 1971; Freedman, 1971; Green, 1980, 1986, 1987).

In one extensive study of the development of sexual preference, the parent–child relationships of heterosexual and homosexual males and females were compared (Bell, Weinberg, & Hammersmith, 1981). Among white males, 52 percent of heterosexuals and 23 percent of homosexuals gave a generally or entirely positive description of their fathers; in contrast, 48 percent of homosexuals and 29 percent of heterosexuals expressed negative feelings such as anger, resentment, or fear toward their fathers. More homosexuals than heterosexuals viewed their fathers as detached, hostile, rejecting, or unfair (52 percent versus 37 percent). With respect to identification, a considerably larger percentage of homosexuals said that they had felt "very little" or "not at all" like their fathers while growing up (72 percent versus 34 percent); and many more homosexuals said that they had felt more similar to their mothers than to their fathers (72 percent versus 37 percent).

Although heterosexual and homosexual males did not differ in the extent of positive or negative feelings they expressed toward their mothers, more homosexuals reported feeling particularly close to their mothers while growing up (47 percent versus 21 percent). They also saw their mothers as stronger and more dominant than their fathers (53 percent versus 30 percent) and felt that their mothers had been overprotective (43 percent versus 21 percent).

Among white females in the Kinsey Institute's study of nonclinical participants, 73 percent of heterosexuals and 36 percent of homosexuals gave generally or entirely positive descriptions of their fathers. Forty-five percent of homosexuals and 23 percent of heterosexuals expressed such negative feelings as anger, fear, or resentment toward their fathers. In contrast to the findings for males, more homosexual than heterosexual females viewed their relationships with their mothers as generally or entirely negative (49 percent versus 21 percent). More homosexuals than heterosexuals described their mothers as "bitter," "uncommunicative," or "frustrated" (48 percent versus 20 percent), and fewer described them as warm, pleasant, relaxed, and adequate as mothers (19 percent versus 40 percent). With respect to maternal identification, significantly more homosexual women recalled not feeling at all similar to their mothers while they were growing up (45 percent versus 15 percent) and not wanting to be at all like them (47 percent versus 15 percent).

In another study of the parental background of nonclinical samples of homosexual and heterosexual women who scored low on measures of neuroticism, homosexuals described their fathers as less loving and more rejecting (Siegelman, 1974). They also depicted their mothers as less loving, more demanding, and more distant, but not as more rejecting. In turn, the homosexual daughters reported less closeness than the heterosexuals both to their fathers and to their mothers.

Several considerations need to be kept in mind in attempting to evaluate the results of these and other studies:

1. Although problems in parent–child relationships are generally reported more frequently in the development of male and female homosexuals than in that of heterosexuals, virtually all studies have found significant numbers of homosexuals who had satisfactory parent–child relationships, as well as significant numbers of nonhomosexuals who had disturbed relations.
2. Associations between perceived parent–child relationships (e.g.,

mother–son closeness and father–son distance) and the development of a homosexual orientation do not in themselves indicate causality. "Some consideration must be given to the likelihood that the child's innate characteristics at least partially determine parental reactions and attitudes toward him" (Evans, 1971, p. 170).

3. Most of the studies conducted to date have been retrospective, making it difficult to determine the accuracy of the individual's recollections and the extent to which they may have been influenced by the sexual orientation he or she ultimately adopted.

In sum, much remains to be learned about the factors that are likely to lead to the development of a predominately homosexual or heterosexual orientation. At present no definitive conclusions can be reached regarding the role of biological or experiential sets of influences or of interactions among them. Moreover, just as homosexuals, like heterosexuals, differ enormously from one another as individuals, they may also differ in terms of the roots—biological, psychological, and/or social—of their homosexual orientation (Bell & Weinberg, 1978). Several studies, for example, suggest that "feminine" males and "masculine" females who are exclusively homosexual may develop a more deep-seated predisposition toward homosexuality early in life than some other homosexuals or bisexuals (Green, 1980, 1986, 1987; Bell et al., 1981). This appears to be reflected in early gender nonconformity in interests and activities and in more frequent feelings of "being different" during childhood (Green, 1987). It may also be seen in early emergence of homosexual feelings and lack of heterosexual arousal during childhood and adolescence. The sexual preferences of bisexuals and some other homosexuals, in contrast, may be "more subject to influence by social and sexual learning" (Bell et al., 1981, p. 201). In this connection, it is interesting to note that individuals who are more or less exclusively homosexual in their orientation, and have not experienced significant heterosexual arousal, are less likely to find their homosexuality "ego-dystonic," to seek changes in sexual orientation through therapy, and to accomplish this goal if they do try (Green, 1980).

Sexual Orientation and Psychopathology

Members of groups like the Gay Liberation movement assert that homosexuality is as normal as heterosexuality. They argue that labeling homosexual behavior "psychopathological" is not only incorrect but a form of discrimination and oppression. They point out that there have been cultures, such as that of the ancient Greeks, in which homosexual behavior was accepted along with heterosexual behavior. They also note that significant numbers of successful artists, scientists, and leaders in all walks of life have been homosexually oriented, and that although some homosexuals may be personally miserable, sexually unsatisfied, and socially ineffective, so are many heterosexuals.

Many of these protests are valid. The labeling of homosexually oriented individuals as "sick" or "pathological" *is* often done pejoratively, for a variety of reasons such as hostility, fear, and as a way of reassuring oneself of one's own "normality." It is often true, as a homosexual-movement leader has stated, that "calling homosexuality sick is like calling it sinful" (Freedman, 1971, p. 93). In response to such protests, the American Psychiatric Association has removed homosexuality as such from its diagnostic manual of mental disorders, retaining only a category entitled "ego-dystonic homosexuality" for those individuals who experience "sustained distress" as a result of homosexual arousal and who want to acquire or increase heterosexual arousal but have difficulty doing so (American Psychiatric Association, 1987).

An extensive study of homosexual and heterosexual men and women concluded that homosexual adults who have come to terms with their homosexuality, do not regret their sexual orientation, and can function effectively sexually and socially, are no more distressed psychologically than heterosexual men and women (Bell, Weinberg, & Hammersmith, 1981; Green, 1980). Clearly, there are many homosexually oriented individuals who, in terms of overall adjustment and contributions to society, are at least as successful as many heterosexually oriented individuals.

Nevertheless, a predominantly or exclusively homosexual orientation is likely to present significant problems of adaptation, at least in our society. Despite increased tolerance for differences in sexual preference, large segments of the population, including younger as well as older Americans, still consider homosexual behavior wrong or disturbed, even though they may oppose legal regulation of homosexual behavior. Among college freshmen, over 45 percent state that they favor prohibition of homosexual behavior (Astin, Korn, & Berz, 1989). A majority of American adolescents do not favor employment of homosexuals as schoolteachers, clergy, or physicians (Gallup, 1979). AIDS, with its high incidence among male homosexuals and intravenous drug users, has not only brought tragedy into the lives of gay people and their friends but also appears to have increased discrimination against homosexuals in employment, social life, and health care.

It seems unlikely that an individual would be motivated to accept the personal restrictions and social difficulties imposed by a homosexual life-style in the absence of strong attraction to members of the same sex, together with a lack of heterosexual attraction. As Alan Bell and his colleagues at the Kinsey Institute have observed,

> Neither homosexuals nor heterosexuals are what they are by design. Homosexuals, in particular, cannot be dismissed as persons who simply refuse to conform. There is no reason to think it would be any easier for homosexual men or women to reverse their sexual orientation than it would be for heterosexual readers to become predominantly or exclusively homosexual (Bell & Weinberg, 1978, p. 222).

In view of this fact, legal and social harassment of homosexuals and attempts to picture them as "perverted" are both cruel and unjustified. In addition, they make it even more difficult for the homosexually oriented individual to achieve self-esteem and social adaptation.

Today, gay young people have more reliable sources of support than in the past (Bell, 1987). Social, professional, religious, and political support groups for gay males and lesbians are expanding, as are groups of parents of gays and other interested nongay organizations. More health and mental-health professionals are developing special knowledge and skills (as well as abandoning myths and misconceptions) that will enable them to deal more effectively with the psychological and physical problems of gay persons. Expert legal and other services are more available, although more are needed.

With further research, we may gain a better understanding of the genesis of sexual orientation. In the meantime, however, it should be possible, given greater self-understanding and understanding of others, for both homosexuals and heterosexuals to enjoy mature, constructive, and rewarding lives.

SUMMARY

The physical changes associated with sexual maturation require a variety of adjustments by the adolescent and produce changes in his or her self-image. Integrating sexuality with other aspects of the self and relationships with others is a major developmental task for both boys and girls.

Although there is a significant increase in sexual interest and behavior in both sexes during adolescence, sexual activity is more prevalent among boys than among girls, although the size of the difference has narrowed in recent years. Girls are also more likely than boys to stress the importance of love in sexual relationships. A number of theories have been advanced to explain such differences; some are primarily physiological, others primarily cultural.

The role of cultural factors is evidenced both by changes in sexual attitudes and behavior within our own society and by marked variations from one culture to another. Some cultures restrict sexual activity in childhood and adolescence; others are more permissive. Still others are restrictive during some age periods but permissive during others. Sexual training practices may be generalized to affect other aspects of social behavior, but they are also affected by and reflect broader cultural attitudes.

Although most adolescents and their parents favor comprehensive sex education, the subject remains highly controversial. In the view of a minority of Americans, sex education is dangerous and premature, even in high school, and is likely to lead to promiscuity. Some believe that sex education should be left to parents. In light of current statistics on premarital intercourse, pregnancy, and abortion, as well as the general social climate, it is difficult to see how sex education for adolescents could be viewed as premature. Moreover, there is no consistent evidence that sex education increases the likelihood that an adolescent will become sexually active. Although parental participation in sex education is clearly desirable, many parents are not providing the knowledge their children need.

Today's adolescents tend to be more open about sex and to view decisions about sexual behavior as a private concern. Among entering college freshmen, two-thirds of males, but only one-third of females, agree that "sex is OK if people like each other." However, when there is deep involvement, as in living together prior to marriage, differences are much smaller.

Changing attitudes and values are reflected in higher rates of sexual activity among adolescents—including masturbation, petting, and premarital intercourse. For example, among American women who were teenagers in the late 1950s and early 1960s, slightly over 7 percent reported having had premarital sexual intercourse by age 16 and less than one-third by age 19. By 1988, these figures had increased to over one-third by age 16 and four out of five by age 19. It appears that widespread dissemination of information about AIDS since 1987 has led to increasing condom use.

Overall trends in sexual attitudes and behavior do not reveal the diversity that exists in various sections of the population. More females than males are *serial monogamists* while more males are *sexual adventurers*, although sexual adventurers constitute a minority of both sexes. Economically privileged adolescents are more liberal in their sexual attitudes, but not in their level of sexual activity. Younger adolescents are more conservative than older adolescents, and blacks are more sexually active than whites. Significant cultural differences between nations also exist. The influence of peers on attitudes toward premarital sex is stronger than that of parents.

Among sexually active female adolescents, less than half consistently use some form of contraception. As a result, about 11 percent of 15–19-year-old girls become pregnant each year, a higher rate than is found in any other developed country. Adolescent pregnancies pose threats to the health of both mother and child. In addition, teenage mothers are more likely to face other problems; many drop out of school, are unemployed, and must depend on welfare. They also are less likely to get married, and if they do marry, they are more likely to divorce. With proper support, however, significant numbers of adolescent mothers are able to succeed. Reasons for failure to use contraceptives include: incorrect information; unavailability of contraceptives when they are needed; emotional deprivation; low self-esteem and fatalistic attitudes; and persistence of the double standard. Adolescents who have high self-esteem, are doing well in school, and accept their sexuality and are able to discuss sex with their parents are more likely to use contraceptives. High rates of adolescent pregnancy could be reduced by sex education and family life planning, greater access to contraceptive methods, and more opportunities to build a successful and self-sufficient future for themselves.

Despite dire predictions in the past, neither masturbation, petting to orgasm, nor premarital intercourse reduces an adolescent's chances for successful adaptation to marital sex. Although a significant number of boys and a much smaller percentage of girls have had sexual contacts with members of the same sex, only about 5 or 6 percent go on to establish a basically homosexual orientation in adulthood. Much remains to be learned about the factors that are likely to lead to the development of a predominantly homosexual or heterosexual orientation. At present no definitive conclusions can be reached regarding the role of biological (e.g., genetic or hormonal) or experiential (e.g., parental or peer) influences or of interactions among them. With additional research, we may gain a better understanding of the genesis of sexual orientation. In the meantime, however, it should be possible, given greater self-understanding and understanding of others, for both homosexuals and heterosexuals to enjoy mature, constructive, and rewarding lives.

REVIEW QUESTIONS

1. How do the sexual attitudes and behavior of adolescent males and females differ? What theories have been proposed to account for those differences?
2. How do the sexual attitudes, values, and behavior of contemporary adolescents differ from those of earlier generations of adolescents?
3. Does sex education increase sexual activity among adolescents? Does it lead to increased pregnancy rates? How do rates of premarital intercourse and pregnancy among American adolescents compare with those found in other developed countries? Why?
4. Has sexual activity among adolescent males and females increased, decreased, or remained steady during the 1970s and 1980s? Discuss trends for younger and older adolescents, males and females, and blacks and whites.
5. Describe the differences between *serial monogamists* and *sexual adventurers*. Which group is better adjusted psychologically?
6. Discuss the relative influence of parents and peers on adolescent sexual attitudes and behavior.
7. Discuss current trends in pregnancy and contraceptive use among American adolescents. Why do so many adolescent girls and younger women fail to use contraceptive measures? How does pregnancy affect the lives of adolescent mothers and their babies?
8. Discuss what is known about the effects of biological and experiential factors on sexual orientation.

RECOMMENDED READINGS

Bell, R. (1987). *Changing bodies, changing lives: A book for teens on sex and relationships* (Rev. Ed.). New York: Random House.

Bell, A. P., Weinberg, M. S., & Hammersmith, S. K. (1981). *Sexual preference: Its development in men and women.* Bloomington, IN: Indiana University Press.

Brooks-Gunn, J., & Furstenberg, F. F., Jr. (1989). Adolescent sexual behavior. *American Psychologist, 44,* 249–257.

Chilman, C. S. (1983). *Adolescent sexuality in a changing American society:* *Social and psychological perspectives* (2nd ed.). Washington, DC: U.S. Government Printing Office.

Furstenberg, F. F., Jr., Brooks-Gunn, J. R., & Chase-Lansdale, L. (1989). Teenaged pregnancy and childbearing. *American Psychologist, 44,* 313–320.

Hayes, D. (Ed.) (1987). *Risking the future: Adolescent sexuality, pregnancy, and childbearing, Vol. 1.* Washington, DC: National Academy Press.

Luria, Z., Friedman, S., & Rose, M. D. (1987). *Human sexuality.* New York: Wiley.

CHAPTER

8

ADOLESCENTS AND THEIR PEERS

P eers play a crucial role in the psychological and social development of most adolescents, especially in age-segregated, technologically advanced societies in which entry into the adult world of work and family responsibility is increasingly delayed. Of course, peer influences do not begin in adolescence. From early childhood on, the peer group provides opportunities to learn how to interact with others, control social behavior, develop age-relevant skills and interests, and share problems and feelings (Berndt & Ladd, 1989; Hartup, 1983, 1989; Mussen et al., 1990; Parker & Gottman, 1989). But the role of peers is especially critical during adolescence. Relations with both same- and opposite-sex peers during the adolescent years come closer to serving as prototypes for adult relationships—in social relations, work, and interactions with members of the opposite sex. The young man or woman who has not learned how to establish satisfactory relationships with peers by the time he or she reaches adulthood is likely to face serious obstacles in the years ahead.

Adolescents are also more dependent on peer relations than younger children because their ties to parents become looser as they gain greater independence. In addition, their relations with family members are likely to be charged with conflicting emotions. Especially in the early years of adolescence dependent yearnings exist alongside independent strivings; hostility is mixed with love; and conflicts occur over cultural values and social behavior. Consequently, many areas of the adolescent's inner life and outward behavior cannot readily be shared with parents.

In several related studies, more than two out of three adolescents expressed the belief that a close friend understood them better than their parents did; that they felt more "themselves" with that friend; and that they could learn more at this time in their life from that friend than from their parents (Youniss & Smollar, 1985). Parents, in turn, having managed to repress the emotional ups and downs of their own adolescence, may have difficulty understanding their adolescent children's problems, even though they make an effort to do so and are truly interested in the welfare of their children.

In some cases parental warmth and understanding may be lacking, as in the case of a 16-year-old girl who said of her relationship with her father, "I get along, but, I mean, we're really not that close. Like he's got his business and I've got my school work. He just doesn't seem interested in what I do" (Konopka, 1976, p. 69). In other cases there may be parental hostility, neglect, or exploitation. In such circumstances interested and competent peers may provide not only a means of escaping from a difficult family situation but a source of understanding and support as well. They may also serve as role models for achieving mutually rewarding interactions with others (Conger, 1971, 1979; Hartup, 1970, 1983). As Peter Blos (1979), Anna Freud (1958), and others have observed, adolescence may sometimes provide the last major opportunity for repairing psychological damage incurred during early and middle childhood and developing new and more rewarding relationships both with oneself and with others.

A mature, warm, interested, and above all, nonexploitive adolescent peer may play a crucial role in helping a boy or girl gain a clearer self-concept, a feeling of personal worth, and renewed hope for the future. For example, a warm and supportive girl may show the son of a demanding, manipulative mother that relations with women can be rewarding and nonthreatening. A girl whose father has acknowledged her worth only when she has achieved some socially approved goal, such as high grades in school, may learn from a male peer that it is possible to be appreciated for who she is rather than for what she can do. Just by being himself and by being interested, a male friend may demonstrate to the son of a competitive, authoritarian father that relationships between males need not be characterized by competition and by patterns of domination and submission.

We do not wish to minimize the handicaps that distorted family relations in childhood may impose on an adolescent. In many such cases there is a clear need for psychotherapy. But it is extremely difficult to treat an adolescent successfully, even in intensive individual psychotherapy, when the experiences of therapy cannot be reinforced in relationships with peers. In such instances it is difficult to promote discrimination learning (i.e., the learning of *different* responses to *similar* stimuli; see pages 41–42, and the inappropriate responses learned in interactions with parents are more likely to generalize and be carried over into relationships with others.

Of course, there is another side to the coin. Relations with peers during this vulnerable stage of development may also be harmful. For example, the boy or girl who is put down, laughed at, or rejected in his or her initial efforts to establish heterosexual relationships or to join a high school clique may acquire anxious, avoidant responses that are difficult to extinguish. Moreover, adolescents may be pressured by peers into suspending their own better judgment and engaging in behaviors that they may later regret. Such behaviors range from relatively minor improprieties to more serious, sometimes tragic, incidents such as wanton destruction of school property, unplanned involvement in group sexual activities, or attacks on members of other social or ethnic groups. In such situations the adolescent's autonomy, self-confidence, and personal values may be severely tried.

During adolescence, more than at any other time in life, the young person needs to be able to share emotions, doubts, and dreams (Kniesel, 1987; Parker & Gottman, 1989). Adolescence is typically a time of sociability, but it can also be a time of loneliness (Avery, 1982; Brennan, 1982; Marcoen, Goosens, & Coes, 1987; Moore & Schultz, 1983). Consequently, being accepted by peers generally, and especially having one or more close friends, may make a great difference in the young person's life.

Finally, the role of the peer group in helping an individual define his or her own identity becomes particularly important during adolescence because at no other stage of development is one's sense of identity so fluid. No longer a child, but not yet fully accepted as an adult, the adolescent must prepare to meet society's demands for social independence, new kinds of relationships, vocational competence, a responsible role as a citizen, and in many cases, marriage and parenthood.

For all these reasons, adolescents need the guidance, support, and communion of their peers. No matter how understanding parents and other adults may be, their role is limited by the fact that they are already adults, whereas the adolescent and his or her peers are struggling to achieve adult status. Young people often do not know how they are going to accomplish this task. But they know that previous generations of adolescents have done so, and they reason that if they can stick with their peers—who, after all, are "all in the same boat"—they too will succeed.

CONFORMITY

Because of the heightened importance of the peer group during adolescence, the motivation to conform to the values, customs, and fads of the peer culture increases during this period. Although evidence of a need for such conformity is clearly observable in middle childhood, and although there are wide individual differences in the strength of this need at all ages, most studies indicate that there is a rather rapid rise in need for conformity during the preadolescent and early-adolescent years, followed by a gradual but steady decline from middle through late adolescence (Berndt, 1979; Hartup, 1983; Mussen et al., 1990; Steinberg & Silverberg, 1986). Although the need for conformity may vary, depending on such factors as sex, socioeconomic background, relationships with adults, school environment, and personality, variations are likely to occur in the extent of conformity or the exact age at which it peaks, rather than in the overall developmental pattern (Brownstone & Willis, 1971; Clasen & Brown, 1985; Coleman, 1980; Cooper & Ayers-Lopez, 1985; Costanzo & Shaw, 1966; Steinberg & Silverberg, 1986). For example, children and adolescents with a strong tendency toward self-blame scored significantly higher on measures of conformity than those who were less likely to blame themselves, but the pattern of increased conformity followed by a decrease was quite similar in each case (Costanzo, 1970).

Similar studies have found that young people with low status among peers are more conforming than those with high status; that boys and girls differ little in need for conformity, except when group norms favor misconduct (in which case boys are more susceptible); and that children and adolescents with favorable attitudes toward adults are less subject to peer pressure than those with negative attitudes toward adults (Berndt, 1979; Bixenstine, DeCorte, & Bixenstine, 1976; Brown, Clasen, & Eicher, 1986; Hartup, 1983; Steinberg & Silverberg, 1986). Adolescents with high self-esteem and strong feelings of competence are less conforming than their peers (Cooper & Ayers-Lopez, 1985; Hartup, 1983; Lanelsbaum & Willis, 1971).

Recent findings regarding adolescent conformity are generally similar to those obtained some years ago. In short, whereas the *manifestations* of peer group conformity change rapidly in our society, there can be little doubt that most adolescents, particularly younger ones, have a strong need to conform to peer group norms and pressures, and that this need is reflected in behavior (Berndt, 1979; Clasen & Brown, 1985; Coleman, 1980; Hartup, 1983).

Of course, adolescents may deny or fail to recognize what an outside observer may perceive as excessive conformity to peer pressure. What looks like conformity to the observer may seem to the young person to be a bold exercise in individuality. The explanation of this paradox lies in the different perspectives of the observer and the adolescent: The adolescent may perceive his or her behavior as highly individual because it differs markedly from that of parents and other adults; in contrast, the observer's attention is likely to focus on the similarities between the adolescent's behavior and that of peers.

Needless to say, conformity is not an exclusively adolescent phenomenon. Parallels exist in the conforming behavior of adults, who may also fail to recognize it. Self-conscious liberal or conservative adults may see themselves as paragons of rugged individualism because their attitudes, beliefs, and behaviors differ from those of the "silent majority" of their fellow citizens. What they fail to recognize is that they are conforming to the myths, customs, fads, and philosophical cliches of their own cultural subgroup.

Having left the world of childhood forever without yet being admitted to the world of adults, adolescents are virtually forced to create at least a semblance of an interim culture of their own. Obviously, it is important that this culture, whatever form it may take, be clearly recognizable as different from that of adults. Once adults have recovered from their initial dismay and incorporated adolescent fashions and tastes into their own culture (as has happened to dress, hairstyles, music, and even language), adolescents need to create new fads to preserve their separateness.

Parents are often mystified, and in some cases threatened, by the shifting trappings of adolescent peer culture—from fashions in clothes and music to special and rapidly changing vocabularies. They may wonder why adolescents need to behave in such a "bizarre" manner. Yet that is one of the main reasons for the existence of adolescent fads: They establish a clear line of demarcation from adults. Parents and other adults might actually take some comfort from these outward indicators of the "differentness" of adolescents. By achieving a group identity of their own in these relatively superficial ways, adolescents may partially satisfy the need to be different from their parents in more fundamental matters. Although, as we shall see, adolescent values and behavior are different from those of adults, there is also a fundamental, and often overlooked, continuity in many of the values and beliefs of parents and their children (Conger, 1971, 1979; Cooper & Ayers-Lopez, 1985; Bachman, Johnston, & O'Malley, 1987; National Association, 1983).

PARENTAL AND PEER INFLUENCES—A FALSE DICHOTOMY?

We should not be misled by superficial differences between parents and adolescents, however conspicuous they may be. Although it is commonly asserted that parental and peer group values are incompatible and that an inevitable consequence of heightened dependence on peers during adolescence is a sharp decline in parental influence, this is not true for most adolescents.

In the first place, there is usually a considerable overlap between the values

Parents are often mystified by the shifting trappings of adolescent peer culture—from fashions in clothes and music to special and rapidly changing vocabularies.

of parents and peers because of commonalities in their social, economic, religious, educational, even geographic backgrounds. For example, boys from an Irish-American, Catholic, blue-collar neighborhood in a large city are more likely to share the values of their parents and peers than to share those of boys (or parents) from an upper-middle-class WASP background in the same city (Conger, 1971, 1975; Lerner & Knapp, 1975; Youniss & Smollar, 1989).

Another factor that limits potential conflicts between parental and peer influences is the uncertainty of some parents about the behavior they should expect from adolescents. Parents may feel that social change has occurred so rapidly that they lack the experience to teach their children how to deal with today's world. This was particularly true in the late 1960s and early 1970s, but it is still true of a significant number of parents in the 1990s.

Such a view can easily become a self-fulfilling prophecy. While bemoaning the adolescent's conformity to the peer group, parents may be encouraging the child to turn to the peer group for guidance. Moreover, many parents, particularly upper- and middle-class parents, place great emphasis on popularity and success, thereby strengthening the adolescent's motivation to conform to peer expectations.

Another important consideration that is frequently overlooked is that neither the influence of parents nor that of peers extends to all areas of adolescent decision making and behavior (Berndt, 1979; Clasen & Brown, 1985; Hartup,

1983; Larson, 1972a, 1972b; Wilks, 1986). The weight given to parental or peer opinion depends to a significant degree on the adolescent's appraisal of its relative usefulness in a specific situation. For example, the influence of peers (especially same-sex peers) is more likely to dominate in such matters as tastes in music and entertainment, fashions in clothing and language, patterns of interaction with same- and opposite-sex peers, and the like. Parental influence is more likely to dominate in such areas as educational plans and aspirations, moral and social values, and understanding of the adult world (Brittain, 1966, 1969; Conger, 1971; Davies & Kandel, 1981; Kandel, 1985; Sebald & White, 1980; Wilks, 1986).

Similarly, adolescents are likely to turn to other significant adults, such as grandparents and teachers, for advice in areas in which "expert" knowledge of the adult world is viewed as relevant (Steinberg, 1985; Wilks, 1986; Young & Ferguson, 1979). One must also recognize that when the peer group assumes an unusually dominant role in the lives of adolescents, it is due as much to lack of attention and concern at home as it is to the attractiveness of the peer group (Bronfenbrenner, 1970; Devereux, 1970; Galambos & Silbereisen, 1987).

Parents of strongly peer-oriented adolescents are likely to show passive neglect (i.e., a relative lack of concern and affection) rather than active punitiveness. Indeed, they appear to neither support nor control their children to any significant degree, hence leaving them to seek approval and affection elsewhere (Condry & Siman, 1974; Conger & Petersen, 1984). In contrast, the parents of more adult-oriented adolescents are more active: more nurturant, more demanding, providing more companionship and discipline—and more consistent.

In one study, parental influence was found to be greatest when there was a high level of "parent–adolescent affect" as measured by parental interest and understanding, willingness to be helpful, amount of shared family activity, and so on. Moreover, adolescents in families with high parent–adolescent affect were significantly less likely than those in families with low affect to see a need to differentiate between the influence of their parents and that of their best friends (Larson, 1972a, 1972b).

As psychologist Laurence Steinberg (1985) points out, investigations that are designed to force adolescents to choose between parental and peer influence do not allow them to demonstrate autonomy with respect to both. However, several recent investigations have undertaken to measure the extent of adolescents' conformity to parents and to peers separately (Berndt, 1979; Steinberg & Silverberg, 1986). Such studies have found that, on average, conformity to parents tends to decline during preadolescence and early adolescence while conformity to peers rises. Not until middle and late adolescence do increases in overall autonomy occur, for only then does conformity both to parents *and* to peers decline for a majority of young people—most dramatically with respect to peer pressure to engage in antisocial behavior (see Figure 8.1).

However, at all ages *some* adolescents demonstrate a relatively high degree of autonomy with respect to both parents and peers (Devereux, 1970; Stein-

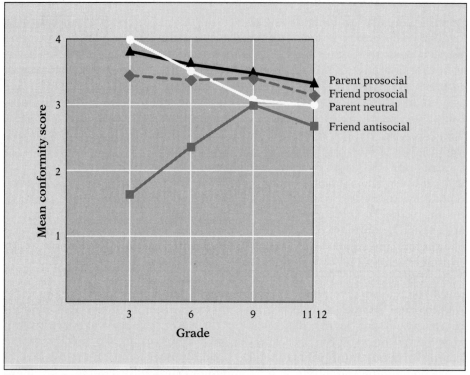

Figure 8.1 Changes in conformity to peers and to parents during adolescence. (From T. J. Berndt (1979). Developmental changes in conformity to peers and parents. *Developmental Psychology,* **15,** 606–616. Copyright 1979 by the American Psychological Association. Reprinted by permission.)

·berg & Silverberg, 1986). Figures 8.2 and 8.3 show the percentage of adolescent males and females in grades 5–9 in one study who were (1) *autonomous* (high in both parent and peer autonomy); (2) *nonautonomous* (low in both parent and peer autonomy); (3) *parent-oriented* (low in parent autonomy but high in peer autonomy); and (4) *peer-oriented* (high in parent autonomy but low in peer autonomy). As can be seen, even in the early years of adolescence a significant minority of adolescents in this study (more girls than boys) demonstrated a relatively high degree of autonomy (Steinberg & Silverberg, 1986).

Finally, we tend to overlook the fact that the need for rigid conformity to either parents or peers varies enormously from one adolescent to another (Berndt, 1979; Conger, 1971, 1979; Larson, 1972a, 1972b; Steinberg & Silverberg, 1986). More self-confident, autonomous adolescents may be able to profit from the views and learning experiences provided by both parents and peers without being strongly dependent on either. Nor are they unduly troubled by differences between the views of parents and peers (Cooper & Ayers-Lopez, 1985; Hartup, 1983; Stone & Church, 1973). Ironically, an adolescent who has gained confidence in his or her own self-image, and is relatively individualistic and unconcerned about popularity, may find that peers flock to him or her as a tower of strength.

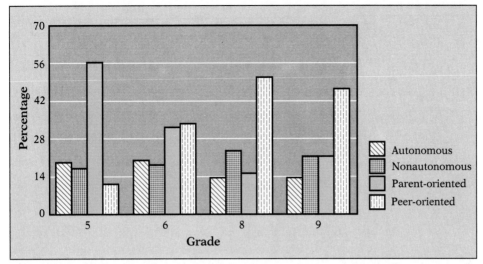

Figure 8.2 Proportions of autonomous, nonautonomous, parent-oriented, and peer-oriented adolescent males across four grade levels. (From L. Steinberg & S. B. Silverberg. (1986) The vicissitudes of autonomy in early adolescence. *Child Development,* **57,** 841–851. By permission.)

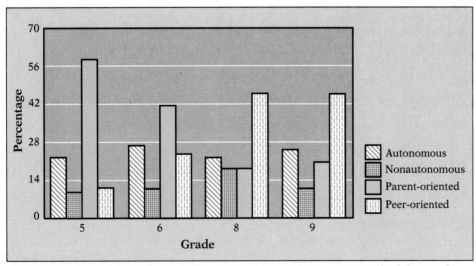

Figure 8.3 Proportions of autonomous, nonautonomous, peer-oriented adolescent females across four grade levels. (From L. Steinberg & S. B. Silverberg. (1986) The vicissitudes of autonomy in early adolescence. *Child Development,* **57,** 841–851. By permission.)

Sources of Difficulty

There are four conditions in which serious difficulties are most likely to arise and parents are most likely to find themselves feeling helpless. Briefly, they are as follows:

1. There is a very strong, homogeneous peer group, with patterns of behavior and attitudes that differ markedly from those of the adolescent's parents.
2. The parents lack interest in and understanding of the adolescent and are unwilling to be helpful; and few family activities are shared.
3. The parents' own values and behaviors are inconsistent, uninformed, unrealistic, maladaptive, or obviously hypocritical.
4. The adolescent lacks either the self-confidence (based on a positive self-image) or the independence training to act autonomously without undue concern (Conger, 1971, 1977).

In most cases in which young people have forsaken or renounced family values for those of deviant peer groups, one or more of these conditions is likely to be present.

As indicated earlier, the parents' task may be easier in the traditional small-town culture, which is characterized by extended kinship and neighborly ties and by continual interaction between parents and other adults, peers, the schools, and other social institutions. Under such circumstances fundamental values and customs are more firmly held and widely shared among adults and adolescents. The parents' task may be much more difficult in other settings, such as a large city, in which both the nuclear family and the peer group may be relatively isolated from interaction or even communication with other individuals and groups in the community. When such an isolated peer group becomes involved in experimentation with drugs, sexual activities, or delinquent behavior, parents may be confronted with seemingly insurmountable problems—especially if the group is homogeneous and exerts strong pressure for conformity.

It is often assumed that such situations either do not exist or are exaggerated—or, conversely, that they are universal, which is not the case. But when they do exist, it is most often in areas in which the sense of community has been dissipated, such as urban ghettos and affluent suburbs.

The more discrepant or deviant the peer group setting, however, the more important it is for parents to attempt to take the democratic authoritative approach to child rearing described earlier. Equally crucial are efforts to communicate with, understand, and interact actively with the adolescent. Both the laissez-faire parent, who provides neither guidance nor a strong model of basic standards and values, and the authoritarian parent, who neither understands nor feels any need to understand the views and problems of the adolescent, are likely to lose whatever influence they might have had and to leave the adolescent vulnerable to deviant peer group influences.

THE CHANGING NATURE OF ADOLESCENT PEER GROUPS

Although we have spoken of the adolescent peer group or peer culture as if each were a single entity, this is not actually the case. In reality, the adolescent interacts in different ways with a number of overlapping peer groups that vary in size and in the degree of intimacy among their members. In addition, the nature of these groups and the functions they serve change with age. During middle childhood and preadolescence peer relations tend to center on neighborhood play groups and same-sex "gangs" (Hartup, 1983; Mussen et al., 1990). Largely informal at first, these groups become more highly structured with increasing age (from about age 10 on). Aspects of formal organization, such as special membership requirements and elaborate rituals for conducting meetings, appear. Even so, the personnel may change frequently and the group itself may not last long.

There are a number of reasons for the predominance of same-sex groups during this period. Chief among these is the presence of differences in interests and activities that are more easily served by same-sex peer groups (Huston, 1983; Mussen et al., 1990). Also, from about age 9 through 11 children tend to be anxious about associations with members of the opposite sex or expressions of interest in them.

Throughout the middle-childhood and preadolescent years, boys are more likely than girls to participate in gangs. However, girls tend to have more intimate interpersonal relationships than boys even at these ages (Hartup, 1983; Hunter & Youniss, 1982; Youniss & Smollar, 1985). The peer relations of both boys and girls during the middle-childhood years tend to be limited to neighborhood acquaintances and schoolmates (who tend to come from the same or adjoining neighborhoods). However, as the young person enters junior high school and spends less and less time at home, the range of peer relations broadens to include a much wider circle of casual acquaintances (Csikszentmihalyi & Larson, 1984).

In general, the adolescent's peer relations fall into three broad categories: the **crowd** or "set," the **clique,** and individual friendships. Thus, a pioneering study of adolescent peer groups in an urban setting found two basic types of groups: relatively large crowds and much smaller cliques (Dunphy, 1963, 1980). The most inclusive and least personal of these categories is the crowd. In a sense, a crowd is a "forced group" made up of individuals who share interests, likes, and social ideals. The members meet on the basis of shared activities, not because of mutual attraction (Brown, 1989; Coleman, 1980; Dunphy, 1972; Hartup, 1983). The crowd is essentially an association of cliques; clique membership appears to be a prerequisite for crowd membership (Coleman, 1980). No subject in the study just mentioned was found to belong to a crowd without also belonging to one of its component cliques. On the other hand, an individual might well be a member of a clique without also belonging to the crowd. Girls' cliques tend to be smaller, more restricted in age range, and more intimate than those of boys (Brown, 1989; Hartup, 1983; Lever, 1976; Savin-Williams, 1980a, 1980b).

Cliques and crowds perform different functions for their members. The smaller clique encourages far more intimacy and group cohesion than the larger crowd. In fact, that cohesion is made possible by the limited membership of cliques. The similarity in size between the family and the clique may facilitate the transfer of allegiance to the clique and allows it to provide an

Girls' cliques tend to be smaller, more restricted in age range, and more intimate than those of boys.

alternative center of security. Clique interactions consist largely of talking, especially on the telephone. An analysis of the content of these conversations showed that the clique performs an important practical function in the preparation of activities, the dissemination of information about them, and subsequent evaluation.

The crowd, on the other hand, provides for larger and more organized social activities such as parties, which are a setting for interaction between the sexes. The crowd "acts as a reservoir of acceptable associates who can be drawn on to the extent required by any social activity. Thus cliques and crowds are not only different in size; they are also different in function" (Dunphy, 1963, p. 235).

Stages of Peer Group Development

As adolescence proceeds, structural changes in the nature of peer groups take place; these, in turn, are related to the changes that occur in the course of adolescent development, particularly the development of heterosexual relationships (Blyth, Hill, & Thiel, 1981; Csikszentmihalyi & Larson, 1984; Dunphy, 1963, 1972, 1980). As the young person enters adolescence, same-sex cliques or "gangs" of preadolescents predominate (Hallinan, 1981; Hartup, 1983). Gradually, however, single-sex cliques begin to interact with cliques of the opposite sex, leading to the formation of the adolescent crowd. At least initially, such heterosexual interactions are tentative and are usually undertaken in the group setting, where the individual is supported by the presence of his or her same-sex friends.

Only in the next stage of peer group development do we see the formation of genuinely heterosexual cliques, in which heterosexual interactions between individuals are begun (usually by higher-status clique leaders). However, adolescents who belong to these emerging heterosexual groups maintain their membership in the same-sex clique; in other words, they possess dual membership in two intersecting cliques.

In the following stage of adolescent group development the situation shifts, and we see the emergence of the fully developed adolescent crowd made up of a number of heterosexual cliques in close association. Finally, in late adolescence couples and loosely associated groups of couples are frequently seen; same-sex friendships continue but become more stable and less intense (see Figure 8.4). The importance of the crowd begins to diminish as the need for conformity to peers lessens and the perceived need to establish an individual identity grows (Coleman, 1980; Csikszentmihalyi & Larson, 1987; Dunphy, 1963, 1980).

Although adolescents currently tend to enter these stages at somewhat younger ages, the sequence of stages seems to have persisted, despite individual variations and occasional regressions. One of the principal functions served by the crowd is to make possible the transition from the same-sex

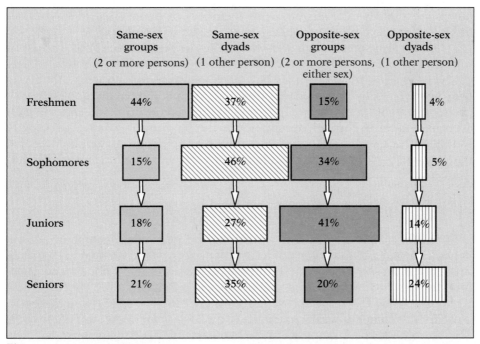

Figure 8.4 The shift from same-sex to opposite-sex friends during high school years. The diagram shows the percentage of time with friends that students in each grade spent with different types of friends. (From M. Csikszentmihalyi & R. Larson (1984). *Being adolescent: Conflict and growth in the teenage years.* New York: Basic Books. By permission.)

cliques of early adolescence to the heterosexual cliques of later adolescence. At the same time, associations with same-sex individuals and groups continue in somewhat muted form throughout adolescence and into adult life. Such associations may be seen in small circles of friends, individual friendships, fraternities and sororities, clubs, or interest groups.

Socioeconomic status plays a significant role in determining crowd and clique membership. There is usually little cutting across class lines, particularly in the case of girls, whose cliques tend generally to be closer, more exclusive, more impregnable to outsiders, and somewhat more enduring (Coleman, 1980). There is somewhat more democracy and flexibility in male cliques, in which athletic skills and overall sociability have a leveling influence. Other influences may also play a role in crowd or clique formation. Among these are shared interests and hobbies; social and athletic skills, academic goals; personal and sexual maturity; traditionalism versus rebellion in cultural values; participation in or avoidance of drug use, sexual experimentation, or delinquent behavior; degree of academic involvement; personality characteristics; ethnic group membership; and residential proximity (Berndt, 1982; Coleman, 1980; Hartup, 1983).

Cliques may exhibit considerable intolerance or contempt for nonmembers who are different in various ways. Individuals—particularly girls—who are personally secure and emotionally mature are most likely to be able to reach out and establish relationships with members of other cliques. In general, older students are also more likely to cross clique boundaries.

There are also some individuals who, either through choice or as a result of rejection by peers, belong neither to cliques nor to crowds. Although adolescents today seem to have somewhat more tolerance for difference than was true in some earlier generations, the fact remains that many adolescents—preoccupied with themselves, uncertain of their own worth, and eager to gain security and status through acceptance by the "in-group"—can be remarkably indifferent or even cruel toward those who do not fit in. As we shall see, for many isolated young people the adolescent years can be a lonely and difficult time.

FRIENDSHIPS AND IDENTITY DEVELOPMENT

Friendships hold a special place among the peer relationships of adolescents. Compared to more general interactions with peers, friendships typically are more intimate, involve more intense feelings, are more honest and open, and are less concerned with social acceptance (Berndt, 1982; Hartup, 1989; Konopka, 1976, 1985; Tesch, 1983; Youniss & Smollar, 1985). Consequently, close friends frequently can contribute to an adolescent's development in ways that the broader peer group cannot. "The particular advantage of the adolescent friendship is that it offers a climate for growth and self-knowledge that the family is not equipped to offer, and that very few persons can provide for themselves" (Konopka, 1976, p. 174). At the same time, because it plays such a vital role in adolescence, friendship gains an importance and intensity that are lacking in earlier and later stages of development. Thus, in his study of adult development in men, Daniel Levinson (1978) observes that as adults most of the participants did not have the kinds of intimate friends that they recalled fondly from their youth.

The young person who is attempting to adjust to a changing self (psychologically and physiologically) and to meet rapidly changing societal demands may experience doubts, anxieties, and resentments. In most situations these reactions must be concealed. To admit them to any but one's closest friends is to open the door to the possibility of misunderstanding, lack of acceptance, amusement, scorn, or rejection. In a meaningful friendship, however, such defensiveness is no longer required.

In one intensive study, middle-class adolescents of both sexes selected "close friend" as the person they were most likely to "talk openly" with and share "true feelings" with. Moreover, the relationship was viewed as reciprocal: Close friends "are not afraid to talk about [their] doubts and fears"; they "depend on each other for advice"; and even when they disagree, they listen to each other's reasons (Youniss & Smollar, 1985, p. 103). In the words of one adolescent girl, "A friend is someone who I can talk to, who'll understand, and don't turn you down and say they don't want to listen and they don't want to hear what you're saying" (Konopka, 1976, p. 85).

In view of the sensitivity of adolescents to the dangers associated with revealing their inner feelings, it is not surprising to find that they emphasize the need for security in a true friendship: They want the friend to be loyal, trustworthy, and a reliable source of support in any emotional crisis (Berndt, 1982; Cooper & Ayers-Lopez, 1985; Hartup, 1983; Youniss & Smollar, 1985). Indeed, untrustworthy behavior is cited by adolescents as the primary cause of serious conflict between close friends (see Table 8.1). As one 14-year-old girl from an urban ghetto stated, "A friend don't talk behind your back. If they are a true friend they help you get out of trouble and they will always be right behind you and they help you get through stuff. And they never snitch on you. That's what a friend is" (Konopka, 1976, p. 85).

Under favorable circumstances, adolescents may reveal a talent for friendship that is not shared by younger children or most adults. A major distinction between the adolescent and the child or adult is that the adolescent often enters friendships with a considerable degree of flexibility and readiness for change. Younger children may not be happy with themselves as they are, but they tend to accept the situation as a fact of life. However, with the beginning of adolescence and formal-operational thinking, young people become more aware of themselves as having a social persona that can be changed by conscious intent (Douvan & Adelson, 1966; Tesch, 1983; Youniss & Smollar, 1985). (Indeed, their readiness for change has become the basis for an enormous and sometimes rather cynically motivated "self-improvement" industry, ranging from grooming aids to magazine columns on manners and morals.) Close friends can often help each other identify and change behaviors that may turn off others, develop new ta⁢ s and social skills, and learn to express ideas effectively.

T A B L E 8.1 ISSUES DESCRIBED AS CAUSING THE MOST SERIOUS CONFLICT IN A CLOSE FRIENDSHIP

Issues	Frequencies per Category Sex of Subjects[a]	
	Females	Males
1. *Untrustworthy acts* (doesn't keep secrets, talks behind back, gets other into trouble, breaks promises, lies, takes a job away, takes opposite-sex friend away, goes out with other's opposite-sex friend)	59	43
2. *Lack of sufficient attention* (leaves other out, ignores other, doesn't come to party, doesn't call, spends time with others, doesn't include in plans, wants to be with opposite-sex friend, ignores when opposite-sex friend is around)	28	13
3. *Disrespectful acts* (is snotty, is rude, calls names, puts down, makes fun of, bossy, uses other, hits, argues with, fights with, breaks something of others, steals something from other)	17	39
4. *Unacceptable behaviors* (talks too much, too moody, drinks too much, has a bad temper, is conceited, lies, quit school, is stubborn, is spoiled, brags, acts stupid, smokes pot)	18	14
5. *Miscellaneous*	6	5
6. *No answer*	30	40

Source: J. Youniss and J. Smollar. *Adolescent relations with mothers, fathers, and friends.* Chicago: University of Chicago Press, 1985. By permission.
[a]Sex difference: $x^2(3) = 16.45$; $p < .01$ with categories 5 and 6 excluded.

Along with openness to change, adolescents show greater openness to inner states of experience. They have not yet defined the boundaries of the self or made the commitment to a particular way of life that, while resulting in a sharper definition of the self, also tends to limit the individual's openness to other possibilities. As a result, they often exhibit "a psychic flexibility, or vulnerability to conflict, an affective lability which together give adolescent intimacies so much of their characteristic flavor" (Douvan & Adelson, 1966, p. 180).

At their best, friendships may help young people learn to deal with their own feelings and those of others. They can serve as a kind of therapy by allowing freer expression of suppressed anger or anxiety and by providing evidence that others share many of the same doubts, hopes, fears, and feelings. As one 16-year-old girl expressed it, "My best friend means a lot to me. We can talk about a lot of things I could never talk about with my parents or other kids—like hassles we're getting or problems we're worried about, and like ideals and things. It really helps to know you're not the only one that has things that bother them" (Conger, 1979, p. 70).

At their best, friendships help young people to learn to deal with their own feelings and those of others.

Similar thoughts are expressed by a 13-year-old boy:

A best friend to me is someone you can have fun with and you can also be serious with about personal things, about girls, what you're going to do with your life or whatever. My best friend, Jeff, and I can talk about things. His parents are divorced too, and he understands when I feel bummed out about the fights between my mom and dad. A best friend is someone who's not going to make fun of you just because you do something stupid or put you down if you make a mistake. If you're afraid of something or someone, they'll give you confidence (Bell, 1987, p. 64).

Finally, close friendships may play a crucial role in helping young people develop a sense of their own identity. By sharing their experiences, plans, hopes and fears—in short, by explaining themselves to each other— adolescent friends are also learning to understand themselves. There is an implicit awareness that self-definition and a coherent view of external reality cannot be achieved solely by reflection, that without the corrective functions of an external voice, one "risks self-delusion or egoism" (Youniss & Smollar, 1985, p. 167). In the words of one adolescent, "You can't always decide what you want to do yourself. You need a second opinion" (Youniss & Smollar,

1985, pp. 164–165). There is also an awareness that mutual understanding is a reciprocal process: "You have to give a friend advice when he has a problem because a lot of times when a person is involved in a problem, he can't see it too well" (Youniss & Smollar, 1985, p. 164). Moreover, when a friend who "really understands" the adolescent still likes and values him or her, the young person's confidence and self-esteem are bolstered (Bell, 1987; Erikson, 1978; Osterrieth, 1969; Parker & Gottman, 1989). In sum, under favorable circumstances friendships may help the adolescent both to define his or her own identity and to have confidence and pride in it.

Unfortunately, the circumstances of adolescent friendship are not always so favorable. By virtue of their very intensity, these friendships are more easily imperiled than those of most adults, which are likely to involve more modest demands (and yield more modest returns). Even the more stable and rewarding adolescent friendships are likely to blow hot and cold in response to the rise and fall of feelings in oneself and others.

Similarity in Friendship Pairs

Friendships are most likely to develop between adolescents with similar demographic characteristics—age, school grade, sex, socioeconomic status, and ethnic background (Epstein, 1989; Hartup, 1979, 1983; Kandel, 1985). The percentage of a person's close friends who are members of the opposite sex increases with age, but even in late adolescence same-sex friendships predominate, particularly in the case of "best friends" (Blythe, Hill, & Thiel, 1982; Duck, 1975; Fischer, 1981; Kandel, 1978). The behaviors and attitudes of best friends are not as similar as their demographic characteristics; nevertheless, best friends tend to be more similar than acquaintances in intelligence, educational and career aspirations, sociability, cooperative activities, school behavior and grades, conformity to adult expectations, amount of participation in peer group activities, and use of drugs and alcohol.

Although similarities in the personality and behavior of adolescent friends are generally more evident than differences, this is not always the case (Berndt, 1986; Epstein, 1989). Indeed, parents sometimes find it difficult to understand their adolescent children's choices of friends. What, they may ask, does their Sally, who has always been so neat, quiet, and studious, see in noisy, extroverted Barbara, who seems more interested in being constantly on the go than in her schoolwork, or indeed in any serious activity? When such an attraction of opposites occurs, it is usually because the young person finds in the friend something that is felt to be desirable but is lacking in the self. Thus, extroverted Barbara may be helping Sally become less inhibited and self-conscious and learn to get along more easily with peers. Barbara, in turn, may find in Sally someone who can help her understand some of her own previously hidden feelings—someone who is really willing to listen (Storr, 1975).

The fact that in many instances friends tend to be similar in behavior, values, and interests could have two sources: It could be that individuals who share personally relevant similarities are attracted to each other, or it could be that the friendship itself has a socializing effect—that similarity between friends results from the influence they have on each other. Although it seems likely that both processes are involved, most studies have not provided a clear answer to the question because they have been conducted at a single point in time. However, in a longitudinal investigation of high school students in New York State, Denise Kandel and her colleagues were able to study individuals before they became friends, during the course of their friendship, and in some cases after their friendship had broken up (Kandel, 1978a, 1978b, 1981, 1985; Kandel & Andrews, 1987). They found that both factors played a part. The adolescents tended to choose as friends others who were similar to them in such characteristics as use of legal and illegal drugs, academic interests (educational aspirations, grades, willingness to cut classes, and school program), and participation in peer activities. However, the researchers also found that friends tended to resolve imbalances in such characteristics by becoming more like each other. In instances in which this did not happen, friendships were more likely to be dissolved. Other investigators have found that these two sets of influences also play a part in the formation and maintenance of adolescent cliques (Cohen, 1972; Epstein, 1988; Tuma & Hallinan, 1977).

Variations in Friendship Patterns

The function, quality, and content of friendship patterns vary with age and sex. Before puberty, friendships tend to be more superficial than they will be later (Dorval et al., 1987; Hartup, 1983; Mussen et al., 1990; Parker & Gottman, 1988). The young person wants a friend who is readily available, is fun to be with, and can share interests, activities, and possessions. It is expected that friends will cooperate with and help each other, and there is growing emphasis on equality in relations between friends. What tends to be lacking is "the sense that friendship can be emotionally relevant" (Douvan & Adelson, 1966, p. 186). As the young person moves through adolescence, however, there is increasing emphasis on mutual understanding, empathy, emotional investment, and eventually a sense of shared identity, in which "I and you" become "we" (Reisman & Shorr, 1978; Selman, 1980; Youniss, 1980; Youniss & Smollar, 1985).

By middle adolescence the personality of the friend and his or her response to the self become the central themes of the friendship. During this period the opportunity for shared thoughts and feelings may help ease the transition toward heterosexual relations and a newly defined sex role identity (Dorval, Brannan, Duckworth, & Smith, 1987; Douvan & Adelson, 1966). This is the age when emphasis on a friend's loyalty, trustworthiness, and respect for confidences reaches its peak and when the emotional intensity and vulnerability of friendships are likely to be at their height. One study found that emphasis on intimacy, shared activities, and loyalty increase until about the eighth grade (Reisman & Shorr, 1978).

In contrast, by late adolescence the passionate quality of friendship tends to recede and to be replaced by a more equable "autonomous interdependence," in which friends can still be close yet at the same time grant each other autonomy and independence (Selman, 1981). In the words of one older adolescent, "If you are really close friends and trust each other, you can't hold on to everything. You gotta let go once in a while. Give each other a chance to breathe" (Selman & Selman, 1979, p. 74). Although having someone to share confidences with is still important, there is a greater, more objective emphasis on the friend's personality and talents—on what he or she can bring to the relationship in the way of interest and stimulation—and a greater degree of tolerance for, and even appreciation of, individual differences. As the adolescent begins to define herself or himself, to find a basis for his or her identity, and to develop fairly secure psychological defenses, dependence on identification with close friends is reduced. In addition, more meaningful heterosexual relationships have begun to develop, further diluting the exclusiveness of the adolescent's reliance on same-sex friends.

Adolescent friendship patterns also vary with sex. Girls' friendships typically are more numerous, deeper, and more interdependent than those of boys; moreover, in their friendships girls reveal a greater need for nurturance, desire for and ability to sustain intimate relationships, and concern about defection (Bigalow & La Gaipa, 1980; Berndt, 1982; Cooper & Grotevant, 1987; Dorval et al., 1987; Sharbany, Gershoni, & Hoffman, 1981; Youniss & Smollar 1985). Boys, in contrast, tend to place relatively more stress on the results of friendship, such as having a congenial companion with whom one shares an interest in sports, hobbies, or other activities.

In one study of middle and late adolescence (Fischer, 1981), two major aspects of friendships were identified: a *friendship* factor (voluntary involvement in mutual activities with a unique other) and *intimacy* (closeness, ease of communication, attachment and affection, lack of egocentrism). On the basis of these two dimensions, male and female adolescents were divided into four categories: relatively *uninvolved* (below the median on both friendship and intimacy), *friendly* (above the median on friendship, below the median on intimacy), *intimate* (the reverse of *friendly*), and *integrated* (above the median on both intimacy and friendship). The investigators found that male high school students were most likely to be classified as either relatively uninvolved or friendly in their relationship styles, whereas female college students were most likely to be classified as integrated or intimate (see Table 8.2). Interestingly, when the gender of the subject and his or her friend was taken into account, female–male friendships showed the highest incidence of integrated relationships, followed in order by male–female, female–female, and male–male friendships (see Table 8.3). On the basis of these findings, it appears possible that "late adolescent females socialize the males for heterosexual relationships on the basis of their practice in intimacy with their girlfriends" (Fischer, 1981, p. 21).

The differences in emphasis between girls' and boys' friendships are not surprising, because throughout adolescent and adult life women have traditionally tended to maintain a stronger interpersonal orientation in adjusting to life. A girl or woman is more likely than a man to be strongly motivated by the need for love and nurturance; when threatened, she is generally less reluctant to appeal to others for support and nurturance. Adolescent and adult males, on the other hand, are more likely than females to be motivated by a need for

T A B L E 8.2 COMPARISON OF MALE AND FEMALE HIGH SCHOOL AND COLLEGE STUDENTS (PERCENT)[a]

Relationship Style	Male		Female	
	High School	College	High School	College
Uninvolved	39	28	31	17
Friendly	24	23	26	11
Intimate	15	23	15	30
Integrated	22	26	28	42

Source: J. L. Fischer. Transitions in relationship style from adolescence to young adulthood. *Journal of Youth and Adolescence.* 1981. **10,** 11–23. By permission.

[a]School $\times$ gender $\times$ style: $x^2(9) = 21.76.$ $p < 0.01.$

autonomy and to rely on oneself or on a group of peers (the gang or the clique) in dealing with competitive demands (Huston, 1983; Newman, 1975a, 1975b; Savin-Williams, 1980a). Adolescent boys tend to be more competitive and more hesitant about expressing support or warmth in all-male discussion groups than do girls in female groups; as the study just described might suggest, boys are somewhat freer in talking about personal feelings in mixed-sex groups than in same-sex groups (Aries, 1974; Newman, 1975a, 1975b; Youniss & Smollar, 1985). Apparently, despite recent social changes, group discussions centering on interpersonal intimacy are somewhat more threatening to males than to females.

It is important to note that there are still significant differences *within* each sex in friendship patterns (Cooper & Grotevant, 1987; Fischer, 1981; Sharbany et al., 1981). Some men are more interpersonally oriented, concerned with intimacy, and willing to express emotion than others. By the same token, some women are more concerned with autonomy and meeting the competitive demands of society, and less concerned with intimacy and self-disclosing com-

T A B L E 8.3 COMPARISON OF GENDER OF PERSON AND GENDER OF TARGET PERSON BY RELATIONSHIP STYLE (PERCENT)[a]

Relationship Style	Gender of Subject–Gender of Target Person			
	Male–Male	Male–Female	Female–Male	Female–Female
Uninvolved	46	12	15	28
Friendly	22	27	22	16
Intimate	17	24	15	28
Integrated	15	36	48	29

Source: J. L. Fischer. Transitions in relationship style from adolescence to young adulthood. *Journal of Youth and Adolescence,* 1981. **10,** 11–23. By permission.

[a]$x^2(9) = 28.91.$ $p < 0.001.$

munication. Such individual variations may be strongly influenced by prior experiences and patterns of interaction within the family (Cooper & Ayers-Lopez, 1985; Cooper & Grotevant, 1987; Huston, 1983; Sroufe & Fleeson, 1986). Thus, parental encouragement of individuality and "separateness" (see page 210) appears to play an important part in fostering the development of autonomy and independence in girls, probably because the broader society encourages these traits more in boys (Hauser et al., 1987; Hauser, Leaper, & Block, 1986; Huston, 1983). Conversely, high levels of parental warmth, support, and "connectedness," particularly in a boy's relationship with his father, appear to be important in encouraging boys to develop close friendships with peers (Baumrind, 1979; Cooper & Grotevant, 1987; Grotevant & Cooper, in press; Huston, 1983).

SOCIAL ACCEPTANCE, NEGLECT, AND REJECTION

As we have implied, an adolescent's personality characteristics, cognitive skills, and social behaviors affect his or her chances of being accepted by peers. In general, adolescents who are accepted by their peers are perceived as liking other people and as being tolerant, flexible, and sympathetic. They are portrayed as lively, cheerful, good-natured, and possessing a sense of humor; low in anxiety and having a reasonable level of self-esteem; acting naturally and self-confidently without being conceited; and possessing initiative, enthusiasm, and drive. Adolescents who are viewed favorably tend to make others feel accepted and involved, to promote constructive interaction between peers, and to plan and initiate interesting or enjoyable group activities. They are adept at interpersonal understanding, know how to communicate effectively, are knowledgeable about peer group norms and values, and are able to infer and vicariously experience their peers' moods and feelings (Allen, Weissberg, & Hawkins, 1989; Asher & Renshaw, 1981; Coleman, 1980; Kurdek & Krile, 1982; Mannerino, 1976).

The characteristics that are least admired and most likely to lead to neglect or outright rejection are in many ways the opposites of those leading to acceptance and popularity. The adolescent who is ill at ease and lacking in self-confidence and who tends to react to discomfiture with timidity, nervousness, or withdrawal is likely to be neglected by peers and to become a social isolate. In contrast, the young person who is self-centered and inconsiderate and who reacts to discomfiture with overaggressiveness, conceit, or demands for attention is likely to court active dislike and rejection. Similarly, the adolescent who is self-centered and unable or unwilling to perceive and meet the needs of others, who is sarcastic, tactless, and inconsiderate and contributes little to the success of group efforts, is likely to receive little consideration in return (Asher, 1978; Asher & Renshaw, 1981; Hartup, 1983, 1989).

There are, of course, many other factors that may affect an adolescent's chances of being accepted or rejected by peers. These include intelligence and ability, physical attractiveness, special talents, socioeconomic status, and

Athletic ability among boys and social skills among girls contribute to an individual's status in most adolescent peer groups.

ethnic-group membership. Athletic ability among boys (Cavior & Dokecki, 1973; Hartup, 1970, 1983) and social skills among girls contribute significantly to an individual's status in most adolescent peer groups (Coleman, 1980). Some characteristics, such as physical size, athletic ability, and physical assertiveness, are more strongly related to group status among younger adolescents than among older ones; conversely, intelligence, creativity, and social skills play a relatively larger role among older adolescents.

Few adolescents are unaffected by social neglect or rejection (Conger, 1977, 1975; Hartup, 1983, 1989; Parker & Asher, 1987; Price & Dodge, 1989). A few individualists, confident of their own goals and interests and having a strong sense of ego identity, may neither need nor seek the approbation of peers. But most adolescents, judging their own worth largely in terms of others' reactions to them, are dependent on the approval and acclaim of prestigious peers.

Unfortunately, an unpopular adolescent is likely to be caught in a vicious cycle. The emotionally troubled, self-preoccupied, and insecure individual is likely to meet with rejection or indifference from peers. In turn, awareness of lack of acceptance, coupled with lack of opportunities to participate in and learn from peer group activities, further undermines the adolescent's self-confidence and increases his or her sense of social isolation, leading to further inappropriate behavior with peers.

Other things being equal, social acceptance by peers is desirable, particularly if it is based on mutual helpfulness and shared interests. However, many

Few adolescents are unaffected by social neglect or rejection. Most are dependent for feelings of self-worth on the approval and acclaim of their peers.

parents—particularly upper- and middle-class parents—place undue emphasis on the pursuit of popularity. Greater emphasis on the importance of being oneself and remaining faithful to individual values and goals, and less on the importance of popularity and superficial appearances—of fitting in at all costs—would be more beneficial to the child in the long run.

But as we have already noted, it would be unrealistic to expect the average adolescent—unsure of his or her own identity and unclear about the demands made by a rapidly changing society—to be immune to the favor of peers. Most adolescents, at one time or another, feel that they do not belong, and the pain, however temporary, can be very real; parents' insistence on popularity can only compound the young person's difficulties.

RELATIONS WITH OPPOSITE-SEX PEERS

Before the middle years of adolescence, peer relationships—especially close friendships—tend to be restricted largely to members of the same sex. To some extent, these patterns are culturally imposed and hence are subject to variation and modification. For example, among preadolescents in some coeducational

Box 8.1 PEER RELATIONS AND SUBSEQUENT ADJUSTMENT

In view of the importance of peer relations in our society, it should not be surprising to find that relationships with peers in childhood and adolescence are significantly related to subsequent adjustment during adolescence and adulthood. A review of research on this subject found that more than thirty studies revealed positive correlations between rejection in childhood and problems later in life (Parker & Asher, 1987). Poor peer relations are predictors of adult neurotic and psychotic disturbances, as well as conduct disorders, delinquency, and disturbances in sexual behavior and adjustment (Elliott, Huzingo, & Ageton, 1985; Hartup, 1983, 1989; Roff, Sells, & Golden, 1972; Rutter & Giller, 1984). For example, in one investigation a wide variety of measures were obtained for third-grade children, including intelligence test scores, school grades, achievement test scores, school attendance, and ratings by teachers and peers. Eleven years later those who were using mental-health services were identified through community mental-health registers. Of all the measures originally obtained, the best predictors of adult mental health were the peer ratings (Cowen et al., 1973).

In a comprehensive longitudinal study of schoolchildren in a large metropolitan area, differences between future delinquents and nondelinquents (matched for age, social class, IQ, school attended, residence area, and ethnicity) emerged as early as the period from kindergarten to the third grade. Future delinquents showed "more difficulty in getting along with peers, both in individual one-to-one contacts and in group situations, and they were less willing or able to treat others courteously, tactfully, and fairly. In return, they were less well liked and accepted by their peers" (Conger & Miller, 1966, p. 68).

In brief, there is reason to believe that poor peer relations are a central factor in the development of a variety of emotional and social maladjustments (Hartup, 1983, 1989; Rutter & Giller, 1984). Whether poor peer relations simply reflect general differences in development or whether they contribute to the development of maladaptive behavior cannot be resolved solely through such "natural experiments." However, experimental studies of monkeys are suggestive: Stephen Suomi (1978) and others have found that early disturbances in peer relations can have significant adverse effects on long-term adjustment (Boccia et al., 1989; Suomi, 1978).

boarding schools cross-sex friendships are more common than is generally the case. To a large extent, however, these patterns appear to reflect the needs of young people themselves. Before the years in which sex drive increases, the young person is more likely to find others with similar concerns, interests, talents, and skills among same-sex peers. Learning culturally sanctioned behaviors (other than those that are specifically heterosexual) may be more easily accomplished in company with others engaged in similar efforts. During a period of rapid physical and psychological change, finding out about one's changing self, and discovering (often with considerable relief) that one is not so different or peculiar, may be facilitated by communication with same-sex peers.

Moreover, the awakening of sexual impulses and related physiological and psychological changes is likely to provoke at least a temporary period of self-consciousness and anxiety about sex in general and about opposite-sex peers. The sex antagonisms that are common in the preadolescent years appear to be at least partly defensive, as though the young person were saying, "I must be a real boy (or girl) because I'm certainly not like those strange persons of the opposite sex." Partly, too, such antagonisms appear to facilitate avoidance of premature heterosexual relationships, with which the adolescent is unprepared to cope.

At this stage of development, when family ties and preoccupations with the self are still strong, seeking to achieve a sense of identity through identification with others of the same sex (through friendship or "crushes") appears to be a precondition for later cross-sex friendships, infatuations, and eventually, mature love (Blos, 1971, 1979; Feinstein & Ardon, 1973).

As maturation continues, boys and girls begin to pay more attention to one another. Earlier sex antagonisms and crushes begin to wane, and heterosexual interests increase. Nevertheless, in their early stages heterosexual relationships reflect many preadolescent characteristics (Conger, 1979). Self-preoccupation remains strong; deep emotional involvement with opposite-sex peers is rare; and heterosexual interactions usually have a superficial, gamelike quality. During this period heterosexual group activities are common and may offer the security of having familiar same-sex peers present. Such activities provide graduated opportunities to learn ways of relating to opposite-sex peers and ensuring that one will not be alone on a date with an opposite-sex peer before one is ready to begin dating.

Gradually, however, experiences in heterosexual cliques promote increasing confidence in one's ability to relate to individual peers of the opposite sex. At the same time, greater maturity—reduced self-preoccupation, a clearer sense of self, and increased concern for others—increases the likelihood that such relationships will themselves be more mature and involve not only sexual attraction but feelings of mutual trust and confidence, a genuine sharing of interests, and a serious involvement in the well-being of the other person.

Dating

In our society the traditional vehicle for individual heterosexual relationships is dating. Although dating clearly provides a ritualized structure for learning heterosexual interactions, it may also promote superficiality and, at times, dishonesty and competitiveness in relations between the sexes. Because dating is ubiquitous in America, we often take it for granted, neglecting the fact that dating tends to occur earlier and to play a more dominant role in adolescent peer relations here than in many other countries. Although there are regional, ethnic, and socioeconomic variations, most girls in the United States begin dating between the ages of 13 and 14 and most boys between the

In the United States, dating tends to occur earlier and to play a more dominant role in adolescent peer relations than in many other countries.

ages of 14 and 15 (Dornbusch et al., 1981; Hansen, 1977; McCabe, 1984). In a national survey of high school seniors carried out in 1989, approximately half indicated that they went out on a date at least once a week, and about one-third said that they dated at least two or three times a week (see Table 8.4).

Under favorable conditions dating serves a number of functions in addition to recreation. It aids in the development of social and interpersonal skills in relations with members of the opposite sex; it provides opportunities to meet opposite-sex peers within a social framework that allows for terminating unwanted relationships (and finding new ones) with minimal loss of face; it offers a means for finding and testing identity; and it provides occasions for sexual experimentation and discovery within mutually acceptable limits (Bell, 1987; Cooper & Grotevant, 1987; McCabe, 1984). Perhaps most important as

FREQUENCY OF DATING AMONG U.S. HIGH SCHOOL SENIORS, 1989				
	Sex		College-Bound	
	Male	Female	Yes	No
Never	13.6	14.4	12.5	14.8
Once a month or less	19.9	17.4	20.2	15.1
Two or three times a month	17.6	15.8	17.6	14.3
Once a week	17.1	15.5	16.3	16.5
Two or three times a week	21.9	22.4	21.8	23.2
Over three times a week	9.8	14.5	10.5	16.1

Source: L. D. Johnston, J. F. Bachman, & P. M. O'Malley. *Monitoring the future: Questionnaire responses from the nation's high school seniors, 1989.* Ann Arbor, MI: Institute for Social Research, forthcoming. By permission.

far as future marriage is concerned, dating may permit the development of genuine trust, love, and mutual concern between opposite-sex peers.

Middle-class dating patterns in this country do in fact appear to serve at least some of these functions. Compared with their European contemporaries, American adolescents exhibit considerably greater poise, nonchalance, and lack of shyness. If the adolescent does not begin going steady too early and for too long a time, dating allows him or her to gain experience with a variety of opposite-sex peers.

Whether dating encourages depth and maturity in interpersonal relationships is more open to question. Particularly in the earlier years of adolescence, there seems to be less emphasis on the development of warm, spontaneous, meaningful interactions between two individuals and more emphasis on the development of the so-called dating personality. Many aspects of the "good" date (superficial social and conversational skills; charm; a bright, interested manner, regardless of one's true feelings; sexual attractiveness) seem irrelevant if not inimical to the development of deeper, more honest and complex emotional relationships, particularly if dating is begun too early. As noted earlier, overly eager pursuit of popularity can sometimes work against the development of a richer personal identity and inner resourcefulness.

Current Dating Patterns

Although dating is considerably less formal and structured today than it was in earlier generations, the characteristics adolescents look for in a prospective date, the doubts and anxieties they share, and the "rules of the dating game" are not nearly as new and different as one might expect (Bell, 1987). Young people are still concerned with such issues as "Does he like me?" "If I ask her to go out with me, will she turn me down?" "Will he call?" "Will I know what to say and how to act if I go out with her?" "What about making out?"

For a young person who is shy, socially inexperienced, or fearful of rejection, asking someone for a first date is not easy. In the words of one 16-year-old boy,

> The way you think about yourself really has a lot to do with how you act. Like you might stop yourself from going up to someone you might want to meet because you think, Oh, I'm not attractive enough or I don't have a good enough personality. You think you won't make a good impression so you're afraid to make an effort. For me, it was always that I was afraid I'd be rejected or—even worse than that—ignored. But what I've learned is that you may have something inside you that the other person would like very much. You have to give yourself a chance because if you put yourself down too quick you never get anywhere (Bell, 1987, p. 67).

Despite the so-called sexual revolution and the women's movement, many traditional stereotypes about dating appear to be alive and well. Thus, most girls are reluctant to ask a boy out first, although in national surveys most boys say they would welcome it (Bell, 1987; Gaylin, 1978, 1979). According to one 17-year-old boy, "I think it's great when a girl calls up a guy to ask him out. A lot of guys are shy, like I was shy for a long time. It was hell for me to ask a girl out. And a lot of the girls I know are much less shy than I am, so it makes me feel wonderful when one of them asks me out" (Bell, 1987, p. 69). Nevertheless, the average adolescent still feels constrained by traditional sex role expectations:

> I think boys have it really hard. Once you get to be a teenager, suddenly everybody expects you to start calling up girls and going out with them. But, hey, I think it takes a lot of courage to call a girl up and ask her out. You know, you always worry that she'll say no. . . . It's not so easy for me to just pick up the phone and act cool. I get nervous (Bell, 1987, p. 68).

Nor is the situation easier for the girl who has been taught to wait to be asked:

> Sitting around waiting for the phone to ring is a big part of my life—you know, wondering if some boy's going to call and ask you out for the weekend. Like on Monday night I'll sit there and say to myself, Well, the phone's going to ring by the time I count to twenty-five. Then if it doesn't ring I count to a new number. It makes me so nervous I can't concentrate on anything else and I'm always yelling at everybody else in the family to get off the phone if they're using it (Bell, 1987, p. 68).

Although nearly 40 percent of boys and nearly 50 percent of girls still think the boy should pay all the expenses of a date, the picture is changing. Today, especially among older adolescents and youth, there is a more egalitarian approach to the costs of dating.

Many contemporary adolescents, like their peers of an earlier day, are concerned about what kinds of sexual activity are or are not appropriate at various stages of the dating process, and about how to initiate or respond to sex-related behavior. Although sexual standards are generally more liberal than they were in earlier decades, most adolescents still expect the boy to take the lead in "making out." Nearly two out of three adolescent girls say that they prefer to have the boy take the lead, even though less than one boy in four says that he would be "turned off" by the girl taking the lead (Bachman, Johnston, & O'Malley, 1990; Bell, 1987; Bell & Wildflower, 1983; Gaylin, 1978, 1979; Lindsay, 1985).

Dating Preferences. In one national survey, adolescent American girls between the ages of 16 and 21 were asked what qualities in boys "turned them on"—or off (Gaylin, 1979). Rated as most important (90 percent or more) were good personality, kindness, good manners, and a sense of humor; these were followed by compassion, good looks, and charm (over 70 percent). In contrast, the following were the most frequently cited "turn-offs": heavy drinking, inability to communicate feelings, profanity, and drug use (all over 70 percent), followed by indecisiveness, "super-jock," and "don't kiss goodnight" (40 percent or more). Apparently, these young women wanted boys to be somewhat androgynous—sensitive and compassionate but also reasonably assertive and decisive.

In a similar survey of boys in the same age range, a number of interesting findings emerged. Three-quarters of the boys said that the first thing that attracts them to a girl is her looks—whether she has an attractive figure and a pretty face. However, when asked what they considered most important in a girl, or what would lead them to want to continue dating her, personality and a sense of humor ranked first, followed by beauty, intelligence, and personal warmth (Gaylin, 1978).

In other surveys, desirable qualities that were frequently mentioned by members of both sexes included good looks; kindness and honesty; responsible and dependable behavior; intelligence; friendliness, confidence without conceitedness; conversational skill; a sense of humor; and a pleasant personality ("fun to be with") (Hass, 1979; Lloyd, 1985; Roscoe, Diana, & Brooks, 1987). Older adolescents were more likely to rate "shares same interests" and "has set goals for the future" as important personal characteristics in choosing a dating partner (Roscoe, Diana, & Brooks, 1987). Conversely, younger adolescents gave greater weight to characteristics associated with popularity and social prestige, such as "dresses fashionably," "approved of by parents," "well-liked by many people," "gets along well with others," and "does not take drugs" (Roscoe, Diana, & Brooks, 1987).

Going Steady. The adolescent who begins going steady at too early an age is likely to miss a number of important developmental experiences. For one thing, the young person may never achieve the benefits of like-sex friendships discussed in the preceding section. Such friendships play a vital role in helping the adolescent learn how to get along with members of the same sex. Same-sex friends can be very important in adult life, even after marriage. They can make life richer, fuller, and more rewarding, as well as providing support during times of stress. As we have also seen, identification with friends of the same sex helps the adolescent come to a deeper understanding of himself or herself and aids in identity formation.

Moreover, when adolescents begin going steady while they are still emotionally and socially immature, the relationship itself is likely to have these qualities. In addition, progress toward becoming mature, self-reliant persons in their own right may be jeopardized. They may use their relationship as a way of avoiding other developmental tasks. And, of course, they miss out on valuable opportunities to know, understand, and enjoy a wide variety of acquaintances of both sexes.

Girls who begin dating very early (ages 11–14) and those who do not date at all, even in late adolescence, are at a developmental disadvantage. One study found that adolescent girls who begin dating very early tend to be active, energetic, and self-confident but also immature, superficial, unimaginative, and limited in their interests and friendships, especially with other girls (Douvan & Adelson, 1966). Older adolescent girls who have had little experience with dating may also be penalized, though in different ways. The same study found that those who do not date at all tend to be retarded in their social development, overly dependent on parents, insecure, and self-absorbed. Clearly, these personality characteristics are not attributable solely to the dating pattern. Preexisting personality characteristics are at least as likely to influence dating practices as the reverse. But once the patterns are established, a vicious cycle may be set in motion, further reinforcing the girls' particular liabilities.

Stages in Dating Behavior. In early adolescence dating functions largely as a source of recreation and enjoyment, a means of achieving or maintaining status with peers, and a way of developing social and interpersonal skills; younger adolescents are often self-conscious and somewhat anxious in their relationships with opposite-sex peers (Bell, 1987; Roscoe, Diana, & Brooks, 1987; Schofield, 1981). Only in late adolescence, with the advent of greater cognitive and emotional maturity, are genuinely intimate relationships likely to develop—relationships characterized by sensitivity and mutual understanding, freedom to reveal thoughts and feelings, emotional involvement, and trust and commitment (Berndt, 1982; Roscoe, Diana, & Brooks, 1987; Sharbany, Gershoni, & Hoffman, 1981).

Among girls, the capacity for intimacy in relationships with both opposite- and same-sex peers usually develops earlier and more intensely than among boys (see Figure 8.5) (Blyth, Hill, & Thiel, 1982; Kacerguis & Adams, 1980; Sharbany et al., 1980). However, adolescent girls tend to place somewhat greater emphasis on the intimate, emotional, interpersonal aspects of boy-girl relationships, while boys are more likely to emphasize shared activities and interests (McCabe & Collins, 1975; Roscoe, Diana, & Brooks, 1987). Even in late adolescence, however, most dating relationships tend to be rather stereotyped and superficial and do not involve a high degree of intimacy (Hodgson & Fisher, 1980; Kacerguis & Adams, 1980; Steinberg, 1985).

Adolescent Love. When American adolescents were asked whether they had ever been in love, 56 percent replied that they had, 39 percent that they had not, and 5 percent that they were not sure (Gallup, 1979). Boys between the ages of 12 and 15 were least likely to say that they had been in love (47 percent); girls between the ages of 16 and 18 were most likely to say that they had been in love. Among those who said that they had been in love at some point, slightly over half (52 percent) said that they were currently in love. Girls were more likely than boys to say that they were currently in love (61 percent versus 42 percent), with older girls having the highest frequency (69 percent) and younger boys the lowest (38 percent).

In some cases adolescent romances evolve gradually into stable, committed, long-term relationships; more frequently they involve an "intense emotional experience that lasts a while and then changes" (Bell, 1987, p. 70). Nevertheless, during the relationship the feelings can be just as vital, and the capacity for joy or despair just as great, as in adult love affairs. To be in love with someone who does not reciprocate is painful; it is "even more painful when you are still in love with someone who's no longer in love with you" (Bell, 1987, p. 71). For adults to dismiss adolescent "puppy love" as not serious (or even as amusing) indicates lack of sensitivity—as well as a short memory. Breaking up

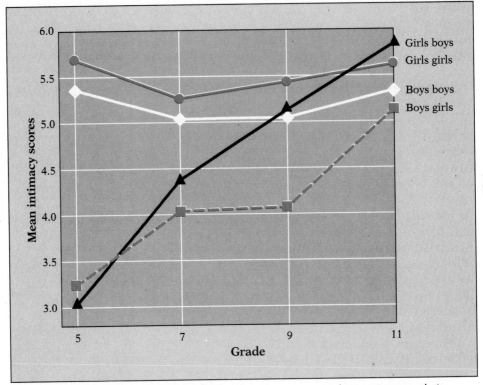

Figure 8.5 Age differences in reported intimacy in same- and opposite-sex relationships. (From R. Sharabany, R. Gershoni, & J. Hoffman (1981). Girlfriend, boyfriend: Age and sex differences in intimate friendship. *Developmental Psychology*, **17**, 800–808. Copyright 1981 by the American Psychological Association. Reprinted by permission)

with a boyfriend or girlfriend can lead to genuine depression; one 17-year-old girl described her feelings as follows: "I just feel like my life's over, like there's never going to be anything to smile about again" (Bell, 1987, p. 71). Fortunately, in most cases the hurt gradually fades, but having a close friend to talk to can be very helpful at such a time.

On the other hand, adolescents sometimes seek to maintain a relationship simply for the security involved, thereby limiting their own continued development: "It's comforting to know that you'll always have a date for the weekend and that someone cares about you and is choosing to spend time with you. But fear—fear of being alone, fear of going out with new people, fear of hurting the other person's feelings, fear of being rejected—is not a healthy basis for a relationship" (Bell, 1987, p. 72).

In brief, it appears that the young person who is best prepared for the responsibilities of adult life and for the emotional demands of marriage will have been able to try out a variety of social and personal roles during adolescence. This involves establishing and maintaining relationships both with opposite-sex peers and with close friends of the same sex in the early years of adolescence and, in the later years of adolescence, having opportunities to develop meaningful, trusting, and mutually supportive relationships with an opposite-sex peer.

ADOLESCENT MARRIAGES

In our society the role requirements associated with marriage are complex and often difficult to fulfill. And they appear to be becoming more so as societal rewards for marriage have diminished and traditional role relationships have become less clearly defined and more controversial, particularly among more advantaged youth (Astin, Green, Korn, 1987; Astin, Korn, & Berz, 1989; Johnston, Bachman, & O'Malley, forthcoming). Among American high school seniors in 1989, only about one-third agreed that "most people will have fuller and happier lives if they choose legal marriage, rather than staying single, or just living with someone"—an idea that was virtually an article of faith in their parents' generation (see Table 8.5).

Nevertheless, more than three-fourths of contemporary adolescents and youth plan to marry, and less than 6 percent think they are not likely to marry, with the remainder uncertain (Johnston et al., forthcoming; America's youth, 1988). Moreover, although the importance attached to being married and raising a family declined dramatically between the late 1960s and the middle 1970s, it increased steadily in the 1980s.

For example, among all first-year female college students in the United States, the percentage citing "raising a family" as an essential or very important value declined from 77.8 percent in 1970 to only 56.8 percent in 1976; by 1989 it had risen to 69.0 percent. The corresponding figures for males were 63.5 percent in 1970, declining to 53.3 percent in 1974, and rising to 68.5 percent in 1989. As may be seen, while significantly more women than men considered raising a family very important or essential in 1970, by 1988 this

TABLE 8.5 HIGH SCHOOL SENIORS RESPONSES ON IMPORTANCE OF MARRIAGE FOR HAPPINESS

	Sex		College-Bound	
	Male	Female	Yes	No
Disagree	19.3	26.7	23.8	22.3
Mostly disagree	10.6	13.9	13.0	11.6
Neither	32.2	29.3	31.6	27.6
Mostly agree	17.4	13.1	14.6	16.8
Agree	20.6	17.0	17.0	21.6

Source: L. D. Johnston, J. F. Bachman, & P. M. O'Malley. *Monitoring the future: Questionnaire responses from the nation's high school seniors, 1989.* Ann Arbor, MI: Institute for Social Research, forthcoming. By permission.

difference had almost vanished. Both the greater decline among women in the first half of the 1970s and the smaller subsequent increase probably reflect the increased importance of careers in women's value systems during the past two decades (Astin et al., 1989). (The percentage of women who desire administrative responsibility more than doubled during this period, and there were large increases in the number who wish to succeed in their own businesses, to be an authority in their field, or to be well off financially.)

Among the small minority of young people between the ages of 13 and 18 who are planning not to marry, half of adolescent males, but only 4 percent of females, say that they do not want the responsibility of marriage (Norman & Harris, 1981). In contrast, twice as many girls as boys fear loss of freedom in marriage (44 percent versus 22 percent); similarly, more than twice as many girls as boys express concern that marriage would interfere with their career plans (19 percent versus 9 percent).

Marriage is likely to be more difficult for married adolescents, who may still be struggling to complete their education, establish themselves in a vocation, or complete the process of identity formation.

The burdens of marriage are likely to be greatest for married adolescents, who may still be struggling to complete their education, establish themselves in a vocation, or complete the process of identity formation. Typically, married adolescents are also economically insecure or dependent on parents for financial assistance—situations that may create additional problems.

Young married couples are under greater pressure than their single peers to meet complicated cultural demands, both in social relationships with others and in the increasingly complex and changing world of work. Along with the rapid increase in two-job families in recent years has come the need to juggle jobs, household work, and child rearing; the result may be increased stress on the family. This is especially likely for wives without extended-family support; even among young couples with an egalitarian view of marriage, in which the husband makes an effort to share household tasks and child care, the burden of these responsibilities is still likely to fall most heavily on the wife, whether she is employed or not (Lindsay, 1985; Smith, 1979).

In any marriage both husband and wife have to learn to cope with new restrictions on personal freedom, adjust their personal wishes and habits to those of their partner, and shift much of their emotional concern from themselves to their spouse and children. This can be particularly difficult for young people who are still preoccupied with the formation of their own identity. In the words of a young woman who married while still in high school,

> Sometimes I wish I would have never married, had my baby and gotten older. I'm doing fine, I guess. I've never known any years that passed me by so very fast. I went straight from having to be in the house when the lights went on to having to be in when the child cried or the husband called.
>
> I don't know what's going on with me. Dick treats me good and we never really fight. He's always there when I need him but he's never there when I don't. Please try to tell me what's wrong. I still love him very much (Lindsay, 1985, p. 46).

In addition, our society's emphasis on marriage as a continuing romantic affair may attach unrealistic expectations to what is already a difficult emotional interaction. Considerable personal maturity and integration into other adult roles enhance a couple's chances of achieving a successful marriage. Adolescents themselves tend to agree with this statement; in one national survey, more than eight out of ten young people expressed the belief that a person should be over 20 before marrying (Lindsay, 1985).

Adolescent marriages are often complicated by the fact that they are likely to have resulted from pregnancy. The great majority of all premaritally pregnant brides are in their teens; nearly half of all marital births to teenagers are conceived premaritally, despite the fact that more than half of all births to adolescents today are occurring outside marriage—up from one-third in 1970 (Hayes, 1987). Premarital pregnancy may lead young people to marry someone they otherwise would not have chosen. Even when the choice is one that they would ultimately have made, however, they have less time to become adjusted to each other and to the demands of marriage before undertaking the responsibilities of parenthood. Most young people would prefer to wait at least two years after marriage before having children, and a majority actually do so (Johnston, Bachman, & O'Malley, forthcoming; U.S. Bureau of the Census, 1989).

When we add to these considerations the facts that young marrieds are statistically more likely than persons marrying at later ages to have lower intelligence test scores, lower school grades, and lower educational levels, to drop out of school, and to be employed at unskilled and semiskilled jobs, it is not surprising to find that adolescent marriages are two to three times more likely to break up than those of couples who marry in their twenties (Hayes, 1987; Edelman, 1987; Norton & Moorman, 1986). The younger the adolescent partners are when they marry, the greater the likelihood of divorce or legal separation. In 1985 one-third of women who had married before age 20 were divorced; the proportion declined steadily with increasing age at first marriage, reaching a low of 12 percent among women who first married at 30 or older (Norton & Moorman, 1986).

Box 8.2 AGE TRENDS IN MARRIAGES AMONG YOUTH

In the past two decades there has been a steady increase in age at first marriage among both males and females (from 20.6 years for women and 22.5 years for men in 1970 to 23 years for women and 24.8 years for men in 1985, the last year for which data were available). In 1985 more than 86 percent of 19-year-old young women were single, compared to a little over two-thirds in 1970. Among 20–24-year-olds, 58 percent were single in 1985, compared to only a little over one-third in 1970 (U.S. Bureau of the Census, 1989).

For most young people, these figures reflect postponement of marriage, and not, as some have suggested, abandonment of marriage as an institution. What accounts for the delay? One factor that clearly plays a role is the greater social and personal acceptability of sexual relationships between unmarried youth and young adults, especially those who are going steady or engaged (see page 246). Many more young couples are living together or involved in fairly stable premarital relationships than ever before (Glick, 1984; Lindsay, 1985; Risman et al., 1981; U.S. Bureau of the Census, 1979, 1989). Increased rates of high school and college attendance also appear to contribute to the reduction in rates of adolescent marriage (Cherlin, 1980). Between 1970 and 1985 college enrollment among males increased by 38 percent, while among females it increased by nearly 50 percent (U.S. Bureau of the Census, 1989).

In addition, growing concern with material values and "making it", combined with the increased difficulty of achieving financial stability and such goals as home ownership in the face of increased costs, are leading many young people to postpone the responsibilities of marriage until they feel more secure.

Moreover, for many young people, especially young women, there is less pressure from peers to rush into marriage and parenthood and increased concern with achieving financial and social independence and becoming well established in a career—that is, developing a social and vocational identity—before taking on the commitments of marriage and family life. One national study found that young women in their early twenties who planned to be working outside the home later in life (age 35) were more likely to postpone marriage than those who planned to be full-time homemakers (Cherlin, 1980).

Finally, the rise in divorce rates and the amount of marital conflict observed by young people, not only among members of their parents' generation but among married peers who are struggling with their new responsibilities, may cause young people to want to be quite sure of their decision before committing themselves to marriage.

Paradoxically, however, recent changes in the life-styles and values of young people may portend greater marital stability within the next decade. Insofar as low income, low education, and early age at marriage increase the probability of eventual divorce, current trends away from these conditions are consistent with a favorable prognosis for future marital stability (Glick, 1984; Norton & Moorman, 1986). Indeed, there are indications that this may already be happening. The prevalence of divorce among women in their thirties rose steadily throughout the past decade (and is currently higher than for any other age group, including women twenty years older). In contrast, the proportion of divorce among women in their twenties increased between 1975 and 1980 but then remained the same through 1985 (Norton & Moorman, 1986).

Premaritally pregnant adolescent girls are even more likely to suffer marital breakups (*Eleven million teenagers*, 1977; Furstenberg, Brooks-Gunn, & Morgan, 1987; Hayes, 1987; Jones et al., 1985). One Baltimore study found that three out of five premaritally pregnant mothers age 17 or younger were separated or divorced within six years of the marriage. One-fifth of the marriages were dissolved within twelve months, two and one-half times the proportion of broken marriages among classmates of the adolescent mothers who were not pregnant premaritally (Furstenberg et al., 1987). Even at the end of three years, the premaritally pregnant teenage brides were nearly twice as likely to have separated as their classmates. Those teenage mothers who married the father prior to the child's delivery were more likely to stay married than those who did not marry until after the birth.

Nevertheless, significant numbers of adolescent marriages are successful. What makes the difference between those that end in divorce and the larger number that succeed despite the difficulties involved? A number of factors appear to differentiate successful young marriages from those that end in failure (see Table 8.6). Obviously, the larger the number of positive factors operat-

T A B L E 8.6 HYPOTHESIZED RELATIONSHIPS BETWEEN SELECTED CHARACTERISTICS AND OUTCOMES OF YOUNG MARRIAGES: FORECAST OF MARITAL COMPETENCE AND SATISFACTION

Characteristic	Poorest
Ages at marriage	Both 17 or younger
Educational attainment	Both school dropouts
Pregnancy	Premarital pregnancy
Acquaintance before marriage	Less than six months, no engagement period, formal or informal
Previous dating patterns	Limited number of dating partners, went steady immediately, or short period between first date and first date with fiancé
Personality dynamics	Generally poor interpersonal skills, lacking maturity, limited interests, poor personal and social adjustment
Motivation for marrying	Drift into marriage, because of pregnancy, seemed like the thing to do, just wanted to, or other impulsive reasons with no strong emphasis on marital and parental roles
Status of families of orientation	Both lower
Parental attitudes before marriage	Stongly opposed
Wedding	Elopement and civil ceremony
Economic basis	Virtually completely dependent upon relatives
Residence	Always lived with in-laws or other relatives
Postmarriage parental views	Rejecting or punitive, assistance provided as a method of controlling the marriage

Source: L. G. Burchinal. Trends and prospects for young marriages in the U.S. *Journal of Marriage and the Family,* May 1965. Copyright 1965 by the National Council on Family Relations, 3989 Centry Ave., N.E., Suite # 550, Minneapolis, MN 55421. Reprinted by permission.

ing in a particular adolescent marriage, the greater its chances of survival; conversely, the larger the number of negative factors, the greater the likelihood of additional problems arising from the marriage (Burchinal, 1965; Lindsay, 1985).

Intermediate	Best
Female 17, male 20 or older	Female at least 18, male 20 or older
Female dropout, male high school graduate	Both high school graduates, male, at least, with some post-high school education
No premarital pregnancy, pregnancy immediately following marriage	Pregnancy delayed until at least 1 year following marriage
One year, at least, with at least six months engagement or understanding to marry	Several years, with at least six months engagement or understanding to marry
Some dating experience before first dating fiancé	Numerous different dates, played the field, some previous experience with going steady
Mixed	Generally competent in interpersonal relations, flexible, mature, maintaining healthy and pleasurable relations with others
Mixed, marriage as preferred to career, though had previous post-high school educational aspirations and for females perhaps tentative plans to work, etc.	No post-high school educational aspirations and, for females, marriage, family, and homemaking preferred as career over working, living independently; positive emphasis upon role as wife and mother
Mixed, lower, and middle or high	Both middle or high
Mildly opposed or resigned acceptance	Supportive once the decision was clear
	Conventional, hometown, and church-sanctioned
Low dependence upon relatives, mostly independent income, even if near hardship level	At least assured income above self-perceived hardship level
Doubled up with relatives some of the time, independent other periods of time	Always maintained own independent place of residence
Cool	Psychologically supportive, sincerely want to help the young couple, assistance provided with no strings attached

The formidable obstacles faced by many young marriages, their demonstrably higher divorce rates, and the less easily documented identity foreclosure that may sometimes result offer considerable justification for not encouraging adolescent marriages. At the same time, it is important to realize that no matter what the circumstances and no matter how ill advised it may seem, adolescent marriage is not a crime and, "if used as grounds for punitive reactions, probably will only promote the completion of the self-fulfilling prophecy of greater risks of young marriages" (Burchinal, 1965, p. 253).

Nevertheless, many well-meaning people have been prompted to take actions that only serve to increase the problems confronting young married couples. For example, some school boards still require the withdrawal or suspension of pregnant girls or married students. Such policies are intended to prevent marriages among high school students. However, the few available studies indicate that they have little, if any, effect on high school marriage rates. Instead, they may only help ensure that young married people will be prevented from acquiring the education necessary for employment (Edelman, 1986).

Far more appropriate are the efforts of some high schools to make all students aware of the realistic problems and demands of marriage. In one experimental program senior high school students "married" for a trimester, during which they learned to face such problems as working out a budget, obtaining housing, providing child care, facing random crises delivered by a "wheel of misfortune" (e.g., coping with the death of a young child), and even—at the end of the course—obtaining a divorce (*Wall Street Journal,* 1975). Most of the participants reported becoming deeply involved in the course and believed that it had increased their understanding of the realities of marriage. A number of couples who were planning to marry in real life decided to defer marriage until they were more mature and more financially secure.

SUMMARY

Peers play an important role in the psychological and social development of most children and adolescents. Relationships with peers during the adolescent years serve as prototypes for adult relationships in social relations, work, and interactions with members of the opposite sex. Adolescents are also more dependent on peer relations than younger children because ties to parents become looser as the young person gains greater independence. More than two out of three adolescents believe that a close friend understands them better than their parents do.

Adolescence may provide opportunities for repairing psychological damage incurred earlier. However, relations with peers during this vulnerable stage of development may also be harmful. The young person may be put down, laughed at, rejected, or pressured into behaviors he or she may regret.

Because of the heightened importance of the peer group during adolescence, motivation for conformity to the values, customs, and fads of peer culture increases during the preadolescent and early adolescent years, followed by a gradual but steady decline from middle through late adolescence. The need to conform may also vary with sex, socioeconomic status, relationships with parents, and personality factors.

Although it is commonly asserted that parental and peer group values are incompatible and that an inevitable result of heightened dependence on the peer group is a sharp decline in parental influence, this is not generally true. For one thing, there is usually considerable overlap between the attitudes of an adolescent's parents and those of his or her peers. Also, neither the influence of parents nor that of peers is all-encompassing. Peers are likely to be more influential in such matters as fashions in music, dress, and language, and patterns of peer interaction. Parental influence is likely to be predominate in educational plans and underlying moral and social values. Recent studies have shown that, on average, during preadolescence and early adolescence conformity to parents tends to decline while conformity to peers rises. Not until middle and late adolescence do increases in overall autonomy occur, for only then does conformity both to parents and to peers decline. Even at an early age, however, some adolescents show a relatively higher degree of overall autonomy than their peers.

During middle childhood and preadolescence, peer relations tend to center on neighborhood play groups and same-sex "gangs." The adolescent's peer relations fall into three broad categories: the broader "crowd" or "set," the smaller, more intimate clique, and individual friendships. As adolescence proceeds, the nature of peer groups changes, and so do the functions they serve. Gradually cliques of one sex begin to interact with cliques of the opposite sex, leading to the formation of the adolescent crowd. Only in the next stage do we see the formation of genuinely heterosexual cliques, in which heterosexual interactions between individuals are initiated. Finally, in late adolescence couples and loosely associated groups of couples are formed. Same-sex friendships are maintained but become more stable and less intense.

Among the peer relationships of adolescents, friendships hold a special place: They are typically more intimate, involve more intense feelings, and are more open and honest than the friendships of earlier and later stages of life. Close friends can contribute to an adolescent's development in ways in which the broader peer group cannot. Adolescents of both sexes name "close friends" as the individuals with whom they are most likely to "talk openly" and share "true feelings." Thus, it is not surprising to find that the main requirements for a friend are to be loyal and trustworthy and to provide support when it is needed. At their best, friendships may help young people learn to deal with their own feelings and those of others; they may also contribute to identity formation.

Friendships are most likely to develop between adolescents who are similar in terms of background, personality characteristics, and interests. However, sometimes an attraction of opposites occurs, in which an adolescent finds in a friend qualities that are felt to be desirable but are lacking in the self. Adolescent friendship patterns also vary with age and sex. Friendships become more intimate and empathic in middle adolescence and more "autonomously interdependent" in late adolescence. Girls' friendships are typically deeper and more interdependent than those of boys.

An adolescent's personality characteristics, cognitive skills, and social behaviors affect his or her chances of being accepted by peers. Adolescents who are viewed favorably tend to make others feel accepted and involved, promote constructive interaction between peers, or plan and initiate interesting or enjoyable group activities. In contrast, a young person who is self-centered and inconsiderate and reacts to discomfiture with overaggressiveness, conceit, or demands for attention is likely to meet with active dislike and rejection.

Under favorable conditions dating may serve a number of useful functions; among other things, it provides opportunities to meet members of the opposite sex and develop social and interpersonal skills. On the other hand, many of the characteristics of the so-called "good date" (e.g., superficial conversational skills and a bright, interested manner) appear to be irrelevant to the development of more genuine emotional relationships. Despite recent social changes, many traditional stereotypes (and many traditional anxieties) about dating appear alive and well.

Adolescents who begin going steady too early may not achieve some of the continuing benefits of like-sex friendships and may also limit their chances of developing into mature, self-reliant individuals. The young person who is best prepared for social and vocational responsibilities in adult life, and also for the emotional demands of marriage, has been able to try out a variety of social and personal roles during adolescence. This involves establishing and maintaining relationships both with opposite-sex peers and with close friends of the same sex in the early years of adolescence and, in the later years, opportunities to develop a meaningful, trusting, and mutually supportive relationship with an opposite-sex peer.

Adolescent marriages are two to three times more likely to fail than those of couples in their twenties because of a variety of social, psychological, and economic stresses (including, in some instances, premarital pregnancy). Nevertheless, a significant number of adolescent marriages can succeed if the young people receive appropriate parental and social support, including a chance to complete their education.

REVIEW QUESTIONS

1. Discuss the role played by peers in helping or hindering the adolescent's psychological and social development.
2. Why does conformity to peers tend to increase during the early years of adolescence? Why are some adolescents more susceptible to peer pressure than others? Give examples.
3. Are parental and peer influences on adolescent values and behavior dichotomous? In which areas are the influences of parents likely to be stronger? In which are the influences of peers likely to be stronger?
4. Describe the structural changes in the nature of peer groups that occur as adolescence proceeds.
5. How may close friendships help young people develop a sense of identity? How do friendship patterns vary with age and sex?
6. What personality characteristics and behaviors are likely to lead to social acceptance by peers or, conversely, to neglect or rejection?

7. What qualities do boys and girls look for in a date? Do these change with age during the adolescent years?
8. What factors differentiate successful adolescent marriages from those that fail?

RECOMMENDED READINGS

Bell, R. (1987). *Changing bodies, changing lives: A book for teens on sex and relationships* (2nd ed.). New York: Random House.

Csikszentmihalyi, M., & Larson, R. (1984). *Being adolescent: Conflict and growth in the teenage years.* New York: Basic Books.

Hartup, W. W. (1983). Peer relations. In E. M. Hetherington (Ed.), & P. H. Mussen (Series Ed.), *Handbook of child psychology: Vol. 4. Socialization, personality, and socil development* (4th ed.) (pp. 103–196). New York: Wiley.

Konopka, G. (1985). *Young girls: A portrait of adolescence.* New York: NY: Harrington Park Press (paperback).

Youniss, J., & Smollar, J. (1985). *Adolescent relations with mothers, fathers, and friends.* Chicago: University of Chicago Press.

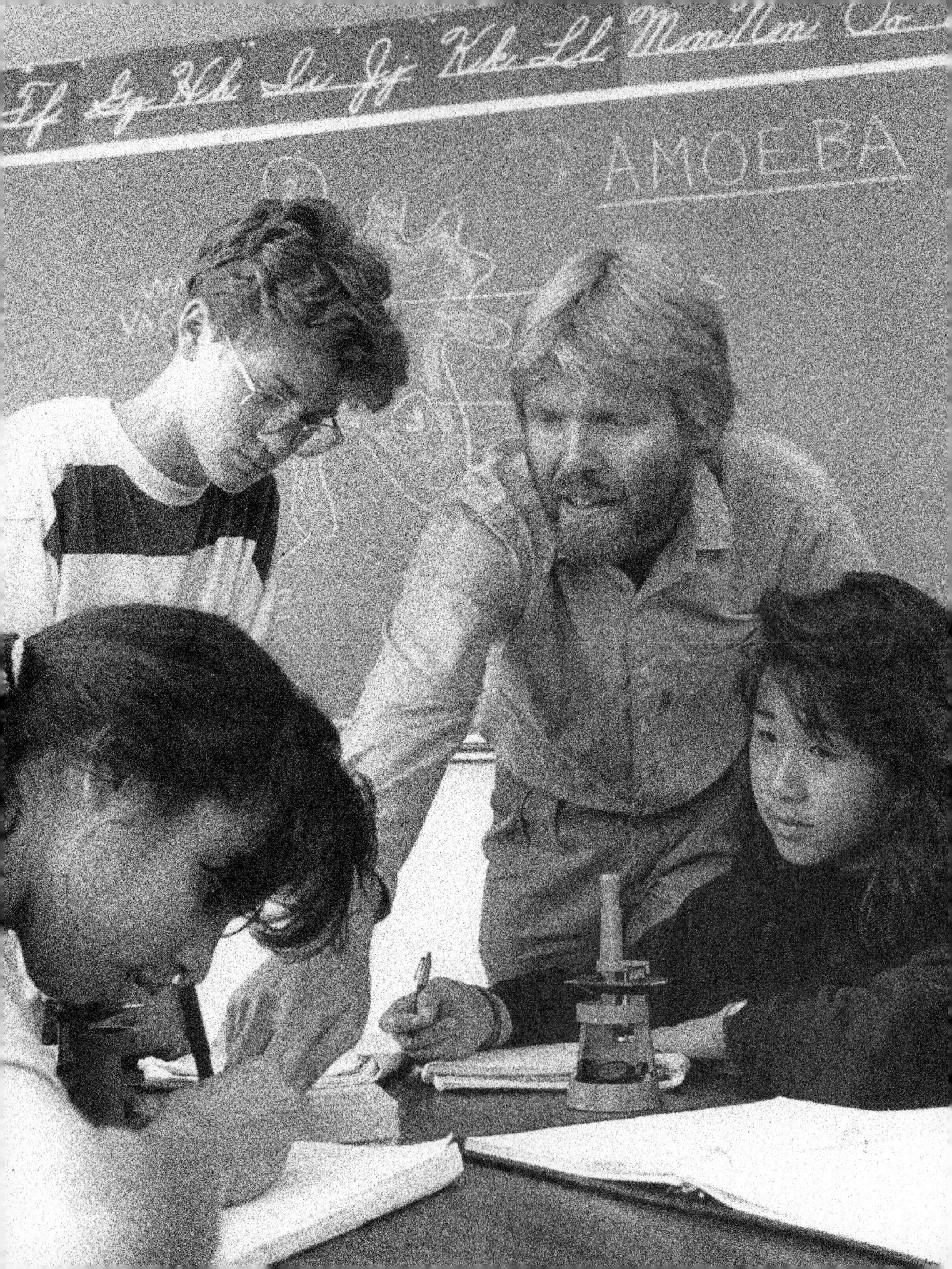
AMOEBA

ADOLESCENTS AND THE SCHOOLS

In America today, the school is the one major social institution other than the family with which nearly everyone is involved during the critical years of childhood and adolescence. Although this may seem entirely normal, in fact it is a relatively recent development. When the United States was primarily an agrarian society, the level of educational skills required for economic survival was generally lower, while the need for young people to help with farm work and other tasks was greater. In 1890, less than 7 percent of all 14–17-year-olds were enrolled in school; by 1900, this figure had risen, but only to 11.4 percent (U.S. Department of Education, 1980). The primary institutional settings in which most young people grew up were the home and the workplace. There were fewer occupations among which to choose, and children typically followed in their parents' footsteps. In short, "the task of socialization was resolved by early and continual interaction with the parents and nearby adults" (Coleman et al., 1974, p. 1).

As our society has become more complex, the influence of other social institutions, including the family, the work place, and the church, on young people's development has been reduced. Responsibility for the development not only of academic skills but also of other vital capabilities—including the ability to manage one's own affairs and life plans effectively—has increasingly shifted to the schools. How well the schools are meeting these varied responsibilities, and indeed, whether they can reasonably be expected to accomplish such a diverse mission, are crucial questions in today's rapidly changing world.

THE QUALITY OF AMERICAN EDUCATION

Let us begin by asking how well the schools are meeting their traditional responsibility for developing basic academic skills.[1] According to a number of widely publicized reports issued in the 1980s, the answer is that they are not performing this task well enough (Carnegie, 1989; Congressional Budget Office, 1987). In 1983 the report of the National Commission on Excellence in Education, *A Nation at Risk*, stated that "the educational foundations of our society are presently being eroded by a rising tide of mediocrity that threatens our very future as a nation and a people. What was unimaginable a generation ago has begun to occur—others are matching and surpassing our educational attainments" (National Commission, 1983, p. 5). And in 1986 another influential report, *A Nation Prepared: Teachers for the 21st Century*, demanded "an improved supply of young people with the knowledge . . . and skills to make the nation once again fully competitive" (Task Force, 1986, p. 2).

These reports and others pointed to a series of studies indicating that American youth were performing more poorly on a wide variety of measures of

[1] For most adolescents "the schools" mean one type of organization: public comprehensive junior and senior high schools. Fewer than 10 percent of adolescents attend private or parochial institutions; fewer still attend so-called alternative schools, private or public.

academic performance, both in relation to the youth of other industrialized countries and, in some cases, to earlier generations of American youth (Boyer, 1983; Congressional Budget Office, 1987). For example, in the 1970s international comparisons of student achievement on a wide variety of academic tasks indicated that Americans were never first or second compared with other industrialized nations and in fact were last more than one-third of the time (Comber & Keeves, 1973; National Commission, 1983). On most standardized tests, American high school students scored lower in the 1970s than they had when Sputnik, the Russian satellite, was launched in the late 1950s (Boyer, 1983; College Entrance Examination Board, 1982; Congressional Budget Office, 1987). Among 17-year-olds who were still enrolled in school in the 1970s, only 50–60 percent (depending on the year of assessment) were able to solve simple problems involving percentages (e.g., "A hockey team won 5 of its 20 games. What percent of the games did it win?) (National Assessment, 1979).

More qualitative findings were also a source of concern. An intensive nationwide investigation conducted by the National Assessment of Educational Progress (1981) found evidence of a continuing decline in reading and writing skills between 1970 and 1980 among both 13- and 17-year-olds. (In each instance girls performed slightly better than boys.)

Recent Trends

Has academic performance improved in the years since 1980? In some respects it has, but not nearly enough to meet the nation's increasing need for informed citizens and productive workers who can compete effectively in the world of the 1990s and beyond (Carnegie, 1989; Congressional Budget Office, 1987). Let us look at the record.

Science. Although the science achievement scores of 17-year-olds improved between 1982 and 1986 following a steady decline in the 1970s, current scores remain well below those of 1969 (Mullis & Jenkins, 1988). More than half of the nation's 17-year-olds are "inadequately prepared either to perform competently jobs that require technical skills or to benefit substantially from on-the-job training" (Mullis & Jenkins, 1988, p. 6). Only 7 percent have the knowledge needed to undertake college-level science courses.

These findings are reinforced by the results of a recent international science assessment, which found that U.S. high school students are among the lowest achievers in all of the participating countries (International Association, 1988; Lapointe, Mead, & Phillips, 1989). Perhaps most discouraging, the further students progress in school, the greater the discrepancy in their performance compared to that of students in other countries.

Mathematics. The 1986 national assessment of mathematics performance, *The Mathematics Report Card: Are We Measuring Up?* obtained only slightly more encouraging results (Dossey, Mullis, Lindquist, & Chambers, 1988). Although average performance had improved since 1978, the gains were confined primarily to lower-order skills. "Most students, even at age 17, do not possess the breadth and depth of mathematics proficiency needed for advanced study in secondary school mathematics" (Dossey et al., 1988, p. 10). The most recent international mathematics assessment found that the *average* Japanese high school student demonstrated a higher level of achievement than the top 5 percent of American students enrolled in college preparatory mathematic courses (McKnight et al., 1987).

American high school students still study only about one-half to one-third as much science and mathematics as their counterparts in Japan, West Germany, and other developed countries, including the Soviet Union, and consequently they know far less about these subjects (Carnegie, 1989; Fiske, 1987a). A National Science Teachers Association survey found that 7,000 of the nation's high schools offer no courses in physics; 4,000 offer no courses in chemistry and 2,000 offer no courses in biology (Fiske, 1987b).

Reading and Writing. In reading and writing, the performance of the nation's 17-year-olds improved modestly in the 1980s—especially among black and Hispanic students—but again, not nearly enough to meet the demand for young people who can understand, analyze, and communicate relatively complicated information (Applebee, Langer, & Mullis, 1986; Daniels, 1990; National Assessment 1986, 1990). According to the chairman of the

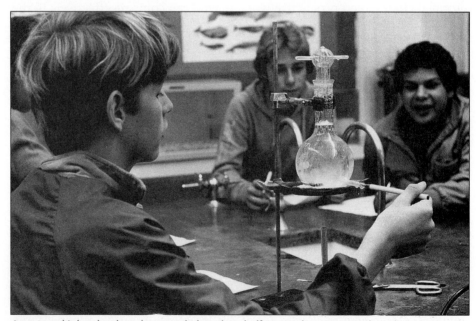

American high school students study less than half as much science and mathematics as their counterparts in other developed countries, and consequently know far less about these subjects.

Xerox Corporation, one out of three major corporations already must provide new workers with basic reading, writing, and arithmetic courses, at a cost of $25 billion a year (Kearns, 1987, cited in Dossey et al., 1988, p. 8).

A national assessment of literacy conducted in 1986 found that less than 40 percent of young adults (ages 21–25) could synthesize the main argument of a lengthy newspaper article, and only 43 percent could follow directions using a street map. When shown a simple menu and asked to say how much change they would get back from a given amount of money if they ordered two specific items, and how much would be required for a 10 percent tip, only 40 percent of respondents could answer both questions correctly (National Assessment, 1986).

A Common Culture? Finally, if we believe that an informed citizenry should share a common culture and some knowledge of our nation's roots and the forces that have shaped it, the picture is at best ambiguous. A national assessment of eleventh-grade students' knowledge of history and literature was conducted in 1986 (Ravitch & Finn, 1987). The results can be interpreted as indicating that "the glass is half full or half empty." Although the questions dealt with "fundamental material that students of this age might reasonably be expected to know" (Ravitch & Finn, 1987, p. 7), only 54 percent of the history questions and 52 percent of the literature questions were answered correctly (see Box 9.1).

Possible Reasons for These Trends

The reasons for the declines in academic performance during the 1960s and 1970s, and for subsequent limited improvements, are not completely clear (Congressional Budget Office, 1987). Among the factors that have been cited as contributing to declining test scores and performance are the following:

A decline in academic standards (e.g., watered-down curricular requirements, less homework, grade inflation, easier textbooks, lower teacher expectations).

Fallout from the societal crisis of the 1960s and early 1970s, including a decline in the authority and perceived relevance of schools and other social institutions; increased alcohol and drug use, school violence, and delinquency; and increased family turmoil, separation, divorce, and single parenthood.

Less mental stimulation in the home and other nonschool settings, including many thousands of hours spent watching television at the expense of reading (see Figure 9.1).

Changes in the socioeconomic mix of students attending school, particularly at the upper secondary school and college levels.

Increases in the percentage of all students who choose to take tests like the Scholastic Aptitude Test (see Box 9.2), thereby diluting the scores of the highest-scoring students (Boyer, 1983; College Entrance Examination Board, 1988; Congressional Budget Office, 1987; Putka, 1988).

Box 9.1 WHAT DO 17-YEAR-OLDS KNOW?

In 1986 Diane Ravitch and Chester E. Finn, Jr., in collaboration with the National Assessment of Educational Progress, conducted a national survey of 8,000 eleventh-graders' core knowledge in the areas of history and litera-ture. As noted in the text, only 54 percent of the history questions and 52 percent of the literature questions were answered correctly. Among the sur-vey's findings were the following:

In the area of history, four out of five students knew that the Bill of Rights guarantees free speech and religion. Sixty to 80 percent identified Lincoln as the author of the Emancipation Proclamation; knew the meaning of the term *Holocaust;* and knew that the United States had been provoked into entering World War I by German submarine attacks on American ships. On the other hand, less than one-third knew in what twenty-year period Lincoln was president or in what half-century the Civil War occurred. Fewer than six in ten knew that World War I occurred after 1900. And only about half knew that Josef Stalin was the leader of the Soviet Union when the United States entered World War II. Closer to the present, only four in ten knew that the controversy surrounding Senator Joseph P. McCarthy focused on investiga-tions of individuals whom he suspected of engaging in Communist activi-ties. Perhaps most surprising, only 22 percent of girls and 23 percent of boys recognized Betty Friedan and Gloria Steinem as leaders of the women's movement in the 1970s.

In literature, two-thirds or more of the adolescents surveyed were familiar with *Robinson Crusoe, The Adventures of Huckleberry Finn, Uncle Tom's Cabin,* and *Romeo and Juliet.* But only 20–25 percent could associate De Tocqueville, Dostoyevsky, Joseph Conrad, Ibsen, William James, or Thomas Hardy with their principal works. Less than 40 percent were familiar with the best-known works of Steinbeck, Orwell, and Hemingway. Contrary to the researchers' expectations, only one in five knew that Salinger's *A Catcher in the Rye,* long considered a classic among high school and college stu-dents, is a novel in which a 16-year-old boy who was expelled from school goes to New York City to find himself.

Thomas Jefferson was convinced that history "by apprising [people] of the past will enable them to judge of the future" (quoted in Ravitch & Finn, 1987, p. vii). He also believed that literature has "a moral dimension," which can "carry home to the heart every moral rule of life" (quoted in Ravitch & Finn, 1987, p. vii). Similar convictions pervade the writings of Winston Churchill and Martin Luther King, Jr. If they are right, we—and the nation's 17-year-olds—have a considerable way to go in preparing youth for the continuing demands of personal growth and responsible citizenship in a democracy.

Source: D. Ravitch & C. E. Finn, Jr. (1987). *What do our 17-year-olds know? A report on the first national assessment of history and literature.* New York: Harper & Row. By permission.

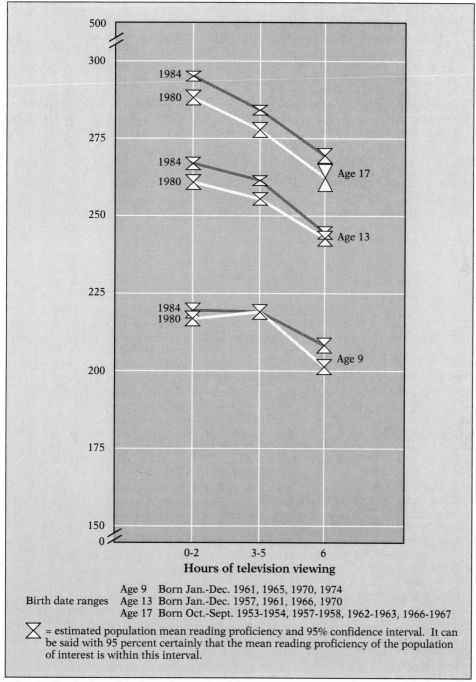

Age 9   Born Jan.-Dec. 1961, 1965, 1970, 1974
Birth date ranges   Age 13   Born Jan.-Dec. 1957, 1961, 1966, 1970
Age 17   Born Oct.-Sept. 1953-1954, 1957-1958, 1962-1963, 1966-1967

☒ = estimated population mean reading proficiency and 95% confidence interval. It can be said with 95 percent certainly that the mean reading proficiency of the population of interest is within this interval.

Figure 9.1 National reading proficiency for 9-, 13-, and 17-year-olds by hours of television viewing daily (1986). (From *The reading report card: Progress toward excellence in our schools*. Princeton, NJ: Educational Testing Service. By permission.)

Box 9.2 HAVE HIGH SCHOOL TEST SCORES STOPPED RISING?

In the 1985 school year [and in subsequent years], average SAT scores remained at [approximately] the level of the previous year, seemingly ending an erratic but appreciable rise that had been under way for half a decade. Some analysts quickly seized on this as evidence that the rise of achievement at the senior high school level had stagnated, even though no other major source of data suggests that scores have stopped rising in those grades.

A closer look at the SAT scores, however, shows that the current stability of average scores probably does not indicate that student performance has become stagnant. Beginning in the mid-1970s, the share of high school graduates taking the SAT grew sharply, from 31 percent in 1976 to 38 percent in 1985 (see Figure B9.2). Just as a similar growth in the test-taking

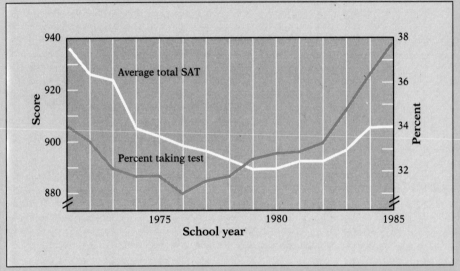

Figure B9.2 The SAT: Average scores and the percent of graduates taking the test.

group exacerbated the SAT decline in the 1960s, the current increase probably impeded the rise in SAT scores substantially. That is, as the pool of test-takers grows, it generally also becomes less selective, and the addition of lower-scoring students depresses average scores. If the proportion of graduates taking the test had remained constant, SAT scores would have been a better gauge of changes in student performance—but they also probably would have risen more, and 1985 scores might well have been higher than those of 1984.

Source: Educational achievement: Explanations and implications of recent trends. Washington, DC: Congressional Budget Office, August, 1987, p. 19.

Conversely, factors that are cited as contributing to recent limited gains include larger recent percentage increases in the scores of blacks and Hispanics (see Figure 9.2), though absolute score averages remain lower; delayed positive effects of Head Start and other early-childhood education programs; more rigorous academic demands; and improved student attitudes and motivation (College Entrance Examination Board, 1988; Congressional Budget Office, 1987; Putka, 1988).

Schooling for What?

While much remains to be learned about the educational effects, positive or negative, of these and other factors, one thing seems clear: No single factor in itself is adequate to explain recent trends. But whatever the ultimate findings regarding the academic performance of American students and the variables

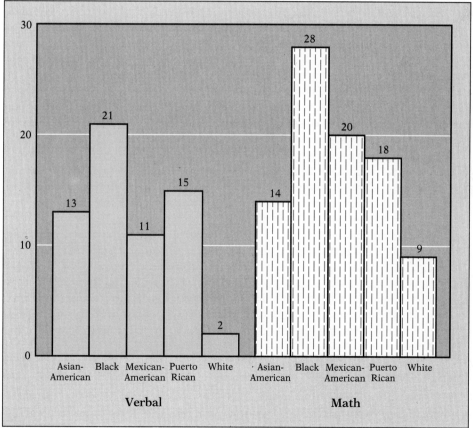

Figure 9.2 Average point increases in Scholastic Aptitude Test scores, 1979–1989. (Source: The College Entrance Examination Board. *National College-Bound Seniors*. New York: The College Board, various years.)

contributing to them, there is widespread agreement that the school experience of many young people leaves much to be desired (Boyer, 1983; Carnegie, 1989; Gross & Osterman, 1971; Ravitch & Finn, 1987; Sarason, 1983). This is so not only for the poor, who are generally at the greatest disadvantage, but for more advantaged students as well.

Many public schools, including many middle-class schools, tend to concentrate on what Charles Silberman called education for docility. They place excessive emphasis on order, discipline, and conformity at the expense of self-expression, intellectual curiosity, creativity, and the development of a humane, sensitive individual (Carnegie, 1989; Sarason, 1983; Silberman, 1970). The situation is most pronounced at the junior high school and high school levels: "Because adolescents are harder to 'control' than younger children, secondary schools tend to be even more authoritarian and repressive than elementary schools; the values they transmit are the values of docility, passivity, conformity, and lack of trust" (Silberman, 1970, p. 324).

The fact that such dulling and repressive emphases are stronger at the junior high school level is ironic, since it is during these years that cognitive changes open up new intellectual and cultural horizons for the developing person. Yet as Seymour Sarason (1983) notes in *Schooling in America,* too many schools are "uninteresting places," at least partly because schooling has traditionally been viewed as something to be imposed on children rather than as a joint venture in intellectual exploration.

Obviously, not all schools fit this rather dismal picture. A growing number (though still too few) are developing competency-based curricula and innovative learning programs designed to meet the needs of students from a variety of backgrounds. They are attempting to combine the development of core knowledge and skills with exciting and creative experiences in the arts and humanities, and are challenging students to work at the peak of their capacities, to think for themselves, and perhaps most important, to learn how to learn (Boyer, 1983; Carnegie, 1989; Sarason, 1983).

One of the mistakes that some critics make is to assume that improving basic skills requires conformity, docility, and the elimination of creative activities such as art, music, and theater. Yet recent comparative studies of Japanese and American secondary education indicate that the one area in which American students have an edge over their Japanese peers is creativity and the ability to think for themselves (Tharp, 1987). As the results of some innovative programs are demonstrating, creativity and high academic standards are not incompatible.

Education for Inequality

More troubling than inadequacies in the average school is the disparity among schools in numerous important characteristics, ranging from physical facilities, equipment, and curricular strength to teacher and pupil composition (Boyer, 1983; Schorr, 1988; Silberman, 1970). Prior to the rapid increases in urbanization and geographic mobility that have occurred in recent decades, a majority of young people lived in smaller cities and towns and on farms, where

Junior high school class being held in a makeshift hallway classroom. Differences between a wealthy suburban school and its counterpart in an inner-city ghetto are so great that they make blanket statements about the quality of American education misleading or irrelevant.

the quality of education was more evenly distributed geographically and socio-economically (if not always racially). Students from varying socioeconomic backgrounds were more likely to attend the same or similar high schools, to interact socially and academically, and to receive similar educational experiences. This is no longer the case: The differences between a wealthy suburban high school and its counterpart in the city ghetto are so great as to make broad statements about what is wrong with contemporary American education misleading and even, in some cases, irrelevant.

Later in the chapter we will consider the needs and school experiences of adolescents from disadvantaged backgrounds and what may be done to improve their chances of survival in "a world they never made," despite current cutbacks in federal, state, and local funding for education. First, however, the findings of research on factors affecting the school adjustment and academic progress of students generally will be examined. Those factors include the school environment itself, the influence of parents and peers, and the personality of the student.

DO SCHOOLS MAKE A DIFFERENCE?

In the 1970s a number of studies concluded that schools make no difference, or only a minimal difference, in the subsequent educational and occupational attainments of students (Averch et al., 1974; Bachman & O'Malley, 1978; Coleman et al., 1966; Jencks et al., 1972). Instead, these studies asserted, what makes a difference are the home environment, genes, and whatever else a child brings to school in the first place.

As we shall see, there can be little argument that factors other than the school itself play an important role both in the educational stimulation of children and adolescents and in their subsequent educational and vocational opportunities. Socioeconomic status, home and community background, parents' educational level and involvement, and other factors are clearly related to educational and vocational aspirations and accomplishments (Bachman & O'Malley, 1978; Comber & Keeves, 1973; Dossey et al., 1988; Hess & Holloway, 1984; Mullis & Jenkins, 1988; National Assessment, 1986). This does not mean, however, that schools may not also play a crucial role.

One reason why a number of studies have found little effect of schools may be in the similarities among many public elementary and secondary schools (Good & Weinstein, 1986; Goodlad, 1984; Sizer, 1984). The content and approaches to teaching (e.g., teacher-dominated instruction, little group work, similar grading methods, the division of schooling into subjects and periods) and even the basic structural features of schools (e.g., course offerings, laboratories, libraries, and classrooms) are often very similar from one school to another (Bachman & O'Malley, 1978, p. 51), making it more difficult to find measures that differentiate schools enough to produce varied student outcomes.

School Processes

Another possible explanation, however, has to do with the *kinds* of school variables employed in these studies. Most have dealt with what Patricia Minuchin and Edna Shapiro (1983) call "distal variables," such as socioeconomic status, school size, teacher-student ratios, and physical facilities. However, when the potential effects of other kinds of school variables have been examined, differences in educational outcomes have been found (Brookover et al., 1979; Good & Weinstein, 1986; Rutter, Maughan, Mortimore, & Ouston, 1979). For example, in a large-scale study of twelve schools in inner London, child psychiatrist Michael Rutter and his colleagues found that **school processes**—what goes on in schools—appeared to be more important than any other set of variables in explaining secondary-school student outcomes (Rutter et al., 1979). This important study showed that schools *do* make a difference in what happens to their students. Although it is clear that some characteristics of education are quite different in London and in the United States, the educational dimensions studied are for the most part universal. The study measured characteristics of pupils at the time of entry into secondary school ("intake") so as to separate these factors from effects of secondary schooling. Intake factors included verbal reasoning skill, parental occupation, and teachers' ratings of student behavior. Outcome measures—a much broader set than were measured in most previous studies—included behavior in school, regularity of attendance, the proportion of students who stayed in school beyond the required age, success on public examinations, and delinquency rates.

Several specific school processes turned out to be quite important predictors of student outcomes. They included homework assignments, teachers' expectations, total teaching time spent on lessons, percent of teacher time spent in interaction with the class, provision of rewards and incentives (coupled with less emphasis on punishment), provision of a pleasant and comfortable environment, provision of opportunities for responsibility in school life, and continuity of teachers and staff. As the authors point out, all of these factors may be controlled by the school staff.

A key aspect of Rutter's study is its focus on *processes,* or the ways in which various factors may directly influence students. It was also the first study to provide information on the interactions among various factors and their relative importance. Recent studies by other investigators have provided further evidence of the importance of a variety of school processes (Brookover et al., 1979; Good & Weinstein, 1986; Purkey & Smith, 1983).

Attributes of the School Environment

School Size. As the number and percentage of students enrolled in public secondary schools have grown over the past fifty years, so too has school size. Whereas the number of students enrolled in public high schools has more than tripled, the number of schools has remained largely unchanged (Garbarino, 1980; Minuchin & Shapiro, 1984). In part, this has been a function of population concentration due to urbanization. In considerable measure, however, it has been the result of an explicit educational philosophy. In his widely heralded 1959 report, *The American High School Today,* J. B. Conant maintained that small high schools could not economically provide the variety and intensity of coursework required in today's world (Boyer, 1983; Conant, 1959).

But is bigness really better? Studies by Roger Barker, Paul Gump, and others have found that because of more opportunities and greater encouragement students in smaller high schools are more likely than those in large high schools to participate in a variety of school activities and to hold positions of responsibility in school organizations (Barker & Gump, 1964; Hamilton, 1983; Wicker, 1968).

What are the consequences of greater student involvement in more activities? Students in small schools were more likely than those in large schools to report that involvement in school activities had helped them develop skills or abilities, gain more confidence in themselves, prove themselves, feel needed, gain a sense of accomplishment, and learn how to work closely with others (Wicker, 1968). These results are consistent with findings that in all instances *performers* (students who were actively and responsibly involved in an activity) reported more gains than *nonperformers* (students who were only marginally involved or were spectators) in both large and small schools. Because small schools have a larger percentage of performers participating in a larger number of activities (Gump, 1966), it could be predicted that they would show more gains.

Students in small schools also reported different kinds of satisfactions than did those in large schools. "Satisfactions in the small schools are more related to improvement of one's capacity, to challenge and action, to close cooperation among peers, and to 'being important'" (Gump, 1966, p. 3). These students were likely to make comments like "Acting in the play gave me more confidence," "It was a lot of work organizing the dance, but we all thought it was worth it," and "Going on trips with the team helps you learn how to adjust yourself to different surroundings" (Gump, 1966, p. 3). In contrast, the satisfactions of students in large schools "tended to be more passive; that is, they were derived from somebody else's action. These satisfactions were also connected with belonging to 'something big.'" These students tended to make statements like "I like to watch a good, suspenseful game," "It was very interesting to hear the ideas and arguments of the debaters," and "Pep rallies give you a feeling of school spirit" (Gump, 1966, p. 3).

Probably partly because of their greater participation in school activities and their greater sense of being needed and being important to the success of those activities, marginal students in small schools are less likely to drop out of school than marginal students in large schools (despite comparable IQs, grades, and home backgrounds). They are also more likely to feel a sense of obligation to support their classmates by participating.

Finally, small schools are more orderly and coherent than large schools and tend to have lower crime rates (Boyer, 1983; Garbarino, 1980). Another study found that anomie and victimization increase as school size increases (Blyth, Hill, & Smyth, 1978).

The principal advantage of large schools is the greater variety of information they offer (see Figure 9.3). However, it takes a lot of added size to yield a little added variety. As may be seen, a 100 percent increase in size may yield only a 17 percent increase in variety. "Since size increase, by itself, pays relatively poor dividends, it might be well for educational planners to consider other maneuvers for increasing the richness of the small school's curriculum" (Gump, 1966, p. 1). In the matter of school size, as in so many other areas of contemporary society, it appears that the slogan "bigger is better" is open to considerable question.

A possible answer for schools that are already too big may be to organize themselves into smaller units—"schools-within-a-school"—in order to "establish a more cohesive, more supportive social setting for all students" (Boyer, 1983, p. 235). Rosemont High School, a suburban school with 2,000 students, has taken this approach:

> A community of 100 students and 5 teachers is organized within the larger setting. This arrangement started about thirteen years ago. It has survived its critics and is well-established. Students become a part of the school-within-a-school for a variety of reasons. One young woman talked about feeling lost and faceless during her freshman year in the "downstairs school" (the term used to refer to the total school). Feeling that in the smaller unit she had gained the self-confidence to thrive in a more competitive setting, she applied to a string of elite colleges (Boyer, 1983, p. 235).

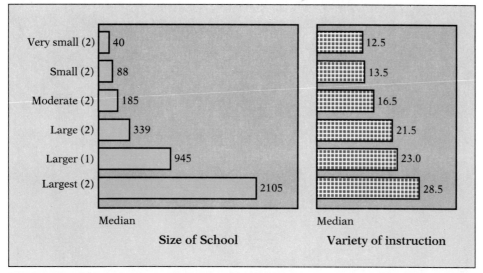

Figure 9.3 Does increasing school size produce a corresponding increase in variety of instruction? (From P. V. Gump, *Big schools, small schools.* Moravia, N.Y.: Chronicle Guidance Publications, 1966. Source: R. Barker & P. V. Gump. *Big school, small school.* Stanford, Calif.: Stanford University Press, 1964. By permission.)

The Principal

Good principals with clear goals have often been cited as a key factor in creating effective schools (Benjamin, 1981; Boyer, 1983; Rutter, 1983; Schorr, 1988). A strong principal, one who acts as an educational leader, appears to be especially important in schools where the majority of students are socially and economically disadvantaged. In many schools it is the principal who sets the tone, maintains school values, and reinforces school practices with respect to everything from academic expectations to support services and codes of behavior.

Although the principal bears a great deal of responsibility, he or she is also subject to the will of the school board, parents, and teachers and their unions— a position that frequently results in diminished authority (McAndrew, 1981). A study of 1600 principals found that fully one-quarter intended to quit in the near future (Boyer, 1983). Many complained of being caught in a bureaucratic web:

> Far too many of our school systems are top-heavy with administration; they are administered to within an inch of their lives. School leadership is crippled by layer upon layer of administration. And, while control is rooted in the need for accountability, the reality is that it makes change in many schools all but impossible (Boyer, 1983, p. 224).

Morgan Freeman as Joe Clark, real-life principal of Eastside High School, in the film "Lean on Me." A strong, dedicated principal with clear goals is a key factor in creating effective schools.

Principals who are lacking in vision and incapable of educational leadership—who view themselves as "middle managers"—are unlikely to satisfy their varied, and sometimes conflicting, constituencies. But even principals who possess the necessary interpersonal skills, energy, commitment, and academic vision will have limited success unless they are given essential resources and sufficient freedom and flexibility in using them (Boyer, 1983). However, when an inspired principal has the resources required for educational leadership, the results can be astonishingly successful, even against seemingly overwhelming odds (see pages 367–369).

Teachers

Teachers play a highly influential role in schools, since they have the most direct contact with students. The kinds of teachers encountered by an adolescent determine in great measure whether the school experience will foster the young person's overall development or simply increase his or her problems and frustrations. The right teachers may help young people overcome handicaps and make the most of their talents and interests, whereas teachers who are ill suited for working with young people may cause serious consequences. This is especially true in the case of teachers working with economically disadvantaged, ethnically diverse young people.

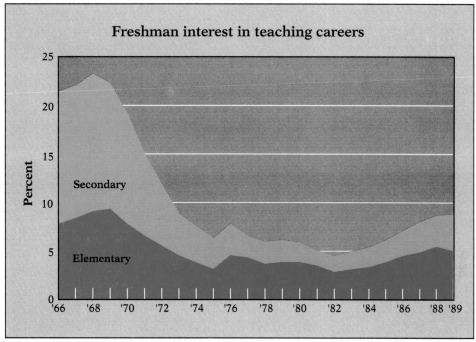

Figure 9.4 Freshman interest in teaching careers. (From W. Astin, K. C. Green, W. S. Korn, N. Schalit, & E. R. Berz, *The American Freshman: National norms for fall, 1988, 1989.* Los Angeles, CA: Higher Education Research Institute, University of California at Los Angeles. By permission.

Teachers, as well as schools themselves, have come in for increasingly harsh criticism in recent years (Boyer, 1983; Tifft, 1988). Although there are many skilled and intellectually challenging teachers, there are also significant numbers who lack minimal competency, even in basic communication skills (National Commission, 1983; Tifft, 1988). Despite a modest renewal of interest in teaching (see Figure 9.4), the SAT scores of high school seniors planning to major in education remain below those of students generally and well below those planning to major in fields like English, health-related fields, and the physical and social sciences (Evangelauf, 1988).

Obstacles to Learning. It should be recognized that in many instances in which teachers appear to be failing to meet the needs of students the source of the difficulty may lie elsewhere. Overly large classes, impossible work loads, rigid curricula and administrative regulations, poorly prepared or poorly motivated students, problems in the larger community, shortages of teaching materials, and lack of agreement among various constituencies as to the proper goals of education—all of these factors may frustrate the efforts of even the most sensitive, imaginative, and dedicated teacher. Moreover, in a growing number of instances, particularly in large metropolitan areas, violence and vandalism have been making the jobs of teachers and administrators increasingly difficult (Boyer, 1983; Tifft, 1988).

As is often true of social institutions, a specific component of the system— such as teachers—is seldom the sole cause of a problem. Many experts feel that the solution must be sought in the priorities of society itself. As one prominent educator has put it, "By and large, society gets what it deserves out of its school system. It gets what it expects. If you don't value things, you don't get them" (*Time*, 1980, p. 63).

Effective Teachers. Despite the problems confronting teachers, many are able to teach effectively. Students like and respond to some kinds of teachers better than others. There are also individual differences in the kinds of teachers to whom different kinds of students respond favorably. In general, adolescents prefer and respond more favorably to teachers who are warm, enthusiastic, sympathetic, adaptable, and responsive to their concerns (Baird, 1973; Jersild, 1963; Norman & Harris, 1981). They also want teachers who are firm yet fair and impartial. Not least, they want their teachers to be effective *as teachers*: able to plan and organize, to explain things clearly, and to be knowledgeable and enthusiastic about their subjects (Bennett, 1978; Brophy, 1986; Feeney, 1980; Norman & Harris, 1981). And they want them to have a teaching style that actively involves students in the learning process (Mullis & Jenkins, 1988; Rutter et al., 1979).

Young people respond more favorably to teachers who are warm, enthusiastic, and responsive to their concerns, but who are also firm, fair, and effective as teachers.

In a national survey of 160,000 American adolescents between the ages of 13 and 18, young people were asked, "What do you like about a teacher?" (Norman & Harris, 1981). The characteristic that was mentioned most often was fairness ("Is fair. Grades fairly and doesn't pick on certain kids"). This was followed in order of frequency by: knowledge of the subject taught; enthusiasm about the subject; willingness to help students with schoolwork or other problems, even after school; positive attitude toward students; avoidance of homework; and ability to maintain discipline in the classroom. In contrast, adolescents respond negatively to teachers who are harsh, unkind, and sarcastic ("makes fun of you"); who are unfair, inconsistent, or overly rigid in their discipline; or who, in their teaching, are ill prepared ("don't know much"), dull, poorly organized, or lacking in enthusiasm and commitment to the subject.

The emotional climate of the classroom affects not only the preferences of students but also their achievement. Studies have consistently found negative relationships between student achievement and measures of teacher criticism, threat, ridicule, or punishment of students. Often such negative indicators of emotional climate are associated with poor classroom management skills (Brophy, 1986). Conversely, classrooms that produce high achievement gains are most frequently described as pleasant and convivial (Brophy, 1986; Evertson et al., 1980; Berliner & Tikunoff, 1977).

Although there are general characteristics that distinguish effective teachers from ineffective ones, it would be a mistake to conclude that the successful teacher fits some sort of bland stereotype. Most readers will agree that the teachers who influenced them most were unique human beings. It is also clear that there are group and individual differences among pupils in the kinds of teachers to whom they respond most favorably or most negatively.

Teacher–Student Interactions

Specific characteristics of students or teachers may enhance or inhibit the effectiveness of the interactions between them. Class, race, or sex stereotypes may create initial barriers to effective communication. More important, there is mounting evidence that teachers' expectations for students exert a powerful influence on student behavior (Minuchin & Shapiro, 1983; Parsons, Kaczala, & Meece, 1983). If those expectations are based on **stereotypes** rather than on the student's actual ability and potential, student behavior will be shaped in the direction of the expectations.

It is quite clear that different children can have quite different experiences in the same classroom.

> Teachers are generally more attached to students who are achieving, conforming, and make few demands. They show concern for students who make demands appropriate to classroom activity but are indifferent to the invisible and silent children and have little interaction with them. They reject children who make demands considered illegitimate or who tend to be "behavior problems" (Minuchin & Shapiro, 1983, p. 84).

In several studies, education majors and student teachers were more likely than others (e.g., psychology majors, Teacher Corps interns) to have a high regard for pupils who were described as rigid, conforming, and orderly, and a lower opinion of those who were described as independent, active, and assertive (Minuchin & Shapiro, 1983). Similar results have been found for both male and female teachers, and at varying grade levels.

Teachers may also be influenced by stereotypes rather than by students' actual behavior. Consequently, the teacher's expectations may not correspond with the students' abilities. Several studies have shown that teachers are likely to have relatively low expectations for academic achievement by disadvantaged minority children and adolescents (Mullis & Jenkins, 1988). However, when teachers believe that these young people can achieve, and when they convey their expectations to their students and adapt their teaching to meet the students' needs, performance often improves dramatically (Hirshorn, 1987, 1988).

Boys and girls are also likely to be treated differently. Girls generally receive less criticism than boys, but they also receive less praise (Fine, 1981; Parsons, Kaczala, & Meece, 1982). Girls who were in classrooms where they were treated differently than boys had lower expectations for their own achievement.

Stereotyping is a major deterrent to the participation of female and minority students in science courses and science-related activities (Dweck, 1986; Malcolm, 1986; Mullis & Jenkins, 1988). Science teachers generally have higher expectations for boys than for girls and ask them higher-level questions (Matyas & Kahle, 1986). Textbooks may imply that the most notable accomplishments in science are those of white males (Mullis & Jenkins, 1988). Parents, peers, and the media may reinforce the idea that only certain roles are appropriate for female or minority students (Malcolm, 1986; Mullis & Jenkins, 1988).

Taken together, the studies just described clearly show that teacher time, attention, and involvement are likely to be distributed unequally among students and that differential treatment produces differential outcomes. If these patterns are to be reversed, teachers, parents, and other influential adults need to become "aware of the more subtle behaviors that communicate low expectations to particular students" (Mullis & Jenkins 1988, p. 9). In addition, students need to be exposed to a variety of appropriate sex, racial, and ethnic role models in books, films, and videotapes, and in person.

Variations in Teaching Methods

The effectiveness of different teaching methods may vary from one student to another (Brophy, 1986; Snow, 1986). In a study of college students, two kinds of instruction were distinguished: those that were formally structured and stressed conformity (e.g., classes with formal lectures, assigned papers, and regular examinations) and those that were more informal and placed a premium on student independence and initiative (e.g., small seminars stressing independent planning and study) (Domino, 1968). The students' needs for achievement were then determined independently through psychological testing. Two types of achievement motivations were identified: a need for achievement through being independent (Ai) and a need for achievement through conforming (Ac).

Students who were high in achievement motivation, regardless of its sources, performed better in their overall college work than students who were low in such motivation. Moreover, students who were high on the Ai dimension and low on the Ac dimension did not differ in *overall* academic performance from students who scored high on Ac and low on Ai. Of particular interest, however, was the finding that the Ai group performed significantly better in the more informal settings stressing self-reliance and independence, whereas the Ac group performed significantly better in the more formal, structured settings.

Students who feel secure and confident have different needs in the classroom than those who are anxious or alienated (Brophy, 1986). Students who are low in manifest anxiety perform better in more informal, student-centered classes (in which active student participation is encouraged at all times); students who are high in manifest anxiety perform better in more formal, structured, teacher-centered classes (Dowaliby & Schumer, 1971).

Similarly, socioeconomically advantaged students are more likely to be self-confident, eager to participate, and responsive to challenge: "They want respect and require feedback but usually do not need frequent encouragement or praise. They thrive in an atmosphere that is academically stimulating and somewhat demanding" (Brophy, 1986, p. 1073). In contrast, students from less advantaged backgrounds are more likely to require warmth and support, encouragement for their efforts, and praise for their successes, as well as good instruction (Brophy, 1986).

Studies like these demonstrate that different teaching methods may well have very different effects on different kinds of children and adolescents. They also serve as a needed corrective to the tendency of both students and teachers to assume that a technique that seems to work for them individually (or for their school) would automatically be better for others as well.

SOCIOECONOMIC STATUS, EDUCATIONAL ASPIRATIONS, AND EDUCATIONAL ATTAINMENT

Socioeconomic status is significantly related to the level and nature of students' educational aspirations and to their actual educational attainment (Applebee, Langer, & Mullis, 1986; Bachman, O'Malley, & Johnston, 1978; Mussen et al., 1990; National Assessment, 1986). Upper-middle- and upper-class youth have traditionally aspired to higher levels of educational attainment than lower-middle- and lower-class youth (Bachman, 1970; Brophy, 1986; Burton & Jones, 1982; Mullis & Jenkins, 1988). Young people from upper-class families are highly unlikely to drop out of high school (see Figure 9.5). And they are more than fifteen times as likely to gain a bachelor's degree

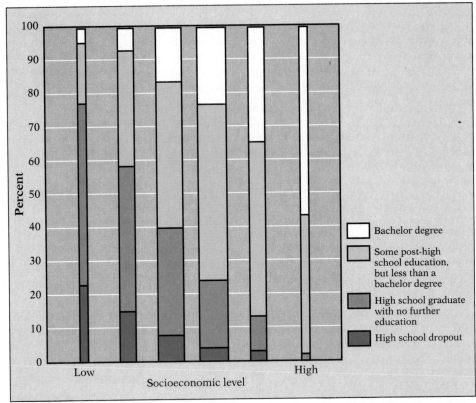

Figure 9.5 Educational attainment related to parental socioeconomic level. (From J. G. Bachman, P. M. O'Malley, & J. Johnston. *Youth in transition, Vol. VI: Adolescence to adulthood—Change and stability in the lives of young men.* Ann Arbor, Mich.: Institute for Social Research, 1978. By permission.)

as students from lower-class families (Bachman et al., 1978). At any particular educational level, socially and economically favored youth, as a group, score somewhat higher than their working-class peers—and much higher than those who are seriously deprived socially and economically—both in school grades and on standard tests of academic skills (Dossey et al., 1988; Johnson, 1975; Mullis & Jenkins, 1988; National Assessment, 1986).

Adolescents and youth from highly educated, affluent suburban families have a marked advantage in terms of achievement in reading, writing, science, and mathematics over young people whose parents are poorly educated, and who come from poverty areas of inner cities. These differences tend to be clearly established by age 9 and change little thereafter (Johnson, 1975; Mullis & Jenkins, 1988; National Assessment, 1986).

Some of the reasons for these persisting disparities are fairly clear, others are more subtle. A lower-class young person is more likely to face serious economic problems in continuing his or her education. Government and private assistance is grossly inadequate to meet the needs of many students and is becoming more so (Conger, 1988; Schorr, 1988). Moreover, disadvantaged adolescents are more likely to have had poor academic preparation throughout their schooling. Typically, their schools are physically inferior and poorly equipped, with inadequate curricula and severe shortages of trained teachers and auxiliary personnel.

Because of poor nutrition and inadequate health care, many more children at the lowest socioeconomic levels have serious health problems that may interfere with their ability to do academic work (Bryant et al., 1978; Scanlon, 1975; Schorr, 1988). Moreover, many thousands of children still go to school hungry—a condition that interferes with alertness and attention to studies. Other, more subtle factors also operate to limit the educational aspirations and accomplishments of poor and working-class youth, including broad, class-related customs and values and the influence of parents and peers.

Parental Aspirations and Rewards for School Achievement

Parents at different socioeconomic levels vary in their views of schooling for their children. Middle- and upper-class parents are more likely to value schooling for the sake of the education—both academic and social—it provides. Lower-class parents, in contrast, have traditionally looked upon school as necessary for vocational success because of the skills gained and credentials earned. However, except for the very lowest socioeconomic groups (particularly those subject to ethnic discrimination), all groups of parents have reinforced the value of school to some degree because they have expected the school to do something for their children (Mussen, Conger, Kagan, & Huston, 1984).

Several factors seem to be meaningfully related to the more positive attitudes toward academic success shown by both young people and adults from higher socioeconomic backgrounds. For one thing, most school programs have actually been more relevant to the needs, customs, and expectations of individuals in these classes. Indeed, one of their principal functions has traditionally been to prepare succeeding generations of young people for admission to a society that is dominated by the middle class. As psychologist Boyd McCandless commented, "schools succeed relatively well with upper- and middle-class youngsters. After all, schools are built for them, staffed by middle-class people, and modeled after middle-class people" (1970, p. 295).

Other factors also play a role in the development of the more positive attitudes traditionally displayed by upper-class parents and their children. School success is more important in maintaining class membership in the higher socioeconomic classes than in the lower classes. Middle- or upper-class adolescents can readily see the delayed rewards of academic achievement by noting the important part it plays in the success of a doctor-father, a scientist-aunt, or an accountant-older brother. Of course, we would not expect these anticipated future rewards to be effective if the young person's immediate experiences were highly unfavorable, but when they are favorable, the prospects of additional future rewards may provide increased motivation to try to do well in school.

Moreover, better-educated, more affluent parents are more likely to encourage their children to work hard in school; they also tend to take an active interest in their children's schoolwork (Davies & Kandel, 1981; Dossey et al., 1988; Mullis & Jenkins, 1988; National Assessment, 1986). For example, eleventh-graders whose parents are college graduates are almost twice as likely as those whose parents did not graduate from college to report that their parents talk to them about what they are learning (Mullis & Jenkins, 1988). Parents with higher levels of education are also more likely to provide access to books, magazines, newspapers, and reference materials at home; to discuss ideas with their children; to help them with school projects; and to take them to museums and cultural events (Dossey et al., 1988; National Assessment, 1986). Not too surprisingly, parental interest and involvement in schoolwork and greater exposure to reading and reference materials in the home are positively associated with proficiency in reading, mathematics, and science (Dossey et

Better-educated, more affluent parents are more likely to provide their children with books and magazines, to help them with school projects, and to take them to museums and cultural events.

al., 1988; Mullis & Jenkins, 1988; National Assessment, 1986). In contrast, academic proficiency is negatively related to number of hours spent watching television.

Despite popular stereotypes, social-class differences and attitudes cut across membership in racial, ethnic, and other minority groups. For example, among middle- and upper-class blacks, the concern of parents for their child's scholastic success and, consequently, their approval of his or her successful efforts are, if anything, stronger than among middle-class whites.

Perhaps most important of all, there are wide individual differences in orientation to education within all socioeconomic, ethnic, racial, and other subgroups. When parents are truly interested in their children and motivated to help them succeed academically, and when relevant educational opportunities exist in the community, the effects of parental influences may override the otherwise limiting effects of lower socioeconomic status or the negative influences of peers. A study of high school boys demonstrated that although middle-class boys, as a group, had higher educational and vocational aspirations than their working-class peers, working-class boys with parents who encouraged and supported educational and occupational mobility had higher aspirations than middle-class boys with parents who did not encourage such striving (Simpson, 1967).

Another study found that parents' educational aspirations for their children were equaled only by the young person's academic ability as predictors of adolescents' educational aspirations. Interestingly, the parents' actual aspirations were higher than their adolescent children's *perceptions* of those aspirations. "These findings are important, for they document that the interpersonal influences of parents are exerted in subtle ways, and not necessarily with the awareness of the adolescent being influenced" (Davies & Kandel, 1981, p. 376). In addition, a national study of tenth-grade boys found that family relations were a better predictor of school attitudes than socioeconomic status. Boys whose family relations were positive and rewarding showed more positive attitudes and fewer negative attitudes toward school (Bachman et al., 1967).

FAMILY INFLUENCES ON EDUCATIONAL ASPIRATIONS AND ACHIEVEMENT

As these studies indicate, parents may have an important influence on the academic aspirations and achievement of their children—an influence that can, under favorable circumstances, transcend the otherwise limiting effects of such factors as lower socioeconomic status. One of the most important factors is the expectations that parents have for their children's educational attainment (Baumrind, 1975; Clark, 1983; Hess & Holloway, 1984; Parsons, Kaczala, & Meece, 1987; Seginer, 1983). For example, one study showed that parents' expectations are strongly related to the child's attitudes about and performance in mathematics (Hess & Holloway, 1984). Despite the fact that prior to the study the boys and girls had performed equally well in mathematics courses and on their most recent standardized test, parents reported sex differences in the abilities of their children. Parents of daughters were more likely than parents of sons to report that their children had to work hard at mathematics and science. In addition, parents of sons were more likely than parents of daughters to feel that mathematics and science are important. The belief that success for girls is due to effort rather than ability, together with the lesser importance placed on these subjects for girls than for boys, is likely to decrease girls' motivation to continue in these courses (Anderson, 1980; Fennema, 1980).

Clearly, parental expectations are a function of their own attitudes, values, and motivations, all of which may be expressed in the parents' achievement behavior. The models of achievement that parents present can influence their children's achievement, but this may be a less potent factor than the parents' expectations. In addition, positive identification with parents undoubtedly plays a role in fostering achievement (Dornbusch et al., 1987; L. W. Hoffman, 1984; Marjoribanks, 1979; Shaw & White, 1965; Weinhert & Trieber, 1982).

What kinds of parents have academically motivated, achieving children? Such parents are likely to place a high value on autonomy and independence and on mastery, competence, and achievement in general (Baumrind, 1971, 1973, 1975; Hess & Holloway, 1984; Marjoribanks, 1979). They tend to be democratic and to interact actively with their children (Dornbusch et al., 1988; Kelly & Worrell, 1977; Steinberg, Elmen, & Mounts, 1989). They also exhibit curiosity and respect for knowledge (Bell, 1963; Hess & Holloway, 1984; Kelly & Worrell, 1977). The parents of children with low aspirations and achievement do not share these values or characteristics even if they are similar to the parents of achieving children in socioeconomic status and intelligence.

Taken together, these positive parental attributes are generally characteristic of authoritative parents (see pages 204–205). A recent study of nearly 8000 high school students in the San Francisco Bay area examined the relationship between school achievement and parental child-rearing styles, using Baumrind's three main categories: authoritarian, authoritative, and permissive (Dornbusch et al., 1987). Authoritative parenting was most closely associated with good grades, while authoritarian, permissive, and inconsistent styles (e.g., fluctuating between authoritarian and permissive styles) were associated with poorer school performance (see Table 9.1). Similarly, granting young people autonomy in family decision making too early is associated with poorer school performance (Dornbusch, Ritter, Mont-Reynau, & Chen, 1990). Joint decision making, involving both parents and children, is more effective than decision making by either youth alone or parents alone during the formative years of adolescence.

It is clear that the parents of children and adolescents with relatively high educational aspirations and achievement tend to exhibit those attributes themselves. Various studies indicate that the parents of academic achievers also possess personality characteristics that facilitate educational attainment in their children. Specifically, such parents give their children more praise and approval, show more interest and understanding, are closer to their children,

T A B L E 9.1 MEAN GRADE OF EACH COMBINATION OF HIGH ON PARENTING STYLE INDICES, BY SEX

Indices on Which Household Is High	Male Mean Grade	N	Female Mean Grade	N	Total Mean Grade	N
All indices high	2.34 (.73)	92	2.42 (.79)	54	2.37 (.75)	146
Authoritarian and permissive	2.42 (.82)	349	2.49 (.83)	328	2.45 (.83)	677
Authoritarian and authoritative	2.54 (.77)	444	2.65 (.77)	303	2.58 (.77)	747
Permissive and authoritative	2.84 (.76)	129	2.94 (.69)	133	2.89 (.72)	262
Authoritarian only (pure)	2.62 (.79)	555	2.68 (.79)	509	2.65 (.79)	1,064
Permissive only (pure)	2.61 (.90)	673	2.70 (.85)	648	2.66 (.87)	1,321
Authoritative only (pure)	2.96 (.77)	552	3.08 (.72)	666	3.02 (.75)	1,218
No index high	2.80 (.82)	917	3.00 (.74)	908	2.90 (.79)	1,825

Source: S. M. Dornbusch, P. L. Ritter, P. H. Leiderman, D. F. Roberts, & M. J. Fraleigh. The relation of parenting style to adolescent school performance. *Child Development,* 1987, **58,** 1244–1257. Copyright 1987 by The Society for Research in Child Development. By permission.

and give them a greater feeling of family belongingness (Hess & Holloway, 1984).

One of the better-controlled studies of these attributes compared the family relations of bright high-achieving and underachieving high school boys equated for grade in school, socioeconomic status, and intelligence (Morrow & Wilson, 1961). As Table 9.2 shows, the families of high achievers were significantly more likely to do things together, to share ideas, and to involve their children in family decision making. They were also more likely to display parental approval, confidence, and trust, and less likely to engage in overrestrictive controls and overly severe discipline. Overall morale in these families was far higher than in the families of underachieving boys.

In contrast, the parents of underachieving children and adolescents have been found to be more domineering, more restrictive, more likely to engage in severe and arbitrary punishment, and more likely either to be overly protective of their children or to pressure them excessively for achievement (Bachman, O'Malley, & Johnston, 1978; Dornbusch et al., 1987; Hess & McDevitt, 1984; Morrow & Wilson, 1961; Steinberg et al., 1989). Family tensions and parental disagreement over the behavior expected of their children were greater in the families of underachieving children and adolescents.

As indicated earlier, a potential factor in the extent to which parents influ-

T A B L E 9.2 FAMILY RELATIONS SCALES: MEDIAN TESTS

		Percent Above Median		
Scale Title	r^a	Highs (N = 48)	Lows (N = 48)	p
Family sharing of recreation	.76	69	44	.02
Family sharing of confidence and ideas	.84	63	35	.01
Family sharing in making decisions	.88	60	44	ns
Parental approval	.56	73	33	.001
Parental affection	.88	60	42	ns
Parental trust	.73	60	25	.001
Parental approval of peer activities	.94	71	42	.01
Student acceptance of parental standards	.69	52	25	.01
Student affection and respect toward parents	.91	58	44	ns
Lack of parental overrestrictiveness	.63	56	29	.01
Lack of parental severity of discipline	.70	69	42	.01
Lack of parental overprotection	.77	52	56	ns
Lack of parental overinsistence on achievement	.75	63	46	ns
Parental encouragement of achievement	.74	60	40	.05
Harmony of parents (N = 40)	.72	63	48	ns
Regularity of home routine	.76	52	46	ns
Overall family morale	.97	67	33	.001

Source: W. R. Morrow and R. C. Wilson. Family relations of bright high-achieving and underachieving high school boys. *Child Development,* 1961, **32,** 501–510. Copyright 1961 by The Society for Research in Child Development. By permission.

Note: Tests are two-tailed.
[a]Odd-even reliability coefficient, corrected by Spearman-Brown formula.

ence their adolescent children is the response of the adolescent to each parent. A strong and positive parent–child relationship is surely important. On the other hand, an adolescent may find it difficult or impossible to identify with either parent. Under these circumstances the parent's potential influence is reduced. Indeed, in the search for a workable identity the young person may even attempt, consciously or unconsciously, to be as *unlike* the parent as possible, and consequently may reject the parent's academically oriented values.

Every therapist has encountered young people who, in spite of their basic inclinations and abilities, somehow manage to fail academically because they are so involved in rejecting the academic values and aspirations of their parents. Conversely, an adolescent may identify strongly and positively with a parental model; but if that model is indifferent to, or suspicious and critical of, educational values and goals, the young person may adopt the parent's attitudes and motivations. These considerations may help explain some apparently contradictory findings regarding the role of parental identification in academic aspirations and achievement.

PEER INFLUENCES ON EDUCATIONAL ASPIRATIONS

Adolescents have a strong need for acceptance by peers. Depending on the particular values of the peer group in general and of close friends in particular, the adolescent's educational aspirations may be either strengthened or reduced. The educational aspirations of adolescents are clearly consonant with those of their peers (Berndt, 1982; Davies & Kandel, 1981; Kandel & Lesser, 1969). Moreover, degree of agreement with peer values is directly related to intimacy of peer relations. One extensive study of high school students used three indicators of intensity of friendship: (1) whether or not the friendship choice was reciprocated, (2) how frequently the adolescent saw the friend out of school, and (3) whether the best school friend was also the best friend overall (Kandel & Lesser, 1969). Friendship pairs characterized by greater intimacy and greater frequency of contact were expected to show greater concordance in academic aspirations.

As shown in Table 9.3, friends whose choices were reciprocated were in somewhat greater agreement about educational goals than friends whose choices were not reciprocated. Adolescents were in greater agreement with friends whom they saw frequently out of school than with those whom they saw rarely. And "agreement is higher with school friends who are also the adolescent's very best friend overall (outside school as well as in school) than with those school friends who are not" (Kandel & Lesser, 1969, p. 221).

In this investigation the degree of friendship was refined further by considering simultaneously whether the choice was reciprocated and whether the friend in school was the best friend overall. The "very best friend" was defined as the best friend overall whose choice was reciprocated. Concordance on

T A B L E 9.3 CONCORDANCE ON EDUCATIONAL PLANS BETWEEN ADOLESCENT AND BEST SCHOOL FRIEND, BY STRENGTH OF FRIENDSHIP (DYADS)

Strength of Friendship	Tau-Beta	N
Reciprocity of choice		
Reciprocated	.390	(438)
Not reciprocated	.346	(622)
Frequency of contact out of school		
More than once a week	.369	(732)
Once a week–month	.350	(213)
Never	.316	(114)
School friend is best friend overall		
Yes	.406	(710)
No	.291	(338)

Source: D. B. Kandel and G. S. Lesser. Parental and peer influences on educational plans of adolescents. *American Sociological Review,* 1969, **34,** 213–223. By permission.

Note: Concordance as measured by tau-beta, all significant beyond .001 level.

educational plans with reciprocated best friends overall was higher than for any other category of friendship.

A subsequent study by the same investigators shows that one should be cautious in assuming that similarity in peer aspirations is solely, or even primarily, a result of peer influence (Davies & Kandel, 1981; Kandel, 1978a, 1978b). Similarities in educational aspirations (and other attitudes and behavior, such as drug use) tend to lead to the development of friendships in the first place. Only subsequently does interaction with the friend strengthen or reduce the young person's existing aspirations or beliefs; moreover, such peer influences are reciprocal. In many situations, also, educational aspirations are widely shared in the peer group (largely because of socioeconomic homogeneity). Finally, peer influences on educational aspirations appear to be considerably greater for girls than for boys, reaching a peak at the ninth grade and then declining (Davies & Kandel, 1981).

Relative Influence of Parents and Peers

It is often assumed that with educational aspirations as with most other values, irreconcilable differences are likely to arise between parents and peers, and that in any such confrontation peer values will win out over those of parents (see page 283). As we have seen, however, there is usually considerable overlap between the values of parents and those of peers because of commonalities in their backgrounds. With respect to educational goals, in many middle- and upper-class groups scholastic success—or at least the absence of scholastic failure—is positively valued and explicitly rewarded not only by teachers and parents but also by young people themselves. Among middle-class children and adolescents, those who were most popular in school were also better students and were rated as more conforming and cooperative (Mussen et al., 1990). Lower-class children (especially in ghetto neighborhoods) are less likely to be rewarded by either parents or peers for scholastic achievement.

In one study, parental influence on adolescent educational aspirations exceeded peer influence by ratios ranging from 2:1 to 8:1, depending on the measure of educational aspirations used (Davies & Kandel, 1981). Contrary to the popular view, parental influences increased more for girls than for boys during the high school years. However, there are exceptions to this general finding, as in cases in which deviant peer group pressures are unusually strong and homogeneous, or in which communication between parents and their children has broken down and parental influence has diminished accordingly.

PERSONALITY CHARACTERISTICS, INTELLIGENCE, AND SCHOOL ACHIEVEMENT

Intellectual level is clearly related to school success, with correlations between intelligence and measures of academic achievement generally ranging from about .50 to .70 or .75 (Snow & Yalow, 1988). The results of one investigation are typical (Kavrell & Petersen, 1984). The correlations between IQ scores and achievement test scores for a longitudinal sample of boys and girls in the sixth and eighth grades are shown in Table 9.4. While the correlations are quite similar for boys and girls in the sixth grade, by the eighth grade IQ is less related to achievement for boys than for girls.

When grades given by teachers are used as a measure of achievement, the correlations are usually lower (Kavrell & Petersen, 1984; McCandless, 1970). Although boys and girls generally have similar IQ test scores, there are sex differences in scores on achievement tests; boys tend to score higher than girls on mathematics and some science tests, while girls tend to score higher than boys on verbal and language tests (Dossey et al., 1988; Mullis & Jenkins, 1988; National Assessment, 1986). Girls often earn higher grades overall than boys until college (Kavrell & Petersen, 1984; Maccoby & Jacklin, 1974). This may be explained at least partly by girls' greater conformity and boys' more active and disruptive behavior in the classroom (Fine, 1981).

As these findings suggest, intelligence is not the only determinant of school achievement, and indeed, among some students it may be far less important than many other factors, such as motivation, interest, work habits, and personality characteristics (Lao, 1980; Snow, 1986). In one investigation of 475 high school seniors, students were divided into three subgroups: those whose academic performance (in English, science, mathematics, and social science) exceeded what would have been anticipated statistically on the basis of their IQs (**overachievers**); those whose performance was about what would have been anticipated (**normal achievers**); and those whose performance fell below expected levels (**underachievers**). When these three groups were compared, a number of significant differences emerged.

Overachievers demonstrated significantly better work habits, greater interest in schoolwork generally, and more persistence in carrying out assignments, and they tended to be more grade conscious. They also emerged as more responsible, conscientious, and likely to plan than normal achievers, although

T A B L E 9.4 CORRELATIONS FOR BOYS AND GIRLS BETWEEN GROUP INTELLIGENCE TEST SCORES AND STANDARDIZED ACHIEVEMENT TEST SCORES

Achievement Test Score	Sixth Grade		Eighth Grade	
	Boys	Girls	Boys	Girls
Reading	.72	.77	.58	.75
Mathematics	.70	.79	.52	.72
Total achievement[a]	.82	.75	.59	.78

Source: S. M. Kavrell and A. C. Petersen (1984). Patterns of achievement in early adolescence. In M. L. Maehr and M. W. Steinkamp (Eds.), *Women and science.* Greenwich, Conn.: JAI Press. By permission.

[a]Based on other areas besides those listed.

they were similar to them in many other respects. Underachievers differed markedly from normal achievers and overachievers. They appeared to have more difficulty in "self-regulation" and were more impulsive, uninhibited, pleasure seeking, and interested in immediate rewards. They also seemed to have greater difficulty in interpersonal relationships with peers and appeared to be less cooperative, more selfish, less dependable, less sociable, and "less diligent in their efforts to attain socially acceptable goals" (Gawronski & Mathis, 1965, p. 153). They enjoyed both school and home less than normal achievers, manifested more "defensive and resentful" behavior, and were more likely to become disorganized, particularly under pressure. Despite these characteristics, underachievers were less likely than either overachievers or normal achievers to report not having enough time for their studies. Finally, they displayed greater pessimism about their future opportunities.

Other studies reveal that overachievers, compared with underachieving peers, are more likely to have the following characteristics:

1. *Positive self-value* (e.g., optimism, self-confidence, self-acceptance, high self-esteem).
2. *Acceptance of authority* (e.g., conformity to expectations of teachers and parents, eagerness to please them).
3. *Positive interpersonal relations* (e.g., interest in, and responsiveness to, the feelings of others).
4. *Little conflict over independence versus dependence* (e.g., freedom to make choices and initiate activities and to lead, although within a generally conforming context).
5. *An academic orientation* (e.g., orderly study habits, high motivation for academic achievement, interest in academic values and subject matter).
6. *Realistic goal orientation* (e.g., a drive to organize and plan, basic seriousness of purpose, ability to delay short-term pleasures for longer-term goals, efficiency and energy).
7. *Better control over anxiety* (e.g., direction of inner tensions into organized task-related activities) (Schuer & Kuna, 1987; Taylor, 1964; Weiner, 1970, 1980).

In contrast, underachieving students are more likely to be characterized by a high level of free-floating anxiety; negative self-concepts; hostility toward authority; difficulty in relating to peers, combined with excessive dependence on the peer group; a high level of conflict over independence versus dependence; a social, pleasure-seeking orientation, rather than an academic one; and unrealistic goals or no long-term goals at all.

Obviously, these findings represent only general trends, and there are many exceptions. For example, whereas many high-achieving students are well adjusted, self-confident, and mature, significant numbers have feelings of inadequacy and unworthiness, are overly worried about the impressions they make on others, are concerned about loss of parental love if they do not measure up to expectations, and are overly dependent and conforming (Conger & Petersen, 1984). For such young people, overachieving may be a way of compensating for self-doubts and warding off potential rejection by parents and others. By the same token, some students who are classified as underachieving in the usual academic sense—and history provides some distinguished examples, such as Darwin, Churchill, and Einstein—may merely be marching to the beat of a different drummer. It is also clear that the fact of achievement or underachievement can influence the developmental course of self-esteem and academic self-concept (Kifer, 1975). Therefore, achievement can be as much a *cause* of psychological characteristics as a *result* of such characteristics.

DROPPING OUT OF SCHOOL

Approximately one in every four students drops out of school before graduation (Bickel & Papagiannis, 1988; High School, 1989), although there are marked regional variations (see Figure 9.6). Dropping out usually begins in junior high school; the dropout rate reaches a peak of about 10 percent among high school juniors. In an era when the number of unskilled jobs is declining steadily while the number of jobs requiring high levels of education and tech-

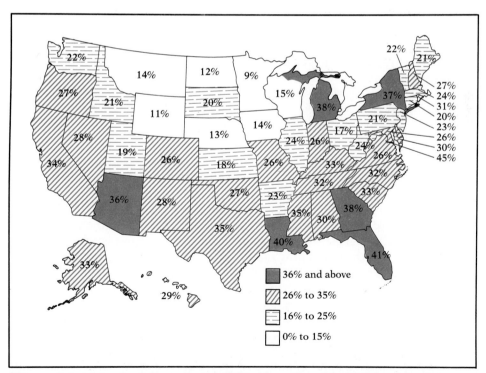

Figure 9.6 High school dropout rates, 1987. (From *Chronicle of Higher Education Almanac,* September 6, 1989. By permission.)

Employment prospects for most school dropouts are increasingly bleak.

nical skills is rising rapidly, the employment prospects for most dropouts are increasingly bleak (see Chapter 11). Even if they find a job, it is likely to be menial work with the lowest pay and few chances of advancement (Boyer, 1983; Rumberger, 1981, 1983; *The forgotten half*, 1988).

Why Do Young People Drop Out?

Both sociological and psychological factors are involved in adolescents' decisions to drop out. The dropout rate is highest among young people living in ethnically segregated urban and rural slums; many schools in poor inner-city neighborhoods have dropout rates exceeding 50 percent (Schorr, 1988). Dropping out is more frequent among the poor in general than among the more well-to-do. At the highest socioeconomic level, dropping out is extremely rare (probably one youth in fifty). At the lower end of the socioeconomic ladder, nearly one-quarter drop out, and at the very bottom of the ladder as many as one in two young people may drop out of high school (Bachman, O'Malley, & Johnston, 1978; Mensch & Kandel, 1988; Sebald, 1984; U.S. Bureau of the Census, 1989).

Overall, however, economic need is not the major reason for dropping out (Cervantes, 1965; Fagan & Pabon, 1990; Rumberger, 1981, 1983). Most males cite school-related reasons, including dislike of school, poor performance, and suspension or expulsion (see Table 9.5). Among females, the most frequently cited reasons are pregnancy and marriage (Rumberger, 1983).

T A B L E 9.5 PRIMARY REASON HIGH SCHOOL STUDENTS DROP OUT, AGES 14 TO 21, BY RACE AND SEX (IN PERCENTS)

	Female				Male				Overall
Reason for leaving school	Black	Hispanic	White	Total	Black	Hispanic	White	Total	Total
School Related	**29**	**21**	**36**	**32**	**56**	**36**	**55**	**53**	**44**
Poor performance	5	4	5	5	9	4	9	9	7
Disliked school	18	15	27	24	29	26	36	33	29
Expelled or suspended	5	1	2	2	18	6	9	10	7
School too dangerous	1	1	2	1	0	0	1	1	1
Economic	**15**	**24**	**14**	**15**	**23**	**38**	**22**	**24**	**20**
Desired to work	4	7	5	5	12	16	15	14	10
Financial difficulties	3	9	3	4	7	9	3	5	4
Home responsibilities	8	8	6	6	4	13	4	5	6
Personal	**45**	**30**	**31**	**33**	**0**	**3**	**3**	**2**	**17**
Pregnancy	41	15	14	19	0	0	0	0	9
Marriage	4	15	17	14	0	3	3	2	8
Other	**11**	**25**	**19**	**20**	**21**	**23**	**20**	**21**	**19**
Total percent	**100**	**100**	**100**	**100**	**100**	**100**	**100**	**100**	**100**

Source: National Longitudinal Survey of Youth Labor Market Experience. In R. W. Rumberger, "Dropping Out of High School: The Influence of Race, Sex, and Family Background," American Educational Research Journal (Summer 1983):201. Copyright 1983 by the American Educational Research Association. Reprinted by permission of the publisher.

School Experience and Dropping Out

Adolescents with below-average intelligence drop out of school in significantly greater numbers than those with average or higher IQs, especially early in junior high school (Voss, Wendling, & Elliott, 1966). However, intelligence per se is not a decisive factor in many instances, since a majority of dropouts are of at least average intelligence (Bachman, O'Malley, & Johnston, 1978).

On the other hand, school difficulties, both academic and social, play a prominent role in the histories of most dropouts. The typical dropout, despite an average IQ, is two years behind in reading and arithmetic by the time he or she reaches the seventh grade; moreover, dropouts are likely to have failed one or more school years. Although dropouts tend to fall further behind in academic skills during the course of their school experience, future dropouts and graduates differ significantly even in the early school years (Lloyd, 1978; Mensch & Kandel, 1988; Pallas, 1984). In tests given in the second grade, for example, only about 10 percent of future graduates scored below their grade level on measures of reading and spelling, whereas the figure was about 90 percent for future dropouts. Students dropped out earlier and more abundantly in direct ratio to their low scholastic ranks and in direct proportion to the number of times they had been held back in grade level. Other research has shown that future high school dropouts could be identified by the end of third grade with 75 percent accuracy, using such factors as school grades, scores on intelligence and achievement tests, family characteristics, and socioeconomic status (Lloyd, 1978).

In addition, for many lower-class youth school is an unrewarding experience socially as well as academically. They do not participate to the same degree as other youth in the social life and activities of the school; they do not share the values of their largely middle-class teachers; and they are likely to feel inadequate or resentful when confronted with the social demands of the school setting. Similar reactions may affect dropouts from other social classes; they also appear to affect the lower-class dropout more than the lower-class youth who stays in school. Even while they are still in school, future dropouts are more likely than nondropouts to avoid participating in school activities and to associate with peers who have already dropped out (Cervantes, 1965, 1966; Elliott, Voss, & Wendling, 1966; *The forgotten half*, 1988).

These findings clearly indicate that the school experience is failing to meet the needs—personal, social, and vocational—of an increasing number of young people, particularly in large urban ghettos. And unless remedial actions are taken soon, the situation for these young people will continue to deteriorate (see pages 365–369).

Psychological Characteristics of Dropouts

Compared with graduates, dropouts are more likely to be emotionally troubled, to lack confidence in their own worth, to have low self-esteem, to lack a clearly defined self-image and sense of identity, and to lack structured values and goals (Bachman, Green, & Wirtanen, 1972; Bachman et al., 1978; Berry, 1974; Jones, 1977). Dropouts report higher rates of drug use and delinquency prior to dropping out (Mensch & Kandel, 1988). They are more likely to have hostile, angry feelings and to resent authority in any form—"home authority, civil authority, intellectual authority, occupational authority" (Cervantes, 1965a, p. 192). Influenced more by frustrations from which they are trying to escape than by longer-term goals toward which they are striving, these adolescents tend to live for the moment: responding impulsively, planning little, showing little sustained, goal-directed activity, and seeking immediate gratification.

Dropouts are more likely to view the world as an unpredictable place characterized by violence and exploitation of other people. In such a world longer-term goals are relatively meaningless and plans are likely to go astray or to be doomed from the start (Cervantes, 1965a).

Consequences of Dropping Out

A special focus of the Youth in Transition project at the University of Michigan's Institute for Social Research was an effort to distinguish between the causes and consequences of dropping out of high school (Bachman, Green, & Wirtanen, 1972). The participants were a national sample of over 2000 young men who were studied longitudinally until one year after most had graduated from high school. Among the findings of this investigation were that compared to nondropouts, dropouts were characterized by lower self-esteem; higher rates of delinquency; higher use of cigarettes, alcohol, and drugs; and greater fear of unemployment. The differences in self-esteem, delinquency, and drug use, however, predated dropping out from school. Increases in self-esteem among dropouts over the eight years of the study (from the tenth grade on) paralleled those seen among young men who completed high school, except in the immediate post-high school period (see Figure 9.7). This result contradicts the common belief that the self-esteem of dropouts suffers as a result of their leaving school. Similarly, differences in delinquency were stable over the years of the study; if anything, the gap between dropouts and high school graduates decreased over the eight years of the study.

Dropping Out—Problem or Symptom?

It appears clear from these findings that many of the problems that dropouts are likely to encounter after leaving high school—unemployment, personality problems, low aspirations, a higher incidence of delinquency—are at least as likely to reflect the kinds of problems that led to dropping out in the first place as they are to result from the act of dropping out itself (Bachman, Green, & Wirtanen, 1972; Mensch & Kandel, 1988). The greatest challenge is not to keep a young person in a school situation that is unrewarding or irrelevant but to

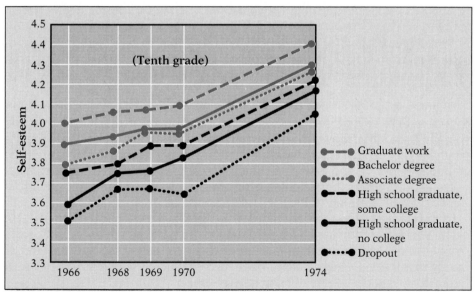

Figure 9.7 Self-esteem related to educational attainment in young males during the transition from adolescence to young adulthood. (From J. G. Bachman, P. M. O'Malley, and J. Johnston. *Youth in transition, Vol. VI: Adolescence to adulthood—Change and stability in the lives of young men.* Ann Arbor, Mich.: Institute for Social Research, 1978. By permission.)

ameliorate the conditions that lead to dropping out, beginning as early as possible in the child's life.

SCHOOLS FOR YOUNGER ADOLESCENTS

The transition from elementary to junior high school is an important event in the lives of most younger adolescents. Instead of having one main teacher and a relatively small, stable set of classmates, new seventh-graders are catapulted into a large bureaucratic maze "with teachers, classrooms, and often classmates constantly changing over the course of the day" (Simmons, Burgeson, Carlton-Ford, & Blyth, 1987). Many are likely to feel anonymous—that they know nobody and are known by nobody (Blyth, Simmons, & Carlton-Ford, 1983).

To further complicate matters, this educational transition is likely to coincide with other major changes in the young person's life, including the onset of puberty and changing social expectations (Carnegie, 1989; Conger, 1979; Lipsitz, 1977; Simmons et al., 1979, 1987). In one study, adolescents making the transition to junior high school were compared with peers who remained in elementary and middle school through the ninth grade. Girls in transitional groups were found to suffer a decrease in self-esteem, while boys' grade point averages decreased. Both girls and boys engaged in fewer extracurricular activities compared with nontransitional students (Simmons, Blyth, VanCleave, & Bush, 1979). Other studies have found an initial decline in grades but not in "global self-esteem" (Berndt & Hawkins, 1985; Hirsch & Rapkin, 1987). There is broad agreement, however, that the transition leads to a dramatic reduction in the perceived quality of junior high school life, as well as a decrease in commitment to school and a deterioration in the social climate of the classroom (Berndt & Hawkins, 1985; Epstein & McPartland, 1976; Hirsch & Rapkin, 1987).

Of greatest interest, however, is recent research showing that the transition to junior high school does not occur in isolation from other events in the young person's life. How stressful or difficult the junior high transition is depends largely on how many other potential stresses the young person is encountering and on the extent to which he or she finds social support from peers and others in the school setting (Berndt & Hawkins, 1985; Hirsch & Reischl, 1985; Mittman & Packer, 1982; Simmons et al., 1987).

In a well-designed study of students in the Milwaukee public schools, Roberta Simmons and her colleagues demonstrated that the more other life stresses (early individual dating, moving to a new neighborhood, and major family disruptions such as death or divorce) coincide with the transition to junior high school, the greater the adverse effect (Simmons et al., 1987). For example, among seventh-grade girls self-esteem, grade point average, and participation in extracurricular activities were all lowest for those who were facing the greatest number of life transitions (see Figures 9.8, 9.9, and 9.10). Similar results were obtained for boys, except in the area of self-esteem, where no significant relationship was found.

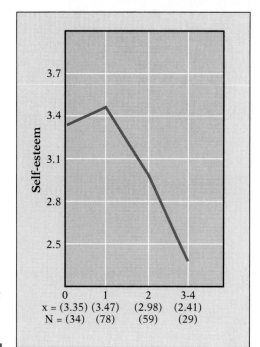

Figure 9.8 Self-esteem, by number of life transitions for grade 7 girls (N = 200). (From R. G. Simmons, R. Burgeson, S. Carlton Ford, & D. A. Blyth. The impact of cumulative change in early adolescence. *Child Development*, 1987, **58** (5), 1220–1234. By permission.)

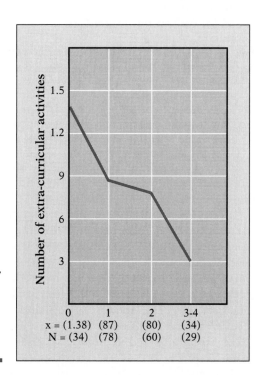

Figure 9.9 Extracurricular participation, by number of life transitions for grade 7 girls (N = 201). (From R. G. Simmons, R. Burgeson, S. Carlton Ford, & D. A. Blyth. The impact of cumulative change in early adolescence. *Child Development*, 1987, **58** (5), 1220–1234. By permission.)

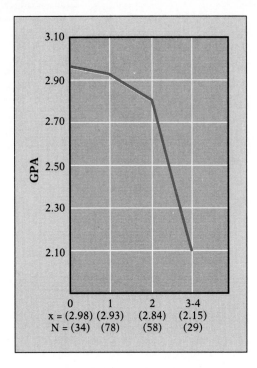

Figure 9.10 GPA by number of life transitions for grade 7 girls (N = 199). (From R. G. Simmons, R. Burgeson, S. Carlton Ford, & D. A. Blyth. The impact of cumulative change in early adolescence. *Child Development,* 1987, **58** (5), 1220–1234. By permission.)

In discussing their results the investigators call attention to the adolescent's need for an "arena of comfort":

> If the child is comfortable in some environments, life arenas, and role relationships, then discomfort in another arena should be able to be tolerated and mastered. Children appear less able to cope if at the same time they are uncomfortable with their bodies because of physical changes, with family because of changes in family constellation, with home because of a move, with school because of great discontinuity in the nature of the school environment, and with peers because of the emergence of opposite-sex relationships and the disruption of prior peer networks. There needs to be some arena of life or some set of role relationships with which the individual can feel relaxed and comfortable, to which he or she can withdraw and become reinvigorated (Simmons et al., 1987, pp. 1231–1232).

A number of authorities on adolescence have argued that the seventh grade may be too early for a major shift in the school environment. They believe that for many young people this change may occur too close in time to other major life changes (Hamburg, 1974; Lipsitz, 1977; Simmons et al., 1987). They point out that "many youngsters are forced to cope simultaneously with dramatic changes in biology, social definition, and organizational context" (Simmons et al., 1987, p. 1221). An increasingly popular way of avoiding this problem is the middle school (grades 5–7, 5–8, or 6–8). Whereas junior high schools are likely to be modeled after high schools, with a primary focus on subject matter, middle schools tend to focus more on the specific developmental needs of young adolescents (Eichorn, 1980). Middle schools may have an additional advantage: their relative isolation from the influence of older students. The results are likely to include a decrease in feelings of anonymity, less concern with being picked on or beaten up, increased participation in school activities, decreased substance abuse, an increase in dating (but less sexual intercourse), less premature sophistication, and an increase in self-esteem (Blythe, Hill, & Smythe, 1981).

NEW DIRECTIONS FOR THE NATION'S SCHOOLS

The available evidence indicates that the American educational system is failing to meet the needs either of society or of young people themselves. As a whole, the nation's youth are not being well enough prepared in reading and writing skills, in science and mathematics, or in history and the social sciences to provide the highly skilled work force that will be required if the United States is to compete effectively in an increasingly global economy. Nor are today's youth being adequately prepared to assume their responsibilities as informed citizens (Carnegie, 1989; *The forgotten half,* 1988; Ravitch & Finn, 1987). As we have seen, calls for educational reform have yielded some gains in recent years, but much more remains to be done.

If reform efforts have produced limited gains for students generally, they have had even less impact on the increasing number of poor and minority children growing up in urban and rural ghettos. Terrell H. Bell, who commissioned *A Nation at Risk* when he was Secretary of Education in the Reagan administration, recently commented: "The school reform movement has had no significant impact on the 30 percent of our students who are low income minority students. We are still not effectively educating them" (quoted in Schorr, 1988, p. 220). Indeed, while improvements are being made in a number of economically advantaged schools, urban schools with economically disadvantaged, largely minority students are getting worse (Boyer, 1983; Levin, 1985; Schorr, 1988). As Lisbeth Schorr recently noted in her compelling book *Within Our Reach: Breaking the Cycle of Disadvantage,*

> The failure of our education system to provide all American youngsters with basic skills exacts a high price, whether measured in personal, moral, or economic terms. There is also increasing recognition that early school experiences, especially for disadvantaged youngsters, impact powerfully not only on educational outcomes, but, because of the centrality of schooling in children's lives, also on rates of delinquency and early childbearing (1988, p. 221).

Recommendations for Educational Reform

Recommendations for reform have focused largely on three issues: what needs to be taught, how it should be taught, and the kinds of support that are needed if educational efforts are to succeed.

What Should Be Taught? Many schools fail to provide sufficiently advanced courses (or sometimes any courses) in important curricular areas. This is perhaps most apparent in the sciences and mathematics, but it is frequently true in other areas as well, including foreign languages, history, literature, and the arts. In an era of mass education and multiple-choice tests, too few students gain proficiency in the written and spoken word, even though "clear writing leads to clear thinking; clear thinking is the basis of clear writing" (Boyer, 1983, p. 302).

In his report on secondary education in America, Ernest Boyer, president of the Carnegie Foundation for the Advancement of Teaching, proposes a core high school curriculum that includes two-year sequences in mathematics and in the biological and social sciences and at least two years of foreign-language study, as well as coursework in literature, history, civics, and the arts. Few schools currently provide such comprehensive curricular opportunities and in many of those that do, few students participate fully (Fiske, 1987a, 1987b). For example, only about 6 percent of all U.S. high school students take advanced courses in biology, compared with 45 percent of the students in Finland and 28 percent of the students in English-speaking Canada (International Association, 1988, cited in Mullis & Jenkins, 1988, p. 10). Very few students in U.S. schools study advanced chemistry and physics; in other countries, one-sixth to one-fourth of students takes these courses.

How Should Students Be Taught? The effectiveness of what is taught frequently depends on how it is taught. One reason that school is often "an uninteresting place" (Sarason, 1983) is teachers' heavy reliance on lecturing *to* students, with minimal give-and-take between teacher and student. Teachers also tend to convey "facts" rather than stimulating questions and to encourage the regurgitation of rote answers—frequently on multiple-choice tests—as a measure of what a student has learned. In brief, students tend to be cast in the role of passive recipients of knowledge.

Such a one-sided approach flies in the face of what we know about both the nature of children and adolescents and the nature of intellectual accomplishment. Children are naturally curious; adolescents, with their greater cognitive development, are increasingly capable of raising questions (hypotheses), considering possible answers (solutions), and testing each against the available evidence (Carnegie, 1989; Keating, 1988; see page 143). It is this same spirit of inquiry, of relentless curiosity, that motivates scientists, artists, writers, entrepreneurs, and indeed, innovators in any field of endeavor.

In a recent report by the National Assessment of Educational Progress on the status of science learning in the nation's schools, the authors state:

> As active rather than passive participants in the learning process, students can strengthen their full range of mental processes, from formulating hypotheses, explaining observations, and interpreting data to other thinking skills used by scientists in their efforts to build understanding. For the classroom to mirror the real-world practice of science, the teacher should be an active model, spending less time lectur-

ing and more time engaging students in hands-on activities and asking open-ended questions than do teachers in general (Mullis & Jenkins, 1988, pp. 13–14).

The need to encourage an active approach to learning is not limited to scientific subjects. In *The Reading Report Card*, a report assessing the status of reading in the nation's schools, the authors conclude that "improvements in higher-level reading skills cannot come about simply by an emphasis on reading instruction in isolation from the other work students do in school. To foster higher-level literacy skills is to place a new and special emphasis on thoughtful, critical elaboration of ideas and understandings drawn from the material students read and from what they already know" (National Assessment, 1986, p. 8).

The Context of Teaching. Teaching and learning do not take place in a vacuum. If curricula are to be upgraded and if more innovative, student-oriented approaches to teaching are to succeed, the support of school boards, principals, and parents is essential (Boyer, 1983; Schorr, 1988). As we have already noted (page 338), school boards need to give principals greater administrative flexibility, and principals in turn need to give teachers greater freedom to teach in creative ways that are responsive to the needs and potential of their students. Parents need to be encouraged to participate as active partners in the education of their children wherever possible—understanding, supporting, and, when necessary, questioning the efforts of teachers and administrators (Comer, 1984; Rich, 1985; Schorr, 1988).

The High-Risk Student

New approaches to learning are also required for students who, by virtue of poverty, minority status, or both, have the greatest need for appropriate education but are least likely to receive it. A 1985 study found that about 30 percent of the public school population was educationally disadvantaged and that this percentage was rising (Levin, 1985). Moreover, most proposed reforms "have relatively little to offer educationally disadvantaged students" (Levin, cited in Schorr, 1988, p. 221), many of whom are growing up in socially disorganized inner-city ghettos or in rural slums, with parents (often one parent) who are poor and have little education themselves. It is these students who are most likely to become dropouts as adolescents, although their school difficulties usually become evident many years before—often as early as the third grade.

Economically disadvantaged young people are most likely to be poorly prepared for academic work (at least by traditional middle-class standards) even at the time that they enter elementary school. The discrepancy continues and in many cases widens during the elementary-school years (Applebee, Langer, & Mullis, 1986; Mullis & Jenkins, 1988). These young people are likely to feel inadequate, have a poor self-concept, be less motivated, and have lower educational aspirations than their middle-class counterparts. Moreover, they often receive little academic encouragement from either parents or peers.

Another problem that is likely to arise in any attempt to deal adequately with disadvantaged children or adolescents in the school setting, particularly in inner-city environments, is transiency and, increasingly, homelessness (Levine, Wesolowski, & Corbett, 1966; Roberts, 1987). In New York City alone over 7,000 homeless students are living in shelters and welfare hotels (Roberts, 1987). Many other homeless school-age children and adolescents may not even be registered. Often students are lodged far from the school they attend, a situation that results in frequent absences. "Regular non-attendance is how I would characterize it," said one official (Roberts, 1987, p. B1).

When one considers the problems that disadvantaged young people face in meeting traditional academic, social, and vocational demands, it seems reasonable that they should be given more assistance in school than better-prepared, more advantaged middle-class youth. Yet the reverse is typically the case.

It would be a mistake, however, to conclude that what disadvantaged children and adolescents need is simply more of the traditional educational programs provided for the average middle- and upper-class young person. Certainly, like all children they need decent physical surroundings and educational facilities and dedicated, skillful teachers. But they also need new and imaginative approaches to psychological development in general and educational development in particular. They need curricula and programs geared

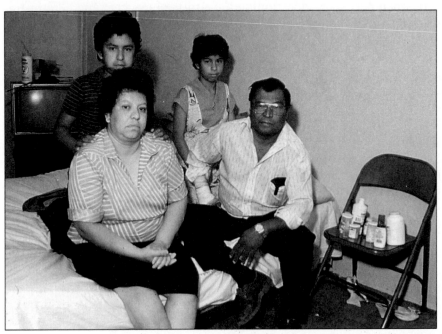

A problem likely to arise in attempts to provide adequately for disadvantaged children and adolescents in the school setting, particularly in inner-city environments, is transiency, and increasingly, homelessness.

Box 9.3 MIDDLE COLLEGE HIGH SCHOOL: A MODEL PROGRAM

"It was one of the most depressing days I ever had," Cecila L. Cullen recalls.

One Monday last winter, the high school principal was interviewing the forty students who had done most poorly during the just-completed academic cycle. "One story after another was more horrendous than the last," she says, her voice rising with emotion. "Parents dying—and we're talking about young teenagers 14 and 15 years old—and a brother being killed in a drug bust over the summer and he couldn't get over it and his girlfriend's expecting a baby."

To Ms. Cullen and the other administrators who run the Middle College High School here, those students are not lost causes.

For nearly fifteen years, the Middle College High [administered by La-Guardia Community College of the City University of New York under a joint city–state agreement] has run on the principle that underprivileged children are not to blame for their underachievement—the system is. And by changing the high school to fit the needs of New York City's minority and lower-class high-school students, the program has had remarkable success in taking children who were on the verge of dropping out and turning them into high school graduates. Middle College boasts a graduation rate of 85 percent—which makes its dropout rate about half the city average—by working with students who are academically, socially, or emotionally troubled. . . .

The Middle College program has succeeded through a combination of intensive counseling, small classes, a job-internship program, direct access to college facilities and classes, and a system that makes students answer to their peers for their actions.

Middle College was also at the forefront of what is now called the "teacher empowerment" movement, giving teachers great leeway to determine what is taught and how. . . . The program admits students who have completed the ninth grade and have been identified by counselors or teachers as students who have potential but who are not performing for any of a number of reasons: alcohol, drugs, pregnancy, family problems, poverty, emotional problems.

The school's 500-odd students are taught in classes of about twenty. . . . A number of past and current Middle College students say the small classes and the counseling saved them from dropping out and helped them weather personal crises. Many recall large and impersonal public schools where they did not know their neighbors and where teachers did not care if they came to class or not.

"At my old school I would ask myself, 'What is this, a jail cell?'" says Rubiel Cordoba, a 1985 graduate of Middle College.

"I would have ended up barefoot and pregnant," recalls Lynn Kraemer, a 1987 graduate of Middle College and now a student at LaGuardia Commu-

(Continued on next page)

nity College. "My father passed away in 1985, and I wouldn't have made it without the guidance counselors." . . .

Every day at Middle College, counselors meet with about a dozen students for group counseling—known as "group" to the students—in which the students discuss personal problems, drugs, sex, classes, or anything else that's on their minds. The program works on the principle that the students care most about what their peers think of them and will respond more readily when a fellow student tells them to stop taking drugs or drinking. . . .

The Middle College program also hopes that by exposing its students to college life and to the working world, it will help students learn to raise their sights.

The school requires students to participate in three work internships during their stay at Middle College, and they must take courses in career education.

After the tenth grade, selected students are also allowed to enroll free in LaGuardia Community College courses, which administrators hope will lessen the mystery of college life and make further education an enticing prospect.

To Mr. Brown [Nevin C. Brown, assistant director of special programs and urban affairs] of the National Association of State Universities and Land Grant Colleges, that connection is crucial in an age when a college diploma is increasingly important in determining a student's future socioeconomic status. "Ultimately, the goal is to get them into four-year colleges," says Mr. Brown. "If you want kids in Long Island City to be thinking about a future, especially in today's economy, you have to be thinking about how do you give them the maximum amount of skills.

"The problem is that if you don't go on to college, you end up in low-wage, low [status]-service jobs," he says. "That's why you've got to have a postsecondary institution involved in the collaboration."

To Janet Lieberman, the guiding light behind the program, Middle College should serve as a model to the public-education system. . . .

One idea that can be transferred, she says, is the emphasis on small size, even in schools with thousands of students. "There are different ways of doing it," she says, "in mini-schools or by dividing grades into mini-houses. The anonymity of the big institutions is one of the reasons for the high dropout rate."

The other factor, she says, is the human one. "Making school into a pleasant place, a place to learn and a place where people care," she says, "those things are transferable."

Source: M. W. Hirschorn, City U. of New York's Middle College High School helps troubled youths, serves as model program. *The Chronicle of Higher Education*, June 1, 1988, pp. 37–38. Copyright 1988, *The Chronicle of Higher Education*. Reprinted with permission.

to their specific talents, needs, and problems (academic and social) and skilled academic, vocational, and personal guidance.

Despite the difficulties involved, educational programs that are successful—not only in developing essential academic, social, and vocational skills but also in fostering self-pride and a sense of meaningful and rewarding cultural identity—are being instituted in many communities (see Box 9.3). An equally important, though little acknowledged, fact is that these programs can make learning and living joyful and exciting (Boyer, 1983; Hirschorn, 1987).

How are such results achieved? A number of factors appear to play a major role (Boyer, 1983; Carnegie, 1989; Comer, 1980, 1984; Schorr, 1988; Silberman, 1970; Tyack & Hansot, 1987, 1988; Urich & Batchelder, 1979). They include the following:

> An emphasis on academics; classroom management that maximizes academic learning time; routines that discourage disorder and disruptions.
>
> A safe, orderly, disciplined—but not rigid—school environment.
>
> A principal who exercises vigorous instructional leadership; makes clear, consistent, and fair decisions; has a vision of what a good school is and systematically strives to bring that vision to life; and visibly and actively supports a climate of learning and achievement. Teachers with high expectations that all their students can and will learn; collegiality among teachers in support of student achievement.
>
> Regular and frequent review of student progress; modification of instructional practices in light of information about student progress; public ceremonies honoring student achievement.
>
> Agreement among principals, teachers, students, and parents on the goals, methods, and content of schooling; the belief that each student is capable of making academic progress; and recognition of the importance of a coherent curriculum, of promoting a sense of school tradition and pride, and of protecting school time for learning (Schorr, 1988, p. 227).

Innovative schools like these demonstrate that it is possible to reach even seriously disadvantaged students. But unless the number of such schools is expanded significantly, and soon, the capacity of the United States to compete effectively in today's global economy will be endangered, and millions of adolescents will enter adulthood unprepared to lead reasonably happy, self-sufficient, and productive lives (Carnegie, 1989; *The forgotten half*, 1988).

SUMMARY

In contemporary America the school is the one major social institution, other than the family, to which everyone is exposed during the critical years of childhood and adolescence. As society has become more complex, the importance of the school has grown, while that of other social institutions has diminished. However, schools are not meeting their traditional responsibility for developing basic academic skills. American youth perform poorly in science, mathematics, and reading and writing compared with young people in other industrialized countries and, in some cases, earlier generations of American youth. A variety of reasons for this situation have been cited, ranging from declining academic standards to excessive exposure to television, less mental stimulation in the home, and changes in the socioeconomic mix of students attending school. Although some progress has been made in the past few years, particularly among black and Hispanic students, much remains to be done.

Some theorists have asserted that schools make little or no difference in the subsequent educational and occupational attainments of students. However, more recent research indicates that some aspects of school do indeed make a difference. These include teachers' expectations, amount of teacher time spent in interaction with the class, opportunities for responsibility in school life, and continuity of teachers and staff.

School size also has important effects. Students in small schools are involved in more activities and are given more responsibility than students in large schools. Students in small schools are more likely than those in large schools to report that involvement in school activities has helped them develop skills or abilities, gain self-confidence, feel needed, gain a sense of accomplishment, and work closely with others.

Good principals with clear goals are a key factor in creating effective schools. But to be successful they need sufficient resources and more freedom and flexibility in using them. Teachers also play a vital role because they have the most direct contact with students. Recently teachers have come under increasing criticism. However, it should be recognized that much of the responsibility for failure to meet the needs of students lies elsewhere. Among the factors that interfere with teacher effectiveness are overly large classes, rigid curricula, poorly prepared or poorly motivated students, shortages of materials, violence, and vandalism.

Nevertheless, many teachers are effective; such teachers are perceived as warm, enthusiastic, knowledgeable, well prepared, and firm, but also as fair and impartial. The emotional climate of the classroom is also important. Specific characteristics of students or teachers, including class, race, or gender stereotypes, may enhance or inhibit student–teacher interactions. The effectiveness of different teaching methods may also vary from one student to another; some students profit more from formally structured teaching, while others benefit from greater independence and initiative.

Socioeconomic status is significantly related to educational aspirations and attainment. Middle- and upper-class youth score higher, on the average, than their working-class peers, and much higher than seriously disadvantaged youth, for a variety of reasons. Nevertheless, there are wide individual differences within all socioeconomic, ethnic, and other subgroups in aspirations and accomplishments. When parents are motivated to help their children succeed academically, and when relevant educational opportunities are available, the effects of parental influence may override the otherwise limiting effects of lower socioeconomic status or negative peer influence. In general, children of warm, academically motivated, authoritative parents who spend time with their children do better than children of authoritarian, permissive, or neglectful parents.

Depending on the values of the peer group, especially close friends, adolescents' educational aspirations may be either strengthened or reduced. The educational values of parents and peers often overlap; when they do not, parental influence is likely to be greater if parent–child interactions are positive.

Intelligence, motivation, interests, work habits, and personality characteristics are all related to school achievement. Overachievers, for example, have greater interest, better work habits and more persistance, and are more self-confident, responsible, and conscientious. Underachievers have more difficulty controlling their impulses, are more anxious and less cooperative, and are more "pleasure-seeking" and interested in immediate rewards.

Approximately one in four students drops out of school before graduation—a significant problem in an era when the number of jobs for unskilled workers is declining while the number of jobs that require a high level of educational ability and technical skills is increasing. Dropout rates are highest in the inner cities and rural slums. The reasons given for dropping out include dislike of school, poor academic performance, and pregnancy. Compared with students who graduate, dropouts are more likely to be emotionally troubled, to be less self-confident, to have lower self-esteem, to be more resentful of authority, and to have less structured values and goals. They also exhibit higher rates of delinquency and drug use. In most cases these difficulties are among the factors that lead to dropping out, rather than being consequences of failure to finish high school.

The transition from elementary to junior high school is a major one for adolescents and coincides with other important life changes and stresses, including puberty and new social expectations. An increasingly popular—and promising—means of reducing the number of pressures that the young person must cope with during this age period is the middle school.

If schools are to meet the needs of contemporary adolescents, curricula need to be upgraded and more innovative, student-oriented approaches to teaching are needed. In addition, the combined support of school boards, principals, teachers, parents, and the community is essential if such changes are to be effective. This is particularly critical in the case of disadvantaged students, who have the greatest need for appropriate education but are least likely to receive it.

REVIEW QUESTIONS

1. How well are America's schools meeting their responsibility for the development of basic academic skills? How does the performance of students in the United States compare with that of students in other industrialized countries? Discuss possible reasons for these trends.
2. Some theorists assert that schools make little or no difference in students' subsequent educational and occupational attainments. Others disagree. How can these differences be explained?
3. How does school affect students' self-confidence, development of skills and abilities, and participation in school activities? Are marginal students more likely to drop out of small schools or large ones?

4. What personal and professional attributes do students look for in teachers? What teacher characteristics are most likely to evoke negative responses from students?
5. Discuss the relationship between socioeconomic status and the educational aspirations and attainment of adolescents and youth.
6. What kinds of parents are most likely to have academically motivated, achieving children?
7. How do the personal characteristics of overachievers, normal achievers, and underachievers differ?
8. What sociological, educational, and psychological factors are related to dropping out of school?
9. Why have middle schools been recommended by some psychologists and educators as an alternative to junior high school?
10. What reforms in the American educational system are needed if schools are to meet the needs both of society and of young people themselves, including economically disadvantaged children and adolescents?

RECOMMENDED READINGS

Boyer, E. L. (1983). *High school: A report on secondary education in America*. New York: Harper & Row

Carnegie Council on Adolescent Development, Task Force on Education of Young Adolescents (1989). *Turning points: Preparing American youth for the 21st century*. Washington, DC: Carnegie Council on Adolescent Development (11 Dupont Circle NW, Washington, D.C., 20036).

Dornbusch, S. M., Ritter, D. L., Leiderman, P. H., Roberts, D. F., & Fraleigh, M. J. (1987). The relation of parenting style to adolescent school performance. *Child Development*, **58**, 1244–1257.

Freedman, S. G. (1990). *Small victories: The real world of a teacher, her students & their high school*. New York: Harper & Row.

Ravitch, D. O., & Finn, C. E., Jr. (1987). *What do our 17-year-olds know? A report on the first national assessment of history and literature*. New York: Harper & Row.

Rutter, M., Maughan, B., Mortimore, P., & Ouston, J. (1979). *Fifteen thousand hours: Secondary schools and their effects on children*. Cambridge, MA: Harvard University Press.

CHAPTER

10

VOCATIONAL CHOICE IN A CHANGING WORLD

The problem of choosing and preparing for a vocation is one of the major developmental tasks of adolescence. Indeed, some theorists assert that adolescence can end only with practical experience in the working world. Before then the vocational goals of adolescents tend to have a highly theoretical quality. When they go to work, however, young people begin to learn whether they can in fact resolve the inevitable conflicts between their ideals, values, and goals, on the one hand, and the sometimes harsh realities of adult life, on the other. In the process, they begin to reassess the adult world, as well as their own assets and limitations, and tend to become more accepting of both (Herr & Cramer, 1979).

Opportunities for constructive and appropriate work experience can give adolescents a sense of purpose and responsibility and a feeling that they are participating meaningfully in the broader society. At the same time, such opportunities may reduce communication barriers between adults and young people. Work experience may also give young people a chance to learn about vocational possibilities, develop their interests, and test their developing skills and talents against the demands of the so-called real world. "If a child is to become a responsible person, he not only must be exposed to adults engaged in demanding tasks, but must himself participate in such tasks" (Bronfenbrenner, 1974, p. 60).

In an earlier era such issues seldom arose. Before 1925, for example, most teenagers entered the work force by age 15; only the most affluent young people were likely to continue their education without interruption (Kett, 1977; Greenberger & Steinberg, 1986). Currently, however, well over 85 percent of young people complete high school, and another 10 percent have from one to three years of high school (U.S. Bureau of the Census, 1985). One result of this shift is that many young people are not given opportunities for meaningful interaction with working adults. However, this need not be the case. A limited number of programs around the country are providing high school (and college) students with well-planned exposure to the kinds of work involved in careers in health, industry and business, the arts, and local government and social-service agencies.

In Denver, a joint program sponsored by a local high school and a building trades union enabled students to gain on-the-job experience in housebuilding while learning related academic skills in the classroom. Other students work with research scientists in their laboratories or with business executives; tutor younger students who are having problems in school; provide services to children, the elderly, or the handicapped; or work in business-funded training programs, such as renovating buildings in the community (Greenberger & Steinberg, 1986; Hamilton, 1981; Hamilton & Crouter, 1980; Hirsch, 1974; Bacas, 1986).

If such programs are to be of value in helping adolescents make the transition to the world of work, the experiences provided should be meaningful and relevant to the young person's goals (Greenberger & Steinberg, 1986). Recent studies suggest that the kinds of jobs that are most frequently available to adolescents attending school, such as working at fast-food outlets, washing cars, or packing groceries, may promote greater understanding of money matters, increased work orientation, and a somewhat greater feeling of independence, but they do little to encourage higher educational and vocational aspirations and planning for future employment. Indeed, for some young people, especially those who work long hours and are poorer students to begin with, such employment may interfere significantly with school performance (Greenberger & Steinberg, 1982, 1986).

Interestingly, part-time employment for high school students is far more common in the United States than in other industrialized countries. This is due partly to scheduling conflicts (longer school days and shorter business hours) in those countries and partly to the fact that opportunities for part-time employment are not as readily available there as in this country. To a large extent, however, it is a function of the much greater after-school demands placed on students in other countries. Many European and Japanese students, for example, are assigned four to five hours of homework nightly (Steinberg, 1985). In contrast, as we saw in Chapter 9, less than one-third of American students reported spending an hour or more on homework, while 40 percent said that they spend no time at all on homework (National Assessment of Educational Progress, 1981).

If the goals set for American education in recent reports are to be achieved, the question of how much time young people can afford to spend in academically unproductive part-time employment may need to be readdressed; currently, "well over half of high-school seniors hold at least the equivalent of a half-time job" (Greenberg & Steinberg, 1986, p. 17). Of course, substantial

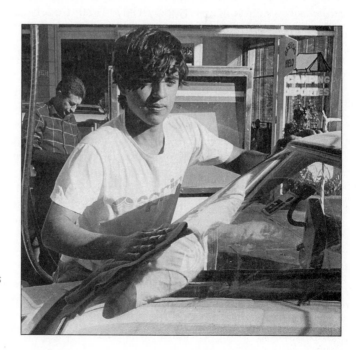

Part-time employment for high school students is far more common in the United States than in other industrialized countries.

part-time employment may be essential for some students to help support themselves or their families. A majority of students, however, spend none of their income on family living expenses or future educational needs (Greenberg & Steinberg, 1986). Moreover, long hours, poor or hazardous working conditions, and a high degree of stress may interfere with a young person's health. One study found that rates of alcohol, cigarette, and marijuana use were highest among adolescents who worked long hours or under stressful conditions (Greenberger, Steinberg, & Vaux, 1981).

Under favorable conditions work experience may help an adolescent interact more effectively with others, including employers. However, in many of the jobs available to adolescents opportunities to learn from or model oneself after a successful adult mentor are rather limited (Greenberger & Steinberg, 1986; Hamilton & Crouter, 1980). Moreover, in some shoddy or unchallenging work settings, adolescents may become more cynical about the intrinsic rewards of work and more accepting of questionable business practices (Steinberg, Greenberger, Vaux, & Ruggero, 1981; Stephenson, 1979). Finally, although having had such jobs during adolescence appears to have a positive effect on the adult employability of high school dropouts, it is unclear how much difference employment makes in the case of full-time students (Greenberger & Steinberg, 1986; Hamilton & Crouter, 1980; Stevenson, 1978).

THE PSYCHOLOGICAL SIGNIFICANCE OF WORK

In our society the choice of a vocation may help crystallize and reinforce an adolescent's self-concept (Super, 1967, 1980; Super, Starishevsky, Matlin, & Jordaan, 1963). Indeed, for most people, young and old alike, vocational identity is an important part of overall identity (Erikson, 1968; Marcia, 1980). Consequently, it is not surprising that having a job that society values—and doing it well—enhances self-esteem and aids in the development of an increasingly secure, stable sense of identity. Conversely, being given the message that one is not needed and that meaningful employment is not available fosters self-doubt, resentment, and loss of self-esteem, and increases the likelihood of identity confusion or even a negative identity (see pages 62–63).

A very important aspect of most people's working lives is the fact that "working gives them a feeling of being tied into the larger system of society, of having something to do, of having a purpose in life" (Morse & Weiss, 1968, p. 7). In 1989 American high school seniors were asked, "If you were to get enough money to live as comfortably as you'd like for the rest of your life, would you want to work?" Seventy-three percent stated that they would want to work, with girls outnumbering boys (79 percent versus 67 percent) (Johnston, Bachman, & O'Malley, forthcoming).

Recent research indicates that women who are employed outside the home are more likely to indicate overall satisfaction with their lives than those who are employed full time as homemakers. Among both white-collar and blue-collar working women, employment may enhance feelings of self-worth and provide a sense of challenge (L. W. Hoffman, 1984, 1986; Moos, 1986). At the same time, work that is unrewarding, frustrating, or extremely stressful, or that leads to failure, can have a negative effect on an individual's self-concept as well as creating stresses in other areas (Conger, 1984; Kessler & McRae, 1982; Moos, 1986). Thus, when maternal employment involves excessive strain resulting from the hassle of juggling two roles, the effects may be disruptive for the family and the child as well as for the mother herself (L. W. Hoffman, 1984, 1986; Warr & Parry, 1982).

A major ongoing epidemiological study of coronary heart disease (CHD) found that, overall, women clerical workers were no more susceptible to CHD than homemakers (Haynes & Feinleib, 1980). But working women who had three or more children were more likely to develop CHD than working women without children (11% versus 6.5%) or homemakers with the same number of children (4.4%). Differences were greatest for the wives of blue-collar workers; presumably this is due to less cultural acceptance of women working outside the home, stronger emphasis on traditional sex roles in the family, and greater economic strain than in professional and white-collar families. In short, the involvement of women in multiple roles does not detract from their physical and mental health unless the totality of demands they face is too great or they lack support from important people in their lives or evaluate their work role negatively (Haw, 1982; Moos, 1986).

In addition to helping to crystallize the young person's sense of identity and feelings of self-esteem, the choice of a particular vocation may offer socially approved ways of satisfying motives that may not have been satisfied during earlier stages of development. For example, motives such as desire for dominance, aggression, nurturance, and, occasionally, sexual curiosity can be at least partially gratified in certain occupations (e.g., army officer, police officer, social worker, physician, or nurse).

VOCATIONAL CHOICE AND SOCIAL CHANGE

In traditional societies and earlier periods, the problem of vocational choice was considerably simpler than it is in advanced societies today. Traditional societies typically offered fewer vocations, and adolescents were likely to be familiar with most of them through either observation or apprenticeship. In earlier periods in our own society, particularly in rural areas and small towns, young people were far more likely to have observed parents or other adults pursuing the occupations that they themselves were considering, and to have opportunities for early apprenticeships, whether informal and occasional (e.g., summer or after-school work) or formal and sustained.

Ellen Greenberger and Laurence Steinberg note that "three occupations historically have provided continuity in young people's passage from adolescent to adult employment: the skilled trades and crafts, factory work, and farm work" (1986, p. 50). In each of these occupational groups adolescent jobs have clear adult counterparts. In the past fifty years, however, adolescent work in these fields has diminished significantly and has been largely replaced by employment in service and sales jobs. Figure 10.1 dramatically illustrates the shift from the "old" workplace (crafts, factory, and farm) to the "new" workplace (service and sales) that occurred among 16- and 17-year-old workers between 1940 and 1980 alone; since then this trend has continued (see page 405). Moreover, for most adolescents many of these newer jobs have little continuity with their eventual adult employment, even in the same field; "wrapping hamburgers at the local fast-food franchise is less likely to lead to a management position in the food service industry than is a master's degree in business administration" (Greenberger & Steinberg, 1986, p 50).

Vocational Problems of Contemporary Adolescents

Today many adolescents, especially in cities and suburbs, have only a vague conception of the work that their parents and those of their friends actually do, or of the nature of the many different kinds of jobs available. They do not know which jobs they would be able to do successfully and would enjoy doing. They are not aware of the training required for a specific job or of the demand for workers in various occupations. This problem is becoming increasingly prevalent as our society grows more complex, more specialized, and more technologically oriented. The *Dictionary of Occupational Titles* now lists more than 47,000 different occupations and it is probably safe to say that many of them are unfamiliar not only to contemporary adolescents and their parents but to

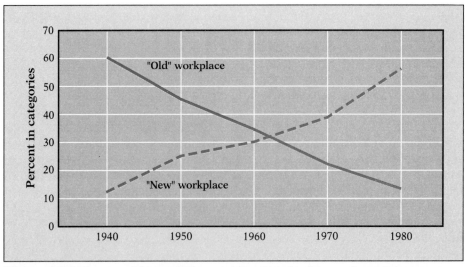

Figure 10.1 Percent of 16- and 17-year-old workers (students and nonstudents combined) employed in the "new" (service and sales) versus the "old" (crafts, factory, and farm) adolescent workplace, 1940–1980. (Source: U.S. Bureau of the Census, *Characteristics of the Population,* Washington, D.C.: U.S. Department of Commerce, 1940, 1950, 1960, 1970, 1980).

The need for well-informed vocational counsellors is becoming increasingly vital as the world grows more complex, more specialized, and more technologically oriented.

most vocational counselors as well (Super & Hall, 1978). Moreover, the kinds of skills required by employers are changing rapidly as new technologies are developed. As a result of increasing automation, there are few opportunities for unskilled or semiskilled workers; prior education and training are becoming increasingly necessary for admission to the world of work (Schorr, 1988).

DEVELOPMENT OF VOCATIONAL GOALS

As the time approaches when young people must support themselves, they are likely to spend more time thinking about vocational goals. They also become progressively more realistic about those goals. According to Eli Ginzberg (1972) and Donald Super (1967, 1980), before adolescence occupational goals tend to reflect fantasy more than reality; children are likely to select occupations that seem active and exciting, such as cowboy or cowgirl, actor, baseball player, astronaut, firefighter, airline pilot or flight attendant, and explorer (Ginzberg, 1972; Super, 1967, 1980; Tiedman & O'Hara, 1963). With the advent of more mature cognitive ability, young people tentatively begin to balance their interests against actual job opportunities and their own capabilities. At about age 15 or 16, adolescents enter a period of exploration: They become increasingly aware of the need to make career decisions, and they are likely to seek out relevant occupational information (Ginzberg, 1972; Jepsen, 1975; Super, 1967). As the young person's self-concept becomes more mature and more clearly defined, he or she searches for a workable match between that self-concept and the actual demands and opportunities of various careers

(Gottfredson, 1981; Herr & Cramer, 1979; Osipow, 1986; Super, 1967, 1980). As young people become more concerned with articulating their values and beliefs, they are likely to look for occupations that allow for the expression of these values (Ginzberg, 1972). Interest in service to others is also likely to arise at this time (Fuhrman, 1986).

Between the ages of 18 and 21 career choices tend to become increasingly *crystallized* (Ginzberg, 1972) and *specific* (Super, 1967). Decisions made during this period can have important consequences for the young person's career. A general interest in, for example, a job that would involve service to others or a career in business evolves into specific consideration of being, say, a medical social worker or a corporate lawyer. The individual determines the specific education and training required for such a career and tailors his or her educational plans and job experiences accordingly.

Empirical studies support the notion of a steady but gradual maturation in vocational thinking during the adolescent years (Borow, 1966; Herr & Cramer, 1979; Osipow, 1983, 1986). Whereas the younger child is not likely to be influenced very much by the social status of a particular occupation, as he or she grows older occupational prestige becomes a more important consideration. Finally, as adulthood approaches, young people are likely to settle on an occupation that represents a realistic reconciliation between what they would like to do and what they think they might actually be able to do.

As vocational interests become progressively more realistic, they also become more stable. For example, the older the adolescent, the less changeable his or her vocational interests, as measured by repeated vocational-interest tests. By late adolescence vocational interest tends to become fairly stable, though changes may still occur (Borow, 1966).

Until recently, developmental theorists believed that vocational stability was achieved upon actual entrance into and experience with a job (Borow, 1976; Ginzberg, 1980). Probably reflecting major changes in society as a whole, most now believe that there is no fixed cutoff point and that occupational choice is a lifelong decision-making process. In this view, the individual continually attempts to find the optimal fit between his or her career goals and the changing realities of the world of work. In brief, as circumstances, job experience, and characteristics of the person change over the years, new choices may be made, though such choices may entail financial, social, or personal costs (Borow, 1966; Herr & Cramer, 1979; Osipow, 1983, 1986).

As a number of theorists have noted, "Occupational choice is clearly an implementation of the self-concept, and self-identity is a necessary precursor to career commitment" (Fuhrman, 1976, p. 376). Conversely, as we noted in Chapter 2, difficulty in choosing a career can be viewed as a problem in the development of a clear sense of identity (Osipow, 1983, 1986; Herr & Cramer, 1979; Lunneborg, 1975). Nevertheless, there is considerable evidence that most adolescents cannot simply be left to their own devices in coping with vocational problems. In a society as complex as ours, in which the actual requirements of most jobs and their availability in the labor market are not matters of common knowledge, young people clearly need help. However, the availability of knowledgeable, skilled assistance is extremely limited. As a result, the young person's vocational interests usually develop in a rather unsystematic fashion, guided by such influences as parental desires, relationships with parents, suggestions by school counselors, contact with people in various occupations, and the kinds of jobs friends are choosing. Class- and sex-based standards also play a role, as we shall see in the following sections.

SUBCULTURAL INFLUENCES ON VOCATIONAL CHOICE

Two broad subcultural influences have a significant effect on adolescents' vocational goals: social class and sex. Social-class membership influences vocational goals in a variety of ways. For one thing, it helps determine the kinds of occupations to which the young person is exposed and hence is likely to consider. In addition, it plays an important role in determining the social acceptability (i.e., reward value) of particular occupations. Certain types of occupations are considered appropriate to the members of a particular social class, while others are felt to be inappropriate. The individual who deviates from these expectations is likely to evoke the disapproval of peers, particularly if the chosen occupation is associated with lower-class status.

The very young upper-class child who wants to be an ice cream vendor or truck driver may be indulged or even encouraged. During adolescence, however, when the problem of vocational choice takes on practical implications, the child's parents are not likely to find such notions amusing. Choices of lower-status occupations run counter to the parents' ideas about appropriate behavior for a member of their social class, and consequently are likely to be discouraged.

If the reader harbors any doubts that this indeed is the case, just observe the reactions of many otherwise tolerant and reasonably flexible upper- and upper-middle-class parents to an adolescent daughter's announcement that she intends to raise vegetables and take in sewing on a communal farm, or a son's statement that he intends to take part-time laboring jobs or drive a cab in order to devote as much time as possible to painting or writing poetry. Parents may fear that such choices will lead to social disapproval both of their child and of themselves. Moreover, when the economic rewards of the selected occupation are meager, parents may fear that the child will not be able to live in the same kind of neighborhood as other members of his or her social class, or to afford the same social, recreational, and educational advantages.

Conversely, aspirations toward higher-status occupations may also lead to social disapproval (particularly if they are flaunted), since such aspirations may be viewed as a threat by other members of the individual's social class. In this case, however, the disapproval is likely to be less strong and, in the adolescent's view, may be more than outweighed by the prospect of higher rewards.

The relationship between social-class membership and vocational aspirations was demonstrated in a study of graduating seniors in Wisconsin's public and private high schools (Little, 1967). The students were asked to state the occupations that they hoped to enter. Their choices were then assigned "prestige scores." The investigators found that subjects in the lower third of the student population in terms of socioeconomic status aspired to high-prestige occupations significantly less often than would be expected by chance; conversely, students in the upper third aspired to such occupations significantly more often than would be expected. Moreover, the later occupational attainments of lower-status students were close to their expectations (see Table 10.1).

Several hypotheses have been offered to account for social-class differences in vocational goals. One is that there are class differences in the evaluation of the relative values assigned by adolescents to various occupations, and that these differences account largely for social-class differences in vocational goals (Caro, 1966). Other theorists argue that both middle-class and working-class youth agree on the relative desirability and prestige of various occupations, and that differences in goals stem not primarily from values but from class-associated perceptions of differences in opportunities and general life chances (Borow, 1976; Harvey & Kevin, 1978).

Although many adolescents may be somewhat unrealistic about their vocational goals, they nevertheless possess some awareness of practical obstacles that may modify their vocational aspirations, and these are certainly affected by social-class status. A working-class girl whose parents are unable to help or uninterested in helping her go to college is less likely to aspire to be a doctor than one whose parents encourage such a vocational choice and are in a position to help her. Similarly, a boy whose parents expect him to go to work after the ninth grade is not likely to spend much time contemplating the idea of becoming an engineer.

One study found that working-class students, perceiving high-prestige occupations as less accessible to them, tended to protect themselves from possible disappointment by placing relatively less value on high-prestige positions and more value on medium-prestige occupations (Rodman, 1962). Nevertheless, they still tended to view high-prestige positions as more desirable, although the differences were not nearly as great as they were for middle-class students.

The Growing Underclass. The vocational outlooks of both middle- and working-class students are quite different from that of a growing **underclass**—individuals who have, in effect, been, and see themselves as, excluded from participation in the system (Lemann, 1986). The desperately poor, largely minority young person growing up in the heart of a socially disorganized, crime-ridden inner city who sees that the great majority of his or her peers are out of work—with virtually no prospect of future employment—are likely either to have no sustainable vocational hopes, or, more rarely, to have highly unrealistic aspirations (Borow, 1976; Freeman, 1986). The size of this group has grown steadily since the early 1950s (see pages 403–407).

Women and Work: The New American Revolution

One of the most dramatic and significant changes in American society since the end of World War II has been the precipitous rise in the number of women

TABLE 10.1 CHARACTERISTICS OF GRADUATES IN HIGH- AND LOW-PRESTIGE OCCUPATIONS

Characteristics	High Prestige			Low Prestige		
	(1) %	(2) %	(3) Diff.	(1) %	(2) %	(3) Diff.
1. Size of community						
Countries with cities:						
Not over 10,000	38	30	−8	38	48	+10
10,000–24,999	7	7	0	7	8	+1
25,000–49,999	22	22	0	22	22	0
Metropolitan areas	33	41	+8	33	22	−11
2. Socioeconomic status						
Lower third	33	20	−13	33	40	+7
Middle third	34	33	+11	34	40	+6
Higher third	33	47	+14	33	20	−13
3. Father's occupation						
Farming	22	15	−7	22	35	+13
Unskilled	39	35	−4	39	42	+3
Skilled	10	10	0	10	9	−1
White collar	20	25	+5	20	11	−9
Professional	9	15	+6	9	3	−6
4. Father's education						
No high school	46	34	−12	46	58	+12
Some high school	16	13	−3	16	17	+1
High school graduate	26	32	+6	26	19	−7
Some college	12	21	+9	12	6	−6
5. Scholastic aptitude						
Lower half	52	32	−20	52	67	+15
Higher half	48	68	+20	48	33	−15
6. High school achievement						
Lower half	62	41	−21	62	77	+15
Higher half	38	59	+21	38	23	−15
7. Level of education						
High school only	43	18	−25	43	76	+33
Vocational school	16	14	−2	16	13	−3
Some college	41	68	+27	41	11	−30

Source: J. K. Little. The occupations of non-college youth. *American Educational Research Journal,* 1967, **4,** 147–153. Copyright 1967 by the American Educational Research Association, Washington, D.C. Reprinted by permission of the publisher.

Note: Column (1), percentage of all graduates in sample; column (2), percentage of all graduates who attained high- or low-prestige occupations; column (3), difference and direction of difference.

entering the job market. More young women are working before marriage, delaying marriage, and returning to work after the birth of children. In 1947, only one-third of all women over age 16 were employed outside the home; beginning in 1984, for the first time a majority of married women from intact families with children under the age of 6 were employed outside the home, and their numbers continue to grow (see Table 10.2).

T A B L E 10.2 MARRIED, SEPARATED, AND DIVORCED WOMEN: LABOR FORCE STATUS, BY PRESENCE AND AGE OF CHILDREN, 1960–1988 (PERCENT)

Item	Participation Rate[a]			
	1960	1970	1980	1988
Married, husband present, total	30.5	40.8	50.2	56.5
No children under 18	34.7	42.2	46.1	48.9
Children 6–17 only	39.0	49.2	61.8	72.5
Children under 6	18.6	30.3	45.0	57.1
Separated, total	(NA)	52.3	59.4	60.9
No children under 18	(NA)	52.3	58.7	60.1
Children 6–17 only	(NA)	60.6	66.4	69.3
Children under 6	(NA)	45.4	51.8	53.0
Divorced, total				
No children under 18	(NA)	67.7	71.4	73.0
Children 6–17 only	(NA)	82.4	82.3	83.9
Children under 6	(NA)	63.3	68.0	70.1

Source: U.S. Bureau of Labor Statistics, 1989; and U.S. Department of Commerce, Bureau of the Census, Statistical abstract of the United States, 1986. Washington, D.C.: U.S. Government Printing Office, 1989 (109th ed.).

Note: NA = Not available.
[a]Percent of women in each specific category in the labor force.

The reasons for these profound social changes are both economic and social. They include a sharply declining birthrate, increased employment opportunities and higher salaries for women, changing social and sex roles, and families' desire for two incomes (Wessel, 1986). Recent studies indicate that in the past fifteen years the percentages of upper-income families (above $50,000) and of families with incomes below the poverty line have both expanded significantly while the size of the middle class, which had remained fairly stable since World War II, has decreased (Wessel, 1986). In part, these changes may be due to structural changes in the economy, such as the decline in the number of high-paying factory jobs. In part, however, they have resulted from changing family employment patterns. When both spouses have reasonably good jobs, their combined income may well total over $50,000. "At the same time, divorce and unwed motherhood are creating more households headed by women—and half of the 7.2 million poor families in America are headed by women with no husband present" (Wessel, 1986, p. 20). Moreover, unemployment of one spouse is likely to be far less devastating in two-earner families.

For all of these reasons, the percentage of working mothers can be expected to continue to grow—out of choice or out of necessity or both. However, combining full-time employment and the responsibilities of home and family is seldom easy (see page 408). Thus, it is not surprising that although the majority (52 percent) of working mothers are currently employed full time, most of those with younger children would prefer to work part-time, to have more flexible hours, or to work from their homes if it were economically feasible (Kantrowitz, 1986; Taylor, 1986).

In a continuing national survey (Bachman, Johnston, & O'Malley, 1981; Herzog, Bachman, & Johnston, 1979; Johnston, Bachman, & O'Malley, forthcoming), the attitudes of high school seniors toward various working arrangements of couples were investigated. For couples without children, the most widely preferred working arrangements are those in which the husband is employed full time and the wife is employed either full time or half-time, with a higher percentage of females preferring that both partners work full time and a higher percentage of males preferring that the wife work only half-time (Johnston et al., forthcoming). Less than 9 percent of the males and less than 7 percent of the females view as desirable the traditional pattern in which the husband is employed full time and the wife is not employed outside the home. (Except for a very small minority, neither males nor females considered a reversal of this traditional sex role pattern desirable or even acceptable.)

The presence of preschool children changes the picture significantly. In such cases the most preferred arrangement among both males and females is for the husband to work full time while the wife remains at home or, at most, works part time. Fifty-one percent of males and 44 percent of females considered an arrangement in which both husband and wife work full time to be unacceptable, and less than 9 percent of members of both sexes considered such an arrangement desirable. Interestingly, regardless of the type of working arrangement they prefer, both males and females prefer an equal division of labor in child care, although many consider a somewhat greater proportion of care by the wife acceptable, particularly when the husband is working full time (Bachman et al., 1987; Johnston et al., forthcoming).

Despite a significant liberalization in attitudes toward male and female roles in marriage, it appears that for the majority of young people the responsibility for the financial stability of the family rests more with the husband while the responsibility for child care rests more with the wife. But the picture is not static. For example, in 1980 nearly two-thirds (63.4 percent) of seniors considered it unacceptable for both parents to work full time when there are preschool children in the home (even though many will do so); by 1989 this figure had declined to 51 percent. Similarly, the percentage of seniors considering half-time work acceptable or desirable for wives with preschool children increased from 60 percent to over 69 percent between 1980 and 1989 (Bachman et al., 1981, 1987; Johnston et al., forthcoming). Further changes may well occur as the number of working women continues to grow.

Sex Differences in Vocational Goals

Despite women's increased participation in the labor force, the influence of the women's movement, and decreased sex role stereotyping, the career choices of many teenage Americans of both sexes still reflect relatively traditional, sex-related occupational aspirations, such as secretary or teacher for females and skilled worker for males (America's youth, 1988). However, nearly equal numbers of male and female high school seniors aspire to managerial and professional occupations, such as office manager, lawyer, physician, dentist, or college professor (Bachman et al., 1987; Johnston et al., 1986).

Upon entering college more young women than men are planning to enter such occupations as clinical psychologist, nurse, teacher, and physical or occupational therapist (see Table 10.3). Conversely, more young men are planning to enter such occupations as engineer, business owner, the military, and skilled trades (Astin et al., 1989). Although more young men than women are still planning to enter such traditionally male fields as business executive, lawyer or judge, and physician, the gap has narrowed dramatically in recent years, and these trends show every sign of continuing.

Moreover, more girls than boys are currently choosing nontraditional jobs; that is, more girls than boys choose jobs that were traditionally filled by members of the opposite sex (Astin et al., 1989). This trend is due partly to the greater economic and other rewards associated with many traditionally male occupations, partly to the greater number and variety of traditionally male jobs in our society, and partly to girls' relative freedom from inhibitions about aspiring to nontraditional occupations. Middle- and upper-class girls, and those whose mothers have nontraditional jobs themselves, are most likely to choose atypical occupations (Franken, 1983; Reid & Stephens, 1985; Shapiro & Crowley, 1982).

T A B L E 10.3 SEX DIFFERENCES IN PROBABLE CAREER OCCUPATIONS OF FIRST-YEAR COLLEGE AND UNIVERSITY STUDENTS, 1989

Probable Career Occupation	All Men	All Women
Accountant or actuary	5.2	6.3
Architect or urban planner	3.0	0.8
Business executive	12.8	9.9
Business owner or proprietor	5.0	2.0
Clinical psychologist	0.6	2.6
Computer programmer or analyst	3.5	1.9
Engineer	16.5	2.6
Law enforcement officer	1.9	0.4
Lawyer or judge	5.3	5.3
Military service or career	1.7	0.2
Nurse	0.3	4.8
Physician	4.0	3.6
Social, welfare, or recreation worker	0.3	2.1
Therapist (physical, occupational, speech)	1.2	3.8
Teacher (elementary)	0.7	8.7
Teacher (secondary)	2.8	3.5
Writer or journalist	1.6	2.9
Skilled trades	2.5	0.3

Source: A. W. Astin, W. S. Korn, & E. R. Berz. *The American freshman: National norms for fall, 1989.* Los Angeles: Higher Education Research Institute, University of California at Los Angeles, 1989. By permission.

More girls than boys are currently choosing nontraditional jobs— jobs traditionally filled by members of the opposite sex.

Family Values, Sex Role Attitudes, and Vocational Goals

Vocational theorists have tended to ignore the role of values regarding family life and parenthood in determining adolescents' vocational orientation. This has occurred partly because those values appear to be related less strongly to the vocational aspirations and behavior of males than to those of females (Fitzgerald & Crites, 1980; L. W. Hoffman, 1984). Several studies indicate that the occupational aspirations of young women are closely related to their views about marriage and parenthood, and that this is much less true of young men (Areshansel & Rosen, 1980; Leslie, 1986).

Young women with high-status occupational expectations, typically in full-time careers and often in traditionally male fields, are likely to have less traditional sex role attitudes than peers with more conventional expectations (L. W. Hoffman, 1989; Zaslow, 1987). If they are among the more than 90 percent who plan to marry, they are likely to plan to marry later, to have fewer children, and to work while their children are young. Although most want to combine a career and child rearing, they are somewhat less likely to view having children and having "someone to rely on" as important needs or satisfactions in deciding to marry (Areshansel & Rosen, 1980; Cerra, 1980; L. W. Hoffman, 1973, 1980, 1989; Marini, 1978; Marini & Greenberger, 1978).

Other studies have shown that young women who plan to enter nontraditional careers typically score higher on measures of academic ability (particularly in the physical and biological sciences and in mathematics) and have higher grades. They are also likely to be more independent and assertive and more concerned with exhibiting competence. Their mothers are more likely to work outside the home and to have a positive orientation toward working (Areshansel & Rosen, 1980; Cerra, 1980; L. W. Hoffman, 1973, 1980; Marini, 1978).

In contrast, the minority of young women who plan to become full-time homemakers are likely to strongly endorse traditional values with respect to occupational and domestic roles of men and women. They also have more traditional perceptions of male and female behavior generally. They plan to marry younger and have more children, have lower educational aspirations, and view children and "having someone to rely on" as important family values (Areshansel & Rosen, 1980; Tittle, 1980, 1981).

Occupying a middle ground between these two extremes are adolescent girls who plan to stay at home while their children are young but to work before having children and when their children are older. On most variables (e.g., desired family size, relative importance of children and jobs, occupational and domestic values, sex role attitudes), their scores fall between those of full-time homemakers and high-status career seekers. These young women are likely to have relatively traditional occupational expectations.

PARENTAL INFLUENCES ON VOCATIONAL CHOICE

Parents and siblings play a significant role in a young person's vocational choice. In general, if parents set high educational and occupational goals and reward good schoolwork, their children have high levels of aspiration. Working-class adolescents are more likely to choose advanced education and occupational mobility if their parents urge them to do so (L. W. Hoffman, 1984, 1986). In one study, *ambitious middle-class males* reported the highest degree of parental support and encouragement for educational and vocational achievement. *Upwardly mobile working-class males* ranked a close second (Simpson, 1962). In contrast, *unambitious middle-class males* and *nonmobile working-class males* ranked far behind in level of parental support. A major reason for the superior academic success of many Asian students, including children of recent immigrants, lies in the great importance their families attach to education and hard work, together with the high credibility of parental values in the eyes of their children (Brand, 1987).

Father's Occupation and Work Experience

Parents' occupations and the way parents view their work can significantly influence the career choices of their children. To date most research dealing with the influence of parental occupation on adolescent career choices has involved fathers; most studies of mothers' influence have dealt with the effects of employment per se (L. W. Hoffman, 1984, 1986). The number of sons following in their father's footsteps greatly exceeds what one would expect by chance, even if social-class influences are taken into account (L. W. Hoffman, 1984, 1986; Mortimer, 1974, 1976, 1982; Werts, 1968). For example, sons of physicians, lawyers, and scientists are far more likely to enter these occupations than other young men of similar socioeconomic status. When the occupational categories are broadened to include the same or similar kinds of occupations, the strength of the relationship between the vocational choices of fathers and sons increases.

These findings can probably be explained partly in terms of such obvious factors as greater opportunity to become familiar with one's father's occupation, greater access to that occupation, and at least in some cases (e.g., physicians), strong parental motivation—and sometimes pressure—for the son to enter the occupation. However, recent research suggests that more subtle factors also play a part; one such factor is the communication of values from parent to child (Mortimer, 1976, 1982).

Several theorists believe that "through one's job one develops notions of what qualities and values are important for success, and these ideas are embodied in child-rearing patterns" (L. W. Hoffman, 1986, p. 184). For example, fathers in middle-class white-collar occupations that involve manipulation of ideas, symbols, and interpersonal relations and require considerable flexibility, thought, and judgment place a high value on self-direction and independence (Kohn, 1959a, 1959b, 1969; Kohn & Schooler, 1978, 1982). Accordingly, they emphasize achievement, independence, and self-reliance in child-rearing. In contrast, lower-class or blue-collar fathers whose occupations are more standardized, less complex, more closely supervised, and more likely to require manipulation of physical objects than of ideas or interpersonal relationships are more likely to value obedience and conformity in their child-rearing practices.

Although other factors clearly play a role in determining the values and practices emphasized by parents, there are indications that on-the-job experiences make an important contribution (L. W. Hoffman, 1986). In one study, workers in a plant that actively engaged workers in management decision making were asked about some of the effects of their experiences (Crouter, 1984). Many described how their personal experiences on the job had led them to use similar methods with their children:

> I have a 16-year-old son and I use some of the things we do at work with him instead of yelling. We listen better here, we let people tell their side.
> I say things to my 8-year-old daughter that I know are a result of the way we do things at work. I ask her, "What do you think about that?" or "How would you handle this problem?"
> In terms of dealing with my family, I'm more willing to get their opinions. We hold "team meetings" at home to make decisions (Crouter, 1984, pp. 81–82).

In an interesting series of studies, Mortimer (1974, 1976) investigated the hypothesis that value differences between business and professional subcultures and work activities are transmitted from fathers to sons and influence their sons' subsequent occupational choices. Professional occupations were seen as placing greater emphasis on *intrinsic* work satisfactions such as autonomy, expert knowledge, and opportunities for service; business occupations, in turn, were found to place more emphasis on such *extrinsic* rewards as high income and advancement. This investigator examined the occupational choices of college students whose fathers were (1) professionals (e.g., physician, scientist, lawyer, teacher); (2) high-prestige businessmen; and (3) lower-prestige businessmen. In addition, the degree of closeness between father and son was measured. A number of interesting findings emerged. As predicted, sons of professionals were indeed more likely than sons of businessmen to choose a profession, while the latter were more likely to choose business. However, sons were far more likely to choose a vocation similar to that of the father when the father's job had high prestige and the son had a close relationship with his father (see Table 10.4). When the prestige of the father's job was low, even sons who felt close to their fathers apparently were motivated to look elsewhere to find their life's work. "The father's prestigious occupation alone, however, is not enough to motivate occupational inheritance if the relationship between the father and son is not conducive to strong parental identification and value transference" (Mortimer, 1976, p. 252).

For example, among the sons of high-prestige businessmen, those who were close to their fathers were almost twice as likely to choose a career in business as those who were not close to their fathers. Other studies have found this combination of a close relationship with a prestigious father and the choice of similar occupation to be associated with sons' patterns of identification and modeling (Bell, 1969; L. W. Hoffman, 1984).

Vocational Adjustment. The kinds of role models—both positive and negative—that parents provide affect not only career choice but also overall vocational adjustment. In addition, the relevance of parental models may vary

The kinds of role models that parents provide can have an important influence, not only on occupational choice but also on overall vocational adjustment.

T A B L E 10.4 PERCENTAGE DISTRIBUTIONS OF SENIOR CAREER CHOICES BY CLOSENESS TO FATHER IN BUSINESS AND PROFESSIONAL ORIGIN GROUPS

	Senior Career Choice^a								Total	
	Doctor	Dentist	Scientist	Teacher	College Professor	Government	Lawyer	Business	%	N
A. Lower-prestige business origin										
Close	16.9	4.8	9.6	8.4	19.3	4.8	12.0	24.1	48.8	83
Not close	14.9	1.1	3.4	6.9	20.7	10.3	12.6	29.9	51.2	87
Total	15.9	2.9	6.5	7.6	20.0	7.6	12.4	27.1	100.0	170
B. Higher-prestige business origin										
Close	17.8	4.1	4.1	5.5	4.1	4.1	20.5	39.7	56.6	73
Not close	17.9	7.1	3.6	5.4	21.4	7.1	16.1	21.4	43.4	56
Total	17.8	5.4	3.9	5.4	11.6	5.4	18.6	31.8	100.0	129
C. Professional origin										
Close	48.4	3.1	1.6	4.7	20.3	1.6	7.8	12.5	71.1	64
Not close	30.8	7.7	11.5	3.8	19.2	0.0	11.5	15.4	28.9	26
Total	43.3	4.4	4.4	4.4	20.0	1.1	8.9	13.3	100.0	90

Source: J. T. Mortimer. Social class, work, and the family: Some implications of the father's occupation for familial relationships and sons' career decisions. *Journal of Marriage and the Family*, 1976, **38**, No. 2, 241–256. By permission.

^aStudents making other, less popular choices are deleted from the table.

considerably with age. Both of these possibilities were investigated in a longitudinal study of male adolescents during the ninth grade (average age 15) and again when they had been out of high school for seven years (age 25) (Bell, 1969).

Using semistructured interviews, the investigators attempted to determine the adolescent's primary role models "overall" and in various "life spheres" (i.e., educational, occupational, personal), as well as the position occupied by the model on a dimension ranging from highly positive to negative. Vocational adjustment was measured by a variety of criteria, including fulfillment of original occupational goal, job stability, reasons for changing jobs, occupational level, job competence and success, job satisfaction, and the like. The following interesting findings emerged:

1. The most frequently mentioned role model, both in ninth grade and in young adulthood, was the father. However, with age the importance of the father decreased and that of other figures, including peers, teachers, adult relatives, employers, and other adults, increased.

2. Of all the role models that subjects possessed when they were in the ninth grade (e.g., father, mother, siblings, adult relatives), only the father's role modeling (both occupational and overall) was related to the sons' vocational adjustment and behaviors ten years later.

3. In general, boys who at age 15 had fathers as strong and positive role models tended to achieve higher levels of vocational adjustment than those for whom fathers were either weak or nonexistent role models or negative models.

4. The differences in vocational adjustment were generally greater in the former cases (weak or nonexistent role model) than in the latter (negative role model). It appears that both identification *and* rejection of role models may serve as determinants of career patterns. "Their importance may be more similar than it has been commonly realized. Each may serve as important occasions for self-definition" (Bell, 1969, p. 34).

5. Interestingly, the kinds of relationships obtained between father-modeling at age 15 and vocational adjustment at 25 are no longer found when father-modeling at age 25 and vocational adjustment at 25 are examined. Indeed, at age 25 *moderate* use of the father as a positive role model is significantly more often associated with successful vocational adjustment than either strong, positive modeling or negative modeling. The researchers concluded:

> It would appear that what may be appropriate with regard to the use of fathers as role models in adolescence is no longer so in young adulthood. The latter period has been thought of as involving a trend toward increasing autonomy, as the giving up of internalized parents, as the opportunity for the nonparents emerging as increasingly significant role models as the adolescent subjects moved into young adulthood. And those subjects whose fathers were moderate or even nonscoring role models at this period and whose statuses appeared to denote a disengagement with them on the part of their sons appeared to function

more effectively in young adulthood than those subjects whose relationship with their fathers represented a continuing and negative involvement. It may be that adolescents need their fathers as important sources on self-definition even into adolescence but most move on, in young adulthood, to new and different but important experiences of others (Bell, 1969, p. 34).

Effects of Maternal Employment on Adolescent Vocational Attitudes

Studies of fathers' influence on adolescents' vocational values and goals have tended to focus on the idea that the father's occupation affects the child because the traits required for success in that occupation are valued and passed on to the child (L. W. Hoffman, 1984). In contrast, in studies of the mother's influence the focus has been primarily on her employment status per se (Bronfenbrenner & Crouter, 1982; Greenberger & Goldberg, 1989; Hoffman, 1986). Moreover, until recently it was assumed that maternal employment outside the home was most likely to have an adverse effect not merely on vocational orientation but on development generally.

Recent research suggests, however, that neither is the case. There is little evidence that maternal investment in work occurs at the expense of child rearing (Greenberger & Goldberg, 1989). Indeed, maternal employment is more likely to have positive effects, particularly for adolescent girls. And as maternal employment becomes the norm and social and economic arrangements accommodate this shift, it seems likely that this trend will continue (L. W. Hoffman, 1986). A number of studies have indicated that the views of girls and young women (and, in some investigations, males as well) regarding appropriate roles for women are influenced by the kinds of maternal role models to which they are exposed (Baruch, 1972; L. W. Hoffman, 1984, 1986; Vogel et al., 1970). In the middle-childhood years, girls whose mothers work outside the home are more likely than those with nonemployed mothers to view both men and women as typically engaging in a wider variety of adult activities, including those that have traditionally been stereotyped as masculine or feminine. They are also more likely to say that they approve of maternal employment (Hartley, 1960; L. W. Hoffman, 1984; Marantz & Mansfield, 1977).

Girls and young women whose mothers are employed outside the home also are more likely to view work as something they will want to do if and when they themselves become mothers (Banducci, 1967; L. W. Hoffman, 1974; Huston, 1983; Smith, 1969). In a study of the sex role perceptions of college students, one team of investigators found that young women and young men with employed mothers perceived smaller male–female differences compared with children of nonemployed mothers on such generally sex-stereotyped attributes as competence and warmth-expressiveness, with females being more affected by maternal employment than males (Vogel et al., 1970). In a related study (Baruch, 1972), college women were given a number of scholarly articles and asked to judge the quality of the article and of the author. Half the articles were attributed to female authors and half to male authors. Daughters of working mothers were less likely than those of nonemployed full-time homemakers to assume lower competence on the part of female authors.

Employed mothers are more likely to encourage independence in their children (L. W. Hoffman, 1974, 1986), and indeed, daughters of working mothers tend to be more autonomous, active, self-reliant, and achievement oriented (Almquist & Angrist, 1971; Gold & Andres, 1978; Hock, 1978; L. W. Hoffman, 1974, 1986, 1989). They also are somewhat more likely to view their mothers as people whom they admire and want to be like; however, the self-esteem of girls does not seem to be related to their mothers' employment status (Baruch, 1972; Douvan, 1963).

Finally, the vocational attitudes, aspirations, and accomplishments of girls are influenced not simply by the fact of maternal employment as such but by the mother's attitude toward employment, her degree of satisfaction and accomplishment in her work, and her ability to successfully combine the roles of worker, mother, and wife (Gottfried, Gottfried, & Bathurst, 1988; Guidubaldi & Nastasi, 1987; L. W. Hoffman, 1986, 1989). One study found that whether a girl expresses positive attitudes toward employment combined with home-making depends on "whether her mother endorses it and, if the mother works, upon how successfully she has integrated her two roles. Thus, if a subject's mother had worked but had also experienced negative personal consequences because of her career, the subject evaluated women's competence highly but was unfavorable to the dual role pattern" (Baruch, 1972, p. 37). The girl's attitudes were also influenced by whether or not her father expressed acceptance of his wife's career orientation.

A variety of investigations have found that "highly achieving women and women who aspire to careers, particularly to less conventionally feminine careers, are more likely to be the daughters of educated women and the daughters of employed women. The high-achieving woman has a high-achieving daughter" (L. W. Hoffman, 1973, p. 213). Lois Hoffman (1973, 1984, 1986) suggests several reasons for this. First, the mother provides a model of achievement for her daughter. Second, such mothers are more likely to encourage independence in their daughters; this is particularly important because many girls are handicapped by overprotection and encouragement of dependency. And finally, optimum conditions include a good relationship with the father, who encourages the girl's independence and achievement while accepting her as a female.

Although encouragement of independence by employed mothers is likely to have positive effects on daughters, it is not clear whether it is an advantage or a disadvantage to sons. Sons traditionally have received more independence training than daughters, and while this seems to be an advantage in families with nonemployed mothers, it may be too much in those in which the mother is employed (L. W. Hoffman, 1986). Among middle-class boys, in contrast to girls, maternal employment is associated with somewhat lower IQ scores, lower school performance, and, possibly, a greater incidence of aggressive behavior and adjustment problems (Gold & Andres, 1978; L. W. Hoffman, 1980, 1986; Montemayor, 1984; Montemayor & Clayton, 1983). Some theorists have suggested that the sons of working mothers, perhaps because of their greater independence, may be more likely to become involved in peer groups which may undermine adult socialization (Bronfenbrenner & Crouter, 1982; Montemayor, 1984). Conversely, sons of full-time homemakers were more inhibited and conforming in early adolescence, but they also performed better in school (Moore, 1975). It may be that employed mothers place too much pressure for independence on their adolescent sons, while mothers who are full-time homemakers unwittingly encourage conformity and place too little emphasis on independence training (L. W. Hoffman, 1986).

Investigators have also found that working mothers (and their husbands) have more positive views of their daughters than of their sons, whereas the reverse is true for nonworking mothers (Bronfenbrenner, Alvarez, & Henderson, 1984). While working mothers tend to view their daughters as self-reliant and helpful, they are more likely to complain about their sons' noncompliance and aggressiveness. In turn, adolescent sons (but not daughters) report more frequent, longer, and more intense conflicts with working mothers than with nonemployed mothers (Montemayor, 1984). It may be that working mothers are less tolerant than nonemployed mothers of the greater aggressiveness and rebellious tendencies of adolescent boys. It is also possible that the lack of supervision and greater peer group involvement of sons of working mothers tends to foster increased conflicts with parental values and expectations (Bronfenbrenner & Crouter, 1982; Montemayor, 1984). Considerably more research will be needed before firm conclusions can be reached on this subject (L. W. Hoffman, 1986).

In brief, full-time involvement of mothers in careers that they enjoy and do well appears to have positive effects on the educational and vocational aspirations of adolescent girls, particularly when the father provides encouragement and support. However, the picture is not as clear or as positive in the case of middle-class sons of working mothers.

Ordinal Position and Sibling Sex Status

Vocational values and goals may also be influenced by the adolescent's ordinal position in the family. For example, firstborn children are likely to receive more training in achievement and responsibility than children who are born later, as well as more attention from their parents (Altus, 1965; Chemers, 1970; Gandy, 1973). They are more likely to prefer occupations that involve the direction, control, and supervision of others (Oberlander, Frauenfelder, & Heath, 1970; Very & Prull, 1970). This may result from the fact that parents generally assign more responsibility to the oldest child. They are more likely to be put in charge of other children and given household chores, and in general get more experience at playing adult surrogate roles than later-born children do (Gandy, 1973; Sutton-Smith, Roberts, & Rosenberg, 1964). Among college students in two-child families, firstborns (especially females) are significantly more likely than second-borns to score high on vocational-interest patterns associated with teaching. In contrast, second-borns appear to be more inclined toward activities that require sociable, empathic, and sympathetic behavior

(Schacter, 1964), possibly because "these characteristics are related to the more relaxed relationship the second child has with his parents as well as the opportunity to seek more varied relationships" (Gandy, 1973, p. 406).

The sex of siblings also appears to play a role. In general, traditionally masculine vocational interests occur more frequently in all-male dyads (i.e., among both the older and the younger brother in two-child families). Similarly, there appears to be a tendency for girls in all-female dyads to score highest on interest patterns associated with traditionally feminine occupations (Sutton-Smith et al., 1964). On the other hand, a study of women in top management found that none had brothers; they were either only children or the first child in a family in which all the children were female, reflecting the importance of ordinal position (Henning & Jardin, 1983).

Opposite-sex siblings have been found to affect masculinity-femininity scores in the direction of the sibling's sex. Interestingly, "the most expressively creative occupations of artist, music performer, author, and architect were preferred most by subjects with opposite-sex siblings" (Sutton-Smith et al., 1964, pp. 34–35).

PERSONALITY CHARACTERISTICS AND INTEREST PATTERNS

Clearly, personality characteristics, interests, and needs are related to vocational interests. Adolescent boys with vocational interests in artistic fields are more likely than boys with other interests to perceive themselves as introspective, intuitive, disorderly, imaginative, original, sensitive, unconventional, enthusiastic, rebellious, and impractical (Holland, 1963a, 1963b). In contrast, boys who express interest in scientific vocations are more likely to perceive themselves as analytical, curious, "hard-headed," imaginative, quiet and reserved, and scholarly. Those with entrepreneurial interests (e.g., sales manager) are more likely to perceive themselves as aggressive, striving, dominant, conventional, energetic, extraverted, industrious, practical, persuasive, and not particularly interested in artistic, idealistic, scholarly, or scientific pursuits.

Youth who are not anxious and do not fear failure, and who have a strong need for achievement, tend to choose high-prestige occupations on tests of vocational choice. In contrast, those with a high level of anxiety and fear of failure, but a weak need for achievement, tend to make lower-prestige choices (Burnstein, 1963; Elder, 1968).

Among college women, those majoring in science have been found to have the strongest motives for achievement; those majoring in languages score in the midrange and those majoring in education score lowest. Conversely, the latter group score highest in need for affiliation with others (Sundheim, 1963). Women who are most anxious or least achievement oriented may not complete a degree at all.

Certain fields require a stronger commitment to success than others. Young women who choose an atypical vocation—particularly one with high status that has traditionally been reserved for men—are more likely to be independent, self-confident and able to assert themselves (Areshansel & Rosen, 1980; L. W. Hoffman, 1984; Tangri, 1972). In view of the fact that they are likely to be subjected to greater competitive and sex role stresses than their peers in many more traditional occupations, this would appear fortunate.

An adolescent may not consciously recognize all of the motives that influence his or her selection of a career. However, most adolescents have a fantasy or a stereotyped picture of what an engineer, army officer, physicist, actor, or psychiatrist is like and what he or she does—a daydream that contains some of the gratifications sought by the young person and usually has at least some relationship to reality. To illustrate, the most frequent attributes assigned to engineers by high school seniors of superior ability were found to be (in order of frequency): practical, builders, useful, intelligent, inventive, important, interesting, and hardworking (Holland, 1963a). Teachers, in contrast, were seen as underpaid, dedicated, indispensable to society, patient, and helpful. Accountants were seen as dull, precise, mathematically inclined, boring, methodical, and unimaginative, but also as necessary. Such stereotypes obviously can be misleading, and the chances of a student's selecting an occupation that is consonant with his or her own needs (consciously or unconsciously) will be greatly enhanced by actual knowledge about a variety of careers. Unfortunately, such knowledge is all too limited and frequently influenced by stereotyped thinking, even among vocational counselors.

CURRENT TRENDS IN VOCATIONAL VALUES

The vocational values and attitudes of young people today differ in a number of important respects from those of their counterparts in the late 1960s and early 1970s (Conger, 1981, 1988; Conger & Petersen, 1984). Reflecting the "youth culture" of the time, young people in the 1960s (particularly college students) became more concerned than their predecessors with finding work that provided opportunities for individuality, self-expression, and personal growth. Moreover, the number who felt that this could not be done "within the system" reached an all-time high (Yankelovich, 1974). So, too, did the number who sought "alternative occupations"—as a means of self-expression (e.g., in art, music, or skilled crafts), as a way of achieving a new life-style (e.g., through communal living), or to promote social change (e.g., by working as counsellors of runaway children or organizers of the poor in ghettos).

Nevertheless, a majority planned to and eventually did enter relatively traditional careers, although they remained more critical of business values and practices than their predecessors. The 1960s and early 1970s led to significant changes in the vocational values of adolescents and youth, particularly those from upper- and middle-class background. However, the extent of these changes was often exaggerated by the media and their meaning distorted.

In the intervening years there have been profound changes in social values, rapid and often unpredictable shifts in patterns of occupational demand, and perhaps most significant, declining productivity and a dramatic rise in the cost of goods and services. In contrast to the situation in earlier periods, even a "good," reasonably well-paying job no longer provides assured access to such elements of the American Dream as a home of one's own, a college education for one's children, or financial security during retirement. Consequently, it is hardly surprising that the percentage of strongly "career-minded" college students has increased steadily in recent years while the number of students who view their college experience as a period of self-discovery and change has declined considerably (Astin, Green, & Korn, 1987; Astin et al., 1988; Astin, Korn, & Berg, 1989; Yankelovich, 1974, 1981). Between 1969 and 1989 the percentage of first-year college students in the United States who cited "being very well off financially" as an "essential or very important objective" increased from slightly less than half to more than three out of four (80 percent of males and 72 percent of females) (see page 490). Among high school seniors, too, there have been parallel but less dramatic increases in the number for whom "the chance to earn a good deal of money" and to have "a predictable, secure future" was rated as very important in a job (Bachman & Johnston, 1979; Bachman et al., 1981, 1987, 1990; Evangelauf, 1989). In accordance with these changing concerns and values, the percentages of college students enrolling in

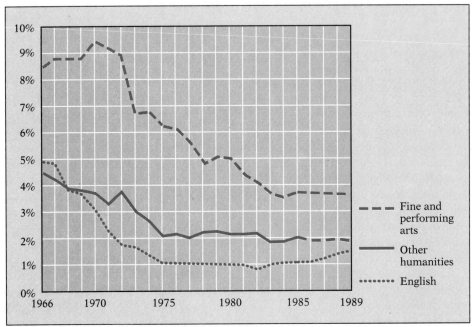

Figure 10.2 Interest in humanities majors (percentages, 1966–1989). (From A. W. Astin, K. C. Green, W. S. Korn, M. Schalit, & E. R. Berz, *The American freshman: National norms for fall, 1966–1989.* Los Angeles: Higher Education Research Institute, University of California at Los Angeles, 1989. By permission.)

the arts and humanities and the sciences have declined steadily while the percentages enrolling in such fields as business and preprofessional programs increased. Although interest in business declined moderately between 1987 and 1989, interest in graduate professional programs reached an all-time high in 1989. (Astin et al., 1987, 1988, 1989; see Figures 10.2 and 10.3).

These changes have been particularly evident among women. For example, while the number of first-year college women aspiring to be teachers declined by more than two-thirds in the past decade and a half (from 38 percent to 12.2 percent), the number planning to become business executives tripled (from less than 4 percent to over 12 percent) (Astin et al., 1987, 1988, 1989). Do these changes mean, as some observers have suggested, that contemporary adolescents and youth are engaged in a return to pre-1960s vocational values and goals? The answer is no. A study of college students in the late 1950s found them to be "models of the status quo," with few real commitments and a rather uncritical acceptance of the values and practices of social institutions generally, including those of government and big business (Goldsen, Rosenberg, Williams, & Suchman, 1960; Wolensky, 1977).

In contrast, today's adolescents and youth, though they are generally more willing to adjust to the demands of the workplace and more ready to accept compromise than their predecessors, are far less willing than the youth of the 1950s to suppress their individuality and need for self-expression. Nor are they

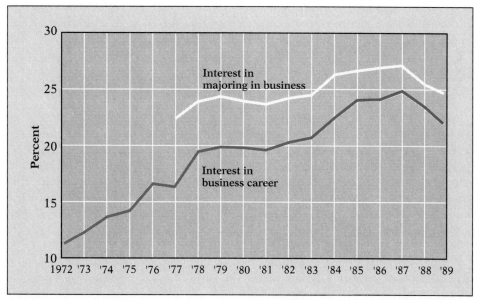

Figure 10.3 Trends in freshman interest in business careers (percentages, 1972–1989). (From A. W. Astin, W. S. Korn, & E. R. Berz, *The American freshman: National norms for fall, 1989.* Los Angeles: Higher Education Research Institute, University of California at Los Angeles, 1989. By permission.)

as ready or willing to accept a sharp dichotomy between their private lives and their work, and they do not see a great need to do so. Although they acknowledge an interest in economic security and "getting ahead," they are also concerned that their work be personally rewarding (Conger, 1981, 1988; Johnston et al., forthcoming). When 1989 college-bound American high school seniors were asked what things they rated very important in a job, the three most frequent responses were having "interesting things to do" (89 percent), "using skills and ability" (72 percent), and "not having to pretend to be the type of person you are not" (71 percent). In comparison, 58 percent cited having "a chance to earn a great deal of money" as very important (up from 41 percent a decade ago). Only 35 percent stressed "high status, prestige," but two-thirds wanted "good chances for advancement" and a "predictable, secure future" (Johnston et al., forthcoming).

Nor do today's youth share the unquestioning faith in big business (and other social institutions) that characterized their counterparts in the 1950s, although their views were somewhat more favorable in the late 1980s than they were at the beginning of the decade. For example, in 1989 two-thirds of high school seniors agreed that there is at least moderate dishonesty and immorality in the leadership of large corporations, and less than half believed that corporations are doing a good or very good job for the country (Johnston et al., forthcoming). Less than one-third thought that corporations should have less influence on people's lives (down from 55 percent in 1980).

In brief, today's young people want to combine challenging work, self-expression, and time for family, friends, and outside interests with at least a moderately high income, economic security, and the chance to get ahead. How successful they will be in achieving these goals remains to be seen.

VOCATIONAL PROSPECTS IN A CHANGING WORLD

What, then, are the prospects for today's adolescents and young adults, in terms of the numbers and kinds of jobs that are likely to be available? Between 1960 and 1980 the number of youth of working age increased by nearly 50 percent. Together with the dramatic increase in the participation of women in the labor force during the same period (from 38 percent to 52 percent), this produced a surge in available workers that could not easily be absorbed by the labor market (Fullerton, 1986; Smith, 1979). Teenage unemployment rates increased accordingly, reaching a high of over 20 percent for all teenagers by 1980.

Since 1980, however, the number of young people has been declining steadily, and it will continue to do so for the next few years. As a consequence, young people between the ages of 16 and 24, who made up nearly one-quarter of the total work force in 1980, accounted for only 19 percent of all workers in 1987; this figure is projected to drop further, to 16 percent, by 1995 before turning up again (Bacas, 1986; Brannigan, 1986; U.S. Bureau of the Census,

1989; U.S. Department of Labor, 1988). Thus, whereas the postwar baby-boom generation faced a growing shortage of jobs, the employers of the "baby-bust" generation are encountering a growing shortage of entry-level workers.

At present, the problem for employers is most acute in retail and service businesses such as fast-food restaurants, gasoline stations, department and convenience stores, and sectors of the lodging and recreation industries, which have traditionally relied heavily on younger workers. But many employers who look to graduates of colleges and skilled training programs will increasingly feel the impact as this shrinking population group moves through the economy behind the baby-boom generation (who are now in the 30–45 age bracket).

These population trends appear to augur well for the vocational prospects of the generation of young people who are now coming of age. However, a number of cautions are necessary. In the past twenty years automation and rapid technological change (especially in the development and application of computer technology), the consolidation of small businesses and farms into larger ones, and increased urbanization have produced significant shifts in employment patterns. Even for qualified workers, there will be significant variations in the kinds of skills that are in demand at any one time, as well as marked regional variations in overall employment rates, as the economy continues to shift away from the production of goods to the provision of services.

The number of jobs available to unskilled industrial workers and farm workers declined during the 1970s and 1980s; meanwhile the number of jobs for professional and technical workers, and for workers engaged in service occupations and clerical and sales positions, rose significantly (Persanick, 1986). These trends are expected to continue well into the 1990s (see Figure 10.4). In particular, occupations involving trade and services will continue to employ many more people than those involving the production of manufactured goods (see Figure 10.5). Industries providing services will account for nearly 4 out of 5 jobs by the year 2000 (U.S. Department of Labor, 1988). It is clear from these trends that poorly educated youth with few skills will find themselves increasingly penalized in the years ahead. For example, among 16–21-year olds who were seeking work and not in college in 1985, more than twice as many dropouts as high school graduates were unemployed (31 percent versus 15 percent) (U.S. Bureau of the Census, 1989).

Even more critical, however, is the fact that large segments of poor and minority youth have become increasingly isolated not only from participation in the economy but from the mainstream of American society. Although the current economic recovery and the shrinking youth population have contributed to a substantial decline since 1983, in the unemployment rate among black youth in late 1989 it was still nearly 33 percent, sharply higher than the rate for white teenagers. In some inner-city areas the teenage minority unemployment rate still runs as high as 70 percent or more. What is particularly troubling is that the discrepancy between whites and blacks has increased steadily. In 1954 teenage unemployment rate for blacks exceeded that for

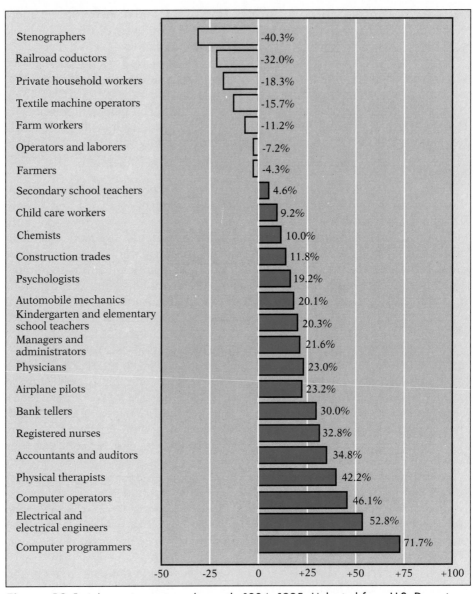

Figure 10.4 Job requirements and growth, 1984–1995. (Adapted from U.S. Department of Labor, Bureau of Labor Statistics. Occupational projections and training data, April 1986. Bulletin 22511. Washington, D.C.: U.S. Government Printing Office, 1986.)

whites by only 4.5 percent (16.5 percent versus 12 percent), but by 1989 unemployment among black youth was more than two and a half times the rate for whites (see Figure 10.6). Our society is in real danger of creating a permanent underclass of poor minority youth (Freeman, 1986; Lemann, 1986; U.S. Department of Labor, 1989).

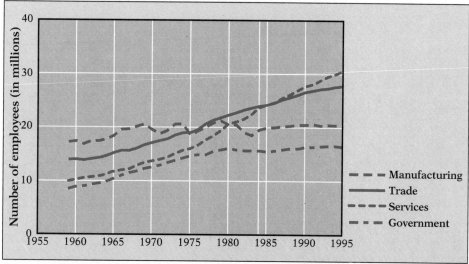

Figure 10.5 Total employment in selected major economic sectors, 1959–84, and projected, 1985–95. (From U.S. Bureau of Labor Statistics, 1986.)

Prisoners of the City. Why have young blacks fared so badly in the labor market, even during periods of prosperity? One reason for high unemployment among young blacks is that they tend to be concentrated in the inner-city areas of larger, and often poorer, cities. As a result, they are likely to be exposed to inadequate and inappropriate educational facilities and to a climate of social disorganization (Conger, 1980). In many of these areas conditions have deteriorated steadily since the 1950s and early 1960s as people who were able to move away did so. Those who left included community leaders who

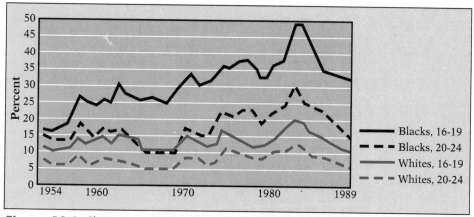

Figure 10.6 Changes in teenage unemployment among black and white youth, 1954–1989. (From U.S. Bureau of Labor Statistics, 1983, 1986, 1988, 1989.)

One reason that so many young blacks have fared badly in the labor market is that they tend to be concentrated in inner-city areas of larger, and often poorer, cities with inadequate schools, a climate of social disorganization, and few job opportunities.

had played an important role in creating and maintaining stability in social institutions like schools, churches, businesses, theaters, social clubs, and political organizations (Lemann, 1986; Lerman, 1986).

As neighborhoods have eroded, crime, unemployment, inadequate education and high dropout rates, drug use (especially use of crack cocaine), and gang violence have all escalated. Not surprisingly, young people growing up in such an environment are less likely to view conventional employment as a workable alternative to crime or welfare dependency; even when this is not the case, many inner-city teenagers lack the minimum skills in reading, arithmetic, and interpersonal interaction necessary to master even entry-level jobs (Freeman, 1986).

At the same time, new job opportunities keep moving farther away from the inner-city areas where they are needed. For many inner-city youth, their only realistic chance of breaking out of the cycle of poverty and depression lies in specifically targeted, adequately funded educational and training programs and accessible initial employment opportunities (Bacas, 1986; Brannigan, 1986; Schorr, 1988; *The forgotten half*, 1988; Williams & Kornblum, 1985).

Unfortunately, governmental policies and practices have been moving in the opposite direction in the past decade, although a number of private employers have attempted to deal with some of these problems. More companies are hiring unqualified central-city young people and training them for entry-level jobs, sometimes busing them to work (Brannigan, 1986). Exodus, a business-backed program in Atlanta, is designed to provide disadvantaged youth with fundamental skills needed for employment and to place them in jobs where they can gain experience with the hope of advancement (Bacas, 1986). However, a great deal more needs to be done, both by government and by the private sector.

It is doubtful that job-related activities alone can be effective on a broad scale unless some effort is also made to address social conditions that have created many of the problems just described. In the words of Neil Shorthouse, director of Exodus, "These kids are imprisoned in social and educational bondage, and they're not going to get free unless we help them" (Bacas, 1986, p. 20).

Women in the Work Force: New Opportunities and Old Realities

As we have seen, women are entering the labor market in numbers that far outstrip all earlier projections, and there is no sign of a letup in the current decade. Approximately 60 percent of all women between the ages of 16 and 64 (compared to 76 percent of men) currently work outside the home for pay, and their ranks are increasing at the rate of 2 million per year (U.S. Bureau of the Census, 1989; U.S. Department of Labor, 1983, 1986a, 1986b). Through the mid-1990s women will account for over three-fifths of the growth of the labor force (see Figure 10.7).

What are the vocational prospects for women entering the labor force? If one looks only at current statistics for women as a whole, one may conclude that the prospects are not very good. Full-time earnings for women are still

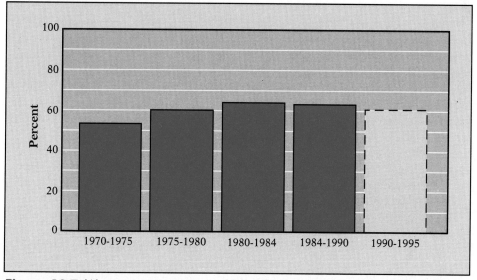

Figure 10.7 Women as a percentage of labor force growth. (From Bureau of Labor Statistics, 1986.)

only about 64 percent of those for men. Moreover, the great majority of working women still hold jobs in the fields in which women have traditionally been employed. Indeed, almost two out of every five women workers are employed in just ten occupations: secretary, bookkeeper, sales clerk (retail trade), cashier, waiter, registered nurse, elementary-school teacher, private household worker, typist, and nursing aide (U.S. Bureau of the Census, 1989; U.S. Department of Labor, 1983, 1988).

Nevertheless, the opportunities for women with appropriate education or training are expanding. For example, during the 1970s and 1980s the percentages of female lawyers and judges, economists, accountants and auditors, bank officials, financial managers, scientists, engineers, computer systems analysts, sales managers, electricians and carpenters, telephone installers and line workers, firefighters, police officers, and detectives more than doubled and in some instances increased sixfold (U.S. Department of Labor, 1983, 1988; U.S. Bureau of the Census, 1989). During these years the proportion of women accountants and auditors rose from 21.7 to 45.7 percent; the proportion of women sales managers in retail trade has risen from 15.6 percent to 31.8 percent, and that of female computer systems analysts has increased from 16.8 to 37.1 percent.

The age at which women begin working and the continuity of their work experience play important roles. "A large part of career development is a function of continuity and experience on the job. If a woman doesn't work from age 28 to 43, she loses relative position in the competition" (Bennetts, 1979, p. 59). But reconciling the demands of work and family life can be difficult, particularly when the children are small and when the job demands great flexibility and long hours, as is the case for many corporate executives (Kantrowitz, 1986; Taylor, 1986).

Several recent studies have shown that significantly more women MBAs than men who are parents leave jobs in corporate management ten years after graduation from business school. They do so in order to assume less all-consuming jobs or to start businesses of their own, either full or part time, that involve more flexible hours (Taylor, 1986). Even in less demanding jobs, however, juggling job, children, and household responsibilities is seldom easy. The myth of Supermom, who handles all of these demands smoothly and skillfully without stress or fatigue, is fading fast (Cowan, 1989; Dionne, 1989; Kantrowitz, 1986). If women are to succeed in combining these multiple responsibilities greater support is needed, not simply from other family members but from society as a whole.

The United States does less than many European countries to accommodate working parents through family support systems such as paid leaves, child allowances, subsidized day care, and free health services. For example, currently only 40 percent of working women in the United States are entitled to six weeks or more of paid disability leave on the occasion of a child's birth (Taylor, 1986). More companies are instituting programs such as temporary part-time or at-home work after a child is born (Kantrowitz, 1986; Taylor, 1986), as well as more flexible hours, job sharing, unpaid child care leaves, and

The myth of supermom, who juggles a demanding job, children, and household responsibilities smoothly and skillfully without stress or fatigue, is fading fast.

company-operated day care facilities. Nevertheless, in the words of former Labor Secretary William Brock, "It's just incredible that we have seen the feminization of the work force with no more adaptation than we have had. It is a problem of sufficient magnitude that everybody is going to have to play a role: families, individuals, businesses, local government, state government" (Kantrowitz, 1986, p. 47).

College Graduates: Demand and Supply in the 1990s

Although in the 1990s there will be more job opportunities for youth with more skills and education, this does not mean that graduation from college will guarantee a high-level job—even with smaller numbers of young people coming into the job market. A major reason for this is the unprecedented rise in the number of college graduates, which more than doubled between 1960 and 1985. The number of professional, technical, and managerial occupations did not expand rapidly enough to absorb this increase. Roughly one out of five college graduates who entered the labor market between 1970 and 1984 took a job that does not usually require a degree (U.S. Department of Labor, 1986, 1988; U.S. Bureau of the Census, 1989).

The oversupply of college graduates is likely to continue through the mid-1990s. Not all occupations that require a college degree will be overcrowded, however. For example, there will be good opportunities for systems analysts, nurses, elementary-school teachers, and electrical engineers. Despite the generally competitive job market for college graduates, a college degree is still needed for most high-paying and high-status jobs. Moreover, unemployment rates are consistently lower for college graduates (U.S. Department of Labor, 1986, 1988).

One of the economic problems of a high-technology society is that, on the one hand, it demands highly specialized, often nontransferable skills, whereas on the other hand it also generates rapid shifts in technology and in the economy that may make those skills obsolete in a relatively short period. The problem of preparing young people for the vocational demands of tomorrow is not a simple one. If anything, it is likely to become more difficult in the future as our society grows more complex, more specialized, more technologically oriented, and more subject to the effects of forces beyond our immediate control. Nevertheless, it is a problem that can be solved if society is willing to increase its commitment to the well-being of the nation's youth.

SUMMARY

Deciding on and preparing for a vocation is one of the major developmental tasks of adolescence. Constructive work experience can give adolescents a sense of purpose and a feeling that they are participating in the broader society. However, many of the jobs that are most commonly available to adolescents, such as working at a fast-food outlet, do little to encourage educational and vocational planning. In some instances they may also interfere with schoolwork.

Having a job that society values enhances self-esteem and contributes to a person's sense of identity. Conversely, getting the message that one is not needed and that meaningful employment is not available fosters self-doubt and resentment.

In earlier times choosing a vocation was much simpler than it is in today's complex, rapidly changing society. In the past fifty years there has been a marked shift from the "old workplace" (crafts, factory, farm) to the "new workplace" (service and sales). As a result of automation there is less and less opportunity for unskilled or semiskilled workers.

Before adolescence a child's occupational goals are likely to reflect fantasy more than reality (e.g., explorer, firefighter, movie actor). With the advent of more mature cognitive ability, young people begin to balance their interests against actual job opportunities and their own capabilities. In the late teens career choices tend to become increasingly crystallized and specific, as well as more stable.

Class- and sex-typed standards also play a role. Adolescents from lower-socioeconomic families are less likely to aspire to high-prestige occupations. Those in the growing underclass of poor families living in the inner cities, with few prospects of meaningful future employment, are likely to have no sustainable vocational hopes.

One of the most significant changes in American society since World War II has been the rapid increase in the number of women entering the job market. In 1947, only one-third of all women over 16 were employed outside the home. At present, a majority of married women with children under 6 are employed outside the home, and their numbers are continuing to grow.

Although the career choices of many young people still reflect traditional sex-related aspirations, many more young women are planning to enter traditionally male fields such as business executive, lawyer or judge, or physician. Young women with high-status occupational expectations are likely to have less traditional sex role attitudes. In contrast, the minority of young women who plan to be full-time homemakers tend to strongly endorse traditional sex roles. Occupying a middle ground are adolescents who plan to stay home while their children are young but work before having children and after their children are in school.

Parents play a significant role in vocational choice. If they set high educational and occupational goals, their children are likely to have high aspirations. Fathers are likely to have the strongest influence on both the career choices and vocational values of their children (particularly sons) when there is a close relationship with the father and when the father's job has high prestige. Adolescents of both sexes whose mothers are employed are less likely to have stereotyped views regarding appropriate sex and vocational roles for women.

Employed mothers are more likely than nonemployed mothers to encourage independence in their children, and indeed, their daughters are likely to be more autonomous, self-reliant, and achievement-oriented. Whether encouragement of independence by employed mothers has a similarly positive effect on sons is more open to question. Among middle-class boys maternal employment is associated with lower school performance and, possibly, a greater incidence of aggressive behavior and adjustment problems. Adolescent sons (but not daughters) report more frequent conflicts with working mothers. Vocational values and goals may also be influenced by the adolescent's ordinal position within the family and by the sex of his or her siblings.

Personality characteristics, interests, and needs are related to vocational interests. For example, the personality characteristics of boys with artistic vocational interests differ significantly from those of boys with scientific or entrepreneurial interests. Women majoring in science are more independent and achievement oriented than those majoring in education.

The percentage of strongly career-oriented college students has increased steadily in recent years, whereas the number who view college as a period of self-discovery has declined. Among both high school and college students, "getting ahead" and making money have become increasingly important goals; accordingly, the percentages of students enrolling in the arts and humanities have declined steadily while the percentages enrolling in business and preprofessional programs have increased. At the same time, although contemporary youth are willing to work hard, they are not willing to suppress their individuality and need for self-expression. In brief, today's young people want to combine challenging work, self-expression, and time for family, friends, and outside interests with at least a moderately high income, economic security, and the chance to get ahead.

The reduced number of young people who will be entering the job market in the 1990s generally augurs well for their vocational prospects. However, poorly educated youth with few skills will find themselves increasingly penalized in the years ahead. The situation is most critical for poor and minority youth in the nation's inner cities, who have become increasingly isolated from the mainstream of American society. In some such areas unemployment rates still run as high as 70 percent or more. Although a majority of women continue to enter traditional occupations, opportunities for appropriately educated and trained women are expanding. The percentages of female lawyers and judges, economists, financial managers, computer systems analysts, and scientists more than doubled during the 1970s and 1980s. Nevertheless, reconciling the demands of work and family can be difficult, and much greater support is needed from society in the form of paid leaves, subsidized day care, more flexible hour, and the like.

Although in the 1990s more jobs will be available for youth with more skills and education, a college degree will not guarantee a high-level job. While the number of college graduates doubled in recent decades, the number of professional, technical, and managerial occupations did not expand rapidly enough to absorb the increase. Even so, unemployment rates will remain consistently lower for college graduates.

REVIEW QUESTIONS

1. Some authorities maintain that work experience during adolescence promotes personal growth and aids in the transition to the adult world; others disagree. Can these opposing views be reconciled? Discuss.
2. Describe the development of vocational interests and goals from childhood through adolescence.
3. In what ways does social-class status influence vocational goals in adolescence, and why?
4. What effects has the women's movement had on the participation of women in the work force?
5. In what ways do fathers and mothers influence the vocational attitudes and goals of female and male adolescents?
6. Are personality characteristics, interests, and psychological needs related to vocational interests. If so, how?

7. How have the vocational values and goals of male and female adolescents and youth changed in the past three decades?

8. What are the vocational prospects for male and female adolescents and youth in the 1990s? Discuss the changes in teenage unemployment patterns among black youth and white youth since the 1950s. Are these trends encouraging or discouraging? How important is graduation from college?

RECOMMENDED READINGS

Greenberger, E., & Steinberg, L. (1986). *When teenagers work: The psychological and social costs of adolescent employment.* New York: Basic Books.

Hoffman, L. W. (1984). Work, family, and socialization of the child. In R. D. Parke et al. (Eds.), *The review of child development research, Vol. 7: The family: An interdisciplinary perspective.* Chicago: University of Chicago Press.

Hoffman, L. W. (1986). Work, family, and the child. In M. Pallak & R. O. Perloff, *Psychology and work: Productivity, change, and employment* (pp. 171–220). Washington, DC: American Psychological Association.

Hoffman, L W. (1989). Effects of maternal employment in the two-parent family. *American Psychologist,* **44,** 283–292.

Osipow, S. H. (1983). *Theories of career development* (3rd ed.). Englewood Cliffs, NJ: Prentice-Hall.

Osipow, S. H. (1986). Career issues through the life span. In M. Pallak & R. O. Perloff, *Psychology and work: Productivity, change, and employment* (pp. 141–168). Washington, DC: American Psychological Association.

Smith, R. E. (1979) (Ed.). *The subtle revolution: Women at work.* Washington, DC: Urban Institute.

11

ADOLESCENTS AND DRUGS

Until the 1980s American adults tended to view increased drug use as a phenomenon limited to adolescents—a product of the youth culture of the late 1960s and early 1970s. But the picture has changed: Excessive drug use has come to be viewed as a major problem not only of adolescents and youth but of society as a whole. In the mid-1980s reports of extensive drug use among professional athletes, stockbrokers, young executives, actors, and even physicians and nurses, train crews, and pilots and air traffic controllers began to be widely publicized in national news magazines, newspapers, and television documentaries, alarming the general public as well as parents and politicians (Clymer, 1986; Kerr, 1988; Lamar, 1986a).

More recently, the widespread social disorganization and violence generated by the mounting use of cocaine—especially in its least expensive form, crack—has produced increased political pressure for a more realistic national "war on drugs" (Berke, 1989). Drug dealers are terrorizing entire urban neighborhoods (indeed, entire countries). Drug-related homicides are escalating exponentially (at present a majority of murders in some large cities are drug related). And thousands of neurologically impaired babies are being born to drug-dependent mothers. In the face of such developments, the appeal of a former First Lady to "Just say no" to drugs, while commendable, is clearly insufficient.

In an August 1989 survey, 27 percent of all Americans cited drugs as the most serious problem facing the nation, eclipsing the budget deficit, pollution, homelessness, and other issues (Gallup, 1989). Thirty percent of adolescents agreed that drugs are the most serious problem facing the nation as a whole, and 60 percent said that drugs are the number one problem confronting their age group (an additional 12 percent listed alcohol use). Three-fourths of the teenagers and half of the adults surveyed said that they would be willing, if asked, to join in a volunteer program aimed at preventing or treating drug abuse. (By September 1989 the percentage of adults citing drugs as the most important problem facing the nation had increased sharply, to 64 percent) (The N.Y. Times/CBS News, 1989).

Since 1986 there have been a number of ill-fated congressional efforts to deal seriously with the drug problem (before 1986 the administration steadily reduced federal funds for drug treatment and education). In 1989, however, the new President proposed, and Congress approved, a multibillion-dollar legislative package intended to provide a program of stepped-up law enforcement, education, and treatment aimed at reducing both the supply of and the demand for drugs (Berke, 1989). In view of funding difficulties, the economic power of the illicit drug industry, and the unresolved societal problems that foster drug dealing and drug abuse, it remains to be seen how successful the program will be.

THE NATURE OF THE PROBLEM

Widespread drug use and abuse are not restricted to adolescents and did not have their origins in the youth culture of the 1960s. Although there are significant differences between generations in patterns of drug use, the broader society has been developing into a drug culture for many years. For example, one-quarter to one-third of all prescriptions currently written in the United States are for pep or diet pills (amphetamines) or tranquilizers such as Xanax and Valium (which are now the two most widely prescribed drugs in the nation). Television and radio bombard viewers with insistent messages that relief for almost anything—anxiety, depression, restlessness, or any of numerous other ailments—is "just a swallow away." In the words of one 13-year-old, "We're not supposed to take drugs, but TV is full of commercials showing people running for a pill because something is bugging them." Moreover, adult use of a number of drugs has increased as members of the baby-boom generation and their immediate successors have aged, replacing older adults who, while frequent users of alcohol and tobacco, were infrequent users of many other drugs, such as marijuana, cocaine, and hallucinogens (Johnston, O'Malley, & Bachman, 1989, 1990).

In a continuing study of drug use among young adults, representative samples of American high school graduates have been followed annually beginning with the class of 1976 (Johnston et al., 1989, 1990; O'Malley, Bachman, & Johnston, 1984). The survey reveals that over the years drug use among these young adults has tended to parallel use among high school seniors, except in the case of cocaine, which is used significantly more by young adults (Johnston, 1985; Johnston, O'Malley, & Bachman, 1989, 1990). However, adult drug use among high school graduates has been declining in recent years. Indeed, since 1987 usage rates for a number of drugs, including LSD, stimulants, methaqualone ("Quaalude" or "ludes"), and cocaine, have declined faster among young adult graduates than among high school seniors.

Two Worlds of Drugs

In addition to recognizing that drug use and abuse have been endemic in our society for many years and have not been restricted to post-1960s youth, we also need to recognize that "the drug problem" is not, in reality, a single problem. In terms of root causes, severity of the problem, or prospects for change, the drug problem among economically favored, well-educated youth and young adults is not the same as the drug problem among impoverished, poorly educated young people growing up in the socially disorganized, crime-ridden sections of large cities. As we shall see, this disparity accounts in large measure for seemingly contradictory reports in the press that drug use among young people is declining *and* that the drug problem is steadily getting worse.

Adolescent Drug Use

Although far too many adolescents become high-risk drug users, the majority do not. While use of marijuana, alcohol, and tobacco is still widespread among high school students, and about one-quarter have tried amphetamines (stimulants) at one time or another, use of other substances on the youthful drug scene has never exceeded one person in five in the United States (less in most other Western countries), and many former occasional users appear to have quit—as indicated by "no use in the past year" (see Figure 11.1). Moreover, from 1981 through 1989 adolescent use of various drugs either reached a plateau or declined (Johnston et al., 1990). Use of marijuana within the past thirty days, which had been rising steadily for fifteen years, showed a steady decline (from 37.1 to 16.7 percent) from 1978 through 1989 (see Table 11.1). In the same period daily use declined from 10.7 to 2.9 percent (see Table 11.2). Decreases also occurred in the annual, monthly, and daily use of inhalants, hallucinogens, barbituates, tranquilizers, cigarettes, and alcohol. Use of cocaine among high school seniors reached a peak in 1985 and has since de-

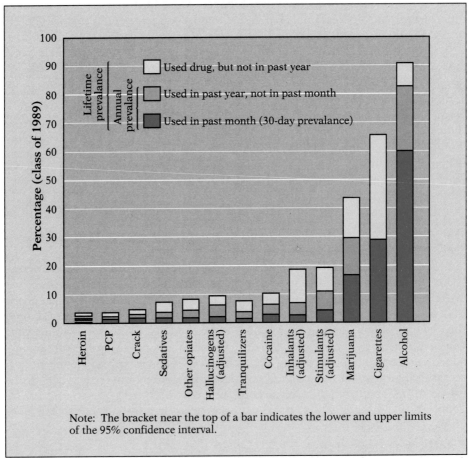

Note: The bracket near the top of a bar indicates the lower and upper limits of the 95% confidence interval.

Figure 11.1 Prevalence and recency of use of thirteen types of drugs, class of 1989. (Based on data from L. D. Johnston, J. G. Bachman, & P. M. O'Malley. *Drug use, drinking, and smoking: National survey results from high school, college, and young adults populations, 1975–1989.* Washington, DC: National Institute on Drug Abuse, 1990. Reprinted with permission.)

creased sharply—apparently as a result of increased perceptions of the high risk associated with any use of this drug (Johnston et al., 1990; see page 441). Rates of heroin use, never large, remained relatively steady.

Despite these generally encouraging trends, there is little room for complacency. For one thing, in 1989 one in six high school seniors still reported use of marijuana within the past thirty days. Over 10 percent reported having at least tried cocaine at some time in their lives (down, however, from a high of over 17 percent in the class of 1985), and nearly 5 percent had tried crack at least once. One-third reported having had five or more drinks in a row during the past two weeks (down from over 40 percent in 1983), and over 4 percent reported daily use of alcohol.

Since 1984 there has been little further progress toward reducing cigarette smoking, despite the associated risks of disease and preventable death (see pages 430–434). For most drugs other than cocaine, between 40 and 50 percent of eventual users begin using the drug before the ninth grade (Johnston, O'Malley, & Bachman, 1986; Johnston et al., 1988, 1990).

Moreover, we cannot lose sight of the fact that rates of illicit drug use are significantly higher among school dropouts, although accurate figures are more difficult to obtain (Johnston, 1989; Mensch & Kandel, 1988). This is especially true in the case of out-of-work young people living in deteriorated, crime-ridden neighborhoods in large metropolitan areas. In such surroundings participation in drug dealing may appear to provide the easiest, and by far the most lucrative, way out of poverty. For other young people, vulnerability to drug use is greatly increased by easy accessibility, peer influence, and a pervasive sense of hopelessness and despair.

One of the most frightening aspects of drug abuse at all economic levels is the number of young women who use drugs during pregnancy, often causing permanent neurobiological impairment, and sometimes death, in their infants. In a national study of thirty-six hospitals encompassing varied socioeconomic levels, the researchers found that over 11 percent of babies were born to mothers who had used drugs during pregnancy; in one hospital the rate was 27 percent (Brody, 1988). And these figures do not include alcohol abuse, which many experts view as an even more widespread danger (see page 430).

As we shall see, there are many other reasons for serious concern. The rapid spread of "crack" or "rock," an extremely potent and addictive form of cocaine, has created major problems for drug treatment centers and law enforcement officials in New York, Los Angeles, Chicago, Detroit, and other cities, and is rapidly spreading to other communities across the country. The greatest danger for those of us who work with adolescents is the adolescent or youth who turns repeatedly to drugs in order to cope with insecurity, stress, tension, low self-esteem, feelings of rejection or alienation, conflicts with parents, or problems of daily living. One of the important developmental tasks of adolescence is to learn how to cope with stress, conflict, and frustration; others include the development of cognitive, social, and vocational skills and the establishment of rewarding interpersonal relationships with peers and adults. Failure to master these essential developmental demands during adolescence because of re-

T A B L E 11.1 **TRENDS IN THIRTY-DAY PREVALENCE OF EIGHTEEN TYPES OF DRUGS**

	Percent who used in last thirty days						
Approx. $N=$	Class of 1975 (9,400)	Class of 1976 (15,400)	Class of 1977 (17,100)	Class of 1978 (17,800)	Class of 1979 (15,500)	Class of 1980 (15,900)	Class of 1981 (17,500)
Any Illicit Drug Use[a]	30.7	34.2	37.6	38.9	38.9	37.2	36.9
Adjusted Version[b]	—	—	—	—	—	—	—
Any Illicit Drug Other Than Marijuana[c]	15.4	13.9	15.2	15.1	16.8	18.4	21.7
Adjusted Version[b]	—	—	—	—	—	—	—
Marijuana/Hashish	27.1	32.2	35.4	37.1	36.5	33.7	31.6
Inhalants[d]	NA	0.9	1.3	1.5	1.7	1.4	1.5
Inhalants Adjusted[e]	NA	NA	NA	NA	3.2	2.7	2.5
Amyl & Butyl Nitrites[f,g]	NA	NA	NA	NA	2.4	1.8	1.4
Hallucinogens	4.7	3.4	4.1	3.9	4.0	3.7	3.7
Hallucinogens Adjusted[h]	NA	NA	NA	NA	5.3	4.4	4.5
LSD	2.3	1.9	2.1	2.1	2.4	2.3	2.5
PCP[f,g]	NA	NA	NA	NA	2.4	1.4	1.4
Cocaine	1.9	2.0	2.9	3.9	5.7	5.2	5.8
"Crack"[i]	NA	NA	NA	NA	NA	NA	NA
Other cocaine[f]	NA	NA	NA	NA	NA	NA	NA
Heroin	0.4	0.2	0.3	0.3	0.2	0.2	0.2
Other opiates[i]	2.1	2.0	2.8	2.1	2.4	2.4	2.1
Stimulants[i]	8.5	7.7	8.8	8.7	9.9	12.1	15.8
Stimulants Adjusted[b,i]	NA	NA	NA	NA	NA	NA	NA
Sedatives[i]	5.4	4.5	5.1	4.2	4.4	4.8	4.6
Barbiturates[i]	4.7	3.9	4.3	3.2	3.2	2.9	2.6
Methaqualone[i]	2.1	1.6	2.3	1.9	2.3	3.3	3.1
Tranquilizers[i]	4.1	4.0	4.6	3.4	3.7	3.1	2.7
Alcohol	68.2	68.3	71.2	72.1	71.8	72.0	70.7
Cigarettes	36.7	38.8	38.4	36.7	34.4	30.5	29.4

NOTES: Level of significance of difference between the two most recent classes: $s = .05$, $ss = .01$, $sss = .001$. NA indicates data not available.

[a]Use of "any illicit drugs" includes any use of marijuana, hallucinogens, cocaine, and heroin, or any use of other opiates, stimulants, sedatives, or tranquilizers not under a doctor's orders.

[b]Based on the data from the revised question, which attempts to exclude the inappropriate reporting of non-prescription stimulants.

[c]Use of "other illicit drugs" includes any use of hallucinogens, cocaine, and heroin, or any use of other opiates, stimulants, sedatives, or tranquilizers not under a doctor's orders.

[d]Data based on four questionnaire forms in 1976–1988; N is four-fifths of N indicated. Data based on five questionnaire forms in 1989; N is five-sixths of N indicated.

[e]Adjusted for underreporting of amyl and butyl nitrites.

	Percent who used in last thirty days								
Class of 1982 (17,700)	Class of 1983 (16,300)	Class of 1984 (15,900)	Class of 1985 (16,000)	Class of 1986 (15,200)	Class of 1987 (16,300)	Class of 1988 (16,300)	Class of 1989 (16,700)	'88–'89 change
33.5	32.4	—	—	—	—	—	—	
32.5	30.5	29.2	29.7	27.1	24.7	21.3	19.7	−1.6s
19.2	18.4	—	—	—	—	—	—	
17.0	15.4	15.1	14.9	13.2	11.6	10.0	9.1	−0.9
28.5	27.0	25.2	25.7	23.4	21.0	18.0	16.7	−1.3
1.5	1.7	1.9	2.2	2.5	2.8	2.6	2.3	−0.3
2.5	2.5	2.6	3.0	3.2	3.5	3.0	2.7	−0.3
1.1	1.4	1.4	1.6	1.3	1.3	0.6	0.6	0.0
3.4	2.8	2.6	2.5	2.5	2.5	2.2	2.2	0.0
4.1	3.5	3.2	3.8	3.5	2.8	2.3	2.9	+0.6
2.4	1.9	1.5	1.6	1.7	1.8	1.8	1.8	0.0
1.0	1.3	1.0	1.6	1.3	0.6	0.3	1.4	+1.1sss
5.0	4.9	5.8	6.7	6.2	4.3	3.4	2.8	−0.6s
NA	NA	NA	NA	NA	1.3	1.6	1.4	−0.2
NA	NA	NA	NA	NA	4.1	3.2	1.9	−1.3s
0.2	0.2	0.3	0.3	0.2	0.2	0.2	0.3	+0.1
1.8	1.8	1.8	2.3	2.0	1.8	1.6	1.6	0.0
13.7	12.4	NA	NA	NA	NA	NA	NA	NA
10.7	8.9	8.3	6.8	5.5	5.2	4.6	4.2	−0.4
3.4	3.0	2.3	2.4	2.2	1.7	1.4	1.6	+0.2
2.0	2.1	1.7	2.0	1.8	1.4	1.2	1.4	+0.2
2.4	1.8	1.1	1.0	0.8	0.6	0.5	0.6	+0.1
2.4	2.5	2.1	2.1	2.1	2.0	1.5	1.3	−0.2
69.7	69.4	67.2	65.9	65.3	66.4	63.9	60.0	−3.9ss
30.0	30.3	29.3	30.1	29.6	29.4	28.7	28.6	−0.1

[f]Data based on a single questionnaire form; N is one-fifth of N indicated in 1979–1988 and one-sixth of N indicated in 1989.
[g]Question text changed slightly in 1987.
[h]Adjusted for underreporting of PCP.
[i]Data based on two questionnaire forms; N is two-fifths of N indicated in 1987–1988 and two-sixths of N indicated in 1989.
[j]Only drug use which was not under a doctor's orders is included here.

Source: L. D. Johnston, P. M. O'Malley, and J. G. Bachman. *Drug use, drinking, and smoking: National survey results from high school, college, and young adults populations, 1975–1990.* Washington, DC: National Institute on Drug Abuse, 1990.

T A B L E 11.2 **TRENDS IN THIRTY-DAY PREVALENCE OF** *DAILY* **USE OF EIGHTEEN TYPES OF DRUGS**

	Percent who used in last thirty days						
Approx. N =	Class of 1975 (9,400)	Class of 1976 (15,400)	Class of 1977 (17,100)	Class of 1978 (17,800)	Class of 1979 (15,500)	Class of 1980 (15,900)	Class of 1981 (17,500)
Marijuana/Hashish	6.0	8.2	9.1	10.7	10.3	9.1	7.0
Inhalants[a]	NA	0.0	0.0	0.1	0.0	0.1	0.1
Inhalants Adjusted[b]	NA	NA	NA	NA	0.1	0.2	0.2
Amyl & Butyl Nitrites[c,d]	NA	NA	NA	NA	0.0	0.1	0.1
Hallucinogens	0.1	0.1	0.1	0.1	0.1	0.1	0.1
Hallucinogens Adjusted[e]	NA	NA	NA	NA	0.2	0.2	0.1
LSD	0.0	0.0	0.0	0.0	0.0	0.0	0.1
PCP[c,d]	NA	NA	NA	NA	0.1	0.1	0.1
Cocaine	0.1	0.1	0.1	0.1	0.2	0.2	0.3
"Crack"[f]	NA	NA	NA	NA	NA	NA	NA
Other cocaine[c]	NA	NA	NA	NA	NA	NA	NA
Heroin	0.1	0.0	0.0	0.0	0.0	0.0	0.0
Other opiates[g]	0.1	0.1	0.2	0.1	0.0	0.1	0.1
Stimulants[g]	0.5	0.4	0.5	0.5	0.6	0.7	1.2
Stimulants Adjusted[g,h]	NA	NA	NA	NA	NA	NA	NA
Sedatives[g]	0.3	0.2	0.2	0.2	0.1	0.2	0.2
Barbiturates[g]	0.1	0.1	0.2	0.1	0.0	0.1	0.1
Methaqualone[g]	0.0	0.0	0.0	0.0	0.0	0.1	0.1
Tranquilizers[g]	0.1	0.2	0.3	0.1	0.1	0.1	0.1
Alcohol							
Daily	5.7	5.6	6.1	5.7	6.9	6.0	6.0
5+ drinks in a row/ last 2 weeks	36.8	37.1	39.4	40.3	41.2	41.2	41.4
Cigarettes							
Daily	26.9	28.8	28.8	27.5	25.4	21.3	20.3
Half-pack or more per day	17.9	19.2	19.4	18.8	16.5	14.3	13.5

NOTES: Level of significance of difference between the two most recent classes: s = .05, ss = .01, sss = .001. NA indicates data not available.
[a]Data based on four questionnaire forms in 1976–1988; N is four-fifths of N indicated. Data based on five questionnaire forms in 1989; N is five-sixths of N indicated.
[b]Adjusted for underreporting of amyl and butyl nitrites.
[c]Data based on a single questionnaire form; N is one-fifth of N indicated in 1979–1988 and one-sixth of N indicated in 1989.
[d]Question text changed slightly in 1987.
[e]Adjusted for underreporting of PCP.
[f]Data based on two questionnaire forms; N is two-fifths of N indicated in 1987–1988 and two-sixths of N indicated in 1989.

	Percent who used in last thirty days							
Class of 1982 (17,700)	Class of 1983 (16,300)	Class of 1984 (15,900)	Class of 1985 (16,000)	Class of 1986 (15,200)	Class of 1987 (16,300)	Class of 1988 (16,300)	Class of 1989 (16,700)	'88–'89 change
6.3	5.5	5.0	4.9	4.0	3.3	2.7	2.9	+0.2
0.1	0.1	0.1	0.2	0.2	0.1	0.2	0.2	0.0
0.2	0.2	0.2	0.4	0.4	0.4	0.3	0.3	0.0
0.0	0.2	0.1	0.3	0.5	0.3	0.1	0.3	+0.2
0.1	0.1	0.1	0.1	0.1	0.1	0.0	0.1	0.0[i]
0.2	0.2	0.2	0.3	0.3	0.2	0.0	0.3	+0.2ss[i]
0.0	0.1	0.1	0.1	0.0	0.1	0.0	0.0	0.0
0.1	0.1	0.1	0.3	0.2	0.3	0.1	0.2	+0.1
0.2	0.2	0.2	0.4	0.4	0.3	0.2	0.3	+0.1
NA	NA	NA	NA	NA	0.1	0.1	0.2	+0.1
NA	NA	NA	NA	NA	0.2	0.2	0.1	−0.1
0.0	0.1	0.0	0.0	0.0	0.0	0.0	0.1	+0.1
0.1	0.1	0.1	0.1	0.1	0.1	0.1	0.2	0.0[i]
1.1	1.1	NA	NA	NA	NA	NA	NA	NA
0.7	0.8	0.6	0.4	0.3	0.3	0.3	0.3	0.0
0.2	0.2	0.1	0.1	0.1	0.1	0.1	0.1	+0.1[i]
0.1	0.1	0.0	0.1	0.1	0.1	0.0	0.1	0.0[i]
0.1	0.0	0.0	0.0	0.0	0.0	0.1	0.0	0.0[i]
0.1	0.1	0.1	0.0	0.0	0.1	0.0	0.1	0.0[i]
5.7	5.5	4.8	5.0	4.8	4.8	4.2	4.2	0.0
40.5	40.8	38.7	36.7	36.8	37.5	34.7	33.0	−1.7
21.1	21.2	18.7	19.5	18.7	18.7	18.1	18.9	+0.8
14.2	13.8	12.3	12.5	11.4	11.4	10.6	11.2	+0.6

[g]Only drug use which was not under a doctor's orders is included here.
[h]Based on the data from the revised question, which attempts to exclude the inappropriate reporting of nonprescription stimulants.
[i]Any apparent inconsistency between the change estimate and the prevalence estimates for the two most recent classes is due to rounding error.

Source: L. D. Johnston, P. M. O'Malley, and J. G. Bachman. Drug use, drinking, and smoking: National survey results from high school, college, and young adults populations, 1975–1989. Washington, DC: National Institute on Drug Abuse, 1990.

Box 11.1 A SCHOOL PROGRAM FOR CHILDREN OF DRUG-ADDICTED MOTHERS

As children born to drug-addicted mothers are starting school, some schools are making an effort to meet their needs. The task is not easy, not only because the children may be suffering to varying degrees from neurobiological problems but also because many have been exposed to severe neglect. Drugs and violence are often a familiar part of their environment. Many have been abused by their biological parents and shifted from one foster home to another.

Most schools are poorly prepared to assist such children (Trost, 1989). Although they may look normal initially, their ability to learn and to relate to others may be impaired. "Fine motor skills may be hampered. A child may have difficulty developing strong attachments for others. Extremes of behavior are common, from apathy to aggression, passivity to hyperactivity, indiscriminate trust to extreme suspicion" (Trost, 1989, p. 1).

In an effort to understand and meet the needs of such children, investigators at the University of California School of Medicine have started a pilot project at the Salvin Special Education School in Los Angeles. Only a small number of children who are referred to the program can be accepted because of the amount of attention required. The twenty-four children currently enrolled are assigned three teachers and five aides.

All the children are seen regularly by a social worker, a psychologist, a pediatrician, a speech and language therapist, and a physical education teacher. Parents and care-givers are invited to attend a support program.

Caring for drug-damaged children demands an extraordinary commitment from the staff—in and out of the classroom. Some ferry children to after-school parties they normally would have missed for lack of transportation. Others spend long hours with the children's families or caseworkers . . . Among the lessons gleaned from the two-year project: Routine is crucial. Abrupt transitions from one activity to another can be unsettling. Lots of old-fashioned love helps immeasurably" (Trost, 1989, p. A8).

A 6-year-old boy is now able to sit on the floor with the other students happily singing an alphabet song. "Two years ago, he used to throw hour-long tantrums. He would build a tower of blocks, then shout that it was on fire and knock it down. Last year, while classmates watched the space shuttle blast off on television, he banged on his desk and cried" (Trost, 1989, p. 1). When one girl first came to the program, "she went to 20 different toys in 20 minutes," flinging them around. Now, says her teacher, "She has whole themes in her play" (Trost, 1989, p. A8). It also helps that her sixth foster home has been successful.

Vicky Ferrara, a kindergarten teacher, says that one of the biggest changes is that children "are now able to discuss their feelings, needs, and wants," rather than misbehaving out of frustration (Trost, 1989, p. 8).

Source: Trost, C. Second chance: As drug babies grow older, schools strive to meet their needs. *The Wall Street Journal*, December 27, 1989, p. 1. Reprinted by permission of *The Wall Street Journal*. © Dow Jones & Company, Inc. 1989. All rights reserved worldwide.

Because crack is so easy to prepare, so addictive, and so profitable, "crack houses" have proliferated, especially in urban ghettos. Crack use and dealing, and the large numbers of other crimes associated with these activities, are rapidly becoming the principal threat to survival among children and adolescents in America's inner cities.

peated escapes into the world of drugs leaves the young person ill prepared to meet the additional demands of responsible adulthood (Baumrind & Moselle, 1985; Kandel et al., 1986; Newcomb & Bentler, 1988). Unfortunately, a significant number of vulnerable adolescents are finding that drug use becomes a psychological crutch that is increasingly difficult to renounce. In addition, a highly addictive drug like crack produces such an intense rush (high) and such a powerful subsequent crash that it may lead to compulsive repetitive behavior, even among first-time users.

Our principal aim in this chapter will be to examine the various reasons that adolescents take drugs. But first it is necessary to examine the range of drugs available to young people, and their effects.

ALCOHOL

A few years ago clinicians and others who work with young people often heard parents make comments like "I'm becoming concerned that Johnny (or Susie) may be drinking a bit too much. But at least it's better than drugs." What these parents were failing to realize, of course, is that alcohol is just as much a **psychoactive drug** as, for example, marijuana, and its dangers have been far more clearly established. Moreover, use of alcohol provides no assurance that other drugs will not be used; indeed, prior and concomitant use of alcohol (and tobacco) is more common among marijuana and other drug users than among nonusers (Kandel & Faust, 1975; Yamaguchi & Kandel, 1984a, 1984b).

What many such parents appeared to be saying was that alcohol use was a more familiar phenomenon, was more socially acceptable, and consequently seemed less mysterious and frightening and less likely to indicate a rejection of parental or societal values. As generational conflicts subsided in the late 1970s, and as public awareness of the severity of alcohol problems among adolescents increased, parental attitudes began to change. In recent polls adults have expressed as great (or greater) concern with alcohol use among adolescents as with marijuana use.

On many college and university campuses, administrators, faculty, and students cite excessive use of alcohol as a major problem and have instituted programs to deal with it more effectively. Indeed, the prevalence of occasions of heavy drinking (five or more drinks in a row in the past two weeks) is higher for college students than for others in their age group (Johnston et al., 1989).

Another area of significant concern is drunken driving. Most states have increased, or are planning to increase, their legal drinking age to 21. Although the greatest concern is the minority of youth who will become serious problem drinkers, there is also concern about the potentially adverse effects of heavy social drinking. Nine percent of all automobile fatalities involve drunken drivers under 20 years of age; research has consistently shown that between 45 and 60 percent of all fatal crashes with a young driver are alcohol related.

Adolescent Use of Alcohol

How widespread is the use of alcohol among adolescents? Virtually all studies agree that the vast majority of young people have at least tried alcoholic beverages by the end of adolescence (Johnston et al., 1989, 1990; Parry, 1979; Rachal et al., 1984). Among high school seniors in the United States in 1989, over 90 percent acknowledged having used alcohol at some time—a higher overall incidence than for any other psychoactive drug, including marijuana. Frequency of alcohol use has been found to vary with such factors as age, sex, social-class status, religious affiliation, ethnic background, geographic area (including rural and urban settings), and personal and social characteristics (DeLuca, 1981; Friedman & Humphrey, 1985; Jessor, 1984b; Johnston et al., 1989, 1990). For example, the results of a nationwide study indicated that among seventh-graders, 60 percent of boys and 47 percent of girls had at least tried drinking; by the twelfth grade these figures increased to 95 percent for boys and 92 percent for girls (Donovan & Jessor, 1978). Students who do not plan to complete four years of college drink more than those who do, as do school dropouts (Johnston et al., 1989, 1990; Mensch & Kandel, 1988). At all ages from 14 to 18, adolescents living in large metropolitan areas drink more than their rural and small-town peers. Those living in the Northeast and the West drink the most, followed closely by those in the north central states; those

On many college campuses, excessive use of alcohol has become a major problem, and programs are being initiated to deal with it more effectively. Although most students will not become problem drinkers, the prevalence of heavy drinking is higher among college students than for others in their age group.

living in the South drink the least (Hamburg, Elliott, & Parron, 1982; Johnston et al., 1989, 1990; Rachal et al., 1984).

Alcohol use among adolescents increased dramatically between 1966 and 1975. For example, in 1966 only 19 percent of adolescents reported ever having been drunk; by 1975 the proportion had increased to 45 percent (Noble, 1978). Between 1975 and 1981, overall alcohol use increased modestly, with slightly more adolescents drinking each year and at slightly younger ages. Since 1980, however, alcohol use has been dropping slowly; for example, by 1989, 60 percent of high school seniors had used alcohol in the last month, down from a high of 72.0 percent in 1980 (see Table 11.1). Sex differences in alcohol use are decreasing, as are rural–urban and regional differences.

It should be emphasized that the majority of adolescents who drink are temperate in their use of alcohol and are likely to remain so. What is of far greater concern to clinicians and others who work with young people is the relatively small but important minority who continue to drink frequently and heavily: 4.2 percent of 1989 high school seniors reported daily use of alcohol in the past month (down from 6.0 in 1980), and one-third reported having had more than five drinks in a row in the past two weeks (see Table 11.2). In an earlier national study, 4.3 percent of 13-year-olds and 9.7 percent of 14-year-olds were already heavy drinkers (Rachal, 1975).

In brief, it appears clear that most adolescents are not problem drinkers and are unlikely to become so; nevertheless, the fact that, for example, nearly 10 percent of 14-year-olds are already heavy drinkers can hardly be viewed as reassuring. Moreover, these nationwide findings are restricted to young people who are still in school. The incidence of problem drinking is known to be much higher among school dropouts.

Characteristics of Student Drinkers

In general, adolescent abstainers are more likely than either moderate or heavy drinkers to be conservative, controlled, responsible, studious, cautious, religious, and interested in solitary pursuits. They are less likely to be adventurous, outgoing, socially assertive, impulsive, socially and sexually active, subject to mood swings, critical of society, or tolerant of socially deviant behavior (Braucht, 1984; Donovan & Jessor, 1978; Jessor, Donovan, & Widmer, 1980; Rachal et al., 1984). Abstainers are more likely to come from close-knit families with conservative, religious, hardworking, nondrinking parents who place a high value on education (Barnes, 1984; Braucht, 1984; Harburg et al., 1990; Jessor, 1984b; Jessor & Jessor, 1973; Rachal et al., 1984). In contrast, young people who are heavy or problem drinkers are more likely than either abstainers or moderate drinkers to place a high value on independence; to engage heavily in social activities such as dances, parties, and dating; to be impulsive and engage in socially disapproved or deviant behavior (e.g., cutting classes, cheating on examinations, driving too fast, and using other drugs); and to be dominant and outgoing (Braucht, 1984; Donovan & Jessor 1978; Jessor & Jessor, 1977).

Compared to abstainers or moderate drinkers, heavy drinkers are more likely to experience feelings of exuberance and excitement. However, they are also more likely to be pessimistic, bored, impulsive, distrustful, and irresponsible, and to have low self-esteem (Clark & Midanik, 1984; Rachal et al., 1984; Yanish & Battle, 1985). "Male and especially female drinkers reported more frequent feelings of an inability to get going, of boredom, and of vague uneasiness. Furthermore, significantly greater proportions of female heavy drinkers reported feeling lonely or remote from people, angry at some minor frustration, depressed or unhappy, and restless" (Moos, Moos, & Kulik, 1976, p. 357).

At all levels from junior high school to college, problem or heavy drinkers report more difficulties in relations with their parents. They are also less likely to value academic achievement; they expect less academic success and do, in fact, obtain lower grades (Braucht, 1980, 1984; Jessor, 1984a, 1984b; Kandel,

---

Box 11.2 DO GENETIC FACTORS PLAY A ROLE IN ALCOHOL USE AND ABUSE?

A number of twin studies and adoption studies suggest that genetic factors may play a role in alcohol use and abuse (Bolman, Sigvardsson, & Cloringer, 1981; Goodwin et al., 1974; Vandenberg, Singer, & Pauls, 1986). For example, a Swedish study of identical and fraternal twins found that extent of alcohol use (ranging from complete abstention to chronic alcoholism) was much more alike for identical twins than for fraternal twins (Kaij, 1960).

Several adoption studies have found that adopted-away children with biological parents who were alcoholic were more than three times as likely to become alcoholic as adoptees whose biological parents were not alcoholic (Bolman, Sigvardsson, & Cloringer, 1981; Goodwin et al., 1973, 1974). In a study involving foster parents, when children of nonalcoholic biological parents were raised by alcoholic foster parents they were more likely to become alcoholic than if the foster parents were nonalcoholic (14 percent versus 8 percent), indicating that environmental factors can exert an important influence. However, if the biological parents were alcoholic, approximately half of the foster children became alcoholic, regardless of whether the foster parent drank or not (Schuckit, Goodwin, & Winokur, 1972). Recent research suggests that a specific gene (dopamine D_2 receptor gene located on chromosome 11) may play a role in susceptibility to some forms of alcoholism, although much more research is needed (Blum, K., Noble, E. P., Sheridan, P. J. et al., 1990; Gordis et al., 1990).

Such studies indicate that among individuals who become alcoholic, genetic factors may play a significant role. But this is not the same as saying that genetic factors drive us to drink; what is inherited is probably an absence of brakes (Plomin, 1986). In the words of one prominent investigator, "large numbers of people are more or less 'protected' from becoming alcoholic because of genetically determined adverse physical reactions to alcohol. Possibly, if anything is inherited in alcoholism, it is *a lack of intolerance* for alcohol" (Goodwin, 1979, p. 60).

Kessler, & Margulies, 1978; Rachal et al., 1984; Reeves, 1984). At the college level, they exhibit higher rates of academic failure and dropping out. Finally, heavy drinkers are more likely to have parents who drink, in a disproportionate number of cases, heavily, as well as friends and best friends who also drink.

Effects of Alcohol

Despite the popular notion that alcohol serves as a stimulant, it has a depressant effect on the central nervous system. This depressant effect increases in proportion to the percentage of alcohol in the blood and is greater for more complex and unfamiliar tasks than for simpler and well-learned tasks. Even in small doses, alcohol impairs perception and time estimation; reduces reasoning, learning ability, and memory; and produces a relative impoverishment of thought content. Consequently, it is not surprising that alcohol plays a major role in half of all fatalities in automobile accidents.

In higher dosages alcohol impairs basic brain functions, resulting in abnormality of gross bodily functions and mental faculties and ultimately in coma. In extreme instances—as in "chugalug" drinking contests—alcohol intake may even cause death (although usually the individual passes out before consuming enough alcohol to suspend the brain functions that regulate breathing, heart action, and the like). In addition to its direct effects on the central nervous system, alcohol may adversely affect action of the adrenal glands, and hormonal activity of the pituitary gland and gonads (in males, testosterone is reduced and estrogen increased), as well as kidney, cardiovascular, brain, and liver functioning (DeLuca, 1981; Hamburg, Elliott, & Parron 1982). In combination with smoking, excessive use of alcohol appears to be related to the development of certain cancers.

Heavy drinking during pregnancy can adversely affect fetal development. It is currently estimated that **fetal alcohol syndrome** (characterized by retarded growth, physical abnormalities, and intellectual defects) may result from maternal consumption of 3 ounces of absolute alcohol per day (i.e., about six drinks). Even smaller doses (1 ounce or more a day) increase the likelihood of low birthweight, developmental delays, physical difficulties (e.g., in breathing and sucking ability), and spontaneous abortion (DeLuca, 1981; Hamburg et al., 1982; Kliegman & King, 1983; Moore, 1982).

TOBACCO

Cigarette smoking among adolescents appears to have reached a peak in 1976–1977, after which it declined until 1984 (Johnston et al., 1988, 1990; National Institute, 1987). Since that time there has been little overall change, although there was a slight increase among high school seniors in 1985.

One-third fewer seniors engaged in daily use of cigarettes in 1989 than in 1976 (Johnston et al., 1988, 1990). However, this overall decline masks different patterns among girls and boys: Between 1975 and 1977, girls increased their smoking rate more than boys did, essentially closing the gap between them. Between 1977 and 1982, there were significant decreases for both sexes; however, these decreases were slightly greater for boys, resulting in slightly lower current smoking rates for boys than for girls.

Among senior high school students in 1988, 31 percent of girls and 27 percent of boys reported smoking in the past thirty days (11.6 percent of girls and 10.7 percent of boys reported smoking at least a half-pack daily) (Johnston, Bachman, & O'Malley, 1988; Johnston et al., 1989). Also noteworthy is the fact that seniors who did not plan to complete four years of college were more than twice as likely to smoke as those who planned to complete college. Among young people who do not graduate from high school, smoking rates are higher for both boys and girls (Johnston et al., 1989; Kandel, Raveis, & Kandel, 1984; National Institute, 1989).

In the past fifteen years, girls closed the gap with boys in cigarette smoking, and now have a slightly higher smoking rate than boys.

Why Do Adolescents Smoke?

It has been clearly established that smoking substantially increases the risk of heart disease, lung cancer, chronic bronchitis, emphysema, and other ailments, and that it decreases longevity (Hamburg, Elliott, & Parron, 1982, *Smoking and health*, 1989; Surgeon General, 1988). Moreover, smoking by pregnant women lowers their infants' birthweight and resistance to illness. It also increases the chances of spontaneous abortion, premature birth, and long-term problems in the physical and intellectual development of their children. In the words of former U.S. Surgeon General Julius Richmond, "Smoking is the largest preventable cause of death in America" (*Smoking and health*, 1979, p. ii).

Why, then, do adolescents begin and continue smoking, and why has the rate increased so dramatically among girls? Clearly it is not because of ignorance of the associated health hazards, at least for the great majority. Seventy-seven percent of teenage smokers believe that it is better not to start smoking than to have to quit; 84 percent believe that smoking is habit forming; and 78 percent believe that it can cause lung cancer and heart disease (Evans, Henderson, Hill, & Raines, 1979). Over two-thirds believe that regular smoking entails great personal risk (Johnston et al., 1989).

Such findings suggest that a majority of adolescent smokers do so not out of ignorance but despite the personal dangers. Why? In approaching this question, it is necessary to consider *initiation* of smoking separately from *continuation* of the habit. Once established, dependence on cigarettes can be very difficult to overcome, both physiologically and psychologically. Largely because of its nicotine content, tobacco is physiologically addictive, and cessation of smoking can produce symptoms of withdrawal that are comparable in many ways to those of withdrawal from narcotics (Institute of Medicine, 1980). Psychological dependence is fostered by continued use of tobacco in specific circumstances, such as when one is anxious or bored, trying to concentrate, or attempting to deal with a difficult social situation, or in association with alcohol or coffee.

Neither type of dependence exists initially, however. What factors encourage initiation of use? Although we still have much to learn, a number of factors increase the likelihood of smoking. One is parental influence. In families in which both parents smoke, 22.2 percent of boys and 20.7 percent of girls also become smokers, compared to 11.3 percent and 7.6 percent, respectively, in families in which neither parent smokes (Evans, 1984; Evans, Henderson, Hill, & Raines, 1979; Hamburg et al., 1984). Siblings may exert a similar influence; indeed, if an older sibling *and* both parents smoke, a child is four times as likely to smoke as when there is no model for smoking in the family.

Among younger adolescents in particular, peer pressure and conformity to group norms exert a strong influence on smoking behavior. Indeed, several surveys have identified peer influence as the single most significant factor in the initiation of smoking (Evans, 1979, 1984; Evans, Smith, & Raines, 1985; Kozlowski, 1974). In one such study, having a best friend or group of friends who smoke was found to be the best predictor of smoking in children and adolescents from the fifth through the twelfth grade (Levitt & Edwards, 1970). Other factors that may play a role in encouraging smoking include nonparental adult models, such as teachers, and advertising, which portrays smoking as sophisticated, sexy, masculine, and so on. The extent of media influence is open to some question, however, since adolescents tend to view cigarette advertising as "hypocritical" and "least liked" of all advertisements (Evans et al., 1978).

Individual Characteristics. Attempts to find personality characteristics that may predispose a young person to become a smoker have had only limited success (Evans et al., 1978; Gerber & Newman, 1989). Compared with young people who do not smoke, those who become smokers are slightly more likely to be extraverted, tense and anxious, inclined to take risks, and rebellious. They are also more likely to believe that their fate is determined by external events and chance rather than by their own efforts, and to have lower academic expectations (Evans, 1986; Evans et al., 1978; Gerber & Newman, 1989).

Other variables include low self-esteem, poor social skills, and social anxiety (Hamburg et al., 1982). However, it appears that personality characteristics are more strongly related to the amount smoked than to who will begin to smoke. For example, in several studies of smokers, amount smoked has been found to be directly related to degree of anxiety (Evans, Henderson, & Raines, 1979; Thomas, 1973).

Sex Differences. A variety of explanations have been offered for the earlier dramatic rise in smoking among girls at the same time that it was declining among boys. Girls may have felt that they were less likely to develop diseases associated with smoking, such as lung cancer and heart disease, because the incidence of these diseases was lower in women (Hamburg et al., 1982; Molotsky, 1986; U.S. Bureau of the Census, 1989). More recently, however, there has been an alarming increase in smoking-related diseases among women as rates of smoking among women have increased. The incidence of lung cancer in women, for example, has shown a fivefold increase since the early 1960s, and among women with comparable smoking experiences it is rapidly approaching the levels found in men. In the words of the former surgeon general, "it is becoming clear that women who smoke like men die like men who smoke" (*Smoking and health*, 1979, p. 1).

Another possibility is that changing sex roles and greater similarity between the sexes is involved. Smoking was once considered more socially acceptable for men than for women, particularly in public; clearly, this is no longer the case. The manufacturer of one brand of cigarettes targeted toward younger women proclaims, "You've come a long way, baby!" It would be ironic to find that the women's movement has "freed" adolescent girls to develop the same future disabilities as their male peers. At any rate, as we have seen, females are not only smoking more than males but are smoking earlier and more heavily. One can only hope that this trend can be reversed—especially because there is evidence that women suffer more severe withdrawal symptoms than men (*Women and smoking*, 1980).

Prevention

In view of the difficulties involved in giving up smoking, prevention appears to offer the brightest prospect for significantly decreasing tobacco use. Although many traditional approaches to prevention (e.g., lectures on the health risks linked to smoking) have proved relatively ineffective, some newer approaches seem promising (Evans, 1984; Flag, 1985; Matarazzo, 1984; Lichtenstein & Mermelstein, 1984). Generally, these efforts have been directed toward adolescents, beginning in about the seventh grade; if a person succeeds in avoiding smoking during the adolescent years, his or her chances of smoking in adulthood are significantly reduced (Conger, 1987; Evans, 1984; Institute of Medicine, 1980). Although they differ in their content, most of these programs tend to emphasize active involvement by the young person in developing strategies to handle pressure to smoke, whether from peers, the media, or adults. In the case of cigarette advertising, content analyses of ads may be used to reveal the techniques used by advertisers. In some instances filmed vignettes showing peer pressure to smoke are presented; the class may then discuss appropriate ways to respond (Evans, 1984; Evans, Smith, & Raines, 1985; Hurd et al., 1980). For example, if a young adolescent is called "chicken" for refusing an offer of cigarettes, he or she might reply, "If I smoke to prove to you that I'm not chicken, all I'll really be showing is that I'm afraid not to do what you want me to do. I don't want to smoke" (McAlister, Perry, & Maccoby, 1979, p. 653).

Related approaches may involve role playing of smoking situations and counseling of junior high school students by high school students. More general techniques for dealing with a variety of stressful situations that may increase vulnerability to smoking may also be employed. These include development of social skills, efforts to improve self-esteem and self-confidence, and assertiveness training. Several studies using these newer approaches have shown significant differences in subsequent smoking between experimental and control groups over two- to three-year follow-up periods (Institute of Medicine, 1980; Evans et al., 1981; Evans, 1984). There is also some preliminary evidence suggesting that "inoculation" against smoking may extend to use of other drugs, including alcohol (McAlister et al., 1979).

MARIJUANA

Except for tobacco and alcohol, marijuana is by a considerable margin the drug that is most frequently used by young people. The active chemical ingredients in marijuana—primarily tetrahydrocannabinols, or THC—are contained in a resin found in the topmost leaves and flower clusters of the female plant (the male plant contains similar substances, but in much smaller amounts). These chemicals are the principal cause of the so-called marijuana high. The strength of the drug may vary considerably, depending on growing conditions, climate, degree of cultivation, the portions of the plant used, and manner of preparation.

An increasing concern of public health officials is that most marijuana is now two to five times more potent than it was in the early 1970s; in some highly developed varieties, such as sinsemilla samples tested by researchers for the National Institute on Drug Abuse, levels of THC were found to be thirteen times more potent (Kerr, 1986). These officials are concerned that parents who were able to smoke a joint and then drive a car or go to class when they were students may not realize that at current dose levels driving is far more dangerous and impairment of short-term memory is far more disruptive.

Since 1978–1979, when it reached an all-time high, marijuana use among adolescents has declined significantly (National Institute, 1989; Johnston et al., 1990). For example, among high school seniors marijuana use within the past thirty days decreased from 36.5 percent in 1978 to 25.2 percent in 1984 and 16.7 percent in 1989. The decline is apparently largely a function of a steady increase in perceived risk, since availability of the drug remains high (Bachman, Johnston, O'Malley, & Humphrey, 1988; Johnston et al., 1990) (see

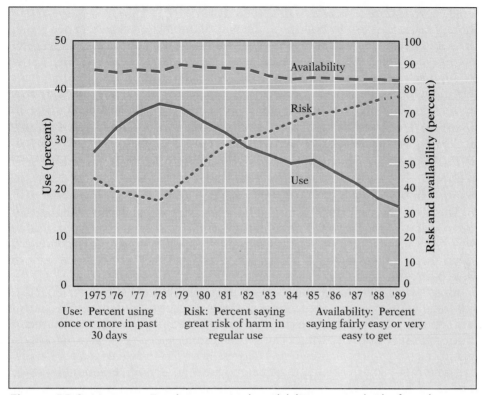

Figure 11.2 Marijuana: Trends in perceived availability, perceived risk of regular use, and prevalence of use in past thirty days. (From L. D. Johnston, P. M. O'Malley, & J. G. Bachman. *Drug use, drinking and smoking: National survey results from high school, college, and young adults populations, 1975–1989.* Washington, DC: National Institute on Drug Abuse, 1990. By permission.)

Figure 11.2). *Daily* use dropped by 75 percent in the decade from 1978 to 1989 (from 10.7 percent to 2.9 percent) (see Table 11.2).

In addition, a trend toward earlier use of marijuana appears to have halted. For example, the proportion of 12- and 13-year-olds reporting any experience with marijuana was 6 percent in 1971 and rose to 8 percent in 1977; however, since 1977 it appears to have remained constant at about 8 percent (Johnston et al., 1984, 1988, 1989, 1990; National Institute, 1989).

As in the case of alcohol, marijuana use among high school seniors is more frequent among males and among those who do not plan to go on to four years of college. Geographically, use is still most frequent in the Northeast and least frequent in the South; it also is most frequent in large metropolitan areas and least frequent in rural areas (Johnston et al., 1989).

As "forerunners of the youth revolution" (Yankelovich, 1969, 1974), American college students in the late 1960s and early 1970s were far more likely to use marijuana than their noncollege contemporaries (Abelson, 1977; Johnston et al., 1989; *Marihuana and health*, 1980; Parry, 1979). Thus, it is interesting to note that current use by college students is about average for their age group; indeed, their rate of daily use is below that of their noncollege agemates (Johnston et al., 1989, 1990). College students' marijuana use is also similar to that of high school seniors (Johnston, 1989; Johnston et al., 1989, 1990).

Among both adults and young people, the largest percentage of marijuana users are experimenters or occasional users, and the smallest percentage are heavy users. However, as will become evident, it is this minority of chronic users who are most likely to have significant drug problems and about whom psychologists and others who work with young people are most concerned.

Subjective Effects of Marijuana

The subjective effects of a marijuana high are extremely variable, particularly at low dosage levels. Many first-time marijuana smokers report feeling only very limited effects, such as difficulty concentrating and remembering what they were saying or thinking; others say that the initial experience provoked anxiety, while still others found it pleasurable and relaxing.

Most social users and clinical observers agree that the subjective effects of marijuana are extremely dependent not only on the strength of the dosage but also on the user's expectations and psychological and physical characteristics, both transient and enduring. The physical and social setting in which use occurs also plays a role. An already depressed or seriously anxious person may become more so after using marijuana. One who is more emotionally stable and is looking forward to a pleasant, relaxing experience with good friends may indeed have such an experience. On the other hand, a suspicious individual taking marijuana furtively in an ugly or distracting setting, or in one where there is a possibility of being arrested, may become more suspicious or even paranoid.

At very mild dosage levels, the most common responses are alterations in mood, especially feeling happy, silly, and relaxed. At higher levels, colors seem brighter and hearing keener, the body feels lighter, and alterations in time perception are frequently reported. At still higher levels, these subjective effects are more pronounced and a majority of users report changes in body image, illusions, delusions, and hallucinations—toxic reactions that occur with excessive dosages of many chemicals that affect the nervous system (*Committee*, 1982).

Adverse Effects of Marijuana: Fact or Fiction?

Despite assertions to the contrary, marijuana is not a narcotic and is not physiologically addictive; nor is marijuana use likely for most users to lead to the use of hard drugs such as heroin (*Committee*, 1982; Carroll, 1985; Hollister, 1986; Kandel & Faust, 1975). Marijuana's short-term physical effects at normal dosage levels are not particularly remarkable: There is an increase in pulse rate, some alteration of blood pressure, and some minimal loss in muscle strength and steadiness. Perhaps the most dramatic physical effect is a marked increase in appetite 30–60 minutes after ingestion. The degree of impairment of cognitive and psychomotor performance is related to dosage, although there are wide individual differences. At low dosage levels and on simple or familiar tasks, impairment is usually minimal, but clearly impaired performance is observable on complex or unfamiliar tasks at higher dosage levels.

Even at relatively low dosage levels, however, such perceptual and psychomotor functions as signal or cue detection (e.g., ability to perceive a brief flash of light) and tracking (e.g., ability to follow a moving stimulus) are significantly and consistently impaired; evidence of such impairment may last from four to eight hours beyond the feeling of intoxication (Carroll, 1985). Such impairments present a very real danger for drivers, pilots, or users of machinery (Yesavage et al., 1985). Experiments have shown that subjects can usually remember previously learned material while under the influence of marijuana about as well as control group subjects who have been given a placebo. When subjects perform learning tasks while under the influence of moderate dosages of marijuana, their short-term, immediate memory seems to be relatively unaffected; however, their longer-term memory is impaired. With large doses, both short- and long-term memory are impaired.

As already noted, consumption of marijuana under unfavorable circumstances may lead, at least temporarily, to suspiciousness, terror, paranoia, or depression. Personality factors are also important. A person who believes that affairs in life never work out well or that he or she is not liked by others may experience brief spells of paranoia when under the influence of marijuana. Moreover, at larger doses marijuana may produce changes in body image, subjective sensations, and a feeling of loss of bodily boundaries or fusion with surroundings (Carroll, 1985; *Committee*, 1982). Many users may view this as pleasurable, but in those with conscious or unconscious fear of loss of control or those whose contact with reality is tenuous, this experience may produce extensive psychological distress.

Although marijuana is not physiologically addictive, psychological dependence on the drug can become a serious problem for a minority of users. Probably not more than 5–10 percent of young people are chronic heavy users. However, for them marijuana can present real dangers that are comparable in severity to those faced by chronic alcoholics. It can also result in serious pulmonary problems (Hollister, 1986). Moreover, if an adolescent is using marijuana chronically to escape from stress, his or her psychological growth is likely to be impaired because he or she is not learning how to deal with frustration and with daily problems (Newcomb & Bentler, 1988).

In addition, as we have noted, marijuana can reduce performance on cognitive tasks and longer-term memory. Thus, the minority of students who come to school stoned or become stoned during the school day are endangering their academic performance. Indeed, consistent users eventually do appear to suffer academically. Whether prolonged heavy use of marijuana actually damages the brain's capacity to function or produces genetic or prenatal damage to unborn children is still a matter of scientific debate. We simply do not yet know enough about the long-term effects of marijuana use (Braude & Ludford, 1984; Carroll, 1985; *Committee*, 1982; Hollister, 1986). Some recent research suggests that THC, the active ingredient in marijuana, may affect the structure of the brain in much the same way that aging does (Bales, 1986; Study, 1986).

There is still considerable controversy about whether chronic heavy marijuana use produces "burnout." Professionals who work with young people, as well as parents, have reported that such prolonged use may cause the user to become mentally blunted, dulled, and mildly confused, with a diminished attention span, as well as passive and lacking in goal-directed activity (what has been termed the *amotivational syndrome*) (Baumrind, Moselle, & Martin, 1985; Newcomb & Bentler, 1988). Although there is little doubt that such effects are seen in a minority of "potheads," it is difficult to establish causality. Did chronic marijuana use lead to the personality changes, or did the personality changes accelerate marijuana use? To complicate matters further, heavy marijuana use is almost always accompanied by multiple use of other drugs (Kandel, 1980; Single, Kandel, & Faust, 1974).

At present, the most reasonable conclusion appears to be that the final chapter on marijuana use has yet to be written. It may be that many fears of physical or physiological damage will prove groundless. But long experience with drugs and chemicals of all sorts that were once considered harmless—ranging from aspirin to thalidomide, from DDT to food additives and estrogenic compounds such as stilbestrol—cannot help but dictate caution, particularly in the case of women who are or might be pregnant (Carroll, 1985; Hollister, 1986; Petersen, 1980). The following statement by an advisory committee of the National Academy of Sciences in 1982 remains valid today:

> The scientific evidence published to date indicates that marijuana has a broad range of psychological and biological effects, some of which, at least under certain conditions, are harmful to human health. Unfortunately, the available information does not tell us how serious this risk may be. Our major conclusion is that what little we know for certain about the effects of marijuana on human health—and all that we have reason to suspect—justifies serious national concern (*Committee*, 1982; quoted in *The New York Times*, 1982, p. 9).

Personal Characteristics of Marijuana Users

A variety of investigations have attempted to determine whether marijuana users and nonusers differ in their personal characteristics. Although there are many differences among individuals in any category of marijuana users, a number of fairly consistent findings emerge if we differentiate among categories of users.

Early Users, Late Users, and Nonusers.
One might expect that young people who begin using marijuana early in adolescence, when it is less common and less sanctioned, would differ significantly from late users as well as from nonusers. In a large-scale longitudinal study of over 12,000 students in grades 4–12 in the greater Boston area, this indeed proved to be the case

(Smith & Fogg, 1978). Both in peer ratings and on personality test responses, the greatest differences were found between nonusers and early users (before the ninth grade), with late users (tenth grade or later) falling between the two extremes. Nonusers were described as most orderly, curious, hard working, self-confident, determined, persistent, tender-hearted, achievement oriented, and obedient, and as most likely to feel valued and accepted and in control of their lives. In contrast, early users were most likely to be perceived as impulsive, dependent, not responsible or considerate, unable to be trusted consistently, immature in their interests, emotional, talkative, sociable, and pessimistic.

Extent of Marijuana Use. Even more salient is the extent of marijuana use. Clearly, the occasional experimenter and the chronic "pothead" are using marijuana in very different ways and may be expected to differ significantly in personality and behavior as well. Experimenters (those who have tried marijuana a few times and either given it up completely or engaged in subsequent use only very infrequently) appear to be basically similar to nonusers, especially in peer groups in which marijuana use is not a rarity. Experimenters may be slightly more open to experience, less conventional and concerned with rules, more interested in creative pursuits, less reserved, less authoritarian, more adventuresome, and more interested in novel experiences (Jessor, 1979; Kandel, 1980; Kovach & Glickman, 1986). In general, however, experimenters tend to be motivated primarily by curiosity or the desire to share a social experience and are as "disciplined, optimistic, self-confident, . . . responsible, goal-oriented as nonusers" (Robins, 1979, p. 44).

As a group, moderate or intermittent users are less conventional, more adventuresome, more independent, less authoritarian, more impulsive, more sensation seeking, less inclined to delay gratification, more concerned with self-expression, and generally more open to experience than either experimenters or nonusers (Jessor, 1979; Kandel, 1980; Wogan & Elliott, 1972). They are also more likely to be uncertain of their future identity, somewhat more anxious, more rebellious, and more critical of existing social institutions. Studies of high school and college students indicate that moderate users are more likely to manifest anti-Establishment views regarding politics, religion, restraints on personal freedom, and the success ethic. They are also likely to be less religious and more tolerant of deviant behavior generally (Jessor, 1979; Jessor & Jessor, 1977; Kandel, 1980; Slappy, 1985).

The clearest differences from nonusers or experimenters, however, occur among chronic heavy users. It is among the latter group that fairly consistent indications of significant psychological and social disturbance are observed. Significantly, but perhaps not surprisingly, it is in this group that multiple drug use is more frequent and most extensive (see Figure 11.3). In a number of studies, heavy marijuana use has been found to be associated with "poor social and work adjustment, increased hostility, greater difficulty in mastering new problems, and the desire for a 'psychotomimetic' experience in marijuana use, rather than simple tension reduction or pleasurable stimulation" (Victor,

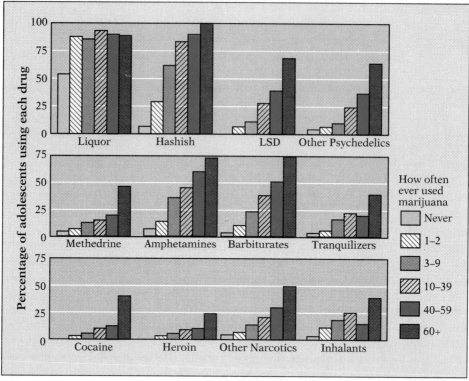

Figure 11.3 The use of other drugs by frequency of marijuana use (total New York State weighted sample, Wave 1, fall 1971). (From E. Single, D. Kandel, & R. Faust. Patterns of multiple drug use in high school. *Journal of Health and Social Behavior*, 1974, **15,** 344–357. By permission.)

Grossman, & Eiseman, 1973, p. 78). Heavy users score significantly higher (in the direction of pathology) than control subjects on psychological tests (Brill, Crumpton, & Grayson, 1971), and they tend to be anxious, restless, depressed, insecure, irresponsible, immature, or incapable of sustained intimate relationships with others (Carroll, 1985; *Marihuana and health,* 1980).

Very heavy users tend to lose interest in activities other than drug use, and they may exhibit extreme lethargy and inappropriate social behavior. It should be noted, however, that in American society heavy marijuana use is typically associated with multiple use of other drugs. One therefore cannot infer that psychological disturbance in this group is a direct result of heavy marijuana use. Moreover, studies of multiple drug users suggest that heavy drug use is primarily a result of psychological and social disturbances rather than their cause, although once such drug use has begun, a vicious cycle may become established.

OTHER DRUGS

Although young people still are more likely to use marijuana than other drugs (except for alcohol and tobacco), smaller percentages of youth have used other drugs as well. Those drugs include cocaine, "the pills" (barbiturates, tranquilizers, amphetamines), hallucinogens (morning glory seeds, mescaline, LSD, PCP), and hard narcotics (heroin). In addition, some adolescents have sniffed glue and other volatile hydrocarbons ranging from gasoline and paint thinner to dry-cleaning fluid.

Among all high school seniors in 1989, a substantial majority disapproved of ever experimenting with the more serious illicit drugs. They also disapproved of *regular* use of all nonprescription drugs, including marijuana, alcohol, and cigarettes (see pages 458–459); friends were perceived as having similar views (Johnston et al., 1989, 1990).

Cocaine

Once confined largely to ghetto residents, cocaine use increased rapidly during the 1970s, especially among middle-class youth and affluent young adults who could afford its mounting costs (Johnston et al., 1990). Between 1975 and 1985 the proportion of high school seniors who reported having tried cocaine increased from 9 percent to 17 percent; the number who reported having used it during the past month increased from 1.9 percent to 6.7 percent (see Table 11.1). Among 22-year-old high school graduates, 10–12 percent reported use in the past thirty days, and by age 27, 40 percent acknowledged at least having tried cocaine (Abelson, 1977; Johnston et al., 1988). Moreover, its use broadened to include ever-larger segments of society. As members of the "youth culture" of the 1960s and 1970s grew older the upper age limit for significant use of cocaine rose accordingly. Of the 21 million Americans who have tried cocaine and the estimated 2.9 million who are regular cocaine users (down from 5.8 million in 1985), the overwhelming majority are under 40 (National Institute, 1989). Ironically, what had become a drug of the privileged and affluent in the 1960s returned to the urban ghettos in the 1980s in a particularly lethal form: "crack" or "rock."

Since 1986, however, use of cocaine among high school seniors, college students, and other young adults has dropped markedly—despite greater availability—as the perceived danger of cocaine use has risen (Johnston et al., 1989, 1990; National Institute, 1989). Among high school seniors, the percentage who said that there is "great risk" associated with even *experimenting* with cocaine rose from 34 percent to 55 percent between 1986 and 1989, while the percentage who saw great risk associated with occasional use rose from 54 percent to 69 percent during the same period (see Figure 11.4). Despite these encouraging trends, however, the number of hard-core (weekly) users of cocaine in the United States increased from 647,000 in 1985 to at least 862,000 in 1988 (National Institute, 1989). Disapproval of cocaine use also increased among all these groups, reaching a level of well over 90 percent for regular use.

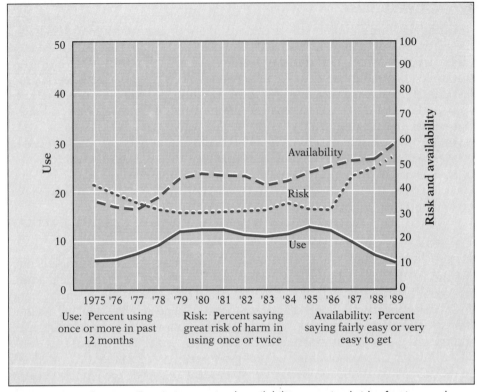

Figure 11.4 Cocaine: Trends in perceived availability, perceived risk of trying, and prevalence of use in past year among high school seniors. (From L. D. Johnston, J. G. Bachman, & P. M. O'Malley. *Drug use, drinking, and smoking: National survey results from high school, college, and young adults populations, 1975–1989.* Washington, DC: National Institute on Drug Abuse, 1990. By permission.)

In 1989 reported use of crack cocaine within the past year—never high—declined from 4.0 percent to 3.1 percent among high school seniors and from 2.0 percent to 1.9 percent among college students.

Cocaine is a powerful stimulant to the central nervous system, producing a general activation or excitement that is similar in many respects to the effects of amphetamines (Grabowski, 1984; Lamar, 1986; Woods & Downs, 1973). Heart rate and blood pressure increase. In high doses, cocaine may cause heart rate to suddenly decrease or become irregular and may depress respiration, sometimes resulting in delirium, convulsions, and cardiovascular collapse.

Although further work is necessary, research with rats at the National Institute of Mental Health suggests that extended use of cocaine may have a "kindling" effect that makes the brain more sensitive to the drug (Bales, 1986). It appears that the brain becomes more susceptible to lethal convulsions from repeated cocaine use than from a single large dose (which can also cause fatal seizures). Consequently, it is possible that what was previously a normal dose for a particular user could become a fatal dose.

Repeated high dosages of cocaine may produce both visual and (more frequently) tactile hallucinations. Paranoia—reflected, for example, in fear of being spied upon by police ("bull horrors")—is often associated with chronic cocaine use and can even result from an episode of high-dose use lasting several hours. Increasing hostility, impulsiveness, social withdrawal, and general deterioration of behavior may also result (Crowley, 1987; Grabowski, 1984; Washton & Gold, 1984). Prolonged use can inflame or destroy nasal tissue or cause perforation of the septum separating the nostrils, although this occurs less frequently than was previously thought.

The most striking initial effect of a moderate dose of cocaine is a state of euphoria (which may be accompanied or followed by anxiety or apprehension). Feelings of enhanced mental and physical abilities are characteristic. However, as the individual comes down from the immediate effects of the drug, euphoria is followed by depression and irritability. It appears that cocaine triggers the simultaneous release of a number of chemical transmitters in the brain (chiefly, dopamine, serotonin, and epinephrine), leading to euphoria in the experienced user. But cocaine also blocks the return of these neurotransmitters to the brain for reuse, leading to depression, irritability, and a craving for further stimulation (Crowley, 1987; Grabowski, 1984; Washton & Gold, 1984; Washton & Tartarsky, 1984).

"Crack" or "Rock." Crack is an inexpensive, extremely potent, and highly addictive form of cocaine that is rapidly becoming a major public health and crime problem, particularly in the inner cities of large metropolitan areas like New York and Los Angeles, but increasingly in other parts of the United States as well (Johnson, 1986; Kolata, 1989; Lamar, 1986). It is made by mixing ordinary coke with baking soda and water; the resulting solution is then heated, dried, and broken into tiny chunks or "rocks."

Unlike regular cocaine, which has traditionally been sniffed or "snorted," crack is smoked, and the resulting intoxication is far more rapid and intense. The immediate euphoria produced is much greater; the subsequent depression, irritability, and craving are also much greater.

The National Institute on Drug Abuse estimates that an addiction to regular coke typically develops after three to four years, whereas crack users are usually hooked after only six to eight weeks, sometimes sooner. In the words of one expert, James Hall, "It's an extremely compulsive drug, much more so than regular cocaine. The rush is so intense and the crash so powerful that it keeps users—even first time users—focused on nothing but their next hit" (quoted in Lamar, 1986, p. 17). Or, as a psychopharmacologist at a drug treatment center puts it, "There is *no such thing* as the recreational use of crack" (Morganthau, 1986, p. 58).

Crack is simply a form of **"freebasing,"** in which sniffable cocaine is converted into a smokable "base" form. Before crack was developed, ether was

used in this process. Since ether is highly flammable, freebasing was a dangerous way to get high, as comedian Richard Pryor discovered when he set himself on fire "freebasing." With crack, ether is no longer needed and the conversion process is simple and relatively inexpensive. As a result, "crack houses" or
"base houses," where crack can be purchased and smoked, have proliferated in
urban ghettos and to a much lesser extent, in middle-class neighborhoods.
Ironically, some crack houses were formerly shooting galleries for heroin.

Currently, a majority of the cocaine arrests are for crack dealing, and there
are no signs of a letup in the foreseeable future. Because crack is so easy to
prepare and so highly addictive, and because of the large profits that can be
made by dealing in crack, it is rapidly becoming the principal threat to survival
among disenfranchised children and adolescents in America's inner cities.
However, the rising number of crack-addicted mothers poses an even greater
threat to their offspring, both because of neurobiological damage during prenatal development and because of the inability or even desire of many of these
mothers to care for their children (Brody, 1988).

The Pills

The problems posed by the pills—barbiturates, tranquilizers, and amphetamines—vary, although all of these substances are overused both by adolescents and by adults. In this section we will discuss the effects of each of these
substances and the problems associated with them.

Sedatives. *Barbiturates* ("downers," "yellows," "phennies," "reds"), or
sleeping pills, account for over 3000 accidental or intentional deaths a year in
this country alone, but habituation and addiction are far more common problems. Barbiturate intoxication is characterized by intellectual impairment,
self-neglect, slurred speech, tremor, defective judgment, drowsiness, mood
swings, bizarre behavior, and **ataxia.** Contrary to popular opinion, withdrawal
symptoms are more serious for barbiturate addiction than for heroin; if withdrawal is abrupt, they may include nausea, high fever, delirium, hallucinations, convulsions, stupor, and sometimes fatal coma.

Except when they are used as part of a dangerous cycle of "uppers" and
"downers"—amphetamines to get high, barbiturates to come down—or for
conventional medical reasons (which may also lead to addiction), barbiturates
are taken by adolescents out of naivete or because other drugs are not available. Because they are nonspecific general depressants (Noble, 1978), they do
not provide a true high, and after a brief period of relaxation in which tension
may seem to disappear, they provide only physical and mental lassitude. Although reliable figures are not available, it appears that the notion of taking
barbiturates for kicks is most prevalent among younger, more indiscriminate
users. In 1989 less than 4 percent of high school seniors reported using barbiturates in the previous 12 months, and less than 1.5 percent had done so in the
previous thirty days, a marked decrease from the figures for earlier years
(Johnston et al., 1986, 1990).

Methaqualone, usually known on the street as Quaalude (one of its commercial names) or "Ludes," is a nonbarbiturate sedative hypnotic. "As a 'downer,' methaqualone appears to have an inordinate capacity to produce a dissociative 'high' and ultimately a compelling addiction. Users describe a loss of physical and mental self" (Pascarelli, 1973, p. 103). As one adolescent stated, "It's like being hit with four joints at once." The drug also has a reputation among some young people as an aphrodisiac and has been referred to as "the love drug." The feeling of well-being it produces is associated with ataxia and paresthesia of the legs, arms, fingers, lips, and tongue. A sense of invulnerability can lead to accidents.

At least initially, most youthful users did not believe that methaqualone was addictive ("It's not a barbiturate"). But in fact it is, and it may produce serious withdrawal symptoms. Moreover, the user develops a tolerance for the drug, and as this occurs the quantity needed for a "high" gets closer to the lethal dose. Overdoses may result in coma, heart failure, convulsions, and death. Fortunately, in recent years use of this drug has declined sharply, largely because legal manufacture and distribution in the United States has been stopped, but partly also because youthful users and potential users have come to understand the serious dangers of the drug. In 1988, only 1.3 percent of high school seniors reported having used methaqualone in the past year, compared to a peak of 7.6 in 1981 (Johnston et al., 1989). Among college students and other young adults, the decline was even greater.

Amphetamines. The *amphetamines* ("bennies," 'dex," "meth," "ice," "speed," "copilot," "pep pills") belong to a class of drugs known as sympathomimetics, which "produce effects resembling those resulting from stimulation of the sympathetic nervous system, a part of the nervous system which has primary control over bodily functions" (Noble, 1978, p. 141). In various forms, such as Benzedrine, and the more potent Dexedrine (dextroamphetamine) and Methedrine (methamphetamine), they may be used to suppress appetite, restore energy, or elevate mood.

Withdrawal from amphetamines can produce depression, lassitude, drowsiness, increased appetite, and intense or frightening dreams. It can also be extremely dangerous. Overdoses may result in convulsions, coma, and cerebral hemorrhage; as the hippies of the late 1960s succinctly stated, "Speed kills." In contrast to the majority of central nervous system stimulants, amphetamines may produce a high degree of tolerance (i.e., rapid physiological adaptation) that affects various systems selectively. Thus, although increased dosage levels may be necessary to maintain feelings of energy and well-being, the same dosage level may result in marked increases in nervousness and insomnia. An alternating vicious cycle between amphetamines and barbiturates ("runs and crashes") frequently characterizes heavy users. Continued heavy usage may produce impairment of judgment and intellectual function, aggressive or violent behavior, lack of coordination, and hallucinations, as well as extreme irritability and suspicious or paranoid feelings (Carroll, 1986; Crowley & Rhine, 1985; Noble, 1978).

In 1989 almost no college students and 10.8 percent of senior high school students reported use of amphetamines in the past year. No college students and only 4.2 percent of high school seniors reported having used them in the past thirty days (Johnston et al., 1988, 1989). At present, however, there is a resurgence in street sales of methamphetamines ("ice"), especially among chronic users of cocaine and other drugs. This trend is at least partly due to the relative ease and low cost of manufacturing this drug.

LSD and Other Hallucinogens

The hallucinogens (i.e., drugs that can produce hallucinations or distortions of reality in one or more sensory systems) vary in strength from mild (e.g., marijuana, nutmeg) to moderate (e.g., psilocybin, mescaline, peyote) to highly potent (e.g., LDS-25). LSD in its pure form is an odorless, tasteless white crystalline powder that is readily soluble in water and highly potent. It was originally derived from a fungus growing on wheat and rye.

Youthful experimentation with LSD and other hallucinogens increased rapidly in the late 1960s, appeared to reach a plateau in the early 1970s, and has since declined steadily (Abelson et al., 1977; Johnston et al., 1989, 1990; National Institute, 1989; Shafer et al., 1973). In 1989 only about 8 percent of high school seniors had ever used LSD, and less than 5 percent had used it in the past year; similar downward trends are apparent for other hallucinogens, such as mescaline, psilocybin, and peyote. Many former users have discontinued use of LSD because of fear of physical damage or psychological harm and because they have had upsetting experiences with the drug (Johnston et al., 1989, 1990).

In the late 1960s, at the height of the hippie era, many LSD users viewed hallucinogenic experiences as a way of "expanding their consciousness." For them the sense of timelessness, vivid panoramic hallucinations, and heightening or blocking of sensory experiences gave them the feeling that they were achieving lasting insights and that their individual identity was being merged with that of other human beings, animals, and even inanimate objects and the universe in general (Blum, 1979; *Committee,* 1982). Today's users are more likely to view LSD simply as an explosive way of becoming high or having a novel experience.

For some individuals at some times, LSD may be predominately a positive experience; for other individuals, or at other times, however, an LSD trip may produce bizarre and frightening images, a sense of isolation and depersonalization, acute panic, and paranoia. LSD use also carries with it danger of subsequent unanticipated "flashbacks," and in psychologically unstable individuals it sometimes precipitates acute psychosis (Wikler, 1970).

The possible long-term physiological or psychological effects of LSD, including brain damage or genetic or prenatal damage to one's offspring, are still not clearly understood (Carroll, 1985; Jacobs & Trulson, 1979). Some long-term users of LSD tend to view themselves as less constricted, less anxious, more relaxed, more creative, more loving, and generally more open to experience. However, these presumed assets are viewed differently by outside observers, who describe long-term users as showing poor judgment, unresponsiveness to danger, and inappropriate euphoria (Blum, 1979; Yablonsky, 1969). Other naturally occurring drugs, such as mescaline (from the mescal bud of the peyote cactus), psilocybin (from the Mexican mushroom of the same name), and morning glory seeds, also act as hallucinogens. In addition, a seemingly endless number of synthetic hallucinogens (e.g., DMT, MDA, STP, DOB) have appeared in the past decade (Carroll, 1985). Some are similar to mescaline or peyote in their effects at the dosage levels in which they are usually consumed; others are far more dangerous and more similar to LSD.

PCP (phencyclidine). Also known as angel dust, Krystal, or DOA (dead on arrival), PCP is another street drug that achieved notoriety in the late 1960s. It was originally developed as an experimental anesthetic, but its use was stopped when patients developed psychoses after receiving it. It now has no known medical function for humans. One of its principal dangers is the variability of its effects, which may range from a pleasant, dreamlike state to extreme confusion, paranoia, psychotic states, and assaultive behavior. PCP may also lead to loss of orientation in space, muscle rigidity, lack of coordination, and inability to sense imminent danger (Carroll, 1985; Crowley & Rhine, 1985; Peterson & Stillman, 1979; National Institute, 1983). Significant numbers of homicides, suicides, and accidental deaths have been related to PCP use. In large doses PCP has also been known to produce coma and death when combined with other drugs. There are some indications that long-term use may produce memory loss and inability to concentrate, and withdrawal may lead to depression.

Among adolescents between the ages of 12 and 17, PCP use doubled, from 3 percent to approximately 6 percent, between 1976 and 1977; use among 18–25-year-olds increased from 9.5 percent to 14 percent in the same period (Abelson, 1977). PCP use has declined in the past decade (National Institute, 1989). Among high school seniors in the United States, annual use of PCP dropped from 7 percent in the class of 1979 to 1.3 percent in the class of 1988; unfortunately, it increased to 2.4 percent in 1989 (Johnston et al., 1989, 1990).

Inhalants

Inhalants fall into three broad categories (Carroll, 1985). Sniffing of *commercial solvents,* such as glue and other volatile hydrocarbons (gasoline, cleaning fluid, paint thinner), is largely confined to younger adolescents and children—some as young as 8 or 9. Although such substances may sometimes produce a sense of euphoria and dizziness, they may also cause severe headache and vomiting. In addition, many of them can cause permanent damage to organs like the kidneys, brain, and liver; acute poisoning can cause death (Cohen, 1979; *Committee,* 1982).

Aerosols are particles suspended in gas, as in hair sprays. They include amyl nitrite capsules, which are used in treating some heart patients and produce a flushing sensation and light-headedness through dilation of the arteries, and butyl nitrite, a room deodorizer that produces a short high (Carroll, 1985). *Anesthetics,* such as chloroform, ether, and nitrous oxide (laughing gas), may produce the euphoria of intoxication but pose the dangers of confused behavior or a potentially lethal overdose.

About 7 percent of high school seniors used inhalants in 1989 (down slightly from 8.9 percent in 1979); 1.7 percent have used amyl or butyl nitrites (down from 6.5 percent in 1979). Almost 40 percent of all inhalant users began use before the ninth grade (although nitrite users typically began somewhat later) (Johnston et al., 1989, 1990).

Heroin

Until the 1960s the use of heroin and other hard narcotics was confined largely to the most depressed sectors of our society. In fact, heroin has been described as the drug of despair—a drug that is used not to "turn on" to one's surroundings or to expand one's consciousness, but rather to shut out physical pain, mental anguish, and a sense of emptiness. The drug produces a brief euphoria and release of tension that is characterized externally by apathy, listlessness, and inertia.

Heroin traditionally had little appeal for adolescents or adults outside the ghetto, although its use among physicians, nurses, and pharmacists was higher than among other professionals, such as teachers and lawyers. Beginning in the second half of the 1960s, however, experimentation with heroin spread to middle-class suburban schools (*Committee* 1982; Shafer, 1973; Single, Kandel, & Faust, 1973). By 1972 approximately 1.5 million persons, or 6 percent of all young people between the ages of 12 and 17, acknowledged having at least tried heroin (Josephson & Carroll, 1974; Shafer, 1973). Fortunately, this figure has gone down over the years. In 1989 the number of high school seniors who had ever used heroin dropped to about 1.3 percent, and over half of them had not used it in the past year (Johnston, O'Malley, & Bachman, 1989, 1990).

When dissolved in water and injected into a vein (a method termed **mainlining**), heroin may produce an acute episode of nausea and vomiting ("a good sick") and heightened feelings of physical warmth, peacefulness, and increased self-esteem and confidence; some users have described the initial feelings as similar to a prolonged orgasm (*Committee*, 1982; Crowley & Rhine, 1985). In the words of a young San Francisco user, heroin is

> the mellowest downer of all. You get none of the side effects of speed and barbs. After you fix you feel the rush, like an orgasm if it's a good dope. Then you float for about four hours; nothing positive, just a normal feeling, nowhere. It's like being half asleep, like watching a movie: Nothing gets through to you, you're safe and warm. The big thing is, you don't hurt. You can walk around with rotting teeth and a busted appendix and not feel it. You don't need sex, you don't need food, you don't need people; you don't care. It's like death without permanence, life without pain (Luce, 1970, p. 10).

After about four hours the effects taper off. If the individual is not already addicted, the aftereffects may be confined to a slight irritability. However, if the individual is strongly addicted, within twelve hours or so he or she will begin to experience withdrawal symptoms: yawning, sweating, sniffling, and watering of the eyes, followed within another twenty-four hours by twitching and shaking, cramps, chills, vomiting, and diarrhea. The experience is much like an attack of the flu.

The potential danger of addiction to heroin is very real, despite the fact that, contrary to public opinion, not all users become addicts (Robins, 1979). Tolerance for the drug develops quickly, and ever-larger doses may be needed to maintain its effects and avoid withdrawal symptoms. Heroin acts as a strong depressant, and large doses may slow respiration to as little as two or three breaths a minute, thereby starving the brain of oxygen and leading to deep sleep, coma, shock, and even death. Other complications may include pneumonia or edema (i.e., waterlogging) of the lungs (Carroll, 1985; *Committee,* 1982).

Use of dirty needles, which is common among intravenous users of heroin and other drugs, is one of the causes of the spread of AIDS (acquired immuno-

Use of dirty needles, which is common among users of heroin and other drugs, is a major cause of the spread of AIDS.

deficiency syndrome), a fatal viral disease that destroys the ability of the immune system to ward off disease, as well as directly attacking the brain and possibly other organs. The overwhelming majority of cases of AIDS are transmitted through sexual relations and through the use of dirty needles (Turner, Miller, & Moses, 1989). Only a small number of cases result from blood transfusions or through transmission from mother to infant, although such transmission is more frequent in parts of Africa.

Psychological Characteristics. Heroin-dependent individuals have been variously described as immature, resentful of authority, passive–aggressive, emotionally labile, sexually inadequate, anxious, and socially isolated. They are also likely to have a low tolerance for frustration and a need for immediate gratification, as well as low self-esteem and a tendency to manipulate others (characteristics that are often associated with antisocial personality disorder) (Crowley & Rhine, 1985). It is sobering to find that the median age of of initial heroin experience in some urban ghettos is about 14 for males and 15 or 16 for females (Bernstein & Shkuda, 1974; Brunswick, Mergel & Messeri, 1985). Moreover, young people are usually introduced to the drug by peers rather than by adult pushers.

PATTERNS OF MULTIPLE DRUG USE

Thus far we have discussed the use of each of a variety of drugs separately. However, there is increasing evidence of multiple drug use among adolescents (Donovan & Jessor, 1983; Kandel, 1980; Kandel, Kessler, & Margulies, 1978; Keyes & Block, 1984; Welte & Barnes, 1985; Yamaguchi & Kandel, 1984). In general, users of one drug are more likely to use another drug that is similar with respect to its legal status and pharmacological properties than they are to use a dissimilar drug. Thus, in one extensive study (Single, Kandel, & Faust, 1974), the correlation between marijuana use and use of hashish was .78 and that between heroin use and cocaine use was .48. In contrast, the correlation between use of beer or wine and use of heroin was only .046. Heavy use of any drug markedly increases the likelihood of use of any other drug, legal or illegal (Kandel & Faust, 1975; Single, Kandel, & Faust, 1974; Yamaguchi & Kandel, 1984).

Young people who have used marijuana only once or twice are unlikely to use any other drugs, with the exception of alcohol. However, as marijuana use increases, the likelihood of using other drugs increases rapidly. Thus, in the 1970s among heavy marijuana users (sixty or more times) 84 percent also reported use of the pills (methedrine, amphetamine, barbiturates, or tranquilizers), 78 percent used LSD or other psychedelics, and 62 percent used cocaine, heroin, or narcotics other than heroin (Single, Kandel, & Faust, 1974). Other investigators have obtained similar results (Johnston, 1973; Josephson, 1974; Yamaguchi & Kandel, 1984).

Young people who become involved in the use of a variety of drugs appear to follow a chronological progression. Most users of heroin or other hard drugs have previously used marijuana; indeed, this fact was interpreted for many years by federal authorities and others as indicating that marijuana use leads to use of heroin. Two points need to be made in this regard, however: (1) Few adolescent marijuana users (9 percent or less) have ever tried heroin, and (2) prior use of marijuana among heroin users does not establish a causal relationship. It seems more likely that a person who is predisposed to heroin use, for whatever reasons, will also be predisposed to trying other drugs.

Nevertheless, it is interesting to note that when multiple use occurs there is a statistically significant pattern (Donovan & Jessor, 1983; Kandel, 1975; Kandel & Logan, 1984; Yamaguchi & Kandel, 1984a, 1986; Welte & Barnes, 1985). Beer and wine are most likely to be tried first, tobacco and hard liquor second, and marijuana third—followed in chronological order by the pills, psychedelics, tranquilizers, methamphetamine, cocaine, and heroin. If one were to accept the "first fatal step" theory that was formerly asserted by narcotics authorities, it would appear that cigarettes and alcohol would lead the way to, or at least share the limelight with, marijuana. However, for reasons more political and social than scientific, this was not the case historically, despite the fact that use of marijuana rarely takes place without prior use of liquor, tobacco, or both.

WHY DO ADOLESCENTS TAKE DRUGS?

The reasons that adolescents take drugs vary widely. So does the seriousness of their drug use. There is a world of difference between the curious young adolescent who has tried marijuana at a party and the lonely, despairing young person who has become hooked on heroin as "an escape to nowhere," in the words of a 14-year-old ex-addict, or the crack-dependent young mother who has abandoned her newborn infant or stopped caring for her other children (a problem whose frequency has more than doubled in less than two years) (Morning edition, PBS, 1989).

One reason adolescents may try a drug is simply because it is there. As noted at the beginning of the chapter, our entire society has, to a large extent, become a drug culture. We take drugs to relax, to restore energy, to sleep, to relieve anxiety and depression, to relieve boredom, and for many other purposes. It is no surprise that many adolescents, like adults, conclude that they can find "better living through chemistry."

Moreover, all kinds of drugs are readily available to young people (Johnston et al., 1989, 1990). Almost nine out of ten high school seniors in the United States recently reported that they could easily obtain marijuana, and the same can be said for amphetamines, cocaine, tranquilizers, and barbiturates (Johnston et al., 1989, 1990). In the inner cities of some metropolitan areas, drugs are virtually endemic. Unlike the average young person of fifty years ago, for whom opportunities for illicit drug use were limited to alcohol and tobacco, today's adolescent may choose from a cornucopia of drugs, both those sold in pharmacies and those available only on the street.

Adolescents characteristically are curious about their expanding world and far more inclined than most adults to take risks. They do so partly to prove their boldness ("not being chicken") and sense of adventure, and partly because they do not believe that anything disastrous can really happen to *them*. Thus, many adolescents may experiment with drugs merely because of curiosity, a sense of adventure, and opportunity (Johnston & O'Malley, 1986).

Parental Influences

Parents influence drug use through their own attitudes, values, and behavior and through the kinds of relationships they have with their children. Parents who believe strongly that drug use is harmful, socially unacceptable, or morally wrong, and who convey these attitudes to their children, are less likely to have children who engage in drug use (Brook, Lukoff, & Whiteman, 1980; Jessor, 1979, 1984b; Kandel, 1980). Parental use of tranquilizers, amphetamines, or barbiturates, as well as alcohol and tobacco, is positively correlated with use of marijuana and other illegal drugs by their children (Ellis & Stone, 1979; Kandel, 1980; Kandel, Kessler, & Margulies, 1978).

Some young people try drugs as a way of rebelling against the constraints imposed by adults, particularly parents. At one time or another all adolescents need ways of asserting independence from their parents. But whether this takes the form of serious drug use appears to depend to a large extent on the kind of relationship the adolescent has with his or her parents (Newcomb &

Box 11.3 WHAT CAN PARENTS DO?

In an era when the availability and use of drugs is widespread, even the most enlightened, sensible parents cannot guarantee that their children will not become involved in some experimentation with drugs. There are, however, a number of steps that parents can take to minimize the likelihood of adolescent drug use or to limit its seriousness. In particular, they can seek to keep open the lines of communication between themselves and their children, to be fair, and to encourage their children to participate in family decision making, while still retaining ultimate responsibility and expecting adherence to reasonable standards of behavior (Bell & Wildflower, 1983; Conger, 1979). In brief, parents should be authoritative, rather than authoritarian on the one hand, or permissive or neglectful on the other hand (see pages 203–207).

One study found that parents of drug-abusing adolescents were far more inclined than parents of normal adolescents to engage in *scapegoating*—blaming family problems and difficulties in decision making on the adolescent (Gantman, 1978). Moreover, they were far less likely to consult with the young person about his or her views; instead, they simply told the adolescent what to do. In addition, in the normal families all members were free to express themselves openly and there was greater clarity of communication and more equal participation by all family members.

Parents can also encourage their children long before the onset of adolescence, to begin learning to become more independent and to take increasing responsibility for their own actions. Obviously, such learning experiences should be geared to the age of the child and should be expanded only as the child becomes more mature. Parents who think that they can continue—sometimes indefinitely—to run the lives of their adolescent children and to protect them from any adverse consequences of their actions are not preparing them to cope with exposure to drugs—or with life itself.

In addition, parents need to remember that they are role models and that children take their cues from what parents do as well as from what they say. If parents present models of stable, responsible, problem-solving behavior, their children are likely to behave in those ways (see pages 213–214). With respect to drug use, we have already seen that drug-using parents are more likely to have drug-using children, even though the actual drugs may differ. If parents use drugs rarely, and only for responsible, well-defined purposes, their adolescents are much more likely to do the same than if the parents are constantly running from one drug to another to help them sleep, stay awake, relax, or cope with anxiety or pressure.

It is important for young people to know that their parents have basic values and that they are making a real effort to live by them. Whether the young person disagrees with some of those values is far less important than the knowledge that the values exist. In the end, this knowledge provides young people with a sense of trust and security, encourages them to think through their own basic values, and promotes respect for parents and willingness to listen to their views.

Finally, adolescents need to know that their parents really care about them, not just in the abstract but in concrete, demonstrated ways: through shared family activities, and by knowing about and taking an interest in their children's schoolwork, hobbies, friends, social life, goals, and dreams. None of these parental efforts can guarantee that a young person will not experiment with drugs, but they can do much to lessen its likelihood and to minimize its seriousness should it occur.

Bentler, 1988; Stone, Miranne, & Elliot, 1979). For a child of democratic, authoritative, loving parents (especially those with relatively traditional values) who give their children age-appropriate opportunities to test their wings, the risk of serious drug use is generally low (Bachman, 1970; Barnes, 1984; Jessor, 1984a, 1984b; Jessor & Jessor, 1977; Rees & Wilborn, 1983). But for a child whose parents have not been loving and are neglectful, overly permissive, or authoritarian and hostile, the risk of drug abuse is much greater (Barnes, 1984; Blum, 1970, 1972; Kovach & Glickman, 1986). One angry adolescent said of his parents, "They're always telling me what to do, like I don't have any mind of my own. And like my father is sitting around having his third martini before supper, and telling me like he's some big expert, and I'm an idiot, about how marijuana will destroy my brain. Well, the hell with him!" (Conger, 1979,

p. 82). Another adolescent, in contrast, seemed to be trying to get some response—any response—from her parents as a sign that they cared: "I've been on drugs since I was 12. My parents think I'm rebelling about something, but they don't know what. It's them. Not that they're strict. It's just that they're not really there and you feel you have to jump up and down and scream before they really notice" (Child Study Association, 1971, p. 24).

Peer Pressure

Peers play a major part in adolescent drug use (Brook, Lukoff, & Whiteman, 1980; Brunswick & Boyle, 1979; Elliott, Huizinga, & Ageton, 1985). Indeed, one of the best predictors of whether an adolescent will use a drug, and how heavily, is use of that drug by friends, especially the young person's best friend (Jessor, 1979; Kandel, 1980; Kovach & Glickman, 1986; Yamaguchi & Kandel, 1984).

For example, in a comprehensive study of drug use among public secondary school students in New York State, Denise Kandel (1973, 1974, 1980) and her associates found that involvement with other drug-using adolescents is a more important correlate of adolescent marijuana use than parental use of psychoactive drugs, including alcohol. For example, among participants whose best school friends had never used marijuana, only 15 percent reported using the drug themselves; in contrast, among subjects whose best school friends reported using marijuana sixty times or more, reports of use increased to 79 percent. However, parental use of these drugs (especially alcohol) also played a role, though a more modest one. The highest rates of marijuana usage were found among adolescents whose parents *and* best school friends were drug users (see Table 11.3).

T A B L E 11.3 ADOLESCENT MARIJUANA USE BY BEST SCHOOL FRIEND MARIJUANA USE AND PARENTAL PSYCHOACTIVE DRUGS USE

Parental Psychoactive Drug Use	Adolescents Having Ever Used Marijuana Best School Friend Marijuana Use	
	Never Used	Used
Never used:	13%	56%
Total N	(385)	(185)
Used:	17%	67%
Total N	(327)	(165)

Source: D. Kandel. Inter- and intragenerational influences on adolescent marijuana use. *Journal of Social Issues,* 1974, **30,** 107–135. By permission.

Note: Use patterns for each group are self-reported.

In Kandel's view, findings on the relative influence of parents and peers on adolescent drug use fit a "cultural deviance" model of behavior: The family can potentially lead the young person toward some form of socially disapproved behavior (e.g., drug use or delinquency) either because the family engages in the behavior itself and the young person imitates that behavior, or because the family creates a negative climate in the home and the young person seeks to escape from it. Yet even though either or both of these factors may characterize the family, the young person usually will not engage in deviant behavior unless such behavior is present in the immediate peer culture. "Peer behavior is the crucial determining factor in adolescent drug use; parental behavior becomes important when such behavior exists in the peer group" (Kandel, 1974, p. 126).

Because peers play such an important role in adolescent life, any evidence of changes in adolescent attitudes toward drugs is significant. Fortunately, in the last few years adolescent attitudes toward drug use have become much more critical (Bachman, Johnston, O'Malley, & Humphrey, 1988; Johnston et al., 1989, 1990). These shifts in attitudes closely parallel declines in the actual rates of use of most drugs in recent years (see Table 11.4 and 11.5).

At the same time, we should not forget the other side of the coin: Adolescents who have drug-using friends are more likely to use drugs. And finally, there are young people for whom drug use is a private response to stress, feelings of social isolation, low self-esteem, anxiety, depression, or alienation and hence is not directly related to peer group values and behavior (Conger, 1979; Kovach & Glickman, 1986; Slappy, 1985).

Escape from the Pressures of Life

Another reason adolescents give for using drugs is to escape from tension and the pressures of life, or from boredom (Conger, 1979; Johnston & O'Malley, 1986). Ironically, this is also a major reason why adults use drugs. The bored, depressed suburban homemaker who has a few drinks to get her through the day, and the highly pressured corporate executive who takes alcohol and barbiturates to relax or sleep and pep pills to combat fatigue, have much in common with the tense, jittery, insecure adolescent girl who tries to relax with marijuana, downers (barbiturates), and alcohol, or the boy who takes a few bennies (amphetamines) or cocaine to relieve his feelings of inadequacy and low self-esteem and give himself—if only briefly—a feeling of power, competence, and well-being.

When high school seniors were asked their reasons for using drugs, infrequent users tended to stress social or recreational reasons reflecting positive affect, such as "to have a good time with my friends" or "to feel good or get high." Heavy users (particularly daily users), while also acknowledging social or recreational reasons, were far more likely to cite reasons that involved coping with negative affect and stress, such as "to get away from my problems," "to deal with anger and frustration," "to relax and relieve tension," "to get through the day" (Johnston & O'Malley, 1986).

T A B L E 11.4 **TRENDS IN HARMFULNESS OF DRUGS AS PERCEIVED BY SENIORS**

Q. How much do you think people risk harming themselves (physically or in other ways) if they . . .	Percentage saying "great risk"[a]				
	Class of 1975	Class of 1976	Class of 1977	Class of 1978	Class of 1979
Try marijuana once or twice	15.1	11.4	9.5	8.1	9.4
Smoke marijuana occasionally	18.1	15.0	13.4	12.4	13.5
Smoke marijuana regularly	43.3	38.6	36.4	34.9	42.0
Try LSD once or twice	49.4	45.7	43.2	42.7	41.6
Take LSD regularly	81.4	80.8	79.1	81.1	82.4
Try PCP once or twice	NA	NA	NA	NA	NA
Try cocaine once or twice	42.6	39.1	35.6	33.2	31.5
Take cocaine occasionally	NA	NA	NA	NA	NA
Take cocaine regularly	73.1	72.3	68.2	68.2	69.5
Try "crack" once or twice	NA	NA	NA	NA	NA
Take "crack" occasionally	NA	NA	NA	NA	NA
Take "crack" regularly	NA	NA	NA	NA	NA
Try cocaine powder once or twice	NA	NA	NA	NA	NA
Take cocaine powder occasionally	NA	NA	NA	NA	NA
Take cocaine powder regularly	NA	NA	NA	NA	NA
Try heroin once or twice	60.1	58.9	55.8	52.9	50.4
Take heroin occasionally	75.6	75.6	71.9	71.4	70.9
Take heroin regularly	87.2	88.6	86.1	86.6	87.5
Try amphetamines once or twice	35.4	33.4	30.8	29.9	29.7
Take amphetamines regularly	69.0	67.3	66.6	67.1	69.9
Try barbiturates once or twice	34.8	32.5	31.2	31.3	30.7
Take barbiturates regularly	69.1	67.7	68.6	68.4	71.6
Try one or two drinks of an alcoholic beverage (beer, wine, liquor)	5.3	4.8	4.1	3.4	4.1
Take one or two drinks nearly every day	21.5	21.2	18.5	19.6	22.6
Take four or five drinks nearly every day	63.5	61.0	62.9	63.1	66.2
Have five or more drinks once or twice each weekend	37.8	37.0	34.7	34.5	34.9
Smoke one or more packs of cigarettes per day	51.3	56.4	58.4	59.0	63.0
Approx. N =	(2804)	(2918)	(3052)	(3770)	(3250)

Note: Level of significance of difference between the two most recent classes: $s = .05$, $ss = .01$, $sss = .001$, NA indicates data not available.
[a]Answer alternatives were: (1) No risk, (2) Slight risk, (3) Moderate risk, (4) Great risk, and (5) Can't say, drug unfamiliar.

Source: L. D. Johnston, P. M. O'Malley, and J. G. Bachman, Drug use, drinking, and smoking: National survey results from high school, college, and young adults populations, 1975–1988. Washington, DC: National Institute on Drug Abuse, 1989. By permission.

	Percentage saying "great risk"[a]							
Class of 1980	Class of 1981	Class of 1982	Class of 1983	Class of 1984	Class of 1985	Class of 1986	Class of 1987	Class of 1988
10.0	11.4	11.5	12.7	14.7	14.8	15.1	18.4	19.0
14.7	19.1	18.3	20.6	22.6	24.5	25.0	30.4	31.7
50.4	57.6	60.4	62.8	66.9	70.4	71.3	73.5	77.0
43.9	45.5	44.9	44.7	45.4	43.5	42.0	44.9	45.7
83.0	83.5	83.5	83.2	83.8	82.9	82.6	83.8	84.2
NA	NA	NA	NA	NA	NA	NA	55.6	58.8
31.3	32.1	32.8	33.0	35.7	34.0	33.5	47.9	51.2
NA	NA	NA	NA	NA	NA	54.2	66.8	69.2
69.2	71.2	73.0	74.3	78.8	79.0	82.2	88.5	89.2
NA	NA	NA	NA	NA	NA	NA	57.0	62.1
NA	NA	NA	NA	NA	NA	NA	70.4	73.2
NA	NA	NA	NA	NA	NA	NA	84.6	84.8
NA	NA	NA	NA	NA	NA	NA	45.3	51.7
NA	NA	NA	NA	NA	NA	NA	56.8	61.9
NA	NA	NA	NA	NA	NA	NA	81.4	82.9
52.1	52.9	51.1	50.8	49.8	47.3	45.8	53.6	54.0
70.9	72.2	69.8	71.8	70.7	69.8	68.2	74.6	73.8
86.2	87.5	86.0	86.1	87.2	86.0	87.1	88.7	88.8
29.7	26.4	25.3	24.7	25.4	25.2	25.1	29.1	29.6
69.1	66.1	64.7	64.8	67.1	67.2	67.3	69.4	69.8
30.9	28.4	27.5	27.0	27.4	26.1	25.4	30.9	29.7
72.2	69.9	67.6	67.7	68.5	68.3	67.2	69.4	69.6
3.8	4.6	3.5	4.2	4.6	5.0	4.6	6.2	6.0
20.3	21.6	21.6	21.6	23.0	24.4	25.1	26.2	27.3
65.7	64.5	65.5	66.8	68.4	69.8	66.5	69.7	68.5
35.9	36.3	36.0	38.6	41.7	43.0	39.1	41.9	42.6
63.7	63.3	60.5	61.2	63.8	66.5	66.0	68.6	68.0
(3234)	(3604)	(3557)	(3305)	(3262)	(3250)	(3020)	(3315)	(3276)

T A B L E 11.5 TRENDS IN PROPORTIONS OF SENIORS DISAPPROVING OF DRUG USE

Q. Do you disapprove of people (who are 18 or older) doing each of the following?[b]	Percentage "disapproving"[a]				
	Class of 1975	Class of 1976	Class of 1977	Class of 1978	Class of 1979
Try marijuana once or twice	47.0	38.4	33.4	33.4	34.2
Smoke marijuana occasionally	54.8	47.8	44.3	43.5	45.3
Smoke marijuana regularly	71.9	69.5	65.5	67.5	69.2
Try LSD once or twice	82.8	84.6	83.9	85.4	86.6
Take LSD regularly	94.1	95.3	95.8	96.4	96.9
Try cocaine once or twice	81.3	82.4	79.1	77.0	74.7
Take cocaine regularly	93.3	93.9	92.1	91.9	90.8
Try heroin once or twice	91.5	92.6	92.5	92.0	93.4
Take heroin occasionally	94.8	96.0	96.0	96.4	96.8
Take heroin regularly	96.7	97.5	97.2	97.8	97.9
Try amphetamines once or twice	74.8	75.1	74.2	74.8	75.1
Take amphetamines regularly	92.1	92.8	92.5	93.5	94.4
Try barbiturates once or twice	77.7	81.3	81.1	82.4	84.0
Take barbiturates regularly	93.3	93.6	93.0	94.3	95.2
Try one or two drinks of an alcoholic beverage (beer, wine, liquor)	21.6	18.2	15.6	15.6	15.8
Take one or two drinks nearly every day	67.6	68.9	66.8	67.7	68.3
Take four or five drinks nearly every day	88.7	90.7	88.4	90.2	91.7
Have five or more drinks once or twice each weekend	60.3	58.6	57.4	56.2	56.7
Smoke one or more packs of cigarettes per day	67.5	65.9	66.4	67.0	70.3
Approx. N =	(2677)	(2957)	(3085)	(3686)	(3221)

Note: Level of significance of difference between the two most recent classes: $s = .05$, $ss = .01$, $sss = .001$.
[a]Answer alternatives were: (1) Don't disapprove, (2) Disapprove, and (3) Strongly disapprove. Percentages are shown for categories (2) and (3) combined.
[b]The 1975 question asked about people who are "20 or older."

Source: L. D. Johnston, P. M. O'Malley, and J. G. Bachman, *Drug use, drinking, and smoking: National survey results from high school, college, and young adults populations, 1975–1988.* Washington, DC: National Institute on Drug Abuse, 1989. By permission.

	Percentage "disapproving"[a]							
Class of 1980	Class of 1981	Class of 1982	Class of 1983	Class of 1984	Class of 1985	Class of 1986	Class of 1987	Class of 1988
39.0	40.0	45.5	46.3	49.3	51.4	54.6	56.6	60.8
49.7	52.6	59.1	60.7	63.5	65.8	69.0	71.6	74.0
74.6	77.4	80.6	82.5	84.7	85.5	86.6	89.2	89.3
87.3	86.4	88.8	89.1	88.9	89.5	89.2	91.6	89.8
96.7	96.8	96.7	97.0	96.8	97.0	96.6	97.8	96.4
76.3	74.6	76.6	77.0	79.7	79.3	80.2	87.3	89.1
91.1	90.7	91.5	93.2	94.5	93.8	94.3	96.7	96.2
93.5	93.5	94.6	94.3	94.0	94.0	93.3	96.2	95.0
96.7	97.2	96.9	96.9	97.1	96.8	96.6	97.9	96.9
97.6	97.8	97.5	97.7	98.0	97.6	97.6	98.1	97.2
75.4	71.1	72.6	72.3	72.8	74.9	76.5	80.7	82.5
93.0	91.7	92.0	92.6	93.6	93.3	93.5	95.4	94.2
83.9	82.4	84.4	83.1	84.1	84.9	86.8	89.6	89.4
95.4	94.2	94.4	95.1	95.1	95.5	94.9	96.4	95.3
16.0	17.2	18.2	18.4	17.4	20.3	20.9	21.4	22.6
69.0	69.1	69.9	68.9	72.9	70.9	72.8	74.2	75.0
90.8	91.8	90.9	90.0	91.0	92.0	91.4	92.2	92.8
55.6	55.5	58.8	56.6	59.6	60.4	62.4	62.0	65.3
70.8	69.9	69.4	70.8	73.0	72.3	75.4	74.3	73.1
(3261)	(3610)	(3651)	(3341)	(3254)	(3265)	(3113)	(3302)	(3311)

As noted earlier, one of the greatest dangers of drug use by adolescents is that it can interfere with the developmental task of learning to deal with the daily problems and inevitable frustrations of living (see page 419). Persistent use of drugs to ward off reality and avoid this and other essential developmental tasks is likely to compromise the young person's ability to meet the demands of adulthood in a complex society (Baumrind, Moselle, & Martin, 1985; Kandel et al., 1986; Newcomb & Bentler, 1988).

Emotional Disturbance

For other young people, particularly heavy users of multiple drugs, reliance on drugs may reflect emotional disturbance and inability to cope with the demands of living or to find a meaningful personal identity. In some such cases we need to look to significant disturbances in family relationships during the course of development for clues to the young person's difficulties (Conger, 1979; Glynn, 1981; Konopka, 1976). Among adolescents in residential treatment centers and halfway houses for alcohol and drug users, common themes are feelings of parental rejection or indifference, lack of acceptance by peers, emotional isolation, and low self-esteem concealed behind a defense of appearing "cool" (Conger & Peterson, 1984).

In some cases a genetic predisposition may contribute to an adolescent's vulnerability to use of alcohol or other drugs. As we have seen, children and adolescents whose parents have a history of alcohol abuse are somewhat more likely than other children to become problem drinkers themselves, even if they have been separated from their parents at an early age. Although convincing evidence of genetic influences is lacking in the case of other drugs, such as cocaine, genetic factors may play a part in the development of some personality characteristics that are more frequently found in adolescents and adults who become heavy drug users. Such individuals tend to be impulsive, sensation seeking, restless, and emotionally labile (Kagan, Reznick, & Snidman, 1988; Plomin, 1986; Scarr & Kidd, 1983). In this way, genetic influences *might act indirectly* to increase an individual's likelihood of trying drugs or continuing to use them. In addition, excessive alcohol or drug use can *sometimes* be symptomatic of an underlying emotional disturbance (e.g., severe depression) in which genetic influences may play a part (Klerman, 1988; Puig-Antich, 1986; Vandenberg, Singer, & Pauls, 1986).

Some young people who have been using alcohol or drugs steadily since preadolescence acknowledge that they have never known any other way to cope with anxiety, boredom, depression, fear of failure, or lack of purpose. An important aim of one treatment program, in addition to helping young people learn to deal with their problems and establish genuine friendships with peers, was simply to teach them something many did not know how to do: how to have fun without using drugs!

Societal Rejection

In some cases of adolescent drug abuse, an indifferent society must share much of the blame. Many disadvantaged adolescents face the future without hope. Confronted with economic, social, and racial discrimination, with impossible living conditions, often with untreated physical ills, and with disorganization in their social environment and in their own families, they may give up the search for meaning and identity and seek escape in drugs like crack cocaine, methamphetamines, hard narcotics, or other drugs that have yet to come upon the scene.

In sum, unless our society becomes willing to match the rhetoric of the "war on drugs" with a far greater commitment to action—not only in law enforcement efforts but in education, treatment, and above all, prevention—hundreds of thousands of children will be permanently lost to society and to any hope of a productive, rewarding existence.

SUMMARY

Drug use and abuse did not begin with the "youth revolution" of the 1960s. Although there are significant generational differences in patterns of drug use, our society has been developing into a "drug culture" for many years. It is also important to recognize that the "drug problem" is actually twofold. The problem among economically favored, well-educated adolescents, youth, and young adults is not the same as the problem among impoverished, poorly educated young people growing up in economically depressed, socially disorganized, crime-ridden sections of large cities. The drug problems in these two groups differ significantly in terms of root causes, severity of the problem, and prospects for change.

Overall, drug use by young people has been declining in recent years. Nevertheless, there is little room for complacency: Nearly 20 percent of high school seniors still report using marijuana in the past thirty days; 5 percent have tried "crack"; and one-third report that they had five or more drinks in a row in the past two weeks.

The problem is far worse, however, for young people living in deteriorated crime-ridden neighborhoods in large metropolitan areas. For many of them drug dealing may appear to be the easiest, most lucrative escape from poverty. For others, vulnerability to drug use is increased by easy accessibility, peer influence, and a pervasive sense of hopelessness and despair.

One of the most frightening aspects of drug abuse is the number of young women using cocaine, alcohol, amphetamines, and other drugs during pregnancy, often causing neurobiological impairment in their infants. The rapid spread of "crack," a cheap, extremely potent, highly addictive form of cocaine, has created major problems for drug treatment centers and law enforcement officers, especially in large metropolitan areas.

Despite the widespread public concern about other drugs, alcohol is by far the most widely used and abused drug (distantly followed by cigarettes and marijuana). Although use of alcohol has decreased in recent years, nearly 10 percent of 14-year-olds are problem drinkers. Heavy drinking during pregnancy can result in fetal alcohol syndrome; even smaller doses increase the likelihood of low birthweight and developmental delays.

Cigarette smoking among adolescents reached a peak in 1976–1977, after which it declined until 1989. At present smoking is slightly more prevalent among girls than among boys (31 percent versus 27 percent), a reversal of traditional patterns. Because smoking is "the largest preventable cause of death," there is an urgent need for further reduction in rates of smoking. Adolescents who smoke are aware of the dangers, but the addictive properties of nicotine make it difficult to quit. Prevention therefore appears to offer the greatest promise.

Marijuana use reached an all-time high in 1978–1979 and has since declined markedly. For example, the number of high school seniors using marijuana during the past month decreased from 36 percent to 16.7 percent between 1978 to 1989, largely as a function of a steady increase in perceived risk associated with the drug.

Other drugs, including cocaine, barbiturates, tranquilizers, amphetamines, hallucinogens, inhalants, and narcotics (e.g., heroin), were used far less frequently than alcohol, tobacco, and marijuana, and use of those drugs generally declined throughout the past decade. An exception is use of cocaine, which reached a peak among adolescents and young adults in the mid-1980s but has since declined sharply, primarily because of increased awareness of the dangers associated with it. In contrast, among inner-city adolescents and young adults, use of cocaine, particularly "crack," has increased rapidly in recent years.

Adolescents take drugs for a wide range of reasons, and the seriousness of their drug use also varies widely. One reason that adolescents may try a drug is simply its easy availability. Adolescents are curious about their expanding world and more inclined than adults to take risks. Other important reasons include parental influences, peer pressure, desire to escape from the pressures of life, emotional disturbance, and societal rejection.

Unless our society becomes willing to match the rhetoric of the "war on drugs" with a far greater commitment to effective action, hundreds of thousands of children will be permanently lost to society and to any hope of a productive, rewarding existence.

REVIEW QUESTIONS

1. What are the "two worlds of drugs," and how do they differ?
2. Did overall drug use among high school students increase, decrease, or remain steady during the 1980s? Were these exceptions to the overall pattern? Which three drugs are most frequently used by adolescents?
3. What have been the effects of the rise in the use of "crack," especially among young people in inner cities? Why has "crack" use spread so rapidly? How does "crack" differ from "regular" cocaine?
4. How do adolescents who are heavy drinkers, moderate drinkers, or abstainers differ from one another in personality characteristics and behavior?
5. What causes fetal alcohol syndrome, and what are its effects?

6. What is known about the short- and long-term consequences of heavy marijuana use?
7. How do the personality characteristics of early marijuana users, late users, and nonusers differ?
8. Name five reasons why adolescents take drugs. Discuss each briefly.

RECOMMENDED READINGS

Bachman, J. G., Johnston, L. D., O'Malley, P. M., & Humphrey, R. H. (1988). Explaining the recent decline in marijuana use: Differentiating the effects and perceived risks, disapproval, and general lifestyle factors. *Journal of Health and Social Behavior,* **29,** 92–112.

Baumrind, D., Moselle, K. A., & Martin, J. A. (1985). Adolescent drug abuse research: A critical examination from a developmental perspective. *Advances in Alcohol and Substance Abuse,* **4,** 41–67.

Crowley, T. J. (1987). Clinical issues in cocaine abuse. In S. Fisher, A. Raskin, & E. H. Uhlenhuth (Eds.), *Cocaine: Clinical and Behavioral Aspects* (pp. 193–211). New York: Oxford University Press.

Johnston, L. D., O'Malley, P. M., & Bachman, J. G. (1990). *Drug use, drinking, and smoking: National survey results from high school, college, and young adults populations, 1975–1989.* Washington, DC: National Institute on Drug Abuse.

Kandel, D. B. (1985). On processes of peer influences in adolescent drug use: A developmental perspective. *Advances in Alcohol and Substance Abuse,* **4,** 139–163.

Newcomb, M. D., & Bentler, P. M. (1988). *Consequences of adolescent drug use: Impact on the lives of young adults.* Newbury Park, CA: Sage.

HAPPY BIRTHDAY PLANET EARTH!

MORAL DEVELOPMENT AND VALUES

At no time in life is a person as likely to be concerned about moral values and standards as during adolescence. This should not be surprising. In the first place, rapid cognitive development tends to make adolescents more aware of moral questions and values and better able to deal with them in a relatively sophisticated way. In addition, the social expectations and demands confronting young people, and the experiences they are undergoing, change at an accelerated rate during these years. As Erik Erikson noted, this is especially true in the United States: "This is the country of changes; it is obsessed with change" (Erikson, 1968, p. 29). And seldom has change, and our preoccupation with it, been greater than in the last two decades (Conger, 1981, 1988).

As a consequence, the developing adolescent is likely to be exposed to a multiplicity of shifting, sometimes conflicting, values and standards of behavior. The task of choosing among these values and standards is complicated by the fact that there is a discrepancy between adolescents' increased capacity for comprehending moral issues, on the one hand, and their limited experience in dealing with moral issues and their consequences in everyday life, on the other hand.

Nevertheless, moral choices must be made. Under circumstances in which diversity and change are the order of the day, the problem of developing a strong sense of identity cannot be separated from the problem of values. If young people are to maintain some stability in their conception of self and in their internal guides to action, they must be faithful to some basic values. They may have to adopt new ways of implementing those values to meet changing circumstances. But if the values are there and are sound, young people will be able to adapt to change while remaining constant in their conceptions of self and faithful to their central values (Conger, 1988; Erikson, 1983; Logan, 1980).

Although there is little debate about the importance of moral issues and values to adolescents, there is considerable controversy about the nature of **moral development,** its maturational course, and the factors influencing it. Three basic approaches have been taken toward understanding moral development: cognitive, affective, and social (Youniss, 1981). The cognitive view of moral development focuses on moral reasoning and considers cognitive development to be the necessary stimulus for changes in moral development, with changes occurring in predictable stages paralleling the stages of cognitive development. The affective perspective on moral development focuses primarily on the role of empathy, sympathy, and guilt, which are thought to be influenced by socialization. The social perspective views morality as linked primarily to peer experiences and the related sense of community. Although each of these aspects is probably involved in moral development, each is based on somewhat different assumptions and theoretical orientations, as we shall see.

Morality is a complex phenomenon. A fully developed individual morality has been described as involving four elements: (1) recognition of, and sensitivity to, a given social situation, leading to an awareness that a moral problem exists; (2) moral judgment, in order to determine what ought to be done in a given situation; (3) values and influences that affect one's plan of action consistent with moral ideals, but that consider nonmoral values and goals that the situation may activate, as well as the influence of situational pressures; and (4) execution and implementation of moral action, involving behavior consistent with one's goals despite distractions, impediments, and incidental adjustment (Carroll & Rest, 1982; Rest, 1986).

Too often there has been a tendency to view morality in terms of a single component. For example, some have argued that morality involves the ability to think adequately about a moral situation. Others have construed morality as primarily involving values. Still others have argued that it has to do mainly with what people do, rather than what they think or believe.

It seems clear, however, that morality involves all of these components. A person may fail to act morally because of lack of sensitivity to the needs of others, because of limited cognitive capacities, because of constraints in the situation (e.g., threats from others), or because of some limitation that prevents him or her from carrying out the appropriate behavior (e.g., not knowing how to swim and hence, not rescuing someone who is drowning).

COGNITIVE GROWTH AND STAGES OF MORAL DEVELOPMENT

Jean Piaget's conceptualization of moral development stimulated much further research in this area. Piaget (1948) argued that the organizing principles of the child's world, though different from those of the adult's world, have a coherent structure of their own. This view contrasted sharply with the dominant view of the time, in which moral development was viewed primarily as a process of socialization whereby the moral standards of the adult world were taught to children and eventually internalized by them (Durkheim, 1961). Although Piaget did not dispute the importance of socialization, he maintained that the organization of moral thought in younger children is quite distinct from that found in older children and adults. According to Piaget, younger children base their moral judgments largely on the consequences of one's actions, whereas older children are more likely to take intentions into account.

One method Piaget used in his investigations of morality was to present subjects with a pair of hypothetical stories. One such story depicted a boy who knocked over fifteen cups while coming to dinner; the other story depicted a boy who broke one cup while attempting to sneak some jam out of a cupboard. Younger children were more likely to consider the first boy naughtier because he broke fifteen cups while the second boy broke only one. Older children consistently viewed the second boy as naughtier because he was trying to sneak some jam.

While generally supporting Piaget's position, recent research has shown that the situation is more complex than Piaget thought (Karniol, 1978; Rest, 1983). In the example cited earlier, Piaget confounded *consequences* (the number of broken cups) with *intentions* (trying to sneak jam versus an accident). However, when children are presented with stories in which intent can be separated from outcome, even 6-year-olds are able to use intentions as a basis for their moral judgments (Feldman, Klosson, Parsons, Rholes, & Ruble, 1976).

Kohlberg's Stages of Moral Development

Piaget's work was extended and refined by the late Lawrence Kohlberg, a psychologist at Harvard and his associates (Colby and Kohlberg, 1987; Colby et al., 1980; Kohlberg, 1976, 1979, 1984). They expanded Piaget's method by presenting a more complicated set of moral dilemmas that involve twelve basic moral concepts, values, or issues. Subjects are asked to describe what the actor in the moral dilemma ought to do, and to justify that course of action. For example, in order to gain information about a subject's conceptualization of "the basis of moral worth of human life," he or she is asked such questions as whether a druggist should give a life-saving drug to a dying woman when her husband cannot pay for it, and whether it is better to save the life of one important person or the lives of a large number of unimportant people.

On the basis of the responses obtained, the investigators concluded that children and adolescents tend to progress through six stages of moral thought, which are divided into three major levels: **preconventional, conventional,** and **postconventional** or autonomous (Kohlberg & Gilligan, 1971).

During the preschool years the child is governed mostly by whatever he or she wants to do at a particular moment. With the advent of concrete-operational thinking, however, the child may enter the first of two preconventional stages of moral development (see Table 12.1). During this stage the child is responsive to cultural labels of "good" and "bad" but interprets these labels largely in terms of their physical consequences (i.e., reward or punishment). Behaviors that are punished are perceived as bad and to be avoided, and there is likely to be an "unquestioning deference to superior power" (Kohlberg & Gilligan, 1971, p. 1067).

During the second preconventional stage some progress is made beyond this rather simplistic notion. At this juncture the child is more likely to conform in order to obtain rewards, have favors returned, and the like. "Human relations are viewed in terms like those of the market place. Elements of fairness, reciprocity, and equal sharing are present, but they are always interpreted in a physical, pragmatic way. Reciprocity is a matter of 'you scratch my back and I'll scratch yours,' not of loyalty, gratitude, or justice" (Kohlberg & Gilligan, 1971, p. 1067). For example, when asked, "Should Joe tell on his older brother to his father?" (for going somewhere he was not supposed to go), one boy replied, "I think he should keep quiet. He might want to go someplace like that, and if he squeals on Alex [the older brother], Alex might squeal on him" (Kohlberg, 1969, p. 243).

In our society, by the time the average child reaches adolescence his or her thinking about moral issues has already shifted away from the most basic preconventional mode, in which the child is governed by literal obedience to rules and authority with the aim of avoiding punishment. A majority of children have also begun to shift away from the second preconventional stage, which is characterized by a rather simply conceived doctrine of reciprocity— acting to meet one's own needs and letting others do the same, and doing what is "fair" or what constitutes an equal exchange. The moral orientation in this stage is still primarily individualistic and egocentric, and the rights of others are seen rather concretely as coexisting with one's own (Kohlberg, 1976).

During adolescence, conventional moral thinking tends to be dominant. In conventional morality a focus on societal needs and values takes precedence over individual interests. Initially this is likely to involve a strong emphasis on being "a good person in your own eyes and those of others" (Kohlberg, 1976, p. 34), which means having good motives and showing concern about others. Typically, there is considerable emphasis on conformity to stereotypical images of majority or "natural" behavior. Reflecting increased cognitive development, the intentions behind behavior, not simply the behavior itself, take on greater importance; one seeks approval by "being good." This approach is subsequently expanded to include an

> orientation toward authority, fixed rules, and the maintenance of the social order. Right behavior consists of doing one's duty, showing respect for authority, and maintaining the given social order for its own sake. At this stage, a *social perspective* takes precedence; there is concern not only with conformity to one's social order, but also with maintaining, supporting, and justifying this order (Kohlberg & Gilligan, 1971, p. 1067).

Contrary to earlier assumptions, it appears that many adolescents (and adults) may not advance beyond this level (Edwards, 1980; Kohlberg, 1971; Rest, 1983, 1986; Turiel, Edwards, & Kohlberg, 1978). Some, however, do advance to what Kohlberg calls postconventional or principled thinking. At this level, particular societal arrangements are seen as deriving from a broader moral perspective, which the rational, moral individual has to develop for herself or himself; Kohlberg calls this a "prior-to-society" perspective (Colby, Kohlberg, Gibbs, & Lieberman, 1980; Kohlberg, 1976). Reflecting the acquisition of formal-operational thinking, this level is characterized by a "major thrust toward abstract moral principles which are universally applicable, and not tied to any particular social group" (Kohlberg & Gilligan, 1971, pp. 1066–1067). In the most advanced, and least often achieved, stage of formal principled thinking, there is an effort to formulate abstract ethical principles that appeal to logical comprehensiveness, universality, and consistency.

With more advanced, less concrete cognitive and moral development, the adolescent may no longer be able to adopt without question, the social or political beliefs of his or her parents' conviction that solely because the parents have particular beliefs all right-thinking persons must necessarily share them (Elkind, 1968, 1984). There is a new-found "relativism of personal values and opinions and a corresponding emphasis upon procedural rules for reaching consensus" (Kohlberg & Gilligan, 1971, p. 1067). Thus, when asked whether a husband should steal an expensive black-market drug from an exploitive druggist to save his wife's life, Steve, age 16, answered, "By the law of society he was wrong but by the law of nature or of God the druggist was wrong and the husband was justified. Human life is above financial gain. Regardless of who was dying, if it was a total stranger, man has a duty to save him from dying"

T A B L E 12.1 SIX STAGES OF MORAL DEVELOPMENT

Level and Stage	What is Right	Reasons for Doing Right	Social Perspective of Stage
Level 1: Preconventional			
Stage 1: Heteronomous morality	To avoid breaking rules backed by punishment, obedience for its own sake, and avoiding phyical damage to persons and property.	Avoidance of punishment, and the superior power of authorities.	*Egocentric point of view.* Doesn't consider the interests of others or recognize that they differ from the actor's; doesn't relate two points of view. Actions are considered physically rather than in terms of psychological interests of others. Confusion of authority's perspective with one's own.
Stage 2: Individualism, instrumental purpose, and exchange	Following rules only when it is in someone's immediate interest; acting to meet one's own interests and needs and letting others do the same. Right is also what's fair, what's an equal exchange, a deal, an agreement.	To serve one's own needs or interests in a world where you have to recognize that other people have their interests, too.	*Concrete individualistic perspective.* Aware that everybody has his own interest to pursue and these conflict, so that right is relative (in the concrete individualistic sense).
Level II: Conventional			
Stage 3: Mutual interpersonal expectations, relationships, and interpersonal conformity	Living up to what is expected by people close to you or what people generally expect of people in your role as son, brother, friend, etc. "Being good" is important and means having good motives, showing concern about others. It also means keeping mutual relationships, such as trust, loyalty, respect, and gratitude.	The need to be a good person in your own eyes and those of others. Your caring for others. Belief in the Golden Rule. Desire to maintain rules and authority which support stereotypical good behavior.	*Perspective of the individual in relationships with other individuals.* Aware of shared feelings, agreements, and expectations which take primacy over individual interests. Relates points of view through the concrete Golden Rule, putting yourself in the other guy's shoes. Does not yet consider generalized system perspective.
Stage 4: Social system and conscience	Fulfilling the actual duties to which you have agreed.	To keep the institution going as a whole, to avoid the	*Differentiates societal point of view from interpersonal*

	What is right	Reasons for doing right	Social perspective of stage
		breakdown in the system "if everyone did it," or the imperative of conscience to meet one's defined obligations. (Easily confused with Stage 3 belief in rules and authority.)	*agreements or motives.* Takes the point of view of the system that defines roles and rules. Considers individual relations in terms of place in the system.

Level III: Postconventional, or autonomous

	What is right	Reasons for doing right	Social perspective of stage
Stage 5: Social contract or utility and individual rights	Being aware that people hold a variety of values and opinions, that most values and rules are relative to your group. These relative rules should usually be upheld, however, in the interest of impartiality and because they are the social contract. Some nonrelative values and rights like *life* and *liberty,* however, must be upheld in any society and regardless of majority opinion.	A sense of obligation to law because of one's social contract to make and abide by laws for the welfare of all and for the protection of all people's rights. A feeling of contractual commitment, freely entered upon, to family, friendship, trust, and work obligations. Concern that laws and duties be based on rational calculation of overall utility, "the greatest good for the greatest number."	*Prior-to-society perspective.* Perspective of a rational individual aware of values and rights prior to social attachments and contracts. Integrates perspectives by formal mechanisms of agreement, contract, objective impartiality, and due process. Considers moral and legal points of view; recognizes that they sometimes conflict and finds it difficult to integrate them.
Stage 6: Universal ethical principles	Following self-chosen ethical principles. Particular laws or social agreements are usually valid because they rest on such principles. When laws violate these principles, one acts in accordance with the principle. Principles are universal principles of justice: the equality of human rights and respect for the dignity of human beings as individual **persons.**	The belief as a rational person in the validity of universal moral principles, and a sense of personal commitment to them.	*Perspective of a moral point of view* from which social arrangements derive. Perspective is that of any rational individual recognizing the nature of morality or the fact that persons are ends in themselves and must be treated as such.

Source: L. Kohlberg. Moral stages and moralization. In T. Lickona (Ed.). *Moral development and behavior.* New York: Holt, Rinehart and Winston, 1976. By permission.

(Kohlberg, 1969, p. 244). A number of studies have shown that a certain level of cognitive development is necessary, but not sufficient, for a given level of moral reasoning (Rowe & Marcia, 1980; Walker, 1980; Walker & Richards, 1979).

Because the method of scoring the moral dilemmas developed by Kohlberg is so complicated and requires a great deal of training, another method of assessment, called the Defining Issues Test (DIT), was developed by James Rest, a psychologist at the University of Minnesota. It is based on the same theoretical perspective as Kohlberg's method, but it uses a multiple-choice format and can be objectively scored (Rest, 1979, 1983, 1986). In addition to these format differences, the DIT is a *recognition task* that involves identifying the way of thinking most like the subject's, whereas Kohlberg's test is a *production task* that requires subjects to generate a line of reasoning on their own. Consequently, these two methods tend to yield similar, but not identical, results.

The six-stage model of moral judgment has been validated in both cross-sectional and longitudinal studies using both of these methods (Colby & Kohlberg, 1987; Colby et al., 1980; Holstein, 1976; Rest, 1979, 1986). Change from one stage of moral development to another appears to be gradual and slow, with considerable overlap between stages (Carroll & Rest, 1982; Walker, 1989). Although some longitudinal studies indicate that about 7 percent of the participants actually move downward in moral level at some juncture, most of the movement is upward. In a twenty-year longitudinal study, Kohlberg and his colleagues found a gradual change in all subjects, with all subjects showing the same sequence of stages and no subjects skipping a stage (Colby et al., 1980). Similar results have been found in societies as diverse as Mexico, Turkey, Britain, Canada, and New Zealand. However, development tends to be slower and more limited in more traditional, lower-class, and rural areas (Colby et al., 1980; Edwards, 1977; Turiel, Edwards, & Kohlberg, 1978).

Although level of moral judgment is strongly related to level of cognitive development, these two dimensions are not identical. A certain level of cognitive development may be necessary but not sufficient for a given level of moral reasoning (Walker, 1980). Thus, children who have advanced cognitive capacity will not necessarily demonstrate moral reasoning at the corresponding level (Rowe & Marcia, 1980).

Influences on Moral Development

Piaget suggested that moral development was influenced by cognitive disequilibrium and by experiences of cooperation with peers (Piaget 1970). Kohlberg emphasized the importance of social experiences, particularly opportunities for role playing, in which the individual is able to take the viewpoint of another person, as in the case of shared confidences among friends in childhood and adolescence (Kohlberg, 1969; Rest, 1986). Others have stressed the importance of breadth and diversity in life experiences (Deemer, in press; Rest, 1986; Spickelmier, 1983).

There is support for each of these assertions. Moral judgment is strongly correlated with level of formal education and degree of involvement in educational activities generally, which increase opportunities to be exposed to diverse and sometimes conflicting views (cognitive disequilibrium) and to peer influences (Barnett & Volker, 1985; Colby et al., 1983; Deemer, in press; Rest, 1979, 1986). For most people, it is not specific moral experiences (e.g., moral education programs, or being confronted with moral crises) that foster moral development, "but rather becoming more aware of the social world in general and one's place in it" (Rest, 1986, p. 177; Carroll & Rest, 1982). Parental support and encouragement, exposure to stimulating and challenging social and cultural environments, and meeting new and different kinds of people all appear to foster a higher level of moral development (Mischel & Mischel, 1976; Rest, 1986). Of course, an individual must also be prepared to profit from such opportunities: "The people who develop in moral judgment are those who love to learn, who seek new challenges, who enjoy intellectually stimulating environments, who are reflective, who make plans and set goals, who take risks, who see themselves in the larger social contexts of history and institutions and broad cultural trends, who take responsibility for themselves and their environs" (Rest, 1986, p. 57).

CHANGING SOCIETAL DEMANDS

Changing societal demands during adolescence are likely to increase preoccupation with moral values. The younger child lives in a world that is relatively more homogeneous, more immediate, and more limited than that of the adolescent. As a result, there are fewer occasions for making moral choices. Living according to a fairly circumscribed set of rules established for the most part by parents, the child and his or her peers learn to satisfy their needs within this context. Granted, the child must establish internal controls as a necessary part of socialization, and controls are related to the problem of values. But establishing controls is not synonymous with learning to make value decisions, often under ambiguous circumstances.

In contrast, adolescents *must* make choices. Not only are they changing, but the immediate social world, and their relations with it, are changing too. As they progress through adolescence, young people are confronted with an increasingly diverse world in which the opportunities and the necessity for choice are multiplied. They find, for example, that there are many ways to live their lives and that they must make choices. How will they earn a living? What sort of person do they eventually want to marry—if, in fact, they want to marry at all?

Such choices cannot be made independently from personal values, although of course many other factors are also involved. An adolescent who is strongly convinced of the importance of helping others, may make a different career choice than one who places a high value on material success. If he or she believes more in freedom and autonomy than in security, different choices

City Year, a privately funded youth service program in Boston whose members' ethnic, economic and social diversity is a source of pride to the city, work together to help Boston's most vulnerable residents. Members—some from affluent suburbs and others from inner-city neighborhoods—spend a year sharing their lives with and helping the poor, homeless, and physically and mentally disabled. Here, they are removing debris from the Berkley Community Garden, where food is grown in Boston's South End.

may be also made. If young people believe that honesty is the best policy, they may be less likely to enter certain occupations than if they believe that there's a sucker born every minute and that an individual's main responsibility is to survive in a social jungle.

As we have seen, the time perspective of adolescents, in contrast to that of children, becomes greatly extended (particularly into the future); this, too, increases the urgency of developing a set of values (Erikson, 1968, 1983). The adolescent who is beginning to think about an entire lifetime is much more in need of a set of guiding moral principles to lend a semblance of order, consistency, and meaning to life than a child whose chief concern at a given moment may be whether he or she will be going to an amusement park or to the dentist the next day.

Moreover, the adolescent is confronted with a wider range of conflicting pressures for the adoption or modification of personal values than is the case for the younger child. The peer group may be urging one set of values and the parents another. The adolescent may be motivated to conform to the values of peers in order to gain acceptance or to avoid rejection. Increasingly, too, other influences enter the arena of moral choice—including teachers, books, television, and representatives of conflicting groups in the broader society.

Such conflicting pressures have always been part of adolescence, but they appear to have increased significantly during recent decades as the divisions among both adults and adolescents have been magnified and society has been confronted with more issues on which consensus is difficult to attain. This has made it more difficult for young people to progress from a "father knows best" sort of preadolescent moral thought to the beginning of postconventional thought, with its emphasis on social consensus (Turiel, 1974, 1983). And it appears to have increased the danger that some adolescents will fall into an extreme and chronic kind of moral relativism at this critical juncture in their development. There is also the danger, on the other hand, that adolescents will adopt a very rigid moral stance, as is seen among some cults that are popular with a small percentage of adolescents.

INTRAPSYCHIC CONFLICT, MORAL VALUES, AND MORAL DEVELOPMENT

To complicate matters further, the adolescent may need to wrestle with moral value judgments not simply for their own sake but also as a way of coping with personal problems (Conger & Petersen, 1984; A. Freud, 1965, 1969; Mussen, Conger, Kagan, & Huston, 1990). Value conflicts are often "chosen" by adolescents for internal and usually unconscious reasons (Douvan & Adelson, 1966). For example, preoccupation with the moral issues of war and peace, or the nature of aggression, may reveal a rational concern with these matters for their own sake. But they may also reflect concern with being able to handle aggressive feelings, a concern that is related to greater size and strength as well as to increased expectations of assertion and dominance, particularly for boys.

Similarly, the involvement of adolescents in cults or restrictive religious groups may be a way of resolving moral dilemmas by letting the group dictate the adolescent's values and behavior. Differences with parents over moral or political values and beliefs may reflect the adolescent's efforts to establish an independent identity or to express a deep resentment toward parental hostility or indifference.

In brief, the increased preoccupation with moral values and beliefs that characterizes many adolescents is likely to have its roots in expanded cognitive development, increased—and often contradictory—societal demands, and intimate (often unconscious) intrapsychic concerns and conflicts.

Moral Relativism, Identity, and Social Change

During adolescence the young person progresses from conventional moral reasoning—with its rather simplistic, absolute concepts of what is right and true, and its dependence on socially accepted stereotypes and respect for authority—to principled moral reasoning. The ability to make this progression depends on the development of the capacity for formal-operational thought, which includes the ability to think hypothetically, that is, to consider a variety of possible solutions rather than simply looking for the "right" answer.

The ability to think hypothetically, so obvious in intellectual problem solving, extends equally to moral problems. In some ways it is a two-edged sword. On the one hand, it can help free the young person from rigid, arbitrary, stereotyped thinking and promote flexibility and adaptability in the search for values that will be internally consistent and principled. On the other hand, it can be overwhelming. Freed from conventional morality, the adolescent may find himself or herself adrift in a sea of possible alternatives and may conclude that there is no way of choosing among them—that one set of beliefs or values is no better or worse than another.

The danger of this transitional period in cognitive and moral development, then, is one of what Kohlberg calls *extreme relativism.* It is well illustrated in the following statement by one of Kohlberg's subjects, an upper-middle-class high school student:

> I don't think anybody should be swayed by the dictates of society. It's probably very much up to the individual all the time and there's no general principle except when the views of society seem to conflict with your views and your opportunities at the moment and it seems that the views of society don't really have any basis as being right and in that case, most people, I think, would tend to say forget it and I'll do what I want (Kohlberg & Gilligan, 1971, p. 1074).

Relativism and Identity. Some adolescents go through a period of **moral relativism;** others do not. For those who do, this stage may be transitional and brief, or prolonged and, in a few cases, chronic. As might be anticipated, these varying response patterns are related to the problem of identity. In one study of identity development, college students were divided into four categories based on identity status: (1) identity achievement (those who had gone through an identity crisis, resolved it, and found new commitments); (2) psychosocial moratorium (those who were still in an identity crisis, with only vague commitments); (3) identity foreclosure (those who had experienced no crisis but were committed to the goals and values of parents or significant others); and (4) identity diffusion (those who had no commitment, regardless of whether they had experienced crisis) (Podd, 1972).

Subjects were also grouped according to level of moral development: conventional (stages 3 and 4), principled (stages 5 and 6), and transitional. The last group was further subdivided into those who manifested a combination of conventional and principled thinking and those who were extreme relativists (i.e., rejected conventional thought and appeared to be operating on the basis of stage 2 "instrumental hedonism").

The investigators found that two-thirds of the principled subjects were in the identity achievement category. Forty percent of conventional subjects also fell into this group, and the remainder fell primarily into the identity foreclosure group. None of the morally transitional subjects fell into the identity achievement group, and very few fell into the identity foreclosure group. It appears that "to have questioned conventional morality you must have questioned your identity as well, though you may continue to hold a conventional moral position after having done so" (Kohlberg & Gilligan, 1971, p. 1078). However, as this research also indicates, many morally conventional students have never encountered a period of identity crisis or questioning. "An adolescent stage of identity crisis and its resolutions," the researchers concluded, "is a picture dependent upon attainment of formal logical thought and of questioning of conventional morality. It fits best, then, the picture of adolescence in the developmentally elite and needs further elaboration for other adolescents" (Kohlberg & Gilligan, 1971, p. 1078).

Subsequent studies obtained similar results (Rowe & Marcia, 1980). In one study, however, students in the moratorium category also had high moral reasoning scores, like those of students in the identity achievement category; both groups of students had higher moral-reasoning scores than those with foreclosed or diffused identities (Hult, 1979).

SOCIALIZATION TECHNIQUES AND MORAL DEVELOPMENT

Thus far the primary emphasis has been on factors that sensitize adolescents to questions related to moral values and influence the degree of sophistication with which they conceptualize moral problems. But there is another side to the issue of moral development: the extent to which, and the manner in which, cognitive understanding is reflected in behavior (Blasi, 1980; M. L. Hoffman, 1970; Hogan, 1975; Rest, 1980, 1983). It is clear that a person may be able to conceptualize moral issues with considerable sophistication and to formulate the proper moral course to take, yet may not always act in accordance with that formulation (Blasi, 1980, 1984; Rest, 1983, 1986). In addition, morality may be distinct from understanding of and adherence to social convention (Turiel, 1983).

In one study (Tapp & Levine, 1972), subjects were first asked, "Why should people follow rules?" and were then asked, "Why do *you* follow rules?" In responding to the latter question, most middle-school children and adolescents showed a shift toward earlier, more "primitive" levels of moral development, although they were cognitively capable of understanding loftier reasons and subscribed to them. For example, although only 3 percent of older adolescents said that people *should* follow rules "to avoid negative consequences (see Table 12.2), 25 percent said that they personally *would* do so.

Similarly, in another study adolescents were asked to respond to one of two kinds of stories: one in which they were asked to take the perspective of a fictitious other or one in which they were to respond as they would do themselves (Weiss, 1982). Those responding from the self-involved perspective demonstrated increased concern about punishment and consequences as well as less mature moral reasoning than those responding from the fictitious-other perspective.

Some adolescents show a reasonable degree of adherence to personal moral principles, even under duress, whereas others yield rather quickly to tempta-

T A B L E 12.2 WHY SHOULD PEOPLE FOLLOW RULES? (PERCENTAGES BY AGE)[a]

| Categories | Educational Group | | | Comparisons (by T Test) | |
	Primary (1)	Middle School (2)	College (3)	(1) × (2)	(2) × (3)
Avoid negative consequences	50%	13%	3%	$p < .01$	$p < .05$
Authority	5	—	—		
Personal conformity	35	13	9	$p < .05$	
Social conformity	10	53	25	$p < .01$	$p < .01$
Rational/beneficial/ utilitarian	5	27	51	$p < .05$	$p < .05$
Principled	—	—	5		

Source: J. L. Tapp and F. J. Levine, Compliance from kindergarten to college: A speculative research note. *Journal of Youth and Adolescence.* 1972. **1,** 233–249. By permission.

[a]This question is multiple coded; therefore, percentages may total over 100 percent. Where answers were idiosyncratic or uncodable, the categories were omitted from the table.

tion or group pressure. Still others appear to be guided almost solely by the possibility of external sanctions rather than by internalized standards. In short, knowledge alone, even sophisticated knowledge of moral standards, does not guarantee an effective conscience (M. L. Hoffman, 1975a).

Whether people will do what they know to be right depends on the extent to which morality is central to their self-concept and sense of identity. For a person whose moral convictions are an important part of his or her self, to violate those convictions is to betray one's identity (Blasi, 1980, 1984). "The resulting feeling of guilt is a direct effect of perceiving one's inconsistency, one's lack of intactness and wholeness, one's lack of integrity" (Moshman, Glover, & Bruning, 1987, p. 555).

Factors Affecting the Development of Conscience

The development of conscience begins long before adolescence. Indeed, even during the preschool years the child begins to develop a set of standards for acceptable behavior, generally acts in accordance with those standards, and feels guilty if he or she violates them (Mussen et al., 1990).

How does conscience develop? In Freud's view, conscience is a product of identification (see pages 56–59). The young child's behavior is determined largely by external rewards and sanctions. Gradually, however, the child begins to *internalize* moral standards and prohibitions in the same way that he or she adopts other parental attributes. The adoption of parental standards makes the child feel similar to his or her parents and, therefore, to identify more strongly with them. Children who have internalized moral standards will punish themselves, or feel anxious or guilty, whenever they do (or think) something for which they believe their parents might punish them (Freud, 1964; Whiting & Child, 1953).

Many researchers have investigated and elaborated on various elements that are implicit in Freud's basic formulation (e.g., cognitive aspects, modeling, social learning). It has been found, for example, that the kind of model a parent provides, and the kind of discipline he or she employs, will influence the extent and nature of the child's developing conscience (M. L. Hoffman, 1980). In general, as we shall see, parents who appeal to positive, growth-enhancing motives in the child through their disciplinary techniques appear to foster positive identification and genuine moral maturity to a greater extent than those who appeal to negative motivations such as fear of losing the parent's love or fear of parental aggression (M. L. Hoffman, 1980).

Effects of Child-Rearing Practices

Martin Hoffman, a psychologist at New York University, distinguishes between two basic parental disciplinary patterns that affect moral orientation. They are termed **power-assertive** and *nonpower-assertive* (M. L. Hoffman, 1970, 1979, 1980, 1982). Non–power-assertive discipline can be divided into two main subtypes: **love withdrawal** and **induction** (in which the parent provides explanations or reasons for requiring certain behaviors from the child).

A parent who uses power-assertive techniques does not rely on the child's inner resources (e.g., guilt, shame, dependency, love, or respect) to influence the child's behavior; nor does the parent give the child information necessary for the development of such resources. Instead, the parent seeks to accomplish this end by punishing the child physically or materially or by relying on fear of punishment. Power assertion tends to be related to "a moral orientation based on fear of external detection and punishment" (M. L. Hoffman, 1980, p. 322). The child or adolescent is less likely to act on the basis of internalized moral norms and more likely to continue to be influenced by external sanctions. Not surprisingly, a pattern of power assertion is frequently found among the parents of some kinds of delinquents (see pages 527–529).

Parents who employ love withdrawal give psychological but not physical expression to their anger or disapproval of the child for engaging in some undesirable behavior. They may ignore the child, refuse to speak to him or her, express dislike, or threaten abandonment. As Hoffman observes, "Like power assertion, love withdrawal has a highly punitive quality. Although it poses no immediate physical or material threat to the child, it may be more devastating emotionally than power assertion because it poses the ultimate threat of abandonment or separation" (M. L. Hoffman, 1970, p. 285). Love withdrawal is not consistently related to the child's development of internalized moral standards, although the child is more likely than children of power-assertive parents to confess to violations and to accept blame. Moreover, love withdrawal disrupts communication (and, hence, learning opportunities) between child and parent, and fails to make use of the child's capacity for empathy. There is some evidence that love withdrawal may contribute to inhibition of anger (M. L. Hoffman, 1980).

Induction involves using techniques in which the parent gives explanations or reasons for requiring certain behaviors of the child, such as pointing out the practical realities of a situation or explaining how inappropriate behavior may be harmful to the child or others. Unlike either of the other two approaches, induction is also likely to include appeals to the child's pride and his or her desire for maturity or to be "grown up." Inductive techniques, in addition to promoting positive identification, "help foster the image of the parent as a rational, nonarbitrary authority. They provide the child with cognitive resources needed to control his own behavior" (M. L. Hoffman, 1970, p. 331). Not surprisingly, inductive discipline, combined with affection, has been found to be most likely to result in advanced moral development, as evidenced

Inductive discipline, combined with affection, has been found to be most likely to result in advanced moral development.

by an internal moral orientation and self-induced guilt about violations of internal standards (M. L. Hoffman, 1970, 1979, 1980).

Few parents employ one type of discipline exclusively. For example, even a parent who endorses the use of inductive techniques is likely at times to resort to power assertion (e.g., "Stop that, right this minute!" "Go to your room!") or to express strong disapproval (e.g., "How could you do an irresponsible thing like that?" "You can't treat your sister like that. It's hurtful, and wrong and I won't have it!"). As Hoffman points out, such disciplinary techniques may be necessary to get children to stop what they are doing and pay attention. "Having attended, children will often be influenced cognitively by the information contained in the inductive component and thus experience a reduced sense of opposition between their desires and external demands" (M. L. Hoffman, 1980, p. 324).

Mature moral development involves not only avoidance of prohibitions but also motivation toward positive, altruistic, helpful, or *prosocial* behavior (Boehnke et al., 1989; Eisenberg, Lennon, & Roth, 1983; Eisenberg-Berg & Mussen, 1989). Much recent research on moral development has focused on factors leading to prosocial motivation and behavior. It is not enough, in an impersonal, directionless, and morally confusing world, simply to avoid prohibited behaviors. Individuals need to be secure in their own personal values and standards, resistant to deviant pressures, and concerned with the welfare of others as well as their own. Parents who serve as models for altruistic behavior, who encourage positive identification through unconditional love, and who employ inductive disciplinary techniques are most likely to produce children who go on to become truly inner-directed, concerned, and morally mature (M. L. Hoffman, 1975, 1980; Leahy, 1981; Mussen et al., 1990).

The personal histories of unusually altruistic adults provide impressive evidence of the contribution of parental modeling and identification to the development of prosocial behavior. Non-Jews who risked their lives trying to rescue Jews from the Nazis during World War II characteristically identified strongly with parents who held strong moral convictions and acted in accordance with those convictions (London, 1970). In a recent study, the participants were volunteers at a crisis counseling center who underwent rigorous training and worked very hard, at a great sacrifice of time and effort. Those who had had warm, positive relationships with altruistic parents during childhood completed their six-month commitment to this prosocial work even if they found the training difficult and unrewarding. However, those who had poor early relationships with nonaltruistic parents sustained their crisis work only if they found the training situation personally rewarding (Clary & Miller, 1986).

Sex Differences in Moral Development

For Carol Gilligan, a psychologist at Harvard, the conceptions of moral development adopted by Piaget and Kohlberg reflect a similar orientation. In each instance, the primary emphasis is on morality as a sense of justice based on abstract, rational principles (Gilligan, 1977, 1979, 1982). In her view, this conception of moral development unduly favored males because the socialization of males places greater emphasis on such a conception of morality. In contrast, she maintained, women are brought up to view morality in more personal terms—as a matter of caring and showing compassion for others, especially for those with whom one is intimately connected. Consequently, when women are assessed by "justice-oriented" measures, their level of moral development will appear to be less mature than that of men.

In an effort to redress this perceived imbalance, Gilligan developed a series of stages based on the moral aspects of interpersonal relationships. Level one involves an orientation to self and individual survival. It is followed by a transition from selfishness to responsibility, leading to a second level involving moral judgment that relies on shared norms and expectations requiring self-sacrifice. This level is followed by a transition from concern with conformity to a new inner judgment. The third level of moral reasoning involves elevating nonviolence—the injunction against hurting—to a principle governing all moral judgment and action. But do boys and girls actually differ in level of moral reasoning? Although Gilligan cited some research supporting her position (Kohlberg & Kramer, 1969; Holstein, 1976), the vast majority of recent studies show no difference in the stages of moral development reached by males and females (Friedman, Robinson, & Friedman, 1987; Gibbs, Arnold, & Burkhart, 1984; Rest, 1986; Walker, 1985, 1989; Thoma, 1984). How, then, can we evaluate Gilligan's assertions?

One possibility is that although females and males may not differ on abstract tests of their moral reasoning skills, they may still differ in their responses to the events of daily living. On average, women *may* be more intimately involved with and concerned about the welfare of individuals they know about; men *may* be more concerned with the establishment of laws and broad social policies. This would be consistent with other studies indicating that females tend to be more interpersonally oriented and more immediately concerned with the well-being of others.

Martin Hoffman (1975a, 1975b) has found that mothers tend to express more affection toward girls, as well as more induction and less power assertion, which together may be more likely to foster an internalized, humanistic moral orientation. He also suggests that such sex differences may be partially explained by "differentiated sex role socialization as well as by increasing pressure on males over the life cycle to achieve and succeed, which may often be in conflict with concerns about the welfare of others" (M. L. Hoffman, 1975b, p. 720).

In the long run, Gilligan's principal contribution may be not so much an explication of sex differences as a broadened conception of morality (Baumrind, 1986; Gilligan, 1987; Moshman et al., 1987; Nunner-Winkler, 1984). Effective morality needs to include *both* justice and rights *and* care, compassion, and responsibility for others (Brabeck, 1983). Indeed, although Kohlberg continued to view justice as central to morality, he maintained that the development of justice and the development of caring and compassion are interrelated. He noted that the Golden Rule of the New Testament encompassed both

Mothers tend to express more affection toward girls, as well as more induction and less power assertion.

orientations: "Do unto others as you would have them do unto you" and "Love thy neighbor as thyself" (Kohlberg, Levine, & Hewer, 1983).

THE DEVELOPMENT OF POLITICAL IDEAS

As in the case of moral and religious values, the development of political thought in adolescence is significantly influenced by the young person's cognitive development (Adelson, 1971, 1975, 1982; Adelson & O'Neil, 1966; Gallatin, 1980). In order to explore the processes by which the transformation in political ideas takes place, Joseph Adelson and his colleagues conducted an ingenious series of investigations in the United States, West Germany, and England. To avoid conventional stereotypes and differing degrees of factual information, and to make the results from different countries more comparable, they avoided questions about existing political systems and presented subjects with the premise, "Imagine that a thousand people venture to an island in the Pacific to form a new society; once there they must compose a political order, devise a legal system, and in general confront the myriad problems of government" (Adelson, 1971, p. 1014). They then explored their subjects' thinking on a variety of relevant issues (e.g., the purpose of government, law, and political parties). Proposed laws were suggested and problems of public policy explored.

Changes in Cognitive Mode

The results of the study showed that there is a significant developmental shift in the direction of greater abstractness of thought. For example, when asked the purpose of laws, one 12-year-old replied, "If we had no laws, people could go around killing people." In contrast, a 16-year-old replied, "To insure safety and enforce the government." Another commented, "They are basically guidelines for people. I mean like this is wrong and this is right and to help them understand" (Adelson, 1971, p. 1015).

Lacking the capacity to clearly formulate abstract concepts such as law, society, equal representation, individual rights, and the like, the younger adolescent's political thought tended to be personalized: "When we ask him about the law, he speaks of the policeman, the judge, the criminal. . . . When we mention government, he speaks of the mayor, or the President, or the congressman, and much of the time none of these but rather a shadowy though ubiquitous set of personages known as "they" or "them." ("They do it, like in schools, so that people don't get hurt") (Adelson, 1971, pp. 1015–1016).

The older adolescent's ability to employ abstract thought was well illustrated by a question in which the subjects were told that 20 percent of the people on the island were farmers and that they were concerned that laws might be passed contrary to their interests. The subjects were asked what might be done about this situation. The youngest adolescents could usually do little more than assert that people wouldn't want to hurt farmers or that the farmers should fight or move to another part of the island—if, indeed, they could give any answer at all. Slightly older adolescents made suggestions like "The farmers should talk to the rest of the people and make their problems understood."

By mid-adolescence, however, many subjects were able to suggest such solutions as forming a union to press for their collective rights or electing legislators to defend their interests. Older adolescents were also able to take an extended time perspective (i.e., to look ahead to future as well as present consequences of various political alternatives) and to take motivation into account as a significant factor in social and political behavior.

Adelson evaluates the cognitive transitions that occur during adolescence in terms of five characteristics: abstractness, time, change, costs and benefits, and principles. Abstractness in political thought appears to be strongly linked to the development of abstract reasoning. The concept of time—the shift from focus on the present to consideration of past and future time—also is strongly linked to cognitive development. The consideration of change becomes more central as the adolescent "increasingly recognizes and accepts the tractability of all things human, of human disposition, of the laws men make and the social forms they create. Politics and government become, increasingly, exercises in experiment" (Adelson, 1975, p. 69). The young adolescent also has little sense of relative costs and benefits, whereas the older adolescent recognizes that politics involves competing interests and the need for compromise. Finally, older adolescents, but not younger ones, have developed a grasp of principles, based not only on increasing knowledge of political principles but also on increased cognitive capacity to consider specific situations in terms of universals.

Authoritarianism is characteristic of younger adolescents' political thinking. For example, "On questions of crime and punishment, they were able—without seeming to bat an eyelash—to propose the most sanguinary means of achieving peace and harmony across the land. Here, for example, is the view of one clean-cut middle-class American 13-year-old boy on the control of crime: [On the best reason for sending people to jail] "Well, these people who are in jail for about five years and are still on the same grudge, then I would put them in for triple or double the time. I think they would learn their lesson then" (Adelson, 1982, p. 9).

This view of society gradually gives way to an entirely different view of the purpose of law. Generally, by the time adolescents are 15 or 16 years old, and certainly by age 18, the emphasis on arbitrary punishment has diminished markedly. The idea that laws are a code guiding human conduct becomes more prevalent in the later years of adolescence.

Participants in the National High School Model United Nations, United Nations, New York. Older adolescents are more likely to see laws as providing a means for achieving harmony among individuals, social groups, and nations with competing interests.

T A B L E 12.3 RESPONSES TO "WHAT IS THE PURPOSE OF LAWS?" OVER ADOLESCENCE[a]

	Grade			
Category	5	7	9	12
Restriction	73%	68%	44%	20%
Restrictional benefit	12	18	33	38
Benefit	7	9	20	41

Source: J. Adelson. Rites of passage. Personal communication. 1982. By permission.
[a]N = 326, cross-national sample.

Two other motifs also signal the end of the early-adolescent view of laws. One is the tendency to see laws as benevolent rather than restrictive, as designed to help people. Another motif links law to the larger notion of community and sees laws as providing a means for achieving interpersonal harmony, either among competing social groups or in the nation or state as a whole. These changes, which range from a purely restrictive to a benevolent or normative view of law, appear to be as predictable as the cognitive shift from the concrete to the abstract. This shift, showing the gradual abandonment of an authoritarian, punitive view of morality and law, is illustrated in Table 12.3.

COGNITIVE DEVELOPMENT AND CHANGING RELIGIOUS BELIEFS

In most religions adolescence is marked by some kind of ritual that recognizes that an important developmental transition is taking place. Thus, it is during adolescence that many Christian youth formally enter into church membership through *confirmation* ceremonies. Similarly, Jewish youth become adult members of their congregations through *Bat* or *Bar Mitzvah* ceremonies.

As in the case of moral values generally, the religious beliefs of adolescents also reflect their cognitive development (Elkind, 1978; Mussen et al., 1990; Nelsen, Potvin, & Shields, 1977). The young person's religious beliefs are likely to become more abstract and less literal between the ages of 12 and 18 (Elkind, 1978; Farel, 1982; Fowler, 1981). For example, God comes to be seen more as an abstract power and less as a fatherly human being. Religious views also become more tolerant and less dogmatic. There also appears to be some decline in the stated importance of religion—at least formal religion—during adolescence, although more than nine out of ten adolescents continue to believe in God (*America's youth,* 1988). Significantly more young people of high school age than of college age believe that religion is important to them, and more of them attend church regularly (Bachman, Johnston, & O'Malley, 1981; Johnston, Bachman, & O'Malley, forthcoming; Potvin, Hoge, & Nelsen, 1976; Yankelovich, 1974, 1981).

Cultural Changes

Cultural as well as age changes in religious values appear to be at work (Caplow & Bahr, 1979; Dickinson, 1982). Although most young people still express a general belief in God or a universal spirit, during the 1960s and 1970s there was a steady decline in the percentage of young people who view religion as "a very important personal value" (Yankelovich, 1974). This trend continued through the 1980s. In 1980, 32 percent of American high school seniors stated that religion was very important in their lives; by 1989 this figure had declined to 27 percent (Bachman et al., 1981; Johnston et al., forthcoming). Interestingly, the decline was greatest among the part of the population in which religious concerns formerly were highest, namely, young people who are not attending and not planning to attend college. Although more non-college than college-bound youth continue to consider religion very important, the magnitude of the difference has decreased dramatically. As with other values (see pages 495–497), during the past two decades there has apparently been a rather rapid diffusion of religious values from a minority of economically and socially privileged youth to the majority of their working-class peers.

At least part of this relative decline of interest in religion is clearly related to changing values among young people and a perception on the part of many that religion—at least formal, institutionalized religion—is failing to reflect these changes (*America's youth*, 1988; Farel, 1982; Mussen et al., 1990). For example, rightly or wrongly, approximately half of all adolescents believe that churches are not doing their best to understand young people's ideas about sex. Contemporary adolescents are more likely to state that God has understanding attitudes about sex than to attribute such attitudes to institutionalized religion.

A number of young people, particularly in the women's movement, also feel that the Catholic church and some Protestant denominations are not according full status and recognition to women. A majority of Catholic youth disagree with their church's positions on birth control, annulment and divorce, and the right of priests to marry.

At the same time, an increased interest in more fundamentalist religious traditions can be seen in a significant number of young people. Nearly half of all Protestant teenagers, and 22 percent of their Catholic peers, report having had a "born-again" experience—a turning point in their lives involving personal commitment to Christ (Gallup, 1978; Norback, 1980). These figures are similar to those obtained among adults.

Sects and Cults. Another trend that was especially evident among young people in the past decade and a half was the emergence of new religious sects such as the Jesus Movement, Hare Krishna, Children of God, and the Unification Church (Galanter, 1980; Gallup & Poling, 1980; Mussen et al., 1990; Swope, 1980). Some of these groups are informal and loosely structured. They are held together principally by concern for others, disillusionment with materialistic values (or the apparent absence of strong personal values) in contem-

Prayer time for a Christian biking ministry, New Hartford, Connecticut. A growing interest in more fundamentalist religious traditions can be seen in a significant number of young people.

porary society, and a belief—often simple, direct, and sometimes fundamentalist—in personal salvation.

Other groups have highly authoritarian structures. They may require the surrender of individual autonomy and complete conformity in both behavior and belief to the dictates of leaders. Some young people enlist in such groups as a result of a sudden conversion experience following a period of rootlessness and identity confusion. There is often a prior history of difficulties in parent–child relations, extensive drug use, sexual exploration, and life "on the road" (Adams & Gullota, 1983; Conger & Petersen, 1984; Dean, 1982; Galanter et al., 1980). Still other young people, particularly in less authoritarian groups, seem to be expressing the need for a satisfying and, for them, workable set of simple, straightforward values in an otherwise chaotic society.

CURRENT TRENDS IN ADOLESCENT VALUES

As with so many other aspects of adolescent development, the greatest danger in discussing trends in adolescent values is overgeneralization. In the middle and late 1960s much was made of a so-called revolution in the values of young people. Adolescents were, it was said, developing a **counterculture**—a set of values, beliefs, and life-styles so different from that of their more traditional elders that a profound "generation gap" had developed. There is no question that the troubled, violence-ridden decade of the 1960s produced major changes in the values of some adolescents. Significant minorities of young people became disillusioned by a society that they viewed as unjust, cruel, hypocritical, impersonal, overly competitive, or, in the broadest sense of the term, immoral. They reacted in a variety of ways. Some simply "dropped out" of society; others engaged in vigorous efforts to bring about social change—efforts that ran the gamut from conventional political activity to extreme revolutionary tactics (see Chapter 13).

Where many observers of that era erred was not in identifying a significant change in values, beliefs, and behavior among young people but in their assessment of the numbers involved and the extent of the change. In its most dramatic manifestations, the counterculture of the 1960s was largely confined to a conspicuous, articulate minority of young people on high school and college campuses, in the streets, and in films and the arts. However, social commentators, like many parents and even adolescents themselves, tended to view adolescent culture as monolithic even while acknowledging the growing diversity and polarization of beliefs within adult society. Consequently, they often attributed to young people in general the values, attitudes, beliefs, and modes of behavior of a highly visible minority.

In reality, however, adolescent culture was as heterogeneous as that of adults. During the late 1960s and early 1970s in particular, diversity was at least as great among adolescents as among adults. And although the values of the average adolescent did change in a number of important respects, the extent of the changes was far more circumscribed than popular stereotypes suggested. Indeed, in many ways the values, attitudes, and beliefs of the majority of adolescents remained surprisingly conventional.

Today we are in danger of falling into another trap of overgeneralization. Whereas social observers of the 1960s tended to exaggerate the impact of the so-called youth revolution on the average young person, many contemporary commentators are misinterpreting the meaning of recent trends toward greater concern with materialism and financial security, a sharp decline in political activism, and diminishing interest in the welfare of others. In the minds of some critics, these trends are the harbingers of an across-the-board return to pre-1960s attitudes, values, and beliefs. This is not the case, however, if for no other reason than that the world of the 1990s, in which young people are coming to maturity, is vastly different from the world of the 1950s and early 1960s.

What are the facts regarding contemporary adolescent values?

College Students and College-Bound Youth

Although college (or college-bound) young people constitute a minority of all young people, they tend to be trend setters; any shifts in the values of this group are likely to influence the values of young people generally. What, then, do we know about the value trends of this important minority?

In many respects, contemporary adolescents and youth have needs and values that are far from new. They want self-esteem; feelings of competence; respect from parents, peers, and society; recognition for their accomplishments; growing independence; some close friendships; someone to love; and some idea of where they are headed and what they are going to do with their lives. However, the ways in which these needs and values are expressed, and the importance they are given, may vary with social, economic, and political change. Indeed, what sometimes seem to be dramatic changes in values may actually represent newly aroused concerns brought on by social changes. At any rate, it would be difficult to make progress toward understanding recent changes in expressed attitudes and values without reference to changing social and economic conditions.

Social and Economic Values. Although the extent of the shift is sometimes exaggerated, over the past two decades there has clearly been a significant increase in young people's concern for personal well-being, together with a decrease in their concern for the welfare of others—particularly the disadvantaged—and of society itself (Astin, Green, & Korn, 1987; Astin et al., 1986, 1987; Astin, Korn, & Berz, 1989; Bachman & Johnston, 1980; Conger, 1981, 1988; Johnston, Bachman, & O'Malley, forthcoming). This concern with material values and success is much higher among high school and college students today than it was twenty or even ten years ago. For example, "being very well off financially" was cited as "a very important objective" by only 39 percent of entering college students in the United States in 1970; by 1980 that figure had increased to 63 percent, and by 1989 it was over 75 percent (Astin et al., 1989). In contrast, "developing a meaningful philosophy of life" declined as a very important objective from 82.9 percent in 1967 to 50.4 percent in 1980 and 40.8 percent in 1989—a record low (1988 not included for technical reasons) (see Figure 12.1).

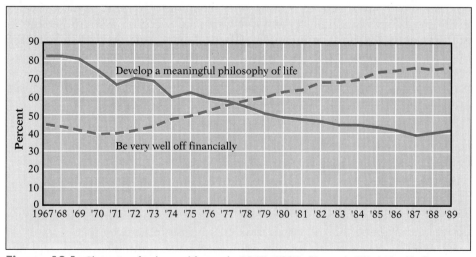

Figure 12.1 Changing freshman life goals, 1967–1989. (From A. W. Astin, K. C. Green, & W. S. Korn. *The American freshman: Twenty year trends;* and A. W. Astin et al., *The American freshman: National norms for fall 1985–1989.* Los Angeles: Higher Education Research Institute, University of California at Los Angeles, 1985, 1989. By permission.)

Similarly, in 1971 slightly less than half of all entering students said that "being able to make more money" is a very important reason for going to college; in 1989 over 72 percent considered it very important. In contrast, the proportion who emphasized the importance of going to college "to gain a general education" fell to just over 62 percent, down from a peak of almost 71 percent in 1977 (see Figure 12.2). Gaining recognition from peers, having administrative responsibility, and being an authority in one's field were all considered significantly more important in the past decade (Astin, 1980; Astin et al., 1986, 1988, 1989).

Among high school seniors there have been parallel but less dramatic increases in the proportion who rated "the chance to earn a good deal of money" and to have "a predictable, secure future" as very important in a job (Bachman, 1971; Bachman & Johnston, 1980; Bachman et al., 1981, 1987; Johnston, Bachman, & O'Malley, 1986, forthcoming). The percentage of college-bound high school seniors who felt that it would be desirable to work for a large corporation increased from 14 percent to 34 percent between 1976 and 1989. Conversely, the number who would consider working for a social-service organization desirable dropped from 23 percent to 11 percent between 1976 and

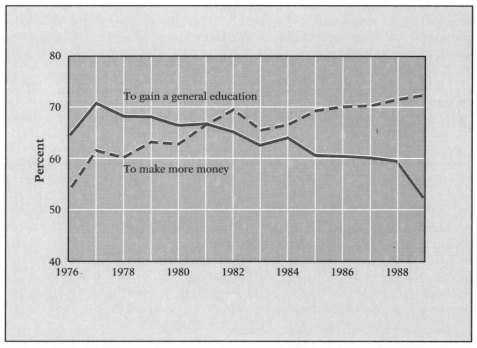

Figure 12.2 Reasons noted as very important in deciding to go to college (percentages). (From A. W. Astin, W. S. Korn, & E. R. Berz. *The American freshman: National norms for fall 1989.* Los Angeles: Higher Education Research Institute, University of California at Los Angeles, 1989. By permission.)

1980, although it increased to almost 17 percent by 1989. Only 20 percent now consider such a job unacceptable.

Along with increasing concern with personal well-being and material success, the 1970s and 1980s witnessed a marked decline in political and social activism (see Chapter 13). The limited activist movements that have emerged recently have tended to emphasize issues that are directly related to immediate personal concerns (e.g., student financial aid) or are broadly shared (e.g., environmental pollution, Central American policy, nuclear proliferation) (Astin et al., 1989).

In 1989, fewer than one in five college-bound high school seniors considered "making a contribution to society" or "working to correct social and economic inequities" a very important value (Johnston et al., forthcoming). Among entering college students, "keeping up with political affairs" was cited as very important by 41 percent fewer young women in 1988 than in 1969 (29.4 percent versus 50 percent) and by 27 percent fewer young men (38.2 percent versus 52.5 percent) (Astin et al., 1988). However, in 1989 these figures *increased* to 36 percent for women and 43 percent for men (Astin et al., 1989).

Among students entering college in 1987, record lows were recorded for interest in "participating in community action programs," "participating in programs to clean up the environment," and "promoting racial understanding"; however, there was an upturn in 1988 and 1989 (Astin et al., 1987, 1988, 1989). Even at a more personal level, the number of college students who considered "helping others in difficulty" to be a very important objective declined in a decade from 58 percent to 49 percent among males and from 75 percent to 68.7 percent among females (Astin et al., 1989).

Consistent with these shifts was a continuing movement toward business careers and away from science, humanities, and the arts. Student interest in most of the "human services" occupations, such as the clergy, social work, nursing, allied health professions, and teaching also declined significantly in the past decade (see Chapter 10). Teaching has shown a mild recovery since 1982, but it is still far less popular than it was in the late 1960s and early 1970s (Astin et al., 1986, 1988, 1989).

The relative shift in emphasis from social to personal concerns was accompanied by an overall decline in political liberalism and an increase in the proportion of young people who view themselves as "middle of the road." A decade and a half ago one-third of all students described themselves as liberals; in 1981 less than one in five did so, although this figure increased to nearly one in four by 1989 (Astin et al., 1989). This increase was accompanied by a slight decline in the middle-of-the-road group and in the proportion of entering students who identified themselves as "conservative" or "far right" (see Figure 12.3).

Does the dramatic shift in political and social values during the past decade and a half indicate, as some have suggested, an across-the-board retreat from the so-called new values that rose to prominence in the 1960s and early 1970s, together with a return to the values that were characteristic of the 1950s? The available evidence clearly indicates otherwise.

Despite a significant increase in positive attitudes during the first half of the

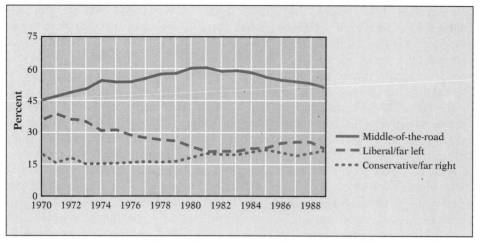

Figure 12.3 Trends in general political attitudes (percentages). (From A. W. Astin, W. S. Korn, & E. R. Berz. *The American freshman: National norms for fall 1989*. Los Angeles: Higher Education Research Institute, University of California at Los Angeles, 1989. By permission.)

1980s, today's young people (and adults as well) remain more, not less, skeptical about the infallibility or even the morality of major social institutions and their values—including big business, big labor unions, Congress, the executive branch of government, the courts, the schools, law enforcement agencies, and so on—than they were in the late 1960s. For example, less than one-third of college-bound high school seniors currently (1989) think that Congress has been doing a good job on the whole, and over 60 percent think that there is at least a moderate amount of dishonesty and immorality in Congress (Johnston et al., forthcoming). Big business, big labor unions, and the executive branch of government do not fare much better. Colleges and universities, churches, the press, and the military are viewed more favorably; at least half of all students think that they are doing at least a pretty good job (Bachman, 1971; Bachman & Johnston, 1980; Bachman et al., 1987; Johnston et al., 1986, forthcoming).

Similarly, among students entering college a strong majority agree that government is not protecting the consumer, controlling pollution, or promoting disarmament; that a national health care plan is needed; that military spending should not be increased; and that the wealthy should pay more taxes. Interestingly, however, less than one-third percent think that taxes should be raised in order to reduce the federal deficit (Astin et al., 1986, 1988, 1989).

Personal and Moral Values. In personal and moral values, too, today's young people show little resemblance to those of the 1950s. The so-called sexual revolution among middle- and upper-class adolescents and youth was a major aspect of the "new morality" of the late 1960s, and one of the most enduring (see Chapter 8). Not only has there not been a return to traditional sexual morality, but previous trends have accelerated, at least until recently.

For example, in 1971 about 28 percent of all 15–19-year-old girls had engaged in premarital intercourse (Hayes, 1987). But by 1988 the rate had increased to four out of five (Child Trends, 1989; London et al., 1989). The number of unmarried couples under age 25 living together in a household, though still relatively small, increased more than sevenfold between 1970 and 1987 (U.S. Bureau of the Census, 1981, 1989).

The trend toward considering sexual behavior more a matter of personal decision than a subject for socially imposed moral codes intensified during the past decade and a half. In 1989 American high school seniors were asked their reactions to "a man and woman who live together without being married"; slightly over half stated that such a couple were "doing their own thing and not affecting anyone else" (Johnston et al., forthcoming). And as noted earlier, beginning in 1986 and continuing throughout the 1980s a slight majority of first-year college students endorsed the proposition that people should live together before getting married (see pages 245–247). Moreover, the percentage of high school seniors and first-year college students who support legalized abortion or consider having children outside marriage to be morally wrong declined between 1969 and 1989 (Astin, 1980; Astin et al., 1986, 1988; Bachman & Johnston, 1979; Bachman et al., 1981, 1987; Johnston et al., 1986, forthcoming).

In other respects, however, adolescents were less permissive in their personal and moral values in the late 1980s than just a few years earlier. Thus, in 1989 support for legalization of marijuana among students entering college continued a precipitous decline, to an all-time low of 16.7 percent from a high of 52.9 percent in 1977. In addition, support for abolishing capital punishment declined to an all-time low of 21.3 percent in 1989 (down from 26.6 in 1985 and 57.6 percent in 1971).

Most adolescents and youth still look forward to getting married and having children, but their numbers have declined slightly in the past fifteen years. Perhaps more significant, having children is increasingly seen as a matter of individual choice—not as a duty to society or an indispensable value (Astin et al., 1986, 1988; Yankelovich, 1974, 1981). Between 1969 and 1989 the percentage of students entering college who considered raising a family to be a very important objective declined from 78 percent to 69 percent for females. For males, it increased by one and one-half percentage points (to 68.5 percent), with the result that males and females now have similar views (Astin, 1980; Astin et al., 1987, 1988, 1989).

More broadly, fulfilling oneself as a person and having opportunities for self-expression (two other important values of the 1960s) have also remained strong. Support for freedom, self-determination, and equality for women—an issue that was only beginning to emerge among young people in the 1960s—became increasingly widespread in the 1970s and early 1980s (Conger, 1981, 1988). Discrimination on the basis of age (which affects both the young and the old) is also under siege politically, culturally and legally. In accordance with the continuing emphasis on "freedom to be me," many young people have shown heightened interest in physical health and well-being, while others have become involved in self-improvement programs and a variety of psychological "therapies" (Conger, 1981, 1988; National Association, 1983). Self-realization—physical, psychological, or material—appears to be the predominant message.

The appropriate question is not whether today's adolescents and youth are engaged in an across-the-board retreat from the values of the 1960s and early 1970s. Rather, it is whether the extension and expansion of such values as self-fulfillment and self-expression is psychologically growth-enhancing without a corresponding sense of commitment to the welfare of others and of society itself.

Social Values in the 1990s: A Turning Point? As America enters the 1990s, will the trends that characterized the 1970s and 1980s continue, or will there be a shift toward less preoccupation with narrow self-interest and a greater concern for the welfare of others and for society itself? There are no clear answers, but there are some signs of a possible shift. Increased numbers of college freshmen in 1989 (41 percent) said that "influencing social values" was a very important goal (up from 36 percent in 1987) (Astin et al., 1989). More 1989 students (26.1 percent) expressed a desire to become involved in cleaning up the environment (up from only 15.9 percent in 1986) (see Figure 12.4). Between 1986 and 1989 there were also modest increases in the num-

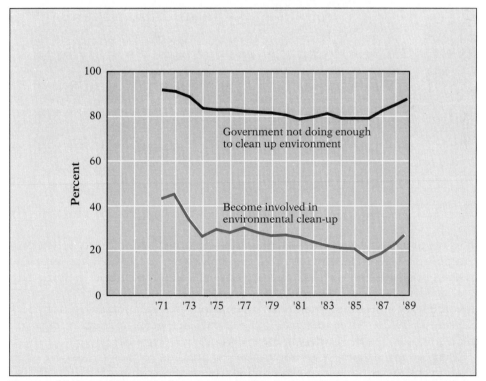

Figure 12.4 Freshman attitudes on environmental issues. (From A. W. Astin, W. S. Korn, & E. R. Berz. *The American freshman and follow-up survey: 1989 freshman survey results.* Los Angeles, CA: Higher Education Research Institute, University of California at Los Angeles, 1989. By permission.)

Increasing numbers of young people are expressing a desire to become involved in cleaning up the environment.

bers of students strongly interested in "participating in community action programs" (23.3 percent, up from 18.5 percent in 1986) and "helping promote racial understanding" (35.3 percent, up from 27.2 percent), and "helping others in difficulty" (59.7 percent, up from 56.4 percent). Fewer 1989 students favored laws prohibiting homosexual behavior (45.4 percent, down from 53.1 percent in 1987). Three-fourths (75.8 percent) support a national health care plan to cover health care costs for everyone, up from 60.5 percent in 1985.

More young people—and adults—are expressing an active concern with such problems as homelessness, child abuse, increased hunger and malnutrition, and inadequate educational, health, and social services for poor children and adolescents (Conger, 1988). And the percentage of students who consider it desirable to work for a social service organization has risen from 11 percent in 1980, and 13 percent in 1986, to 17 percent in 1989 (Bachman et al., 1987; Johnston et al., forthcoming). Whether such stirrings presage a significant shift in social values in the decade ahead remains to be seen.

One thing appears clear, however: Self-realization and self-awareness can be positive goals, "but if they become a person's only goals they can lead only to the kind of banality that has characterized so many of the recent fads in religion, self-improvement books and seminars, and so-called therapies—or even worse, to self-destructiveness" (Conger, 1981, p. 1480).

THE BLUE-COLLAR "REVOLUTION"

As noted earlier, a major error made by many social observers in the 1960s was a tendency to ascribe to the majority of young people the values and behaviors of a relatively small avant-garde minority. Even on college campuses, although the views of the great majority of students were influenced by those of social activists, the New Left, and advocates of alternative life-styles, they changed more slowly and remained somewhat more traditional. In turn, the views of noncollege working-class youth remained markedly more conservative than those of college youth in many areas, ranging from attitudes toward sexual freedom, use of drugs, and conformity in dress to views on the Vietnam War, business and government, minority rights, and law and order. Clearly, in the late 1960s young people, like adults, had their own "silent majority" (Conger, 1981; Yankelovich, 1969, 1974, 1981).

Interestingly, however, a significant change occurred during the 1970s, so that by the mid-1970s the values of noncollege adolescents and youth were "to an almost uncanny degree" just about where those of college youth were in the late 1960s in many areas, including sexual morality, religion, patriotism, politics, work, family, and attitudes toward business and government (Yankelovich, 1974). For example, in 1969 the traditional belief that "hard work always pays off" was held by only 56 percent of college students but by 79 percent of noncollege youth. By the mid-1970s, however, the percentage of noncollege youth who subscribed to this belief had decreased dramatically, to 56 percent—a figure identical to the 1969 figure for college students. In short, there was a rapid transmission of values from a minority of college youth to young people in general.

These trends appear to have continued through the 1980s. In most areas differences between the values of college students or college-bound young people and those of their noncollege peers remain considerably smaller than was the case in the 1960s. For example, high school seniors, whether or not they plan to attend a four-year college, share generally similar views on race relations, drug use, the role of women in the work force, living together before marriage, and the importance of marriage and family life (Bachman et al., 1990; Bachman et al., 1987; Johnston et al., forthcoming). However, the noncollege group (especially males) still tend to hold somewhat more traditional views about appropriate family roles for men and women. Members of this group also express considerably less interest or concern about "what's going on in government" or about "social problems of the nation and the world and about how they might be solved," although interest in these subjects among both groups continued to decline throughout the 1980s (Bachman, 1990; Bachman et al., 1981, 1987; Johnston et al., 1986, forthcoming).

Of particular interest is the fact that college and noncollege youth show increasingly similar vocational values (see Chapter 10). Overwhelming majorities of both groups say that it is very important to have a job that is interesting, makes the best use of one's skills and abilities, and provides opportunities to learn new skills (Bachman, 1990; Bachman et al., 1987; Johnston et al., 1986, forthcoming; Miller & Simon, 1979).

The diffusion of many of the values of college students in the late 1960s and 1970s to noncollege youth in the 1980s and beyond poses a potential problem. Noncollege youth are less likely than better-educated youth to find work that satisfies their needs for personal fulfillment, creativity, and self-expression. Only about one-quarter of employed noncollege youth express the view that "my work is more than just a job," and only one-third feel that they have a chance to develop their skills and abilities. As we noted in Chapter 10, a major challenge of our era is to find work for young people that offers some opportunity for self-fulfillment and personal growth, as well as adequate pay and economic security. For minority youth, particularly in the nation's inner cities, the problem is reaching epidemic proportions.

The task will not be easy, and it will require a far greater societal commit-

Teenage volunteers helping with a city park cleanup and newspaper recycling project.

ment to the welfare of youth than has been evident to date. Nevertheless, neither college nor noncollege youth have given up (*America's youth,* 1988; Bachman, 1990; Bachman et al., 1987; Johnston et al., 1986, forthcoming). Although fewer young people in the latter group feel that they are in control of their future, nearly two-thirds still do. And among both groups over three-quarters feel that, all in all, "my own life is going well"; two-thirds say that they are "pretty happy," with an additional 19 percent saying that they are "very happy." Six out of ten state that they anticipate "no difficulty in accepting the kind of life society has to offer."

In short, the majority of young people do not at present appear to be deeply alienated, either within themselves or in their relations with society. However, as we shall see in the following chapter, although their numbers have decreased markedly since the height of the youth revolt of the late 1960s, a significant minority still feel alienated to varying degrees.

SUMMARY

At no time in life is a person as likely to be concerned about moral values and standards as during adolescence. This is due partly to the multiplicity of shifting, sometimes conflicting values and standards to which the adolescent is exposed, and partly to the adolescent's increasingly sophisticated ability to comprehend moral issues.

Theorists have taken three basic approaches to moral development: cognitive, affective, and social. Some have argued that morality involves the ability to think adequately about a moral situation. Others have construed morality as primarily involving values. Still others have argued that morality is mainly a matter of what people do, rather than what they think or believe. It seems clear, however, that morality involves all of these components.

Jean Piaget's conceptualization of moral development stimulated much subsequent work on this topic. Piaget asserted that the organization of moral thought is quite different in younger children than in older children and adults, largely because children are at earlier stages of cognitive development. Lawrence Kohlberg extended Piaget's conceptualization by positing three major levels of moral development: preconventional, conventional, and postconventional, each of which is divided into two substages.

During adolescence conventional moral thinking tends to become dominant: Right behavior is seen as doing one's duty, showing respect for authority, and maintaining the existing social order. Contrary to earlier assumptions, many adolescents may not progress beyond this level. Some, however, do advance to postconventional levels. Postconventionality reflects the acquisition of formal-operational thinking and is characterized by "a major thrust toward abstract moral principles which are universally applicable, and not tied to any particular social group."

Preoccupation with moral values is fostered by the changing and varied societal demands confronting adolescents. In contrast to younger children, adolescents face an increasingly diverse world in which opportunities for choice are multiplied. Moreover, these choices cannot be made independently from personal values: An adolescent who is strongly concerned with helping others may make a different career choice than an adolescent who places a high valuation on material success. Intrapsychic conflicts may also play a part. In the face of varied and conflicting pressures—from parents, peers, teachers, and the larger society—some adolescents may be in danger either of falling into an essentially directionless moral relativism or of adopting the rigid kind of moral stance seen in some cults.

Intellectual understanding of moral values does not guarantee that individuals will always act in accordance with them. Whether people will do what they know to be right depends on the extent to which morality is central to their self-concept and sense of identity. The development of strong internalized moral values is fostered by parents who use *inductive* techniques to enforce restrictions. Such techniques include explanations of the reasons for the parents' actions and appeals to the child's pride and growing maturity. In contrast, neither *power-assertive* disciplinary techniques (based largely on fear of punishment) nor *love withdrawal* (based ultimately on fear of abandonment or separation) encourage moral (or emotional) maturity.

Carol Gilligan has observed that Piaget's and Kohlberg's conceptions of moral development emphasize justice, based on abstract moral principles, rather than seeing morality as a matter of caring and compassion. In an effort to redress this perceived imbalance, Gilligan has developed a series of stages involving the moral aspects of interpersonal relationships. Effective morality needs to include *both* justice and rights *and* care, compassion, and responsibility for others.

Like moral development, the development of political thought in adolescence is significantly influenced by the young person's level of cognitive development. With increasing age, political thinking becomes more abstract, less authoritarian, more concerned with motivation, and more aware of the need to reconcile competing interests. Similarly, the religious beliefs of adolescents become more abstract and less literal between the ages of 12 and 18. Since the early 1960s there has been a decline in the number of young people who view religion as "a very important value"; at the same time, however, there has been increased interest in fundamentalist religious traditions among a significant minority.

Although today's adolescents and youth share many of the needs and values of earlier generations, they show greater concern for their own well-being and material success (including "being very well off financially") and diminished concern for the welfare of others—particularly the less advantaged—and of society itself. (Fewer than one in five of today's high school seniors consider "making a contribution to society" or "working to correct social and economic inequities" to be "very important values.") In contrast, emphasis on fulfilling oneself as a person and having opportunities for self-expression (two of the "new values" of the 1960s) remains strong, as does support for self-determination and equality between the sexes.

REVIEW QUESTIONS

1. Why are young people particularly likely to be concerned with moral values and standards during the adolescent years?
2. Describe the three basic theoretical approaches to moral development.
3. Describe Kohlberg's six stages of moral development.
4. What does Kohlberg mean by *extreme relativism*? Why does he say that it is a particular danger during the transition from conventional to post-conventional moral reasoning?
5. Martin Hoffman has identified three parental disciplinary patterns that affect moral orientation: *power assertion, love withdrawal,* and *induction.* Define each. Which pattern is most likely to result in advanced moral development, and why?
6. What are Carol Gilligan's objections to Piaget's and Kohlberg's conceptions of moral development? What alternative series of stages does she propose? Can these two approaches be reconciled?
7. In what ways is the development of political thinking in adolescence influenced by cognitive development? Illustrate with examples.
8. What kinds of personal needs and values do contemporary adolescents and youth share with earlier generations of young people?
9. In what ways have the personal, social, political, and economic values of American adolescents and youth changed since the late 1960s?

RECOMMENDED READINGS

Adelson, J. (1971). The political imagination of the young adolescent. *Daedalus,* **100,** 1013–1050; also in J. Kagan & R. Coles (Eds.), *12 to 16: Early adolescence* (pp. 106–144). New York: W. W. Norton.

Colby, A., Kohlberg, L., Gibbs, J., & Lieberman, M. (1980). *A longitudinal study of moral development.* Cambridge, MA: Center for Moral Education.

Conger, J. J. (1988). Hostages to fortune: Youth, values, and the public interest. *American Psychologist,* **43,** 291–300.

Gilligan, C. (1982). *In a different voice: Psychological theory and women's development.* Cambridge, MA: Harvard University Press.

Hoffman, M. L. (1980). Moral development in adolescence. In J. Adelson (Ed.), *Handbook of adolescent psychology.* New York: Wiley.

Rest, J. R. (1986). *Moral development: Advances in research and theory.* New York: Praeger.

Turiel, E. (1983). *The development of social knowledge: Morality and convention.* New York: Cambridge University Press.

ALIENATION AND DELINQUENCY

As noted in the preceding chapter, despite their disenchantment with some of the policies, practices, and values of government and other social institutions, most young people do not appear to be deeply troubled and most feel that their own lives are going reasonably well (*America's youth*, 1989). Most feel "pretty happy," have a positive attitude toward themselves, and feel that they will be able to be successful in life. When asked if they thought their lives would be better in five years, nearly nine out of ten American high school seniors said that they would (Johnston, Bachman, & O'Malley, forthcoming). Although many young people wish they had more good friends (not just acquaintances) and would like more opportunities for self-expression and self-fulfillment, the majority expect to be able to find a rewarding life for themselves within the existing social order (Astin, Green, & Korn, 1987; Astin, Korn, & Berg, 1989; Conger, 1987; Johnston et al., forthcoming). For some, this appears to involve a more pragmatic emphasis on achieving a rewarding life-style, with less concern about the well-being of society in general, and the poor and otherwise disadvantaged in particular (Astin et al., 1987, 1989; Bachman & Johnston, 1980; Conger, 1981, 1988; Yankelovich, 1981).

Nevertheless, there remain significant minorities of young people who do not share these relatively optimistic feelings, who are deeply dissatisfied with either themselves or society or both. As we shall see in this chapter, these include young people who for one reason or another are alienated from society and its values, emotionally isolated, dependent on drugs, or delinquent. It also includes the growing number of young people who have attempted suicide, are runaways or "throwaways," or suffer from serious psychological or psychophysiological disturbances (Calabrese, 1987).

At least 10 percent of high school seniors feel that their lives are not very useful, that they have few friends they can spend time with or turn to for help, and that there is little sense in planning for the future because plans hardly ever work out anyway (Johnston et al., forthcoming). Over 20 percent of college-bound high school seniors (and almost 40 percent of those who do not plan to attend a four-year college) agree or mostly agree that "Every time I try to get ahead, something or somebody stops me" (Johnston et al., forthcoming).

Although distrust of governmental and other social institutions has actually increased since the late 1960s among both youth and adults, responses to this general disenchantment have changed markedly. For example, among high school seniors, confidence in social institutions—ranging from the executive, legislative, and judicial branches of government to business, the press, labor unions, and law firms—has declined since the mid-1960s (Bachman, 1971; Bachman et al., 1987; Johnston et al., forthcoming).

Studies by polling expert Louis Harris show that the number of Americans sharing at least a mild form of alienation—"what I think doesn't count," "most people with power try to take advantage of people like myself"—rose inexorably from one-third in the 1960s to two-thirds recently (Harris, 1987). In recent polls a majority (55 percent) of Americans expressed the belief that "the people running the country don't care about you and me"; more than one-third (37

Significant minorities of young people are deeply dissatisfied either with themselves and their lives or with society and its values—or both.

percent) stated that they feel "left out of things going on around me"—more than four times the number who felt that way in 1966. But instead of responding to this perceived state of affairs with social and political activism aimed at changing "the system," or by "dropping out" in favor of an alternative life-style, both young people and adults are more likely to respond with political apathy and diminished social concern.

There are still young people—and adults—who feel sufficiently disturbed by current social policies to engage actively in efforts to change them. For some, the primary issue is women's rights; for others, it is opposition to nuclear proliferation or destruction of the environment; for still others, it is the rights of the have-nots—children, minority adolescents, the homeless, the elderly, the handicapped, or the mentally ill (Conger, 1988; Edelman, 1987; Moynihan, 1986). Although young activists differ in their views on the nature of society's ills and the appropriate responses to them, they are united in the belief that the American dream is being tarnished. And they are not happy about it.

THE ROOTS OF ALIENATION

In Western culture the term **alienation** came into its own during the cold-war years and reached its peak in popular usage during the 1960s. It was used to "explain" all manner of events characterizing that turbulent decade—from student demonstrations and inner-city riots to increased use of drugs and the rise of the hippie movement (Conger, 1976; Gitlin, 1989). However, the concept of alienation is far from new (Schacht, 1971). Hegel discussed the "self-alienated spirit" in his first book, *Phenomenology of the Spirit*, published in 1807 (Hegel, 1952). Subsequently the term was employed in a variety of ways by psychologists and psychoanalysts. Some, like Durkheim, Marx, and Robert Merton, emphasized the anomie that results from political and economic exploitation and the separation of people from personally meaningful, productive work. Existentialist philosophers and theologians such as Kierkegaard, Tillich, and Sartre emphasized the painful estrangement of the individual from God, from other people, or from the self. Others have employed the term in still other ways; in fact, it has been used in different, and sometimes conflicting, ways by the same writer (Conger, 1976; Keniston, 1971; Seeman, 1975; Stokols, 1975).

What is clear, as the philosopher Richard Schacht has pointed out, is that because the term *alienation* is employed in connection with so many different phenomena, it has no special association with any of them. "Using the term 'alienation' without explaining any further what one has in mind communicates little more today than does tapping one's glass with one's spoon at a banquet; neither does much more than attract attention" (Schacht, 1971, p. 245).

Schacht's observation is as relevant to developmental psychology as it is to philosophy, theology, or sociology. In the late 1960s it became fashionable to refer to young people who did not fit in as being alienated. Through such labeling we gained the illusion that we were saying something significant about them. But as Kenneth Keniston noted at the time, all we were really doing was implying that something was wrong and suggesting the loss or absence of a previously desirable relationship (Keniston, 1960). Unless we can go on to specify what relationships the individual has lost—what he or she is alienated *from*—we have accomplished little. Moreover, it is important to know whether the alienation has been imposed on the individual largely by external forces, as in the case of the disenfranchised poor and some minority groups, or whether it is largely chosen by the individual, as in the case of some militant middle- and upper-class youth of the 1960s (Conger, 1976).

Viewed in this manner, it becomes clear that alienation among young people may differ in important ways. Some aspects of alienation are relatively widespread in a particular culture; others tend to be limited to smaller subgroups. As a result of the decline in clearly defined religious faith in the past century, many adolescents and adults feel alienated from what previously appeared to be a meaningful and orderly universe with a personal God at its center. This feeling of "existential outcastness," of lack of meaning in the universe as a whole, can be painful indeed, and can result in feelings of deprivation and outrage. This is especially true of adolescents because of their sensitivity, their need for absolute values, and their relative lack of repressive defenses (Conger, 1976; Keniston, 1960; Seeman, 1975).

Many adolescents also share what Keniston has called "developmental estrangement": a sense of alienation or loss that comes with the abandonment of ties to one's childhood self and indeed the whole world of childhood—an egocentric world that, as many of us can recall, seemed to have been created specifically for us—with us at its center. How difficult this sense of estrangement will be to deal with depends in great measure both on the particular kinds of childhood experiences the individual has had and also on what he or she finds to take their place. The other side of the coin of childhood dependence is emancipation, and for the young person who can find new emotional ties and new challenges and rewards, the loss of the world of childhood will be much less painful.

In a period of rapid social change such as our own, there is likely to be another keenly felt alienation: an acute sense of historical loss. "Most social innovations replace customs, outlooks, or technologies that are in that measure left behind; and those who are most firmly attached to what has been replaced inevitably mourn their loss" (Keniston, 1960, p. 461). The persistent American myth of the small town and the currently popular nostalgia revival bear at least superficial witness to contemporary feelings of historical loss.

Alienation may also take the form of a sense of estrangement from what is vaguely felt to be one's real self, as Karen Horney, Eric Fromm, and others noted many years before the "youth revolution" of the 1960s (Fromm, 1955; Horney, 1950; Seeman, 1975). Whether as a result of unfortunate developmental experiences or because of the demands of society, some young people feel that they have somehow lost touch with the inner core of their being and that much of what they do is empty, flat, and devoid of meaning. Such feelings characterize some instances of adolescent depression (see Chapter 14).

Young people may show all of these and other forms of alienation to varying degrees. In the 1960s the most prominent form of alienation involved explicit rejection of traditional societal values and practices. Although they were often alienated in other ways as well, significant numbers of young people became disillusioned with the goals, values, and practices of American society. They reacted against what they perceived as the ultimate futility of an obsessive preoccupation with materialistic rewards and social status, as well as the shallowness and hypocrisy of many of the values and practices of contemporary society. Although the intensity and extent of this sort of alienation among privileged youth have decreased sharply in recent years, other, more subtle forms of alienation have emerged.

ALIENATION AMONG MINORITIES AND THE POOR

As noted earlier, there can be important differences in the sources of alienation and the ways in which it is expressed. Among minorities and the poor—

and especially among people who are members of both of these categories—alienation is largely imposed from without. Quite simply, these young people are prevented from sharing in the affluent society that they see around them, both in the real world and on television. The vast majority of adolescents in these disadvantaged groups (i.e., blacks, Hispanics of Mexican-American or Puerto Rican origin, Appalachian whites, and Native Americans) are born into a "culture of poverty," whether they grow up in urban ghettos, in rural slums, or on reservations. Even at birth the odds are against them: The infant mortality rate among Americans living below the poverty level is far higher than among those living above it (Hughes et al., 1989; U.S. Bureau of the Census, 1989). Among blacks alone, the infant mortality rate is nearly twice the rate for whites (see Figure 13.1).

In their developing years poor minority youth are often exposed to hunger and malnutrition; inadequate or nonexistent health care; overcrowded, vermin-infested housing that often lacks heat, electricity, or adequate plumbing; and harassment both by police and other authorities and by petty criminals, drug dealers, youth gangs, slum landlords, and gyp merchants. Their parents (often a mother with no husband present) are frequently so poorly educated, so worn down, or so powerless that they can do little to help their children cope with an increasingly complex society (although some do manage to survive—and to help their children to survive—what would seem to most middle- and upper-class adults to be insurmountable obstacles).

Poorly prepared intellectually, psychologically, and socially, disadvantaged children are likely to enter overcrowded, rundown schools. Under these condi-

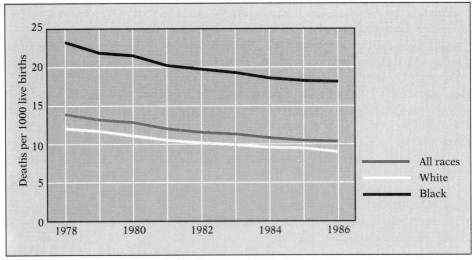

Figure 13.1 Infant mortality rates, by race, United States, 1978–1986. (From D. Hughes, K. Johnson, S. Rosenbaum, and J. Liu (1989). *The health of America's children: Maternal and child health data book.* Copyright 1989 by the Children's Defense Fund. By permission.)

tions they may fail to make normal school progress and may drop out of school as soon as they can. Few jobs are available at their skill level, and they may find themselves discriminated against even in jobs for which they are qualified.

Today more than 12 percent of white youth in the job market and two and a half times that number of blacks are unemployed—not counting those who have given up and are no longer actively seeking work. For those living in the socially and economically disorganized ghettos in large cities, unemployment may exceed 70 percent (see pages 403–407). This situation shows little sign of change in the near future. For such young people, the idea of the American dream can become a nightmare.

It should hardly be surprising that among all major subgroups in the population in recent surveys a higher percentage of blacks generally (71 percent) have stated that they feel alienated from the power centers of society. In contrast, in 1966, just after President Johnson led the drive to pass basic civil-rights legislation, only one-third of blacks expressed this sense of powerlessness (Harris, 1987). Not surprisingly, among young blacks living in poverty the sense of alienation is highest of all, and in some areas it is virtually universal.

Alienation, Identity, and Self-Esteem

Still worse, under such circumstances, young people not only may become alienated from the dominant American culture; in some cases they may also be cut off from the possibility of developing a clearly defined, self-confident personal and cultural identity. Although the ascendance of racial and ethnic pride in recent decades, particularly among young people, played an important part in stemming the development of a negative sense of identity (see pages 62–63) and increasing self-esteem, one wonders how long truly disenfranchised youth can persevere in the face of pervasive societal rejection.

This situation was aggravated in the past decade by massive federal cutbacks in social, vocational, health, educational, and other programs that are desperately needed by the poor and the near-poor, while taxes for the wealthy were being sharply lowered. Among the programs that were eliminated or reduced, a number are of particular concern for young people. They include youth training and employment programs, nutritional programs for pregnant women and infants, food stamps, Medicaid, child abuse and runaway centers and services, family planning services and counseling for adolescents, and educational and training programs for handicapped children and youth, as well as basic health, mental health and rehabilitative services (Conger, 1988; Edelman, 1987; Moynihan, 1986).

ALIENATION AMONG PRIVILEGED YOUTH

In contrast to alienation among the poor and victims of racial or ethnic discrimination, which is largely imposed by society, another kind of alienation became increasingly apparent during the turbulent decade of the 1960s: alienation among middle- and upper-class youth. Alienation among members of this group was not as entirely new as it was sometimes proclaimed to be; there were parallels in earlier youth movements in other countries as well as in the United States. Throughout history such movements have arisen when there is a "perceived discrepancy between the individual needs or aspirations of young people and the existing social and political conditions" (Braungart, 1980, p. 560).

During the late 1700s and the early 1800s, for example, the generational continuity of the family was diminished by the advent of the industrial revolution (Gillis, 1974). "Large numbers of young people were cut adrift from their homes and occupations as the economy moved from the traditional guild system toward a capitalist society." They were forced to migrate to the cities looking for work, and many began roaming aimlessly across the face of Europe "in search of a more permanent identity" (Braungart, 1980, p. 560–561). The historian Samuel Eliot Morison described the American university student of the 1790s as an "atheist in religion, an experimentalist in morals, a rebel to authority" (Morison, 1936, p. 585).

Alienated middle- and upper-class youth have long played an important part in the overthrow of political regimes from which they felt alienated. Nevertheless, the behavior of alienated young people in the late 1960s and early 1970s represented a dramatic departure from that of the "silent generation" of the 1950s; moreover, the visibility of their alienation was heightened by the rapid increase in the numbers of these young people, their unprecedented concentration in age-segregated high schools and colleges, and the attention they were given by the media (Conger, 1981).

There were significant variations in the sources of these privileged youths' alienation and the ways in which it was manifested. For some, their alienation had its roots in particular kinds of developmental experiences, such as disturbed parent–child relations. For others, the special characteristics and conflicts of American society played a dominant role. Specific injustices were often involved, including racial oppression, economic discrimination, violations of personal freedom, and the bitterly opposed war in Vietnam.

In other instances alienation was both deep and pervasive, amounting to rejection of society as a whole, a society that was viewed as inimical to the young person's most deeply held values: intimacy ("love," both individual and communal), individuality (freedom to know and be oneself), autonomy (freedom from coercion and freedom to act independently), and honesty (lack of pretense and dissimulation). As they saw it, this meant rejecting relentless competition, obsessive status seeking, and manipulative role playing. It also meant rejecting respect for authority based on power rather than on competence or morality, along with the traditional Protestant ethic of sacrificing current enjoyment for the sake of a presumably brighter tomorrow (Conger, 1976; Paulson & Lin, 1972; Yankelovich, 1969). In their view, the goals of technological progress and economic affluence were being pursued without regard to the costs in terms of human needs or the quality of the environment. But in the second half of the 1960s all other concerns were overshadowed by the Vietnam War.

Some alienated youth chose to work for change within the system, while smaller numbers became committed radicals (Gitlin, 1989; Jones, 1980; Keniston, 1971; Kerpelman, 1972; Yankelovich, 1969, 1974). Still others withdrew entirely from society. Sometimes this withdrawal involved despair, apathy, or defeat, without any alternative commitment; among these young people were some of the psychiatric casualties of the time. In other cases there was continued searching for meaningful alternatives, either within oneself or within a subculture of like-minded individuals. The latter might involve becoming a member of a self-sustaining urban or rural collective or joining the hippie culture.

For the most part, such alienated youth came from higher-income families in which the parents were highly educated (Pittel et al., 1971; Pittel & Miller, 1976). Those who became left-oriented activists were found, on average, to be more autonomous, assertive, sensitive, and socially concerned than nonactivists, as well as less conforming and less in need of nurturance and support (Block, Haan, & Smith, 1969). But contrary to the assertions of some social critics, *as a group* activists were neither more nor less intelligent or emotionally stable than their nonactivist peers, nor were they any more or less likely to have positive relationships with their parents (Block et al., 1969; Braungart, 1980; Sampson & Korn, 1970; Yankelovich, 1977).

Clearly, the notion that activists were unusually intelligent, mature, and psychologically resilient—or, conversely, that they were—as the psychoanalyst Bruno Bettelheim argued—immature, deeply troubled young people "fixated at the stage of the temper tantrum" (Dempsey, 1970, p. 23)—was simplistic and misleading. "A variety of individuals with highly diverse talents and motivations are bound to be involved in any social movement; global descriptions are certain to be oversimplified" (Sampson, 1970, p. 182).

Recent Trends in Activism and Dissent

Political and social activism and dissent declined markedly in the past two decades (see pages 490–493). Among students who entered college in 1989, for example, only about one in five expressed an interest in influencing the political structure and less than one in four considered participating in community action programs to be very important (Astin et al., 1989). Fewer than one in thirteen expressed an interest in such organizations as the Peace Corps or Vista (Astin, Green, Korn, Schalit, & Berz, 1988). Similarly, fewer than one in five high school seniors were interested in working in a political campaign, participating in a lawful demonstration, or engaging in a boycott—and less than 5 percent have done so (Johnston et al., forthcoming).

Nevertheless, many privileged youth, and an increasing number of adults, express views that would have seemed astonishing before the "youth revolution." Thus, among high school seniors in the late 1980s only a little over one-quarter felt that big corporations were doing a good job for the country as a whole; the courts, the justice system, and Congress fared little better, and the president and his administration fared even worse (Johnston et al., forthcoming).

Among entering college students in 1989, more than two-thirds felt that government was not protecting the consumer, and over 85 percent felt that it was not controlling pollution (Astin et al., 1988). In brief, although there has been a significant decline in the proportion of privileged youth who express highly critical views of society, the extent of the decline is not sufficient to account for the rather marked decreases that have occurred both in political activism and in personal feelings of alienation.

The most likely explanation for these trends appears to be an increasing pragmatism and a greater substitution of private for public concerns among adolescents and youth (see pages 490–495). Although they are not enchanted by the state of society and its institutions, these young people seem less inclined to view issues as one-sided, less likely to believe that social change can occur quickly, and more skeptical of the ability of the individual to contribute significantly to social change.

Although one may be grateful that there has been an apparent decrease in the extent of alienation among young people since the late 1960s, some of the best aspects of the activism of that period—its idealism and genuine concern for others and for society as a whole—seem to have been attenuated in the process. The number of young people actively in pursuit of social goals ranging from improving the situation of the poor, the handicapped, or the elderly to enhancing the quality of life steadily declined, at least until recently (see page 495). Again, those who are involved are increasingly effective, but their numbers are limited. Society is still in need of fundamental changes, and *therefore it needs* young people who are willing to make long-term commitments without being discouraged.

A "New" Alienation?

Today a newer form of alienation appears to have taken root among at least a minority of youth and young adults. This form of alienation is more subtle, elusive, and private than the highly public, intense, and strongly articulated alienation and dissent of the 1960s. It is characterized by feelings of loneliness; desire for—but difficulty achieving—intimacy; a sense of rootlessness; a decreased sense of purpose and direction; and a diffuse sense of self (Conger, 1981, 1988; Lasch, 1979; Yankelovich, 1981).

In part, this newer alienation can be traced to new economic and political realities. Young people growing up in the early 1960s were part of a continually expanding economy that promised ever-greater affluence. In the 1970s and early 1980s the situation changed markedly: rapid inflation, declining productivity and technological innovation, increased competition in world markets, and enormous increases in oil prices took a major toll on the economy. As Daniel Yankelovich observed, "In a matter of a few years we . . . moved from an uptight culture in a dynamic economy to a dynamic culture set in an uptight economy." No longer could open and expanding career choices, future job security, money for one's children's education and a comfortable retirement—or even for the purchase of a home—be taken for granted (Yankelovich, 1981).

Although new economic realities were unsettling and doubtlessly played a role in this newer alienation, its roots appear to lie considerably deeper (Conger, 1981). As we noted in Chapter 5, the greater "freedom to be me," with its emphasis on self-fulfillment, that was a legacy of the 1960s can be a two-edged sword. Efforts to reexamine old stereotypes about personal, family, social, and vocational roles—"to realize oneself"—can be valuable and productive. But without a corresponding commitment to others and their well-being (which, for a time, was also a legacy of the 1960s), self-realization is ultimately meaningless. Psychologically, as well as economically, there is, in reality, no free lunch. In the "me decade" adults did little to help young people understand that "self-realization is not synonymous with self-indulgence, that concern for others is a necessary ingredient of concern for self, and that there can be no freedom without responsibility" (Conger, 1981, p. 1484).

As we have seen throughout this book, achieving a sense of identity is a crucial developmental task of adolescence. But as Erik Erikson has emphasized, maturity also requires the development of a capacity for intimacy—a true sharing of oneself with another that involves caring, trust, and sustained commitment "come rain or come shine." This is especially true in love, but it is also true in friendship; a fair-weather friend is just that. However, a large majority of Americans recognize that "while they have many acquaintances they have few close friends—and they experience this as a serious void in their lives" (Yankelovich, 1981, p. 25). Moreover, two out of five state that they have fewer close friends now than they did in the past.

A Sense of Community. Can these trends be reversed? We are beginning to see widespread efforts to develop a greater sense of community as an antidote to the political, economic, psychological, and social isolation that afflicts contemporary life. In addition to traditional clubs and societies based on cultural interests, sports, hobbies, and ethnic or religious affiliations, there are now a multitude of mutual-support groups whose diversity almost defies description. There are groups for children of alcoholics, parents without partners, widows, new parents, adolescent drug abusers, families with severely mentally ill children, ex-prisoners, patients discharged from mental hospitals, overeaters, children with cancer and their parents, paraplegics, Vietnam-era nurses, abusing parents, abused children, people who have had heart attacks or mastectomies, parents of physically or mentally handicapped children, survivors of natural disasters, men over 40 who need jobs, women seeking careers, and many other categories of people. How successful such groups will be in combating the new alienation remains to be seen (Conger, 1987).

Adolescent Runaways

National attention first became focused on the problem of runaway youth during the late 1960s (Janus, McCormack, Burgess, & Hartman, 1987; Weisberg, 1985). Between 1966 and 1968 thousands of alienated "flower children" left home for urban enclaves like the Haight-Ashbury section of San Francisco and, later, Boston and Boulder, Colorado. The hippie movement has long since disappeared from the social scene, but the problem of adolescent runaways has only grown more diffuse and more troubling.

Each year more than 1 million young people run away from home. Of these, perhaps half return after a few days or weeks. Most of the rest become, for all intents and purposes, homeless (Garbarino, Wilson, & Garbarino, 1986b; Janus et al., 1987). Although those who return home after a brief interval are more likely than nonrunaways to have adjustment problems and difficulties in family relationships, it is those who do not return who are of greatest concern to youth workers. These adolescents are in jeopardy for a variety of reasons: They are more likely to come from dysfunctional homes; to have significant adjustment problems; and to be victims of exploitation, neglect, or even death on the streets (Garbarino et al., 1986). Unlike the predominantly middle-class members of the hippie movement, an increasing number are poor. The fact that the hippie culture no longer exists to provide some support and acceptance serves only to heighten their alienation and to leave them even more powerless and vulnerable.

Studies of the families of "serious" runaways typically reveal chronic patterns of family conflict and lack of communication. Often, however, there are even worse problems in these children's homes. They may include parental alcoholism, family violence, physical and sexual abuse (including incest), chronic neglect, and outright rejection (Adams & Munro, 1979; Brennan,

Lacking money, food, or shelter, adolescent runaways who flock to major cities are often ready candidates for exploitation or violence. Many runaways are robbed, physically assaulted, underfed, or lured into prostitution, drug use, or small-time pushing.

Box 13.1 RUNAWAY OR THROWAWAY? ONE RUNAWAY'S RESPONSE TO ABUSE

Marie is a 16-year-old black female, 5 feet, 5 inches tall and weighing 110 pounds; with black, curly hair and a pretty, if overly made-up face. At the beginning of the interview, Marie appeared shy and nervous. She rarely raised her eyes; she spoke in a quiet, somewhat mumbled voice, and she twisted two fingers of her left hand with her right hand.

Marie first ran away from home at age 15 and has run away twice. She last left home about a month before our interview and has been on her own for the last week.

The earliest that Marie remembers being physically abused is at age 6. She says that both her mother and her father beat her at that time. When asked to recall that specific first instance, Marie is unable to do so and says that she thinks she was beaten because she did not do her chores. She recalls that her brother was being hit with a stick and dragged down stairs, and she remembers knowing she was hurt. Marie explains that she has trouble remembering things, as there were so many incidents that she cannot separate them. She was beaten every day that she can remember until she ran away from home.

When questioned about whether she had ever been sexually abused, Marie initially said she had not. However, during the discussions of her relationship with her father, it becomes apparent that her father molested her frequently, often during the physical beatings. Marie remembers his "always pinching my buttocks and touching my breasts." She says that her grandmother once told her that her father had raped his sister and that Marie should try to stay away from him.

When Marie was 15 years old, she told her friends that she could not stand it any more and that she was leaving. Without saying anything to her parents, she left for a babysitting job, called a girlfriend, and after getting permission from her girlfriend's parents, took a bus to her friend's home. She says that being physically abused was the most important reason for running away.

Her girlfriend's parents called the Children's Aid Society, and Marie told them about the abuse. She said that they didn't believe her and that they brought her back home. Her parents were angry with her when she returned home because "I left and because they said I made up stories."

The parental physical abuse continued during her final year at home, and when she could stand it no longer, Marie ran again to the same girlfriend's home. Her father and mother, when contacted by her girlfriend's parents, were angry. Sometime in the next few weeks her mother told her father that Marie was sleeping with a boy at the girlfriend's home. The father became enraged, went to the friend's home, and beat Marie. He "grabbed me by the breasts and threw me into a chair and then a wall." Marie ran away from her friend's home and traveled from her province to Toronto. Marie had arrived at the shelter the day before the interview.

> Marie reports suffering from headaches, dizzy spells, and sleep problems (nightmares) during childhood and at present. She has always felt lonely and has always been afraid of adult men and women. She admits to shyness, nervousness, self-mutilation, and suicidal feelings.
>
> *Source:* From M-D Janus, A. McCormack, A. W. Burgess, and C. Hartman. *Adolescent Runaways: Causes and Consequences* (pp. 50–51). Lexington, MA: Lexington Books, Copyright 1987, D.C. Heath & Co. By permission.

1980; Garbarino et al., 1986b; Janus, Burgess, & McCormack, 1987; Janus et al., 1987; Weisberg, 1985). In a study of homeless runaways in Toronto, for example, 73 percent reported having been physically beaten and 51 percent reported sexual abuse (Janus et al., 1987). Clearly, many "runaways" could more aptly be described as "throwaways," even when parental mistreatment has not included actual ejection of the young person from the home.

In some cases running away from home may constitute a healthy response to an impossible situation (Schulman & Kende, 1988; Silbert & Pines, 1980). Too often, however, the young person already carries the psychological scars of prior mistreatment. These may include low self-esteem, mistrust, lack of social competence, suicidal impulses, emotional isolation, fear of sex, feelings of going crazy, and psychophysiological problems (Brennan, Huizinga, & Elliott, 1978; Edelbrock, 1980; Garbarino et al., 1986b; Janus et al., 1987). Runaways who have been subjected to extremely stressful events, such as rape and assault, may show symptoms of *post-traumatic stress disorder* similar to those found among combat veterans. These symptoms include denial of the traumatic event or obsessive preoccupation with it, unpredictable flashbacks, fears both of social involvement and of being alone, crying spells, suicidal thoughts, sleep problems, and self-deprecating feelings (Janus et al., 1987).

Ironically, "the personal maladjustment, family conflict, and parental mistreatment that often precipitate running away also make the adolescent especially vulnerable to the risks that running away itself produces" (Garbarino et al., 1986b, p. 45). Lacking money, food, or shelter, adolescent runaways who flock to major cities are ready candidates for exploitation (Mussen, Conger, Kagan, & Huston, 1990; Weisberg, 1985). Thousands of adolescent runaways have become involved in prostitution, including homosexual prostitution, and the production of pornographic films and magazines, especially in large metropolitan areas like Los Angeles and New York (Weisberg, 1985). The average age at which adolescent girls enter prostitution is 14, and the great majority are under 16 (Weisberg, 1985). In addition, many runaways are robbed, physically assaulted, underfed, or lured into drug use and small-time pushing. Their need for adequate human services—health care, shelter, protection, and counseling—is often desperate (Janus et al., 1987). Each year more than 5000 young people are buried in unmarked graves because nobody has identified or claimed them.

The need for adequate human services for runaways—health care, shelter, protection, and counseling—is often desperate.

Temporary shelters, such as Under 21, Independence House, and The Door—A Center of Alternatives, make a valiant effort to protect and assist young runaways, but they are typically understaffed and underfunded, and they are forced to turn away many young people (Janus et al., 1987; Scott, 1980; Weisberg, 1985). It is estimated that no more than one in twelve of the runaway and homeless youth who have actually been identified and counted are currently receiving shelter, and no more than one in three are receiving services of any kind. When the large number of such youth who escape the attention of youth workers or police is taken into account, the figures become even more alarming (Janus et al., 1987). There is an urgent need for society to assume far greater responsibility for abused and exploited children and adolescents.

ADOLESCENT DELINQUENCY

Despite the attention it has received in recent years, adolescent delinquency is not a new phenomenon. Three hundred years ago the great English educator John Locke deplored delinquency in much the same way that we do today. Six thousand years ago an Egyptian priest carved on a stone, "Our earth is degenerate. . . . Children no longer obey their parents" (Johnson, 1959, p. 840). Nevertheless, current rates of delinquency are reason for serious concern, not only in the United States but in most other countries as well.

Delinquency is basically a legal concept that is defined in different ways in different times and places. In our society the term **juvenile delinquent** is generally applied to persons under 18 years of age who exhibit behavior that is punishable by law. It is important to recognize that what we call delinquency includes not only serious offenses such as burglary, assault, robbery, and rape but also "status offenses"—acts such as curfew violation, truancy, running away, sexual activity, or "incorrigibility" that would not constitute violation of the law if they were committed by an adult (Binder, 1988).

Incidence of Delinquency

We know a good deal about the incidence of *recorded* delinquency through various governmental and other compilations. After rising rapidly in the 1960s and 1970s, the delinquency rate reached a peak in 1980 and then declined slightly (see Figure 13.2). Whether this relatively steady rate will persist (albeit at a distressingly high level), only time will tell. Even at recent levels, it is estimated that at least 22 percent of boys and 10 percent of girls are likely to turn up in juvenile court records before the end of adolescence (Elliott et al., 1983; Farrington, 1981, 1987; Shannon, 1981; Vishner & Roth, 1980). Although delinquency is most common in adolescence, reaching a peak between the ages of 15 and 17, closer examination reveals that in many cases delinquent behaviors actually began during middle childhood (Farrington, 1987; Gold & Petronio, 1980; Rutter & Giller, 1984).

Since 1960 the incidence of more serious offenses among young people has been rising at a faster rate than that of delinquency in general. Although in 1987 young people between the ages of 14 and 17 comprised only about 6

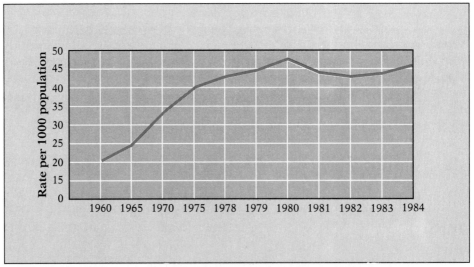

Figure 13.2 Rate (per 1,000 population) of delinquency cases disposed of by juvenile courts involving children and adolescents ages 10–17. (From U.S. Bureau of the Census. *Statistical abstract of the United States, 1989* (109th ed.). Washington, D.C.: U.S. Government Printing Office, 1989.)

percent of the total population, they accounted for a considerably higher proportion of many offenses (see Figure 13.3). Moreover, young people between the ages of 18 and 24, who comprised less than 12 percent of the population, were responsible for 29.1 percent of all serious crimes. Interestingly, however, between 1981 and 1987 the percentage of serious crimes committed by those under 18 and by those age 18–24 declined slightly (from 33.5 percent to a little over 29 percent in both cases). In contrast, 25–44-year-olds became, by a slight margin, the age group with the highest rate of serious crimes (35.8 percent) (U.S. Bureau of the Census, 1981, 1989).

Sex Differences. There are clear sex differences in the incidence of recorded delinquency. Although the male:female ratio has declined in the last half-century both in the United States and in England, boys still exceed girls in juvenile arrests, particularly for serious offenses (Farrington, 1987; U.S. Bu-

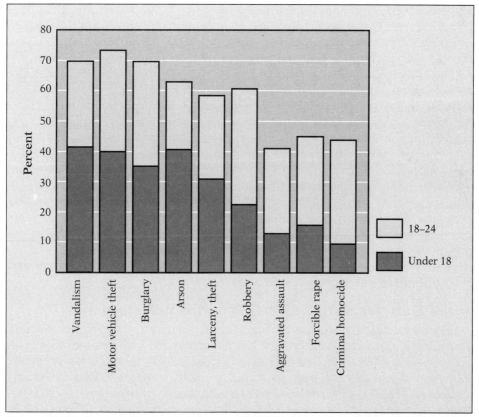

Figure 13.3 Arrests of persons under age 18 and of persons between ages 18 and 24, as a percentage of all arrests. (Adapted from Federal Bureau of Investigation, *Crime in the United States,* annual; and U.S. Bureau of the Census, *Statistical abstract of the United States, 1989* (109th ed.). Washington, D.C.: U.S. Government Printing Office, 1989.)

reau of the Census, 1989; Vishner & Roth, 1986). For example, boys exceed girls in arrests for burglary and robbery by approximately 15 to 1; in contrast, ratios are lowest for offenses like theft and shoplifting (less than 3 to 1). Girls also tend to become involved in delinquency at later ages than boys; the male:female ratio is highest in early adolescence (Elliott et al., 1983; Farrington, 1987; McGarrel & Flanagan, 1985).

In attempting to explain these findings, some investigators have linked the higher prevalence of more serious offenses among males to biologically based differences in aggressiveness and physical strength (Maccoby & Jacklin, 1974; Wilson & Herrenstein, 1985). Not all offenses are linked to aggression or physical strength, however. Another possible explanation for the relationship between delinquency and gender is that boys and girls are socialized differently (Farrington, 1987). Despite recent social changes, delinquent behavior, especially active or aggressive behavior, is still more strenuously discouraged among girls than among boys, not only by parents but by society and even by their peers (Farrington, 1987; Rutter and Giller, 1984). On the other hand, adolescent girls are, if anything, more affected by family conditions than boys (see Chapter 6), and hence they are at least as likely to respond *directly* to unsatisfactory family circumstances through such behaviors as running away, conflict with parents, and sexual acting out. Much sexual delinquency among adolescent girls involves rebellion against parents, a search for substitute sources of affection, or in some cases both (Weiner, 1982).

As David Farrington, an expert on delinquency research, points out, gender differences in sex roles, social habits, and opportunities may all play a part in accounting for male:female ratios for various offenses (Farrington, 1987). For example, boys are more likely to hang around together on the street at night—a situation that is linked to burglary and violence (Elliott, Huizinga, & Ageton, 1985). Girls, on the other hand, are more likely to spend time shopping, which may help explain why shoplifting is the most frequent offense among adolescent girls. The rapid rise in white-collar crime among women in recent years has been linked to increased employment of women in jobs that present opportunities for theft, fraud, or embezzlement. It is still too early to predict what overall effect changing sex roles will ultimately have on the patterns and extent of crime and delinquency.

Social Class, Ethnicity, and Self-Reported Delinquency

Reported delinquency rates are significantly higher among adolescents and youth from lower-income families, particularly those living in urban ghettos (Elliott et al., 1983; Gold, 1987; Gold & Petronio, 1980; Rutter & Giller, 1984). However, a number of surveys based on self-reports show considerably smaller social-class differences than are indicated by official delinquency statistics, and some investigators report finding no social-class differences, at least for overall delinquency (Elliott & Ageton, 1980; Elliott et al., 1983; Gold, 1980, 1987; Rutter & Giller, 1984). This has led some sociologists to conclude that the presumed relationship between social class and delinquency is a myth and that significant social-class differences in official delinquency records are due largely to discrimination against lower-class youth or are a result of inaccurate reporting (Braithwaite, 1981; Elliot et al., 1983).

A careful examination of the available evidence, however, suggests that the presumed myth is itself somewhat mythical. Many self-report studies, especially those showing few or no social-class differences, suffer from several shortcomings: (1) They are based on small numbers and inadequate sampling techniques; (2) they characterize as delinquent relatively minor acts such as cutting classes and disobeying parents (sometimes omitting more serious crimes); (3) they employ broad social-class categories; or (4) they are limited to non-urban youth (Braithwaite, 1981; Farington, 1987).

In contrast, both in the United States and in England self-report studies reveal significant social-class differences when large, representative samples are used, when urban areas are included, when the focus includes the more serious offenses, and when truly lower-class, socioeconomically disadvantaged adolescents and youth are differentiated from their working-class and middle-class peers (Burchard & Burchard, 1987; Elliott & Ageton, 1980; Elliott et al., 1983; Farrington, 1987; Rutter & Giller, 1984). Thus, one representative national survey of adolescents and youth age 11 and 12 found that lower-class youth were two or more times as likely as middle-class youth to become involved in serious and violent offenses (Elliott et al., 1983). Moreover, the higher the level of delinquency (number of offenses per person), the greater the social-class differences (Elliott & Ageton, 1980; Elliott et al., 1983).

Nevertheless, a sizable and growing number of both minor and more serious offenses are committed by middle-class delinquents (Braithwaite, 1981; Gold, 1970; Gold & Petronio, 1979; Quay, 1987b). Consequently, theories of delinquency, while they cannot ignore relationships between poverty or social deprivation and delinquency, cannot be based solely on these relationships. It should also be noted that the majority of low-income young people, even those living in urban ghettos, do not become seriously delinquent (Gold, 1987). In many cases strong parental guidance and supervision appear to play a major role in the young person's resistance to destructive social forces (Patterson, Barsyshe, & Ramsey, 1989; Rutter & Giller, 1983; Snyder & Patterson, 1987).

Delinquency and Ethnicity. Delinquency rates (both recorded and self-reported) also vary with ethnic-group membership. The rates for blacks and Hispanics are somewhat higher than those for whites, particularly for more serious offenses, while the rates for Americans of Japanese or Chinese ancestry are lower (Farrington, 1987; Hindelang, 1981; McGarrell-Flanagan, 1985; Visher & Roth, 1986). In attempting to account for these differences, it has been hypothesized that ethnicity per se is not an important causal factor but that blacks and whites differ in known precursors of delinquency, such as low income, inadequate education, poor parental control and supervision (often in single-parent families), discrimination, and a socially disorganized environment (Farrington, 1986, 1987).

For example, one English study found that black–white differences in reported delinquency did not hold independently of differences in social class or school attainment (Ouston, 1984). In contrast, the relatively low delinquency rate of Asians in the United States and England has been attributed to a close-knit family system with strong family controls on the activities of children and adolescents (Farrington, 1987; Mawby, 1979). Further research on ethnic differences is needed, but it appears likely that both family influences and social and economic conditions play an important role.

Discrimination. In cases in which official statistics show large social-class or ethnic differences in delinquency, one or more of the following factors may be present: differences in *actual* rates of delinquent behavior, discrimination against lower-status youth by juvenile authorities and society generally, greater surveillance by police or citizens in high crime areas, and greater difficulty in finding nonlegal (e.g., parental) solutions to the problems posed by delinquent behavior (Braithwaite, 1981; Farrington, 1987; Gibbons, 1981; Gold, 1987). Not all social-class differences in the way delinquency is treated are a result of discrimination, especially in the case of more serious offenses. In some instances the intent is to protect the young person himself or herself. For example, a lower-class youth may be remanded to the custody of the court because of adverse family conditions (e.g., alcoholic, irresponsible, or delinquent parents) whereas an upper-class youth who has committed a similar offense may be remanded to his or her parents' custody without formal charges.

SOCIAL CHANGE, DEPRIVATION, AND DELINQUENCY

Current high rates of delinquency appear to be related at least in part to changes in the structure of society, including our increased mobility as a people and the consequent disruption of established cultural patterns and family ties; the population growth and social disorganization that has occurred in large metropolitan areas; and the lack of a clear sense of national purpose and concern with social problems. Recent reductions in social programs for the neediest members of society, combined with substantial decreases in taxes and increased benefits for the wealthiest, have increased the sense of frustration, even despair, among those who cannot feed their families properly, find adequate shelter, obtain essential health care, or find a job that pays an adequate wage (Conger, 1981, 1988; Edelman, 1987). Current levels of unemployment among black and Hispanic youth actively seeking work should not be tolerated in a democratic society.

Research has indicated that economic deprivation is most likely to lead to crime and delinquency when it is associated with marked inequality in the distribution of society's resources (Braithwaite, 1981; Gold, 1987; Johnstone, 1978). In one study, several measures of inequality were used to predict average crime rates in 193 cities over a six-year period. "The income gap between the poor and the average income earner was shown to be a significant predictor of crime rates, while the proportion of the population below the poverty line in the city was not" (Braithwaite, 1981, p. 48). In another study, poor children from affluent communities reported *higher* rates of delinquency than those from poor neighborhoods (Johnstone, 1978).

Increases in delinquency, as well as in other adolescent problems, are most likely to occur in situations in which the sense of community and the integrity of the extended family have been seriously disrupted, for example, in urban ghettos and in some affluent suburban communities. They are least likely to occur in situations in which these ties have been preserved, for example, in small, stable relatively isolated towns and cities (Bronfenbrenner, 1974, 1985; Conger, 1971, 1981). In recent years the greatest increase in the juvenile crime rate has occurred in suburbs (more than double the urban increase and more than four times the increase in rural areas). Within the suburbs, the increases have been greatest in communities and families characterized by high rates of social and geographic mobility and lack of stable ties to other people and social institutions (National Center, 1977; U.S. Bureau of the Census, 1982, 1987; U.S. Federal Bureau of Investigation, annual). Nevertheless, absolute rates of delinquency are still highest in deteriorated neighborhoods near the centers of large cities. In such areas, which are characterized by economic deprivation, rapid population turnover, and general disorganization, delinquency is often an approved tradition and there are many opportunities to learn antisocial behavior from delinquent peers (Ouston, 1980; Rutter, 1980; Rutter & Giller, 1983; West & Farrington, 1973, 1977).

Delinquency occurs about twice as frequently among children of immigrants as among children of native-born parents. Among native-born minority groups, it is more frequent among the children of parents who have moved from a relatively simple rural environment to crowded cities than among children of parents who have lived in the city for a long time. Children of parents in both groups experience a great deal of conflict as a result of the contrasting standards of their homes, on the one hand, and the neighborhood and school, on the other. In addition, the prestige of these children and their parents in the community is likely to be lower.

Moreover, such families are more likely to live in deteriorated neighborhoods, and hence the children are more likely to be exposed to delinquent practices. Finally, the parents may themselves lack the knowledge and skill necessary to deal successfully with their environment and therefore serve as inadequate role models for their children. They may also be too preoccupied or defeated by their own problems to give their children adequate attention (Auletta, 1983; Gold, 1987; Reese, 1982).

Peer Influence and Gangs

Recent research has demonstrated the importance of peers in instigating and maintaining delinquent behavior (Elliott et al., 1985; Farrington, 1979, 1986; Patterson et al., 1989; Rutter & Giller, 1984; West & Farrington, 1977). One extensive longitudinal study showed that male and female adolescents who had close ties ("bonding") to delinquent peers and weak bonds to prosocial, nondelinquent peers engaged in delinquent activity with increasing frequency over a three-year period, while those who had only weak or no ties to either group did not (Elliott et al., 1985). For those with strong bonds to both delinquent and prosocial peers, the relationship with prosocial peers appeared to offset, but not negate, the influence of delinquent peers. The authors conclude that bonding with delinquent peers plays a vital role in the development of delinquency.

Gangs. Traditionally, lower-class youth in urban ghettos have been more likely to join delinquent gangs. Although these groups were likely to encourage delinquency, the better organized and less violent gangs often helped meet needs that are common to all youth—the need for a sense of personal worth, a meaningful social life and acceptance by peers, and self-preservation (Campbell, 1984; Cloward & Ohlin, 1960; Gold & Mann, 1972; Truckemiller, 1982).

Youth gangs are typically organized along ethnic, national, and geographic lines. Today's gangs are typically more violent and socially destructive—and better armed—than gangs of the 1950s and 1960s.

Box 13.2 THE GIRLS IN THE GANG

Despite the women's movement and the efforts of female gang members to subscribe to such goals as independence, equality, and "sisterhood," traditional male dominance remains alive and well in today's youth gangs. In her remarkable account of the life of girls in three representative New York gangs, *The Girls in the Gang*, social psychologist Anne Campbell comments:

While some writers have argued for the existence of a set of focal concerns specific to lower-class male life, this should not be parodied into a simplistic belief that gang members are isolated from society at large or hermetically sealed in an alien set of norms. As much as anyone, they are exposed through the media to the images of a life lived with limitless luxury, in which everyone is beautiful and relationships are passionate, stormy, superficial, and ultimately selfish. They subscribe to this as the natural order. There is no counterculture in the gang, only the rehearsal in microcosm of an American belief in consumerism, in the equation of money with power, in competition and success, and in a hierarchy through which the initiate may climb to power and one day become president. All are proud to be American, some have fought for their country, and most would do so enthusiastically if the need arose.

In understanding the fundamentally conservative structure and values of the gang, the position of girls becomes more explicable. Females must accept the range of roles within the gang that might be available to them in society at large. The traditional structure of the nuclear family is firmly duplicated in the gang. In straight society the central, pivotal figure is the male. His status in the world of societal and material success is the critical factor, while the woman supports, nurtures, and sustains him. The gang parodies this state of affairs without even the economic infrastructure to sustain it, for the male rarely works and often it is the female who receives a more stable income through welfare. Nevertheless, the males constitute the true gang. . . .

Nor are the double standards of morality forgotten by gang members. Hell's Angels distinguish promiscuous "sheep" from wifely "old ladies." Girls who sleep around within the gang are disparaged by the males and disciplined by the females. The Sex Girls [part of The Sex Boys and Girls (as in *Essex* Street), a black and Hispanic New York City gang] discuss the girls of rival gangs as only interested in indiscriminate sex with the boys. At the same time, the sexual adventures of the boys are considered an unremarkable aspect of the male character. The perpetuation of such values keeps the girls very firmly in their place.

Source: From *The Girls in the Gang*, by Anne Campbell, pp. 242–243. ©1984 by Anne Campbell. Published by Basil Blackwell Ltd., Oxford and New York. By permission.

Although there is evidence suggesting a decline in the importance of large-scale organized gangs and a rise in small-group and individual crime during the 1960s, any such trend has clearly been reversed (Barich, 1986; Campbell, 1984; Miller, 1975, 1980). Moreover, contemporary gangs have become increasingly violent and socially destructive, particularly in the ghetto areas of cities like New York, Chicago, Los Angeles, Philadelphia, and San Francisco. In Los Angeles County there are an estimated 50,000 gang members, of whom over 580 were murdered in 1989 (*Morning edition*, 1990). And rates are continuing to escalate.

Youth gangs are typically organized along ethnic, national, and geographic lines. In Los Angeles County alone there are hundreds of gangs: most recently, Honduran, Salvadoran, Nicaraguan, and Guatemalan. "There are Samoan gangs in Los Angeles County, and gangs from Tonga, and they feud with each other, just as their ancestors did on the islands" (Barich, 1986, p. 98). In the affluent suburbs there are gangs of white teenagers, who, despite their comfortable environment, nevertheless take to the streets.

Unlike gangs of the 1950s, which typically relied on relatively primitive weapons such as homemade zip guns, today's gangs are likely to be armed with high-quality handguns like the Smith and Wesson .38 caliber police revolver, .357 magnum, or Uzi semiautomatic weapon from Israel (Barich, 1986). As a result, gang violence is more lethal than ever. Although gang members in a number of major cities have terrorized apartment houses and school buildings and killed or wounded scores of teachers, elderly citizens, and nongang youth, most of the victims of gang violence are gang members themselves. What kind of life is this for an adolescent? In the words of a 16-year-old New York boy, "Man, I've been on the outlaw trail most all my life. Can't help it. What else you got for me? . . . The only real world is what I got in my hand. Everything else is makeup." Or, in the words of a 14-year-old, "The human race stinks, man. I'm glad I ain't in it" (Stevens, 1971, p. 91).

Of course, even in high-delinquency areas many adolescents do not become delinquent. Conversely, many adolescents who are not economically deprived, who come from well-established middle-class homes, and whose parents are neither culturally displaced nor members of struggling minority groups, do become delinquent. Indeed, although the absolute rate of delinquency remains lower among middle-class suburban youth, the greatest increases in delinquency rates in recent years have occurred in this group.

PERSONALITY AND DELINQUENCY

Why does one child from a particular neighborhood, school, social class, and ethnic background become delinquent while another, apparently subject to the same environmental influences, does not? In approaching this problem investigators typically use a research design in which delinquents and nondelinquents from the same kind of background are compared with respect to personality characteristics and parent–child relations at various ages. What have been the findings?

Intelligence. The average delinquent scores an average of about eight points lower than nondelinquents on tests of intelligence (Hirchi & Hindelang, 1977; Quay, 1987a). When only recidivists (repeaters) are included, the difference rises to as much as twelve points (Rutter & Giller, 1984). In both instances delinquents consistently score more poorly in verbal skills than in performance skills (Grace & Sweeney, 1986; Hubble & Groff, 1982; Quay, 1987a).

There is also a somewhat higher incidence of mental retardation among delinquents than in the population at large. Nevertheless, most delinquents are not retarded, and low intelligence in and of itself does not appear to have a *direct* impact on delinquency in a majority of cases. It should be noted that the relationship between IQ and delinquency is not simply a reflection of social-class status or ethnic-group membership. Several studies have found that significant IQ–delinquency correlations persist even after controlling for the effects of these variables (Binder, 1988; Hirischi & Hindelang, 1977; Quay, 1987a; Rutter & Giller, 1984).

What, then, accounts for the relationship between delinquency and IQ? One hypothesis has been that lower IQ—particularly verbal IQ—leads to poorer school performance, "which leads to a negative attitude toward school, which in turn leads to delinquency" (Quay, 1987, p. 104). Partial support for this hypothesis is provided by studies showing that improving academic performance may significantly reduce disciplinary problems in the classroom. Researchers have also found a higher incidence of "pure" reading disability among delinquent students (Binder, 1988). It should also be noted that delinquency rates tend to fall after young people leave school (Bachman, O'Malley, & Johnson, 1978; Elliott & Voss, 1974; Phillips & Kelly, 1979; Rutter & Giller, 1984).

Clearly, however, school difficulties are not the whole story. For one thing, antisocial behavior, as well as more general behavioral disturbances, may precede school failure (Patterson et al., 1989; Richman & Lindgren, 1981; Richman, Stevenson, & Graham, 1982; West & Farrington, 1973). Moreover, it is possible that cognitive deficits and conduct disturbances may "to some extent share a common etiology—either in terms of socio-familial variables or temperamental characteristics" (Rutter & Giller, 1984, p. 167; Quay, 1987a). Several studies of children adopted shortly after birth have found that delinquency and adult criminality are related to such behavior in the adoptee's biological parents but not in their adoptive parents, suggesting that genetic factors may play a role in creating a predisposition for delinquent behavior (Robins, 1978; Rutter & Giller, 1984; Trasler, 1987; Wilson & Herrenstein, 1985). However, family and peer relationships, together with other psychological influences, appear to play a far more critical role.

Delinquent Boys. In an extensive study spanning the period from kindergarten through the ninth grade, investigators found that by the end of the third grade, boys who later became delinquents were viewed by their teachers as more poorly adapted than individually matched nondelinquent classmates.

They were less considerate and fair in dealing with others, less friendly, less responsible, more impulsive, and more antagonistic to authority. In return, they were less well liked and accepted by their peers (Conger & Miller, 1966). In school they were much more easily distracted, daydreamed more, and had greater difficulty maintaining attention and sticking to the task at hand. They were less likely to display any special ability or interest. Not surprisingly, these social and academic problems appeared to reflect underlying emotional problems, and in the opinion of their teachers future delinquents more often came from disturbed home environments and were overly aggressive.

Although this general picture continued into the period covering the fourth to sixth grades, some additional differences and changes in emphasis emerged. Thus, in the middle-school years inconsistent academic performance by future delinquents became increasingly evident. These children were more likely to be viewed as underachieving and showed poorer work habits. They demonstrated less leadership ability and had a narrower range of general interests—although, relatively, they were becoming more and more attention seeking. On the other hand, future delinquents and nondelinquents showed similar levels of resentment toward and rejection of school authority, "possibly because problems with authority are *generally* more common at this age than among school beginners" (Conger & Miller, 1966, p. 186).

In the ninth grade delinquents continued to display significantly less respect and consideration for the rights of others than did nondelinquents. Not surprisingly, they were much less cooperative in observing school rules and regulations and meeting their responsibilities as members of a social group. Moreover, at this age delinquents showed much more antagonism toward authority compared with nondelinquent peers than was true in the fourth through sixth grades. Apparently in the years between middle childhood and adolescence the attitudes of the nondelinquents toward authority improved considerably while among delinquents they continued to deteriorate.

Peer relations remained significantly poorer among the delinquents during adolescence. The delinquents were less friendly and pleasant toward classmates and, in return, were less well liked and accepted by their peers. In their academic activities the delinquents continued "to have greater difficulty than their nondelinquent matches. Their work habits were still significantly poorer; they were more careless in their work, appeared more often to be working below their capabilities, and needed much more supervision from teachers. Attendance was more often a problem among these youths" (Conger & Miller, 1966, p. 187). The delinquents were more distractible; they manifested much less capacity for sustained attention, daydreamed more, and tended to give up more easily when challenged academically.

In general, the delinquents were rated as less well adjusted, more lacking in self-confidence and self-respect, less cheerful and happy, less able to get along with members of their own and the opposite sex, and more attention seeking. Again, teachers were much more likely to spontaneously mention a "disturbed home environment" as a significant problem for delinquents. These impressions of poorer adjustment among the delinquents seemed to find support in the reports of the boys themselves, as indicated by the results of psychological testing at the end of junior high school. In the various group tests, the delinquents emerged as clearly less well adjusted.

Delinquent Girls. Somewhat similar results were obtained for girls, with significant differences between future delinquents and nondelinquents becoming evident as early as the period from kindergarten to the third grade (Conger, 1973). Future delinquents were significantly less well adjusted socially, emotionally, and academically than their nondelinquent matches. They were less poised and more emotionally unstable; less likely to be cheerful, happy, or friendly; and less likely to have a sense of humor. They had more difficulty relating to same- and opposite-sex peers and were less likely to show respect and consideration for the rights of others; in return, they were less well liked and accepted by others.

The delinquent girls also displayed significantly more antagonism toward adult authority of any kind, including the school, and were much less cooperative in observing rules and regulations. At the same time, they appeared to have greater difficulty in learning to think for themselves, developing a clear set of values of their own, and setting realistic, planful goals. They showed less creative ability and fewer special abilities or interests. Their work habits were significantly poorer than those of their nondelinquent peers.

Many of these differences are similar to those found in boys. However, there are some variations in emphasis. The largest differences between delinquent and nondelinquent girls were found in the areas of emotional adjustment and conformity; among boys, the largest differences occurred in the areas of conformity, creative ability, self-reliance, and relations with peers.

PARENT–CHILD RELATIONSHIPS OF DELINQUENTS

A representative national study of the family backgrounds of tenth-grade boys found that the single most predictive indicator of actual (not simply recorded) adolescent delinquency is the boy's relationship with his parents: "We . . . find a strong inverse association between family relations and delinquency: The better a boy reports getting along with his parents, the less delinquency" (Bachman, 1970, p. 171). This general finding supports the results of a number of less extensive, but more intensive, studies of the home backgrounds and family influences of delinquents and nondelinquents (Ahlstrom & Havighurst, 1971; Kroupa, 1988; McCord, 1978, 1979; Patterson et al., 1989; Rutter & Giller, 1984; Snyder & Patterson, 1987). With remarkable consistency, these investigations indicate that the early disciplinary techniques to which delinquents have been subjected are likely to be lax, erratic, or overly strict. Moreover, they tend to involve physical punishment rather than reasoning with the child about misconduct and responding consistently and appropriately to both antisocial and prosocial behaviors (Loeber & Dishion, 1983; Olweus, 1980; Patterson et al., 1989; Pulkkinen, 1983; Snyder & Patterson,

1987). Recent research indicates that the extent and adequacy of *parental supervision* may be a particularly critical factor. In a study conducted in England, the family variable that was most strongly associated with delinquency was weak parental supervision, as indicated by characteristics such as not requiring children to say where they were going and when they would return home, allowing children to roam the streets, and not knowing where a child was much of the time (Wilson, 1980).

Similarly, in their work with families of aggressive and delinquent children at the Oregon Social Learning Center (see page 537), Gerald Patterson and his colleagues have found four aspects of family interaction to be associated with delinquency: (1) lack of "house rules" (so that there is neither predictable routine for meals or chores nor a clear set of expectations about what children may and may not do); (2) lack of parental monitoring of their children's behavior (so that the parents do not know what a child is doing or how he or she is feeling, and tend not to respond to deviant behavior because they have not themselves seen it); (3) lack of effective contingencies (so that parents are inconsistent in their responses to unacceptable behavior, tending to shout and nag but not to follow through and not to respond with an adequate distinction between praise for positive activities and punishment for negative or antisocial activities); and (4) lack of ways of dealing with family crises or problems (so that conflicts lead to tension and dispute but do not end up being resolved) (Patterson, 1981a, 1981b; Patterson et al., 1989; Snyder & Patterson, 1987).

The parent–child relationships of delinquents are far more likely than those of nondelinquents to be characterized by lack of communication, understanding, or identification (Canter, 1982; Rutter & Giller, 1984; Wadsworth, 1979; West & Farrington, 1973, 1977). They are also far more likely to be characterized by mutual hostility; lack of cohesiveness; and parental rejection, indifference, dissension, or apathy (Olweus, 1980; Simons, Robertson, & Downs, 1989; Snyder & Patterson, 1987). Parents of delinquents are more likely to have minimal aspirations for their children, to avoid engaging in leisure activities as a family, to be hostile or indifferent toward school, and to have a variety of personal and emotional problems of their own (Canter, 1982; West & Farrington, 1973; Hirschi, 1969; Rutter & Giller, 1984). Parents who have a criminal record—especially one extending into the child-rearing years—are especially likely to have delinquent offspring (Osborn & West, 1979; Robins, West, & Herjanic, 1975; Snyder & Patterson, 1987).

Fathers of delinquents are more likely to be rated by independent observers as cruel, neglecting, and inclined to ridicule their children (particularly sons) and less likely to be rated as warm, affectionate, or passive. In turn, their delinquent children, especially sons, are likely to have few close ties to their fathers and to consider them wholly unacceptable as models. Mothers of delinquents are more likely to be rated as careless or inadequate in supervising their children and as hostile or indifferent; and less likely to be rated as loving (Canter, 1982; Kroupa, 1988; Snyder & Patterson, 1987). Among girls, delinquents, especially recidivists (i.e., repeaters), more frequently acknowledge hostility toward their mothers and report that their mothers spent less time with them (Duncan, 1971). In contrast, democratic, authoritative child-rearing practices can help to increase a young person's resistance to delinquent pressures (see pages 204–207). Such parents are able "to foster a child's skills, to model and encourage normative values, and to provide a caring environment" (Snyder & Patterson, 1987, p. 225).

Finally, in several studies of delinquency a broken home has been found to be significantly associated with a higher incidence of delinquent behavior (Ahlstrom & Havighurst, 1971; Rutter & Giller, 1984; Snyder & Patterson, 1987). However, it has also been shown that the likelihood of adolescent delinquency is far higher in nonbroken homes characterized by mutual hostility, indifference or apathy, and a lack of cohesiveness than in broken homes (usually with only the mother present) characterized by cohesiveness and mutual affection and support (Adams, Milner, & Schrepf, 1984; Ahlstrom & Havighurst, 1971; Rutter & Giller, 1984). It may be that conflict and discord are more critical variables than parental absence or divorce, although clearly the latter events are likely to be stressful in their own right (Hetherington, Cox, & Cox, 1979; Patterson et al., 1989; Rutter, 1971; Snyder & Patterson, 1987).

Adolescent Delinquency and Adult Criminality. Does delinquency during the years of childhood and adolescence lead to criminal behavior in adulthood? The answer appears to be that it depends on how early delinquent behavior begins, the seriousness of the offenses, how often they are repeated, and the extent to which delinquent behavior is part of a generally antisocial life-style (Farrington, 1983; Loeber & Stouthamer-Loeber, 1987; Robins, 1966, 1979, in press; Robins & Ratcliff, 1979). Although it is uncommon for individuals to become seriously criminal for the first time in adulthood, it is also true that most adolescents who have been involved in occasional instances of delinquent behavior—even when they have had to appear in juvenile court—do not progress to criminal careers in adulthood. A number of studies have shown that the younger the age of onset of delinquent behavior, the greater the number of rearrests, the more the delinquent behavior involves a delinquent peer group or parental criminal activity; and the more serious the offenses the adolescent commits, the greater the likelihood that delinquent or criminal activities will continue into adulthood (Farrington et al., 1986; Osborn & West, 1980; Patterson et al., 1989; Rutter & Giller, 1984). In brief, most adolescents' delinquent behavior has only a modest relationship to antisocial behavior in adulthood; in contrast, "a record of extremely delinquent behavior in adolescence is singularly predictive of adult pathology" (Gold & Petronio, 1979, p. 517).

SOCIAL CLASS, DELINQUENCY, AND EMOTIONAL DISTURBANCE

Thus far we have considered overall differences between delinquents and nondelinquents in terms of psychological characteristics and parent–child relationships. However, a number of theorists have argued that there may be social-class differences in the kinds of characteristics that differentiate delinquents from nondelinquents (Conger & Miller, 1966; Rutter & Giller, 1984; Quay, 1987b). For example, one team of investigators has postulated that a non–lower-class youth who becomes involved in delinquency is much more likely to be emotionally disturbed than not, whereas the opposite is true in the case of lower-class children. The basic assumption is that delinquency is much less likely to involve norm-violating behavior in lower-class groups and hence is less likely to be a sign of individual emotional disturbance. They assert that "the preponderant portion of our 'delinquent' population consists of emotionally 'normal' lower-class youngsters" (Kvaraceus, 1945, p. 55).

A related view has been expressed by Adelaide Johnson, who draws a distinction between the "sociologic delinquent" and the "individual delinquent." "What makes the *sociologic delinquent* group is that it is largely molded by community and home forces more or less *consciously* in opposition to the whole other social world" (Johnson, 1959, p. 852). She cites as an example a youngster who grows up in a gypsy society in which stealing from villagers is permissible. In contrast, the individual delinquent's antisocial behavior is seen as stemming not from untroubled conformity to parental and social norms but from disturbed parent–child relations. These frequently include parental attitudes that unconsciously foster defects of conscience and related distortions in the child's capacity to evaluate the environment realistically. Johnson cites clinical examples in which "anti-social acting out in a child is unconsciously fostered and sanctioned by the parents, who vicariously achieve gratification of their own poorly integrated forbidden impulses through a child's acting out" (Johnson, 1959, p. 844).

Other investigators have distinguished among *socialized delinquents* (similar to the sociologic delinquent), *undersocialized aggressive (psychopathic) delinquents*, and *neurotic delinquents*—although these categories are not directly tied to social-class variables (Hewitt & Jenkins, 1946; Peterson, Quay, & Cameron, 1959; Quay, 1987c). One study found that these groups did in fact differ from one another—and from nondelinquents—in terms of parent–child relations (Hetherington, Stouwie, & Ridberg, 1971). In general, the nondelinquents' parents were less hostile and power-assertive (see pages 477–479), had more positive expectations for their children, and were less neurotically involved than the parents of delinquents. Among the latter, the family relations of socialized delinquents appeared to be the most harmonious and stable. Parents of neurotic delinquents tended to be rejecting, highly restrictive, and anxious about any expression of aggression; parents of psychopathic delinquents also attempted to sharply restrict their child's activities, but they encouraged aggression outside the home while suppressing it in the home.

There is little question that many lower-class adolescents—particularly those living in urban ghettos—are subjected to greater cultural pressure toward delinquency than their more privileged peers. But does this mean that lower-class delinquents as a group have fewer emotional problems than middle- and upper-class delinquents? In a seminal study of a large group of delinquents, A. J. Reiss encountered a type of lower-class delinquent youth (the *integrated delinquent*) who tended to come from a stable family and who did not appear to be particularly troubled emotionally (Reiss, 1952). Rather like the sociologic delinquent, the integrated delinquent came from a high-delinquency area and simply tended to adopt the asocial values of the delinquent group with whom he interacted. However, Reiss also found another type of lower-class delinquent who would not usually be described as emotionally normal. This type, the *defective-superego delinquent* (similar to the psychopathic delinquent described earlier), is likely to come from a lower-class background and typically grew up in a very unstable family marked by divorce, desertion, alcoholism, and/or consistent lack of nurturance. He shows very little guilt about his asocial behavior, lacks a well-defined conscience, and has no clearly established goals. He feels a great deal of resentment toward the social environment and expresses his anger through delinquent acts.

Other investigators (Arbuthnot, Gordon, & Jurkovic, 1987; Binder, 1988; Rutter & Giller, 1984; West & Farrington, 1972) have noted signs of poor emotional adjustment and impaired self-concept across a rather wide range of socioeconomic levels of delinquency. One extensive longitudinal study found that *both* lower- and middle-class delinquents were more poorly adjusted than nondelinquents, either deprived or nondeprived (Conger & Miller, 1966). On some traits, at some ages, and at some IQ levels, deprived delinquents scored more poorly than nondeprived delinquents, whereas in some other instances the reverse was true. In general, however, socioeconomically deprived delinquents tended to score more like nondeprived delinquents than like nondelinquents, either deprived or nondeprived.

It would appear to be more meaningful, and probably more accurate, to emphasize the greater accomplishment—emotionally, socially, and academically—of the deprived youth who nevertheless manages to avoid delinquency than to assert that the nondeprived delinquent is much more likely to be emotionally disturbed than the deprived delinquent or that the latter is generally "normal" (i.e., similar to nondelinquents in degree of emotional stability).

PREVENTION AND TREATMENT OF DELINQUENCY

Although a variety of approaches have been employed in efforts to prevent or treat delinquency, the results have not been particularly encouraging (Gordon & Arbuthnot, 1987; Kazdin, 1985; Leitenberg, 1987; Lorian, Tolan, & Wahler, 1987; Martinson, 1974; Rutter & Giller, 1984). Counseling and psychotherapy, transactional analysis, cognitive therapy, institutional treatment in "therapeutic communities," family casework, street corner youth workers, foster-home placement, intensive community-based treatments, recreational programs, educational and vocational programs, youth service bureaus, and combinations of these and other approaches (e.g., health care, legal aid) have not been very successful (Gottschak et al., 1987; Kazdin, 1985; Patterson et al., 1989; Quay, 1987c; Rutter & Giller, 1984).

However, most approaches—even those using a combination of possible solutions—have concentrated largely on young people who are already experiencing serious problems, and for the most part they have been a matter of too little, too late. Moreover, when the data are examined more closely it becomes clear that the intervention techniques used are often of poor quality or inconsistently applied (Sechrest & Rosenblatt, 1987). For example, the effectiveness of a group counseling program cannot be said to have been tested adequately when the counselors are poorly trained and poorly motivated and when the counseling itself is superficial and haphazardly arranged. In other instances studies are so poorly designed that it is impossible to reach valid conclusions about the meaning of the findings—even when they are favorable (Sechrest & Rosenblatt, 1987).

Correctional Institutions. On the other hand, there is considerable evidence that imprisonment in traditional "correctional" institutions makes matters worse by subjecting the young person to traumatic and embittering experiences, frequently including sexual and physical abuse, while providing little or no psychological, educational, or vocational help. Such institutions have been described as "finishing schools" for future criminal behavior (Kaufman, 1979; Prescott, 1981). Not surprisingly, reconviction rates among previously institutionalized youth generally run between 60 and 70 percent (Rutter & Giller, 1984).

Although there are clearly instances in which institutionalization may be the only practical alternative, particularly for violent or "professional" offenders, in many cases suspended sentences, official and unofficial probation, and formal police warnings are at least as effective in terms of recidivism rates. Indeed, several studies indicated that for first offenders such noncustodial alternatives resulted in somewhat lower reconviction rates (Dixon & Wright, 1975; Rutter & Giller, 1984).

Nevertheless, in many states where juvenile courts have considerable discretion in dealing with juvenile offenders, without the strict rule of law and constitutional due process required in adult jurisdictions, adolescents who have committed only status offenses are often institutionalized. Thus, a national study of 722 institutions conducted by the Law Enforcement Assistance Administration (LEAA) in the 1970s found that two-thirds of the girls and one-third of the boys had been confined solely because of status offenses. Many of the girls were institutionalized only for sexual activity (Wooden, 1976).

In contrast, because of the organizational chaos, underfunding, and understaffing of the court system for juveniles in large metropolitan areas like New York City, many adolescents and youth who have committed repeated violent offenses serve little or no time in correctional institutions (Kaufman, 1979). In Chicago, for example, Johnny, a 16-year-old with a long record of arrests for assault, lured a motorist into an alley, drew a .22 caliber pistol, and killed him with six shots. Johnny was arrested but was released when witnesses failed to show up. In New York, a 15-year-old boy recalled why he shot "a dude." "Wasn't nothin'. I didn't think about it. If I had to kill him, I just had to kill him. That's the way I look at it, 'cause I was young. The most I could have got then is eighteen months" (Youth crime plague, 1977, p. 19).

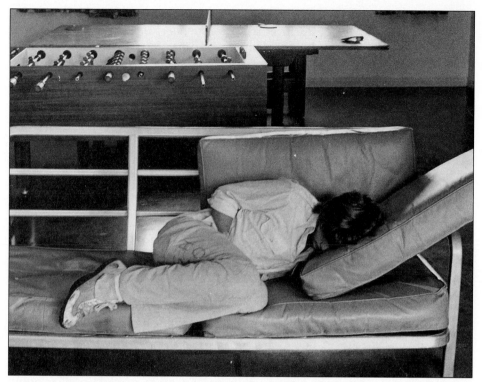

In many states, adolescents who have committed only status offenses are often institutionalized. In one national study, two-thirds of the girls and one third of the boys had been confined solely because of status offenses.

Such incongruities in the system of juvenile justice—or injustice—led Senator Edward Kennedy, chairman of the Senate Judiciary Committee, to comment ironically: "If juveniles want to get locked up, they should skip school, run away from home or be deemed 'a problem.' If they want to avoid jail, they are better off committing a robbery or burglary" (quoted in Kaufman, 1979, p. 58). This situation also led the Juvenile Justice Standards Project of the American Bar Association to conclude, after a decade of research, that juvenile courts, like all other courts, should be bound by the rule of law. Acts that would be crimes if they were committed by adults should be handled in a similar fashion. In the view of Irving R. Kaufman, chief judge of the U.S. Court of Appeals in New York, "Children whose actions do not amount to adult crimes should be dealt with outside the judicial system" (1979, p. 58).

Behavioral Methods

Currently, behavioral approaches appear to have the greatest promise for the treatment of delinquency (Garrett, 1984, 1985; Quay, 1987c; Rutter & Giller, 1984). "The basic assumptions underlying these approaches are that behavior may be modified by its consequences" (Rutter & Giller, 1984, p. 276).

The most frequently employed techniques involve *operant learning* or *behavior modification* (often in the form of a token economy), in which appropriate behavior is systematically rewarded and inappropriate, negative behavior consistently results either in lack of reward or in unpleasant consequences such as temporary loss of some privileges (see pages 36–37). Behavioral methods may be applied in an institutional setting such as a residential treatment center or a correctional institution, in school or community programs, or in the family. Regardless of the setting, however, "an individualized problem-solving approach to intervention is central—meaning that the intervention is planned on the basis of a detailed *functional analysis* of how the individual's behavior is affected by the environment in *actuality* (rather than on the basis of theoretical assumptions)" (Rutter & Giller, 1984, p. 276).

Institutional Applications. One of the most interesting recent developments in the application of behavioral approaches to the treatment of delinquents involves placement in small, community-based group homes under skilled direction. The warm, homelike atmosphere stands in marked contrast to the cold sterility of the typical training school and permits close individual attention and supervision. In one such home, Achievement Place, six to eight boys lived with two professional teaching parents (Fixen, Phillips, & Wolf, 1973; Wolf et al., 1976). Personal interaction and parental warmth were combined with a token economy in which progress toward personal and social responsibility was reinforced with increasing privileges. Compared with similar adolescents who were placed on probation or in a traditional training school, boys who lived in Achievement Place showed markedly lower rates of recidivism, higher rates of school attendance, and better grades during the treatment period. In post-treatment follow-ups, however, graduates of the original Achievement Place (and later replications) fared little better than residents of comparison group homes (Braukmann et al., 1976; Kirigin et al., 1982; Weinrott, Jones, & Howard, 1982). Several investigators have argued that since Achievement Place was genuinely successful in changing behavior during the period of the program, both after-care programs and longer treatment periods might be helpful in maintaining and generalizing these behavioral changes following the youth's return to the community (Braukmann et al., 1976; Hoefler & Bornstein, 1975; Quay, 1987).

In addition to attempts to apply behavioral principles to entire institutions, efforts have been made to apply such principles to individuals within an institutional setting. In one such project the focus was on training in social skills such as those needed in applying for a job, resisting peer pressure to engage in delinquent behavior, personal problem solving, and planning ahead (Sarason, 1978; Sarason & Ganzer, 1973). Strong emphasis was placed on developing behavioral skills that would be widely applicable in everyday life. Modeling, role-playing, and rehearsing appropriate future behaviors in problem situations were among the techniques used. Five years later, young people who had participated in this program while in the institution had a recidivism rate of 23 percent, compared to 48 percent—or more than double—for control individuals who had not been part of the program while they were at the institution.

Family Interactions. Still other behavioral approaches have focused on family interventions. In one carefully designed series of investigations, Gerald Patterson and his colleagues at the Oregon Social Learning Center have employed a behaviorally oriented parental training program (Patterson, 1981; Patterson et al., 1989; Snyder & Patterson, 1987). Parents are helped to use positive, noncoercive methods of control; to interact more positively as a family; to monitor their children's activities better; and to deal more decisively with deviant behavior. They are shown how to negotiate behavioral contracts with their children and to help them develop improved social problem-solving skills. Detailed observations are made of parental behavior, child behavior, and parent–child interactions in the home.

Although these carefully worked out procedures have been found to be remarkably effective in the treatment of overly aggressive children, they appear to have less lasting effects on delinquents. Thus, a follow-up study of twenty-eight families of children who had been caught stealing and had undergone the training program found an impressive reduction in stealing at the end of the treatment; however, by the end of the first year many of the children had reverted to their pretreatment behavior patterns (Patterson, 1981). Another study of young people who had been referred by the courts primarily for status offenses (e.g., truancy, running away, ungovernable behavior) compared the relative effectiveness of three treatment programs: (1) a behavioral approach aimed at improving family communication (and including behavioral contracts), (2) family therapy discussions without behavioral techniques, and (3) a no-treatment group. Over a 6- to 18-month follow-up period, overall recidivism rates for the three groups were 26 percent, 57 percent, and 50 percent, respectively; when only actual criminal offenses were considered, the comparable figures were 17 percent, 21 percent, and 27 percent (Alexander & Parsons, 1973).

In brief, behavioral interventions currently appear to offer the greatest promise of being effective methods of dealing with delinquent behavior. However, several points need to be stressed. It seems clear that significant short-term effects can often be achieved in a particular treatment setting, whether in a residential treatment center, a group home, or a family. To that extent, as the English psychiatrist Michael Rutter notes, "the claim that 'nothing works' is clearly misleading. There are methods that have, at least, a limited degree of success in affecting delinquent behavior. The problem is not so much in bringing about change as in *wanting* change" (Rutter & Giller, 1984, p. 373). Too often, for example, a young person appears to make real progress in modifying self-defeating delinquent behavior in favor of a more socially adaptive behavior while in a treatment-oriented residential facility, only to regress when returned to the home and neighborhood in which the delinquent behavior originally occurred.

Several implications emerge from the findings of recent research on the treatment of delinquency. One is that in the long run efforts at prevention or intervention have little prospect of significant success unless they place major emphasis on changing the child's or adolescent's home environment and existing patterns of parent–child relations. Another is that in most instances efforts

Group homes with caring "house parents" may help emotionally troubled children and adolescents with behavior problems to avoid becoming involved in criminal activities.

to help the delinquent directly need "to be concerned with improving his social problem-solving skills and social competence generally, rather than just seeking to suppress deviant behavior" (Rutter & Giller, 1984, p. 373). Moreover, such efforts have to begin early in life and be part of a comprehensive program of psychological and physical care, education, and training directed toward optimal development (Patterson et al., 1989).

For some, such goals can be realistic. But for many other young people, especially those in the expanding underclass growing up in deteriorated urban slums with defeated, neglectful, or abusing parents (or parents who abandon them), more fundamental social changes will have to come first.

In the final analysis, delinquency is not a disease but a symptom of more serious underlying problems—social, psychological, economic, educational, vocational, physical (e.g., health care, nutrition), and even philosophical. And patchwork approaches—attempts to salvage particular groups of children—appear destined to have limited success as long as society, despite pious rhetoric on the part of political leaders, does little to ameliorate the social conditions that are the breeding ground of delinquency: poverty, urban decay, ethnic and socioeconomic discrimination, the lack of a sense of community among all classes of citizens, paralysis of social institutions, and ever-increasing demands on today's more isolated nuclear families. Without a real commitment to attacking such problems, the rate of delinquency, already staggering, appears likely to rise still higher.

SUMMARY

Despite their disenchantment with some of the policies and practices of government and other social institutions, most adolescents are optimistic and feel that their lives are going reasonably well. However, there remain significant minorities of young people who feel deeply dissatisfied with either themselves or society or both. During the 1960s it became fashionable to refer to such young people as "alienated." But this label says little unless we can specify what the individual is alienated from and whether the alienation has been imposed on the individual by external forces or has been largely chosen by the individual.

Viewed in this way, it becomes clear that alienation among youth has differed in important ways over time. With the decline in clearly identified religious faith in the past century, some youth have a feeling of "existential outcastness." Many adolescents also share a sense of "developmental estrangement"—the feeling of alienation or loss that comes with the abandonment of ties to one's childhood self without finding a rewarding replacement. In a period of rapid social change another kind of alienation may emerge: a sense of *historical loss,* as evidenced by nostalgia for the past. Alienation may also take the form of estrangement from what is vaguely felt to be one's real self; many young people feel that they have somehow lost touch with the inner core of their being and that much of what they do is devoid of meaning. Young people may show all of these forms of alienation and others as well. In the 1960s many middle- and upper-class adolescents and youth became disillusioned with the goals, values, and practices of American society. In response to their alienation, some privileged youth became political activists. Smaller numbers became committed radicals. Still others withdrew from society as a whole—some into despair, others into the search for an alternative way of life, as in the case of the hippie movement. Although these forms of alienation have declined in recent years, other forms of alienation have not.

Much of the alienation among minorities and the poor is largely imposed from outside by an affluent society from which they have been largely excluded—economically, socially, and politically. Recently a "newer," more subtle form of alienation appears to have taken root among a significant number of youth and young adults. It is characterized by feelings of loneliness;

desire for—but difficulty achieving—intimacy; feelings of rootlessness; a decreased sense of purpose and direction; and a diffuse sense of self.

Each year more than 1 million young people move away from home, many permanently. Studies of the families of "serious" runaways typically reveal chronic patterns of family conflict; in many instances, however, the problems are much worse and may include family violence, neglect, and physical and sexual abuse. Adolescent runaways, particularly in large cities, are at risk for robbery, assault, prostitution, drug use and small-time pushing, and physical illness and disease, including AIDS. They urgently need help, but existing facilities are unable to meet their needs adequately.

The adolescent delinquency rate reached a peak in 1980 and has remained relatively stable since then. The incidence of serious offenses has risen more rapidly than that of delinquency in general. Although the male:female ratio has declined, boys still exceed girls in juvenile arrests, particularly for more serious offenses. Delinquency rates are also higher among lower-income youth, including those who are members of minority groups, particularly in urban ghettos. Nevertheless, a growing number of offenses are committed by middle-class youth living in the suburbs. Moreover, within the suburbs the increases are greatest in communities and families characterized by a high degree of social and geographic mobility without stable community ties.

Peers play an important role in instigating and maintaining delinquent behavior. In earlier periods, many gangs—although they encouraged delinquency—often helped meet needs that are common to all youth: a sense of personal worth, a social life, and acceptance by peers. Contemporary gangs are far more violent and socially destructive, particularly in large cities, often terrorizing entire neighborhoods.

The average delinquent scores about eight points lower than nondelinquents on IQ tests. Personality factors also play a role. Even in the early school years future delinquents appear to be more poorly adjusted, less considerate, less friendly, less responsible, more impulsive, and more antagonistic to authority than nondelinquents.

The single best predictor of adolescent delinquency is the young person's relations with his or her parents. The disciplinary techniques to which delinquents were subjected in childhood are likely to have been lax, erratic, or overly strict, and to involve physical punishment rather than reasoning with the child about misconduct and responding consistently and appropriately to both antisocial and prosocial behaviors. The parent–child relationships of delinquents are far more likely than those of nondelinquents to be characterized by mutual hostility; lack of family cohesiveness; and parental rejection, indifference, dissension, or apathy.

Many lower-class youth—particularly those living in urban ghettos—are subjected to greater cultural pressures toward delinquency than middle- and upper-class youth. But this does not mean that lower-class delinquents as a group are more free from emotional problems than middle- and upper-class delinquents.

Although a variety of approaches have been employed in efforts to prevent or treat delinquency, the results have not been particularly encouraging. At present behavioral approaches appear to offer the greatest promise for the treatment of delinquency. These approaches make use of operant-learning or behavior modification techniques. In the long run, however, efforts at prevention or intervention are unlikely to succeed unless they place major emphasis on changing the child's or adolescent's environment and existing patterns of parent–child relations. Moreover, efforts to help delinquents need to be concerned with improving social competence and problem-solving skills rather than just seeking to suppress deviant behavior. If they are to succeed, such efforts need to begin early in life and to be part of a comprehensive program of psychological and physical care, education, and training. Without such a commitment by society, delinquency rates are likely to rise still higher.

REVIEW QUESTIONS

1. Discuss the different forms taken by youthful alienation over the past several decades and how they differ. What is meant by a "new" alienation?

2. How widespread is the problem of adolescent runaways? What are the findings of studies of the families of "serious" runaways? What dangers are runaways likely to encounter?

3. Boys are arrested more often than girls by a ratio of 15:1 for crimes like burglary and robbery, but by a ratio of less than 3:1 for offenses like theft and shoplifting. Girls also tend to become involved in delinquency at later ages than boys. What theories have been advanced to account for these differences?

4. Current high rates of delinquency appear related, at least in part, to changes in our society over the past quarter-century. What are some of these changes, and why may they have led to increases in delinquency?

5. How have urban youth gangs and their role in the lives of their members changed since the 1950s?

6. Research indicates that the personality characteristics and social behavior of children who become delinquents during adolescence are likely to differ from those of their nondelinquent peers during the middle-childhood years. Describe the differences.

7. In what ways do the home backgrounds and parent–child relationships of male and female delinquents differ from those of nondelinquents? Why are the disciplinary techniques used by many parents of aggressive and delinquent children likely to fail?

8. Some theorists have argued that lower-class children who become involved in delinquency are less likely to be emotionally disturbed than middle- and upper-class children. Discuss the rationale for this assertion and whether or not it represents an oversimplification.

9. How successful have efforts to prevent or treat delinquency been? What approaches currently appear to offer the greatest promise for the treatment of delinquency? What social changes will be needed if delinquency rates are to be reduced significantly?

RECOMMENDED READINGS

Garbarino, J., Wilson, J., & Garbarino, A. (1986). The adolescent runaway. In J. Garbarino, C. J. Schellenbach, & J. M. Sebes (Eds.). *Troubled youth, troubled families: Understanding families at risk for adolescent maltreatment.* New York: Aldine de Gruyter.

Janus, M-D, McCormack, A., Burgess, A. W., & Hartman, C. (1987). *Adolescent runaways: Causes and consequences.* Lexington, MA: Lexington Books.

Jones, L. Y. (1990). *Great expectations: America and the baby boom generation* (5th ed). New York: Ballantine.

Patterson, G. R., DeBarsyshe, D. B., & Ramsey, E. (1989). A developmental perspective on antisocial behavior. *American Psychologist, 44,* 329–335.

Quay, H. C. (1987). *Handbook of juvenile delinquency.* New York: Wiley.

Rutter, M., & Giller, H. (1984). *Juvenile delinquency: Trends and perspectives.* New York: Guilford.

PSYCHOLOGICAL AND PSYCHOPHYSIOLOGICAL DISTURBANCES IN ADOLESCENCE

Anxiety, frustration, and conflict are part of the human condition, and every young person will encounter some psychological problems in the course of his or her development. Moreover, there is evidence that psychological problems are more frequent at certain ages than at others (Committee, 1989; Rutter, 1980; Rutter & Garmezy, 1983). For example, referrals to psychiatric and psychological clinics tend to peak in the age ranges of 4–7 and 9–11 during childhood and between the ages of 14 and 16 during adolescence (Anthony, 1970). Each of these periods represents a transitional stage during which accelerations in physical or cognitive development, or rapid changes in parental expectations and general social demands, require new adjustments.

In early adolescence, as we have seen, all of these changes are at work simultaneously. Consequently, by its very nature adolescence in our society involves at least some disruption in whatever psychological equilibrium may have been established previously. There is no doubt that all of adolescence involves important challenges to the individual, requiring change and often stimulating growth.

In some instances, however, the number of changes required in adolescence, particularly if too many of them occur at once, may be overwhelming. And for some vulnerable young people any additional stress may be too much. The extent of the disruption experienced by a majority of adolescents, and the difficulties encountered in reestablishing a new, more mature equilibrium, have often been exaggerated (see Chapter 1); nevertheless, psychological and psychophysiological disturbances do occur in a significant number of young people.

Epidemiological studies in the United States and England indicate that during any one year between 10–15 percent of adolescents are suffering from recognizable disorders (Committee, 1989). When adolescents' own reports of their symptoms and suffering are taken into account, the rate is somewhat higher (Graham & Rutter, 1985; President's Commission, 1978).

Our aim in this final chapter will be to consider the origins, symptoms, and prognosis of some of the more prominent psychological and psychophysiological disturbances encountered in adolescence. As will become apparent, although the roots of these disturbances can usually be found in earlier periods of development, in many cases they are manifested or become worse during adolescence (Ebata, Petersen, & Conger, in press; Graham & Rutter, 1985; Rutter, 1980). For example, eating disorders such as anorexia nervosa, bulimia, and some kinds of obesity; certain kinds of depression; suicide or suicide attempts and accidents; some forms of delinquency; and schizophrenia—all are more likely to emerge during adolescence than in earlier periods. In most instances the emergence or worsening of these disturbances appears to be linked in one way or another to the physical, physiological, sexual, and cognitive changes that take place during adolescence. In this chapter we will also review a number of therapeutic approaches currently employed with adolescents, as well as some of the special problems associated with the treatment of adolescents.

THE NATURE OF SYMPTOMS

Some of the manifestations of psychological problems in adolescence are relatively easily understood. The adolescent whose efforts to establish mutually rewarding relationships with same- or opposite-sex peers have consistently met with rejection or ridicule may become painfully anxious and uncertain in the presence of peers and may tend to withdraw into lonely isolation. The young person who has been subjected to an endless series of injustices or rejection on the part of parents and, at the same time, has had only harsh or inconsistent discipline may become angry and destructive—as occurs in the case of some delinquents (see pages 527–529).

It is not difficult to appreciate the transient depression of a young person who has recently lost a parent, sibling, or close friend, or the acute anxiety and bad dreams of an adolescent who has just been through a terrifying real-life experience. Other kinds of symptoms, however, are not so easily understood: the victim of anorexia nervosa, wasting away while worrying about being fat; a suicide attempt that, on the surface, seems to have been precipitated by a

Adolescents whose efforts to establish rewarding relationships with peers have resulted in rejection or ridicule may withdraw into lonely isolation.

relatively minor disappointment; acute anxiety, or even panic, that seems to have no identifiable source; psychosomatic symptoms of various kinds; and so forth. In many cases, as we saw in Chapter 2, the original source of apparently mysterious or illogical symptoms is anxiety about something—separation or loss of love, angry or hostile feelings, sexual impulses, feelings of inadequacy or concern about having no separate identity of one's own (Conger, 1979). Frequently the anxiety also involves guilt, in that the young person's impulses are unacceptable to his or her conscience—that is, to the internal standards that he or she has developed about what is right and wrong, good and wicked. One of the difficulties in understanding such symptoms lies in the fact that the underlying concerns are not consciously expressed. Instead, the young person may erect psychological defenses against their expression because allowing them to be expressed would produce painful anxiety and guilt. As we have seen, a basic function of defense mechanisms is to help the individual avoid such painful feelings (see pages 48–49). The kinds of defenses that people are most likely to employ will vary, depending on their individual personalities and learning experiences (Horowitz, 1988). A number of defense mechanisms are also likely to be age dependent (A. Freud, 1965, 1968; Smith & Danielsson, 1982; Vaillant, 1987, 1988). Such defenses as intellectualization and asceticism are more common in adolescents than in younger children because they generally depend on a higher level of cognitive development; on the other hand, denial, a more immature defense, is more frequent among younger children (see page 50).

In some cases, of course, defense mechanisms are ineffective or only partially effective. In such instances generalized anxiety, either acute or chronic, may result.

ANXIETY

Anxiety states are characterized by apprehension, fearfulness, and tension and are often accompanied by psychosomatic symptoms such as muscle tension, sometimes leading to shaking, perspiring, headaches, or stomachaches. Unlike both normal fears of realistically dangerous situations and phobias that are intense and unrealistic, anxiety states may occur under any circumstances and are not restricted to specific situations or objects (Barlow, 1988; Hersov, 1985; Nemiah, 1988; Uhde & Nemiah, 1989). Every adolescent will inevitably experience some anxiety in the course of development. It is only when the anxiety is excessively strong and disabling or appears to be chronic that it makes sense to speak of anxiety reaction as a clinically significant disturbance or disorder.

Anxiety reactions are more common in adolescence than in middle childhood, and their frequency appears to increase between the onset of puberty and early adulthood (Chapman, 1974; Nicholi, 1988; Rutter, 1980). The most recent diagnostic manual of the American Psychiatric Association (1987) describes three major categories of **anxiety disorders** during childhood or adolescence: (1) **separation anxiety,** in which the predominant disturbance is excessive anxiety upon separation from major attachment figures or from home or other familiar surroundings (e.g., when leaving home to go away to school); (2) anxiety aroused by contact with strangers or by social situations, which can interfere severely with social functioning with peers; and (3) "**overanxious disorder**," in which the sources of anxiety are generalized and diffuse and lead to unrealistic worry about future events, preoccupation with the appropriateness of one's past behavior, overconcern about one's competence, and "marked feelings of tension or inability to relax" (American Psychiatric Association, 1987, p. 64). In actuality, these categories often overlap (Rutter & Garmezy, 1983).

Acute Anxiety

An adolescent with an acute anxiety reaction feels a sudden fearfulness, as if something bad were about to happen. He or she may become agitated and restless, startle easily, and complain of physical symptoms such as dizziness or headache, sometimes accompanied by nausea and vomiting. The young person may appear distracted and have a limited attention span. Sleep disturbances are common: They include difficulty falling asleep and limited, restless sleep with much tossing and turning, perhaps accompanied by nightmares or sleepwalking (Chapman, 1974; Hersov, 1985a; Nemiah, 1989; Uhde & Nemiah, 1989).

The adolescent suffering from an acute anxiety reaction may be puzzled or alarmed by it or may attribute it to isolated external circumstances or incidents (Barlow, 1988). Upon more careful examination, however, it usually becomes clear that more extensive and fundamental factors are involved, such as disturbed parent–child relations, concern about the demands of growing up, or pervasive fears and guilt regarding sexuality or aggressive impulses, even though the adolescent may not be consciously aware of their role in the disturbance.

For example, an adolescent girl experienced an acute anxiety reaction following a minor automobile accident from which she escaped unhurt (Senn & Solnit, 1968). In the following weeks she suffered from nightmares, complained of being unable to breathe, and became fearful of going anywhere. Obviously, her response was disproportionate to the seriousness of the accident. Upon further exploration it was learned that the girl's parents were on the verge of divorce and family tensions were high. Moreover, it turned out that the girl had recently been upset by menarche, for which she had been poorly prepared by her mother. She had also been apprehended in sexual play with a neighbor boy a few weeks before, and her mother was accusing her of masturbation because she spent long periods in the bathroom—an accusation that she tearfully denied. She had in fact engaged in masturbation, both alone and with her sisters, but largely because of her mother's reaction she felt guilty and "sinful" about it. Reassurance about the normality of her sexual behavior and an opportunity to talk about her difficulties with her mother and her concern for the future of the family resulted in rapid alleviation of the acute anxiety symptoms, although longer-term therapy with both mother and daughter was required to deal with the underlying problems.

Panic Disorder. In some instances acute anxiety may be so intense that it produces almost unbearable panic and terror (Barlow, 1988; Nemiah, 1988; Uhde & Nemiah, 1989). The sufferer is likely to be overwhelmed by a strange sense of dread, a feeling that he or she is about to be engulfed by catastrophe. Such attacks are usually brief (often lasting only minutes) but are likely to recur. Panic attacks often occur completely unexpectedly, thereby increasing the victim's fear of a subsequent attack (Barlow, 1988).

Although **panic disorder** has been observed in children, it usually does not occur before late adolescence (Barlow, 1988). Strong separation anxiety in childhood and "sudden loss of social supports—a disruption of important interpersonal relationships" are thought to predispose an individual to this disorder (American Psychiatric Association, 1987). It also appears that familial influences, including a genetic predisposition, may heighten vulnerability to panic disorder (Barlow, 1988). In some instances psychotherapy is effective in treating this disorder; in other cases relaxation techniques, including meditation, are helpful. Recent research also indicates that several antidepressant drugs may help control panic attacks (Barlow, 1988). Often a combination of these approaches may be effective in dealing both with the immediate effects of this disorder and with its underlying causes (Barlow, 1988; Uhde & Nemiah, 1989).

Chronic Anxiety

Most of what has been said about acute anxiety also applies to chronic anxiety. Indeed, chronic anxiety frequently results from acute anxiety that has not been resolved (Mussen et al., 1990; Nemiah, 1988). An important difference between the anxiety reactions of adolescents and adults is that in adolescents the link between the anxiety reaction and its causative and precipitating factors is usually clearer and more direct. Consequently, attempts at intervention have more chance of success with adolescents (Conger, 1979; Hersov, 1985a). It is essential to begin intervention while the relevance of these causal factors is still apparent and can be dealt with, and before chronic anxiety and the individual's response to it (e.g., psychological withdrawal, impairment of schoolwork, or continuing physical symptoms such as pains, diarrhea, shortness of breath, and fatigue) become a way of life.

FEARS AND PHOBIAS

Fears are, of course, not restricted to any particular age group, although their frequency seems to reach a peak at around age 11 (Fodar, 1984). At age 11, specific fears are reported by 40 percent of boys and 52 percent of girls; by age 13, only 4 percent of boys and 21 percent of girls report such fears. The specific nature of fears is clearly age related. For example, younger children are more likely to manifest fear of the dark, strangers, animals, and ghosts (Bauer, 1976; Hersov, 1985a). Although young people sometimes carry over a childhood fear unchanged into adolescence, other fears are likely to emerge, either for the first time or in a new form.

Many fears arising in adolescence are related to the changing demands of this period (see pages 30–31). The adolescent may have fears related to growing up, meeting new groups of peers, advancing in school, contracting diseases, or starting a job. More advanced cognitive development enables the adolescent to grasp potentially fearful events, such as death, more fully. Adolescents are also more likely than younger children to have fears related to sexuality, partly owing to familial taboos about discussing sex (Bamber, 1979).

Fears may be realistic or unrealistic. An adolescent boy with a recurring illness that has frequently endangered his life may fear death. A girl who has been repeatedly rejected by people close to her may fear further rejection. A young person who has been in an airplane crash may develop a fear of flying. Such fears are not difficult to understand, and within limits they may even be adaptive if the feared person, object, or event is in fact dangerous or threatening.

Other fears, however, are unrealistic and in some cases difficult to understand. Many of the fears expressed by younger children (20 percent) are unrealistic and deal with imaginary creatures, the dark, and being alone (Bauer, 1976; Jersild, Telford, & Sawrey, 1975). Dangerous animals, such as lions and tigers, are also frequently named as objects of fear. Interestingly, in responding to questions about their fears children between the ages of 9 and 12 indicate that they are only moderately afraid of immediate and possible dangers, such as getting hit by a car, but are strongly afraid of remote or impossible events, such as being attacked by lions or ghosts. Unrealistic fears, though less common in adolescence, nevertheless do occur. For example, an adolescent may develop an unrealistic fear of traveling or even of leaving the house, or, conversely, may develop a fear of being in confined spaces (Horowitz, 1988).

Phobias

An intense fear that the individual consciously recognizes as unrealistic is called a *phobia*. When the person is unable to avoid or escape the phobic situation, he or she may become extremely apprehensive and experience faintness, fatigue, palpitations, perspiration, nausea, tremor, and even panic (American Psychiatric Association, 1987).

How can phobias be explained? In general, they can be attributed to fear of some person, object, or event that is too painful and anxiety producing to be given conscious recognition (Horowitz, 1988; Nemiah, 1988). The fear has been displaced onto some other, less unacceptable object or situation, usually one that is in some way symbolic of the original fear. In some cases the basic source of a phobia is readily apparent to the clinician; in others, it is difficult to identify. In younger children, because of their less advanced cognitive development and less complex defense mechanisms, the original source of the phobia is often easier to identify than in the case of older adolescents and adults.

For example, fear of attack by ghosts or giants may clearly symbolize unconscious fears of parental punishment. One adolescent's intense fear of automobiles represented a displaced fear of his father (Chapman, 1974). In cases like these, attempts to reduce the fear of ghosts or automobiles through rational arguments are unlikely to be successful. Unlike realistic fears, unrealistic or symbolic fears can best be reduced by attacking the actual source of the fear, although behavior modification techniques may also be helpful if the displaced fear has acquired independent strength over a period of time (Barlow, 1988; Rachman, 1985). In such cases the antidepressant drug imipramine is sometimes helpful as an adjunct in quelling the anxiety, even panic, produced by being in a phobic situations (Barlow, 1988; Kahn et al., 1986; Yule, 1985).

School Refusal

School refusal (sometimes called school phobia) refers to a fear, which may approach panic, of leaving home and going to school. It is far more common in younger children but may also occur in adolescents (Eisenberg, 1958; Hersov, 1985b; Weiner, 1970, 1982). In many adolescents who are referred for treatment for anxiety, phobia, and **conversion** or **psychophysiologic reactions** (especially headache, abdominal pain, diarrhea, nausea, and vomiting), refusal to attend school is the event that aroused parental concern (Waller & Eisenberg, 1980; Weiner, 1970, 1980). School refusal in an adolescent is likely to be a precursor of work avoidance in adulthood (Gardner & Sperry, 1974).

School refusal should not be confused with the occasional mild reluctance to go to school that can be seen in normal children and adolescents, or with realistic fears of going to school (e.g., fear of the class bully or of abusive treatment by a teacher). In such cases the young person is only too aware of the true source of his or her apprehension and of its realistic nature. School refusal also has little in common with typical truancy (Heath, 1983; Hersov, 1985b; Weiner, 1982). The truant adolescent usually dislikes or does poorly in school, skips classes on an irregular basis as the fancy takes him or her, and spends truant time in pleasurable activities away from home without parental knowledge or consent (Heath, 1988; Herson, 1960). Children and adolescents who suffer from school refusal, in contrast, stay home with their parents' consent if not approval, earn average or better grades, and claim to like school, to have high achievement standards, and to value academic pursuits (Berg et al., 1975; Hersov, 1960, 1985b; Weiner, 1970, 1982). Although many problems may be symbolized by school refusal, it usually indicates a dread of some aspect of the school situation, concern about leaving home, or, perhaps more frequently, both.

"School refusal among young adolescents is frequently one indication of the young adolescent's general inability to cope with the increased demands for an independent existence outside the family, and entry into normal peer relationships" (Hersov, 1985b, p. 384). For example, young people who remain overly dependent and are uncertain about their sexual identity, or who fear heterosexual relationships, may become acutely anxious in school when peers begin to organize their social life around dating, parties, and other heterosexual relationships. Children and adolescents in whom concern about leaving home (i.e., separation anxiety) is strongly related to school refusal are frequently excessively dependent. In such young people school refusal may be precipitated by a move to a new home, absence of the parents on a vacation, or illness of family members. In a minority of children and adolescents, school refusal is accompanied by a depressed mood and even, in some instances, by serious depressive disorder (Hersov 1985b; Weiner, 1982). Consequently, the possibility of significant depression should not be overlooked in the assessment of school refusal.

Many parents of children who refuse to attend school are threatened by the possibility of their children's independence from them. Often this stems from unresolved problems of dependency on their own parents, which may be reflected in an inverted dependency of parent on child (Bowlby, 1973; Eisenberg, 1958; Hersov, 1960, 1985b; Weiner, 1982). Moreover, these parents themselves are likely to see the school as a cold, forbidding place and go to great lengths to protect their children not only from school but also from other painful facts of existence. The child or adolescent, in turn, perceives—at least unconsciously— the parent's underlying desire to maintain the dependent relationship and responds accordingly. The young person is likely to fear separation from the parent because of both dependency and hostility.

When a young person with school phobia is overly dependent on the mother, the father may contribute to the problem by failing to provide a balance to counteract his wife's overprotective approach and by undermining her sense of competence. Some of these fathers are themselves passive, dependent individuals. Others tend to be aggressive and exaggeratedly masculine, deeply involved in their work or outside interests and only minimally interested in their families. Such fathers usually are not informed enough—or interested enough—to intervene in the maladaptive relationship between mother and child (Coolidge, 1979; Weiner, 1982).

School phobias are equally common among boys and girls (Achenbach & Edelbrock, 1981; Fodor, 1984; Hersov, 1985). When it occurs in adolescents school refusal tends to be more resistant to change and to indicate a more serious level of disturbance than is generally the case in younger children (Chapman, 1974; Gardner & Sperry, 1974; Weiner, 1970, 1982).

Forcing a child or adolescent with a genuine, intense school phobia to go back into the dreaded situation will only aggravate the phobia. Prompt therapy to determine and deal with the real source of the youngster's anxiety is essential and in most cases must involve not only the child or adolescent but the parents as well.

ADOLESCENT DEPRESSION

Depressive disorders cover a wide spectrum, from mild, temporary states of sadness, often in response to a life event, to severely disturbed conditions that may involve cognitive as well as affective (mood) disturbances (see pages 575–576) (Committee, 1989; Emde, Harmon, & Good, 1986; Klerman, 1988a; Shaffer, 1985). Until recently it was widely assumed that children and younger adolescents rarely exhibited **depression.** Recent clinical and research studies have demonstrated clearly that this is not the case (Kovacs, 1989). Both major and minor forms of depression have been found during childhood, puberty, and adolescence (Kovacs, 1989; Puig-Antich, 1986; Rutter, Izard, & Read, 1986; Shaw, 1988).

One of the reasons that significant depression in childhood and early adolescence tended to be overlooked is that clinical depression is less common at younger ages (Committee, 1989; Kovacs, 1989; Pearce, 1978; Rutter, 1986). Another reason is that depression may be manifested in different ways at different ages, depending on the individual's level of cognitive, psychological, social, and biological development (Ebata, Petersen, & Conger, in press; Graham & Rutter, 1985; Shaffer, 1985; Shaw, 1988). In early adolescence young people are unlikely to express their feelings openly and tend to deny negative and self-critical attitudes. They are less likely to exhibit the gloom, hopelessness, and self-deprecation that are seen in adult depressives, although these symptoms may occur (Committee, 1989; Shaw, 1988). In a recent national survey of eighth and tenth grade students, 34 percent of girls and 15 percent of boys reported that they often felt sad and hopeless (National Adolescent Student Health Survey, 1988).

In a large study of the population of the Isle of Wight, Michael Rutter and his colleagues found that only one in nine 10- to 11-year-olds reported moodiness, misery, depression, or feelings of self-deprecation, compared to nearly 40 percent of 14- to 15-year-olds (Rutter, 1980; Rutter, Tizard, & Whitmore, 1981). Moreover, when 14–15-year-old boys were subdivided into prepubertal, pubescent, and postpubertal categories, very few of the prepubescent boys showed depressive feelings, whereas about one-third of the postpubescent boys did (Rutter, 1980, 1986) (see Figure 14.1). As the investigators note, "Whether this surprisingly strong association with puberty was a function of

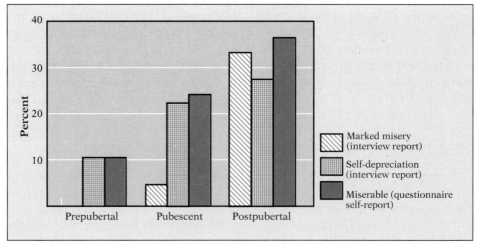

Figure 14.1 Depressive feelings and stage of puberty. (From M. Rutter, C. E. Izard, & P. B. Read (Eds.) (1986). *Depression in young people.* New York: Guilford Press. By permission.)

endocrine changes, psychological responses to sexual maturation, or indeed some other influence remains unknown" (Rutter, Izard, & Read 1986, p. 11). A study of adolescent girls found that those who attain menarche early are more likely to suffer depressed feelings than those who are "on time" or are late maturers (Rierdan & Koff, 1985).

Adolescents, particularly younger adolescents, may manifest feelings of depression through boredom, restlessness, or inability to be alone, coupled with a constant search for new activities (Achenbach & Edelbrock, 1981; Carlson & Cantwell, 1980; Kovacs, 1989; Nicholi, 1978, 1988; Parry-Jones, 1985). Obviously, these characteristics are found in many adolescents at one time or another, but when they become dominant and persistent the possibility of depression should be explored. Escape from feelings of depression and loneliness may also be attempted through frequent and excessive use of alcohol and drugs or through promiscuous sexual activity. Some adolescent delinquents employ the defense mechanism of denial and acting-out behavior as a way of coping with depressed feelings (Nicholi, 1988; Weiner, 1970, 1982).

A depressed adolescent may also reveal his or her feelings through bodily complaints such as waking up tired and fatigued or exhibiting hypochondriacal symptoms and excessive preoccupations with physical conditions (Klerman, 1988a). Difficulty in concentrating and failing school performance are frequently signs of a depressed state in young people (American Psychiatric Association, 1987; Kovacs, 1989; Weiner, 1970, 1982). In one study of college dropouts, it was concluded that depression was the most frequent and most significant causal factor in the decision to drop out of college, either temporarily or permanently (Nicholi, 1988).

Similarities between adolescent and adult symptoms or depression tend to be greater in the case of major affective disorders than in less severe cases of depression (Ryan and Puig-Antich, 1986). As we shall see (pages 575–576), biological, primarily genetic, factors appear to play a more significant part in the major depressive disorders than in less severe instances of depression (Klerman, 1988a; Puig-Antich, 1986; Ryan et al., 1987).

Psychological factors appear to play a particularly important part in two forms of adolescent depression (Josselyn, 1971; Nicholi, 1988). The first is expressed as a lack of feeling and a sense of emptiness. It is as though the childhood self had been abandoned and no growing adult self has replaced it; this vacuum engenders a high level of anxiety. This kind of depression resembles a state of mourning, in which the lost loved one is experienced as a part of the self; it is likely to be the least persistent and most resolvable form of depression.

A second type of adolescent depression is more difficult to resolve. It has its basis in repeated experiences of defeat over a long period. The adolescent may actually have tried hard to solve problems and achieve personally meaningful goals, but without success (Seligman & Peterson, 1986). Perhaps other people fail to accept or understand what the adolescent is trying to do, or perhaps personal inadequacies make the goals impossible to achieve. Many—probably a majority—of adolescent suicide attempts are the result not of a momentary impulse but of a long series of unsuccessful attempts to find solutions to difficulties.

Frequently, the final straw in this type of depression is the loss of a meaningful relationship, whether with a parent, a friend, or someone with whom the adolescent was in love. Telling such an adolescent to "snap out of it," as well-meaning adults often do, is likely to be ineffective because the adolescent feels he or she has no solutions left to try. The young person who has reached this stage of hopelessness is probably most in danger of suicide (Curran, 1987; Inamdar et al., 1979; Jacobs, 1971).

Studies of depressed adolescents who are hospitalized find that they differ from depressed adult patients in that they are less likely to show the usual symptoms of slowed thoughts, irritability, loss of appetite, or diminished libido (Inamdar et al., 1979). Depressed adolescents are more likely than adults to fear social abandonment and experience social frustration, and to engage in

After puberty, depression is more frequent among girls than among boys.

acting-out behaviors such as running away from home and engaging in acts of aggression. Thus, although depression manifests itself in certain basic ways across the life span, depression in adolescence is affected by the demands, tasks, and developmental characteristics of this stage of life.

Sex Differences in Depression

Although psychiatric disorders with depression are more frequent among boys than among girls before puberty, they are more frequent among girls after puberty (Boyd & Weissman, 1981; Klerman, 1988; Pearce, 1982; Weissman et al., 1984). Some investigators and clinicians believe that females are more likely to manifest depression and related difficulties because of the stresses inherent in the female sex role (Gove & Herb, 1974; Radloff, 1975; Weissman & Klerman, 1977). If so, it would make sense for sex differences in depression to appear by the end of adolescence, since gender intensification—the narrowing and intensification of sex roles—tends to occur during this stage (Petersen, 1988). If sex roles continue to shift toward greater flexibility and diversity, we may see a decline in the relatively greater incidence of depression among girls and women.

Box 14.1 IS YOUTHFUL DEPRESSION BECOMING MORE FREQUENT?

Gerald Klerman and Myrna Weissman, experts on the epidemiology of depression, note that the age of onset of major depressive disorders is occurring earlier, and overall incidence is greater, among today's adolescents and younger adults (i.e., the baby-boom generation). As can be seen in Figure

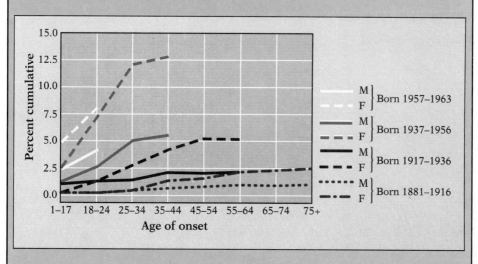

Figure B 14.1 The affective disorders—age at first onset of major depression: Results from the ECA study. (From M. M. Weissman et al. (1984). The epidemiology of depression: An update on sex differences in rates. *Journal of Affective Disorders,* 7, 179–188. By permission.)

B14.1, individuals born between 1957 and 1963 are at greater risk than people in older age cohorts (Weissman et al., 1984).

In Klerman's view, these findings suggest that environmental as well as genetic factors can play a significant role in the onset of major depressive disorders (Klerman, 1988b). But what kinds of factors? While not ruling out the possible role of other environmental factors, such as nutrition, viruses, or chemical agents in the air or water, Klerman considers that the particular stresses to which the baby-boom generation has been subjected constitute a more likely explanation. In support of this contention, he cites parallel increases in youthful suicide and homicides, alcohol and drug abuse, and other health problems.

In contrast, he notes that among the elderly, whose economic security and health care have improved markedly in recent years (owing largely to Social Security and Medicare), rates of depression have changed least.

Suicide

Suicide is rare in children and almost as infrequent among young adolescents. Beginning at about age 15, however, the reported suicide rate increases rapidly. Among white males it reaches a level of over 18 per 100,000 for ages 15–19 and over 28 per 100,000 for ages 20–24; rates for blacks and females are significantly lower, with black females lowest of all (see Table 14.1 and Figure

The reported suicide rate increases rapidly after age 15. Fortunately, this young woman was prevented from jumping to her death.

TABLE 14.1 SUICIDE RATES, BY SEX, RACE, AND AGE GROUP, 1970–1986

Age	Total			Male White			Male Black			Female White			Female Black		
	1970	1980	1986	1970	1980	1986	1970	1980	1986	1970	1980	1986	1970	1980	1986
All ages	11.6	11.9	12.8	18.0	19.9	22.3	8.0	10.3	11.1	7.1	5.9	5.9	2.6	2.2	2.3
10–14 years old	.6	.8	1.5	1.1	1.4	2.4	.3	.5	1.5	.3	.3	.7	.4	.1	.4
15–19 years old	5.9	8.5	10.2	9.4	15.0	18.2	4.7	5.6	7.1	2.9	3.3	4.1	2.9	1.6	2.1
20–24 years old	12.2	16.1	15.8	19.3	27.8	28.4	18.7	20.0	16.0	5.7	5.9	5.3	4.9	3.1	2.4
25–34 years old	14.1	16.0	15.7	19.9	25.6	26.4	19.2	21.8	21.3	9.0	7.5	6.2	5.7	4.1	3.8
35–44 years old	16.9	15.4	15.2	23.3	23.5	23.9	12.6	15.6	17.5	13.0	9.1	8.3	3.7	4.6	2.8
45–54 years old	20.0	15.9	16.4	29.5	24.2	26.3	13.8	12.0	12.8	13.5	10.2	9.6	3.7	2.8	3.2
55–64 years old	21.4	15.9	17.0	35.0	25.8	28.7	10.6	11.7	9.9	12.3	9.1	9.0	2.0	2.3	4.2
65 years and over	20.8	17.8	21.5	41.1	37.5	45.6	8.7	11.4	16.2	8.5	6.5	7.5	2.6	1.4	2.4

Source: U.S. Bureau of the Census. Statistical abstract of the United States, 1989. Washington, DC: U.S. Government Printing Office, 1989.

14.2; Gibbs & Hines, 1989). The overall suicide rate among older adolescents has tripled since 1950, although it has decreased slightly in recent years (*Report*, 1989a; Rosenberg et al., 1987; U.S. Bureau of the Census, 1981b, 1987, 1989).

Females are more likely than males to use passive methods of suicide, such as ingestion of drugs or poisons, and less likely to use active methods, such as shooting or hanging. Among both sexes, firearms or explosives account for the greatest number of *completed* suicides, whereas drugs or poisons account for the greatest number of *attempted* suicides. Although male adolescents outnumber females in completed suicides, attempted suicides are far more common among females (Curran, 1987; Holinger, 1978; *Report*, 1989a; Shaffer, 1986; Shaffer, Philips, & Enzer, 1989; Worden, 1989).

In a national survey, almost four of every ten eighth and tenth grade girls (42 percent) and one-fourth of the boys report having "seriously" thought about committing suicide at some time in their lives; 18 percent of the girls and 11 percent of boys report that they have "actually tried" to commit suicide (National Adolescent Student Health Survey, 1988). Although percentages are higher, similar sex differences have been found among college students who have considered suicide at some time (Bolger et al., 1989).

Reasons for Adolescent Suicide Attempts.

In considering adolescent suicide attempts, it is important to distinguish between immediate precipitating factors and longer-term predisposing factors. Precipitating events may include the breakup or threatened breakup of a romance, pregnancy (real or imagined), homosexual concerns, school failure, conflicts with parents, rejection by a friend, being apprehended in a forbidden or delinquent act, loss of a parent or other loved person, suicide of a friend or relative, and fear of serious illness or imminent mental breakdown (Bolger, Downey, Walker, & Steininger, 1989; Curran, 1987; Jacobs, 1971; Miller, Chiles, & Barnes, 1982). On closer examination, however, it becomes clear that the adolescent's reaction to such events is generally the culmination of a series of mounting difficulties. One study of 154 adolescent suicide attempters found that hopelessness, rather than depression resulting from immediate life situations, was most often the critical factor in the suicide attempt (Wetzel, 1976).

Adolescents who attempt suicide frequently have a long history of escalating family instability and discord (Jacobs, 1971; Kerfoot, 1987; Pfeffer, 1989). They have reached a point at which they feel unable to communicate with their parents or turn to them for support. Early parental loss is also more common among suicidal adolescents (Bolger et al., 1989; Curran, 1987; Shaffer, 1986). Typically, suicidal adolescents have fewer close friends, but their relationships with them are much more intense: "Their relationships become supercharged with a degree of desperation and need that is often not shared by their friends and lovers" (Curran, 1987, p. 30).

Treatment.

Treatment of potentially suicidal adolescents or those who have made suicide attempts must be prompt. Many communities now have

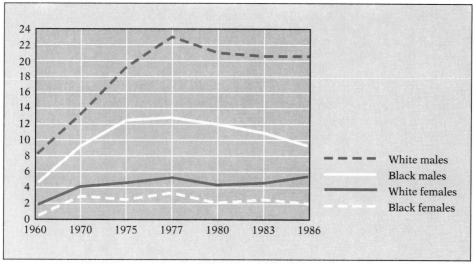

Figure 14.2 Death rates (per 100,000) from suicide among 15- to 24-year-olds, 1960–1983. (From U.S. Bureau of the Census, *Statistical abstract of the United States, 1983–1989*. Washington, DC: U.S. Government Printing Office, 1983–1989.)

hotlines that people who are considering suicide or feeling desperate can call for help. More extended treatment should deal both with the immediate events and life circumstances that are troubling the young person and with long-standing problems and conflicts (Curran, 1987; Kerfoot, 1987; *Report*, 1989a; Tabachnick, 1981). In some instances involving depressive disorders, it may be helpful to combine medication with psychotherapy, although use of drugs with children and adolescents should not be undertaken lightly given the propensity of suicidal adolescents to overdose on drugs and the lethality of antidepressant overdosage (Committee, 1989; Ryan et al., 1987; Shaffer, 1985). In addition, further research on the effects of various drugs in this age group is clearly needed; some anti-depressant drugs such as imipramine, for example, appear to be less effective with adolescents than with children or older adults (Ryan et al., 1987).

PSYCHOPHYSIOLOGICAL PROBLEMS AND HYPOCHONDRIASIS

Psychological disturbance in an adolescent may be reflected in real or imagined physical symptoms. The latter case, called **hypochondriasis** is characterized by excessive preoccupation with the functioning of the body. A hypochondriacal boy may be concerned that there is something wrong with his heartbeat, breathing, or digestion even though these functions are perfectly normal; or he may exaggerate the significance of minor ailments, such as a slightly stuffy nose, a minor stomach upset, or a muscle cramp. Hypochondri-

---

Box 14.2 PREDICTION OF SUICIDE RISK

There is a dangerous myth, not only among the general public but also among some clinicians, that a person who talks about committing suicide will not do so. The tragic fact, however, is that many individuals who have threatened suicide and been ignored—or dismissed as "attention seekers"—have subsequently taken their own lives. Moreover, in talking about suicide adolescents are conveying a message that something is wrong and that they need help, even though they may not yet be seriously intent on suicide as the only remaining solution to their problems.

Talk of suicide should always be taken seriously (Farberow, 1989; Grob, Klein, & Eisen, 1983; Parry-Jones, 1985; *Report*, 1989b; Resnick, 1980; Rotherman, 1987; Shaffer et al., 1989). Predicting suicide risk is not easy, but there are a number of warning signals that can alert the careful observer to the possibility of suicide. Those signals include the following:

1. A persistently depressed or despairing mood (or frantic activity alternating with intolerable boredom and listlessness).
2. Eating and sleeping disturbances.
3. Declining school performance.
4. Gradual social withdrawal and increasing isolation from others.
5. Breakdown in communication with parents or other important people in the young person's life.
6. A history of suicide attempts or involvement in accidents.
7. Seemingly reckless, self-destructive, and uncharacteristic behavior, such as serious drug or alcohol use, reckless driving, sexual acting out, delinquency, or running away.
8. Statements like "I wish I was dead" or "What is there to live for?"
9. Inquiries about the lethal properties of drugs, poisons, or weapons.
10. Unusually stressful events in the young person's life, such as school failure, breakup of a love affair, or loss of a loved one.
11. Having a close friend or family member who attempted or committed suicide.

---

acal symptoms, though they may occur in childhood, are far more prevalent during adolescence (Weiner & Elkind, 1972). In view of the fact that the rapid physical and sexual changes of puberty inevitably focus the adolescent's attention on his or her physical self, this is hardly surprising. Indeed, a certain amount of what might be considered undue bodily preoccupation in an adult may represent a normal developmental phenomenon in an adolescent.

On the other hand, bodily concerns that are excessive and resistant to change may be indicative not of learning about the self but of an underlying disturbance. Hypochondriacal symptoms may serve a number of functions related to handling anxiety. All adolescents experience minor transient states of anxiety, which they are generally able to tolerate. But when anxiety becomes intense, especially when the young person is uncertain of its source, it can be overwhelming, even leading at times to a fear of "going crazy." Being able to find a reason for the anxiety helps make it seem rational and, hence, less mysterious or frightening. For some adolescents, the focus becomes the body. They then will "not be destroyed by some vague monster the nature of which is unknown, but . . . today by tuberculosis, tomorrow by leukemia" (Josselyn, 1971, p. 63).

The focus of the hypochondriacal adolescent's anxiety may also have a realistic component, even though it is not sufficient in itself to account for the degree of concern. General, ill-defined concerns about being unattractive, inadequate, physically immature, or in some way "repulsive" (a persistent term in the lexicon of adolescents) may become linked to some aspect of the body or its functioning. A boy may fear that he will never achieve sexual maturity; a girl may fear that her breasts will be too small or too big. Because of anxiety or guilt regarding sexuality, a mild case of prostatitis may convince an adolescent boy that he has acquired a veneral disease, despite objective evidence to the contrary. Feelings of fatigue may lead boys or girls to fear that they have somehow permanently damaged themselves physically, perhaps as a result of masturbation. Hypochondriacal symptoms may also serve as a face-saving way of avoiding certain activities. One cannot go to a dance or participate in athletic activities because one is "too weak," when the underlying concern is actually fear of rejection or of incompetence.

It is important to keep two considerations in mind when dealing with what appear to be hypochondriacal symptoms among adolescents. One is that the adolescent's concerns may stem simply from ignorance. He or she may not know that a particular "symptom" is actually a normal event or that it indicates a far less serious condition than that which is feared. In such cases reasonable assurances should allay the young person's anxiety. Second, seemingly hypochondriacal symptoms may actually indicate the early stages of a real illness. For example, feelings of fatigue and complaints of a mild sore throat or sensitive glands may actually indicate the presence of that popular adolescent disorder, infectious mononucleosis. Obviously, too, it is important at times to rule out the onset of a more severe psychological disorder, such as schizophrenia, which is sometimes manifested through unusual or peculiar physical complaints.

The adolescent whose hypochondriacal symptoms go beyond normal bodily concerns or are highly resistant to change clearly needs psychological help. Once the underlying problem has been determined and the adolescent has begun to deal with it, the symptoms are likely to disappear surprisingly quickly, in contrast to many adult hypochondriacs (Josselyn, 1971; Nemiah, 1988).

EATING DISORDERS

As noted in Chapter 4, at no other stage in development is the individual as likely to be preoccupied with physical appearance as during adolescence. Adolescents may be concerned about their ultimate height, the adequacy of their sexual development, or their general physical attractiveness. Among female adolescents, however, weight is likely to be the primary concern (Attic & Brooks-Gunn, 1989; Dornbusch et al., 1984; Richards, Boxer, Petersen, & Albrecht, 1990; Striegel-Moore, Silberstein, & Rodin, 1986; Tobin-Richards, Boxer, & Petersen, 1983). This should hardly be surprising. For one thing, puberty normally results in a significantly higher ratio of fat to lean tissue and a lower resting metabolic rate in women than in men (see Chapter 3). Before puberty, girls have 10–15 percent more fat than boys; after puberty, they have almost twice as much fat as boys (Marino & King, 1980).

In addition, there is greater cultural pressure on women to be thin (Russell, 1985; Striegel-Moore, Silberstein, & Rodin, 1986). Ironically, this pressure is greatest in affluent societies, especially during adolescence and young adulthood. Even mild degrees of overweight are likely to be viewed as unattractive and a sign of self-indulgence.

Many adolescents go through brief periods in which their weight deviates upward or downward from generally accepted norms. However, once growth has stabilized, most adolescents will correct their weight through regulation of their diet. A minority, however, will not or cannot do so. In some cases sustained overeating may lead to serious **obesity.** In other cases, pathologically prolonged and extreme dieting may lead to serious, sometimes life-threatening degrees of weight loss. The latter condition, known as **anorexia nervosa,** is most likely to occur during adolescence and is far more common among girls than among boys. Another eating disorder, **bulimia,** involves abnormal eating behavior without abnormal weight loss or gain. In some cases bulimia may be linked to a history of anorexia nervosa; in other instances it may be associated with obesity (Russell, 1985). Each of these conditions, and some of the psychological and psychophysiological factors that may be involved, will be discussed briefly.

Obesity

It is important to recognize that serious obesity is a complex and far from uniform condition (Lomax, 1989; Rodin, 1985; Stunkard, 1985). Biological, psychological, and social factors may all play a role. Obesity in developed countries is far more frequent at lower socioeconomic levels than at upper levels (Stunkard, 1977, 1985). Recent studies using identical twins have shown that hereditary factors can predispose an individual to obesity (Bouchard et al., 1990; Stunkard, Harris, Pedersen, & McClearn, 1990). Obesity may result from disturbances in metabolic functioning or endocrine imbalance and variations in the number and size of cells in the adipose tissues (Hirsch, cited in Kolata, 1988; Ravussin et al., 1988; Striegel-Moore et al., 1986; Stunkard et al., 1985).

Recent research indicates that many people may become obese because their bodies burn calories too slowly owing to a low metabolic rate, not because they eat too much; moreover, low metabolic rates may be inherited (Ravussin et al., 1988; Roberts et al., 1988; Rodin, 1981). In many instances, however, psychological and social problems appear to play a dominant role, and if those problems can be corrected or ameliorated the individual may be able to reach and maintain a reasonable weight level. This is particularly likely in the case of excessive weight gains that begin in adolescence (Bruch, 1973, 1974).

Psychological Factors. It is necessary to distinguish between psychological characteristics that may predispose the adolescent to obesity and those that emerge because of societal reactions to the condition. Many obese adolescents react to social discrimination and criticism with at least partial acceptance of it as valid. In consequence, they tend to be preoccupied with being fat and to become passive or timidly withdrawn, eager to please, and tolerant of abuse (Stunkard, 1985). In brief, sometimes an obese adolescent accepts the negative evaluation of others "and settles down to live with it" (Bruch, 1974, p. 277).

Nevertheless, there are significant individual variations in the reactions of obese adolescents to social criticism. Those who reach adolescence with low self-esteem and a sense of helplessness (often fostered by parental criticism or rejection) will be much less resistant to social criticism than those who have gained self-esteem, competence in a variety of skills, and a sense of autonomy.

The psychological and social factors that may predispose an adolescent to obesity are not uniform. In some cases parents may overfeed their children as a way of showing love or, conversely, of expressing unconscious hostility. The child or adolescent may overeat as a way of avoiding pressures of social interactions, athletic activities, or heterosexual relationships in which he or she feels inadequate. Some may overeat to "fill" a feeling of emptiness or loneliness. Others may do so to give themselves a feeling of "bigness" as a form of compensation for feeling psychologically small or insignificant. Still others may overeat to punish themselves because of guilt feelings or to express hostility toward their parents. Clinical and experimental investigations indicate that obese young people are less likely than their nonobese peers to feel that they are self-directed, separate individuals with the capacity to identify and control their biological urges and to define and present their needs in ways that yield appropriate rewards (Bruch, 1973, 1979; Graham, 1985).

Obese adolescents often cannot discriminate accurately among bodily urges. When exposed to food in a controlled experimental situation, normal students ate considerably less when their stomachs were full than when their stomachs were empty. In contrast, obese students ate as much (and in some instances more) when their stomachs were full as when they were empty (see Figure 14.3). Whereas normal individuals regulate their eating according to physiological cues of hunger, obese individuals do not.

Treatment of Obesity. Therapeutic approaches to the treatment of obesity have focused on attempts (1) to ameliorate the individual's underlying psychological problems and promote personal growth and a sense of identity, autonomy, and control of one's own body; and (2) change the individual's

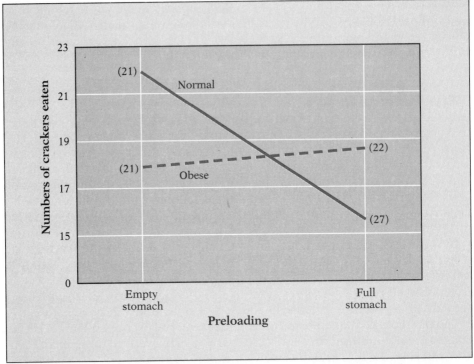

Figure 14.3 Number of crackers eaten by obese and normal subjects under empty stomach and full stomach conditions. (From S. Schacter, *Emotion, obesity and crime.* New York: Academic Press, 1971. Copyright © 1971 Academic Press. By permission.)

specific eating patterns and responses to cues that previously provoked eating behavior. Often these approaches are combined, because although the motivation for continued overeating may have deep psychological roots, the eating itself is likely to become overlearned as a response to a variety of familiar cues, and substantial relearning is required. At the same time, it is important to recognize that for individuals with low metabolic rates, or for whom a heavier weight than others appears to be biologically normal, "it will be a lifelong struggle to lose weight and keep it off and that there are no magic formulas" (Hirsch, cited in Kolata, 1988).

Anorexia Nervosa

Anorexia nervosa is characterized by pathologically prolonged and extreme dieting, which may lead to serious, sometimes life-threatening degrees of weight loss. The condition is particularly puzzling because anorectics have such a distorted body image that they may continue to complain of being too fat even when severely emaciated. Severe undereating and consequent malnutrition and serious weight loss may accompany disorders ranging from some schizophrenic conditions to mental retardation, depression, and a variety of

Because of a distorted body image, anorectics may continue to complain of being too fat even when they are severely underweight.

undiagnosed organic disorders (American Psychiatric Association, 1987). However, the clinical picture in genuine (primary) anorexia nervosa is remarkably similar from one patient to another. The disorder is most likely to begin during adolescence, with peak rates of onset at ages 13–14 to 17–18 (Halmi, Eckert, La Der, & Cohen, 1979). Anorexia is about ten times as likely to occur among females as among males (Herzog, 1988).

Twin studies suggest that genetic factors may increase the risk of developing anorexia, perhaps by impairing the release of gonadotropins from the anterior pituitary gland; another possibility is that there is a defect in the feedback control mechanisms for certain neurotransmitters (e.g., dopamine or norepinephrine) in the brain (Herzog, 1988; Pope & Hudson, 1989). However, psychological influences appear to predominate.

When the backgrounds of anorectic adolescents are examined by researchers, the initial impression is not of pathological disturbance but rather of an unusual freedom from developmental difficulties. As children, these patients appear to have been "outstandingly good and quiet . . . obedient, clean, eager to please, helpful at home, precociously dependable, and excelling in school. They were the pride and joy of their parents and great things were expected of them" (Bruch, 1973, p. 255).

On closer investigation, however, these seemingly positive personality characteristics, and the parents' reactions to them, turn out to have a distinctly negative quality. Most striking is the absence of individual initiative and autonomy—a sense of identity as a separate and distinct individual. Instead, at least unconsciously, anorectics are likely to have had feelings of being "enslaved, exploited, and not being permitted to lead a life of their own" (Bruch, 1973, p. 250). They typically lack a clear sense of emerging selfhood, despite their prolonged struggle to be perfect in the eyes of others (Hood, Moore, & Garner, 1982). Also characteristic is an obsessive need to be in control of every aspect of life, particularly one's own body (Larson & Johnson, 1982).

Not surprisingly, parents of female anorectic adolescents are likely to have exerted such rigid control and regulation that the child had difficulty establishing a sense of identity and confidence in her ability to make decisions by herself. The parents are likely to display intrusive concern, overinvolvement ("enmeshment"), and overprotection and to discourage separation and autonomy (Minuchin, Rosman, & Baker, 1978; Russell, 1985). Discomfort at the idea of separation leads the parent (most frequently the mother) to reinforce the child's reliance on her, thereby hampering the development of a sense of self. Such parents are likely to encourage their children to become perfectionistic overachievers; they also control the child's pleasures. Such a regulated child may become so focused on external cues and controls as determinants of behavior that, like the obese child, she may fail to learn to respond appropriately to differential cues—physiological and psychological—originating within herself.

These results have subsequently been corroborated by a study using very rigorous methods to assess family interactions; in addition, the study suggested that the parents of the anorectic are dependent on her to nurture them as well as to modulate and inhibit conflict between them (Goldstein, 1981). Indeed, there is some evidence that improvement in the adolescent as a result of treatment is likely to exacerbate neurotic problems in the parents (Crisp, 1986; Minuchin et al., 1978, Russell, 1985).

Three basic symptoms of disordered psychological functioning are central in primary anorexia. First is a disturbance of delusional proportions in body image and body concept. Even when her appearance has become skeletonlike, an adolescent girl may deny that she is too thin, and indeed, continue to worry about becoming fat (American Psychiatric Association, 1987; Bruch, 1974; Russell, 1985; Seebach & Norris, 1989). Second is a disturbance in the perception or cognitive interpretation of stimuli arising in the body. Rather than a mere loss of appetite, there is a failure to recognize cues of hunger—a failure similar to that occurring in many obese patients, although the result is very different. Failure to recognize bodily cues indicating fatigue is also likely, and despite severe malnutrition the patient may exhibit hyperactivity (Pope & Hudson, 1989; Russell, 1985). Finally, there is usually a paralyzing sense of ineffectiveness—a feeling of acting only in response to the demands of others, rather than to one's own needs and wishes. This feeling of lack of control is typically masked by a surface negativism and stubborn defiance, making it difficult to treat the disorder effectively (Herzog, 1988).

Treatment of Primary Anorexia Nervosa. In the past about 10 percent of anorectics actually died of starvation, but this seldom occurs today. Proper management requires both psychological and medical intervention. As in the case of obesity, psychological approaches to treatment range from intensive psychotherapy to behavior modification techniques. The primary psychotherapeutic goal is to help the patient see herself or himself as having a separate identity from parents and the right to self-respect (Bruch, 1973, 1974). In behavior modification, patient and therapist may enter into a "contract" spelling out increasing rewards (e.g., access to television, smoking, visits with other patients and family) as progress in eating and weight gain occurs. In instances in which depression is also involved, antidepressant drugs may be helpful as an adjunctive treatment.

The relative long-term success of various treatment approaches is still being evaluated (Herzog, 1988). It appears, however, that long-term success without relapses needs to include the reorganization of maladaptive patterns of family interaction through family therapy (Minuchin, Rosman, & Baker, 1978; Schwartz, Barnett, & Saba, 1985).

Bulimia

During the 1980s there was a dramatic increase in the number of young women who engage alternatively in binge eating and purging. This disorder, which can contain elements both of obesity and anorexia, is called **bulimia** (or *bulimia nervosa*) (Herzog, 1988; Johnson, Lewis, & Hagman, 1984; Russell, 1985). It is characterized by the following: (1) frequent binge eating accompanied by awareness that the eating pattern is abnormal; (2) fear of not being able to stop the pattern voluntarily; (3) self-induced vomiting, use of laxatives or diuretics, or rigorous dieting, fasting, or exercising to prevent weight gain; and (4) persistent concern with body shape and weight (American Psychiatric Association, 1987; Herzog, 1988; Russell, 1985).

A significant number of bulimics also suffer from depression and self-deprecating thoughts; indeed, in some cases bulimia appears to be primarily a consequence of depression and can be alleviated by antidepressant drugs (Herzog, 1988). In instances in which bulimia is preceded by anorexia nervosa, the prognosis is poorer and the disorder is most likely to become chronic (Casper et al., 1980; Garfinkel & Garner, 1983; Russell, 1985).

Typically, however, a bulimic is not also anorectic. She is most likely to be a white, middle-class female in her late teens or early twenties who has tried various diets without much success (Herzog, 1988; Johnson, 1982). Either accidentally or through friends she becomes aware of purging as a method of weight management. Bulimics typically binge on "junk food" that is high in carbohydrates.

In one study almost all of a sample of young women who engaged in binge eating reported doing so at least daily; the average number of calories per binge was estimated at 4800, usually in the form of sweets (94 percent). Of those who reported purging (71 percent of the respondents), 69 percent vomited, 39 percent used laxatives, and 26 percent used both (Johnson, 1982).

After binging, bulimics characteristically feel depressed and out of control; they report having feelings of guilt, shame, and low self-esteem (Herzog, 1988). A bulimic young person is more likely than an anorectic to be distressed by her symptoms and willing to accept help. Unlike anorectics, who are more likely to be isolated and asexual, bulimics are usually outgoing and report normal heterosexual interest and experience (Herzog, 1988; Johnson, 1982). However, they acknowledge that their eating problem has adversely affected their lives in most areas except work, and almost three-quarters report adverse effects on their physical health.

Risk Factors for Bulimia

Why is bulimia primarily a female disorder, why does it appear to be on the increase, and which women are most at risk? Ruth Striegel-Moore, Lisa Silberstein, and Judith Rodin (1986), psychologists at Yale University, explored these questions in an effort to better understand the etiology of bulimia. In addressing the first two questions, they note that contemporary Western society places a high value on thinness, particularly for women (Rodin, Silberstein, & Striegel-Moore, 1985). Adolescent girls are more concerned and more self-critical about their looks than boys, and they are well aware of the premium society places on physical attractiveness in women (Crisp & Kalucy, 1974; Striegel-Moore et al., 1986). Adolescent girls also tend to be more interpersonally oriented than boys. They worry more about what other people think of them and are more concerned with popularity and conforming to social expectations (Hill & Lynch, 1983; Rosenberg & Simmons, 1975; Simmons & Rosenberg, 1975). Finally, physical maturation is more likely to bring boys closer to the current masculine ideal, whereas for girls it is more likely to mean "development away from what is currently considered beautiful" (Striegel-Moore et al., 1986, p. 250).

Which Women Are at Greatest Risk? Silberstein and Rodin (1986) hypothesized that the women who are at greatest risk of bulimia are those "who have accepted and internalized most deeply the sociocultural mores of thinness and attractiveness" (p. 297). As predicted, they found that compared to nonbulimic women, bulimic women express substantially greater acceptance of the idea that "fat is bad," and that "thin is beautiful" and increases the likelihood of success.

Some groups and occupations place a stronger emphasis on thinness than others and thus appear to place their members at greater risk for bulimia and anorexia. For example, schools in which dating is emphasized have a higher incidence of bulimia than schools that are less oriented toward dating (Rodin et al., 1985). Eating disorders, including bulimia, are more frequent among members of certain professions, such as ballet dancers, gymnasts, models, actresses, and athletes (Crago, Yates, Beutler, & Arizmenti, 1985; Striegel-Moore et al., 1986).

It also appears that young women who are genetically programmed "to be heavier than the svelte ideal will be at higher risk for bulimia than those women who are naturally thin" (Striegel-Moore et al., 1986, p. 254; Boskin-White & White, 1983). Similarly, early-maturing girls, because of their earlier increases in body fat, may be at greatest risk for bulimia as well as anorexia (Bruch, 1981; Striegel-Moore et al., 1986).

As in the case of anorexia nervosa, some parents may foster bulimia. In addition to being overly involved emotionally ("enmeshed"), overprotective, and rigid, the families of bulimic patients appear to be unduly conscious of appearance and to attach special meaning to food and eating (Johnson & Flach, 1985; Schwartz, Barrett, & Saba, 1985). However, much more research is needed before firm conclusions can be drawn about the role of family variables in bulimia.

Treatment for bulimia may include individual psychotherapy, group therapy (psychodynamically, cognitively, or educationally oriented), and family therapy (Herzog, 1988). Recently self-help groups have grown rapidly. "These groups usually encourage contact outside the group. Members can develop a sense of self-worth by seeing others who have recovered or improved and can become aware that improvement is possible" (Herzog, 1988, p. 443).

ADOLESCENT PSYCHOSES

The term **psychosis** is applied to disorders that involve severe distortions of cognitive, perceptual, and affective functioning. Frequently, but by no means always, psychotic individuals are unaware of the nature of their illness (even though they may be painfully aware of their suffering), and their ability to make realistic, rational judgments regarding their own condition or events in the world around them is seriously impaired. As a result, they are usually unable to maintain even minimally adequate personal, social, or work relationships or take responsibility for their own welfare. Some psychoses, such as those stemming from toxic drug reactions or disease, are clearly organic in origin; others may be primarily psychological in origin. Still others may involve complex interactions between biological and psychological influences. Included in the latter category are the major **affective disorders,** such as bipolar (manic-depressive) disorders, severe (major) depression, and schizophrenia, a disorder in which cognitive disturbances play a prominent role.

Adolescent Schizophrenia

Among adolescents, **schizophrenia** is by far the most frequently occurring psychotic disorder. Its incidence, though still relatively rare, increases dramatically from age 15 on and reaches a peak during late adolescence and early adulthood, leveling off toward the end of the third decade (Cancro, 1983; Committee, 1989; Graham & Rutter, 1985). Boys are more likely than girls to develop schizophrenia in childhood and adolescence; in adults onset is more frequent among women (Lewine, 1980, 1981).

Symptoms. Like its adult counterpart, adolescent schizophrenia is characterized by disordered thinking; distortions of, or lack of contact with, reality; limited capacity for establishing meaningful relationships with others; and poor emotional control (Graham & Rutter, 1985; Steinberg, 1985; Weiner, 1970, 1982). In its fully developed form, adolescent schizophrenia can usually be identified without much difficulty: The young person's speech is likely to be peculiar—stilted, overelaborate, disconnected, or even incoherent. He or she may display odd facial grimaces or movements; appear distracted, withdrawn, or confused; and manifest inappropriate emotional reactions—either failing to respond with appropriate feeling or overreacting in a poorly controlled fashion. Hallucinations—usually auditory and reflecting control by others (e.g., outside voices telling one what to do)—and intense, bizarre delusions may also be present (Steinberg, 1985).

Proper diagnosis may be difficult in the early stages of this disorder, partly because the symptoms may be far less obvious or dramatic than they tend to be later, and partly because some characteristics that might suggest incipient schizophrenia in adults are likely to occur among nonschizophrenic as well as schizophrenic adolescents. These include circumstantial thinking, abstract preoccupation, and conscious awareness of blatant sexual and aggressive imagery, as well as ideas of reference (belief that others are talking about one), all of which tend to occur more frequently among nonschizophrenic adolescents than among nonschizophrenic adults (Weiner, 1970, 1982).

This should not be too surprising when one realizes that adolescence itself is a period of rapid change during which psychological equilibrium may be temporarily disrupted and controls on thought and psychological defense mechanisms are not yet firmly established. It is important to note, however, that these age-related differences do not extend to other patterns of personality impairment associated with schizophrenia (Weiner, 1970, 1982). In particular, truly disordered thinking and impaired emotional integration and control are equally important clues to schizophrenic disturbance in adolescents and adults.

Precursors. Although schizophrenia is most likely to become manifest after middle adolescence, adolescent schizophrenics, along with adolescents suffering from other emotional disorders, are likely to have displayed greater than average psychological vulnerability in earlier periods (Bromet, Harrow, & Castle, 1974; Garmezy, 1974a, 1974b; Hellgren et al., 1987; Rutter & Garmezy, 1983). Studies of the earlier adjustment of adolescent schizophrenics have found a higher than expected incidence of shyness, social withdrawal, poor social relationships, difficulty in making friends, "peculiar" behavior, stubbornness, sensitivity, lack of humor, difficulties in concentration, fear of demanding situations, and problems in managing daily life (Garmezy, 1987; Holtzman & Grinker, 1974; Rutter & Garmezy, 1983; Steinberg, 1985).

In addition, a number of investigators have found neurodevelopmental problems in the form of poor motor and visual-spatial skills, clumsiness, and attention deficits (including difficulty filtering out relevant stimuli from background "noise") (Asarnow, 1988; Erlenmeyer-Kimling & Cornblatt, 1987; Freedman et al., 1987; Steinberg, 1985; Waldo, Adler, & Freedman, 1988). It should be noted, however, that such "premorbid" characteristics are not manifested by all young people who become schizophrenic or have schizophrenic episodes during adolescence (Rutter & Garmezy, 1983; Steinberg, 1985).

What Causes Schizophrenia? Several generations ago it was thought that traumatic experiences in childhood were the primary cause of schizophrenia. However, recent research indicates that biological and hereditary factors play a major role (Gottesman & Shields, 1982; Kety & Matthysse, 1988; Vandenberg, Singer, & Pauls, 1986). In a number of studies, the incidence of this disorder (or set of disorders with similar symptoms) among the relatives of schizophrenics has been shown to vary according to how closely they are related biologically (Gottesman & Shields, 1982; Plomin, 1986; Rosenthal, Wender, Schulsinger, & Jacobsen, 1975). For example, schizophrenia occurs more frequently in the children of schizophrenics than in their nieces and nephews.

More important from the standpoint of separating genetic from environmental influences, several well-controlled investigations have found that if one identical twin has schizophrenia, the chances are about one in two that the other twin will also develop it (O'Rourke et al., 1981). But if one nonidentical (dizygotic) twin has schizophrenia, the chances of the other twin also developing it are less than one in ten (Gotteson & Shields, 1982; Kety & Matthysse, 1988).

Compelling evidence of a genetic contribution to schizophrenia comes from studies of adopted children (Kety et al., 1978; Kety & Matthysse, 1988; Vandenberg, Singer, & Pauls, 1986). In an extensive study conducted in Denmark, two groups of children who had been adopted early in life were studied after they reached adulthood (Kendler, 1981; Kety, 1978). One group consisted of individuals who had become schizophrenic in the course of their development. The other was a control group that was matched with the first group for age, sex, age at adoption, and socioeconomic status of the adopting family. The incidence of schizophrenia was examined among both the biological and adoptive relatives (parents, siblings, and half-siblings) of each group. There was no significant difference in the prevalence of schizophrenic disorders among the adoptive relatives of the two groups. However, schizophrenia occurred at a rate almost six times higher among the biological relatives of schizophrenics (11 percent) than among their adoptive relatives (about 2 percent). In the control group there was no significant difference in incidence of schizophrenia between biological and adoptive relatives (Kety et al., 1978).

Nongenetic biological factors may also play a part in the development of schizophrenia, as indicated by recent research showing consistent differences in brain structure (e.g., size of cerebral ventricles) between monozygotic twins when one twin has schizophrenia and the other does not (Mesulam, 1990; Suddath et al., 1990).

Note that having close biological relatives with schizophrenia does not mean that one is likely to develop this disorder; in fact, it is unlikely. In the first place, except in the case of identical twins, relatives do not share all of the same genes. Second, the disorder called schizophrenia may in fact be a number of different disorders with similar symptoms (Kety et al., 1978; Kety & Matthysse, 1988; Mesulam, 1990; Scarr & Kidd, 1983). Third, an adequate genetic model for schizophrenia has not yet been developed. At present neither a single gene nor a "polygenic" model (representing a complex combination of interacting genes) appears to be adequate to predict the occurrence of schizophrenia (Plomin, 1986; Scarr & Kidd, 1983).

All in all, it may be more correct to speak of inheriting an increased *vulnerability to schizophrenia* than of inheriting schizophrenia per se. In that case, whether or not the disorder is manifested would depend on two factors: how vulnerable the individual is and how much or what kind of stress he or she is subjected to. Recent longitudinal studies have found that vulnerable individuals are more likely to develop schizophrenia or to suffer relapses after treatment if their families are characterized by high levels of stress, negative expressed emotions, and disturbed communication patterns (Goldstein, 1987; Marcus et al., 1987; Mednick, Parnas, & Schulsinger, 1987; Tienari et al., 1987).

Prognosis. Among hospitalized adolescent schizophrenics, about one-quarter recover, about one-quarter improve but suffer residual symptoms or occasional relapses, and about half make little or no progress and require continuing care (Weiner, 1982). Although comparable data are not available for milder cases in which the individual is not hospitalized, it is reasonable to expect that the proportions who recover or show improvement would be significantly higher.

In general, the older the adolescent is when schizophrenia appears, the better the prognosis. Other favorable indications include sudden, rather than gradual, onset; clear precipitating factors; above-average intelligence; good personal, academic, and social adjustment before onset; and early response to treatment (Steinberg, 1985; Weiner, 1982; Wyatt et al., 1988). Finally, the outlook for improvement is better if the family is able to accept the disturbance and if there is adequate planning for future treatment and for school, work, and living arrangements (Doane et al., 1981; Goldstein, 1987).

Brief Reactive Psychosis

It is important to distinguish between schizophrenia and brief psychotic episodes (American Psychiatric Association, 1987; Feinstein & Miller, 1979). Although during a psychotic episode the individual may exhibit such symptoms as incoherence, disorganized associations or behavior, delusions, or hallucinations, these symptoms appear suddenly and are short-lived (varying from a few hours to at most a couple of weeks). In brief reactive psychosis the psychotic symptoms typically appear immediately following a severe and recognizable psychosocial stressor such as loss of a loved one or a life-threatening event that would evoke symptoms of distress in almost anyone. Invariably, there is emotional turmoil, manifested in rapid, generally depressed and anxious mood swings. This disorder, which usually appears first in adolescence or young adulthood, may be followed by feelings of mild depression or loss of self-esteem. But with psychological assistance and support, the young person may be expected to return fully to his or her previous level of functioning.

Major Affective Disorders

Schizophrenia accounts for the great majority of psychotic reactions found among adolescents (Steinberg, 1985). However, contrary to earlier thinking, major affective disorders can also occur during adolescence (Graham & Rutter, 1985; Klerman, 1988; Kovacs, 1989; Puig-Antich, 1986). Although they are relatively rare, reports of **bipolar (manic-depressive) disorder** among adolescents, particularly older adolescents, have become more frequent (Committee, 1989; Kovacs, 1989; Steinberg, 1985). Severe depression (sometimes referred to as major or **unipolar depression**) may occur at any age, although, like bipolar depression, it is also found most frequently among adults.

Of the major mental disorders, bipolar disorder appears to have the strongest genetic component. This disorder is characterized by periods of excessive euphoria, grandiosity, hyperactivity, and poor judgment, alternating with periods of normality and periods of severe depression, loss of energy, and feelings of worthlessness. If one identical twin has bipolar disorder, the chances are two out of three (65 percent) that the other twin will also suffer from this disorder (Klerman, 1988; Nurnberger & Gershon, 1981; Plomin, 1986). In the case of nonidentical twins, the chances of the other twin also developing bipolar disorder are less than one in sixteen (14 percent).

Although sample sizes are still inadequate, studies of identical twins reared apart show a relatively high incidence of bipolar disorder among the twins of individuals suffering from this disorder. The incidence is not as high as it is for identical-twin siblings reared with the patient, however, indicating that environmental influences also may play a part. Investigators have attempted to identify specific genetic mechanisms involved in manic-depressive disorder (Detera-Wadleigh et al., 1987; Egeland et al., 1987). Thus far, however, results have proved disappointing (Kelsoe et al., 1989; Robertson, 1989).

Genetic factors also appear to play a role, though not as strong a one, in severe (unipolar) depression (Klerman, 1988; Weissman et al., 1984). This disorder is far more common, but less well defined, than manic-depressive illness. It is characterized by a severely depressed mood, loss of interest in activities, lack of energy, and feelings of worthlessness, but without alternating periods of euphoria and manic excitement. In one study of monozygotic (identical) twins reared apart, it was found that if one twin had unipolar depression, the chances were greater than two in five that the other twin also suffered from the disorder. Among dizygotic (nonidentical) twins, the comparable figure was 29 percent (Winokur, 1975).

As in the case of schizophrenia, even an identical twin of a person with bipolar disorder does not necessarily develop the disorder. Despite an apparently strong genetic influence, then, psychological stress or its absence may play an important role (Goldstein, 1987). Current studies suggest that the quality of family interactions may affect the onset and likelihood of relapse in depressive disorders (Goldstein, 1987; Radke-Yarrow & Sherman, 1988).

There are also individuals who develop depressive disorders without a history of disturbance in the family. In this connection it is worth noting that stress alone has been found to produce measurable changes in the levels of certain chemicals in the brain (e.g., norepinephrine) similar to those found in patients with depressive illness (Bunney & Davis, 1965; Davis, 1978; Fawcett, 1975).

WORKING WITH ADOLESCENTS

Like other adolescents, those with significant psychological problems are at a unique stage of development. Their treatment therefore presents special challenges as well as special opportunities (Coleman, 1987; Conger, 1977; Nicholi, 1988; Rutter & Hersov, 1985; Steinberg, 1986). Working with adolescents is more difficult and demanding than working with younger children or adults (Nicholi, 1988). Many adolescent patients, particularly younger adolescents, tend initially to be uncommunicative, skeptical, impatient, uncooperative, and unpredictable, and the course of adolescent therapy, like that of true love, seldom runs smoothly. Acting-out behaviors or threats of such behavior (e.g., running away, becoming involved in a sexual adventure, quitting school, taking drugs, committing delinquent acts, making suicidal gestures) are not uncommon in adolescent therapy and may be a source of considerable concern to the therapist. One discouraged psychotherapist compared adolescent therapy to "running next to an express train" (Anthony, 1974, p. 234).

At the same time, work with adolescents, if it is carried out properly by a skilled and experienced therapist, can be deeply rewarding. Because adolescence itself is a period of change and new beginnings, the young person is less likely than an adult to be already fixed in maladaptive patterns that are resistant to change. Moreover, despite their surface defensiveness and skepticism, at heart many adolescents remain open to experience and eager to learn from it.

Psychotherapy with adolescents is likely to be complicated by the fact that these young people typically are experiencing conflict with their parents over independence and dependence. These conflicts tend to be transferred to the therapist, producing alternating cycles of regressive dependence and unrealistic assertions of independence (Conger, 1977; Lamb, 1987). However, it is important to recognize that problems of dependence and independence in therapy are not merely a matter of transferring parental conflicts to the therapeutic situation. They also represent important reality problems. The establishment of autonomy is a crucial developmental task for all adolescents (see Chapter 6), and the therapist must be alert to the dangers of allowing regressive dependence on therapy to become a substitute for the development of autonomy and self-reliance (Nicholi, 1988). The adolescent psychotherapist—like the wise parent, only more so—must be on guard against the temptation to try to substitute his or her own identity for that of the young person or to prolong therapy unduly.

Qualifications of the Therapist

Therapists who work with adolescents need special knowledge of, and experience with, this age group. In addition, they need a number of personal qualities that specialized training may foster but can rarely create: personal warmth, openness and honesty, confidence in self and the ability to set limits without hostility, lack of defensiveness and overreliance on professional status, and, simple though it may sound, a liking for adolescents.

Adolescents, even more than children, have a talent for spotting phoniness and exploiting it. If the therapist is straightforward, neither minimizing his or her qualifications nor retreating into professional pomposity, the adolescent will usually develop a feeling of trust and respect, though outwardly the young person may still need to make it overly clear that he or she isn't awed by "shrinks." The effective adolescent psychotherapist must also be flexible—prepared to move from listening to questioning, reassuring, clarifying reality, interpreting, even arguing and, when necessary, setting limits. As Irene Josselyn succinctly observes,

> Adolescents not only need but often want limits imposed. They need externally imposed limits because, as a result of their confused state, they are not able to set their own limits. Many adolescents become frightened when they feel that limits have not been defined. They seek a fence beyond which they cannot go, within which they can experiment and by trial and error and accidental success find a self-concept with which they can feel satisfied (1971, p. 146).

Donald Holmes provides an amusing but significant example of setting limits that did more to meet the patient's needs at the time than either logical reasoning or anxious compliance on the part of the therapist:

> A 16-year-old girl says, "I'm going-to-get-out-of-here-and-get-an-apartment-and-get-married-and-you-can't-stop-me!"
> Her doctor replies, "No you're not, and yes I can."
> She acknowledges, quietly enough, "Oh" (1964, p. 110).

Obviously, such directness can be successful only when the young person has basic trust in the therapist and the therapist has already made it clear that he or she respects the individuality and worth of the patient. But if the therapist sets limits only when they are necessary for the well-being of the patient, the young person typically will value the therapist because of the security those limits provide. The patient comes to see the therapist not as a restricting parental figure but as an ally of that side of himself or herself that is striving to establish a confident sense of identity. Conversely, in many instances, failure on the therapist's part to set limits when they are essential is likely to be interpreted by the adolescent as a lack of either real concern or understanding on the part of the therapist.

The Nature of Adolescent Therapy

In most cases psychotherapy with adolescents needs to be directed toward personality development and synthesis—finding new, more adaptive, and less self-defeating ways of handling problems or relating to others; eliminating unnecessary fears and conflicts; and achieving a more workable integration between the young person's basic needs and values and the demands of reality. In helping the adolescent achieve these goals, the therapist may note distortions in the young person's reactions to people and events in everyday life including distortions in the relationship with the therapist. For example, the therapist may observe that an adolescent girl is "turning off" her peers with critical comments not because those peers are basically stupid or hostile, as claimed, but because she fears being rejected if she allows them to come close. Or the therapist may note that an adolescent boy's worry about pleasing a part-time employer appears to stem not from any lack of ability on his own part or from the behavior of the employer (who may have made it clear that he was pleased with the boy's work), but from the fact that nothing he ever did appeared able to satisfy his father. Similarly, the therapist may wonder whether an adolescent's scornful attitude toward the opposite sex really reflects a fear of growing up.

In most cases in which such "limited-insight" techniques are employed to help the adolescent reevaluate unrealistic or self-defeating behavior, the focus is basically on the present (Anthony, 1974; Josselyn, 1971; Lamb, 1986; Nicholi, 1988). Attempts to achieve deep insights, to strip away psychological defenses, and to reconstruct the past are usually avoided. For one thing, most adolescents have little patience with rehashing the past. The adolescent's main developmental task is to cope with the present while moving toward the future: "For an adolescent in search of an identity, overcoming the fears and failures of the moment is much more important than knowing the events which led up to them" (Miller, 1959, p. 774; Nicholi, 1988).

Group Therapy

Group therapy with adolescents, either alone or in combination with individual psychotherapy or behavior therapy, is often an effective way for adolescents to work at "overcoming the fears and failures of the moment." It may be conducted in nonresidential settings such as youth centers, mental-health clinics, private offices, or schools, or as part of the treatment program in a residential treatment center (Berkowitz, 1972; Chapman, 1974; Coleman, 1987; Wilson & Hersov, 1985).

Group therapy with adolescents has "a natural advantage inasmuch as the forces of identification with a potential peer group can be made to work. "The emotional impact of observing one's own experience expressed by someone else in the same situation is usually quite a powerful one and one that facilitates personal involvement and emotional interchanges" (Christ, 1974, p. 350). Group discussions can cover a wide range and will vary according to the nature of the group. For example, some groups may discuss why an adolescent uses drugs, what situations or people tend to provoke this behavior, and its effects on the young person.

Many troubled adolescents, particularly those with more serious disturbances, have had very checkered experiences with parents and other adults. Such experiences may include divorce, death, rejection, exploitation, physical or sexual abuse, even abandonment (actual or psychological). The adolescent may respond with anxiety, distrust, depression, profound feelings of loss, or anger and resentment. Under the guidance of a skilled group therapist or therapists (sometimes a mixed-sex pair), adolescents can often help each other communicate and deal with such feelings and provide mutual support through shared experiences.

In brief, therapeutic work with adolescents, whether individually or in groups, demands skill and extensive experience with young people during these critical years. It also requires personal qualities—of warmth, flexibility,

With the guidance of a skilled group therapist, adolescents can often help each other to communicate and deal with troubling feelings and provide mutual support through shared experiences.

openness and honesty, and a capacity for limit setting without hostility—that training may be able to foster, but rarely to create. Adolescent therapists "need to be worthy of the adolescent's trust and respect, and, in turn, need to demonstrate basic trust in, and respect for, the adolescent as a unique human being" (Conger, 1977, p. 96). The job is seldom easy, but it will be less difficult for those who genuinely like adolescents, which in the last analysis probably means having come to terms with that part of oneself that was once an adolescent.

SUMMARY

Although the rapid physical, psychological, and social changes that occur during adolescence can be a source of stress, most adolescents are able to cope with them successfully. A minority, however, cannot. About 10–15 percent of adolescents suffer from a significant psychological or psychophysiological disorder. Although these disturbances usually have their roots in earlier periods of development, they may be manifested during adolescence.

Some symptoms of adolescent psychological problems are easy to understand, as in the case of the transient depression of a young person who has recently lost a parent or close friend. Other kinds of symptoms are more puzzling, as in the case of an anorexic adolescent who is wasting away while still

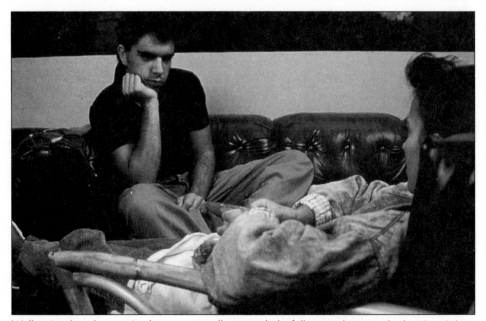

Well-trained and supervised peer counsellors can help fellow students to deal with adolescent problems and to seek professional assistance for serious difficulties. Here, a volunteer listens to a fellow student at Coral Park High School in Miami, Florida.

worrying about being too fat. In many cases the source of apparently illogical symptoms lies in disturbing impulses and feelings that cannot be consciously expressed because they would produce painful anxiety and guilt. A basic function of defense mechanisms is to help the individual avoid such painful feelings.

Anxiety reactions are more common in adolescence than in middle childhood, and their frequency appears to increase between puberty and early adulthood. Anxiety reactions during childhood and adolescence fall into three major categories: separation anxiety, anxiety caused by contact with strangers or social situations, and overanxious disorder. Anxiety states can be either acute or, if left untreated, chronic. Acute anxiety may sometimes be so intense that it produces panic and terror. The treatment of panic disorder may sometimes be aided by a combination of psychotherapy, relaxation techniques, and an antidepressant drug.

An intense fear that the individual consciously recognizes as unrealistic is called a *phobia*. In general, a phobia can be attributed to fear of some person, object, or event that is too painful and anxiety producing to be given conscious recognition. The fear has been displaced onto some other less unacceptable object or situation, usually one that is in some way symbolic of the original fear.

School refusal or "school phobia" refers to a fear (which may approach panic) of leaving home and going to school. Although many problems may be symbolized by school refusal, it usually indicates dread of some aspect of the school situation, concern about leaving home, or, frequently, both. Many mothers of children and adolescents who refuse to attend school are overprotective, and many fathers are either too passive or too uninvolved to intervene in this maladaptive relationship.

Adolescent depression covers a wide spectrum, ranging from mild, temporary states of sadness to severely disturbed, sometimes psychotic conditions. Previous assumptions that children and younger adolescents rarely exhibit depression have been disproved. The ways in which depression may be manifested, however, may differ at different ages. Similarities between adolescent and adult symptoms of depression tend to be greater in the case of the major affective disorders— *manic-depressive (bipolar) disorder* and *severe (unipolar) depression*—in which genetic factors play a significant role. In other forms of adolescent depression psychological factors are more important. Although depressive disorders are more frequent among boys than among girls before puberty, they are more frequent among girls after puberty.

Suicide is rare in childhood and early adolescence. Beginning about age 15, however, the suicide rate increases rapidly, particularly among white males. The overall suicide rate among older adolescents has tripled in the past three decades. Adolescent suicide may initially appear to be a response to a particular event, such as the breakup of a romance. On closer examination, however, it becomes clear that the event represents the culmination of a long history of mounting difficulties, frequently including family instability and discord.

Some *hypochondriacal* symptoms may be due mainly to ignorance or to the heightened awareness of one's body that accompanies puberty. However, when hypochrondrical symptoms go beyond normal adolescent concerns or are resistant to change, psychological help is needed.

Adolescent *eating disorders* include *obesity, anorexia nervosa* (chronic undereating and consequent severe weight loss), and *bulimia* (alternating episodes of binge eating and purging). Although the psychological and physiological factors involved in these disorders vary and are quite complex, in each case our society's obsession with thinness is likely to contribute to the problem. These disorders also tend to involve a feeling of lack of autonomy and control over one's own life and difficulty in establishing a clear sense of self.

The most frequent adolescent psychosis is *adolescent schizophrenia,* which is characterized by disoriented thinking, distortion of reality, difficulty in establishing meaningful relationships, and poor emotional control. Although this disorder is most likely to be manifested after middle adolescence, adolescent schizophrenics are likely to have shown evidence of psychological vulnerability in earlier periods. Twin and adoption studies indicate that genetic influences play a major role in the etiology of schizophrenia; for example, if one identical twin has schizophrenia, the chances are about one in two that the other twin will also develop the disorder. It is important to distinguish between schizophrenia and *brief psychotic episodes* following severe stress. Although they are most likely to be found in adults, *bipolar (manic-depressive) disorder* and *severe (unipolar) depression* can occur in adolescence. As in the case of schizophrenia, genetic factors play an important role, most clearly in the case of bipolar disorder.

Therapeutic work with adolescents, whether individually or in groups, demands skill and extensive experience with young people. It also requires personal qualities—warmth, flexibility, openness and honesty, and a capacity to set limits without hostility—that may be fostered but can rarely be created by training. Adolescent therapists need to be worthy of the adolescent's trust and respect, and, in turn, need to demonstrate basic trust in and respect for the adolescent as a unique human being.

REVIEW QUESTIONS

1. What is the basic function of defense mechanisms?
2. What are the three major categories of anxiety disorders in childhood and adolescence? Can these overlap? What is panic disorder?
3. How can phobias be explained? How can they be treated?
4. What two underlying concerns are most likely to be symbolized by school refusal (school phobia)? What role do parents often play in this disorder?
5. Why was the existence of major depression in children and younger adolescents not recognized until recently? How common are depressed feelings in adolescence?
6. Psychological factors appear to play a particularly important part in two forms of adolescent depression. What are they?

7. Is it true that a person who talks about committing suicide is unlikely to do so? What warning signals can alert careful observers to the possibility of adolescent suicide?
8. What is meant by the term *hypochondriasis?* Are some hypochondriacal symptoms normal during adolescence?
9. Describe the three eating disorders that are most frequently encountered among adolescent and youth. What psychological and social factors are involved in each? Are there any factors that play a role in all three disorders?
10. What symptoms characterize adolescent schizophrenia, and what do we know about the causes of this disorder? How can a brief reactive psychosis be distinguished from schizophrenia?
11. What major mental disorder appears to have the strongest genetic component?
12. What personal and professional qualifications should a therapist have in order to work successfully with adolescents? In what ways does adolescent therapy differ from therapy with younger children or with adults? Why?

RECOMMENDED READINGS

Curran, D. K. (1987). *Adolescent suicidal behavior.* Washington, DC: Hemisphere.

Lamb, D. (1986). *Psychotherapy with adolescent girls* (2nd ed.). New York: Plenum.

Nicholi, A. M., Jr. (1988). The adolescent. In A. M. Nicholi, Jr. (Ed.), *The new Harvard guide to psychiatry* (pp. 637–664). Cambridge, MA: Harvard University Press.

Report of the Secretary's task force on youth suicide, Vols. I and II (1989). Washington, DC: U.S. Government Printing Office.

Rutter, M., & Hersov, L. (1988). *Child and adolescent psychiatry.* London: Blackwell Scientific Publications.

Rutter, M. Izard, C. E., & Read, P. B. (1986). *Depression in young people: Developmental and clinical perspectives.* New York: Guilford.

Striegel-Moore, R. H., Silberstein, L. R., & Rodin, J. (1986). Toward an understanding of risk factors for bulimia. *American Psychologist,* **41,** 246–263.

Weiner, I. B. (1982). *Child and adolescent psychopathology.* New York: Wiley.

EPILOGUE

As we noted at the beginning of the book, our society views the adolescent years and adolescents themselves, in varied and frequently conflicting ways. At this juncture, we hope we can view adolescence with a clearer perspective and greater ability to distinguish myth from reality. Although there is a widespread tendency to exaggerate the extent of adolescent turmoil in our society, adolescence *is* a complex and often difficult period of development both for adolescents and their families.

It could hardly be otherwise. Confronted by rapid physical, psychological, and cognitive changes and by an accelerating series of societal demands, adolescents face formidable challenges as they attempt to decide who they are, what they are going to be, and how they are going to live their lives.

Moreover, the challenges of this period have been increasing, partly as a consequence of continuing changes in the family and other social institutions and partly as a consequence of the accelerated rate of those changes. Much of this book has been devoted to a consideration of the kinds of influences—personal, interpersonal, and societal—that facilitate or hinder the adolescent's struggle toward maturity and a clearly defined sense of identity.

In the course of our discussion we have tried to dispel a number of myths. Among these is the view that today's adolescents and youth are a breed apart, unlike previous generations of young people—or, conversely that apparent generational differences are illusory, a matter of form rather than substance. A related myth is that there is something monolithic about adolescents and youth as a group, in contrast to adults, whose diversity is more readily recognized. We are far more likely to hear blanket statements about "today's youth" than about "today's adults."

In reality, there is nothing homogeneous or monolithic about contemporary adolescents. As we have seen throughout this book, in almost any area one chooses to consider—moral and religious values, social concerns and political beliefs, sexual attitudes and behavior, drug use, intellectual and educational interests, vocational goals, or emotional maturity—there is at least as much diversity among young people as there is among adults. Moreover, in most matters differences *within* both the adolescent and adult populations are far wider than differences *between* the average adolescent and the average adult. Consequently, sweeping generalizations about youth should be treated with caution. It soon becomes clear that what is really being talked about is *some* young people—if indeed the speaker is talking about real people and not simply projecting his or her own hopes and fears.

Nevertheless, there are some important differences between contemporary adolescents and adults. As we have seen, some of these differences reflect differences in the positions adolescents occupy in the life cycle. Others are the effects of very real differences between the worlds into which today's adolescents and their elders were born and in which they developed, as well as profound differences in the futures they face. For example, young people are more likely than older Americans to have liberal views about sexuality, gender equality, and family role relations. They also appear to be more preoccupied with self-fulfillment and less bound by institutional loyalties. Paradoxically, while they seem more cautious about entering into long-term personal relationships, they also express a stronger yearning for intimacy in personal relationships.

In the decade and a half since the first edition of this book appeared, we have witnessed a decline in society's preoccupation with adolescents and youth. During the late 1960s and early 1970s, hardly a week went by without a newspaper or magazine article, a new book, or a television special describing contemporary young people as our last best hope for a more just, more caring, less hypocritical world or, alternatively, as a danger to long-established values, if not to the fabric of society itself. Poll takers vied to keep us abreast of the attitudes and behavior of the nation's youth.

Despite public concern about problems of adolescent drug use, delinquency, pregnancy, and suicide, the kind of broad philosophical preoccupation with the views of youth that characterized the 1960s and 1970s is largely absent as we enter the 1990s. Why? Obviously, there are a variety of reasons, many of which have been addressed in this book: a decline in youthful activism, dissent, and pursuit of alternative life-styles; a narrowing of the so-called generation gap; a shift in the population bulge from adolescents to young adults; a reduced rate of change in social attitudes and behavior, though not in technology; and increased concern about inflation, changes in the job market, and the availability and cost of housing, education, and health care. In all likelihood, too, American society needed a period of cultural integration and equilibrium after the social turmoil of the 1960s and 1970s and the failed "situation ethics" of the 1980s.

In a number of respects, the reduced emphasis on youth can be viewed as positive. In the long run, young people and adults alike may benefit from the recognition that the experience of adolescence is not an end in itself but instead is a challenging and, one hopes, exciting stage in a continuing process of personal and social development. Similarly, a greater sense of generational continuity between parents and children may add meaning to human existence in an unpredictable, often chaotic world.

If this were the full extent of the matter, there would be little cause for concern. Unfortunately, however, the decreased emphasis on youth appears to have an added, more troublesome dimension: a decline in our society's commitment to the well-being of its young people. The self-preoccupation, materialism, and obsession with "the good life" that characterized much of the 1980s encouraged us to turn our backs on the nation's children, youth, and families. We preferred to "feel good about ourselves," even at the cost of shallowness and self-deception. As a result, we accepted assurances of the existence of a "safety net for the truly needy" at the same time that many important health care, nutrition, child care, housing, education, and employment programs were being severely reduced or eliminated—including many programs aimed specifically at adolescents and youth (Conger, 1988, 1989; Edelman, 1987;

Moynihan, 1986; Schorr, 1988). In the process, however, we may have lost more than we bargained for.

Self-deception in one area can lead to self-deception in others; the language of "double-speak," once entered into, can erode the capacity for critical judgment, even in matters of ultimate self-interest. When "the bottom line" becomes the ultimate measure of success, it all too often becomes the only measure, and other values are abandoned. How else can we explain the fall from grace of so many bright and sophisticated government officials, corporate leaders, politicians, investment bankers, stockbrokers, lawyers, research scientists, and members of the electronic clergy during the 1980s?

The danger is not only that a retreat from candor and compassion in the direction of hypocrisy and greed has led us to ignore the vital needs of adolescents but also that it can adversely affect the values, attitudes, and beliefs of young people themselves. As we have seen, in the past decade and a half America's youth became far more concerned with personal well-being and material success and progressively less concerned with the welfare of others—particularly the disadvantaged—and of society itself (Astin et al., 1987, 1990; Bachman et al., 1981, 1987; Conger, 1988; Johnston et al., forthcoming).

Fortunately, however, significant numbers of young people—and adults—are actively trying to create a more human and humane world, whether in personal relations, social-service activities, community participation, school and work, or politics. Moreover, their numbers appear to be increasing. Though still a minority, the percentage of adolescents and youth expressing an interest in influencing social values increased between 1986 and 1989. More young people are expressing concern about such problems as homelessness, child abuse, hunger and malnutrition, and inadequate educational and social services for poor children and adolescents. Whether such stirrings presage a significant shift in social values in the 1990s remains to be seen.

One thing is certain: As a society we can ill afford to abandon the needs and dreams of youth. No matter what the fads or fashions of the moment, or the state of the economy, or the conflicts between nations and the divisions within them, one central fact is inescapable. For better or worse, the future course of our society, and quite possibly of the world itself, rests in the hands of young people.

If this book has in any way helped adults to better understand adolescents, or helped adolescents to gain a deeper understanding of themselves and their peers, it will have served its purpose.

GLOSSARY

A

addiction Physiological dependence on a habit-forming drug.

adolescent growth spurt The accelerated rate of increase in height and weight that accompanies puberty.

adolescent schizophrenia A severe mental disorder characterized by disordered thinking; distortions of, or lack of contact with, reality; limited capacity for relating emotionally to others; and poor emotional control.

alienation Profound rejection of the values of society or isolation from other people that goes well beyond the skepticism of the average adolescent.

androgens Male sex hormones.

androgyny A combination of socially valued "masculine" and "feminine" characteristics in the same individual.

anorexia nervosa A severe eating disorder characterized by a pathological loss of interest in eating, accompanied by a debilitating (sometimes life-threatening) weight loss. Typically the individual has a distorted body image and continues to worry about being too fat even when emaciated.

antecedent–consequent relationships The idea that the effects of events occurring at any one stage of development depend on and proceed from earlier developmental events and will, in turn, influence the individual's responses to future events.

anxiety A state of apprehension, tension, and worry that has both physiological and cognitive components.

anxiety disorders A group of mental disorders characterized by intense anxiety or by defensive maladaptive behaviors aimed at relieving anxiety.

ataxia An inability to coordinate voluntary muscular movements that is symptomatic of some neurological disorders.

authoritative (democratic) parents Parents who value the development of both autonomous self-direction *and* disciplined behavior. Such parents encourage verbal give and take; when they exercise authority in the form of demands or prohibitions they explain their reasons for doing so.

autonomy Self-directed independence; taking responsibility for one's own life.

B

bidirectionality The principle that parent–child influences flow both ways–from parent to child and from child to parent.

bipolar (manic-depressive) disorder A severe affective disorder characterized by alternating episodes of mania and depression.

bulimia An eating disorder characterized by alternating episodes of binge eating and purging. The individual is usually aware that this eating pattern is abnormal but fears being unable to stop it voluntarily.

C

classical conditioning A type of learning process through which a response becomes attached to a previously neutral stimulus.

clique A small, tightly knit social group whose members typically are similar in age, sex, and social status.

cognitive development The changes and advances that occur in cognitive skills during the course of development.

concrete operations According to Piaget, the stage of cognitive development ages (7–11) when children can reason logically about actual objects but are not yet able to engage in hypothetico-deductive, propositional thinking.

conventional level Kohlberg's second level of moral development, during which the focus is on living up to the expectations of family, friends, and society.

conversion reaction Sensory or motor impairment for which there is no organic cause.

counterculture A set of values, beliefs, customs, and behaviors adopted by young people in the 1960s as an alternative to mainstream societal values and behaviors, which were rejected as morally bankrupt.

critical period A stage in development during which the organism is optimally ready to acquire certain response patterns.

crowd A relatively large group made up of individuals who share interests, likes, and social ideals. Members meet on the basis of shared activities, not because of mutual attraction.

crystallized abilities Mental abilities that are influenced primarily by experience and acquired knowledge.

D

defense mechanism A largely unconscious mental process that functions to prevent the emergence into consciousness of anxiety-producing thoughts and feelings.

delinquency See **juvenile delinquent.**

denial A defense mechanism in which the individual treats anxiety-producing realities as if they did not exist.

depression An affective, or mood, disorder characterized by sadness, decreased motivation and interest in life, low energy level, and negative thoughts. See also **bipolar disorder, unipolar disorder.**

development The physical and psychological changes that take place over the lifespan.

developmental stage A period of development characterized by distinctive biological, psychological, and/or behavioral changes.

discrimination Learning to react to differences. Discrimination is brought about by selective reinforcement of responses that have been appropriately generalized, and by the elimination, or *extinction*, of incorrectly generalized responses.

displacement A defense mechanism in which an individual has an appropriate emotional response but attributes it to a source other than its actual source.

dizygotic (DZ) twins Twins that develop from separate ova ("fraternal" twins).

E

ecological psychology The study of the progressive accommodation that takes place over the lifespan between the human organism and the environments in which it grows.

emotion-focused coping Attempts by an individual to reduce anxiety without dealing directly with the anxiety-producing situation. See **defense mechanism.**

estrogens Female sex hormones

F

fetal alcohol syndrome A fetal condition characterized by retarded growth, physical abnormalities, and intellectual defects that results from maternal consumption of alcohol during pregnancy.

field theory Kurt Lewin's theory that behavior (B) is a function (f) of the person (P) and his or her environment (E); hence, $B = f(PE)$.

fluid abilities Mental abilities that depend largely on flexibility, adaptability, and speed of information processing.

formal operations According to Piaget, the stage of cognitive development (about age 12 and up) when the child becomes capable of engaging in abstract reasoning about hypothetical situations.

freebasing Smoking cocaine that has been converted into a smokable "base" form. Smoking cocaine has a more powerful and immediate effect than sniffing it.

G

gender identity Awareness and acceptance of one's biological nature as a male or female.

generalization See **stimulus generalization.**

gradient of generalization A principle of learning that states that the more similar one stimulus is to another, the greater the likelihood that a response learned to one will generalize to the other, and the stronger the response will be.

H

homosexuality (homosexual orientation) Sexual attraction primarily to members of one's own sex.

hormones Secretions of the endocrine glands that circulate in the bloodstream and affect behavior.

hypochondriasis Excessive preoccupation with health and bodily functions.

I

identification The process by which one is led to think, feel, or behave as though the characteristics of another person belonged to oneself.

identity (ego identity) A sense of oneself as a separate, distinct, self-consistent person who has continuity over time.

identity confusion (diffusion) A prolonged period in which an individual is unable to develop a strong, clear sense of identity.

identity foreclosure A premature fixing of an individual's self-image that interferes with the development of other possibilities for self-definition.

imaginary audience The egocentric adolescent belief that others are preoc-cupied with one's behavior and appearance.

induction A non-power-assertive disciplinary technique in which the parent gives explanations or reasons for requiring certain behaviors of the child. Unlike other disciplinary techniques, induction appeals to the child's pride and striving to be "grown up."

information processing An approach to cognition that studies the ways in which people mentally represent and process information.

instrumental conditioning See **operant conditioning.**

intelligence The capacity to learn and use the skills required for successful adaptation to the demands of one's culture and environment.

intelligence quotient (IQ) An intelligence test score, originally based on the ratio between mental age and chronological age. The average intelligence quotient for a person of any age is set at 100.

intimacy A relationship between two people characterized by closeness, ease of communication, attachment, and affection.

IQ See **intelligence quotient.**

J

juvenile delinquent A young person, generally under 18 years of age, who engages in behavior that is punishable by law.

L

laissez-faire parents Parents who give their adolescent child the option of either subscribing to or disregarding parental wishes in making decisions.

learning The process by which behavior (or the potential for behavior) is modified as a result of experience.

love-withdrawal A non-power-assertive disciplinary technique that relies on fear of the loss of parental love to influence the child's behavior.

M

mainlining Injecting a psychoactive drug into a principal vein.

manic-depressive disorder See **bipolar disorder.**

maturation Growth processes that result in orderly physical and behavioral changes and are relatively independent of exercise or experience.

menarche The time of first menstruation, an indication of sexual maturation in a girl.

mental age A person's age as measured by performance on an intelligence test. A person who scores as well as the average 10-year-old has a mental age of 10, regardless of his or her chronological age.

monozygotic (MZ) twins Twins that develop from the division of a single fertilized ovum ("identical" twins).

moral development The acquisition of increasingly sophisticated internalized standards of right and wrong.

moral relativism The belief that there are no absolute standards of right and wrong and that one set of beliefs or values may be no better or worse than another set.

motivation The needs, goals, and desires that provoke an individual to action.

myelination The development of a soft, white, somewhat fatty sheath around certain nerve fibers. Nerve impulses travel faster and with less expenditure of energy in myelinated fibers.

N

normal achiever An individual whose performance is about what would be anticipated on the basis of his or her IQ score or another measure of ability.

O

obesity Weighing more than 20 percent above normal requirements for one's height and skeletal structure.

observational learning Learning by observing the behavior of others.

operant (or instrumental) conditioning A type of learning in which the subject's own response is *instrumental* in producing a reward; that is it *operates* to bring about the reward.

overachiever An individual whose performance exceeds what would be anticipated on the basis of his or her IQ score or another measure of ability.

overanxious disorder An anxiety disorder in which the sources of the anxiety are generalized and diffuse.

P

panic disorder A disorder characterized by acute anxiety that may be so intense that it produces almost unbearable panic and terror. Attacks, though overwhelming, are usually brief but are likely to recur.

peers Individuals who belong to the same age, grade, or status group in society.

perinatal stress Physical or other stress occurring around the time of birth.

permissive parents Parents who permit their adolescent child to assume a more active and influential role than themselves in making decisions that affect him or her.

personal fable The belief that one is somehow special and unique, especially with respect to one's feelings.

phobia An intense fear of a person, object, or situation that the individual consciously recognizes as unrealistic or excessive.

pituitary gland An endocrine gland, located immediately below the brain, that helps regulate growth and the action of other endocrine glands.

postconventional level Kohlberg's third level, during which moral judgments come to be based on broad, abstract principles that are accepted because they are believed to be inherently right rather than because society considers them right.

power-assertive discipline A technique that relies on punishment or fear of punishment to influence the child's behavior, rather than on the child's inner resources.

preconventional level Kohlberg's first level of moral development, during which children judge right and wrong primarily by the consequences of actions.

preoperational stage According to Piaget, the stage of cognitive development (about ages 2–7) when the child's ability to use language begins to dominate intellectual development but the child does not yet comprehend certain rules or mental operations.

problem-focused coping Coping in which the individual confronts and evaluates a stressful situation and then takes steps to deal with it.

progestins Pregnancy-related hormones.

projection A defense mechanism in which anxiety is avoided by ascribing an undesirable thought or action of one's own to another person.

psychoactive drug A drug that affects personality, mood, intellectual functioning, or behavior.

psychophysiologic (psychosomatic) reactions Physical conditions to which psychological factors contribute (e.g., tension headache, gastric ulcer, obesity).

psychosis A severe mental disorder in which cognitive and emotional functioning are so impaired that the individual loses touch with reality and cannot meet the demands of everyday living. See **adolescent schizophrenia.**

psychosocial moratorium A period during which the adolescent has an opportunity to develop an identity while relatively free from other responsibilities.

puberty The initial phase of adolescence, during which the reproductive system matures and secondary sex characteristics develop.

R

reaction formation A defense mechanism in which a person denies an unacceptable motive by strongly expressing its opposite.

recapitulation The theory that during development the individual passes through stages similar to those that occurred during the history of the human race (e.g., from primitive to civilized behavior).

regression The readoption of a response that was characteristic of an earlier phase of development.

repression A major defense mechanism that prevents anxiety-producing thoughts, impulses, and memories from reaching conscious awareness.

S

schizophrenia See **adolescent schizophrenia.**

school phobia See **school refusal.**

school processes What actually goes on in schools; including teacher expectations, amount of teacher time spent interacting with the class, provision of opportunities for responsibility in school life, use of rewards and incentives, and continuity of teachers and staff.

school refusal ("school phobia") A fear, which may approach panic, of leaving home and going to school.

sensorimotor stage According to Piaget, the stage of cognitive development (birth to age 2) when the infant discovers relationships between sensory impressions and motor activities.

separation anxiety A type of anxiety disorder in which the predominant disturbance is excessive anxiety at separation from major attachment figures or from home or other familiar surroundings.

serial monogamists Adolescents and youth who have a relationship with only one partner during a given period.

sex role identity One's perception of oneself as masculine or feminine according to one's own definition of these terms.

sexual adventurers Adolescents and youth who move freely from one sexual partner to another and feel no obligation to be faithful to any one partner.

sexuality The totality of a person's sexual thoughts, feelings, values, beliefs, and relationships.

social cognition The ability of individuals to interpret the social world about them—to infer what others are thinking and feeling, what their intentions are, what their relations with others are, and how they view the world.

status offense An act that is illegal only when it is committed by young people.

stereotyping Uncritically assuming that all members of a group share the same personality traits, abilities, or other characteristics.

stimulus generalization A learning principle stating that when a particular response has been learned to one stimulus, it is likely to occur to similar stimuli.

suppression Dealing with anxiety-producing thoughts, emotional conflicts, or stressors by voluntarily avoiding thinking about them.

T

temperament An inborn bias favoring certain moods and reaction styles.

testosterone The primary male sex hormone, produced by the testes.

U

underachiever An individual whose performance falls below what would be anticipated on the basis of his or her IQ score or another measure of ability.

underclass The growing number of citizens, victims of poverty and discrimination, who feel excluded from society and typically reject commonly accepted values and beliefs.

unipolar depression An affective disorder characterized by episodes of severe depression.

W

withdrawal A defense mechanism in which the individual responds to an anxiety-producing situation by withdrawing from it.

REFERENCES

Abelson, H. I., *et al.* (1977). *National survey on drug abuse, 1977: A nationwide study—Youth, young adults, and older people.* Rockville, MD: National Institute on Drug Abuse. DHEW Publication No. (ADM), 78–618.

Achenbach, T. M., & Edelbrock, C. S. (1981). Behavioral problems and competencies reported by parents of normal and disturbed children aged four through sixteen. *Monographs of the Society for Research in Child Development,* **46,** Serial No. 188.

Ackerman, N. W. (1958). *The psychodynamics of family life.* New York: Basic Books.

Adams, G. R., Abraham, K. G., & Markstrom, C. A. (1987). The relations among identity development, self-consciousness, and self-focusing during middle and late adolescence. *Developmental Psychology,* **23,** 292–297.

Adams, G. R., & Gullota, T. (1983). *Adolescent life experiences.* Monterey, CA: Brooks-Cole.

Adams, G. R., & Munro, G. (1979). Portrait of the North American runaway: A critical review. *Journal of Youth and Adolescence,* **8,** 359–373.

Adams, P. L., Milner, J. R., & Schrepf, N. A. (1984). *Fatherless children.* New York: Wiley-Interscience.

Adelson, J. (1971). The political imagination of the young adolescent. *Daedalus,* **100,** 1013–1050.

Adelson, J. (1975). The development of ideology in adolescence. In S. E. Dragastin & G. H. Elder, Jr. (Eds.), *Adolescence in the life cycle: Psychological change and social context* (pp. 63–78). New York: Wiley.

Adelson, J. (1982, Summer). Rites of passage: How children learn the principles of community. *American Educator,* 6 ff.

Adelson, J., & O'Neil, R. (1966). The development of political thought in adolescence: A sense of community. *Journal of Personality and Social Psychology,* **4,** 295–308.

Adolescent pregnancy: Testing prevention strategies (1986, Summer/Fall). *Carnegie Quarterly,* **31,** Nos. 3 and 4, 1–7.

Ahlstrom, W. M., & Havighurst, R. J. (1971). *400 losers.* San Francisco: Jossey-Bass.

Albert, R. S., & Runco, M. A. (1989). Independence and the creative potential of gifted and exceptionally gifted boys. *Journal of Youth and Adolescence,* **18,** 221–230.

Alessi, N. E., & Magen, J. (1988, November). Panic disorder in psychiatrically hospitalized children. *American Journal of Psychiatry,* **145,** 1450–1452.

Alexander, J. F. (1973). Defensive and supportive communications in normal and deviant families. *Journal of Consulting and Clinical Psychology,* **40,** 223–231.

Alexander, J. F., & Parsons, B. V. (1973). Short-term behavioral intervention with delinquent families: Impact on family process and recidivism. *Journal of Abnormal Psychology,* **81,** 219–225.

Almquist, E. M., & Angrist, S. S. (1971). Role model influences on college women's career aspirations. *Merrill-Palmer Quarterly,* **71,** 263–279.

Alton, I. R. (1982). Nutritional needs and assessment of adolescents. In R. W. Blum (Ed.), *Adolescent health care.* New York: Academic Press.

Altus, W. D. (1965). Birth order and its sequelae. *Science,* **151,** 44–49.

Amabile, T. M. (1983). *The social psychology of creativity.* New York: Springer-Verlag.

America's youth 1977–1988. Princeton, NJ: The George Gallup International Institute, 1988.

Anderson, K. L. (1980). Educational goals of male and female adolescents: The effects of parental characteristics and attitudes. *Youth and Society,* **12,** 173–188.

Anthony, E. J. (1970). The behavior disorders of children. In P. H. Mussen (Ed.), *Carmichael's manual of child psychology* (Vol. 2) (3rd ed., pp. 667–764). New York: Wiley.

Anthony, E. J. (1974). Psychotherapy of adolescence. In G. Caplan (Ed.), *American handbook of psychiatry, Vol. II: Child and adolescent psychiatry, sociocultural and community psychiatry* (pp. 234–249). New York: Basic Books.

Anthony, E. J., & Benedek, T. F. (Eds.) (1970). *Parenthood: Its psychology and psychopathology.* Boston: Little, Brown.

Applebee, A. N., Langer, J. A., & Mullis, I. V. S. (1986). *The writing report card: Writing achievement in American schools.* Princeton, NJ: National Assessment of Educational Progress, Educational Testing Service.

Arbuthnot, J., Gordon, D. A., & Jurkovic, G. J. (1987). Personality. In H. C. Quay (Ed.), *Handbook of juvenile delinquency* (pp. 139–183). New York: Wiley.

Archer, S. L., & Waterman, A. S. (1990). Varieties of identity diffusions and foreclosures: An exploration of subcategories of identity statuses. *Journal of Adolescent Research,* **5,** 96–111.

Areshansel, C. S., & Rosen, B. C. (1980). Domestic roles and sex differences in occupational expectations. *Journal of Marriage and the Family,* **42,** 121–131.

Aries, E. (1974, August 30–September 3). Interaction patterns and themes of male, female, and mixed groups. Paper presented at the annual meeting of the American Psychological Association, New Orleans.

Aries, P. (1962). *Centuries of childhood: A social history of family life* (R. Bladick, trans.). New York: Random House (Vintage Books).

Aristotle (1941). Ethica Nicomachea. In R. McKeon (Ed.), *The basic works of Aristotle* (W. D. Ross, trans.). New York: Random House.

Armsden, G. C., & Greenberg, M. T. (1987). The inventory of parent and peer attachment: Individual differences and their relationship to psychological well-being in adolescence. *Journal of Youth and Adolescence, 16,* 427–451.

Asarnow, J. R. (1988). Children at risk for schizophrenia: Converging lines of evidence. *Schizophrenic Bulletin, 14,* 613–631.

Asher, S. R. (1978). Children's peer relations. In M. E. Lamb (Ed.), *Social and personality development* (pp. 91–113). New York: Holt, Rinehart & Winston.

Asher, S. R., & Renshaw, P. D. (1981). Children without friends: Social knowledge and social skill training. In S. R. Asher & J. M. Gottman (Eds.), *The development of children's friendships.* New York: Cambridge University Press.

Astin, A. W. (1980, June 28). Characteristics and attitudes of first-year college students: A 10-year comparison based on data gathered in national surveys of freshmen in 1969 and 1979. *The Chronicle of Higher Education, 20,* 4–5.

Astin, A. W. (1981). *The American freshman: National norms for fall 1980.* Los Angeles: American Council on Education and Graduate School of Education, University of California at Los Angeles.

Astin, A. W., Green, K. C., & Korn, W. S. (1987). *The American freshman: Twenty year trends.* Los Angeles: Higher Education Research Institute, University of California at Los Angeles.

Astin, A. W., Green, K. C., Korn, W. S., & Schalit, M. (1985). *The American freshman: National norms for fall 1985.* Los Angeles: Higher Education Research Institute, University of California at Los Angeles.

Astin, A. W., Green, K. C., Korn, W. S., & Schalit, M. (1986). *The American freshman: National norms for fall, 1986.* Los Angeles: Higher Education Research Institute, University of California at Los Angeles.

Astin, A. W., Green, K. C., Korn, W. S., & Schalit, M., & Berz, E. R. (1988). *The American freshman: National norms for fall 1988.* Los Angeles: Higher Education Research Institute, University of California at Los Angeles.

Astin, A. W., Korn, W. S., & Berz, E. R. (1989). *The American freshman: National norms for fall, 1989.* Los Angeles: Higher Education Research Institute, University of California, Los Angeles.

Astin, A. W., Korn, W. S., Berz, E. R., & Bailey, R. (1989). *The American freshman and follow-up survey: 1989 freshman survey results.* Los Angeles: Higher Education Research Institute, University of California at Los Angeles.

Atkinson, R. C., & Shiffrin, R. M. (1977). Human memory: A proposed system and its control processes. In G. H. Bower (Ed.), *Human memory: Basic processes.* New York: Academic Press.

Atkinson, R. L., Atkinson, R. C., Smith, E. E., & Hilgard, E. R. (1987). *Introduction to psychology* (9th ed.). New York: Harcourt Brace Jovanovitch.

Attie, I., & Brooks-Gunn, J. (1989). Development of eating problems in adolescent girls. *Developmental Psychology, 25,* 70–79.

Atwater, E. (1988). *Adolescence* (2nd ed.). Englewood Cliffs, NJ: Prentice-Hall.

Ausubel, D. P. (1954). *Theory and problems of adolescent development.* New York: Grune & Stratton.

Avery, A. W. (1982). Escaping loneliness in adolescence: The case for androgyny. *Journal of Youth and Adolescence, 11,* 451–459.

Bacas, H. (1986, August). Where are the teenagers? *Nation's Business,* pp. 18–25.

Bachman, J. G. (1970). *Youth in transition, Vol. II: The impact of family background and intelligence on tenth-grade boys.* Ann Arbor: Institute for Social Research, University of Michigan.

Bachman, J. G. (1971). *Youth looks at national problems: A special report from the youth in transition project.* Ann Arbor: Institute for Social Research, University of Michigan.

Bachman, J. G., Green, S., & Wirtanen, I. (1972). *Dropping out—Problem or symptom.* Ann Arbor: Institute for Social Research, University of Michigan.

Bachman, J. G., & Johnston, L. D. (1979). *Fewer rebels, fewer causes: A profile of today's college freshmen.* Ann Arbor: Survey Research Center, Institute for Social Research, University of Michigan.

Bachman, J. G., Johnston, L. D., & O'Malley, P. M. (1981). *Monitoring the future: Questionnaire responses from the nation's high school seniors 1980.* Ann Arbor: Institute for Social Research, University of Michigan.

Bachman, J. G., Johnston, L. D., & O'Malley, P. M. (1987). *Monitoring the future: Questionnaire responses from the nation's high school seniors, 1986.* Ann Arbor: Institute for Social Research, University of Michigan.

Bachman, J. G., Johnston, L. D., O'Malley, P. M., & Humphrey, R. H. (1988). Explaining the recent decline in marijuana use: Differentiating the effects and perceived risks, disapproval, and general lifestyle factors. *Journal of Health and Social Behavior, 29,* 92–112.

Bachman, J. G., Kahn, R. L., Mednick, M. T., Davidson, T. N., & Johnson, L. D. (1967). *Youth in transition, Vol. I: Blueprint for a longitudinal study of adolescent boys.* Ann Arbor: Institute for Social Research, University of Michigan.

Bachman, J. G., & O'Malley, P. M. (1978). The search for school effects: Some new findings and perspectives. Unpublished manuscript. Ann Arbor: Institute for Social Research, University of Michigan.

Bachman, J. G., O'Malley, P. M., & Johnston, J. (1978). *Adolescence to adulthood: Change and sta-*

bility in the lives of young men. Ann Arbor: Institute for Social Research, University of Michigan.

Bachman, J. G., O'Malley, P. M., & Johnston, J. (1978). *Youth in transition, Vol. VI: Adolescence to adulthood—change and stability in the lives of young men.* Ann Arbor: Institute for Social Research, University of Michigan.

Baird, L. L. (1973). Teaching styles: An exploratory study of dimensions and effects. *Journal of Educational Psychology,* **64,** 15–21.

Bales, J. (1986, November). New studies cite drug use dangers. *The American Psychological Association Monitor,* p. 28.

Baltes, P. B., Reese, H. W., & Lipsitt, L. P. (1980). Life-span developmental psychology. *Annual Review of Psychology,* **31,** 65–110.

Bamber, J. H. (1979). *The fears of adolescents.* London: Academic Press.

Banducci, R. (1967). The effect of mother's employment on the achievement, aspirations, and expectations of the child. *Personnel and Guidance Journal,* **46,** 263–267.

Bandura, A. (1964). The stormy decade: Fact or fiction? *Psychology in the Schools,* **1,** 224–231.

Bandura, A. (1967). The role of modeling processes in personality development. In W. W. Hartup & N. L. Smothergill (Eds.), *The young child: Reviews of research.* Washington, DC: National Association for the Education of Young Children.

Bandura, A. (1977a). Self-efficacy: Toward a unifying theory of behavioral change. *Psychological Review,* **84,** 191–215.

Bandura, A. (1977b). *Social learning theory.* Englewood Cliffs, NJ: Prentice-Hall.

Bandura, A. (1982). Self-efficacy mechanism in human agency. *American Psychologist,* **37,** 122–147.

Bandura, A., & McDonald, F. J. (1963). Influence of social reinforcement and the behavior of models in shaping children's moral judgments. *Journal of Abnormal and Social Psychology,* **67,** 274–281.

Bandura, A., & Walters, R. H. (1959). *Adolescent aggression.* New York: Ronald Press.

Barbach, L. G. (1976). *For yourself: The fulfillment of female sexuality.* New York: Simon & Schuster.

Barclay, A. G., & Cusumano, D. (1967). Father-absence, cross-sex identity, and field-dependent behavior in male adolescents. *Child Development,* **38,** 243–250.

Barich, B. (1986, November 3). A reporter at large: The crazy life. *The New Yorker,* 97–130.

Barker, R. G., & Gump, P. V. (Eds.) (1964). *Big school, small school.* Stanford, CA: Stanford University Press.

Barker, R. G., & Wright, H. F. (1955). *Midwest and its children: The psychological ecology of an American town.* New York: Harper & Row. (Reprinted by Archer Books, Hamden, Conn., 1971.)

Barlow, D. H. (1988). *Anxiety and its disorders.* New York: Guilford Press.

Barnes, G. M. (1984). Adolescent alcohol abuse and other problem behaviors: Their relationships and common parental influences. *Journal of Adolescence and Youth,* **13,** 329–348.

Barnes, H., & Olson, D. H. (1985). Parent-child communication and the circumplex model. *Child Development,* **56,** 438–447.

Barnett, R., & Volker, J. M. (1985). Moral judgment as life experience. Unpublished manuscript. Minneapolis, MN: University of Minnesota.

Barron, F. (1963). *Creativity and psychological health.* Princeton, NJ: Van Nostrand.

Barron, F. X. (1969). *Creative person and creative process.* New York: Holt, Rinehart & Winston.

Barron, F., & Harrington, C. L. (1981). Creativity, intelligence, and personality. *Annual Review of Psychology,* **32,** 439–476.

Barry, H., III, & Schlegel, A. (1984). Measurements of adolescent sexual behavior in the standard sample of societies. *Ethnology,* **23,** 315–329.

Barry, H., III, & Schlegel, A. (1986). Cultural customs that influence sexual freedom in adolescence. *Ethnology,* **25,** 151–162.

Baruch, G. K. (1972). Maternal influences upon college women's attitudes toward women and work. *Developmental Psychology,* **6,** 32–37.

Bauer, D. H. (1976). An exploratory study of developmental changes in children's fears. *Journal of Child Psychiatry and Psychology,* **17,** 69–74.

Baughman, E. E. (1971). *Black Americans.* New York: Academic Press.

Baumrind, D. (1968). Authoritarian vs. authoritative control. *Adolescence,* **3,** 255–272.

Baumrind, D. (1971). Current patterns of parental authority. *Developmental Psychology Monographs,* **4,** No. 1, Part 2.

Baumrind, D. (1973). The development of instrumental competence through socialization. In A. D. Pick (Ed.), *Minnesota symposium on child psychology (Vol. 7,* pp. 3–46). Minneapolis, MN: University of Minnesota Press.

Baumrind, D. (1975). Early socialization and adolescent competence. In S. E. Dragastin & G. H. Elder, Jr. (Eds.), *Adolescence in the life cycle: Psychological change and social context* (pp. 117–143). New York: Wiley.

Baumrind, D. (1979). Sex-related socialization effects. Paper presented at the meeting of the Society for Research in Child Development, San Francisco, CA.

Baumrind, D. (1980). New directions in socialization research. *American Psychologist,* **35,** 639–652.

Baumrind, D. (1986). Sex differences in moral reasoning: Response to Walker's (1984) conclusion that there are none. *Child Development,* **57,** 511–521.

Baumrind, D. (1989, August). *The influence of parenting style on adolescent competence and problem behavior.* G. Stanley Hall Award address presented at the annual meeting of the American Psychological Association, New Orleans, LA.

Baumrind, D. (in press a). Parenting styles and adolescent development. To appear in J. Brooks-Gunn, R. Lerner, & A. C. Petersen (Eds.), *The encyclopedia on adolescence*. New York: Garland.

Baumrind, D. (in press b). Effective parenting during the early adolescent transition. To be published in P. E. Cowan and E. M. Hetherington (Eds.), *Advances in family research, Vol. 2*. Hillsdale, NJ: Lawrence Erlbaum Associates.

Baumrind, D., Moselle, K. A., & Martin, J. A. (1985). Adolescent drug abuse research: A critical examination from a developmental perspective. *Advances in Alcohol and Substance Abuse, 4,* 41–67.

Bayley, N. (1949). Consistency and variability in the growth of intelligence from birth to eighteen years. *Journal of Genetic Psychology, 75,* 165–196.

Bayley, N. (1954). Some increasing parent-child similarities during the growth of children. *Journal of Educational Psychology, 45,* 1–21.

Bayley, N. (1968). Behavioral correlates of mental growth: Birth to thirty-six years. *American Psychologist, 23,* 1–17.

Bayley, N. (1970). Development of mental abilities. In P. H. Mussen (Ed.), *Carmichael's manual of child psychology, Vol. I* (3rd ed., pp. 1163–1209). New York: Wiley.

Bayley, N. (1971). Learning in adulthood: The role of intelligence. In M. C. Jones, N. Bayley, J. W. Macfarlane, & M. P. Honzik (Eds.), *The course of human development*. Waltham, MA: Xerox Publishing Co.

Beach, F. A. (Ed.) (1965). *Sex and behavior*. New York: Wiley.

Beach, F. A. (Ed.) (1977). *Human sexuality in four perspectives*. Baltimore: Johns Hopkins University Press.

Beck, R. D., & Kolakowski, D. (1973). Further evidence of sex-linked major-gene influence on human spatial ability. *American Journal of Human Genetics, 25,* 1–14.

Becker, B. J. (1983). Item characteristics and sex differences on the SAT-M for mathematically able youths. Presented at Annual Meeting of American Educational Research Association, Montreal.

Becker, W. C. (1964). Consequences of different kinds of parental discipline. In M. L. Hoffman & L. W. Hoffman (Eds.), *Review of child development (Vol. I)*. New York: Russell Sage Foundation.

Behrman, R. E., Vaughn, V. C., & Nelson, W. E. (Eds.) (1987). *Textbook of pediatrics* (13th ed.). Philadelphia: W. B. Saunders.

Bell, A. P. (1969). Role modeling of fathers in adolescence and young adulthood. *Journal of Counseling Psychology, 16,* 30–35.

Bell, A. P., & Weinberg, M. S. (1978). *Homosexualities: A study of diversity among men and women*. New York: Simon & Schuster.

Bell, A. P., Weinberg, M. S., & Hammersmith, S. K. (1981). *Sexual preference: Its development in men and women*. Bloomington, IN: Indiana University Press.

Bell, G. D. (1963). Process in the formation of adolescents' aspirations. *Social Forces, 42,* 179–195.

Bell, N., Avery, A. W., Jenkins, D., Feld, J., & Schoenrock, C. J. (1985). Family relationships and social competence during late adolescence. *Journal of Youth and Adolescence, 14,* 109–119.

Bell, R. (1980). *Changing bodies, changing lives: A book for teens on sex and relationships*. New York: Random House.

Bell, R. (1987). *Changing bodies, changing lives: A book for teens on sex and relationships*. (rev. ed.). New York: Random House.

Bell, R., & Wildflower, L. Z. (1983). *Talking with your teenager: A book for parents*. New York: Random House.

Bell, R. Q. (1979). Parent, child, and reciprocal influences. *American Psychologist, 34,* 821–826.

Bell, R. Q., & Herper, L. V. (1977). *The effect of children on parents*. Hillsdale, NJ: Erlbaum.

Bellah, R. N., Madsen, R., Sullivan, W. M., Swidler, A., & Tipton, S. (1985). *Habits of the heart*. New York: Harper & Row.

Belsky, J., & Vondra, J. (1989). Lessons from child abuse: The determinants of parenting. In D. Cicchetti & V. Carlson (Eds.), *Child maltreatment: Theory and research on the causes and consequences of child abuse and neglect* (pp. 153–202). New York: Cambridge University Press.

Bem, S. L. (1975). Sex role adaptability: One consequence of psychological androgyny. *Journal of Personality and Social Psychology, 31,* 634–643.

Bem, S. L. (1981). Gender schema theory: A cognitive account of sex typing. *Psychological Review, 88,* 352–364.

Benbow, C. P., & Stanley, J. C. (1980). Sex differences in mathematical ability. *Science, 210,* 1262–1264.

Benedict, R. (1954). Continuities and discontinuities in cultural conditioning. In W. E. Martin & C. B. Stendler (Eds.), *Readings in child development* (pp. 142–148). New York: Harcourt Brace Jovanovich.

Benjamin, L. S. (1974). Structural analysis of social behavior. *Psychological Review, 81,* 392–425.

Benjamin, L. S. (1977). Structural analysis of a family therapy. *Journal of Consulting and Clinical Psychology, 45,* 391–406.

Benjamin, R. (1981). *Making schools work*. New York: Continuum.

Bennett, S. N. (1978). Recent research on teaching: A dream, a belief, and a model. *British Journal of Educational Psychology, 48,* 127–147.

Bennetts, L. (1979, October 14). Women: New opportunity, old reality. *The New York Times*, National Recruitment Survey.

Berg, I., Collins, R., McGuire, R., & O'Melia, J. (1975). Educational attainment in adolescent school phobia. *Psychological Medicine, 4,* 428–434.

Berke, R. L. (1989, September 12). Poll finds many in U.S. back Bush strategy on drugs. *The New York Times*, p. A14.

Berkowitz, D. A. (1987). Adolescent individuation and family therapy. In J. C. Coleman (Ed.), *Working with troubled adolescents: A handbook* (pp. 19–29). London: Academic Press.

Berkowitz, I. H. (Ed.) (1972), *Adolescents grow in groups: Experiences in adolescent group psychotherapy.* New York: Brunner/Mazel.

Berliner, D., & Tikunoff, W. (1977). Ethnography in the classroom. In G. Borich & K. Fenton (Eds.), *The appraisal of teaching: Concepts and process* (pp. 280–290). Reading, MA: Addison-Wesley.

Bermant, G., & Davidson, J. M. (1974). *Biological bases of sexual behavior.* New York: Harper & Row.

Berndt, T. J. (1979). Developmental changes in conformity to peers and parents. *Developmental Psychology, 15,* 606–616.

Berndt, T. J. (1982). The features and effects of friendship in early adolescence. *Child Development, 53,* 1447–1460.

Berndt, T. J., & Hawkins, J. (1985, April). *The effects of friendships on students' adjustment after the transition to high school.* Paper presented at the annual meeting of the American Educational Research Association, Chicago, IL.

Berndt, T. J., & Ladd, G. W. (Eds.) (1989). *Peer relationships in child development.* New York: Wiley.

Berry, G. L. (1974). Self-concept and need factors of inner city high school adolescents and dropouts. *Child Study Journal, 4,* 21–31.

Bickel, R., & Paporgiannis, G. (1988). Post-high school prospects and district-level dropout rates. *Youth and Society, 20,* 122–147.

Bieber, J. et al. (1962). *A psychoanalytic study of male homosexuals.* New York: Random House (Vintage Books).

Bigalow, B. J., & LaGaipa, J. J. (1980). The development of friendship values and choice. In H. C. Foot, A. J. Chapman, & J. R. Smith (Eds.), *Friendship and social relations in children.* New York: Wiley.

Biller, H. B. (1969). Father-absence, maternal encouragement, and sex-role development in kindergarten-age boys. *Child Development, 40,* 539–546.

Biller, H. B. (1971). *Father, child, and sex-role.* Lexington, MA: Heath.

Biller, H. B. (1974). *Paternal deprivation.* Lexington, MA: Lexington Books.

Biller, H. B. (1981). Father absence, divorce, and personality development. In M. Lamb (Ed.), *The role of the father in child development* (2nd ed.). New York: Wiley.

Biller, H. B., & Bahm, R. M. (1971). Father-absence, perceived maternal behavior, and masculinity of self-concept among junior high school boys. *Developmental Psychology, 4,* 178–181.

Biller, H. B., & Davids, A. (1973). Parent-child rela-

tions, personality development, and psychopathology. In A. Davids (Ed.), *Issues in abnormal and child psychology* (pp. 48–76). Monterey, CA: Brooks/Cole.

Binder, A. (1988). Juvenile delinquency. *Annual Review of Psychology, 39,* 253–282.

Bixenstine, V. E., DeCorte, M. S., & Bixenstine, B. A. (1976). Conformity to peer-sponsored misconduct at four grade levels. *Developmental Psychology, 12,* 226–236.

Blasi, A. (1980). Bridging moral cognition and moral action: A critical review of the literature. *Psychological Bulletin, 88,* 1–45.

Blasi, A. (1984). Moral identity: Its role in moral functioning. In W. M. Kurtines & J. L. Gewirtz (Eds.), *Morality, moral behavior, and moral development* (pp. 128–139). New York: Academic Press.

Block, J. (1971). *Lives through time.* Berkeley, CA: Bancroft Books.

Block, J. (1987). *Longitudinal antecedents of ego-control and ego-resiliency in late adolescence.* Paper presented at the biannual meeting of the Society for Research in Child Development, Baltimore, April 1987.

Block, J., & Turula, E. (1963). Identification, ego control, and adjustment. *Child Development, 34,* 945–953.

Block, J. H. (1973). Conceptions of sex role: Some cross-cultural and longitudinal perspectives. *American Psychologist, 28,* 512–526.

Block, J. H. (1984). *Sex role identity and ego development.* San Francisco: Jossey-Bass.

Block, J. H., Haan, N., & Smith, M. B. (1969). Socialization correlates of student activism. *Journal of Social Issues, 25,* 143–177.

Bloom, B. (1985). *Developing talent in young people.* New York: Ballantine.

Blos, P. (1971, Fall). The child analyst looks at the young adolescent. *Daedalus, 100,* 961–978.

Blos, P. (1979). *The adolescent passage: Developmental issues.* New York: International Universities Press.

Blum, K., Noble, E. P., Sheridan, P. J. et al. (1990). Allelic association of human dopamine D_2 receptor gene in alcoholism. *Journal of the American Medical Association, 263,* 2055–2060.

Blum, R. H. (1979). Youthful drug use. In R. I. Dupont, A. Goldstein, & J. O'Donnell (Eds.), *Handbook on drug abuse* (pp. 257–269). Washington, DC: U.S. Government Printing Office.

Blum, R. H., *et al.* (1972). *Horatio Alger's children.* San Francisco: Jossey-Bass.

Blyth, D. A., Hill, J. P., & Smyth, C. K. (1981). The influence of older adolescents on younger adolescents: Do grade-level arrangements make a difference in behaviors, attitudes, and experiences? *Journal of Early Adolescence, 1,* 85–110.

Blyth, D. A., Hill, J. P., & Thiel, K. (1982). Early adolescents' significant others: Grade and gender differences in perceived relationship with familial and non-familial adults and young people. *Journal of Youth and Adolescence,* **11,** 425–440.

Blyth, D. A., Simmons, R. G., Bulcroft, R., Felt, D., VanCleave, E. F., & Bush, D. M. (1981). The effects of physical development on self-image and satisfaction with body-image for early adolescent males. In R. G. Simmons (Ed.), *Research in Community and Mental Health,* **2,** 43–73. Greenwich, CT: JAI Press.

Blyth, D. A., Simmons, R. G., & Carlton-Ford, S. (1983). The adjustment of early adolescents to school transitions. *Journal of Early Adolescence,* **3,** 105–120.

Blyth, D. A., Simmons, R. G., & Zakin, D. F. (1985). Satisfaction with body image of early adolescent females: The impact of pubertal timing within different school environments. *Journal of Youth and Adolescence,* **14,** 207–225.

Board on Mathematical Sciences/Mathematical Sciences Education Board (1989). *Everybody counts: A report to the nation on the future of mathematics education.* Washington, DC: National Academy Press.

Boccia, M. L., Reite, M., Kaeming, K., Held, P., & Laudenslager, M. (1989). Behavioral and autonomic responses to peer separation in pigtail macaque monkey infants. *Developmental Psychobiology,* **22,** 447–461.

Bodmer, W. F., & Cavalli-Sforza, L. L. (1970). Intelligence and race. *Scientific American,* **4,** 19–29.

Boehnke, K., Silbereisen, R. K., Eisenberg, N., Reykowski, J., & Palmonari, A. (1989). Developmental pattern of prosocial motivation: A cross-national study. *Journal of Cross-Cultural Psychology,* **20,** 219–243.

Bohman, M., Sigvardsson, S., & Cloninger, R. (1981). Maternal inheritance of alcohol abuse. *Archives of General Psychiatry,* **38,** 965–969.

Bolger, N., Downey G., Walker, E., & Steininger, P. (1989). The onset of suicidal ideation in childhood and adolescence. *Journal of Youth and Adolescence,* **18,** 175–190.

Borow, H. (1966). Development of occupational motives and roles. *Review of Child Development Research, Vol. 2* (pp. 373–422). Chicago: University of Chicago Press.

Borow, H. (1976). Career development. In J. F. Adams (Ed.), *Understanding adolescence* (pp. 489–523). Boston: Allyn & Bacon.

Boskia-White, M., & White, W. C. (1983). *Bulimarexia: The binge/purge cycle.* New York: Norton.

Botwinick, J. (1977). Intellectual abilities. In J. E. Birren, & K. W. Schaie (Eds.), *Handbook of the psychology of aging* (pp. 580–605). New York: Van Nostrand Reinhold.

Bouchard, C. et al. (1990). The response to long-term overfeeding in identical twins. *New England Journal of Medicine,* **322,** 1477–1482.

Bouchard, T. J., Jr., & McGee, M. G. (1977). Sex differences in human spatial ability: Not an X-linked recessive gene effect. *Social Biology,* **24,** 332–335.

Bourne, E. (1978a). The state of research on ego identity: A review and appraisal, Part I. *Journal of Youth and Adolescence,* **7,** 223–251.

Bourne, E. (1978b). The state of research on ego identity: A review and appraisal, Part II. *Journal of Youth and Adolescence,* **7,** 371–392.

Bower, G. H., & Hilgard, E. R. (1981). *Theories of learning* (5th ed.). Englewood Cliffs, NJ: Prentice-Hall.

Bowlby, J. (1969). *Attachment, Vol. 1: Attachment and loss.* New York: Basic Books.

Bowlby, J. (1973). *Attachment and loss, Vol. 2: Separation, anxiety and anger.* London: Hogarth Press.

Boyd, J. H., & Weissman, M. M. (1981). Epidemiology of affective disorders: A reexamination and future directions. *Archives of General Psychiatry,* **38,** 1039.

Boyer, E. L. (1983). *High school: A report on secondary education in America.* New York: Harper & Row.

Brabeck, M. (1983). Moral judgment: Theory and research on differences between males and females. *Developmental Review,* **3,** 274–291.

Bradley, R. H., Caldwell, B. M., & Elardo, R. (1977). Home environment, social status, and mental test performance. *Journal of Educational Psychology,* **69,** 697–701.

Braithwaite, J. (1981). The myth of social class and criminality reconsidered. *American Sociological Review,* **46,** 36–57.

Brand, D. (1987, August 31). The new whiz kids. *Time,* pp. 42–51.

Brannigan, M. A. (1986, September 2). Shortage of youths brings wide changes to the labor market. *The Wall Street Journal,* pp. 1, 22.

Braucht, G. N. (1980). Psychosocial research on teenage drinking: Past and future. In F. R. Scarapeteti & S. K. Datesman (Eds.), *Sage Annual Review of Drug and Alcohol Abuse,* **4,** 109–143.

Braucht, G. N. (1984). Problem drinking among adolescents: A review and analysis of psychosocial research. In National Institute on Alcohol Abuse and Alcoholism, *Special Population Issues.* Alcohol and Health Monograph No. 4. Rockville, MD: The Institute.

Braude, M. C., & Ludford, J. P. (1984). *Marihuana effects on the endocrine and reproductive systems.* (NIDA Research Monograph 44) DHHS Publication No. ADM 84–1278. Washington, DC: U.S. Government Printing Office.

Braukmann, C. J., Kirigin, K. A., & Wolf, M. W. (1976). *Achievement Place: The researcher's perspective.* Paper presented at the meeting of the American Psychological Association, Washington, DC.

Braungart, R. G. (1980). Youth movements. In J. Adelson (Ed.), *Handbook of adolescent psychology* (pp. 560–597). New York: Wiley.

Brecher, F. M. (1971). *The sex researchers*. New York: New American Library.

Brennan, T. (1980). Mapping the diversity of runaways: A descriptive multivariate analysis of selected social psychological background conditions. *Journal of Family Issues, 1,* 189–209.

Brennan, T. (1982). Loneliness and adolescence. In L. A. Peplan & D. Perlman (Eds.), *Loneliness: A source book of current research, theory, and practice*. New York: Wiley.

Brill, N., Crumpton, E., & Grayson, H. (1971). Personality factors in marijuana use. *Archives of General Psychiatry, 24,* 163–165.

Brim, O. G., & Kagan, J. (1980). *Constancy and change in human development*. Cambridge, MA: Harvard University Press.

Brittain, C. V. (1966). Age and sex of siblings and conformity toward parents versus peers in adolescence. *Child Development, 37,* 709–714.

Brittain, C. V. (1969). A comparison of rural and urban adolescents with respect to parent vs. peer compliance. *Adolescence, 13,* 59–68.

Brody, E. B. (1968). *Minority group adolescents in the United States*. Baltimore: Williams & Wilkins.

Brody, J. E. (1988, August 30). Widespread abuse of drugs by pregnant women is found. *The New York Times*, pp. 1, 19.

Bronfenbrenner, U. (1960). Freudian theories of identification and their derivatives. *Child Development, 31,* 15–40.

Bronfenbrenner, U. (1970). *Two worlds of childhood: U.S. and U.S.S.R.* New York: Russell Sage Foundation.

Bronfenbrenner, U. (1974). The origins of alienation. *Scientific American, 231,* 53–61.

Bronfenbrenner, U. (1977). Toward an experimental ecology of human development. *American Psychologist, 32,* 513–531.

Bronfenbrenner, U. (1985). Freedom and discipline across the decades. In G. Becker, H. Becker, & L. Huber (Eds.), *Ordnung und Unordnung [Order and Disorder]* (pp. 326–339). Weinheim, West Germany: Beltz Berlag.

Bronfenbrenner, U., Alvarez, W. F., & Henderson, C. R., Jr. (1984). Working and watching: Maternal employment status and parents' perceptions of their three-year-old children. *Child Development, 55,* 1362–1378.

Brofenbrenner, U., & Crouter, A. (1982). Work and family through time and space. In S. B. Kamerman & C. D. Hayes (Eds.), *Families that work: Children in a changing world* (pp. 39–83). Washington, DC: National Academy Press.

Bronfenbrenner, U., Moen, P., & Garbarino, J. (1984). Child, family, and community. In R. D. Parke (Ed.), *Review of child development research, Vol. 7: The family* (pp. 283–328). Chicago: University of Chicago Press.

Brofenbrenner, U., & Weiss, H. B. (1983). Beyond policies without people: An ecological perspective on child and family policy. In E. Zigler, S. L. Kagan, & E. Klugman (Eds.), *Social policy for children and their families: A primer*. Cambridge: Cambridge University Press.

Brook, J. S., Lukoff, J. F., & Whiteman, M. (1980). Initiation into adolescent marihuana use. *Journal of Genetic Psychology, 137,* 133–142.

Brookover, W., Beady, C., Flood, P., Schweitzer, J., & Wisenbaker, J. (1979). *School social systems and students: Schools can make a difference*. New York: Praeger.

Brooks-Gunn, J., & Warren, M. P. (1985). Effects of delayed menarche in different contexts: Dance and nondance students. *Journal of Youth and Adolescence, 14,* 285–300.

Brooks-Gunn, J. (1988). Psychological adaptation to the early adolescent transition: Biological and social contributions. Paper presented at the annual meeting of the American Psychological Association, New York.

Brooks-Gunn, J., & Furstenberg, F. F., Jr. (1989). Adolescent sexual behavior. *American Psychologist, 44,* 249–257.

Brooks-Gunn, J., & Furstenberg, F. F., Jr. (in press). Coming of age in the era of AIDS: Sexual and contraceptive decisions. *Milbank Quarterly*.

Brooks-Gunn, J., & Ruble, D. N. (1978, May). Menstrual related symptomatology in adolescents: The effects of attitudes, first menstrual experience, and parental factors. Paper presented at the second annual Conference on Interdisciplinary Research on the Menstrual Cycle, St. Louis.

Brooks-Gunn, J., & Ruble, D. N. (1983). The experience of menarche from a developmental perspective. In J. Brooks-Gunn & A. C. Petersen (Eds.), *Girls at puberty: Biological, psychological, and social perspectives* (pp. 155–178). New York: Plenum.

Brooks-Gunn, J., & Warren, M. P. (1989). Biological contributions to affective expression in young adolescent girls. *Child Development, 60,* 372–385.

Brophy, J. (1986). Teacher influences on student achievement. *American Psychologist, 41,* 1069–1077.

Brown, A. L. (1975). The development of memory: Knowing, knowing about knowing, and knowing how to know. In H. W. Reese (Ed.), *Advances in child development and behavior, Vol. 10*. New York: Academic Press.

Brown, A. L., Bransford, J. D., Ferrara, R. A., & Campione, J. C. (1983). Learning, remembering, and understanding. In P. H. Mussen (Series Ed.), J. H. Flavell & E. M. Markman (Eds.), *Handbook of child psychology: Cognitive development, Vol. 3.* (pp. 77–166) New York: Wiley (P. H. Mussen, General Editor.

Brown, B. B. (1989). The role of peer groups in adolescents' adjustment to secondary school. In T. J. Berndt & G. W. Ladd (Eds.), *Peer relationships in child development* (pp. 188–216). New York: Wiley.

Brown, B. B., Clasen, D. R., & Eicher, S. A. (1986).

Perceptions of peer pressure, peer conformity, dispositions, and self-reported behavior among adolescents. *Developmental Psychology, 22,* 521–530.

Brown, J. D. (Ed.) (1967). *The hippies.* New York: Time-Life Books.

Brownstone, J. E., & Willis, R. H. (1971). Conformity in early and late adolescence. *Developmental Psychology, 4,* 334–337.

Bruch, H. (1973). *Eating disorders.* New York: Basic Books.

Bruch, H. (1974). Eating disturbances in adolescence. In G. Caplan (Ed.), *American handbook of psychiatry, Vol. II: Child and adolescent psychiatry, sociocultural and community psychiatry* (pp. 275–286). New York: Basic Books.

Brunswick, A. F., & Boyle, J. M. (1979). Patterns of drug involvement: Developmental and secular influences on age of initiation. *Youth and Society, 11,* 139–162.

Brunswick, A. F., & Meseri, P. A. (1984). Origins of cigarette smoking in academic achievement, stress, and social expectations: Does gender make a difference? *Journal of Early Adolescence, 4,* 353–370.

Bryant, T. E. *et. al.* (1978). *Report to the President from the President's Commission on Mental Health, Vol. I.* Washington, DC: U.S. Government Printing Office.

Budzynski, T. H., Stoyva, J. M., & Peffer, K. E. (1980). Biofeedback techniques in psychosomatic disorders. In A. Goldstein & E. B. Foa (Eds.), *Handbook of behavioral interventions: A clinical guide* (pp. 186–205). New York: Wiley.

Bullough, V. L. (1981). Age at menarche: A misunderstanding. *Science, 213,* 365–366.

Burchinal, L. G. (1965). Trends and prospects for young marriages in the U.S. *Journal of Marriage and the Family, 27,* 243–254.

Burgdorff, K. (1980). *Recognition and reporting of child maltreatment: Findings from the National Incidence Study.* Washington, DC: National Center on Child Abuse and Neglect.

Buri, J. R., Louiselle, P. A., Misukanis, T. M., & Mueller, R. A. (1988). Effects of authoritarianism and authoritativeness on self-esteem. *Personality and Social Psychology Bulletin, 14,* 271–282.

Burns, D., & Brady, J. P. (1980). The treatment of stuttering. In A. Goldstein & E. B. Foa (Eds.), *Handbook of behavioral interventions: A clinical guide* (pp. 673–722). New York: Wiley.

Burnstein, E. (1963). Fear of failure, achievement motivation, and aspiring to prestigeful occupations. *Journal of Abnormal and Social Psychology, 67,* 189–193.

Burton, N. W., & Jones, L. V. (1982). Recent trends in achievement levels of black and white youth. *Educational Researcher, 11,* 10–17.

Buss, A. H., & Plomin, R. (1984). *Temperament: Early developing personality traits.* Hillsdale, NJ: Erlbaum.

Calabrese, R. L. (1987). Adolescence: A growth period conducive to alienation. *Adolescence, 22,* 929–958.

Calhoun, J. A., Grotberg, E. H., & Rackey, W. F. (1980). *The status of children, youth, and families 1979.* DHHS Publication No. (OHDS) 80-30274. Washington, DC: U.S. Government Printing Office.

Campbell, A. (1984). *The girls in the gang.* Oxford: Basil Blackwell.

Campbell, A., Converse, P., & Rodgers, W. (1976). *The quality of American life: Perceptions, evaluations, and satisfactions.* New York: Russell Sage Foundation.

Campione, J. C., Brown, A. L., & Ferrara, R. A. (1982). Mental retardation and intelligence. In R. J. Sternberg (Ed.), *Handbook of human intelligence.* New York: Cambridge University Press.

Cancro, R. (1983). History and overview of schizophrenia. In H. I. Kaplan & B. J. Sadock, *Comprehensive textbook of psychiatry Vol. 1* (pp. 631–642). Baltimore: Williams and Wilkins.

Canter, R. J. (1982). Family correlates of male and female delinquency. *Criminology, 20,* 149–160.

Cantrell, V. L., & Prinz, R. J. (1985). Multiple perspectives of rejected, neglected, and accepted children: Relation between sociometric status and behavioral characteristics. *Journal of Consulting and Clinical Psychology, 53,* 884–889.

Caplow, T., & Bahr, H. M. (1979). Half a century of change in adolescent attitudes: Replication of a Middletown survey by the Lynds. *Public Opinion Quarterly,* 1–17.

Carlsmith, J. M., Dornbusch, S. M., & Gross, R. T. (1983). Unpublished study cited in Atkinson *et al.,* 1987.

Carlson, G. A., & Cantwell, D. P. (1980). A survey of depressive symptoms, syndrome and disorder in a child psychiatric population. *Journal of Child Psychology and Psychiatry, 21,* 19–25.

Carmody, D. (1989, September 12). Minority students gain on college entrance tests. *The New York Times,* p. A10.

Carnegie Council on Adolescent Development, Task Force on Education of Young Adolescents (1989). *Turning points: Preparing American youth for the 21st century.* New York: Carnegie Corporation of New York.

Caro, F. G. (1966). Social class and attitudes of youth relevant for the realization of adult goals. *Social Forces, 44,* 492–498.

Carroll, C. R. (1985). *Drugs in modern society.* Dubuque, IA: Wm. C. Brown.

Carroll, J. B. (1982). The measurement of intelligence. In R. J. Sternberg (Ed.), *Handbook of human intelligence* (pp. 29–122). New York: Cambridge University Press.

Carroll, J. B., & Maxwell, S. E. (1979). Individual differences in cognitive abilities. *Annual Review of Psychology, 30,* 603–640.

Carroll, J. L., & Rest, J. R. (1982). Moral development. In B. B. Wolman (Ed.), *Handbook of developmental psychology.* Englewood Cliffs, NJ: Prentice-Hall.

Carron, A. V., & Bailey, D. A. (1974). Strength development in boys from 10 through 16 years. *Monographs of the Society for Research in Child Development,* **39,** No. 4, 1–36.

Carter, L. F. (1984). The sustaining effects study of compensatory and elementary education. *Educational Researcher,* **13,** 4–13.

Casper, R. C., Eckert, E. D., Halmi, K. A., Goldberg, S. C., & Davis, J. M. (1980). Bulimia: Its incidence and clinical significance in patients with anorexia nervosa. *Archives of General Psychiatry,* **37,** 1030–1035.

Cattell, R. B. (1963). Theory of fluid and crystallized intelligence: An initial experiment. *Journal of Educational Psychology,* **105,** 105–111.

Cavaiola, A. A., & Schiff, M. (1988). Behavioral sequelae of physical and/or sexual abuse in adolescents. *Child Abuse and Neglect,* **12,** 181–188.

Cavior, N., & Dokecki, P. R. (1973). Physical attractiveness, perceived attitude similarity, and academic achievement as contributors to interpersonal attraction among adolescents. *Developmental Psychology,* **9,** 44–54.

Cerra, F. (1980, May 11). Study finds college women still aim for traditional jobs. *The New York Times.*

Cervantes, L. F. (1965). *The dropout: Causes and cures.* Ann Arbor: University of Michigan Press.

Chapman, A. H. 91974). *Management of emotional problems of children and adolescents.* Philadelphia: Lippincott.

Chapman, M. (1977). Father absence, stepfathers, and the cognitive performance of college students. *Child Development,* **48,** No. 3, 1155–1158.

Chemers, M. M. (1970). The relationship between birth order and leader style. *Journal of Social Psychology,* **80,** 243–244.

Cherlin, A. (1980). Postponing marriage: The influence of young women's work expectations. *Journal of Marriage and the Family,* **42,** 355–365.

Cherlin, A. (1981). *Marriage, divorce, remarriage.* Cambridge, MA: Harvard University Press.

Chesney, M. A. (1984). Behavior modification and health enhancement. In J. Matarazzo, S. W. Weiss, J. A. Herd, N. Miller, & S. M. Weiss (Eds.), *Behavioral health: A handbook of health enhancement and disease prevention* (pp. 338–350). New York: Wiley.

Child Study Association of America (1971). *You, your child, and drugs.* New York: Child Study Press.

Children and parents: Together in the world (1971). Report of Forum 15, 1970 White House Conference on Children. Washington, DC: Superintendent of Documents.

Chilman, C. S. (1968). Families in development at mid-stage of the family life cycle. *Family Coordinator,* **17,** 297–331.

Chilman, C. S. (1983). *Adolescent sexuality in a changing American society: Social and psychological perspectives* (2nd ed.). Washington, DC: U.S. Government Printing Office.

Chilman, C. S. (1986). Some psychosocial aspects of adolescent sexual and contraceptive behaviors in a changing American society. In J. B. Lancaster & B. A. Hamburg (Eds.), *School-age pregnancy and parenthood: Biosocial dimensions* (pp. 191–217). New York: Aldine De Gruyter.

Christ, J. (1974). Outpatient treatment of adolescents and their families. In G. Caplan (Ed.), *American handbook of psychiatry, Vol. II: Child and adolescent psychiatry, sociocultural and community psychiatry* (pp. 339–352). New York: Basic Books.

Christensen, H., & Gregg, C. (1970). Changing sex norms in America and Scandinavia. *Journal of Marriage and the Family,* **32,** 616–627.

Cicchetti, D., & Carlson, V. (Eds.) (1989). *Child maltreatment: Theory and research on the causes and consequences of child abuse and neglect.* New York: Cambridge University Press.

Clark, B. (1974). Current educational institutions. In J. S. Coleman *et al.* (Eds.), *Youth: Transition to adulthood* (pp. 76–90). Report of the Panel on Youth of the President's Science Advisory Committee. Chicago: University of Chicago Press.

Clark, R. (1983), *Family life and school achievement: Why poor black children succeed or fail.* Chicago: University of Chicago Press.

Clark, W. B., & Midanik, L. (1989). Alcohol use and alcohol problems among U.S. adults. In National Institute on Alcohol Abuse and Alcoholism, *Alcohol consumption and related problems.* Alcohol and Health Mongraphs, No. 1. Rockville, MD: The Institute.

Clarke-Stewart, A., & Friedman, S. (1987). *Child development: Infancy through adolescence.* New York: Wiley.

Clary, E. G., & Miller, J. (1986). Socialization and situational influences on sustained altruism. *Child Development,* **57,** 1358–1369.

Clasen, D. R., & Brown, B. B. (1985). The multidimensionality of peer pressure in adolescence. *Journal of Youth and Adolescence,* **14,** 451–468.

Clausen, J. A. (1975). The social meaning of differential physical and sexual maturation. In S. E. Dragastin & G. H. Elder, Jr. (Eds.), *Adolescence in the life cycle: Psychological change and social context.* New York: Wiley.

Cloward, R. A., & Ohlin, L. E. (1960). *Delinquency and opportunity: A theory of delinquent gangs.* New York: Free Press.

Clymer, A. (1986, September 2). Public found ready to sacrifice in drug fight. *The New York Times,* pp. 1, 16.

Coates, T. J., Petersen, A. C., & Perry, C. (Eds.) (1982). *Promoting adolescent health: A dialog on research and practice.* New York: Academic Press.

Cobb, S., & Kasl, S. (1977). *Termination: The consequences of job loss.* U.S. Department of Health, Education, and Welfare. Washington, DC: U.S. Government Printing Office.

Cohen, D. J., Dibble, E., & Grawe, J. M. (1977). Fathers' and mothers' perceptions of children's personality. *Archives of General Psychiatry,* **34,** 261–282.

Cohen, F. (1984). Coping. In J. Matarazzo, S. W. Weiss, J. A. Herd, N. Miller, & S. M. Weiss (Eds.), *Behavioral health: A handbook of health enhancement and disease prevention* (pp. 261–274). New York: Wiley.

Cohen, J. M. (1972). *Sources of peer group homogeneity. Socioeconomic background and achievement.* New York: Seminar Press.

Cohen, S. (1979). Inhalants. In R. I. Dupont, A. Goldstein, & J. O'Donnell (Eds.), *Handbook on drug abuse* (pp. 213–220). Washington, DC: U.S. Government Printing Office.

Cohler, B. J., & Boxer, A. M. (1984). Settling into the world: Person, time and context in the middle-adult years. In D. Offer & M. Sabshin (Eds.), *Normality and the life cycle.* New York: Basic Books.

Coie, J. D., Dodge, K. A., & Coppotelli, H. (1982). Dimensions and types of social status: A cross-age perspective. *Developmental Psychology,* **18,** 557–570.

Colby, A., & Kohlberg, L. (1987). *The measurement of moral judgment, Vol. I: Theoretical foundations and research validation.* New York: Cambridge University Press.

Colby, A., Kohlberg, L., Gibbs, J., & Lieberman, M. (1980). *A longitudinal study of moral development.* Cambridge, MA: Center for Moral Education.

Coleman, J. C. (1974). *Relationships in adolescence.* Boston: Routledge & Kegan Paul.

Coleman, J. C. (1980). *The nature of adolescence.* London: Methuen.

Coleman, J. C. (Ed.) (1987). *Working with troubled adolescents: A handbook.* London: Academic Press.

Coleman, J. S. (1961). *The adolescent society.* New York: Free Press.

Coleman, J. S., Campbell, E. Q., Hobson, C. J., McPartland, J., Mead, A. M., Weinfeld, F. D., & York, R. L. (1966). *Equality of educational opportunity.* Washington, DC: U.S. Government Printing Office.

Coleman, J. S., *et al.* (1974). *Youth: Transition to adulthood.* Report of the Panel on Youth of the President's Science Advisory Committee. Chicago: University of Chicago Press.

College Entrance Examination Board (1982). *National college-bound seniors.* New York: The College Board.

College Entrance Examination Board (1988). *National college-bound seniors.* New York: The College Board.

Collins, W. A. (Ed.) (1980). *Minnesota symposia on child psychology, Vol. 13: Development of cognition, affect, and social relations.* Hillsdale, NJ: Erlbaum.

Comber, L. C., & Keeves, J. P. (1973). *Science educa-tion in nineteen countries. International studies in evaluation, Vol. 1.* Stockholm: Almquist & Wiksell.

Comer, J. P. (1980). *School power.* New York: Free Press.

Comer, J. P. (1984, May). Home-school relationships as they affect the academic success of children. *Education and Urban Society,* **16,** 323–337.

Comfort, A., & Comfort, J. (1979). *The facts of love: Living, loving, and growing up.* New York: Crown.

Committee for the Study of Research on Child and Adolescent Mental Disorders, Division of Mental Health and Behavioral Medicine, Institute of Medicine (1989). *Research on children and adolescents with mental, behavioral, and developmental disorders: Mobilizing a national initiative.* Washington, DC: National Academy Press.

Committee to study the health-related effects of cannabis and its derivatives. National Academy of Sciences, Institute of Medicine (1982). *Marijuana and health.* Washington, DC: National Academy Press.

Conant, J. B. (1959). *The American high school today.* New York: McGraw-Hill.

Condry, J., & Siman, M. L. (1974). Characteristics of peer- and adult-oriented children. *Journal of Marriage and the Family,* **36,** 543–554.

Conger, J. J. (1971, Fall). A world they never knew: The family and social change. *Daedalus,* **100,** 1105–1138.

Conger, J. J. (1973). *Adolescence and youth: Psychological development in a changing world.* (1st ed.). New York: Harper & Row.

Conger, J. J. (1975). Sexual attitudes and behavior of contemporary adolescents. In J. J. Conger (Ed.), *Contemporary issues in adolescent development* (pp. 221–230). New York: Harper & Row.

Conger, J. J. (1975, April 16). A world they never made: Parents and children in the 1970s. Invited address, American Academy of Pediatrics meeting, Denver.

Conger, J. J. (1976a). Current issues in adolescent development. Master lecture, American Psychological Association: *JSAS Catalog of Selected Documents in Psychology,* **6,** 96. (Ms. No. 1, 334.)

Conger, J. J. (1976b). Roots of alienation. In B. Wolman (Ed.), *International encyclopedia of neurology, psychiatry, psychoanalysis, and psychology.* New York: McGraw-Hill.

Conger, J. J. (1977). Parent-child relationships, social change and adolescent vulnerability. *Journal of Pediatric Psychology,* **2,** 93–97.

Conger, J. J. (1979). *Adolescence: Generation under pressure.* New York: Harper & Row.

Conger, J. J. (1980a). A new morality: Sexual attitudes and behavior of contemporary adolescents. In P. H. Mussen, J. J. Conger, & J. Kagan (Eds.), *Readings in child and adolescent psychology: Contemporary perspectives.* New York: Harper & Row.

Conger, J. J. (1980b). Hostages to fortune: Adolescents and social policy. In H. C. Wallach (Ed.), *Approaches to child and family policy* (pp. 75–100).

AAAS selected symposium 56. Boulder, CO: Westview Press.

Conger, J. J. (1981). Freedom and commitment: Families, youth, and social change. *American Psychologist*, **36**, 1475–1484.

Conger, J. J. (1984, August). Health psychology in a changing world. Invited address presented at the 92nd Annual Convention of the American Psychological Association, Toronto, Canada.

Conger, J. J. (1987). Behavioral medicine and health psychology in a changing world. *Child Abuse and Neglect*, **11**, 443–453.

Conger, J. J. (1988). Hostages to fortune: Youth, values, and the public interest. *American Psychologist*, **43**, 291–300.

Conger, J. J., & Miller W. C. (1966). *Personality, social class, and delinquency*. New York: Wiley.

Conger, J. J., & Petersen, A. C. (1984). *Adolescence and youth: Psychological development in a changing world* (3rd ed.). New York: Harper & Row.

Congressional Budget Office (1987). *Educational achievement: Explanations and implications of recent trends*. Washington, DC: Congressional Budget Office.

Conrad, J. (1968). *Youth: A narrative and two other stories*. Edinburgh and London: Blackwood, 1902. Cited in J. Bartlett, *Familiar quotations* (14th ed., p. 843). Boston: Little, Brown.

Coolidge, J. C. (1979). School phobia. In J. D. Noshpitz (Ed.), *Basic handbook of child psychiatry, Vol. II*. New York: Basic Books.

Cooper, C. R., & Ayers-Lopez, S. (1985). Family and peer systems in early adolescence: New models of the role of relationships in development. *Journal of Early Adolescence*, **5**, 9–21.

Cooper, C. R., & Grotevant, H. D. (1987). Gender issues in the interface of family experience and adolescents' friendship and dating identity. *Journal of Youth and Adolescence*, **16**, 247–264.

Cooper, C. R., Grotevant, H. D., & Condon, S. M. (1983). Individuality and connectedness in the family as a context for adolescent identity formation and role-taking skill. In H. D. Grotevant and C. R. Cooper (Eds.), *Adolescent development in the family* (pp. 43–60). San Francisco: Jossey-Bass.

Corter, C., Trehub, S., Boukydis, C., Ford, L., Celhoffer, L., & Minde, K. (1978). Nurses' judgments of the attractiveness of premature infants. *Infant Behavior and Development*, **1**, 373–380.

Costanzo, P. R. (1970). Conformity development as a function of self-blame. *Journal of Personality and Social Psychology*, **14**, 366–374.

Costanzo, P. R., & Shaw, M. E. (1966). Conformity as a function of age level. *Child Development*, **37**, 967–975.

Cowan, A. L. (1989, August 21). Poll finds women's gains have taken personal toll. *The New York Times*, pp. A1, A8.

Cowen, E. L., Pederson, A., Babijian, H., Izzo, L. D., & Trost, M. A. (1973). Long-term follow-up of early detected vulnerable children. *Journal of Consulting and Clinical Psychology*, **41**, 438–446.

Crago, M., Yates, A., Bentler, L. E., & Arizmendi, T. G. (1985). Height-weight ratios among female athletes: Are collegiate athletics the precursors to an anorexic syndrome? *International Journal of Eating Disorders*, **4**, 79–87.

Crisp, A. H. (1986, April). *Prevention of eating disorders*. Paper presented at the Second International Conference on Eating Disorders. New York, NY.

Crisp, A. H., & Kolucy, R. S. (1979). Aspects of the perceptual disorder in anorexic nervosa. *British Journal of Medical Psychology*, **74**, 349–361.

Crittenden, P. M., & Ainsworth, M. D. S. (1989). Child maltreatment and attachment theory. In D. Cicchetti &V. Carlson (Eds.), *Child maltreatment: Theory and research on the causes and consequences of child abuse and neglect* (pp. 432–463). New York: Cambridge University Press.

Crockett, L. J., & Petersen, A. C. (1987). Pubertal status and psychosocial development: Findings from the early adolescent study. In R. M. Lerner & T. T. Roch (Eds.), *Biological and psychosocial interactions in early adolescence: A life-span perspective* (pp. 173–188). Hillsdale, NJ: Erlbaum.

Cronbach, L. J. (1949). *Essentials of psychological testing*. New York: Harper & Row.

Cronbach, L. J. (1984). *Essentials of psychological testing* (4th ed.). New York: Harper & Row.

Crouter, A. C. (1984). Participative work as an influence of human development. *Journal of Applied Developmental Psychology*, **5**, 71–90.

Crowley, T. J. (1987). Clinical issues in cocaine abuse. In S. Fisher, A. Raskin, & E. H. Uhlenhuth (Eds.), *Cocaine: Clinical and behavioral aspects* (pp. 193–211). New York: Oxford University Press.

Crowley, T. J., & Rhine, M. (1985). The substance use disorders. In R. Simons & H. Pardes (Eds.), *Understanding human behavior in health and illness* (3rd ed., pp. 730–746). New York: Williams and Wilkins.

Csikszentmihalyi, M., & Larson, R. (1984). *Being adolescent: Conflict and growth in the teenage years*. New York: Basic Books.

Curran, D. K. (1987). *Adolescent suicidal behavior*. Washington, DC: Hemisphere Publishing Corporation.

Damon, W., & Hart, D. (1989). *Self-understanding in childhood and adolescence*. Cambridge: Cambridge University Press.

Dan, A. J. (1980). Free-associative versus self-report measures of emotional change over the menstrual cycle. In A. J. Dan, E. A. Graham, & C. P. Beecher (Eds.), *The menstrual cycle, Volume I: A synthesis of interdisciplinary research*. New York: Springer Publishing Co.

Daniels, D., Dunn, J., Furstenberg, F. F., & Plomin, R. (1985). Environmental differences within the family and adjustment differences within pairs of siblings. *Child Development*, **56**, 764–774.

Daniels, L. A. (1990, January 10). Tests show reading and writing lag continues. *The New York Times*, p. B7.

Dare, C. (1985). Family therapy. In M. Rutter & L. Hersov (Eds.), *Child and adolescent psychiatry: Modern approaches* (pp. 809–825). Oxford: Blackwell Scientific Publications.

Darling, C. A., Kallen, D. J., & VanDusen, J. E. (1984). Sex in transition, 1900–1984. *Journal of Youth and Adolescence*, **13**, 385–399.

Datan, N., Rodeheaver, D., & Hughes, F. (1987). Adult development and aging. *Annual Review of Psychology*, **38**, 153–180.

Davies, M., & Kandel, D. B. (1981). Parental and peer influences on adolescents' educational plans: Some further evidence. *American Journal of Sociology*, **87**, 363–387.

Dawson, D. A. (1986). The effects of sex education on adolescent behavior. *Family Planning Perspectives*, **18**, 162–170.

De Beauvoir, S. (1975). *All said and done*. New York: Warner.

Dean, R. A. (1982). Youth: Moonies' target population. *Adolescence*, **17**, 567–574.

Deaux, K. (1985). Sex and gender. *Annual Review of Psychology*, **36**, 49–81.

Deemer, D. (in press). *Life experiences and moral judgment development*. Doctoral dissertation. Minneapolis, MN: University of Minnesota.

Degler, C. (1980). *At odds: Women and the family in America from the Revolution to the present*. New York: Oxford University Press.

Dellas, M., & Gaier, E. L. (1970). Identification of creativity: The individual. *Psychological Bulletin*, **73**, 55–73.

DeLuca, J. R. (Ed.) (1981). Alcohol and health: Fourth special report to the U.S. Congress. Rockville, MD: National Institute on Alcohol and Alcohol Abuse.

Demos, J. (1970). *A little commonwealth: Family life in Plymouth Colony*. New York: Oxford University Press.

Dempsey, D. (1970, January 11). Bruno Bettelheim is Dr. No. *New York Times Magazine*, 22 ff.

Devereux, E. (1970). The role of peer group experience in moral development. In J. Hill (Ed.), *Minnesota Symposium on Child Psychology*, **4**, 94–140.

Dickinson, G. E. (1982). Changing religious behavior of adolescents 1964–1979 (1982). *Youth and Society*, **13**, 283–288.

Dionne, E. J. (1989, August 22). Struggle for work and family fueling women's movement. *The New York Times*, A1, A14.

Dixson, M. C., & Wright, W. E. (1975). *Juvenile delinquency prevention programs: An evaluation of policy-related research on the effectiveness of prevention programs*. Nashville, TN: Office of Education Services, Peabody College for Teachers.

Doane, J. A., West, K. L., Goldstein, M. J., Rodnick, E. H., & Jones, J. E. (1981). Parental communication deviance and affective style: Predictors of subsequent schizophrenic-spectrum disorders in vulnerable adolescents. *Archives of General Psychiatry*, **38**, 679–685.

Dodge, K. A. (1983). Behavioral antecedents of peer social status. *Child Development*, **54**, 1386–1399.

Dollard, J., & Miller, N. E. (1950). *Personality and psychotherapy: An analysis in terms of learning, thinking, and culture*. New York: McGraw-Hill.

Domino, G. (1968). Differential prediction of academic achievement in conforming to independent settings. *Journal of Educational Psychology*, **59**, 256–260.

Donovan, J. E., & Jessor, R. (1978). Adolescent problem drinking: Psychosocial correlates in a national study sample. *Quarterly Journal of Studies on Alcohol*, **39**, 1506–1524.

Donovan, J. E., & Jessor, R. (1983). Problem drinking and the dimension of involvement with drugs: A Guttman scalogram analysis of adolescent drug use. *American Journal of Public Health*, **73**, 543–552.

Donovan, J. M. (1975). Ego identity status and interpersonal style. *Journal of Youth and Adolescence*, **4**, 37–56.

Dornbusch, S. M. (1988, August). Family processes and school achievement. Paper presented at the annual meeting of the American Psychological Association, New York, NY.

Dornbusch, S. M., Carlsmith, J. M., Bushwall, S. J., Ritter, P. L., Leiderman, H., Hastorf, A. H., & Gross, R. T. (1985). Single parents, extended households, and the control of adolescents. *Child Development*, **56**, 326–341.

Dornbusch, S. M., Carlsmith, L., Gross, R. T., Martin, J. A., Jenning, D., Rosenberg, A., & Duke, D. (1981). Sexual development, age, and dating: A comparison of biological and social influence upon one set of behaviors. *Child Development*, **52**, 179–185.

Dornbusch, S. M., Ritter, D. L., Leiderman, P. H., Roberts, D. F., & Fraleigh, M. J. (1987). The relation of parenting style to adolescent school performance. *Child Development*, **58**, 1244–1257.

Dornbusch, S. M., Ritter, P. L., Mont-Reynard, R., & Chen, Z-Y (1990). Family decision making and academic performance in a diverse high school population. *Journal of Adolescent Research*, **5**, 143–160.

Dorner, G. (1976). *Hormone and brain differentiation*. New York: Elsevier.

Dorner, G., Rohde, W., Stahl, R., Krell, L., & Musius, W. (1975). Neuroendocrine predisposition to homosexuality in men. *Archives of Sexual Behavior*, **4**, 1–8.

Dorval, B., Brannan, J., Duckworth, M., & Smith, P. (1987, April). Developmental trends in conceptions of friendship in comparison to the quality of friends' talk and commentary on it. Paper presented at the biennial meeting of the Society for Research in Child Development, Baltimore, MD.

Dossey, J. A., Mullis, I. V. S., Lindquist, M. M., & Chambers, D. L. (1988). *The mathematics report card: Are we measuring up? Trends and achievement based on the 1986 National Assessment.* Princeton, NJ: Educational Testing Service.

Douvan, E. (1963). Employment and the adolescent. In F. I. Nye & L. W. Hoffman (Eds.), *The employed mother in America* (pp. 1421–1464). Chicago: Rand McNally.

Douvan, E. A., & Adelson, J. (1966). *The adolescent experience.* New York: Wiley.

Dowaliby, F. J., & Schumer, H. (1971). Teacher-centered versus student-centered mode of college classroom instruction as related to manifest anxiety. *Proceedings, 79th Annual Convention, American Psychological Association.*

Dreger, R. M., & Miller, K. S. (1960). Comparative psychological studies of Negroes and whites in the United States. *Psychological Bulletin,* **57,** 361–402.

Dreger, R. M., & Miller K. S. (1968). Comparative psychological studies of Negroes and whites in the United States: 1959–1965. *Psychological Bulletin Monograph Supplemental,* **70,** No. 3, Part 2.

Dreyer, P. H. (1982). Sexuality during adolescence. In B. B. Wolman (Ed.), *Handbook of developmental psychology* (pp. 559–601). Englewood Cliffs, NJ: Prentice-Hall.

Dryfoos, J. G. (1988). School-based health clinics: Three years of experience. *Family Planning Perspectives,* **20,** 193–200.

Dryfoos, J. G., & Klerman, L. V. (1988). School-based clinics: Their role in helping students meet the 1990 objectives. *Health Education Quarterly,* **15,** 71–80.

Duck, S. W. (1975). Personality similarity and friendship choices by adolescents. *European Journal of Social Psychology,* **5,** 351–365.

Duncan, P. (1971). Parental attitudes and interactions in delinquency. *Child Development,* **42,** 1751–1765.

Dunphy, D. C. (1963). The social structure of urban adolescent peer groups. *Sociometry,* **26,** 230–246.

Dunphy, D. C. (1972). Peer group socialisation. In F. J. Hunt (Ed.), *Socialisation in Australia* (pp. 200–217). Sydney: Angus & Robertson.

Dunphy, D. C. (1980). Peer group socialization. In R. Muus (Ed.), *Adolescent behavior and society* (3rd ed.). New York: Random House.

Durkheim, E. (1961) (originally published 1925). *Moral education.* New York: Free Press.

Dweck, C. S. (1986). Motivational processes affecting learning. *American Psychologist,* **41,** 1040–1048.

Dwyer, J. (1980). Diets for children and adolescents that meet the dietary goals. *American Journal of Diseases of Children,* **134,** 1077.

Dwyer, J., & Mayer, J. (1967a). Variations in physi-

cal appearance during adolescence. Part 1. Boys. *Postgraduate Medicine,* **41,** 99–107.

Dwyer, J., & Mayer, J. (1967b). Variations in physical appearance during adolescence. Part 2. Girls. *Postgraduate Medicine,* **42,** 91–97.

Earls, F., Robbins, L. N., Stifman, A. R., & Powell, J. (1989). Comprehensive health care for high risk adolescents: An evaluation today. *American Journal of Public Health,* **79,** 999–1010.

East, P. L., Hess, L. E., & Lerner, R. M. (1987). Peer social support and adjustment of early adolescent peer group. *Journal of Early Adolescence,* **7,** 153–163.

Ebata, A. T. (1987). *A longitudinal study of psychological distress during early adolescence.* Ph.D. dissertation. University Park, PA: Pennsylvania State University.

Ebata, A. T., Petersen, A. C., & Conger, J. J. (in press). The development of psychopathology in adolescence. In J. E. Rolf, A. Masten, D. Ciccheti, K. H. Neuchterlein, & S. Weintraub (Eds.), *Risk and protective factors in the development of psychopathology.* New York: Cambridge University Press.

Edelman, M. M. (1987). *Families in peril: An agenda for social change.* Cambridge, MA: Harvard University Press.

Edwards, C. P. (1980). The comparative study of the development of moral judgment and reasoning. In R. W. Monroe, R. Monroe, & B. B. Whiting (Eds.), *Handbook of cross-cultural human development.* New York: Garland.

Egeland, B., Sroufe, L. A., & Erickson, M. (1983). The developmental consequences of different patterns of maltreatment. *Child Abuse and Neglect,* **7,** 459–469.

Ehrhardt, A. A., & Baker, S. (1975). Hormonal aberrations and their implications for the understanding of normal sex differentiation. In P. H. Mussen, J. J. Conger, & J. Kagan (Eds.), *Basic and contemporary issues in developmental psychology* (pp. 113–121). New York: Harper & Row.

Ehrhardt, A. A., & Money, J. (1967). Progestin-induced hermaphroditism: IQ and psychosocial identity. *Journal of Sex Research,* **3,** 83–100.

Eichorn, D. H. (1970). Physiological development. In P. H. Mussen (Ed.), *Carmichael's manual of child psychology Vol. 2,* 3rd ed. New York: Wiley.

Eichorn, D. H. (1975). Asychronizations in adolescent development. In S. E. Dragastin & G. H. Elder, Jr. (Eds.), *Adolescence in the life cycle: Psychological change and social context* (pp. 81–96). New York: Wiley.

Eichorn, D. H. (1980). The school. In M. Johnson (Ed.), *Toward adolescence: The middle school years.* 79th Yearbook of the National Society for the Study of Education. Chicago: University of Chicago Press.

Eisenberg, L. (1958). School phobia: A study in communication of anxiety. *American Journal of Psychiatry,* **144,** 712–718.

Eisenberg, N., Lennon, R., & Roth, K. (1983). Prosocial development: A longitudinal study. *Developmental Psychology, 19,* 846–855.

Eisenberg-Berg, N., & Mussen, P. (1978). Empathy and moral development judgment. *Developmental Psychology, 15,* 128–137.

Eisenberg-Berg, N., & Mussen, P. H. (1989). *Roots of caring, sharing, and helping* (2nd ed.). Englewood Cliffs, NJ: Prentice-Hall.

Ekstrom, R. B., French, J. W., Harmon, H. H., & Derman, D. (1976). *Manual for kit of factor-referenced cognitive tests, 1976.* Princeton, NJ: Educational Testing Service.

Elder, G. H., Jr. (1962). Structural variations in the child-rearing relationship. *Sociometry, 25,* 241–262.

Elder, G. H., Jr. (1963). Parental power legitimation and its effect on the adolescent. *Sociometry, 26,* 50–65.

Elder, G. H., Jr. (1968). Occupational level, motivation, and mobility: A longitudinal analysis. *Journal of Counseling Psychology, 15,* 1–7.

Elder, G. H., Jr. (1974). *Children of the Great Depression.* Chicago: University of Chicago Press.

Elder, G. H., Jr. (1979). Historical change in life patterns and personality. In P. Baltes & O. G. Brim, Jr. (Eds.), *Life-span development and behavior, Vol. II.* New York: Academic Press.

Elder, G. H., Jr. (1980). *Family structure and socialization.* New York: Arno Press.

Elder, G. H., Jr. (1984). Families, kin, and the life course: A sociological perspective. In R. D. Parke (Ed.), *Review of child development research* (Vol. 7) (pp. 80–136). Chicago: University of Chicago Press.

Eleven million teenagers: What can be done about the epidemic of adolescent pregnancies in the United States (1976). New York: Planned Parenthood Federation of America.

Elkin, I. *et al.* (1989). National Institute of Mental Health treatment of depression collaborative research program: General effectiveness of treatments. *Archives of General Psychiatry, 46,* 971–981.

Elkind, D. (1966). Conceptual orientation shifts in children and adolescents. *Child Development, 37,* 493–498.

Elkind, D. (1967). Cognitive structure and adolescent experience. *Adolescence, 2,* 427–433.

Elkind, D. (1968). Cognitive development in adolescence. In J. F. Adams (Ed.), *Understanding adolescence* (pp. 128–158). Boston: Allyn & Bacon.

Elkind, D. (1970). *Children and adolescents: Interpretive essays on Jean Piaget.* New York: Oxford University Press.

Elkind, D. (1971a). *A sympathetic understanding of the child from six to sixteen.* Boston: Allyn & Bacon.

Elkind, D. (1971b). Measuring young minds. *Horizon, 13,* No. 1, 35.

Elkind, D. (1978). *The child's reality: Three developmental themes.* Hillsdale, NJ: Erlbaum.

Elkind, D. (1984). *All grown up and no place to go: Teenagers in crisis.* Reading, MA: Addison-Wesley.

Elkind D., & Weiner, I. B. (1978). *Development of the child.* New York: Wiley.

Elliott, D. S., & Ageton, S. S. (1980). Reconciling race and class differences in self-reported and official estimates of delinquency. *American Sociological Review, 45,* 95–110.

Elliott, D. S., Ageton, S. S., Huizinga, D., Knowles, B. A., & Canter, R. J. (1983). *The prevalence and incidence of delinquent behavior, 1976–1980.* Boulder, CO: Behavioral Research Institute.

Elliott, D. S., Hinzinga, D., & Ageton, S. S. (1985). *Explaining delinquency and drug use.* Beverly Hills, CA: Sage Publications.

Elliott, D. S., & Voss, H. (1974). *Delinquency and dropouts.* Lexington, MA: Heath.

Elliott, G. R., & Eisdorfer, C. (1982). *Stress and human health: Analysis and implications of research.* A study by the Institute of Medicine, National Academy of Sciences. New York: Springer.

Ellis, G. J., & Stone, L. H. (1979). Marijuana use in college: An evaluation of a modelling explanation. *Youth and Society, 10,* 323–334.

Emde, R., Harmon, R., & Good, W. (1986). Depressive feelings in children: A transactional model of research. In M. Rutter, C. E. Izard, & P. B. Read (Eds.), *Depression in young people: Developmental and clinical perspectives* (pp. 135–162). New York: Guilford Press.

Emmerich, J. J. (1978). The influence of parents and peers on choices made by adolescents. *Journal of Youth and Adolescence, 7,* 175–180.

Enright, R. D., Lapsley, D. K., & Shukla, D. G. (1979). Adolescent egocentrism in early and late adolescence. *Adolescence, 14,* 687–695.

Enright, R. D., Shukla, D. G., & Lapsley, D. K. (1980). Adolescent egocentrism-sociocentrism and self-consciousness. *Journal of Youth and Adolescence, 9,* 529–545.

Epstein, J. L. (1989). The selection of friends: Changes across grades and in different school environments. In T. J. Berndt & G. W. Ladd (Eds.), *Peer relationships in child development* (pp. 158–187). New York: Wiley.

Epstein, J., & McPartland, J. (1976). The concept and measurement of the quality of school life. *American Educational Research Journal, 50,* 13–30.

Erikson, E. H. (1950). *Childhood and society.* New York: Norton.

Erikson, E. H. (1956). The problem of ego identity. *Journal of the American Psychoanalytic Association, 4,* 56–121.

Erikson, E. H. (1968). *Identity: Youth and crisis.* New York: Norton.

Erikson, E. H. (1983). Obstacles and pathways in the journey from adolescence to parenthood. In M. Sugar (Ed.), *Adolescent psychiatry: Developmental and clinical studies, Vol. XI.* Chicago: University of Chicago Press.

Erlenmeyer-Kimling, L., & Cornblatt, B. (1987). The New York High Risk Project: A followup report. *Schizophrenia Bulletin,* **13,** 451–461.

Estes, W. K. (1980). Is human memory obsolete? *American Scientist,* **68,** 62–69.

Evangelauf, J. (1986, January 15). Half of all college students now hold jobs as costs rise and financial aid is squeezed. *The Chronicle of Higher Education,* pp. 29, 32.

Evangelauf, J. (1988, September 28). Minority groups continue gains on admissions tests. *The Chronicle of Higher Education,* pp. 1, 32.

Evans, R. B. (1971, April). Parental relationships and homosexuality. *Medical Aspects of Human Sexuality,* pp. 164–177.

Evans, R. I. (1984a). A social inoculation strategy to deter smoking in adolescents. In J. D. Matarazzo, S. M. Weiss, J. A. Herd, N. E. Miller, & S. M. Weiss, *Behavioral health: A handbook of health enhancement and disease prevention* (pp. 765–777). New York: Wiley.

Evans, R. I. (1984b). Smoking prevention: Overview. In J. Matarazzo, S. W. Weiss, J. A. Herd, N. Miller, & S. M. Weiss (Eds.), *Behavioral health: A handbook of health enhancement and disease prevention* (pp. 693–695). New York: Wiley.

Evans, R. I., Henderson, A., Hill, P., & Raines, B. (1979). Smoking in children and adolescents: Psychosocial determinants and prevention strategies. In *Smoking and health: A report of the Surgeon General.* (DHEW Publication No. (PHS) 79-50066, U.S. Department of Health, Education and Welfare) (Chapter 17, pp. 1–30). Washington, DC: U.S. Government Printing Office (No. 017-000-00218-0).

Evans, R. I., Rozelle, R. M., Mittlemark, M. B. *et al.* (1978). Deterring the onset of smoking in children: Knowledge of immediate physiological effects and coping with peer pressure, media pressure, and parent modeling. *Journal of Applied Social Psychology,* **8,** 126–135.

Evans, R. I., Smith, C. K., & Raines, B. E. (1985). Deterring cigarette smoking in adolescents: A psycho-social-behavioral analysis of an intervention strategy. In A. Baum, J. Singer, & S. Taylor (Eds.), *Social psychological aspects of health.* Hillsdale, NJ: Erlbaum.

Eveleth, P., & Tanner, J. (1976). *Worldwide variation in human growth.* Cambridge, MA: Cambridge University Press.

Evertson, C., Anderson, C., Anderson, L., & Brophy, J. (1980). Relationships between classroom behaviors and student outcomes in junior high mathematics and English classes. *American Educational Research Journal,* **17,** 43–60.

Eysenck, H. J. (with Kamin, L.) (1981). *The intelligence controversy.* New York: Wiley.

Fagan, J., & Pabon, E. (1990). Contributions of delinquency and substance abuse to school dropout among inner city youth. *Youth and Society,* **21,** 306–354.

Faiman, C., & Winter, J. S. (1974). Gonadotropins and sex hormone patterns in puberty: Clinical data. In M. M. Grumbach, G. D. Grave, & F. E. Mayer (Eds.), *Control of the onset of puberty.* New York: Wiley.

Farber, E. D., & Kinast, C. (1984). Violence in families of adolescent runaways. *Child Abuse and Neglect,* **8,** 295–299.

Farbero, N. L. (1989). Preparatory and prior suicidal behavior factors. In *Report of the Secretary's task force on youth suicide, Volume 2: Risk factors for youth suicide* (pp. 34–55). Washington, DC: U.S. Government Printing Office.

Farel, A. (1982). *Early adolescence and religion: A status study.* Carrboro, NC: Center for Early Adolescence.

Farley, J. (1979). Family separation-individuation tolerance: A developmental conceptualization of the nuclear family. *Journal of Marriage and Family Therapy,* **5,** 61–67.

Farley, J. (1990). Family developmental task assessment: A prerequisite to family treatment. *Clinical Social Work Journal,* **18,** 85–98.

Farmer, H. S. (1985). The role of typical female characteristics in career and achievement motivation. *Youth and Society,* **16,** 315–334.

Farrington, D. P. (1981). The prevalence of convictions. *British Journal of Criminology,* **21,** 123–135.

Farrington, D. P. (1983). Offending from 10 to 25 years of age. In K. T. Van Dusen & S. A. Mednick (Eds.), *Prospective studies of crime and delinquency* (pp. 17–37). Boston: Kluwer-Nijhoff.

Farrington, D. P. (1986). Age and crime. In M. Tonry & N. Morris (Eds.), *Crime and Justice, Vol. 7* (pp. 29–60). Chicago: University of Chicago Press.

Farrington, D. P. (1987). Epidemiology. In H. C. Quay (Ed.), *Handbook of juvenile delinquency* (pp. 33–61). New York: Wiley.

Faust, M. S. (1960). Developmental maturity as a determinant in prestige of adolescent girls. *Child Development,* **31,** 173–184.

Faust, M. S. (1977). Somatic development of adolescent girls. *Monographs of the Society for Research in Child Development,* **42,** No. 1, 1–90.

Faust, M. S. (1983). Alternative constructions of adolescent growth. In J. Brooks-Gunn & A. C. Petersen (Eds.), *Girls at puberty: Biological, psychological, and social perspectives* (pp. 105–126). New York: Plenum.

Fay, R. E., Turner, C. F., Klassen, A. P., & Gagnon, J. H. (1989). Prevalence and patterns of same-gender sexual contact among men. *Science,* **243,** 338–348.

Feeney, S. (1980). *Schools for young adolescents: Adopting the early childhood model.* Carrboro, NC: University of North Carolina.

Feinberg, J. (1987). Adolescence and mental illness. *Science,* **236,** 507–508.

Feinstein, S. C., & Ardon, M. S. (1973). Trends in dating patterns and adolescent development. *Journal of Youth and Adolescence,* **2,** 157–166.

Feinstein, S. C., & Miller, D. (1979). Psychoses of adolescence. In J. D. Noshpitz (Ed.), *Basic handbook of child psychiatry, Vol. II: Disturbances in development* (pp. 708–722). New York: Basic Books.

Feldman, N. S., Klosson, E. C., Parsons, J. E., Rholes, W. S., & Ruble, D. N. (1976). Order of information presentation on children's moral judgments. *Child Development, 47,* 556–559.

Fennema, E. (1980). Sex-related differences in mathematics achievement: Where and why. In L. H. Fox, L. Brody, & D. Tobin (Eds.), *Women and the mathematical mystique* (pp. 76–93). Baltimore: The Johns Hopkins University Press.

Ferris, B. G., Whittenberger, J. L., & Gallagher, J. R. (1952). Maximum breathing capacity and vital capacity of male children and adolescents. *Pediatrics, 9,* 659–670.

Feshbach, N. D. (1989). The construct of empathy and the phenomenon of physical maltreatment of children. In D. Cicchetti & V. Carlson (Eds.), *Child maltreatment: Theory and research on the causes and consequences of child abuse and neglect* (pp. 349–373). New York: Cambridge University Press.

Fiegelson, N. (1970). *The underground revolution.* New York: Funk & Wagnal.

Fine, J. T. (1981). Sex similarities in behavior in a seventh grade classroom. *Journal of Early Adolescence, 1,* 233–243.

Fine, M. (1988). Sexuality, schooling, and adolescent females: The missing discourse of desire. *Harvard Educational Review, 58,* 29–55.

Fischer, C. S. (1977). *Networks and places: Social relations in the urban setting.* New York: Free Press.

Fischer, J. (1981). Transitions in relationship style from adolescence to young adulthood. *Journal of Youth and Adolescence, 10,* 11–23.

Fischer, J. L. (1980). Reciprocity, agreement, and family style in family systems with a disturbed and nondisturbed adolescent. *Journal of Youth and Adolescence, 9,* 391–406.

Fischer, K. W., & Silvern, L. (1985). Stages and individual differences in cognitive development. *Annual Review of Psychology, 36,* 613–618.

Fischer, S. F., (1973). *The female orgasm: Psychology, physiology, fantasy.* New York: Basic Books.

Fiske, E. B. (1987a, January 4). Searching for the key to science literacy. *The New York Times,* pp. 20–23.

Fiske, E. B. (1987b, August 24). Report warns school reforms may fall short. *The New York Times,* pp. 1, 10.

Fitzgerald, L. F., & Crites, J. O. (1980). Toward a career psychology of women: What do we know? What do we need to know? *Journal of Counseling Psychology, 27,* 44–62.

Fixsen, D. L., Phillips, E. L., & Wolf, M. M. (1973). Achievement place: Experiments in self government with predelinquents. *Journal of Applied Behavioral Analysis, 6,* 31–49.

Flavell, J. H. (1963). *The developmental psychology of Jean Piaget.* New York: Van Nostrand.

Flavell, J. H. (1985). *Cognitive development* (2nd ed.). Englewood Cliffs, NJ: Prentice-Hall.

Flavell, J. H., & Ross, L. (Eds.) (1981). *Social cognitive development.* New York: Cambridge University Press.

Flay, B. R. What do we know about the social influences approach to smoking prevention? Review and recommendations. In C. Bell & R. Battjes (Eds.), *Prevention Research: Deterring drug abuse among children and adolescents,* NIDA Research Monograph. Rockville, MD: U.S. Government Printing Office.

Floderus-Myrhed, B., Pedersen, N., & Rasmuson, I. (1980). Assessment of heritability for personality based on a short form of the Eysenck Personality Inventory: A study of 12,898 twin pairs. *Behavior Genetics, 10,* 153–162.

Fodor, I. G. (1984). Toward an understanding of male/female differences in phobic anxiety disorders. In I. Al-Issan (Ed.), *Gender and psychopathology.* New York: Academic Press.

Ford, C. S. (1961). Culture and sex. In A. Ellis & A. Abarband (Eds.), *The encyclopedia of sexual behavior, Vol. I* (pp. 306–312). New York: Hawthorn Books.

Ford, C. S. & Beach, F. A. (1951). *Patterns of sexual behavior.* New York: Harper & Row.

Ford, M. E. (1982). Social cognition and social competence in adolescence. *Developmental Psychology, 18,* 323–340.

Fort, J. (1969). *The pleasure seekers: The drug crisis, youth and society.* New York: Grove Press.

Fowler, J. W. (1981). *Stages of faith: The psychology of human development and the quest for meaning.* San Francisco: Harper & Row.

Francke, L. B. (1980, February 11). Children of divorce. *Newsweek,* 58–66.

Franken, M. W. (1985). Sex role expectations in children's vocational aspirations and perceptions of occupations. *Psychology of Women Quarterly, 8,* 59–68.

Frazer, F. C., & Nora, J. J. (1986). *Genetics of man.* Philadelphia: Lea & Febiger.

Freedman, J., & Humphrey, R. (1985). Antecedents of college drinking. *Journal of Youth and Adolescence, 14,* 11–22.

Freedman, M. (1971). *Homosexuality and psychological functioning.* Monterey, CA: Brooks/Cole.

Freeman, R. N. (1986, July 20). Cutting black youth unemployment. *The New York Times.*

Freud, A. (1946). *The ego and the mechanisms of defense.* New York: International Universities Press.

Freud, A. (1958). Adolescence. *Psychoanalytic Study of the Child, 13,* 255–278.

Freud, A. (1966). *The ego and the mechanisms of defense* (revised ed.). New York: International Universities Press.

Freud, A. (1968). Adolescence. In A. E. Winder & D.

Angus (Eds.), *Adolescence: Contemporary studies* (pp. 13–24). New York: American Book.

Freud, A. (1969). Adolescence as a developmental disturbance. In G. Caplan & S. Lebovici (Eds.), *Adolescence: Psychosocial perspectives* (pp. 5–10). New York: Basic Books.

Freud, S. (1953). *A general introduction to psychoanalysis* (Joan Riviere, trans.). New York: Permabooks.

Freud, S. (1964). *An outline of psychoanalysis*. Standard edition of the works of Sigmund Freud. London: Hogarth Press.

Friedman, W. J., Robinson, A. B., & Friedman, B. L. (1987). Sex differences in moral judgments: A test of Gilligan's theory. *Psychology of Women Quarterly*, **11,** 37–46.

Frisch, R. E. (1983). Fatness, puberty, and fertility. In J. Brooks-Gunn & A. C. Petersen (Eds.), *Girls at puberty: Biological, psychological, and social perspectives* (pp. 29–50). New York: Plenum.

Frisch, R. E., Gotz-Welbergen, A. V., McArthur, J. W., Albright, T., Witschi, J., Bullen, B., Birnhelz, J., Reed, R. B., & Hermann, H. (1981). Delayed menarche and amenorrhea of college athletes in relation to age of onset and training. *Journal of the American Medical Association*, **246,** 1559–1590.

Frisch, R. E., Wyshak, G., & Vincent, L. (1980). Delayed menarche and amenorrhea in ballet dancers. *New England Journal of Medicine*, **303,** 17–18.

Fromm, E. (1941). *Escape from freedom*. New York: Holt, Rinehart & Winston.

Fromm, E. (1955). *The sane society*. New York: Holt, Rinehart & Winston.

Fry, P. S., & Scher, A. (1984). The effect of father absence on children's achievement motivation, ego-strength, and locus of control orientation: A five-year longitudinal assessment. *British Journal of Developmental Psychology*, **2,** 167–178.

Fuller, F. (1962). Words to give to the young man knowledge and discretion (London, 1685). Cited in P. Aries, *Centuries of childhood: A social history of family life* (p. 498). New York: Random House (Vintage Books).

Fullerton, H. N. (1986). The 1995 labor force: BLS' latest projections. In *Employment projections for 1995: Data and methods* (pp. 16–24). Washington, DC: U.S. Government Printing Office.

Furstenberg, F. F. (1976). *Unplanned parenthood: The social consequences of teenage childbearing*. New York: Free Press.

Furstenberg, F. F., Jr., Brooks-Gunn, J., & Chase-Lansdale, L. (1989). Teenage pregnancy and childbearing. *American Psychologist*, **44,** 313–320.

Furstenberg, F. F., Jr., Brooks-Gunn, J., & Morgan, S. P. (1987). Adolescent mothers in later life. New York: Cambridge University Press.

Gaddis, A., & Brooks-Gunn, J. (1985). The male experience of pubertal change. *Journal of Youth and Adolescence*, **14,** 61–69.

Galambos, N. L., & Silbereisen, R. K. (1987). Influence of income change and parental acceptance on adolescent transgression proneness and peer relations. *European Journal of Psychology and Education*, **1,** 17–28.

Galanter, M. (1980). Psychological induction into the large group: Findings from a contemporary religious sect. *American Journal of Psychiatry*, **137,** 1574–1579.

Galanter, M., Buckley, P., Deutsch, A., Rabkin, R., & Rabkin, J. (1980). Large group influence for decreased drug use: Findings from two contemporary religious sects. *American Journal of Drug and Alcohol Abuse*, **7,** 291–304.

Gallatin, J. (1980). Political thinking in adolescence. In J. Adelson (Ed.), *Handbook of adolescent psychology* (pp. 344–382). New York: Wiley.

Galler, J. R. (Ed.) (1984). *Human nutrition: A comprehensive treatise, Vol. 5: Nutrition and behavior*. New York: Plenum.

Gallup, G. (1978, January 15). Gallup youth survey. *Denver Post*, p. 50.

Gallup, G. (1979, November 20). Gallup youth survey. *Denver Post*, p. 36.

Gallup, G. H. (1989, August 15). Drugs cited as top problem (Gallup Organization Poll, White House press release). *Rocky Mountain News*, p. 3.

Gallup, G., & Poling, D. (1980). *The search for America's faith*. New York: Abingdon.

Gandy, G. L. (1973). Birth order and vocational interest. *Developmental Psychology*, **9,** 406–410.

Gantman, C. A. (1978). Family interaction patterns among families with normal, disturbed, and drug-abusing adolescents. *Journal of Youth and Adolescence*, **7,** 429–440.

Garbarino, J. (1980). Some thoughts on school size and its effects on adolescent development. *Journal of Youth and Adolescence*, **9,** 19–31.

Garbarino, J. (1985). *Adolescent development: An ecological perspective*. Columbus, Ohio: Charles E. Merrill.

Garbarino, J. (1989). Troubled youth, troubled families: The dynamics of adolescent maltreatment. In D. Cicchetti, & V. Carlson (Eds.), *Child maltreatment: Theory and research on the causes and consequences of child abuse and neglect* (pp. 685–706). New York: Cambridge University Press.

Garbarino, J., & Guttman, E. (1986). Characteristics of high risk families: Parental and adolescent perspectives. In J. Garbarino, C. J. Schellenbach, & J. M. Sebes (Eds.), *Troubled youth, troubled families: Understanding families at risk for adolescent maltreatment* (pp. 121–150). New York: Aldine de Gruyter.

Garbarino, J., & Kelly, A. F. (1986). An introduction to troubled youth and troubled families. In J. Garbarino, C. J. Schellenbach, & J. M. Sebes (Eds.), *Troubled youth, troubled families: Understanding families at risk for adolescent maltreatment* (pp. 3–26). New York: Aldine de Gruyter.

Garbarino, J., & Plantz, M. C. (1986). Child abuse and juvenile delinquency: What are the links? In J. Garbarino, C. J. Schellenbach, & J. M. Sebes

(Eds.), *Troubled youth, troubled families: Understanding families at risk for adolescent maltreatment* (pp. 27–40). New York: Aldine de Gruyter.

Garbarino, J., Schellenbach, C. J., & Sebes, J. M. (Eds.) (1986). *Troubled youth, troubled families: Understanding families at risk for adolescent maltreatment.* New York: Aldine de Gruyter.

Gardner, G. E., & Sperry, B. M. (1974). School problems—learning disabilities and school phobia. In G. Caplan (Ed.), *American handbook of psychiatry, Vol. II: Child and adolescent psychiatry, sociocultural and community psychiatry* (pp. 116–129). New York: Basic Books.

Gardner, H. (1983). *Frames of mind: The theory of multiple intelligences.* New York: Basic Books.

Garfinkel, P. E., & Garner, D. M. (1983). *Anorexia nervosa: A multidimensional perspective.* New York: Brunner/Mazel.

Garmezy, N. (1987). Stress, competency and development: Continuities in the study of schizophrenic adults, children vulnerable to psychopathology and the search for stress-resistant children. *American Journal of Orthopsychiatry,* **57,** 159–174.

Garrett, C. J. (1984). *Meta-analysis of the effects of institutional and community residential treatment on adjudicated delinquents.* Unpublished doctoral dissertation, University of Colorado.

Garrett, C. J. (1985). Effects of residential treatment on adjudicated delinquents: A meta-analysis. *Journal of Research and Crime and Delinquency,* **22,** 287–308.

Gawronski, D. A., & Mathis, C. (1965). Differences between over-achieving, normal-achieving, and under-achieving high-school students. *Psychology in the Schools,* **2,** 152–155.

Gaylin, J. (1978, March). What boys look for in girls. *Seventeen,* 107–113.

Gaylin, J. (1979, March). What girls really look for in boys. *Seventeen,* 131–137.

Gelman, R. (1978). Cognitive development. *Annual Review of Psychology,* **29,** 297–332.

Gerber, R. W., & Newman, I. M. (1989). Predicting future smoking of adolescent experimental smokers. *Journal of Youth and Adolescence,* **18,** 191–201.

Gerzon, M. (1970). *The whole world is watching.* New York: Paperback Library.

Gesell, A., Ilg, F. L., & Ames, L. B. (1956). *Youth: The years from ten to sixteen.* New York: Harper & Row.

Gibbons, D. C. (1981). *Delinquent behaviors* (3rd ed.). Englewood Cliffs, NJ: Prentice-Hall.

Gibbs, J. C., Arnold, K. D., & Burkhart, J. E. (1984). Sex differences in the expression of moral judgment. *Child Development,* **55,** 1040–1043.

Gibbs, J. T., & Hines, A. M. (1989). Factors related to sex differences in suicidal behavior among black youth: Implications for intervention and research. *Journal of Adolescent Research,* **4,** 152–172.

Gilligan, C. (1977). In a different voice: Women's conceptions of self and of morality. *Harvard Educational Review,* **47,** 481–517.

Gilligan, C. (1979). Woman's place in man's life cycle. *Harvard Educational Review,* **49,** 431–446.

Gilligan, C. (1981). Moral development. In A. W. Chickering (Ed.), *The modern American college.* San Francisco: Jossey-Bass.

Gilligan, C. (1982). *In a different voice: Psychological theory and women's development.* Cambridge, MA: Harvard University Press.

Gilligan, C. (1987). The origins of morality in early childhood relationships. Paper presented at the biennial meetings of The Society for Research in Child Development, Baltimore, MD.

Gillis, J. R. (1974). *Youth and history.* New York: Academic Press.

Ginzberg, E. (1972). Toward a theory of occupational choice: A restatement. *Vocational Guidance Quarterly,* **20,** 169–176.

Ginzberg, E. (1980). Education, jobs, and all that. *New York University Education Quarterly,* **11,** 10–14.

Ginsburg, H., & Opper, S. (1979). *Piaget's theory of intellectual development* (2nd ed.). Englewood Cliffs, NJ: Prentice-Hall.

Gitlin, T. (1989). *The sixties: Years of hope, days of rage.* New York: Bantam Books.

Gladue, B. A., Green, R., & Hellman, R. E. (1984). Neuroendocrine response to estrogen and sexual orientation. *Science,* **225,** 1496–1499.

Glick, P. C. (1984). Marriage, divorce, and living arrangements: Prospective changes. *Journal of Family Issues,* **5,** 7–26.

Glick, P. C., & Norton, A. J. (1979). Marrying, divorcing, and living together in the U.S. today. *Population Bulletin,* **32,** 1–40.

Glyn, T. J. (1981). *Drugs and the family.* (*Research Issues* 29, National Institute on Drug Abuse.) Washington, DC: U.S. Government Printing Office.

Gold, D., & Andres, D. (1978a). Comparisons of adolescent children with employed and nonemployed mothers. *Merrill-Palmer Quarterly,* **24,** 242–254.

Gold, D., & Andres, D. (1978b). Developmental comparisons between 10-year-old children with employed and nonemployed mothers. *Child Development,* **49,** 75–84.

Gold, M. (1987). Social ecology. In H. C. Quay (Ed.), *Handbook of juvenile delinquency* (pp. 62–105). New York: Wiley.

Gold, M., & Mann, D. (1972). Delinquency as defense. *American Journal of Orthopsychiatry,* **42,** 463–479.

Gold, M., & Petronio. R. J. (1979). Delinquent behavior in adolescence. In J. Adelson (Ed.), *Handbook of adolescent psychology.* New York: Wiley.

Goldfarb, J. L., Mumford, D. M., Schum, D. A., Smith, P. B., Flowers, C., & Schum, D. (1977). An attempt to detect "pregnancy susceptibility" in indigent adolescent girls. *Journal of Youth and Adolescence,* **6,** 127–144.

Goldsen, R., Rosenberg, M., Williams, R., & Suchman, I. (1960). *What college students think.* New York: Van Nostrand.

Goldsmith, H. H. (1983). Genetic influences on personality from infancy to adulthood. *Child Development,* **54,** 331–355.

Goldsmith, H. H. (1984). Continuity of personality: A genetic perspective. In R. N. Emde & R. J. Harmon (Eds.), *The development of attachment and affiliative systems.* New York: Plenum.

Goldsmith, H. H., & Campos, J. J. (1982). Genetic influence on individual differences in emotionality. *Infant Behavior and Development,* **5,** 99.

Goldstein, M. J. (1981). Family factors associated with schizophrenia and anorexia nervosa. *Journal of Youth and Adolescence,* **10,** 385–405.

Goldstein, M. J. (1987). The UCLA high-risk project, 1962–1986. *Schizophrenia Bulletin,* **13,** 505–514.

Goldstein, M. J., Baker, B. L., & Jamison, K. R. (1980). *Abnormal psychology: Experiences, origins, and interventions.* Boston: Little, Brown.

Goldstein, M. J., & Jones, J. E. (1977). Adolescent and familial precursors of borderline and schizophrenic conditions. In *Borderline personality disorders: The concept, the syndrome, the patient.* New York: International Universities Press.

Good, T. L., & Weinstein, R. S. (1986). Schools make a difference: Evidence, criticisms, and new directions. *American Psychologist,* **41,** 1090–1097.

Goodchilds, J. D., & Zellman, G. L. (1984). Sexual signaling and sexual aggression in adolescent relationships. In N. M. Malamuth & E. D. Donnerstein (Eds.), (pp. 233–243), *Pornography and sexual aggression.* New York: Academic Press.

Goodlad, J. I. (1984). *A place called school: Prospects for the future.* New York: McGraw-Hill.

Goodwin, D. W., Schulsinger, F., Hermansen, L., Guze, S. B., & Winokur, G. (1973). Alcohol problems in adoptees raised apart from alcoholic biological parents. *Archives of General Psychiatry,* **28,** 238–243.

Goodwin, D. W., Schulsinger, F., Moller, N., Hermansen, L., Winokur, G., & Guze, S. B. (1974). Drinking problems in adopted and non-adopted sons of alcoholics. *Archives of General Psychiatry,* **31,** 164–169.

Gordis, E., Taborkoff, B., Goldman, D., & Berg, K. (1990). Finding the gene(s) for alcoholism. *Journal of the American Medical Association,* **263,** 2094–2055.

Gordon, D. A., & Arbuthnot, J. (1987). Individual, group, and family interventions. In H. C. Quay (Ed.), *Handbook of juvenile delinquency* (pp. 290–324). New York: Wiley.

Gordon, R. E., & Gordon, K. K. (1960). Social psychiatry in a mobile suburb. *International Journal of Social Psychiatry,* **6,** 1–2.

Gottesman, I. I., & Shields, J. (1982). *Schizophrenia: The enigmatic puzzle.* New York: Cambridge University Press.

Gottfredson, L. S. (1981). Circumscription and compromise: A developmental theory of occupational aspirations. *Journal of Counseling Psychology,* **28,** 545–579.

Gottfried, A. E., Gottfried, A. W., & Bathhurst, K. (1988). Maternal employment, family environment and children's development: Infancy through the school years. In A. E. Gottfried & A. W. Gottfried (Eds.), *Maternal employment and children's development: Longitudinal research* (pp. 11–58). New York: Plenum.

Gottschalk, R., Davidson, W. S., II, Gensheimer, L. K., & Mayer, J. P. (1987). Community-based interventions. In H. C. Quay (Ed.), *Handbook of juvenile delinquency* (pp. 266–289). New York: Wiley.

Gove, W. R., & Herb, T. R. (1974). Stress and mental illness among the young: A comparison of the sexes. *Social Forces,* **53,** 256–265.

Gove, W., & Peterson, C. (1980). An update of the literature on personal and marital satisfaction: The effect of children and the employment of wives. *Marriage and Family Review,* **3,** 63–96.

Goyan, A. J. (1980, April 3). U.S. Food and Drug Administration, cited by United Press International.

Graber, J. A., & Petersen, A. C. (in press). Cognitive changes at adolescence: Biological perspectives. In K. Gibson & A. C. Petersen (Eds.), *The brain and behavioral development: Biosocial dimensions.* New York: Aldine.

Grabowski, J. (Ed.) (1984). *Cocaine: Pharmacology, effects, and treatment* (NIDA Research Monograph 50). Washington, DC: U.S. Government Printing Office.

Grace, W. C., & Sweeney, M. E. (1986). Comparison of the P > V sign on the WISC-R and WAIS-R in delinquent males. *Journal of Clinical Psychology,* **42,** 173–176.

Graham, P. J. (1985). Psychosomatic relationships. In M. Rutter & L. Hersov (Eds.), *Child and adolescent psychiatry: Modern approaches* (pp. 599–613). Oxford: Blackwell Scientific Publications.

Graham, P., & Rutter, M. (1985). Adolescent disorders. In M. Rutter & L. Hersov, *Child and adolescent psychiatry* (pp. 351–367). Oxford: Blackwell Scientific Publications.

Green, R. (1974). *Sexual identity conflict in children and adults.* New York: Basic Books.

Green, R. (1980). Homosexuality. In H. I. Kaplan, A. M. Freedman, & B. J. Sadock (Eds.), *Comprehensive textbook of psychiatry, Vol. 2* (pp. 1762–1770). Baltimore: Williams and Wilkins.

Green, R. (1987). *"The sissy boy syndrome" and the development of homosexuality: A 15-year prospective study.* New Haven, CT: Yale University Press.

Greenberger, E. (1984). Defining psychosocial maturity in adolescence. In P. Karoly & J. J. Steffen (Eds.), *Adolescent behavior disorders: Foundations and contemporary concerns* (pp. 3–39). Lexington, MA: Heath (Revision).

Greenberger, E., & Goldberg, W. A. (1989). Work,

parenting, and the socialization of children. *Developmental Psychology, 25,* 22–35.

Greenberger, E., & Steinberg, L. D. (1982). Sex differences in early labor force experience: Harbinger of things to come. Unpublished manuscript.

Greenberger, E., & Steinberg, L. D. (1986). *When teenagers work: The psychological and social costs of adolescent employment.* New York: Basic Books.

Greenberger, E., Steinberg, L. D., & Vaux, A. (1981). Adolescents who work: Health and behavioral consequences of job stress. *Developmental Psychology, 17,* 691–703.

Grinder, R. E., & Strickland, C. E. (1969). G. Stanley Hall and the social significance of adolescence. In R. E. Grinder (Ed.), *Studies in adolescence: A book of readings in adolescent development* (2nd ed.). New York: Macmillan.

Grinker, R. R., & Werble, B. (1974). Mentally healthy young men (homoclites): Fourteen years later. *Archives of General Psychiatry, 30,* 701–704.

Gross, R., & Osterman, P. (1971). *High School.* New York: Simon & Schuster.

Grotevant, H. D., & Cooper, C. R. (Eds.) (1983). *Adolescent development in the family.* San Francisco: Jossey-Bass.

Grotevant, H. D., & Cooper, C. R. (1985). Patterns of interaction in family relationships and the development of identity exploration in adolescence. *Child Development, 56,* 415–428.

Grotevant, H. D., & Cooper, C. R. (in press). The role of family experience in career exploration: A life-span perspective. In R. M. Lerner & D. Featherman (Eds.), *Life-Span Development and Behavior Vol. 8.* Hillsdale, NJ: Erlbaum.

Guidubaldi, J., & Nastasi, B. K. (1987, April). *Home environment factors as predictors of child adjustment in mother-employed households: Results of a nationwide study.* Paper presented at the biennial meeting of the Society for Research in Child Development, Baltimore, MD.

Guidubaldi, J., & Perry, J. D. (1985). Divorce and mental health sequelae for children: A two-year follow-up of a nationwide sample. *Journal of the American Academy of Child Psychiatry, 24,* 531–537.

Guilford, J. P. (1967). *The nature of human intelligence.* New York: McGraw-Hill.

Guilford, J. P. (1975). Creativity: A quarter century of progress. In I. A. Taylor & J. W. Getzels (Eds.), *Perspectives in creativity* (pp. 37–59). Chicago: Aldine.

Guilford, J. P. (1982). Cognitive psychology's ambiguities: Some suggested remedies. *Psychological Review, 89,* 48–49.

Gump, P. V. (1966). *Big schools, small schools.* Moravia, NY: Chronicle Guidance Publications.

Gunter, N. C., & LaBara, R. C. (1980). The consequences of adolescent childbearing on postnatal development. *International Journal of Behavioral Development, 3,* 191– 214.

Gunzenhauser, N., & Caldwell, B. M. (1986). *Group care for young children: Considerations for child care and health professionals, public policy makers and parents.* Somerville, NJ: Johnson and Johnson.

Gupta, D., Attanasio, A., & Raaf, S. (1975). Plasma estrogen and androgen concentrations in children during adolescence. *Journal of Clinical Endocrinology and Metabolism, 40,* 636–643.

Guttmacher, A. F., & Kaiser, J. H. (1986). *Pregnancy, birth, and family planning.* New York: New American Library.

Haan, N. (1977). *Coping and defending: Processes of self-environment organization.* New York: Academic Press.

Hall, G. S. (1904, 1905). *Adolescence: Its psychology and its relations to physiology, anthropology, sociology, sex, crime, religion, and education, Vol. I.* Englewood Cliffs, NJ: Prentice-Hall.

Hall, G. S. (1923). *Life and confessions of a psychologist.* Englewood Cliffs, NJ: Prentice-Hall.

Hallinan, M. (1981). Recent advances in sociometry. In S. Asher & J. Gottman (Eds.), *The development of children's friendships* (pp. 91–115). New York: Cambridge University Press.

Hamburg, B. (1974). Early adolescence: A specific and stressful stage of the life cycle. In G. Coelho, D. Hamburg, & J. Adams (Eds.), *Coping and adaptation* (pp. 101–124). New York: Basic.

Hamburg, D. A., Elliott, G. R., & Parron, D. L. (1982). *Health and behavior: Frontiers of research in the biobehavioral sciences.* Washington, DC: National Academy Press.

Hamburg, D. A., & Trudeau, M. B. (Eds.) (1981). *Biobehavioral aspects of aggression.* New York: Alan R. Liss, Inc.

Hamilton, S. (1981). Adolescents in community settings: What is to be learned? *Theory and Research in Social Education, 9,* 23–38.

Hamilton, S. F., & Crouter, A. C. (1980). Work and growth: A review of research on the impact of work experience on adolescent development. *Journal of Youth and Adolescence, 9,* 323–338.

Hansen, S. L. (1977). Dating choices of high school students. *Family Coordinator, 26,* 133–138.

Harburg, E. D., Franceisco, W., Webster, D. W., Gleiberman, L., & Schork, A. (1990). Familial transmission of alcohol use. II. Initiation of an aversion to parent drinking (1960) by adult offspring. *Journal of Studies on Alcohol, 51,* 245–256.

Harevan, T. K. (1978). Family time and historical time. In A. S. Ross, J. Kagan, & T. K. Harevan (Eds.), *The family.* New York: Norton.

Harevan, T. K. (1984). Themes in the historical development of the family. In R. D. Parke (Ed.), *Review of child development research, Vol. 7* (pp. 137–178). Chicago: University of Chicago Press.

Harlan, W. R., Crillo, G. P., Cotmoni-Huntley, J., & Leaverton, P. E. (1979). Secondary sex characteristics of boys 12 to 17 years of age: The U.S. Health Examination Survey. *Journal of Pediatrics, 95,* 293–297.

Harlan, W. R., Harlan, E. A., & Grillo, G. R. (1980). Secondary sex characteristics of girls 12–17 years of age: The U.S. Health Examination Survey. *Journal of Pediatrics,* **96,** 1074–1087.

Harlow, H. (1965). Sexual behavior in the rhesus monkey. In F. A. Beach (Ed.), *Sex and behavior* (pp. 234–265). New York: Wiley.

Harrel, T. W., & Harrel, M. S. (1945). Army General Classification Test scores for civilian occupations. *Educational and Psychological Measurement,* **5,** 229–239.

Harris, L. (1971, January 8). Change, yes—upheaval, no. *Life,* **70,** 22–27.

Harris, L. (1987). *Inside America.* New York: Vintage Books.

Harter, S. (1983). Developmental perspectives on the self-system. In P. H. Mussen (Series Ed.), & E. M. Hetherington (Ed.), *Handbook of child psychology, Vol. 4: Socialization, personality, and social development* (4th ed., pp. 275–386). New York: Wiley.

Hartley, R. E. (1960). Children's concepts of male and female roles. *Merrill-Palmer Quarterly,* **6,** 83–91.

Hartup, W. W. (1970). Peer interaction and social organization. In P. H. Mussen (Ed.), *Carmichael's manual of child psychology, Vol. 2* (3rd ed., pp. 361–456). New York: Wiley.

Hartup, W. W. (1979). The social world of children. *American Psychologist,* **34,** 944–950.

Hartup, W. W. (1983). Peer relations. In E. M. Hetherington (Ed.), P. H. Mussen (Series Ed.), *Handbook of child psychology, Vol. 4: Socialization, personality, and social development* (4th ed., pp. 103–196). New York: Wiley.

Hartup, W. W. (1989). Social relationships and their significance. *American Psychologist,* **44,** 120–126.

Harvey, M. G., & Kevin, R. A. (1978). The influence of social stratification and age on occupational aspirations of adolescents. *Journal of Educational Research,* 262–266.

Hass, A. (1979). *Teenage sexuality: A survey of teenage sexual behavior.* New York: Macmillan.

Hauser, S. T., Book, B. K., Houlihan, J., Powers, S., Weiss-Perry, B., Follansbee, D., Jacobson, A. M., & Noam, G. G. (1987). Sex differences within the family: Studies of adolescent and parent family interactions. *Journal of Youth and Adolescence,* **16,** 199–220.

Hauser, S. T., Leaper, C., & Block, B. (1986). Parental discourse in the socialization of adolescent gender differences in individuation. Unpublished manuscript.

Havighurst, R. J. (1953). *Human development and education.* New York: Longmans, Green.

Haw, M. A. (1982). Women, work, and stress: A review and agenda for the future. *Journal of Health and Social Behavior,* **23,** 132–144.

Hayes, D. (Ed.) (1987). *Risking the future: Adolescent sexuality, pregnancy, and childbearing, Vol. 1.* Washington, DC: National Academy Press.

Haynes, S., & Feinleib, M. (1980). Women, work, and coronary heart disease: Prospective findings from the Framingham Heart Study. *American Journal of Public Health,* **70,** 133–141.

Healthy people: The Surgeon General's report on health promotion and disease prevention (1979). Washington, DC: U.S. Government Printing Office.

Heath, A. (1983). *The self-concepts of school refusers.* Doctoral dissertation, University of London.

Hechinger, F. M. (1981, June 16). About education: A warning on the decline of quality in teacher training. *New York Times,* p. 17.

Heckert, R. E. et al. (1984). *High schools and the changing workplace: The employer's view. Report of the panel on secondary school education from the changing work place.* Washington, DC: National Academy Press.

Hegel, G. W. F. (1952). *Phenomenologie des Geistes* (6th ed.). J Hoffmeister (Ed.). Hamburg: Meiner.

Heil, L. M., & Washburne, C. (1961). Characteristics of teachers related to children's progress. *Journal of Teacher Education,* **12,** 401–406.

Heilbrun, A. B., Orr, H. K., & Harrell, S. N. (1966). Patterns of parental childrearing and subsequent vulnerability to cognitive disturbance. *Journal of Consulting Psychology,* **36,** 51–59.

Heiman, J. R. (1977). A psychophysiological exploration of sexual arousal patterns in females and males. *Psychophysiology,* **14,** 266–274.

Heiman, J. R. (1980). Female sexual response patterns. *Archives of General Psychiatry,* **37,** 1311–1316.

Helfer, R. E., & Kempe, R. S. (1987). *The battered child* (4th ed.). Chicago: University of Chicago Press.

Henning, M., & Jardian, A. (1983). *The managerial woman.* New York: Pocket Books.

Herr, E. L., & Cramer, S. H. (1979). *Career guidance through the life span: Systematic approaches.* Boston: Little, Brown.

Hersov, L. (1969). Refusal to go to school. *Journal of Child Psychology and Psychiatry,* *1,* 137–145.

Hersov, L. (1985a). Emotional disorders. In M. Rutter & L. Hersov (Eds.), *Child and adolescent psychiatry: Modern approaches* (pp. 368–381). Oxford: Blackwell Scientific Publications.

Hersov, L. (1985b). School refusal. In M. Rutter & L. Hersov (Eds.), *Child and adolescent psychiatry: Modern approaches* (pp. 382–399). Oxford: Blackwell Scientific Publications.

Herzog, A. R., Bachman, J. G., & Johnston, L. D. (1979). *Paid work, child care, and housework: A national study of high school seniors' preferences for sharing responsibilities between husband and wife.* Ann Arbor: Survey Research Center, Institute for Social Research, University of Michigan.

Herzog, D. P. (1988). Eating disorders. In A. M. Nicholi, Jr. (Ed.), *The new Harvard guide to psychiatry* (pp. 434–445). Cambridge, MA: Harvard University Press.

Hess, E. H. (1970). Ethology and developmental psychology. In P. H. Mussen (Ed.), *Carmichael's manual of child psychology, Vol. I* (pp. 1–38). New York: Wiley.

Hess, R. D., & Halloway, S. D. (1984). Family and school as educational institutions. In R. D. Parke (Ed.), *Review of child development research, Vol. 7: The family* (pp. 179–222). Chicago: University of Chicago Press.

Hess, R. D., & McDevitt, T. M. (1984). Some antecedents of maternal intervention techniques: A longitudinal study. *Child Development, 55,* 2017–2030.

Heston, L., & Shields, J. (1968). Homosexuality in twins. *Archives of General Psychiatry, 18,* 149–160.

Hetherington, E. M. (1967). The effects of familial variables on sex typing, on parent-child similarity and on imitation in children. In J. P. Hill (Ed.), *Minnesota symposia on child psychology, Vol. 1* (pp. 82–107). Minneapolis, MN: University of Minnesota Press.

Hetherington, E. M. (1972). Effects of father absence on personality development in adolescent daughters. *Developmental Psychology, 7,* 313–326.

Hetherington, E. M. (1978). The aftermath of divorce. In J. H. Stevens & M. Mathews (Eds.), *Mother/child, father/child relationships* (pp. 110–155). Washington, DC: National Association for the Education of Young Children.

Hetherington, E. M. (1979). Divorce: A child's perspective. *American Psychologist, 34,* 851–858.

Hetherington, E. M. (1981). Children and divorce. In R. Henderson (Ed.), *Parent-child interaction: Theory, research, and prospect* (pp. 33–58). New York: Academic Press.

Hetherington, E. M. (1989). Coping with family transitions: Winners, losers, and survivors. *Child Development, 60,* 1–14.

Hetherington, E. M., & Camara, K. A. (1984). Families in transition: The process of dissolution and reconstitution. In R. D. Parke (Ed.), *Review of child development research: The family, Vol. 7* (pp. 398–439). Chicago: University of Chicago Press.

Hetherington, E. M., Cox, M., & Cox, R. (1982). Effects of divorce on parents and children. In M. E. Lamb (Ed.), *Nontraditional families: Parenting and child development* (pp. 233–288). Hillsdale, NJ: Erlbaum.

Hetherington, E. M., Cox, M., & Cox, R. (1985). Long-term effects of divorce and remarriage on the adjustment of children: A two-year follow-up of a nationwide sample. *Journal of the American Academy of Child Psychiatry, 24,* 518–530.

Hetherington, E. M., & Parke, R. D. (1986). *Child psychology: A contemporary viewpoint* (3rd ed.). New York: McGraw Hill.

Hetherington, E. M., Stanley-Hagan, M., & Anderson, E. R. (1989). Marital transitions: A child's perspective. *American Psychologist, 44,* 303–312.

Hetherington, E. M., Stouwie, R., & Ridberg, E. H. (1971). Patterns of family interaction and child rearing attitudes related to three dimensions of juvenile delinquency. *Journal of Abnormal Psychology, 77,* 160–176.

Hewitt, L. E., & Jenkins, R. L. (1946). *Fundamental patterns of maladjustment, the dynamics of their origin.* Springfield, IL: State of Illinois.

Higgins, E. T., & Bargh, J. A. (1987). Social cognition and social perception. *Annual Review of Psychology, 38,* 369–425.

Higgins, E. T., Ruble, D. N., & Hartup, W. W. (Eds.) (1983). *Social cognition and social development: A sociocultural perspective.* New York: Cambridge University Press.

High school dropout rates (1989, September 6). *The Chronicle of Higher Education Almanac,* p. 15.

Higham, E. (1980). Variations in adolescent psychohormonal development. In J. Adelson (Ed.), *Handbook of Adolescent Psychology.* New York: Wiley.

Hill, J. P., & Holmbeck, G. N. (1986). Attachment and autonomy during adolescence. In G. Whitehurst (Ed.), *Annals of Child Development, Vol. 3* (pp. 145–189). Greenwich, CT: JAI Press.

Hill, J. P., & Holmbeck, G. (1987). Disagreements about rules in families with seventh grade boys and girls. *Journal of Youth and Adolescence, 16,* 221–246.

Hill, J. P., & Lynch, M. E. (1983). The intensification of gender-related role expectations during early adolescence. In J. Brooks-Gunn & A. C. Petersen (Eds.), *Girls at puberty: Biological, psychological, and social perspectives* (pp. 201–228). New York: Plenum.

Hill, J., & Palamquist, W. (1978). Social cognition and social relations in early adolescence. *International Journal of Behavioural Development, 1,* 1–36.

Hindelang, M. J. (1981). Variations in sex-race-age-specific rates of offending. *American Sociological Review, 46,* 461–474.

Hirsch, B. J., & Rapkin, B. D. (1987). The transition to junior high school: A longitudinal study of self-esteem, psychological symptomatology, school life and social support. *Child Development, 58,* 1235–1243.

Hirsch, B. J., & Reischl, T. (1985). Social networks and developmental psychopathology: A comparison of adolescent children of a depressed, arthritic, or normal parent. *Journal of Abnormal Psychology 94,* 272–281.

Hirsch, S. P. (1974). Study at the top: Executive high school internships. *Educational Leadership, 32,* 112–115.

Hirschi, T. (1969). *Causes of delinquency.* Berkeley, CA: University of California Press.

Hirschi, T., & Hindelang, M. J. (1977). Intelligence and delinquency: A revisionist review. *American Sociological Review, 42,* 571–587.

Hirschorn, M. W. (1987, November 27). Programs

for potential high-school dropouts. *The Chronicle of Higher Education*, pp. A29–30.

Hirschorn, M. W. (1988, January 27). Coalition of 120 colleges hopes to encourage a million students to tutor 'at risk' youths. *The Chronicle of Higher Education*, pp. A35, A38.

Hirschorn, M. W. (1988, June 1). City U. of New York's Middle College High School helps troubled youths, serves as model program. *The Chronicle of Higher Education*, pp. 37–38.

Hocevar, D. (1981). Measurement of creativity: Review and critique. *Journal of Personality Assessment, 45,* 450–464.

Hock, E. (1980). Working and nonworking mothers and their infants: A comparative study of maternal care-giving characteristics and infant social behavior. *Merrill-Palmer Quarterly, 26,* 79–101.

Hodges, W. F., & Bloom, B. (1984). Parent perception of children's adjustment to divorce: A longitudinal study. *Journal of Divorce, 8,* 33–50.

Hodgson, J. W., & Fischer, J. L. (1978). Sex differences in identity and intimacy development in college youth. *Journal of Youth and Adolescence, 7,* 333–352.

Hoefler, S. A., & Bornstein, P. H. (1975). Achievement Place: An evaluative review. *Criminal Justice and Behavior, 2,* 146–168.

Hofferth, S. L. (1987). Trends in adolescent sexual activity, contraception, and pregnancy in the United States. In J. Bancroft (Ed.), *Adolescence and puberty.* New York: Oxford University Press.

Hofferth, S. L., Kahn, J. R., & Baldwin, W. (1987). Premarital sexual activity among U.S. teenage women over the past three decades. *Family Planning Perspectives, 19,* 46–53.

Hoffman, L. W. (1972). Early childhood experiences and women's achievement motives. *Journal of Social Issues, 28,* 129–155.

Hoffman, L. W. (1973). The professional woman as mother. *Annals of the New York Academy of Sciences, 208,* 211–216.

Hoffman, L. W. (1974). Effects of maternal employment on the child—A review of the research. *Developmental Psychology, 10,* 204–228.

Hoffman, L. W. (1977). Changes in family roles, socialization, and sex differences. *American Psychologist, 32,* 644–657.

Hoffman, L. W. (1980). The effects of maternal employment on the academic attitudes and performance of school-aged children. *School Psychology Review, 9,* No. 4, 319–336.

Hoffman, L. W. (1984). Work, family, and the socialization of the child. In R. D. Parke (Ed.), *Review of child development research* (Vol. 7), (pp. 223–282). Chicago: University of Chicago Press.

Hoffman, L. W. (1986). Work, family, and the child. In M. Pallak & R. O. Perloff, *Psychology and work: Productivity, change, and employment* (pp. 171–220). Washington, DC: American Psychological Association.

Hoffman, L. W. (1989). Effects of maternal employ-

ment in the two-parent family. *American Psychologist, 44,* 283–292.

Hoffman, M. L. (1970). Moral development. In P. H. Mussen (Ed.), *Carmichael's manual of child psychology, Vol. 2.* New York: Wiley.

Hoffman, M. L. (1975a). Moral internalization, parental power, and the nature of parent-child interaction. *Developmental Psychology, 11,* 228–239.

Hoffman, M. L. (1975b). Sex differences in moral internalization and values. *Journal of Personality and Social Psychology, 32,* 720–729.

Hoffman, M. L. (1979). Development of moral thought, feeling and behavior. *American Psychologist, 34,* 958–966.

Hoffman, M. L. (1980). Moral development in adolescence. In J. Adelson, (Ed.), *Handbook of adolescent psychology.* New York: Wiley.

Hoffman, M. L. (1982). The role of the father in moral internalization. In M. E. Lamb (Ed.), *The role of the father in child development.* New York: Wiley.

Hogan, R. (1975). The structure of moral character and the exploration of moral action. *Journal of Youth and Adolescence, 4,* 1–15.

Hogan, R. (1980). The gifted adolescent. In J. Adelson (Ed.), *Handbook of adolescent psychology* (pp. 536–559). New York: Wiley.

Holinger, P. C. (1978). Adolescent suicide: An epidemiological study of recent trends. *American Journal of Psychiatry, 135,* 754–756.

Holland, J. L. (1963a). Explorations of a theory of vocational choice: Part I. Vocational images and choice. *Vocational Guidance Quarterly, 11,* 232–239.

Holland, J. L. (1963b). Explorations of a theory of vocational choice: Part II. Self-descriptions and vocational preferences. *Vocational Guidance Quarterly, 12,* 17–24.

Hollingworth, L. S. (1928). *The psychology of the adolescent.* Englewood Cliffs, NJ: Prentice-Hall.

Hollister, L. E. (1986). Health aspects of cannabis. *Pharmacological Reviews, 38,* 1–20.

Holmes, D. J. (1964). *The adolescent in psychotherapy.* Boston: Little, Brown.

Holstein, C. B. (1976). Irreversible, stepwise sequence in the development of moral judgment: A longitudinal study of males and females. *Child Development, 47,* 51–61.

Holzman, P. S., & Grinker, R. R., Sr. (1974). Schizophrenia in adolescence. *Journal of Youth and Adolescence, 3,* 267–279.

Holzman, P. S., & Grinker, R. R., Sr. (1977). Schizophrenia in adolescence. In S. C. Feinstein & P. L. Giovacchini (Eds.), *Adolescent psychiatry: Developmental and clinical studies, Vol. V* (pp. 276–290). New York: Aronson.

Honzik, M. P. (1957). Developmental studies of parent-child resemblance in intelligence. *Child Development, 28,* 215–228.

Honzik, M. P. (1973). The development of intelligence. In B. B. Wolman (Ed.), *Handbook of general psychology* (pp. 644–655). Englewood Cliffs, NJ: Prentice-Hall.

Honzik, M. P., Macfarlane, J. W., & Allen, L. (1948). The stability of mental test performance between two and eighteen years. *Journal of Experimental Education,* **17,** 309–324.

Hood, J., Moore, T. E., & Garner, D. M. (1982). Locus of control as a measure of ineffectiveness in anorexia nervosa. *Journal of Consulting and Clinical Psychology,* **50,** 3–13.

Horn, J. L. (1976). Human abilities: A review of research and theory in the early 1970s. *Annual Review of Psychology,* **27,** 437–485.

Horn, J. L., & Donaldson, G. (1980). Cognitive development II: Adult development of human abilities. In O. G. Brim and J. Kagan (Eds.), *Constancy and change in human development: A volume of review essays* (pp. 445–529). Cambridge, MA: Harvard University Press.

Horney, K. (1937). *The neurotic personality of our time.* New York: Norton.

Horney, K. (1950). *Neurosis and human growth.* New York: Norton.

Hornick, J. P., Doran, L., & Crawford, S. H. (1979). Premarital contraceptives usage among male and female adolescents. *The Family Coordinator,* **28,** 181–190.

Horowitz, F. D., & O'Brien, M. (1985). *The gifted and talented: Developmental perspectives.* Washington, DC: American Psychological Association.

Horowitz, M. J. (1988). *Introduction to psychodynamics.* New York: Basic Books.

Howard, M., & McCabe, J. B. Helping teenagers postpone sexual involvement (1990). *Family Planning Perspectives,* **22,** 21–26.

Hubble, L. M., & Groff, M. (1982). WISC-R Verbal Performance IQ discrepancies among Quay-classified adolescent male delinquents. *Journal of Youth and Adolescence,* **10,** 179–184.

Hughes, D., Johnson, K. Rosenbaum, J., & Lin, J. (1989). *The health of America's children: Maternal and child health data book.* Washington, DC: Children's Defense Fund.

Hult, R. E., Jr. (1979). The relationship between ego identity status and moral reasoning in university women. *The Journal of Psychology,* **103,** 203–207.

Humphrey, L. L., & Benjamin, L. S. (1986). Using Structural Analysis of Social Behavior to assess critical but elusive family processes: A new solution to an old problem. *American Psychologist,* **41,** 979–989.

Hunt, J. McV. (1979). Psychological development: Early experience. In M. R. Rosenzweig & L. W. Porter (Eds.), *Annual Review of Psychiatry, Vol. 30* (pp. 103–144). Palo Alto, CA: Annual Reviews, Inc.

Hunt, M. (1970, July). Special sex education survey. *Seventeen,* 94ff.

Hunt, M. (1974). *Sexual behavior in the 1970s.* Chicago: Playboy Press.

Hunter, F., & Youniss, J. (1982). Changes in func-

tions of three relations during adolescence. *Developmental Psychology,* **18,** 806–811.

Hunter, R. S., & Kilstrom, N. (1979). Breaking the cycle in abusive families. *American Journal of Psychiatry,* **136,** 1320–1322.

Hurd, P. D., Johnson, C. A., Pechacek, T., Bast, L. P., Jacobs, D. R., & Leupker, R. V. (1980). Prevention of cigarette smoking in seventh grade students. *Journal of Behavioral Medicine,* **3,** 15–28.

Huston, A. C. (1983). Sex typing. In E. M. Hetherington (Ed.), P. H. Mussen (Series Ed.), *Handbook of child psychology, Vol. 4.: Socialization, personality, and social development* (4th ed., pp. 387–467). New York: Wiley.

Huston-Stein, A. (1978). Development of females from childhood through adulthood: Career and feminine role orientations. In P. Baltes (Ed.), *Lifespan development and behavior, Vol. I.* New York: Academic Press.

Hyde, J. S. (1981). How large are cognitive gender differences? A meta-analysis using w^2 and d. *American Psychologist,* **36,** 892–901.

Iliff, A., & Lee, V. A. (1952). Pulse rate, respiratory rate, and body temperature of children between two months and eighteen years of age. *Child Development,* **23,** 237–245.

Illingworth, R. S. (1987). *The development of the infant and young child: Normal and abnormal.* Edinburgh: Churchill Livingstone.

Inamdar, S. C., Siomopoulos, G., Osborn, M., & Bianchi, E. C. (1979). Phenomenology associated with depressed moods in adolescents. *American Journal of Social Psychiatry,* **136,** 156–159.

Inhelder, B., & Piaget, J. (1958). *The growth of logical thinking from childhood to adolescence.* New York: Basic Books.

Inoff-Germain, G., Arnold, G. S., Nottelman, E. D., Susman, E. J., Cutler, G. B., Jr., & Chrousos, G. P. (1988). Relations between hormone levels and observational measures of aggressive behavior in young adolescents in family interactions. *Developmental Psychology,* **24,** 129–139.

Institute of Medicine (1980). *Smoking and behavior.* Washington, DC: National Academy of Sciences.

International Association for the Evaluation of Educational Achievement (1988). *Science achievement in 17 countries: A preliminary report.* New York: Teachers College, Columbia University.

Irion, J. C., Coon, R. C., & Blanchard-Fields, F. (1988). The influence of divorce on coping in adolescence. *Journal of Youth and Adolescence,* **17,** 135–145.

Ivey, M. E., & Bardwick, J. M. (1968). Patterns of affective fluctuation in the menstrual cycle. *Psychosomatic Medicine,* **30,** 336–345.

Jacob, T. (1975). Family interaction in disturbed and normal families: A methodological and substantive review. *Psychological Bulletin,* **82,** 33–65.

Jacobs, B. L., & Trulson, M. E. (1979). Mechanisms of action of LSD. *American Scientist,* **67,** 396–404.

Jacobs, J. (1971). *Adolescent suicide.* New York: Wiley.

Janos, P. M., & Robinson, N. M. (1985). Psychosocial development in intellectually gifted children. In F. D. Horowitz & M. O'Brien (Eds.), *The gifted and talented: Developmental perspectives* (pp. 149–195). Washington, DC: American Psychological Association.

Janus, M-D, Burgess, A. W., & McCormack, A. (1987). Histories of sexual abuse in adolescent runaways. *Adolescence,* **22,** 405–417.

Janus, M-D, McCormack, A., Burgess, A. W., & Hartman, C. (1987). *Adolescent runaways: Causes and consequences.* Lexington, MA: Lexington Books.

Jencks, C. S., Smith, M., Acland, H., Bane, M. J., Cohen, D., Gintis, H., Heyns, B., & Michelson, S. (1972). *Inequality: A reassessment of the effects of family and schooling in America.* New York: Basic Books.

Jensen, A. R. (1969). How much can we boost IQ and school achievement? *Harvard Educational Review,* **39,** 1–123.

Jepsen, D. A. (1975). Occupational decision development over the high school years. *Journal of Vocational Behavior,* **7,** 225–237.

Jersild, A. T. (1963). *The psychology of adolescence* (2nd ed.). New York: Macmillan.

Jersild, A. T., Telford, C. W., & Sawrey, J. M. (1975). *Child psychology* (7th ed.). New York: Prentice-Hall.

Jessor, R. (1979). Marihuana: A review of recent psychosocial research. In R. I. Dupont, A. Goldstein, & J. O'Donnell (Eds.), *Handbook on drug abuse* (pp. 337–356). Washington, DC: U.S. Government Printing Office.

Jessor, R. (1984a). Adolescent development and behavioral health. In J. D. Matarazzo, S. M. Weiss, J. A. Herd, N. E. Miller, & S. M. Weiss (Eds.), *Behavioral health: A handbook of health enhancement and disease prevention* (pp. 69–90). New York: Wiley.

Jessor, R. (1984b, November). *Adolescent problem drinking: Psychosocial aspects and developmental outcomes.* Paper presented at the Carnegie Conference on Unhealthful Risk-Taking Behavior Among Adolescents, Stanford, CA.

Jessor, R., Chase, J. A., & Donovan, J. E. (1980). Psychosocial correlates of marijuana use and problem drinking in a national sample of adolescents. *American Journal of Public Health,* **70,** 604–613.

Jessor, R., Donovan, J. E., & Widmer, K. (1980). *Psychosocial factors in adolescent alcohol and drug use: The 1978 national sample study, and the 1974–78 panel study.* Boulder, CO: Institute of Behavioral Science, University of Colorado.

Jessor, R., & Jessor, S. L. (1973). *Problem drinking in youth: Personality, social and behavioral antecedents and correlates.* Publication 144: Boulder, CO: Institute of Behavioral Science, University of Colorado.

Jessor, R., & Jessor, S. L. (1977). *Problem behavior and psychosocial development: A longitudinal study of youth.* New York: Academic Press.

Jessor, S. L., & Jessor, R. (1974). Maternal ideology and adolescent problem behavior. *Developmental Psychology,* **10,** 246–254.

Johnson, A. M. (1959). Juvenile delinquency. In S. Arieti (Ed.), *American handbook of psychiatry* (pp. 840–856). New York: Basic Books.

Johnson, C. (1982). Anorexia nervosa and bulimia. In T. J. Coates, A. C. Petersen, & C. Perry (Eds.), *Adolescent health: Crossing the barriers.* New York: Academic Press.

Johnson, C., & Black, A. (1985). Family characteristics of 105 patients with bulimia. *American Journal of Psychiatry,* **142,** 1321–1324.

Johnson, C., Lewis, C., & Hagman, J. (1984). The syndrome of bulimia. *Psychiatric Clinics of North America,* **7,** 247–274.

Johnson, S. S. (1975). *Update on education: A digest of the National Assessment of Education Progress.* Denver: The Education Commission of the States.

Johnston, L. D. (1973). *Drugs and American youth.* Ann Arbor, MI: Institute for Social Research.

Johnston, L. D. (1985). The etiology and prevention of substance use: What can we learn from recent historical change? In C. L. Jones & R. J. Battjes (Eds.), *Etiology of drug abuse: Implications for prevention.* (NIDA Research Monograph 56) (ADM). Rockville, MD: National Institute of Drug Abuse.

Johnston, L. D., Bachman, J. G., & O'Malley, P. M. (1979). *Drugs and the class of '78: Behavior: attitudes, and recent national trends.* Rockville, MD: National Institute on Drug Abuse. DHEW Publication No. (ADM) 79-877.

Johnston, L. D., Bachman, J. G., & O'Malley, P. M. (1986). *Monitoring the future: Questionnaire responses from the nation's high school students, 1985.* Ann Arbor: Institute for Social Research, University of Michigan.

Johnston, L. D., Bachman, J. G., & O'Malley, P. M. (1987). *Monitoring the future: Questionnaire responses from the nation's high school seniors, 1986.* Ann Arbor: Institute for Social Research, University of Michigan.

Johnston, L. D., Bachman, J. G., & O'Malley, P. M. (forthcoming). *Monitoring the future: Questionnaire responses from the nation's high school seniors.* Ann Arbor: Survey Research Center, Institute for Social Research, University of Michigan.

Johnston, L. D., & O'Malley, P. M. (1986). Why do the nation's students use drugs and alcohol? Self-reported reasons from nine national surveys. *Journal of Drug Issues,* 16, 29–66.

Johnston, L. D., O'Malley, P. M., & Bachman, J. G. (1984). *Highlights from drugs and American high school students, 1975–1983.* (National Institute on Drug Abuse.) Washington, DC: U.S. Government Printing Office.

Johnston, L. D., O'Malley, P. M., & Bachman, J. G. (1986). *Drug use among American high school students, college students, and other young adults:*

National trends through 1985. (DHHS Publication No. ADM 86-1450.) Washington, DC: U.S. Government Printing Office.

Johnston, L. D., O'Malley, P. M., & Bachman, J. G. (1989). *Drug use, drinking, and smoking: National survey results from high school, college, and young adults populations, 1975–1988.* Washington, DC: National Institute on Drug Abuse.

Johnston, L. D., O'Malley, P. M., & Bachman, J. G. (1990). *National trends in drug use and related factors among American high school students and young adults, 1975–1989.* U.S. Department of Health and Human Services. Washington, DC: National Institute on Drug Abuse.

Johnstone, J. W. C. (1978). Social class, social areas, and delinquency. *Sociology and Social Research,* **63,** 49–72.

Jones, E., Forrest, J. D., Goldman, N., Henshaw, S. K., Lincoln, R., Rosof, J. I., Westoff, C. F., & Wulf, D. (1985). Teenage pregnancy in developed countries: Determinants and policy implications. *Family Planning Perspectives,* **17,** 53–63.

Jones, F. (1974). A 4-year follow-up of vulnerable adolescents. *Journal of Nervous and Mental Disease,* **159,** 20–39.

Jones, F. *et al.* (1987). *Teenage pregnancy in industrialized countries.* New Haven, CT: Alan Guttmacher Institute (Yale University Press).

Jones, H. E. (1946). Environmental influence on moral development. In L. Carmichael (Ed.), *Manual of child psychology.* New York: Wiley.

Jones, H. E. (1954). The environment and mental development. In L. Carmichael (Eds.), *Manual of child psychology* (2nd ed., pp. 631–698). New York: Wiley.

Jones, J., Rodnick, E., Goldstein, M. J., McPherson, S., & West, K. (1977). Parental transactional deviance as a possible indicator of risk for schizophrenia. *Archives of General Psychiatry,* **34,** 71–74.

Jones, L. Y. (1980). *Great expectations: America and the baby boom generation.* New York: Ballantine Books.

Jones, M. C. (1957). The later careers of boys who were early or late maturing. *Child Development* **28,** 113–128.

Jones, M. C. (1965). Psychological correlates of somatic development. *Child Development,* **36,** 899–911.

Jones, M. C., & Mussen, P. H. (1958). Self-conceptions, motivations, and interpersonal attitudes of early and late maturing girls. *Child Development,* **29,** 491–501.

Jones, W. M. (1977). The impact on society of youths who drop out or are undereducated. *Educational Leadership,* **34,** 411–416.

Josselyn, I. M. (1954). The ego in adolescence. *American Journal of Orthopsychiatry,* **24,** 223–227.

Josselyn, I. M. (1959). Psychological changes in adolescence. *Children,* **6,** 43–47.

Josselyn, I. M. (1968). *Adolescence.* Washington, D.C.: Joint Commission on Mental Health of Children.

Josselyn, I. M. (1971). *Adolescence.* New York: Harper & Row.

Kacerguis, M., & Adams, G. (1980). Erikson's stage resolution: The relationship between identity and intimacy. *Journal of Youth and Adolescence,* **9,** 117–126.

Kagan, J. (1964). Acquisition and significance of sex typing and sex role identity. In M. L. Hoffman & L. W. Hoffman (Eds.), *Review of child development research, Vol. II* (pp. 137–167). New York: Russell Sage.

Kagan, J. (1971). A conception of early adolescence. *Daedalus,* **100,** 997–1012.

Kagan, J., Reznick, S., & Snidman, N. (1988). Biological bases of childhood shyness. *Science,* **240,** 167–171.

Kagan, J., & Segal, J. (1988). *Psychology: An introduction* (6th ed.). San Diego, CA: Brace Jovanovich.

Kagan, J., Sontag, L. W., Baker, C. T., & Nelson, V. L. (1958). Personality and I.Q. change. *Journal of Abnormal and Social Psychology,* **56,** 261–266.

Kahn, R. J., McNair, D. M., Lipman, R. S., Covi, L., Rickels, K., Downing, R., Fisher, S., & Frankenthaler, L. M. (1986). Imipramine and clordiazepoxide in depressive and anxiety disorders. *Archives of General Psychiatry,* **43,** 79–85.

Kahn, R. L. (1981). *Work and health.* New York: Wiley.

Kamin, L. (with Eysenck, H. J.) (1981). *The intelligence controversy.* New York: Wiley.

Kampter, N. L. (1988). Identity development in late adolescence: Casual modeling of social and familial influences. *Journal of Youth and Adolescence,* **17,** 493–514.

Kandel, D. (1973). The role of parents and peers in adolescent marijuana use. *Science,* **181,** 1067–1070.

Kandel, D. (1974). Inter- and intragenerational influences on adolescent marijuana use. *Journal of Social Issues,* **30,** 107–135.

Kandel, D. B. (1978a). Homophily, selection, and socialization in adolescent friendships. *American Journal of Sociology,* **84,** 427–436.

Kandel, D. B. (1978b). Similarity in real-life adolescent friendship pairs. *Journal of Personality and Social Psychology,* **36,** 306–312.

Kandel, D. B. (1980). Drug and drinking behavior among youth. *Annual Review of Sociology,* **6,** 235–285.

Kandel, D. B. (1985). On processes of peer influences in adolescent drug use: A developmental perspective. In J. Brook, D. Lettieri, & D. Brook (Eds.), *Advances in alcohol and substance abuse,* **4,** 139–163.

Kandel, D. B., & Andrews, K. (1987). Processes of adolescent socialization by parents and peers. *International Journal of Addictions,* **22,** 319–342.

Kandel, D. B., Davies, M., Karus, D., & Yamaguchi,

K. (1986). The consequences in young adulthood of adolescent drug involvement: An overview. *Archives of General Psychiatry*, **43**, 746–754.

Kandel, D. B., & Faust, R. (1975). Sequence and stages in patterns of adolescent drug use. *Archives of General Psychiatry*, **32**, 923–932.

Kandel, D. B., Kessler, R. C., & Margulies, R. Z. (1978). Antecedents of adolescent initiation into stages of drug use: A developmental analysis. In D. B. Kandel (Ed.), *Longitudinal research on drug use: Empirical findings and methodological issues* (pp. 73–99). Washington, DC: Hemisphere Publishing Corporation.

Kandel, D. B., & Lesser, G. S. (1969). Parental and peer influences on educational plans of adolescents. *American Sociological Review*, **34**, 213–223.

Kandel, D. B., & Lesser, G. S. (1972). *Youth in two worlds*. San Francisco: Jossey-Bass.

Kandel, D. B., & Logan, J. A. (1984). Patterns of drug use from adolescence to young adulthood: I. Periods of risk for initiation, continued use, and discontinuation. *American Journal of Public Health*, **74**, 660–666.

Kandel, D. B., Raveis, V. H., & Kandel, P. (1984). Continuity in discontinuities: Adjustment in young adulthood of former school absentees. *Youth and Society*, **15**, 325–353.

Kantner, J., & Zelnik, M. (1973). Contraception and pregnancy: Experience of young unmarried women in the United States. *Family Planning Perspectives*, **5**, 21–35.

Kantrowitz, B. (1986, March 31). A mother's choice. *Newsweek*, pp. 46–51.

Kaplan, H. S. (1974). *The new sex therapy: Active treatment of sexual dysfunctions*. New York: Bruner/Mazel.

Karniol, R. (1978). Children's use of intention cues in excusing behavior. *Psychological Bulletin*, **85**, 76–86.

Kasarda, J. D., & Janowitz, M. (1974). Community attachment in mass society. *American Sociological Review*, **39**, 328–339.

Katchadourian, H. A. (1985). *Fundamentals of human sexuality* (4th ed.). New York: Holt, Rinehart, & Winston.

Kaufman, I. R. (1979, October 14). Juvenile justice: A plea for reform. *New York Times Magazine*, 42–60.

Kaufman, J., & Zigler, E. (1987). Do abusive children become abusive parents? *American Journal of Orthopsychiatry*, **57**, 186–192.

Kavrell, S. M., & Petersen, A. C. (1984). Patterns of achievement in early adolescence. In M. L. Maehr & M. W. Steinkamp (Eds.), *Women and science*. Greenwich, CT: JAI Press.

Kawash, G. F., Kerr, E. N., & Clewes, J. L. (1983). Self-esteem in children as a function of perceived parental behavior. *Journal of Psychology*, **119**, 235–242.

Kazdin, A. E. (1978). The application of operant techniques in treatment, rehabilitation, and edu-

cation. In S. L. Garfield & A. E. Bergin (Eds.), *Handbook of psychotherapy and behavior change: An empirical analysis* (pp. 549–590). New York: Wiley.

Kazdin, A. E. (1985). *Treatment of antisocial behavior in children and adolescents*. Homewood, IL: Dorsey Press.

Keating, D. P. (1980). Thinking processes in adolescence. In J. Adelson (Ed.), *Handbook of adolescent psychology* (pp. 211–246). New York: Wiley.

Keating, D. P. (1988, July). Cognitive processes in adolescence (draft). In G. R. Elliott & S. S. Feldman (Eds.), *Volume on normal adolescent development* (in preparation). Stanford, CA: Stanford University and Carnegie Corporation of New York.

Kelley, K. (1979). Socialization factors in contraceptive attitudes: Roles of affective responses, parental attitudes, and sexual experience. *Journal of Sex Research*, **15**, 6–20.

Kelly, J. A., & Worrell, L. (1977). The joint and differential perceived contribution of parents to adolescents' cognitive functioning. *Developmental Psychology*, **13**, 282–283.

Kelsoe, J. R., Ginns, E. I., Egeland, J. A., *et al.* (1989). Re-evaluation of the linkage between chromosome 11p loci and the gene for bipolar affective disorders in the Old Order Amish. *Nature*, **342**, 238–243.

Kempe, R. S., & Kempe, C. H. (1978). *Child abuse*. Cambridge, MA: Harvard University Press.

Kempe, R. S., & Kempe, C. H. (1984). *The common secret: Sexual abuse of children and adolescents*. New York: W. H. Freeman.

Kendler, K. S., Gruenberg, A. M., & Strauss, J. S. (1981). An independent analysis of the Copenhagen sample of the Danish Adoption Study of Schizophrenia. I. The relationship between anxiety disorder and schizophrenia. *Archives of General Psychiatry*, **38**, 937–977.

Keniston, K. (1960). *The uncommitted: Alienated youth in American society*. New York: Dell.

Keniston, K. (1971). *Youth and dissent*. New York: Harcourt Brace Jovanovich.

Kenney, A. M., Guardado, S., & Brown, L. (1988). Sex education and AIDS education in the schools: What states and large school districts are doing. *Family Planning Perspectives*, **21**, 56–64.

Kerpelman, L. C. (1969). Student political activism and ideology. *Journal of Counseling Psychology*, **16**, 8–13.

Kerr, P. (1986, November 17). Anatomy of an issue: Drugs, the evidence, the reaction. *The New York Times*, pp. 1, 12.

Kessler, R. C., & McRae, J. A., Jr. (1982). The effects of wives' employment on the mental health of married men and women. *American Sociological Review*, **47**, 216–227.

Kett, J. F. (1967). *The universal experience of adolescence*. Boston: Beacon Press.

Kety, S., & Matthysse, S. (1988). Genetic and biochemical aspects of schizophrenia. In A. M. Nicholi, Jr. (Ed.), *The new Harvard guide to psychiatry* (pp. 139–151). Cambridge, MA: Harvard University Press.

Kety, S. S., Rosenthal, D., Wender, P. H., Schulsinger, F., & Jacobsen, B. (1978). The biological and adoptive families of adopted individuals who became schizophrenic: Prevalence of mental illness and other characteristics. In L. C. Wynne, R. L. Cromwell, & S. Matthysse (Eds.), *The nature of schizophrenia: New approaches to research and treatment.* New York: Wiley.

Keyes, S., & Block, J. (1984). Prevalence and patterns of substance abuse among early adolescents. *Journal of Youth and Adolescence, 13,* 1–14.

Kiell, N. (1967). *The universal experience of adolescence.* Boston: Beacon Press.

Kifer, E. (1975). Relationships between academic achievement and personality characteristics: A quasi-longitudinal study. *American Educational Research Journal 12,* 191–210.

Kinsey, A. C., Pomeroy, W. B., & Martin, C. E. (1948). *Sexual behavior in the human male.* Philadelphia: Saunders.

Kinsey, A. C., Pomeroy, W. B., Martin, C. E., & Gebhard, P. H. (1953). *Sexual behavior in the human female.* Philadelphia: Saunders.

Kirby, D. (1985). *School-based health clinics: An emerging approach to improving adolescent health and addressing teenage pregnancy.* Report prepared for the Center for Population Options.

Kirgin, K. A., Braukmann, C. J., Atwater, J. D., & Wolf, M. M. (1982). An evaluation of teaching-family (Achievement Place) group homes for juvenile offenders. *Journal of Applied Behavior Analysis, 15,* 1–16.

Klatzky, R. L. (1980). *Human memory: Structures and processes* (2nd ed.). San Francisco: Freeman.

Klaus, M. H., & Kennell, J. H. (1984). Hunting and gathering societies: An empirical basis for exploring biobehavioral processes in mothers and infants. Paper presented at the International Conference on Infant Studies, New York.

Klerman, G. L. (1988a). Depression and related disorders of mood (affective disorders). In A. M. Nicholi, Jr., (Ed.) *The new Harvard guide to psychiatry* (pp. 309–336). Cambridge, MA: Harvard University Press.

Klerman, G. (1988b). The current age of youth melancholia: Evidence for increase in depression among adolescents and young adults. *British Journal of Psychiatry, 152,* 4–14.

Kliegman, R. M., & King, K. C. (1983). Intrauterine growth retardation: Determinants of aberrant fetal growth. In A. A. Fanaroff, R. J. Martin, & J. R. Merkatz (Eds.), *Berhman's neonatal-perinatal medicine.* St. Louis, Mosby.

Kniesel, P. M. (1987, April). Social support preferences of female adolescents in the context of interpersonal stress. Paper presented at the biennial meeting of the Society for Research in Child Development, Baltimore, MD.

Koff, E., Rierdan, J., & Sheingold, K. (1982). Memories of menarche: Age, preparation, and prior knowledge as determinants of initial menstrual experience. *Journal of Youth and Adolescence, 11,* 1–9.

Kogan, N. (1983). Stylistic variation in childhood and adolescence: Creativity, metaphor, and cognitive styles. In J. H. Flavell & E. M. Markman (Eds.), *Handbook of child psychology, Vol. 3.: Cognitive development* (4th ed., pp. 630–706). New York: Wiley.

Kohlberg, L. (1969). Stage and sequence: The cognitive-developmental approach to socialization. In D. Gostlin (Ed.), *Handbook of socialization theory and research.* Skokie, IL: Rand McNally.

Kohlberg, L. (1971). From is to ought: How to commit the naturalistic fallacy and get away with it in the study of moral development. In T. Mischel (Ed.), *Cognitive development and epistemology.* New York: Academic Press.

Kohlberg, L. (1976). Moral stages and moralization: The cognitive-developmental approach. In T. Lickona (Ed.), *Moral development and behavior.* New York: Holt, Rinehart & Winston.

Kohlberg, L. (1979). *The meaning and measurement of moral development.* Clark Lectures, Clark University.

Kohlberg, L. (1984). *Essays on moral development, Vol. 11: The psychology of moral development.* New York: Harper & Row.

Kohlberg, L., & Gilligan, C. (1971). The adolescent as a philosopher: The discovery of the self in a postconventional world. *Daedalus, 100,* 1051–1086.

Kohlberg, L., & Gilligan, C. (1972). The adolescent as a philosopher: The discovery of the self in a postconventional world. In J. Kagan & R. Coles (Eds.), *12 to 16: Early adolescence.* New York: Norton.

Kohlberg, L. & Kramer, R. (1969). Continuities and discontinuities in childhood and adult development. *Human Development, 12,* 93–120.

Kohlberg, L., Levine, C., & Hewer, A. (1983). *Moral stages: A current formulation and a response to critics.* Basel: S. Karger.

Kohn M. L. (1959a). Social class and the exercise of parental authority. *American Sociological Review, 24,* 352–366.

Kohn, M. L. (1959b). Social class and parental values. *American Journal of Sociology, 64,* 337–351.

Kohn, M. L. (1969). *Class and conformity: A study in values.* Homewood, IL: Dorsey Press.

Kohn, M. L., & Schooler, C. (1978). The reciprocal effects of the substantive complexity of work and intellectual flexibility: A longitudinal assessment. *American Journal of Sociology, 84,* 24–52.

Kohn, M. L., & Schooler, C. (1982). Job conditions and personality: A longitudinal assessment of their reciprocal effects. *American Journal of Sociology,* **87,** 1257–1286.

Kolata, G. (1988, February 25). New obesity studies indicate metabolism is often to blame, *New York Times,* pp. 1, 17.

Kolata, G. (1989, August 11). In cities, poor families are dying of crack. *The New York Times,* pp. 1, 10.

Konopka, G. (1976). *Young girls: A portrait of adolescence.* Englewood Cliffs, NJ: Prentice-Hall.

Konopka, G. (1985). *Young girls: A portrait of adolescence.* New York: Harrington Press (paperback).

Kovach, J. A., & Glickman, N. W. (1986). Levels and psychosocial correlates of adolescent drug use. *Journal of Youth and Adolescence,* **115,** 61–78.

Kovacs, M. (1989). Affective disorders in children and adolescents. *American Psychologist,* **44,** 209–215.

Kozlowski, L. T. (1979). Psychosocial influences on cigarette smoking. In *Smoking and health: A report of the Surgeon General.* (DHEW Publication No. (PHS) 79-50066, U.S. Department of Health, Education, and Welfare) (Chapter 18, pp. 1–31). Washington, DC: U.S. Government Printing Office (No. 017-000-00218-0).

Kratkoski, P. C. (1984). Child abuse and violence against the family. *Child Welfare,* **61,** 435–444.

Kris, E. (1952). *Psychoanalytic explorations in art.* New York: International Universities Press.

Kroupa, S. E. (1988). Perceived parental acceptance and female juvenile delinquency. *Adolescence,* **23,** 171–185.

Kurdek, L., & Krile, D. (1982). A developmental analysis of the relation between peer acceptance and both interpersonal understanding and perceived social competence. *Child Development,* **53,** 1485–1491.

Kyman, W., Berger, D., & Perez, G. (1987). The making of an adolescent clinic. *Adolescence,* **22,** 879–881.

Laboratory of Comparative Human Cognition (1983). Culture and cognitive development. In P. H. Mussen (Series Ed.) & W. Kessen (Ed.), *Handbook of child psychology, Vol. 1: History, theory, and methods* (pp. 295–358). New York: Wiley.

Lamar, J. V., Jr. (1986a, September 27). Rolling out the big guns: The First Couple and Congress press the attack on drugs. *The New York Times.*

Lamar, J. V., Jr. (1986b, June 2). Crack. *Time,* pp. 16–18.

Lamb, D. (1986). *Psychotherapy with adolescent girls* (2nd ed.). New York: Plenum.

Lanelsbaum, J., & Willis, R. (1971). Conformity in early and late adolescence. *Developmental Psychology,* **4,** 334–337.

Lao, R. C. (1980). Differential factors affecting male and female academic performance in high school. *The Journal of Psychology,* **104,** 119–127.

Lapointe, A. E., Mead, N. A., & Phillips, G. W. (1989). *A world of difference: An international assessment of mathematics and science.* Princeton, NJ: Educational Testing Service.

Larson, L. E. (1972a). The influence of parents and peers during adolescence. *Journal of Marriage and the Family,* **34,** 67–74.

Larson, L. E. (1972b). The relative influence of parent-adolescent affect in predicting the salience hierarchy among youth. *Pacific Sociological Review,* **15,** 83–102.

Larson, R., & Johnson, C. (1981). Anorexia nervosa in context of daily living. *Journal of Youth and Adolescence,* **10,** 455–471.

Larson, R., & Lampman-Petraitis (1989). Daily emotional states as reported by children and adolescents. *Child Development,* **60,** 1250–1260.

LaVoie, J. C. (1976). Ego identity formation in middle adolescence. *Journal of Youth and Adolescence,* **5,** 371–385.

Lawrence, T. S., & Velleman, J. D. (1974). Correlates of student drug use in a suburban high school. *Psychiatry,* **37,** 129–136.

Layzer, D. (1974). Heritability analyses of IQ scores: Science or numerology? *Science,* **183,** 1259–1266.

Lazar, I., & Darlington, R. (1982). Lasting effects of early education: A report from the Consortium for Longitudinal Studies. *Monographs of the Society for Research in Child Development,* **47,** 2–3.

Lazarus, R. S., & Folkman, S. (1984) *Stress, appraisal, and coping.* New York: Springer.

Leahy, R. L. (1981). Parental practices and the development of moral judgment and self-image disparity during adolescence. *Developmental Psychology,* **17,** 580–594.

Lebowitz, F. (1978). *Metropolitan life.* New York: Dutton.

Leith, G. (1972). The relationships between intelligence, personality, and creativity under two conditions of stress. *British Journal of Educational Psychology,* **42,** 240–247.

Lemann, N. (1986, June). The origins of the underclass. *The Atlantic,* pp. 31–55.

Lerman, R. I. (1986). Unemployment among low-income and black youth: A review of causes, programs, and policies. *Youth and Society,* **17,** 237–266.

Lerner, R. M., Karabenick, S. A., & Stuart, J. L. (1973). Relations among physical attractiveness, body attitudes, and self-concept in male and female college students. *Journal of Psychology,* **85,** 119–129.

Lerner, R. M., & Karabenick, S. A. (1974). Physical attractiveness, body attitudes, and self-concept in late adolescents. *Journal of Youth and Adolescence,* **3,** 307–316.

Lerner, R. M., & Knapp, J. R. (1975). Actual and perceived intrafamilial attitudes of late adolescents and their parents. *Journal of Youth and Adolescence,* **4,** 17–36.

Lerner, R. M., & Korn, S. J. (1972). The development of body-build stereotypes in males. *Child Development,* **43,** 908–920.

Lerner, R. M., Sorrell, A. T., & Brackney, B. E. (1981). Sex differences in self-concept and self-esteem in late adolescents: A time-lag analysis. *Sex Roles, 7,* 709–722.

Leslie, L. A. (1986). The impact of adolescent females' assessment of parenthood and employment on plans for the future. *Journal of Youth and Adolescence, 15,* 19–28.

Lesser, G. S., & Kandel, D. (1969). Parent-adolescent relationships and adolescent independence in the United States and Denmark. *Journal of Marriage and the Family, 31,* 348–358.

Levin, H. M. (1985). The educationally disadvantaged: A national crisis. *The State Youth Initiatives Project, Working paper No. 6.* Philadelphia: Public/Private Ventures.

Levine, L., Coll, C., & Oh, W. (1984, April). Determinants of mother-infant interaction in adolescent mothers. Paper presented at the International Conference on Infant Studies, New York.

Levine, M., Wesolowski, J. C., & Corbett, F. J. (1966). Pupil turnover and academic performance in an inner city elementary school. *Psychology in the Schools, 3,* 153–158.

Levinson, D. J., Darrow, C. N., Klein, E. B., Levinson, M. H., & McKee, B. (1978). *The seasons of a man's life.* New York: Knopf.

Levitt, E. E., & Edwards, J. A. (1970). A multivariate study of correlative factors in youthful cigarette smoking. *Developmental Psychology, 2,* 5–11.

Lewin, K. (1935). *A dynamic theory of personality.* New York: McGraw-Hill.

Lewin, K. (1946). Behavior and development as a function of the total situation. In L. Carmichael (Ed.), *Manual of child psychology.* New York: Wiley.

Lewin, K. (1951). *Field theory and social science.* New York: Harper & Row.

Lewin, K., Lippitt, R., & White, R. K. (1939). Patterns of aggressive behavior in experimentally created social climates. *Journal of Social Psychology, 10,* 271–299.

Lewine, R. R. J. (1980). Sex differences in age of symptom onset and first hospitalization in schizophrenia. *American Journal of Orthopsychiatry, 50,* 316–322.

Lewis, D. O., Mallouh, C., & Webb, V. (1989). Child abuse, delinquency, and violent criminality. In D. Cicchetti & V. Carlson (Eds.), *Child maltreatment: Theory and research on the causes and consequences of child abuse and neglect* (pp. 707–721). New York: Cambridge University Press.

Lewis, D. O., Shanok, S. S., Pincus, J. H., & Glaser, G. H. (1979). Violent juvenile delinquents: Psychiatric, neurological, psychological, and abuse factors. *Journal of the American Academy of Child Psychiatry, 18,* 307–319.

Lewis, O. (1966). *La Vida.* New York: Random House.

Lichtenstein, E., & Mermelstein, R. J. (1984). Review of approaches to smoking treatment: Behavior modification strategies. In J. Matarazzo, S. W. Weiss, J. A. Herd, N. Miller, & S. M. Weiss (Eds.), *Behavioral health: A handbook of health enhancement and disease prevention* (pp. 695–712). New York: Wiley.

Lindberg, F. H., & Distad, L. J. (1985). Survival responses to incest: Adolescents in crisis. *Child Abuse and Neglect, 9,* 521–526.

Lindsay, J. W. (1985). *Teens look at marriage: Rainbows, role, and realities.* Buena Park, CA: Morning Glory Press.

Linn, M., & Petersen, A. C. (1985). Gender differences and spatial ability: Emergence and characterization. *Child Development, 56,* 1479–1498.

Lipsitz, J. (1977). *Growing up forgotten.* Lexington, MA: Lexington Books.

Lipsitz, J. (1982, March 21). Successful schools for young adolescents: A report on a report. Paper presented at the annual meeting of the American Educational Research Association, New York City.

Litt, I. F., & Vaughn, V. C. III (1987). Growth and development during adolescence. In R. E. Behrman, V. C. Vaughn, & W. E. Nelson (Eds.), *Textbook of pediatrics* (13th ed., pp. 20–24). Philadelphia: W. B. Saunders.

Little, J. K. (1967). The occupations of non-college youth. *American Educational Research Journal, 4,* 147–153.

Livesley, W. J., & Bromley, D. B. (1973). *Person perception in childhood and adolescence.* New York: Wiley.

Livson, N., & Peskin, H. (1980). Perspectives on adolescence from longitudinal research. In J. Adelson (Ed.), *Handbook of adolescent psychology* (pp. 47–98). New York: Wiley.

Lloyd, D. (1978). Prediction of school failure from third-grade data. *Educational Psychological Measurement, 38,* 1193–1200.

Lloyd, M. A. (1985). *Adolescence.* New York: Harper & Row.

Loeber, R., & Dishion, T. (1983). Early predictors of male delinquency: A review. *Psychological Bulletin, 94,* 68–99.

Loeber, R., & Stouthamer-Loeber (1986). Family factors as correlates and predictors of juvenile conduct problems and delinquency. In M. Tonry & N. Morris (Eds.), *Crime and Justice* (Vol. 7, pp. 29–149). Chicago: University of Chicago Press.

Loehlin, J. C., Willerman, L., & Horn, J. M. (1988). Human behavior genetics. *Annual Review of Psychology, 39,* 101–133.

Logan, R. D. (1980). Identity, purity, and ecology. *Adolescence, 58,* 409–412.

Lomax, J. W. (1989). Obesity. In H. I. Kaplan & B. J. Sadock (Eds.), *Comprehensive textbook of psychiatry/V* (5th ed.) (pp. 1179–1186). Baltimore, MD: Williams & Wilkins.

London, K. A., Mosher, W. D., Pratt, W. F., & Williams, L. B. (1989, March). *Preliminary findings from the National Survey of Family Growth, Cycle IV.* Paper presented at the annual meeting of the

Population Association of America, Baltimore, MD.

London, P. (1970). The resources: Motivational hypotheses about Christians who saved Jesus from the Nazis. In J. Macaulay & L. Berkowitz (Eds.), *Altruism and helping behavior.* New York: Academic Press.

Long, N., & Forehand, R. (1987). The effects of parental divorce and marital conflict on children: An overview. *Journal of Developmental and Behavioral Pediatrics, 8,* 292–296.

LoPiccolo, J., & Hogan, D. R. (1979). Sexual dysfunction. In O. F. Pomerleau & J. P. Brady (Eds.), *Behavioral medicine: Theory and practice* (pp. 177–204). Baltimore: Wiliams & Wilkins.

Lorenz, K. Z. (1965). *Evolution and modification of behavior.* Chicago: University of Chicago Press.

Lorenz, K. Z. (1966). *On aggression.* New York: Harcourt Brace Jovanovich.

Lorenz, K. Z. (1981). *The foundations of ethology.* New York: Springer-Verlag.

Lorion, R. P., Tolan, P. H., & Wahler, R. G. (1987). Prevention. In H. C. Quay (Ed.), *Handbook of juvenile delinquency* (pp. 383–416). New York: Wiley.

Lozoff, B. (1989). Nutrition and behavior. *American Psychologist, 44,* 231–236.

Luce, J. (1970, November 8). End of the road. *Behavior: San Francisco Sunday Examiner and Chronicle,* 8–10.

Lunneborg, P. W. (1975). Interest diferentiation in high school and vocational indecision in college. *Journal of Vocational Behavior, 7,* 297–303.

Luria, Z., Friedman, S., & Rose, M. D. (1987). *Human sexuality.* New York: Wiley.

Lynd, H. (1966). *On shame and the search for identity.* New York: Science Editions, Inc.

Lytton, H. (1972). *Creativity and education.* New York: Schocken.

Lytton, H. (1977). Do parents create, or respond to, differences in twins? *Developmental Psychology, 13,* 456–459.

Maccoby, E. E. (Ed.) (1966). *The development of sex differences.* Stanford, CA: Stanford University Press.

Maccoby, E. E., & Martin, A. (1983). Socialization in the context of the family: Parent-child interaction. In P. H. Mussen (Series Ed.), & E. M. Hetherington (Ed.), *Handbook of child psychology: Vol. 4. Socialization, personality and social behavior* (4th ed., pp. 1–102). New York: Wiley.

Maccoby, E. E., & Jacklin, C. (1974). *The psychology of sex differences.* Stanford, CA: Stanford University Press.

MacKinnon, D. W. (1963). Identifying and developing creativity. *Journal of Secondary Education, 38,* 166–174.

MacKinnon, D. W. (1968). Selecting students with creative potential. In P. Heist (Ed.), *The creative college student: An unmet challenge* (pp. 101–116). San Francisco: Jossey-Bass.

MacKinnon, D. W. (1983). Creative architects. In R. S. Albert (Ed.), *Genius and eminence: The social psychology of creativity and exceptional achievement* (pp. 291–301). Elmsford, NY: Pergamon Press.

Magnan, K. S. (1988, September 28). Sexually active students found failing to take precautions against AIDS. *Chronicle of Higher Education, 30,* 1, 32.

Mahoney, E. R. (1979). Sex education in the public schools: A discriminant analysis of characteristics of pro and anti individuals. *Journal of Sex Research, 15,* 276–284.

Malcolm, S., (1986). Why middle school is important to science equity concerns. In I. Weiss (Ed.), *Developing options for managing the National Science Foundation's middle school science education programs.* Research Triangle Park, NC: Research Triangle Institute.

Malina, R. M. (1974). Adolescent changes in size, build, composition and performance. *Human Biology, 46,* 117–131.

Man and woman of the year: The middle Americans (1970, January 5). *Time.*

Mannerino, A. P. (1976). Friendship patterns and altruistic behavior in pre-adolescent males. *Developmental Psychology, 12,* 555–556.

Marantz, S. A., & Mansfield, A. F. (1977). Maternal employment and the development of sex-role stereotyping in five- to eleven-year-old girls. *Child Development, 48,* 668–673.

Marcia, J. E. (1980). Identity in adolescence. In J. Adelson (Ed.), *Handbook of adolescent psychology* (pp. 159–187). New York: Wiley.

Marcoen, A., Goosens, L., & Coes, P. (1987). Loneliness in pre- through late adolescence: Exploring the contributions of a multidimensional approach. *Journal of Youth and Adolescence, 16,* 561–578.

Marcus, J., Hans, S. L., Nagler, S., Auerbach, J. G., Mirsky, A. P., & Aubrey, A. (1987). Review of the NIMH Israel Kibbutz-city study and the Jerusalem infant development study. *Schizophrenia Bulletin, 13,* 425–438.

Marihuana and health (1980). Eighth annual report to the U.S. Congress from the Secretary of Health, Education, and Welfare. Washington, DC: U.S. Government Printing Office.

Marini, M. M. (1978). Sex differences in the determination of adolescent aspirations: A review of research. *Sex Roles, 4,* 723–753.

Marini, M. M., & Greenberger, E. (1978). Sex differences in occupational aspirations and expectations. *Sociology of Work and Occupations, 5,* 147–178.

Marino, D. D., & King, J. C. (1980). Nutritional concerns during adolescence. *Pediatric Clinics of North America, 27,* 125–139.

Marjoribanks, K. (1979). Family environments. In H. J. Walbert (Ed.), *Educational environments and effects* (pp. 15–37). Berkeley, CA: McCuthan.

Marshall, J. M., & Karabenick, S. A. (1975). Self-esteem, fear of success, and occupational choice in female adolescents. In C. Guardo (Ed.), *Readings in adolescence*. New York: Harper & Row.

Marshall, W. A. (1978). Puberty. In F. Falkner & J. M. Tanner (Eds.), *Human growth, Vol. 2: Postnatal growth*. New York: Plenum.

Marshall, W. A., & Tanner, J. M. (1970). Variations in the pattern of pubertal changes in boys. *Archives of Disease in Childhood, 45,* 13.

Marsiglio, W., & Mott, F. L. (1986). The impact of sex education on sexual activity, contraceptive use and premarital pregnancy among American teenagers. *Family Planning Perspectives, 18,* 151–162.

Martin, B. (1975). Parent-child relations. In F. D. Horowitz (Ed.), *Review of child development research* (Vol. 4) (pp. 463–540). Chicago: University of Chicago Press.

Masters, W. H., & Johnson, V. E. (1966). *Human sexual response*. Boston: Little, Brown.

Masters, W. H., & Johnson, V. E. (1970). *Human sexual inadequacy*. Boston: Little, Brown.

Masters, W. H., & Johnson, V. E. (1979). *Homosexuality in perspective*. Boston: Little, Brown.

Masters, W. H., Johnson, V. E., & Kolodny, R. C. (1987). *Human sexuality* (3rd ed.). Glenview, IL: Scott Foresman/Little Brown.

Masterson, J. F. (1967). *The psychiatric dilemma of adolescence*. Boston: Little, Brown.

Masterson, J. F. (1968). The psychiatric significance of adolescent turmoil. *American Journal of Psychiatry, 124,* 1549–1554.

Matarazzo, J. D. (1984). Behavioral health: A 1990 challenge for the health services profession. In J. D. Matarazzo, S. N. Weiss, J. A. Herd, N. E. Miller, & S. M. Weiss (Eds.), *Behavioral health: A handbook of health enhancement and disease prevention* (pp. 3–40). New York: Wiley.

Matarazzo, J. D., Weiss, S. M., Herd, J. A., Miller, N. E., & Weiss, S. M. (Eds.) (1984). *Behavioral health: A handbook of health enhancement and disease prevention*. New York: Wiley.

Matheny, A. P., Jr., Wilson, R. S., Dolan, A. B., & Krantz, J. Z. (1981). Behavior contrasts in twinships: Stability and patterns of differences in childhood. *Child Development, 52,* 579–588.

Matteson, D. R. (1974). Alienation vs. exploration and commitment: Personality and family corollaries of adolescent identity statuses. Report from the Project for Youth Research. Copenhagen: Royal Danish School of Educational Studies.

Matyas, M., & Kahle, J. (1986). *Equitable precollege science and mathematics: A discrepancy model*. Paper presented at the Workshop on Underrepresentation and career differentials of women in science and engineering. Washington, DC: National Academy of Sciences.

Mawby, R. I., McCullough, J. W., & Batta, I. D. (1979). Crime amongst Asian juveniles in Bradford. *International Journal of the Sociology of Law, 7,* 297–306.

McAlister, A. L., Perry, C., & Maccoby, N. (1979). Adolescent smoking: Onset and prevention. *Pediatrics, 63,* 650–658.

McAndrew, G. L. (1981). *Adolescents: Behavior and development*. New York: Holt, Rinehart and Winston.

McCabe, M. P. (1984). Toward a theory of adolescent dating. *Adolescence, 19,* 159–170.

McCabe, M. P., & Collins, J. K. (1979). Sex role and dating orientation. *Journal of Youth and Adolescence, 8,* 407–425.

McCall, R. B., Appelbauam, M. I., & Hogarty, P. S. (1973). Developmental changes in mental performance. *Monographs of the Society for Research in Child Development, 38,* No. 3, 1–84.

McCandless, B. (1970). *Adolescents: Behavior and development*. New York: Holt, Rinehart and Winston.

McCoy, K., & Wibbelsman, C. (1984). *The teenage body book*. New York: Pocket Books.

McGarrell, E. F., & Flanagan, T. J. (Eds.) (1985). *Sourcebook of criminal justice statistics, 1984*. Washington, DC: U.S. Department of Justice.

McGee, M. G. (1979a). *Human spatial abilities*. New York: Praeger.

McGee, M. G. (1979b). Human spatial abilities: Psychometric studies and environmental, genetic, hormonal, and neurological influences. *Psychological Bulletin, 86,* 889–918.

McKnight, C. et al. (1987). *The underachieving curriculum: Assessing U.S. school mathematics from an international perspective*. Champaign, IL: Stipes Publishing Co.

Mead, M. (1970). *Culture and commitment: A study of the generation gap*. Garden City, NY: Doubleday.

Mednick, S. A., Parnas, J., & Schulsinger, F. (1987). The Copenhagen high-risk project. *Schizophrenia Bulletin, 13,* 485–495.

Meikle, S., Peitchinis, J. A., & Pearce, K. (1985). *Teenage sexuality*. San Diego, CA: College-Hill Press.

Meislin, R. J. (1977, November 27). Poll finds more liberal beliefs on marriage and sex roles, especially among the young. *New York Times*, p. 75.

Mensch, B. S., & Kandel, D. B. (1988). Dropping out of high school and drug involvement. *Sociology of Education, 61,* 95–113.

Mesulam, M-M (1990). Schizophrenia and the brain. *New England Journal of Medicine, 322,* 842–844.

Middleton, R., & Snell, P. (1963). Political expression of adolescent rebellion. *American Journal of Sociology, 68,* 527–535.

Miller, D. C. (1959). Short-term therapy with adolescents. *American Journal of Orthopsychiatry, 29,* 772–779.

Miller, G. A. (1983). Personal communication. Cited in Kagan and Segal (1988), p. 281.

Miller, M. L., Chiles, J. A., & Barnes, V. E. (1982). Suicide attempters within a delinquent population. *Journal of Consulting and Clinical Psychology*, **50**, 490–498.

Miller, N. E. (1951). Learnable drives and rewards. In S. S. Stevens (Ed.), *Handbook of experimental psychology* (pp. 435–472). New York: Wiley.

Miller, N. E. (1980). Applications of learning and biofeedback to psychiatry and medicine. In H. J. Kapan, A. M. Freedman, & B. J. Sadock (Eds.), *Comprehensive textbook of psychiatry/III* (pp. 468–484). Baltimore: Williams & Wilkins.

Miller, N. E. (1984). Learning: Some facts and needed research relevant to maintaining health. In J. Matarazzo, S. W. Weiss, J. A. Herd, N. Miller, & S. M. Weiss (Eds.), *Behavioral health: A handbook of health enhancement and disease prevention* (pp. 199–208). New York: Wiley.

Miller, N. E., & Dworkin, B. R. (1977). Effects of learning on visceral functions: Biofeedback. *New England Journal of Medicine*, **296**, 1274–1278.

Miller, N. E., & Dworkin, B. R. (1980). Different ways in which learning is involved in homeostasis. In F. Thompson, L. H. Hicks, & V. B. Shvgrkov (Eds.), *Neural mechanisms of goal-directed behavior and learning*. New York: Academic Press.

Miller, P. Y., & Simon, W. (1968). The development of sexuality in adolescence. In J. Adelson (Ed.), *Handbook of adolescent psychology* (pp. 383–407). New York: Wiley.

Miller, P. Y., & Simon, W. (1979). Do youth really want to work: A comparison of the work values and job perceptions of younger and older men. *Youth and Society*, **10**, 379–404.

Minturn, L., & Lambert, W. W., *et al.* (1964). *Mothers of six cultures: Antecedents of child rearing*. New York: Wiley.

Minuchin, P. (1985). Families and individual development: Provocations from the field of family therapy. *Child Development*, **56**, 289–302.

Minuchin, P. P., & Shapiro, E. K. (1983). The school as a context for social development. In P. H. Mussen (Series Ed.), E. M. Hetherington (Ed.), *Handbook of child psychology*, (4th ed.,). *Vol. 3: Social development*. New York: Wiley.

Minuchin, S. (1974). *Families and family therapy*. Cambridge, MA: Harvard University Press.

Minuchin, S., Rosman, B. L., & Baker, L. (1978). *Psychomatic families: Anorexia nervosa in context*. Cambridge, MA: Harvard University Press.

Mischel, W. (1961a). Father-absence and delay of gratification. *Journal of Abnormal and Social Psychology*, **62**, 116–124.

Mischel, W. (1961b). Preference for delayed reward and social responsibility. *Journal of Abnormal and Social Psychology*, **62**, 1–7.

Mischel, W., & Mischel, H. N. (1976). A cognitive social learning approach to morality and self-regulation. In T. Lickona (Ed.), *Moral development and behavior*. New York: Holt, Rinehart & Winston.

Mittman, A., & Packer, M. (1982). Concerns of seventh-graders about their transition to junior high school. *Journal of Early Adolescence*, **2**, 319–338.

Molotsky, I. (1986, December 16). Surgeon General, citing risks, urges smoke-free workplace. *The New York Times*, p. 14.

Money, J., & Ehrhardt, A. A. (1972). *Man and woman, boy and girl: The differentiation and dimorphism of gender identity from conception to maturity*. Baltimore: Johns Hopkins University Press.

Money, J., Hampson, J. G., & Hampson, J. L. (1955). An examination of some basic sexual concepts: The evidence of human hermaphroditism. *Bulletin of Johns Hopkins Hospital*, **97**, 301–319.

Money, J., Ehrhardt, A. A., & Masica, D. N. (1968). Fetal feminization induced by androgenic insensitivity in the testicular feminizing syndrome: Effect on marriage and maternalism. *Johns Hopkins Medical Journal*, **123**, 105–114.

Money, J., & Schwartz, M. (1977). Dating, romantic and non-romantic friendships, and sexuality in 17 early-treated adrenogenital females, aged 16–25. In P. A. Lee *et al.* (Eds.), *Congenital Adrenal Hyperplasia*. Baltimore: University Park Press.

Montemayor, R. (1984). Maternal employment and adolescents' relations with parents, siblings, and peers. *Journal of Youth and Adolescence*, **13**, 543–557.

Montemayor, R., & Brownlee, J. R. (1987). Fathers, mothers, and adolescents: Gender-based differences in parental roles during adolescence. *Journal of Youth and Adolescence*, **16**, 281–291.

Montemayor, R., & Clayton, M. D. (1983). Maternal employment and adolescent development. *Theory Practice*, **22**, 112–118.

Montemayer, R., & Eisen, M. (1977). The development of self-conceptions from childhood to adolescence. *Developmental Psychology*, **13**, 314–319.

Moore, D., & Schultz, N. (1983). Loneliness at adolescence: Correlates, attributions, and coping. *Journal of Youth and Adolescence*, **12**, 95–100.

Moore, K. A. (1989). *Facts at a glance*. Washington, DC: Child Trends, Inc.

Moore, K. L. (1982). *The developing human: Clinically oriented embryology* (3rd ed.). Philadelphia: Saunders.

Moore, T. W. (1975). Exclusive early mothering and its alternatives. *Scandinavian Journal of Psychology*, **16**, 256–272.

Moos, R. H. (1986). Work as a human context. In M. Pallak & R. O. Perloff, *Psychology and work: Productivity, change, and employment* (pp. 7–52). Washington, DC: American Psychological Association.

Moos, R. H., Moos, B. S., & Kulik, J. A. (1976). College-student abstainers, moderate drinkers, and heavy drinkers: A comparative analysis. *Journal of Youth and Adolescence*, **5**, 349–360.

Morganthau, T. (1986, March 17). Kids and cocaine. *Newsweek*, pp. 58–65.

Morgenthaler, E. (1986, October 7). Although the

scarcities are fewer, some job skills are in short supply. *The Wall Street Journal*, p. 37.

Morison, S. E. (1936). *Three centuries of Harvard.* Cambridge, MA: Harvard University Press.

Morning edition (April 9, 1990). Washington, DC: National Public Radio.

Morrison, D. M. (1985). Adolescent contraceptive behavior: A review. *Psychological Bulletin,* **98,** 538–568.

Morrow, A. J. (1969). *The practical theorist: The life and work of Kurt Lewin.* New York: Basic Books.

Morrow, W. R., & Wilson, R. C. (1961). Family relations of bright high-achieving and under-achieving high school boys. *Child Development, 32,* 501–510.

Morse, B. (1973). Identity status in college women in relation to perceived parent-child relationships. Unpublished doctoral dissertation. Ohio State University.

Morse, N. C., & Weiss, R. S. (1968). The function and meaning of work and the job. In D. G. Zytowski (Ed.), *Vocational behavior* (pp. 7–16). New York: Holt, Rinehart and Winston.

Mortimer, J. T. (1974). Patterns of intergenerational occupational movements: A smallest-space analysis. *American Journal of Sociology, 79,* 1278–1299.

Mortimer, J. T. (1976). Social class, work, and the family: Some implications of the father's occupation for familial relationships and sons' career decisions. *Journal of Marriage and the Family,* **38,** 241–256.

Mortimer, J. T., & Kumka, D. (1982, Winter). A further examination of the "occupational linkage hypothesis." *The Sociological Quarterly,* **23,** 3–16.

Moshman, D., Glover, J. A., & Bruning, R. H. (1987). *Developmental psychology: A topical approach.* Boston: Little, Brown.

Mott, F. L., & Haurin, R. J. (1988). Linkages between sexual activity and alcohol and drug use among American adolescents. *Family Planning Perspectives,* **20,** 128–136.

Mouzakitis, C. (1984). Characteristics of abused adolescents and guidelines for intervention. *Child Welfare,* **63,** 149–157.

Moynihan, D. P. (1986). *Family and nation.* New York: Harcourt Brace Jovanovich.

Mrazek, P. B., & Kempe, C. H. (1981). *Sexually abused children and their families.* Elmsford, NY: Pergamon Press.

Mrazek, P. B., & Mrazek, D. A. (1978). The effects of child sexual abuse. In R. S. Kempe and H. Kempe, *Child abuse* (pp. 223–245). Cambridge, MA: Harvard University Press.

Mueller, E., & Silverman, N. (1989). Peer relations in maltreated children. In D. Cicchetti & V. Carlson (Eds.). *Child maltreatment: Theory and research on the causes and consequences of child abuse and neglect* (pp. 569–578). New York: Cambridge University Press.

Mullis, R. L., & McKinley, K. (1989). Gender-role orientation of adolescent females: Effects on self-esteem and locus of control. *Journal of Adolescent Research,* **4,** 483–505.

Mullis, V. S., & Jenkins, L. B. (1988). *The science report card: Elements of risk and recovery. Trends and achievement based on the 1986 National Assessment.* Princeton, NJ: Educational Testing Service.

Munsinger, H. (1975). The adopted child's IQ: A critical review. *Psychological Bulletin,* **82,** 623–659.

Muraskin, L. D. (1986). Sex education mandates: Are they the answer. *Family Planning Perspectives,* **18,** 170–174.

Murphy, G. (1947). *Personality.* New York: Harper & Row.

Mussen, P. H., Conger, J. J., & Kagan, J. (1974). *Child Development and personality* (4th ed.). New York: Harper & Row.

Mussen, P. H., Conger, J. J., & Kagan, J. (1979). *Child development and personality* (5th ed.). New York: Harper & Row.

Mussen, P. H., Conger, J. J., Kagan, J., & Huston, A. C. (1984). *Child development and personality* (6th ed.). New York: Harper & Row.

Mussen, P. H., Conger, J. J., Kagan, J., & Huston, A. C. (1990). *Child development and personality* (7th ed.). New York: Harper & Row.

Mussen, P. H., & Jones, M. C. (1957). Self-conceptions, motivations, and interpersonal attitudes of late and early maturing boys. *Child Development,* **28,** 243–256.

Mussen, P. H., & Rosenzweig, M. R. *et al.* (1973). *Psychology: An introduction.* Lexington, MA: Heath.

Muus, R. E. (1971). The nature, theory, and historical roots of theories of adolescence. In R. E. Muus (Ed.), *Adolescent behavior and society: A book of readings.* New York: Random House.

Muus, R. E. (1988). *Theories of adolescence* (5th ed.). New York: Random House.

Nash, S. C. (1979). Sex role as a mediator of intellectual functioning. In M. A. Wittig & A. C. Petersen (Eds.), *Sex-related differences in cognitive functioning.* New York: Academic Press.

National adolescent student health survey (1988). Reston, VA: American Alliance for Health, Physical Education, Recreation, and Dance.

National Assessment of Educational Progress (1979). *Changes in mathematical achievement, 1973–1978.* Denver: NAEP/Education Commission of the States.

National Assessment of Educational Progress (1981). *Reading, thinking, and writing: Results from the 1979–80 national assessment of reading and literature.* Denver: Educational Commission of the States.

National Assessment of Educational Progress (1986). *The reading report card: Progress toward excellence in our schools. Trends in reading over four national assessments, 1971–1984.* Princeton, NJ: (NAEP) Educational Testing Service.

National Association of Secondary School Principals (1984). *The mood of American youth.* Reston, VA: Author.

National Center on Child Abuse and Neglect (1981). *Executive summary: National study of the incidence and severity of child abuse and neglect.* (DHHS Publication No. OHDS 81-30329.) Washington, DC: U.S. Government Printing Office.

National Commission on Excellence in Education (1983). *A nation at risk: The imperative for educational reform.* Washington, DC: U.S. Government Printing Office.

National Institute on Drug Abuse (1989, August). "NIDA Capsules" (press release developed from *1988 National Household Survey on Drug Abuse*). Rockville, MD: National Institute on Drug Abuse.

Neimark, E. D. (1975a). Intellectual development during adolescence. In F. D. Horowitz (Ed.), *Review of child development research, Vol. 4.* Chicago: University of Chicago Press.

Neimark, E. D. (1975b). Longitudinal development of formal operations thought. *Genetic Psychology Monographs,* **91,** 171–225.

Neinstein, L. S. (1985). *Adolescent health care: A practical guide.* Baltimore-Munich: Urban & Schwarzenberg.

Nelsen, H. M., Potvin, R. H., & Shields, J. (1977). *The religion of children.* Washington, DC: U.S. Catholic Conference.

Nelson, E. A., & Vangen, P. M. (1971). Impact of father absence on heterosexual behaviors and social development of preadolescent girls in a ghetto environment. *Proceedings, 79th Annual Convention of the American Psychological Association,* **6,** 165–166.

Nemiah, J. C. (1974). Anxiety: Signal, symptom, and syndrome. In S. Arieti & E. B. Brody (Eds.), *American handbook of psychiatry, Vol. III: Adult clinical psychiatry* (pp. 91–109). New York: Basic Books.

Nemiah, J. C. (1988). Psychoneurotic disorders. In A. M. Nicholi, Jr. (Ed.), *The new Harvard guide to psychiatry* (pp. 234–258). Cambridge, MA: Harvard University Press.

Nemiah, J. C., & Uhde, T. W. (1989). Phobic disorders. In H. J. Kaplan & B. J. Sadock, *Comprehensive textbook of psychiatry/V* (5th ed., pp. 972–984). Baltimore, MD: Williams & Wilkins.

New plan keeps students in school (1988, January 27). *The New York Times,* p. 14.

New York Times/CBS Poll (1986, November 14). *The New York Times,* p. 1.

Newcomb, M. D., & Bentler, P. M. (1988). *Consequences of adolescent drug use: Impact on the lives of young adults.* Newbury Park, CA: Sage.

Newcombe, N., & Bandura, M. M. (1983). The effect of age at puberty on spatial ability in girls: A question of mechanism. *Developmental Psychology,* **19,** 215–224.

Newcombe, N., & Dubas, J. S. (1987). Individual differences in cognitive ability: Are they related to timing of puberty? In R. M. Lerner & T. T. Foch (Eds.), *Biological-psychosocial interactions in early adolescence: A Life-span perspective* (pp. 249–302). Hillsdale, NJ: Erlbaum.

Newman, B. M. (1975a). Characteristics of interpersonal behavior among adolescent boys. *Journal of Youth and Adolescence,* **4,** 145–153.

Newman, B. M. (1975b). Interpersonal behavior and preferences for exploration in adolescent boys: A small group study. In J. G. Kelly (Ed.), *The socialization process in the high school years.* New York: Behavioral Publications.

Newsweek Poll (1986, March 31). *Newsweek,* p. 51.

Nicholi, A. M., Jr. (1988). The adolescent. In A. M. Nicholi, Jr. (Ed.), *The new Harvard guide to psychiatry* (pp. 637–664). Cambridge, MA: Harvard University Press.

Nichols, P. L. (1984). Familial mental retardation. *Behavior Genetics,* **14,** 161–170.

Noble, E. P. (Ed.) (1978). *Alcohol and health: Third special report to the U.S. Congress.* Rockville, MD: National Institute on Alcohol Abuse and Alcoholism (preprint edition).

Norback, C. (Ed.) (1980). *The complete book of American surveys.* New York: New American Library.

Norton, A. J., & Moorman, J. E. (1986, April). Marriage and divorce patterns of U.S. women in the 1980s. Paper presented at the annual meeting of the Population Association of America, San Francisco, CA.

Nottelmann, E. D., Susman, E. J., Blue, J. H., Inoff-Germain, G., Dorn, L. D., Loriaux, D. L., Cutler, G. B., & Chrousos, G. P. (1987a). Gonadal and adrenal hormonal correlates of adjustment in early adolescence. In R. M. Lerner, & T. T. Foch (Eds.), *Biological-Psychosocial interactions in early adolescence: A life-span perspective* (pp. 303–324). Hillsdale, NJ: Erlbaum.

Nottelmann, E. D., Susman, E. J., Inoff-Germain, G., Cutler, G. B., Jr., Loriaux, D. L., & Chrousos, G. P. (1987b). Developmental processes in early adolescence: Relations between adolescent adjustment problems and chronological age, pubertal stage, and puberty-related serum hormone levels. *Journal of Pediatrics,* **110,** 473–480.

Nunner-Winkler, G. (1984). Two moralities? A critical discussion of an ethnic of care and responsibility versus an ethic of rights and justice. In W. M. Kurtines & J. L. Gewirtz (Eds.), *Morality, moral behavior, and moral development* (pp. 348–361). New York: Wiley.

Nurnberger, J. I., & Gershon, E. S. (1981). Genetics of affective disorders. In E. Friedman (Ed.), *Depression and antidepressants: Implications for courses and treatment.* New York: Raven.

O'Malley, P. M., Bachman, J. G., & Johnston, L. D. (1984). Period, age, and cohort effects on substance abuse among American youth, 1976–82. *American Journal of Public Health,* **74,** 682–688.

O'Rourke, D. H., Gottesman, I. I., Suarez, B. K., Rice, J., & Reich, T. (1982). Refutation of the general single-locus model for the etiology of schizophrenia. *American Journal of Human Genetics,* **34,** 630–649.

Oates, R. K., Forrest, D., & Peacock, A. (1985). Self-esteem of abused children. *Child Abuse and Neglect,* **9,** 159–164.

Oberlander, M. I., Frauenfelder, K. J., & Heath, H. (1970). Ordinal position, sex of sibling, sex, and personal preferences in a group of eighteen-year-olds. *Journal of Consulting and Clinical Psychology,* **35,** 122–125.

Offer, D., & Offer, J. (1974). Normal adolescent males: The high school and college years. *Journal of the American College Health Association,* **22,** 209–215.

Offer, D., & Offer, J. (1975). *From teenage to young manhood.* New York: Basic Books.

Offer, D., Marcus, D., & Offer, J. L. (1970). A longitudinal study of normal adolescent boys. *American Journal of Psychiatry,* **126,** 917–924.

Offer, D., Ostrov, E., & Howard, K. I. (1981). *The adolescent: A psychological self-portrait.* New York: Basic Books.

Olson, L., & Holmes, W. (1983). *Youth at risk: Adolescents and maltreatment.* Boston, MA: Center for Applied Social Research.

Onat, T., & Ertem, B. (1974). Adolescent female height velocity: Relationships to body measurements, sexual and skeletal maturity. *Human Biology,* **46,** 199–217.

Orlofsky, J. L. (1978). Identity formation, achievement, and fear of success in college men and women. *Journal of Youth and Adolescence,* **7,** 49–62.

Orlofsky, J., Marcia, J., & Lesser, I. (1973). Ego identity status and the intimacy versus isolation crisis of young adulthood. *Journal of Personality and Social Psychology,* **27,** 211–219.

Osborn, S. G., & West, D. J. (1979). Conviction records of fathers and sons compared. *British Journal of Criminology,* **19,** 120–135.

Osborn, S. G. & West, D. J. (1980). Do young delinquents really reform? *Journal of Adolescence,* **3,** 99–114.

Osipow, S. H. (1983). *Theories of career development* (3rd ed.). Englewood Cliffs, NJ: Prentice-Hall.

Osipow, S. H. (1986). Career issues through the life span. In M. Pallak & R. O. Perloff, *Psychology and work: Productivity, change, and employment* (pp. 141–168). Washington, DC: American Psychological Association.

Osofsky, J. D. (1990, Winter). Risk and protective factors for teenage mothers and their infants. *Society for Research in Child Development Newsletter,* pp. 1–2.

Osofsky, J. D., & O'Conell, E. J. (1972). Parent-child interactions: Daughter's effects upon mothers' and fathers' behavior. *Developmental Psychology,* **7,** 157–168.

Osterrieth, P. A. (1969). Adolescence: Some psychological aspects. In G. Caplan & S. Lebovici (Eds.), *Adolescence: Psychosocial perspectives.* New York: Basic Books.

Ouston, J. (1984). Delinquency, family background, and educational attainment. *British Journal of Criminology,* **24,** 2–26.

Packard, V. (1974). *A nation of strangers.* New York: Pocket Books.

Paige, K. E. (1973). Beyond the raging hormone: Women learn to sing the menstrual blues. *Psychology Today,* **7,** 41–46.

Paikoff, R. L., & Brooks-Gunn, J. (in press). Taking fewer chances: Teenage pregnancy prevention programs. *American Psychologist.*

Pallas, A. M. (1984). The determinants of high school dropout. Unpublished Ph.D. dissertation, Johns Hopkins University.

Parke, R. D., & Collmer, C. W. (1975). Child abuse: An interdisciplinary analysis. In E. M. Hetherington, J. W. Hagen, R. Kron, & A. H. Stein (Eds.), *Review of child development research, Vol. 5.* Chicago: University of Chicago Press.

Parker, G., Tupling, H., & Brown, L. B. (1979). A parental bonding instrument. *British Journal of Medical Psychology,* **52,** 1–10.

Parker, J. G., & Asher, S. R. (1987). Peer relations and later adjustment: Are low-accepted children at risk? *Psychological Bulletin,* **102,** 357–389.

Parker, J. G., & Gottman, J. M. (1989). Social and emotional development in a relational context: Friendship interaction from early childhood to adolescence. In T. J. Berndt & G. W. Ladd (Eds.), *Peer relationships in child development* (pp. 95–132). New York: Wiley.

Parlee, M. B. (1980). Positive changes in moods and activation levels during the menstrual cycle in experimentally naive subjects. In A. J. Dan, E. A. Graham, & C. P. Beecher (Eds.), *The menstrual cycle, Volume I: A synthesis of interdisciplinary research.* New York: Springer Publishing Co.

Parry, H. J. (1979). Sample surveys of drug abuse. In R. I. Dupont, A. Goldstein, & J. O'Donnell (Eds.), *Handbook on drug abuse* (pp. 381–394). Washington, DC: U.S. Government Printing Office.

Parry-Jones, W. L. (1985). Adolescent disturbance. In M. Rutter & L. Hersov (Eds.), *Child and adolescent psychiatry: Modern approaches* (pp. 584–598). Oxford: Blackwell Scientific Publications.

Parsons, J E., Kaczala, C. M., & Meece, J. L. (1982). Socialization of achievement attitudes and beliefs: Classroom influences. *Child Development,* **53,** 322–339.

Pascarelli, E. F. (1973). Methaqualone: The quiet epidemic. In R. P. Shafer *et al., Drug use in America: Problem in perspective* (Appendix, Vol. 1) (pp. 102–105). Second report of the National Commission on Marijuana and Drug Abuse. Washington, DC: U.S. Government Printing Office, No. 5266-00004.

Pascual-Leone, J. (1970). A mathematical model for transition in Piaget's developmental stages. *Acta Psychologica,* **32,** 301–345.

Passell, P. (1989, July 16). Forces in society, and Reaganism, helped dig deep hole for poor. *The New York Times*, pp. 1, 12.

Patel, C. (1984). Behavior modification and health enhancement. In J. Matarazzo, S. W. Weiss, J. A. Herd, N. Miller, & S. M. Weiss (Eds.), *Behavioral health: A handbook of health enhancement and disease prevention* (pp. 338–350). New York: Wiley.

Patterson, G. R. (1976). The aggressive child: Victim and architect of a coercive system. In L. A. Hamerlynck, L. C. Handy, & E. J. Mash (Eds.), *Behavior modification and families: 1. Theory and research.* New York: Brunner/Mazel.

Patterson, G. R. (1981). *Coercive family processes.* Eugene, OR: Castalia Publishing Co.

Patterson, G. R. (1982). *Coercive family process.* Eugene, OR: Castalia Press.

Patterson, G. R., DeBarsyshe, B. D., & Ramsey, E. (1989). A developmental perspective on antisocial behavior. *American Psychologist*, **44**, 329–335.

Paulson, M. J., & Lin, T. T. (1972). Family harmony: An etiologic factor in alienation. *Child Development*, **43**, 591–604.

Pearce, J. (1977). The recognition of depressive disorder in children. *Journal of the Royal Society of Medicine*, **71**, 494–500.

Pearce, J. (1982, March). Personal communication. (Cited in Graham, P., & Rutter, M., Adolescent disorders.) In M. Rutter, & L. Hersov (Eds.), *Child and adolescent psychiatry: Modern approaches* (pp. 351–367). Oxford: Blackwell Scientific Publications.

Pearlin, L. J., & Kohn, M. L. (1966). Social class, occupation, and parental values: A cross-national study. *American Sociological Review*, **31**, 466–479.

Pelcovitz, D., Kaplan, S., Samit, C., Krieger, R., & Cornelius, P. (1984). Adolescent abuse: Family structure and implications for treatment. *Journal of Child psychiatry*, **23**, 85–90.

Pelletier, K. R. (1984). *Healthy people in unhealthy places: Stress and fitness at work.* New York: Delacorte Press.

Personick, V. A. (1986). A second look at industry output and employment trends through 1995. In *Employment projections for 1995: Data and methods* (pp. 25–40). Washington, DC: U.S. Government Printing Office.

Peskin, H. (1967). Pubertal onset and ego functioning. *Journal of Abnormal Psychology*, **72**, 1–15.

Peskin, H. (1973). Influence of the developmental schedule of puberty on learning and ego functioning. *Journal of Youth and Adolescence*, **2**, 273–290.

Petersen, A. C. (1979). *Female pubertal development.* In M. Sugar (Ed.), *Female adolescent development* (pp. 23–46). New York: Brunner/Mazel.

Petersen, A. C. (1981). Sex differences in performance on spatial tasks: Biopsychological influences. In H. Ansara, N. Geschwind, A. Galaburda, M. Albert, & N. Gertrell (Eds.), *Sex differences in dyslexia.* Towson, MD: Orton Society.

Petersen, A. C. (1983). Menarche: Meaning of measures and measuring meaning. In S. Golub (Ed.), *Menarche.* Lexington, MA: Heath.

Petersen, A. C. (1988). Adolescent development. *Annual Review of Psychology*, **39**, 503–607.

Petersen, A. C., & Boxer, A. (1982). Adolescent sexuality. In T. Coates, A. Petersen, & C. Perry (Eds.), *Adolescent health: Crossing the barriers* (pp. 237–253). New York: Academic Press.

Petersen, A. C., & Crockett, L. J. (1985). Pubertal timing and grade effects on adjustment. *Journal of Youth and Adolescence*, **14**, 191–206.

Petersen, A. C., & Ebata, A. T. (1987). Developmental transitions and adolescent problem behavior: Implications for prevention and intervention. In K. Hurrelmann (Ed.), *Social Prevention and Intervention.* New York: de Gruyter.

Petersen, A. C., & Gitelson, I. B. (1984). *Toward understanding sex-related differences in cognitive performance.* Unpublished data.

Petersen, A. C., Kennedy, R. E., & Sullivan, P. (in press). Coping with adolescence. In M. E. Colten & S. Gore (Eds.), *Adolescent stress, social relationships and mental health.* New York: Aldine.

Petersen, A. C., Susman, E., & Beard, J. L. (1989). The development of coping responses during adolescence: Endocrine and behavioral aspects. In D. Palermo (Ed.), *Coping with uncertainty: Behavioral and developmental perspectives* (pp. 151–172). Hillsdale, NJ: Erlbaum.

Petersen, A. C., & Taylor, B. (1980). The biological approach to adolescence: Biological change and psychological adaptation. In J. Adelson (Ed.), *Handbook of adolescent psychology* (pp. 117–155). New York: Wiley.

Petersen, R. C. (1980). *Marijuana research findings: 1980.* NIDA Research Monograph 31 (DHHS Publication No ADM 80-1001). Washington, DC: U.S. Government Printing Office.

Petersen, R. C., & Stillman, R. C. (1979). *Phencyclidine (PCP) abuse: An appraisal.* NIDA Research Monograph 21. Washington, DC: U.S. Government Printing Office.

Peterson, D. R., Quay, H. C., & Cameron, G. R. (1959). Personality and background factors in juvenile delinquency as inferred from questionnaire responses. *Journal of Consulting Psychology*, **23**, 392–399.

Peterson, J. L., & Zill, N. (1983, April). Marital disruption, parent/child relationships and behavioral problems in children. Paper presented at the annual meeting of the Society for Research in Child Development, Detroit, MI.

Peterson, J. L., & Zill, N. (1986). Marital disruption, parent-child relationship, and behavior problems in children. *Journal of Marriage and the Family*, **48**, 295–307.

Pfeffer, C. R. (1989). Family characteristics and support systems as risk factors for youth suicidal behavior. In *Report of the Secretary's task force on youth suicide, Volume 2: Risk factors for youth sui-*

cide (pp. 71–87). Washington, DC: U.S. Government Printing Office.

Phillips, C. (1979). The modification of tension headache pain using EMG biofeedback. In J. Stoyva, J. Kamiya, T. X. Barber, N. E. Miller, & D. Shapiro (Eds.), *Biofeedback and self control* (pp. 69–79). Chicago: Aldine.

Piaget, J. (1948). *The moral judgment of the child.* New York: Free Press.

Piaget, J. (1954). *The construction of reality in the child.* New York: Basic Books.

Piaget, J. (1970). Piaget's theory. In P. H. Mussen (Ed.), *Carmichael's manual of child psychology, Vol. 1* (3rd ed., pp. 703–732). New York: Wiley.

Pianta, R., Egeland, B., & Erickson, M. F. (1989). The antecedents of maltreatment: Results of the Mother-Child Interaction Research Project. In D. Cicchetti & V. Carlson, (Eds.), *Child maltreatment: Theory and research on the causes and consequences of child abuse and neglect* (pp. 203–253). New York: Cambridge University Press.

Pikas, A. (1961). Children's attitudes toward rational versus inhibiting parental authority. *Journal of Abnormal and Social Psychology, 62,* 315–321.

Pittel, S. M., Calef, V., Gryler, R. B., Hilles, L., Hofer, R., & Kempner, P. (1971). Developmental factors in adolescent drug use: A study of psychedelic drug users. *Journal of the American Academy of Child Psychiatry, 10,* 640–660.

Pittel, S. M. *et al.* (1971). Developmental factors in adolescent drug use: A study of the psychedelic drug users. *Journal of the American Academy of Child Psychiatry, 10,* 640–660.

Pittel, S. M., & Miller, H. (1976). *Dropping down: The hippie then and now.* Berkeley, CA: Haight Ashbury Research Project, Wright Institute.

Plato (1953). (B. Jewett, trans.). *The dialogues of Plato, Vol. 4* (4th ed.). New York: Oxford University Press (Clarendon Press).

Plomin, R. (1986). *Development, genetics, and psychology.* Hillsdale, NJ: Erlbaum.

Plomin, R., & DeFries, J. C. (1985). A parent-offspring adoption study of cognitive abilities in early childhood. *Intelligence, 9,* 341–356.

Plomin, R., Willerman, L., & Loehlin, J. C. (1976). Resemblance in appearance and the equal environments assumption in twin studies of personality. *Behavior Genetics, 6,* 43–52.

Podd, M. H. (1972). Ego identity status and morality: The relationship between two constructs. *Developmental Psychology, 6,* 497–507.

Pollin, W. (1980, January 16). Health consequences of marijuana use. Statement before the Subcommittee on Criminal Justice, Committee on the Judiciary, U.S. Senate. National Institute on Drug Abuse, Rockville, MD, mimeographed.

Pomeroy, W. B. (1969). *Girls and sex.* New York: Dell (Delacorte Press).

Pope, H. G., Jr., & Hudson, J. I. (1989). Eating disorders. In H. I. Kaplan & B. J. Sadock (Eds.), *Comprehensive textbook of psychiatry/V* (5th ed.,

pp. 1854–1864). Baltimore, MD: Williams & Wilkins.

Popper, C. W. (1986). Child and adolescent pharmacology. In A. J. Solnit, D. J. Cohen, & J. E. Schowalter (Eds.), *Psychiatry, Vol. 6: Child Psychiatry* (pp. 417–439). New York: Basic Books.

Potvin, R. H., Hoge, D. R., & Nelsen, H. M. (1976). Religion and American youth: With emphasis on Catholic adolescents and young adults. Washington, DC: Catholic Conference.

Power, T. G., & Shanks, J. A. (1989). Parents as socializers: Maternal and paternal view. *Journal of Youth and Adolescence, 18,* 203–220.

Prescott, P. S. (1981). *The child savers.* New York: Knopf.

President's Commission on Mental Health (1978). *Report to the President, Vol. 1.* Washington, DC: U.S. Government Printing Office.

Price, J. M., & Dodge, K. A. (1989). Peers contributions to children's social maladjustment: Description and intervention. In T. J. Berndt & G. W. Ladd (Eds.), *Peer relationships in child development* (pp. 341–370). New York: Wiley.

Prinz, R. J., Rosenblum, R. S., & O'Leary, K. D. (1978). Affective communication differences between distressed and nondistressed mother-adolescent dyads. *Journal of Abnormal Child Psychiatry, 6,* 373–383.

Puig-Antich, J. (1986). Psychobiological markers: Effects of age and puberty. In M. Rutter, C. E. Izard, & P. B. Read (Eds.), *Depression in young people: Developmental and clinical perspectives* (pp. 341–382). New York: Guilford Press.

Purkey, S. C., & Smith, M. S. (1983). Effective schools: A review. *Elementary School Journal, 83,* 427–452.

Putka, G. (1988, September 20). SAT scores fall for first time since '80. *Wall Street Journal,* p. 40.

Quay, H. C. (Ed.) (1987a). *Handbook of juvenile delinquency.* New York: Wiley.

Quay, H. C. (1987b). Intelligence. In H. C. Quay (Ed.), *Handbook of juvenile delinquency* (pp. 106–117). New York: Wiley.

Quay, H. C. (1987c). Patterns of delinquent behavior. In H. C. Quay (Ed.), *Handbook of juvenile delinquency* (pp. 118–138). New York: Wiley.

Rachal, J. V. *et al.* (1975). *A national study of adolescent drinking behavior, attitudes, and correlates.* Research Triangle Park, NC: Research Triangle Institute.

Rachal, J. V., Maisto, S. A., Guess, L. L., & Hubbard, R. L. (1984). Alcohol use among adolescents. In National Institute on Alcohol Abuse and Alcoholism, *Alcohol consumption and related problems.* Alcohol and Health Monograph No. 1. Rockville, MD: The Institute.

Rachman, S. J. (1985). The treatment of anxiety disorders: A critique of the implications for psychopathology. In A. H. Tuma & J. D. Maser (Eds.), *Anxiety and the anxiety disorders.* Hillsdale, NJ: Erlbaum.

Radish, E. S., Hofferth, S. L., & Evans, V. J. (1984, August). *Family and household structure fact sheet.* Prepared for the Demographic and Behavioral Sciences Branch, Center for Population Research, National Institute of Child Health and Human Development, Bethesda, MD.

Radke-Yarrow, M., & Sherman, T. (in press). Hard growing. In J. E. Rolf, A. Masten, D. Ciccheti, K. H. Neuchterlein, & S. Weintraub (Eds.) *Risk and protective factors in the development of psychopathology.* New York: Cambridge University Press.

Radloff, L. (1975). Sex differences in depression: The effects of occupation and marital status. *Sex Roles,* **1,** 249–269.

Ramey, E. (1973). Discussion. *Annals of the New York Academy of Sciences,* **208,** 251.

Raskin, P. M. (1986). The relationship between identity and intimacy in early adulthood. *Journal of Genetic Psychology,* **147,** 167–181.

Ravitch, D. O., & Finn, C. E., Jr. (1987). *What do our 17-year-olds know? A report on the first national assessment of history and literature.* New York: Harper & Row.

Ravussin, E., Lillioja, S., Knowler, W. C., Christin, L., Boyce, V., Howard, B. V., & Bogardus, C. (1988). Reduced rate of energy expenditure as a risk factor for body-weight gain. *New England Journal of Medicine,* **318,** 467–472.

Rees, C. D., & Wilborn, B. L. (1983). Correlates of drug abuse in adolescents: A comparison of families of drug abusers with families of nondrug abusers. *Journal of Youth and Adolescence,* **12,** 55–64.

Reeves, D. (1984). Parental power and adolescents' drinking. *Psychological Reports,* **55,** 161–162.

Reid, P. T., & Stephens, D. S. (1985). The roots of future occupations in childhood: A review of the literature on girls and careers. *Youth and Society,* **16,** 267–288.

Reisman, J. M., & Shorr, S. I. (1978). Friendship claims and expectations among children and adults. *Child Development,* **49,** 913–916.

Reiss, A. J. (1952). Social correlates of psychological types of delinquency. *American Sociological Review,* **17,** 710–718.

Report of the Secretary's task force on youth suicide, Vol. 1: Overview and recommendations (1989). Washington, DC: U.S. Government Printing Office.

Report of the Secretary's task force on youth suicide, Vol. 2: Risk factors for youth suicide (1989). Washington, DC: U.S. Government Printing Office.

Rest, J. R. (1979). *Development of judging moral issues.* Minneapolis: University of Minnesota Press.

Rest, J. R. (1983). Morality. In P. H. Mussen, J. Flavel, & E. Markman (Eds.), *Handbook of child psychology, Vol. 3: Cognitive development* (4th ed.). New York: Wiley.

Rest, J. R. (1986). *Moral development: Advances in research and theory.* New York: Praeger.

Reynolds, E. L., & Wines, J. V. (1951). Physical changes associated with adolescence in boys. *American Journal of Diseases of Children,* **82,** 529–547.

Rich, D. (1985). *The forgotten factor in school success—the family.* Washington, DC: Home and School Institute.

Richards, M. H., Boxer, A. M., Petersen, A. C., & Albrecht, R. (1990). Relation of weight to body image in pubertal girls and boys for two communities. *Developmental Psychology,* **26,** 313–321.

Richards, M. H., Petersen, A. C., Boxer, A. M., & Albrecht, R. (1990). Relation of weight to body image in pubertal girls and boys from two communities. *Developmental Psychology,* **26,** 313–321.

Richardson, J. G., & Cranston, J. E. (1981). Social change, parental values, and the salience of sex education. *Journal of Marriage and the Family,* **43,** 547–558.

Richman, L. C., & Lindgren, S. D. (1981). Verbal mediation deficits: Relation to behavior and achievement in children. *Journal of Abnormal Psychology,* **90,** 99–104.

Richman, N., Stevenson, J., & Graham, P. J. (1982). *Pre-school to school: A behavioural study.* London: Academic Press.

Rierdan, J., & Koff, E. (1985a). Timing of menarche and initial menstrual experience. *Journal of Youth and Adolescence,* **14,** 237–244.

Rierdan, J., & Koff, E. (1985b, March). Depression in adolescent girls. Poster presented at the biennial meeting of the Society for Research in Child Development.

Riggs, S., & Cheng, T. (1988). Adolescents' willingness to use a school-based clinic in view of expressed health concerns. *Journal of Adolescent Health Care,* **9,** 208–213.

Ringness, T. A. (1963). *Differences in attitudes toward self and others of academically successful and non-successful ninth-grade boys of superior intelligence.* Madison: University of Wisconsin.

Ringness, T. A. (1967). Identification patterns, motivation, and school achievement of bright junior high school boys. *Journal of Educational Psychology,* **58,** 93–102.

Roberts, J. (1971). *Intellectual development of children by demographic and socioeconomic factors.* Washington, DC: Department of Health, Education and Welfare, Publication No. (HSM) 72-1012 (Data from National Health Survey, Series 11, No. 110).

Roberts, S. (1987, April 23). For homeless struggles include getting to school. *The New York Times,* p. B1.

Roberts, S. B., Savage, J., Coward, W. A., Chew, B., & Lucas, A. (1988). Energy expenditure and intake in infants born to lean and overweight mothers. *New England Journal of Medicine,* **318,** 461–466.

Robertson, M. (1989). False start on manic depression. *Nature,* **342,** 222.

Robins, L. N. (1966). *Deviant children grow up: A*

sociological and psychiatric study of sociopathic personality. Baltimore: Williams & Williams.

Robins, L. N. (1978). Sturdy childhood predictors of adult antisocial behavior: Replications from longitudinal studies. *Psychological Medicine, 8,* 611–622.

Robins, L. N. (1979). Addict careers. In R. I. Dupont, A. Goldstein, & J. O'Donnell (Eds.), *Handbook on drug abuse* (pp. 325–336). Washington, DC: U.S. Government Printing Office.

Robins, L. N. (in press). Changes in conduct disorder over time. In D. C. Farren & J. D. McKinney (Eds.), *Risk in intellectual and psychosocial development.* New York: Academic Press.

Robins, L. N., & Ratcliff, K. S. (1979). Risk factors in the continuation of childhood antisocial behavior into adulthood. *International Journal of Mental Health, 7,* 96–116.

Robins, L., West, P. A., & Herjanic, B. L. (1975). Arrests and delinquency in two generations: A study of black urban families and their children. *Journal of Child Psychology and Psychiatry, 76,* 125–140.

Roche, A. F. (1978). Bone growth and maturation. In F. Falkner & J. M. Tanner (Eds.), *Human growth, Vol. 2: Postnatal growth.* New York: Plenum.

Rodin, J. (1985). Insulin levels, hunger, and food intake: An example of feedback loops in body weight regulation. *Health Psychology, 4,* 1–24.

Rodman, H. (1963). The lower class value stretch. *Social Forces, 42,* 205–215.

Roff, M., Sells, S., & Golden, M. (1972). *Social adjustment and personality development in children.* Minneapolis, MN: University of Minnesota Press.

Rogan, H. (1984, October 30). Executive women find it difficult to balance demands of job, home. *The Wall Street Journal,* pp. 33, 52.

Roscoe, B., Diana, M., & Brooks, R. (1987). Early, middle, and late adolescents' views on dating and factors influencing selection of a dating partner. *Adolescence, 22,* 59–68.

Rosenberg, F. R., & Simmons, R. G. (1975). Sex differences in the self-concept during adolescence. *Sex Roles, 1,* 147–160.

Rosenberg, M. (1965). *Society and the adolescent self-image.* Princeton, NJ: Princeton University Press.

Ross, A. O. (1978). Behavior therapy with children. In S. L. Garfield & A. E. Bergin (Eds.), *Handbook of psychotherapy and behavior change: An empirical analysis* (pp. 591–620). New York: Wiley.

Ross, R. J. (1973). Some empirical parameters of formal thinking. *Journal of Youth and Adolescence, 2,* 167–177.

Rossi, A. S. (1978). A biosocial perspective on parenting. In A. S. Rossi, J. Kagan, & T. K. Harevan (Eds.), *The family* (pp. 11–31). New York: Norton.

Roszak, T. (1969). *The making of a counter culture.* Garden City, NY: Doubleday (Anchor Books).

Rotheram, M. J. (1987). Evaluation of imminent danger for suicide among youth. *American Journal of Orthopsychiatry, 57,* 102–110.

Rowe, I., & Marcia, J. E. (1980). Ego identity status, formal operations, and moral development. *Journal of Youth and Adolescence, 9,* 87–99.

Ruble, D. N. (1977). Premenstrual symptoms. *Science, 197,* 291–292.

Ruble, D. N., & Brooks, J. (1977). Attitudes about menstruation. Paper presented at the Biennial Meeting of the Society for Research in Child Development, New Orleans, March 17–20.

Rumberger, R. W. (1981, April). *Why kids drop out of school.* Paper presented at the annual meeting of the American Educational Research Association, Los Angeles, CA.

Rumberger, R. W. (1983, Summer). Dropping out of high school: The influence of race, sex, and family background. *American Education Research Journal,* 199–200.

Russell, G. F. M. (1985). Anorexia and bulimia nervosa. In M. Rutter & L. Hersov (Eds.), *Child and adolescent psychiatry: Modern approaches* (pp. 625–637). Oxford: Blackwell Scientific Publications.

Rutter, M. (1979). Maternal deprivation 1972–1978: New findings, new concepts, new approaches. *Child Development, 50,* 283–305.

Rutter, M. (1980). *Changing youth in a changing society: Patterns of adolescent development and disorder.* Cambridge, MA: Harvard University Press.

Rutter, M. (1983). School effects on pupil progress: Research findings and policy implications. In L. Shulman & G. Sykes (Eds.), *Handbook of teaching and policy* (pp. 3–41). New York: Longmans.

Rutter, M. (1989). Intergenerational continuities and discontinuities in serious parenting difficulties. In D. Cicchetti & V. Carlson, (Eds.), *Child maltreatment: Theory and research on the causes and consequences of child abuse and neglect* (pp. 317–348). New York: Cambridge University Press.

Rutter, M., & Garmezy, N. (1983). Developmental psychopathology. In P. H. Mussen (Series Ed.) & E. M. Hetherington (Ed.), *Handbook of child psychology, Vol. IV: Socialization, personality and social development* (pp. 775–911). New York: Wiley.

Rutter, M., & Giller, H. (1984). *Juvenile delinquency: Trends and perspectives.* New York: Guilford.

Rutter, M., Izard, C. E., & Read, P. B. (1986). *Depression in young people: Developmental and clinical perspectives.* New York: Guilford Press.

Rutter, M., Maughan, B., Mortimore, P., & Ouston, J. (1979). *Fifteen thousand hours: Secondary schools and their effects on children.* Cambridge, MA: Harvard University Press.

Rutter, M., Tizard, J., & Whitmore, K. (1970/1981). *Education, health and behavior.* Huntington, NY: Krieger (Original work published 1970, London: Longmans).

Ryan, N. D., & Puiz-Antich, J. (1986). Affective illness in adolescence. In A. J. Frances & R. E. Hales (Eds.), *Psychiatry update: American Psychiatric Association Annual Review, Vol. 5.* Washington, DC: American Psychiatric Association Press.

Ryan, N. D., Puig-Antich, J., Ambrosini, P., Rabinovich, H., Robinson, D., Nelson, B., Iyengar, S., & Twomey, J. (1987). The clinical picture of major depression in children and adolescents. *Archives of General Psychiatry, 44,* 854–861.

Sadock, V. A. (1985). Psychosexual dysfunctions and treatment. In H. J. Kaplan & B. J. Sadock (Eds.), *Comprehensive textbook of psychiatry/IV, Vol. I* (4th ed., pp. 1077–1090). Baltimore, MD: Williams & Wilkins.

Sampson, E. E., & Korn, H. A. (Eds.) (1970). *Student activism and dissent: Alternatives for social change.* San Francisco: Jossey-Bass.

Sanders, B., & Soares, M. P. (1986). Sexual maturation and spatial ability in college students. *Developmental Psychology, 22,* 199–203.

Sanders, B., Soares, M. P., & D'Aquila, J. M. (1982). The sex difference on one test of spatial visualization: A nontrivial difference. *Child Development, 53,* 1106–1110.

Santrock, J. W. (1972). The relation of onset and type of father absence to cognitive development. *Child Development, 43,* 455–469.

Santrock, J. W. (1987). *Adolescence: An introduction* (3rd ed.). Dubuque, IA: Wm. C. Brown Publishers.

Santrock, J. W., & Warshak, R. A. (1979). Father custody and social development in boys and girls. *Journal of Social Issues, 35*(4), 112–135.

Santrock, J. W., & Warshak, R. A. (1986). Development, relationships, and legal/clinical considerations in father-custody families. In M. E. Lamb (Ed.), *The father role: Applied perspectives.* New York: Wiley.

Santrock, J. W., Warshak, R., Lindbergh, C., & Meadows, L. (1982). Children's and parents' observed social behavior in stepfather families. *Child Development, 53,* 472–480.

Sarason, I. G. (1978). A cognitive social learning approach to juvenile delinquency. In R. Hare & D. Schilling (Eds.), *Psychopathic behavior: Approaches to research* (pp. 299–317). New York: Wiley.

Sarason, I. G., & Ganzer, V. J. (1973). Modeling and group discussion in the rehabilitation of juvenile delinquents. *Journal of Counseling Psychology, 20,* 442–449.

Sarason, S. B. (1983). *Schooling in America: Scapegoat and salvation.* New York: The Free Press.

Savin-Williams, R. C. (1980a). Dominance hierarchies in groups of late adolescent males. *Journal of Youth and Adolescence, 9,* 75–83.

Savin-Williams, R. C. (1980b). Social interactions of adolescent females in natural groups. In H. C. Foot, A. J. Chapman, & J. R. Smith (Eds.), *Friendship and social relations in children.* New York: Wiley.

Scanlon, J. (1975). *Self-reported health behavior and attitudes of youths 12–17 years.* Washington, D.C.: Department of Health, Education, and Welfare, Publication No. (HRA) 75-1629 (Data from National Health Survey, Series 11, No. 147).

Scarr, S., & Carter-Saltzman, L. (1979). Twin method: Defense of a critical assumption. *Behavior Genetics, 9,* 527–542.

Scarr, S., & Carter-Saltzman, L. C. (1982). Genetics and intelligence. In R. J. Sternberg (Ed.), *Handbook of human intelligence* (pp. 792–896). New York: Cambridge University Press.

Scarr, S., & Kidd, K. K. (1983). Developmental behavior genetics. In M. Haith & J. Campos (Eds.), P. H. Mussen (Series Ed.), *Handbook of child psychology: Vol. 2. Infancy and developmental psychobiology* (pp. 345–435). New York: Wiley.

Scarr, S., & Weinberg, R. A. (1976, October). IQ test performance of black children adopted by white families. *American Psychologist, 31,* 726–739.

Schacht, R. (1971). *Alienation.* Garden City, NY: Doubleday.

Schachter, S. (1964). Birth order and sociometric choice. *Journal of Abnormal and Social Psychology, 68,* 453–456.

Schaefer, E. S. (1959). A circumplex model for maternal behavior. *Journal of Abnormal and Social Psychology, 59,* 226–235.

Schaefer, E. S. (1965). A configurational analysis of children's reports of parent behavior. *Journal of Consulting Psychology, 29,* 552–557.

Schaie, K. W., & Hertzog, C. (1983). Fourteen-year cohort-sequential analysis of adult intellectual development. *Developmental Psychology, 19,* 531–543.

Schaie, K. W., & Willis, S. L. (1986). Can decline in adult intellectual functioning be reversed? *Developmental Psychology, 23,* 223–232.

Schiff, M., Duyme, M., Dumaret, A., & Tomkiewicz, S. (1982). How much could we boost scholastic achievement and IQ scores: A direct answer from a French adoption study. *Cognition, 12,* 165–196.

Schmidt, G. (1975). Male-female differences in sexual arousal and behavior during and after exposure to sexually explicit stimuli. *Archives of Sexual Behavior, 1,* 353–364.

Schmidt, G., & Sigusch, V. (1973). Women's sexual arousal. In J. Zubin & J. Money (Eds.), *Contemporary sexual behavior: Critical issues in the 1970s* (pp. 117–145). Baltimore: Johns Hopkins University Press.

Schofield, J. (1981). Complementary and conflicting identities: Images and interaction in an interracial school. In S. Asher & J. Gottman (Eds.), *The development of children's friendships* (pp. 53–90). Cambridge: Cambridge University Press.

Schorr, L. (Ed.) (1981). *Better health for our children: A national strategy. The report of the Select Panel for the Promotion of Child Health, Vol. I: Major findings and recommendations.* Washington, DC: U.S. Government Printing Office.

Schorr, L. B. with Schorr, D. (1988). *Within our reach: Breaking the cycle of disadvantage and despair.* New York: Doubleday/Anchor.

Schuckit, M., Goodwin, D. W., & Winokur, G. (1972). The half-sibling approach in a genetic study of alcoholism. In M. Roff, L. N. Rolins, & M. Pollack (Eds.), *Life history research in psychopathology, Vol. 2.* Minneapolis, MN: University of Minneapolis Press.

Schuerger, J. M., & Kuna, D. L. (1987). Adolescent personality and school and college performance: A follow-up study. *Psychology in the Schools, 24,* 281–285.

Schulman, R., & Kende, B. (1988). A study of runaways from a short-term diagnostic center. *Residential Treatment for Children and Youth, 5,* 11–31.

Schultz, T. R. (1980). Development of the concept of intention. In W. A. Collins (Ed.), *Minnesota symposia on child psychology* (Vol. 13). Hillsdale, NJ: Erlbaum.

Schwartz, L. A., Barnett, M. J., & Sabor, G. (1985). Family therapy for bulimia. In D. M. Garner & P. E. Garfinkel (Eds.), *Handbook of psychotherapy for anorexia nervosa and bulimia* (pp. 280–307). New York: Guilford Press.

Scott, R. M. (1980). Coordinating services for runaway youth: The case of New York City. *Journal of Family Issues, 1,* 308–312.

Sebald, H. (1984). *Adolescence: A social psychological analysis* (3rd ed.). Englewood Cliffs, NJ: Prentice-Hall.

Sebald, H., & White, B. (1980). Teenagers divided reference groups: Uneven alignment with parents and peers. *Adolescence, 15,* 579–984.

Sechrest, L., & Rosenblatt, A. (1987). Research methods. In H. C. Quay (Ed.), *Handbook of juvenile delinquency* (pp. 417–450). New York: Wiley.

Seebach, S. E., & Norris, R. C. (1989). Brunswikian model for body image research. *Journal of Adolescence Research, 4,* 299–318.

Seeman, M. (1975). Alienation studies. In A. Inkeles, J. Coleman, & N. Smelser (Eds.), *Annual review of sociology, Vol. I.* Palo Alto, CA: Annual Reviews, Inc.

Segal, N. L. (1985). Monozygotic and dizygotic twins: A comparative analysis of mental ability profiles. *Child Development, 56,* 1051–1058.

Seginer, R. (1983). Parent's educational expectations and children's academic achievements: A literature review. *Merrill-Palmer Quarterly, 29,* 1–23.

Seligman, M. E. P., & Peterson, C. (1986). A learned helplessness perspective on childhood depression: Theory and research. In M. Rutter, C. Izard, & P. Read (Eds.), *Depression in young people: Developmental and clinical perspectives* (pp. 223–249). New York: Guilford Press.

Selman, R. L. (1980). *The growth of interpersonal understanding: Developmental and clinical analyses.* New York: Academic Press.

Selman, R. L., & Selman, A. D. (1979). Children's ideas about friendship: A new theory. *Psychology Today, 13,* No. 4, 71ff.

Senn, M. J. E., & Solnit, A. J. (1968). *Problems in child behavior and development.* Philadelphia: Lea & Febiger.

Sennett, R. (1977). *The fall of public man.* New York: Knopf.

Sex education and sex related behavior (1986). *Family Planning Perspectives, 18,* 150, 192.

Shafer, R. P. *et al.* (1972). *Marihuana: A signal of misunderstanding. The official report of the National Commission on Marihuana and Drug Abuse.* New York: New American Library.

Shaffer, D. (1985). Depression, mania, and suicidal acts. In M. Rutter & L. Hersov (Eds.), *Child and adolescent psychiatry: Modern approaches* (2nd ed., pp. 698–719). Oxford: Blackwell Scientific Publications.

Shaffer, D. (1986). Development factors in child and adolescent suicide. In M. Rutter, C. E. Izard, & P. B. Read (Eds.), *Depression in young people: Clinical and developmental perspectives* (pp. 383–398). New York: Guilford Press.

Shah, F., & Zelnik, M. (1981). Parent and peer influence on sexual behavior, contraceptive use, and pregnancy experience of young women. *Journal of Marriage and the Family, 43,* 339–348.

Shannon, L. W. (1981). *Assessing the relationship of adult criminal careers to juvenile careers.* Washington, DC: National Institute of Juvenile Justice and Delinquency Prevention.

Shantz, C. U. (1975). The development of social cognition. In E. M. Hetherington (Ed.), *Review of Child Development Research, (Vol. 5).* Chicago: University of Chicago Press.

Shantz, C. U. (1983). Social cognition. In P. H. Mussen (Series Ed.), J. H. Flavell & E. M. Markman (Eds.), *Handbook of child psychology, Vol. 3: Cognitive development* (pp. 495–555, 4th ed.). New York: Wiley.

Shapiro, D., & Crowley, J. E. (1982). Aspirations and expectations of youth in the United States, Part 2: Employment activity. *Youth and Society, 14,* 33–58.

Shapiro, D., & Surwit, R. S. (1979). Biofeedback. In O. F. Pomerleau & J. P. Brady (Eds.), *Behavioral medicine: Theory and practice* (pp. 45–74). Baltimore: Williams & Wilkins.

Sharabany, R., Gershoni, R., & Hoffman, J. E. (1981). Girlfriend, boyfriend: Age and sex differences in intimate friendship. *Developmental Psychology, 17,* 800–808.

Shaw, J. A. (1988). Childhood depression. *Medical Clinics of North America, 72,* 831–845.

Shaw, M. E., & White, D. L. The relationship between child-parent identification and academic underachievement. *Journal of Clinical Psychology, 21,* 10–13.

Sherman, S. J., Judd, C. M., & Park, B. (1989). Social cognition. *Annual Review of Psychology, 40,* 281–326.

Shinn, M. (1978). Father absence and children's cognitive development. *Psychological Bulletin, 85,* 295–324.

Shorter, E. (1975). *The making of the modern family.* New York: Basic Books.

Siegelman, M. (1974). Parental background of homosexual and heterosexual women. *British Journal of Psychiatry*, **124**, 14–21.

Siegler, R. S., & Richards, D. D. (1982). The development of intelligence. In R. J. Sternberg (Ed.), *Handbook of human intelligence* (pp. 897–970). New York: Cambridge University Press.

Silberman, C. E. (1970). *Crisis in the classroom: The remaking of American education.* New York: Random House.

Silverberg, S. B., & Steinberg, L. (1987). Adolescent autonomy, parent-adolescent conflict, and parental well-being. *Journal of Youth and Adolescence*, **16**, 293–312.

Simmons, R. G., R. Blyth, D. A. (1987). *Moving into adolescence: The impact of pubertal change and school context.* Hawthorne, NY: Aldine de Gruyter.

Simmons, R. G., Blyth, D. A., & McKinney, K. L. (1983). The social and psychological effects of puberty on white females. In J. Brooks-Gunn & A. Petersen (Eds.), *Girls at puberty: Biological and social perspectives* (pp. 229–272). New York: Plenum.

Simmons, R. G., Blyth, D. A., Van Cleave, E. F., & Bush, D. M. (1979). Entry into early adolescence: The impact of school structure, puberty, and early dating on self-esteem. *American Sociological Review*, **44**, 948–967.

Simmons, R. B., Burgeson, R., Carlton-Ford, S., & Blyth, D. A. (1987). The impact of cumulative change in early adolescence. *Child Development*, **58**, 1220–1234.

Simmons, R. G., & Rosenberg, F. R. (1975). Sex, sex roles, and self-image. *Journal of Youth and Adolescence*, **4**, 229–258.

Simmons, R. G., Rosenberg, F., & Rosenberg, M. (1973). Disturbance in the self-image at adolescence. *American Sociological Review*, **38**, 553–568.

Simons, R. L., Robertson, J. F., & Downs, W. R. (1989). The nature of the association between parental rejection and delinquent behavior. *Journal of Youth and Adolescence*, **18**, 297–310.

Simpson, R. L. (1962). Parental influence, anticipatory socialization, and social mobility. *American Sociological Review*, **27**, 517–522.

Single, E., Kandel, D., & Faust, R. (1974). Patterns of multiple drug use in high school. *Journal of Health and Social Behavior*, **151**, 344–357.

Sizer, T. (1984). *Horace's compromise: The dilemma of the American high school.* Boston: Houghton Mifflin.

Slappy, C. A. (1985). College student drug use: A note on some correlates of cessation. *Youth and Society*, **16**, 457–470.

Slater, P. (1971). *Pursuit of loneliness: American culture at the breaking point.* Boston: Beacon Press.

Small, S. A., Eastman, G., & Cornelius, S. (1988). Adolescent autonomy and parental stress. *Journal of Youth and Adolescence*, **17**, 377–391.

Smith, D. E., & Luce, J. (1971). *Love needs care.* Boston: Little, Brown.

Smith, G. J., & Danielsson, A. (1982). *Anxiety and defensive strategies in childhood and adolescence.* New York: International Universities Press.

Smith, G. M., & Fogg, C. P. (1978). Psychological predictors of early use, late use, and nonuse of marihuana among teenage students. In D. B. Kandel (Ed.), *Longitudinal research on drug use: Empirical findings and methodological issues.* Washington, DC: Hemisphere Publishing Corporation.

Smith, H. C. (1969). *An investigation of the attitudes of adolescent girls toward combining marriage, motherhood and a career.* Doctoral dissertation, Columbia University. Ann Arbor, MI: University Microfilms, No. 69-8089.

Smith, R. E. (Ed.) (1979). *The subtle revolution: Women at work.* Washington, DC: The Urban Institute.

Smith, S. R. (1975). Religion and the conception of youth in seventeenth century England. *History of Childhood Quarterly: The Journal of Psychohistory*, **2**, 493–516.

Smith, T. E. (1981). Adolescent agreement with perceived maternal and paternal educational goals. *Journal of Marriage and the Family*, **43**, 85–93.

Smoking and health: A report of the Surgeon General (1979). (DHEW Publication No. (PHS) 79-50066, U.S. Department of Health, Education and Welfare). Washington, DC: U.S. Government Printing Office (No. 017-000-00218-0).

Snow, R. E. (1986). Individual differences and the design of educational programs. *American Psychologist*, **41**, 1029–1039.

Snow, R. E., & Yalow, E. (1982). Education and intelligence. In R. J. Sternberg (Ed.), *Handbook of human intelligence* (pp. 493–585). New York: Cambridge University Press.

Snyder, J., & Patterson, G. R. (1987). Family interaction and delinquent behavior. In H. C. Quay (Ed.), *Handbook of juvenile delinquency* (pp. 216–243). New York: Wiley.

Sonnenstein, F. S., Pleck, J. H., & Ku, L. C. (1989). Sexual acting, condom use and AIDS awareness among adolescent males. *Family Planning Perspectives*, **21**, 152–158.

Sontag, L. W., Baker, C. T., & Nelson, V. L. (1958). Mental growth and personality: A longitudinal study. *Monographs of the Society for Research in Child Development*, **23**, No. 68, 1–143.

Sorensen, R. C. (1973). *Adolescent sexuality in contemporary America: Personal values and sexual behavior ages 13–19.* New York: Abrams.

Spacks, P. M. (1981). *The adolescent idea: Myths of youth and the adult imagination.* New York: Basic Books.

Spanier, G. B., & Furstenberg, F. F. (1982). Adjustment to separation and divorce: A qualitative analysis. In M. B. Sussman & M. Steinmetz (Eds.), *Handbook of Marriage and the Family.* New York: Plenum.

Spearman, C. (1927). *The abilities of man*. London: Macmillan.

Spence, J. T. (1985). Gender identity and its implications for concepts of masculinity and femininity. In T. B. Sonderegger (Ed.), *Nebraska symposium on motivation: Psychology and gender, Vol. 32*. Lincoln: University of Nebraska Press.

Spence, J. T., & Helmreich, R. L. (1978). *Masculinity and femininity: Their psychological dimensions, correlates, and antecedents*. Austin, TX: University of Texas Press.

Spence, J. T., Helmreich, R. L., & Holahan, C. K. (1979). Negative and positive components of psychological masculinity and femininity and their relationships to self-reports of neurotic and acting-out behaviors. *Journal of Personality and Social Psychology, 37,* 1673–1682.

Spickelmeier, J. L. (1983). *College experience and moral judgment development*. Doctoral dissertation. Minneapolis, MN: University of Minnesota.

Spock, B. (1946). *Baby and child care*. New York: Pocket Books.

Sroufe, L. A., & Fleeson, J. (1986). Attachments and the construction of relationships. In W. W. Hartup & Z. Rubin (Eds.), *Relationships and development*. Hillsdale, NJ: Erlbaum.

St. Clair, S., & Day, H. D. (1979). Ego identity status and values among high school females. *Journal of Youth and Adolescence, 8,* 317–326.

Steele, B. (1976). Violence within the family. In R. E. Helfer & C. H. Kempe (Eds.), *Child abuse and neglect: The family and the community* (pp. 3–24). Cambridge, MA: Ballinger.

Steele, B. (1987). Psychodynamics. In R. E. Helfer & R. S. Kempe, *The battered child* (4th ed.). Chicago: University of Chicago Press.

Steinberg, D. (1985). Psychotic and other severe disorders in adolescence. In M. Rutter & L. Hersov (Eds.), *Child and adolescent psychiatry: Modern approaches* (pp. 567–583). Oxford: Blackwell Scientific Publications.

Steinberg, D. (1986). *The adolescent unit: Work and teamwork in adolescent psychiatry*. New York: Wiley.

Steinberg, L. D. (1981). Transformations in family relations at puberty. *Developmental Psychology, 17,* 833–840.

Steinberg, L. (1985). *Adolescence*. New York: Knopf.

Steinberg, L. (1987). Recent research on the family at adolescence: The extent and nature of sex differences. *Journal of Youth and Adolescence, 16,* 191–197.

Steinberg, L. (1988). Reciprocal relation between parent-child distance and pubertal maturation. *Developmental Psychology, 24,* 122–128.

Steinberg, L., Elmen, J. D., & Mounts, N. S. (1989). Authoritative parenting, psychosocial maturity, and academic success among adolescents. *Child Development, 60,* 1424–1436.

Steinberg, L., Greenberger, E., Vaux, A., & Ruggiero, M. (1981). Effects of early work experience on adolescent occupational socialization. *Youth and Society, 12,* 403–422.

Steinberg, L. D., & Hill, J. P. (1978). Patterns of family interaction as a function of age, the onset of puberty, and formal thinking. *Developmental Psychology, 14,* 683–684.

Steinberg, L. D., & Silverberg, S. B. (1986). The vicissitudes of autonomy in early adolescence. *Child Development, 57,* 975–985.

Stephenson, S. P. (1979). From school to work: A transition with job-search implications. *Youth and Society, 11,* 114–133.

Sternberg, R. J. (Ed.) (1982a). *Handbook of human intelligence*. New York: Cambridge University Press.

Sternberg, R. J. (1982b). Reasoning, problem solving, and intelligence. In R. J. Sternberg (Ed.), *Handbook of human intelligence* (pp. 227–351). New York: Cambridge University Press.

Sternberg, R. J. (1985). *Beyond IQ: A triarchic theory of human intelligence*. Cambridge: Cambridge University Press.

Sternberg, R. J., & Nigro, G. (1980). Developmental patterns in the solution of verbal analogies. *Child Development, 51,* 27–38.

Sternberg, R. J., & Powell, J. S. (1983). The development of intelligence. In P. H. Mussen (Series Ed.), J. H. Flavell & E. M. Markman (Eds.), *Handbook of child psychology, Vol. 3: Cognitive development* (pp. 341–419, 4th ed.). New York: Wiley.

Sternberg, R. J., & Rifkin, B. (1979). The development of analogical reasoning processes. *Journal of Experimental Child Psychology, 27,* 195–232.

Stevenson, W. (1978). The relationship between early work experience and future employability. In A. Adams & G. Mangum (Eds.), *The lingering crisis of youth unemployment*. Kalamazoo, MI: W. E. Upjohn Institute for Employment Research.

Stokols, D. (1975). Toward a psychological theory of alienation. *Psychological Review, 82,* 26–44.

Stoller, R. J. (1980). Gender identity disorders. In H. I. Kaplan, A. M. Freedman, & B. J. Sadock (Eds.), *Comprehensive textbook of psychiatry, Vol. 2* (3rd ed., pp. 1695–1705). Baltimore: Williams & Wilkins.

Stone, L. H., Miranne, A. C., & Ellis, G. J. (1979). Parent-peer influence as a predictor of marijuana use. *Adolescence, 14,* 115–121.

Stone, L. J., & Church, J. (1973). *Childhood and adolescence: A psychology of the growing person* (3rd ed.). New York: Random House.

Storr, C. (1975). *Growing up: A practical guide to adolescence for parents and children*. London: Arrow Books.

Stoyva, J. M. (1979). Musculoskeletal and stress-related disorders. In O. F. Pomerleau & J. P. Brady (Eds.), *Behavioral medicine: Theory and practice* (pp. 155–176). Baltimore: Williams & Wilkins.

Striegel-Moore, R. H., Silberstein, L. R., & Rodin, J. (1986). Toward an understanding of risk factors for bulimia. *American Psychologist, 41,* 246–263.

Student survey (1971, September). *Playboy,* 118ff.

Student survey (1976). What's really happening on campus. *Playboy,* **23,** 128–169.

Study finds women smokers try quitting less than men (1986, November 29). *The New York Times,* p. 1.

Study says abuse of cocaine may cause seizures (1986, September 28). *The New York Times,* p. 12.

Stunkard, A. J., Harris, J. R., Pedersen, N. L., & McClearn, G. E. (1990). The body-mass index of twins who have been reared apart. *New England Journal of Medicine,* **322,** 1483–1487.

Stunkard, A. J. (1985). Obesity. In H. I. Kaplan & B. J. Sadock (Eds.), *Comprehensive textbook of psychiatry/IV* (4th ed., pp. 1133–1142). Baltimore, MD: Williams & Wilkins.

Suddath, R. L., Christison, G. W.,Torrey, E. F., Casanova, M. F., & Weinberger, D. R. (1990). Anatomical abnormalities in the brains of monozygotic twins discordant for schizophrenia. *New England Journal of Medicine,* **322,** 789–794.

Sue, D. (1979). Erotic fantasies of college students during coitus. *Journal of Sex Research,* **15,** 299–305.

Sundheim, B. (1963). The relationships between achievement, affiliation, sex role concepts, academic grades, and curricular choice. *Dissertation Abstracts,* **23,** 3471.

Super, D. E. (1967). *The psychology of careers.* New York: Harper & Row.

Super, D. E. (1980). A life-span life-space approach to career development. *Journal of Vocational Behavior,* **16,** 282–298.

Super, D. E., & Hall, D. T. (1978). Career development: Exploration and planning. *Annual Review of Psychology,* **29,** 333–372.

Super, D. E., Starishevsky, R., Matlin, N., & Jordaan, J. P. (1963). *Career development: Self concept theory.* New York: College Entrance Examination Board.

Susman, E. J., Inoff-Germaine, G., Loriaux, D. L., Cutler, G. B., Jr., & Chrousos, G. P. (1987). Hormones, emotional dispositions, and aggressive attributes in young adolescents. *Child Development,* **58,** 1114–1134.

Susman, E. J., Nottelman, E. O., Inoff-Germain, G. E., Dorn, L. D., Cutler, G. B., Loriaux, D. L., & Chrensos, G. P. (1985). The relation of relative hormonal levels and physical development and social-emotional behavior in young adolescents. *Journal of Youth and Adolescence,* **14,** 245–264.

Sutton-Smith, B., Roberts, J. M., & Rosenberg, B. G. (1964). Sibling associations and role involvement. *Merrill-Palmer Quarterly on Behavioral Development,* **10,** 25–38.

Swanson, G. E. (1988). *Ego defenses and the legitimation of behavior.* Cambridge: Cambridge University Press.

Swope, G. W. (1980). Kids and cults: Who joins and why? *Media and Methods,* **16,** 18–21.

Tanfer, K., & Cope, L. (1989). *The national survey of adolescent males.* Philadelphia, PA: Institute for Social Research, Temple University.

Tangri, S. S. (1972). Determinants of occupational role innovation among college women. *Journal of Social Issues,* **28,** 177–199.

Tanner, J. M. (1962). *Growth at adolescence* (2nd ed.). Philadelphia: Davis.

Tanner, J. M. (1968). Growth of bone, muscle and fat during childhood and adolescence. In G. A. Lodge (Ed.), *Growth and development of mammals.* London: Butterworths.

Tanner, J. M. (1970). Physical growth. In P. H. Mussen (Ed.), *Carmichael's manual of child psychology, Vol. I* (3rd ed., pp. 77–156). New York: Wiley.

Tanner, J. M. (1971). Sequence, tempo, and individual variation in the growth and development of boys and girls aged twelve to sixteen. *Daedalus,* **100,** No. 4, 907–930.

Tapp, J. L., & Levine, F. J. (1972). Compliance from kindergarten to college: A speculative research note. *Journal of Youth and Adolescence,* **1,** 233–249.

Tarler-Benlolo, L. (1978). The role of relaxation in biofeedback training. *Psychological Bulletin,* **85,** 727–755.

Task Force on Pediatric Aids, American Psychological Association (1989). Pediatric AIDS and human immunodeficiency virus infection. *American Psychologist,* **44,** 258–264.

Task Force on Teaching as a Profession (1986). *A nation prepared: Teachers for the 21st century.* Washington, D.C.: Carnegie Forum on Education and the Economy.

Taylor, A. III (1986, August 18). Why women managers are bailing out. *Fortune,* pp. 16–23.

Taylor, R. G. (1964). Personality traits and discrepant achievement: A review. *Journal of Counseling Psychology,* **11,** 76–82.

Teenage pregnancy: The problem that hasn't gone away (1981). New York: Alan Guttmacher Institute, Planned Parenthood Federation of America.

Terman, L. M., & Merrill, M. A. (1960). *Stanford-Binet intelligence scale. Manual for 3rd revision.* Boston: Houghton Mifflin.

Tesch, S. (1983). Review of friendship development across the life span. *Human Development,* **26,** 266–276.

Tharp, M. (1987, March 10). High schoolers in U.S. lack drive of Japan's but show spontaneity. *The Wall Street Journal,* pp. 1, 14.

The forgotten half: Pathways to success for America's youth and young families (1988). Washington, DC: Youth and America's Future: The William T. Grant Commission on Work, Family, and Citizenship.

The New York Times/CBS News Poll (1989, September 12). *The New York Times,* p. A14.

The office of Christian parents. Cambridge: 1616. Cited in P. Aries (1962). *Centuries of childhood: A social history of family life* (pp. 18–22). New York: Random House (Vintage Books).

The youth crime plague (1977, July 11). *Time*, pp. 18–28.

Thissen, P., Bock, R. D., Wainer, H., & Roche, A. F. (1976). Individual growth in stature: A comparison of four growth studies in the U.S.A. *Annals of Human Biology*, **3**, 529–542.

Thoma, S. J. (1984). *Estimating gender differences in the comprehension and preference of moral issues.* Unpublished manuscript, Minneapolis, MN: University of Minnesota.

Thomas, C. B. (1973). The relationship of smoking and habits of nervous tension. In W. L. Dunn, Jr. (Ed.), *Smoking behavior: Motives and incentives* (pp. 157–170). Washington, DC: Winston.

Thomas, R. M. (1985). *Comparing theories of child development* (2nd ed.). Belmont, CA: Wadsworth.

Thorndike, R. L., Hagen, E. P., & Sattler, J. M. (1986). *Stanford-Binet Intelligence Scale: Guide for administering and scoring the fourth edition.* Chicago: Riverside.

Thurstone, L. L. (1938). Primary mental abilities. *Psychometric Monographs* (No. 1). Chicago: University of Chicago Press.

Thurstone, L. L., & Thurstone, T. G. (1941). Factorial studies of intelligence. *Psychometric Monographs* (No. 2). Chicago: University of Chicago Press.

Tiedeman, D. V., & O'Hara, R. P. (1963). *Career development: Choice and adjustment.* Princeton, NJ: College Entrance Examination Board.

Tienari, P., Sorri, A., Lahti, I., Naarla, M., Wahlberg, J. M., Pohjola, J., & Wynne, L. C. (1987). Genetic and psychosocial factors in schizophrenia: The Finnish adoptive family study. *Schizophrenia Bulletin*, **13**, 477–484.

Tifft, S. (1988, November 14). Who's teaching the children? *Time*, pp. 58–64.

Time, June 16, 1980, pp. 54–63.

Tittle, C. K. (1980, September). Life plans and values of high school students. Paper presented at the annual meeting of the American Psychological Association, Montreal.

Tittle, C. K. (1981). *Careers and family: Sex roles and adolescent life plans.* Beverly Hills, CA: Sage Publications.

Tobin-Richards, M. Boxer, A., & Petersen, A. C. (1983). The psychological impact of pubertal change: Sex differences in perceptions of self during early adolescence. In J. Brooks-Gunn & A. C. Petersen (Eds.), *Girls at puberty: Biological, psychological, and social perspectives* (pp. 127–154). New York: Plenum.

Toder, N. L., & Marcia, J. E. (1973). Ego identity status and response to conformity pressure in college women. *Journal of Personality and Social Psychology*, **26**, 2878–294.

Torgersen, A. M., & Kringlen, E. (1978). Genetic aspects of temperamental differences in infants: A study of same-sexed twins. *Journal of the American Academy of Child Psychiatry*, **17**, 433–444.

Trasler, G. (1987). Biogenetic factors. In H. C. Quay (Ed.), *Handbook of juvenile delinquency* (pp. 184–215). New York: Wiley.

Trost, C. (1989, December 27). Second chance: As drug babies grow older, schools strive to meet their needs. *Wall Street Journal*, p. 1.

Truckenmiller, J. L. (1982). Delinquency, bread, and books. *Behavioral Disorders*, **7**, 82–85.

Trussell, J. (1988). Teenage pregnancy in the United States. *Family Planning Perspectives*, **20**, 262–272.

Tuma, N. B., & Hallinan, M. T. (1977). The affects of similarity and status on change in schoolchildren's friendships. Unpublished manuscript, Stanford University.

Turiel, E. (1974). Conflict and transition in adolescent moral development. *Child Development*, **45**, 14–29.

Turiel, E. (1983). *The development of social knowledge: Morality and convention.* New York: Cambridge University Press.

Turiel, E., Edwards, C. P., & Kohlberg, L. (1978). Moral development in Turkish children, adolescents and young adults. *Journal of Cross-Cultural Psychology*, **9**, 75–85.

Turner, C. F., Miller, H. G., & Moses, L. E. (Eds.) (1989). *AIDS, sexual behavior, and intravenous drug use.* Washington, DC: National Academy Press.

Tyack, D., & Hansot, E. (1982, April). Hard times, hard choices: The case of coherence in public school leadership. *Phi Delta Kappan*, 511–515.

U.S. Bureau of the Census (1974), Current population reports, Series P-23, No. 49. *Population of the United States, trends and prospects: 1950–1990.* Washington, DC: U.S. Government Printing Office.

U.S. Bureau of the Census (1977). Projections of the population of the United States: 1977 to 2050. In *Current population reports*, Series P-25, No. 704. Washington, DC: U.S. Government Printing Office.

U.S. Bureau of the Census (1978). Current population reports, Series P-220, No. 338. *Marital status and living arrangements: March 1978.* Washington, DC: U.S. Government Printing Office.

U.S. Bureau of the Census (1980). Current population reports, Series P-20, No. 3. *Geographic mobility: March 1975 to March 1979.* Washington, DC: U.S. Government Printing Office.

U.S. Bureau of the Census (1981). Current population reports, Series P-20, No. 363. *Population profile of the United States: 1980.* Washington, DC: U.S. Government Printing Office.

U.S. Bureau of the Census (1978). *Statistical abstract of the United States: 1977* (99th ed.). Washington, DC: U.S. Government Printing Office.

U.S. Bureau of the Census (1985). *Statistical abstract of the United States: 1986* (106th ed.). Washington, DC: U.S. Government Printing Office.

U.S. Bureau of the Census (1986). *Statistical abstract of the United States: 1987* (107th ed.). Washington, DC: U.S. Government Printing Office.

U.S. Bureau of the Census (1989). *Statistical abstract of the United States: 1989* (109th ed.). Washington, DC: U.S. Government Printing Office.

U.S. Bureau of the Census (1990). *Statistical abstract of the United States: 1990* (110th ed.). Washington, DC: U.S. Government Printing Office.

U.S. Department of Education (1980), National Center for Education Statistics. *The condition of education: Statistical report.* Washington, DC: U.S. Government Printing Office.

U.S. Department of Health, Education and Welfare (1969). *Toward a social report.* Washington, DC: U.S. Government Printing Office, pp. 66–70.

U.S. Department of Labor (1983). *Time and change: 1983 handbook on women workers* (Bulletin 298). Washington, DC: U.S. Government Printing Office.

U.S. Department of Labor, Bureau of Labor Statistics (1981). Current population reports, Series P-20, No. 1 363. *Population profile of the United States: 1980.* Washington, DC: U.S. Government Printing Office.

U.S. Department of Labor, Bureau of Labor Statistics (1986a). *Employment projections for 1995: Data and methods,* Bulletin 2253. Washington, DC: U.S. Government Printing Office.

U.S. Department of Labor, Bureau of Labor Statistics (1986b). *Occupational projections and training data,* Bulletin 2251. Washington, DC: U.S. Government Printing Office.

U.S. Department of Labor, Bureau of Labor Statistics (1988). *Occupational outlook handbook,* Bulletin 2300. Washington, DC: U.S. Government Printing Office.

U.S. Department of Labor, Office of the Secretary, Women's Bureau (1983). *Time of change: 1983 handbook on women workers,* Bulletin 298. Washington, DC: U.S. Government Printing Office.

Udry, J. R. (1988). Biological predispositions and social control in adolescent sexual behavior. *American Sociological Review, 53,* 709–722.

Udry, J. R., Billy, J. O. G., Morris, N. M., Groff, T. R., & Raj, M. H. (1985). Serum androgenic hormones motivate general behavior in adolescent boys. *Fertility and Sterility, 43,* 90–94.

Udry, J. R., Talbert, L. M., & Morris, N. M. (1986). Biosocial foundations for adolescence female sexuality. *Demography, 23,* 217–230.

Uhde, T. W., & Nemiah, J. C. (1989). Panic and generalized anxiety disorders. In H. J. Kaplan & B. J. Sadock, *Comprehensive textbook of psychiatry/V* (5th ed., pp. 952–971). Baltimore, MD: Williams & Wilkins.

Urich, T., & Batchelder, R. (1979). Turning an urban high school around. *Phi Delta Kappan, 61,* 206–209.

Vaillant, G. E. (1971). Theoretical hierarchy of adaptive ego mechanisms. *Archives of General Psychiatry, 24,* 107–118.

Vaillant, G. E. (1977). *Adaptation to life.* Boston: Little, Brown.

Vaillant, G. E. (1987). Empirical studies of ego mechanisms of defense. *American Journal of Psychiatry, 48,* 131–135.

Vaillant, G. E. (1988). Defense mechanisms. In A. M. Nicholi, Jr. (Ed.), *The new Harvard guide to psychiatry* (pp. 200–207). Cambridge, MA: Harvard University Press.

Vandenberg, S. G., & Kuse, A. R. (1979). Spatial ability: A critical review of the sex-linked major-gene hypothesis. In M. A. Wittig & A. C. Petersen (Eds.), *Sex-related differences in cognitive functioning.* New York: Academic Press.

Vandenberg, S. G., Singer, S. M., & Pauls, D. (1986). *The heredity of behavior disorders in adults and children.* New York: Plenum.

Vangelisti, A. L. (1988). Adolescent socialization into the workplace. *Youth and Society, 19,* 460–484.

Very, P. S., & Zannini, J. A. (1969). Relationship between birth order and being a beautician. *Journal of Applied Psychology, 53,* 149–151.

Victor, H. R., Grossman, J. C., & Eisenman, R. (1973). Openness to experience and marijuana use in high school students. *Journal of Consulting and Clinical Psychology, 41,* 78–85.

Visher, C. A., & Roth, J. A. (1986). Participation in criminal careers. In A. Blumstein, J. Cohen, J. A. Roth, & C. A. Visher (Eds.), *Criminal careers and "career criminals"* (Vol. 1, pp. 211–291). Washington, DC: National Academy Press.

Vogel, S. R., Broverman, I. K., Broverman, D. M., Clarkson, F., & Rosenkrantz, P. (1970). Maternal employment and perception of sex roles among college students. *Developmental Psychology, 3,* 384–391.

Voss, H. L., Wendling, A., & Elliott, D. S. (1966). Some types of high-school dropouts. *Journal of Educational Research, 59,* 363–368.

Waber, D. P. (1977). Sex differences in mental abilities, hemispheric lateralization and rate of physical growth at adolescence. *Developmental Psychology, 13,* 29–38.

Waber, D. P. (1979). Cognitive abilities and sex-related variations in the maturation of cerebral cortical functions. In M. A. Wittig & A. C. Petersen (Eds.), *Sex-related differences in cognitive functioning.* New York: Academic Press.

Waber, D. P., Mann, M. B., Merola, J., & Moylan, P. M. (1985). Physical maturation rate and cognitive performance in early adolescence: A longitudinal examination. *Developmental Psychology, 21,* 666–681.

Walberg, H. J. (1971). Varieties of adolescent creativity and the high school environment. *Exceptional Children, 38,* 111–116.

Waldo, M. C., Adler, L. E., & Freedman, R. (1988). Defects in auditory sensory gating and their apparent compensation in relatives of schizophrenics. *Schizophrenic Research, 1,* 19–24.

Walker, L. J. (1980). Cognitive and perspective-taking prerequisites for moral development. *Child Development, 51,* 13–139.

Walker, L. J. (1984). Sex difference in the development of moral reasoning: A critical review. *Child Development, 55,* 677–691.

Walker, L. J. (1989). A longitudinal study of moral reasoning. *Child Development, 60,* 157–166.

Walker, L. J., & Richards, B. S. (1979). Stimulating transitions in moral reasoning as a function of stage of cognitive development. *Developmental Psychology, 15,* 95–103.

Wallach, M. A. (1985). Creativity testing and giftedness. In F. D. Horowitz & M. O'Brien (Eds.), *The gifted and talented: Development perspectives* (pp. 99–123). Washington, DC: American Psychological Association.

Wallach, M. A., & Kogan, N. (1965). *Modes of thinking in young children.* New York: Holt, Rinehart & Winston.

Waller, D., & Eisenberg, L. (1980). School refusal in childhood—a psychiatric-paediatric perspective. In L. Hersov & I. Berg (Eds.), *Out of school—Modern perspectives in school refusal and truancy* (pp. 209–249). Chichester, UK: Wiley.

Wallerstein, J. S. (1981). Children of divorce: The long-term impact. *Medical Aspects of Human Sexuality, 15,* 36–47.

Wallerstein, J. S. (1985). Children of divorce: Preliminary report of a ten-year follow-up of older children and adolescents. *Journal of the American Academy of Child Psychiatry, 24,* 545–553.

Wallerstein, J., Corbin, S. B., & Lewis, J. M. (1988). Children of divorce: A ten-year study. In E. M. Hetherington & J. Arasteh (Eds.), *Impact of divorce, single-parenting and stepparenting on children* (pp. 198–214). Hillsdale, NJ: Erlbaum.

Wallerstein, J. S., & Kelly, J. B. (1980). *Surviving the breakup.* New York: Basic Books.

Warr, P., & Parry, G. (1982). Paid employment and women's psychological well-being. *Psychological Bulletin, 911,* 498–516.

Warren, M. P. (1980). The effects of exercise on pubertal progression and reproductive function in girls. *Journal of Clinical Endocrinology Metabolism, 51,* 1150–1157.

Washton, A. M., & Gold, M. S. (1984). Chronic cocaine abuse: Evidence for adverse effects on health and functioning. *Psychiatric Annals, 14,* 737–739.

Washton, A. M., & Tatarsky, A. (1984). Adverse effects of cocaine abuse. In L. S. Harris (Ed.), *Problems of drug dependence, 1983: NIDA Research Monograph Series No. 49* (pp. 247–254). Washington, DC: U.S. Government Printing Office.

Waterman, A. S. (1982). Identity development from adolescence to adulthood: An extension of theory and a review of research. *Developmental Psychology, 18,* 341–358.

Waterman, C. K., & Waterman, A. S. (1974). Ego identity status and decision styles. *Journal of Youth and Adolescence, 3,* 1–6.

Wechsler, D. (1975). Intelligence defined and undefined. *American Psychologist, 30,* 135–159.

Wechsler, D. (1981). *WAIS-R Manual: Wechsler Intelligence Scale Revised.* New York: The Psychological Corporation.

Weiner, I. B. (1970). *Psychological disturbance in adolescence.* New York: Wiley.

Weiner, I. B. (1980). Psychopathology in adolescence. In J. Adelson (Ed.), *Handbook of adolescent psychology* (pp. 447–471). New York: Wiley.

Weiner, I. B. (1982). *Child and adolescent psychopathology.* New York: Wiley.

Weiner, I. B., & Elkind, D. (1972). *Child development: A core approach.* New York: Wiley.

Weinhert, F. E., & Trieber, B. (1982). School socialization and cognitive development. In W. Hartup (Ed.), *Review of child development research* (Vol. 6, pp. 704–758). Chicago: University of Chicago Press.

Weinrott, M. R., Jones, R. R., & Howard, J. R. (1982). Cost-effectiveness of teaching family programs for delinquents: Results of a national evaluation. *Evaluation Review, 6,* 173–201.

Weisberg, D. K. (1985). *Children of the night: A study of adolescent prostitution.* Lexington, MA: Heath.

Weiss, R. J. (1982). Understanding moral thought: Effects on moral reasoning and decision-making. *Developmental Psychology, 18,* 852–861.

Weissman, M. M., et al., (1984a). The epidemiology of depression: An update on sex differences in rates. *Journal of Affective Disorders, 7,* 179–188.

Weissman, M. M., Gershon, E. S., Kidd, K. K., Brusoff, B. A., Leckman, J. F., Dibble, E., Hamovit, J., Thompson, W. D., Pauls, D. L., & Guroff, J. J. (1984b). Psychiatric disorders in the relatives of probands with affective disorders. *Archives of General Psychiatry, 41,* 13–21.

Weissman, M. M., & Klerman, G. L. (1977). Sex differences and the epidemiology of depression. *Archives of General Psychiatry, 34,* 98–111.

Weissman, M. M., Lea, P. J., Holzer, C. E., III, Myers, J. K., & Tischler, G. L. (1984). The epidemiology of depression: An update on sex differences in rates. *Journal of Affective Disorders, 7,* 179–188.

Welsh, G. S. (1975). *Creativity and intelligence: A personality approach.* Chapel Hill, NC: Institute for Research in Social Science.

Welsh, G. S. (1977). Personality correlates of intelligence and creativity in gifted adolescents. In J. C. Stanley, W. C. George, & C. H. Solano (Eds.), *The gifted and the creative: A fifty-year perspective.* Baltimore: Johns Hopkins University Press.

Welte, J. W., & Barnes, G. M. (1985). Alcohol: The gateway to other drug use among secondary school students. *Journal of Youth and Adolescence, 14,* 487–488.

Werner, E. E., & Smith, R. S. (1982). *Vulnerable but invincible.* New York: McGraw-Hill.

Werner, L. M. (1986, November 14). U.S. report asserts administration halted liberal 'anti-family agenda.' *The New York Times,* p. 8.

Werts, C. E. (1968). Paternal influences on career choice. *Journal of Counseling Psychology, 15,* 48–52.

Wessel, D. (1986a, September 22). Growing gap: U.S. rich and poor gain in numbers. *The Wall Street Journal,* pp. 1, 20.

Wessel, D. (1986b, September 22). U.S. rich and poor increase in numbers: middle loses ground. *The Wall Street Journal,* pp. 1, 20.

West, D. J., & Farrington, D. P. (1973). *Who becomes delinquent?* London: Heinemann Educational.

West, D. J., & Farrington, D. W. (1977). *The delinquent way of life.* London: Heinemann.

Whisnant, L., & Zegans, L. (1975). A study of attitudes toward menarche in white middle-class American adolescent girls. *American Journal of Psychiatry, 132,* 809–814.

Whiting, B. B. (Ed.) (1963). *Six cultures: Studies of child rearing.* New York: Wiley.

Whiting, J. W. M., & Child, I. L. (1953). *Child training and personality: A cross-cultural study.* New Haven, CT: Yale University Press.

Whyte, W. (1956). *The organization man.* New York: Simon & Schuster.

Wicker, A. W. (1968). Undermanning, performances, and students' subjective experiences in behavior settings of large and small high schools. *Journal of Personality and Social Psychology, 10,* 255–261.

Wiggins, J. S. (1982). Circumplex models of interpersonal behavior in clinical psychology. In P. C. Kendall and J. K. Butcher (Eds.), *Handbook of research methods in clinical psychology* (pp. 183–221). New York: Wiley.

Wikler, A. (1970). Clinical and social aspects of marihuana intoxication. *Archives of General Psychiatry, 23,* 320–325.

Wilks, J. (1986). The relative importance of parents and friends in adolescent decision making. *Journal of Youth and Adolescence, 15,* 323–334.

Will, D. (1987). Some techniques of working with resistant families of adolescents. In J. C. Coleman (Ed.), *Working with troubled adolescents: A handbook* (pp. 47–60). London: Academic Press.

Willerman, L. (1979). Effects of families on intellectual development. *American Psychologist, 34,* 923–929.

Williams, A. (1970). College problem drinkers: A personality profile. In G. L. Maddox (Ed.), *The domesticated drug: Drinking among collegians.* New Haven, CT: College and University Press.

Williams, T., & Kornblum, W. (1985). *Growing up poor.* Lexington, Massachusetts: Lexington Books.

Wilson, H. (1980). Parental supervision: A neglected aspect of delinquency. *British Journal of Criminology, 20,* 203–235.

Wilson, J. R., & Gold, M. (1985). *Crime and human nature.* New York: Simon and Schuster.

Wilson, P., & Hersov, L. (1985). Individual and group psychotherapy. In M. Rutter and L. Hersov (Eds.), *Child and adolescent psychiatry: Modern approaches* (pp. 826–839). Oxford: Blackwell Scientific Publications.

Wilson, R. S. (1972). Early mental development. *Science, 175,* 914–917.

Wilson, R. S. (1975). Twins: Patterns of cognitive development as measured on the Wechsler Preschool and Primary Scale of Intelligence. *Developmental Psychology, 11,* 126–134.

Wilson, R. S. (1977). Twins and siblings: Concordance for school-age mental development. *Child Development, 48,* 21–216.

Wilson, R. S. (1983). The Louisville twin study: Developmental synchronies in behavior. *Child Development, 54,* 298–316.

Wilson, R. S., & Harpring, E. B. (1972). Mental and motor development in infant twins. *Developmental Psychology, 7,* 277–287.

Wilson, W. C. et al. (1971a). *Technical report of the Commission on Obscenity and Pornography, Vol. 1: Preliminary studies.* Washington, DC: U.S. Government Printing Office.

Wilson, W. C. et al. (1971b). *Technical report of the Commission on Obscenity and Pornography, Vol. VI: National survey.* Washington, DC: U.S. Government Printing Office.

Winokur, G. (1975). Heredity in the affective disorders. In E. Anthony & T. Benedek (Eds.), *Depression in human existence.* Boston: Little, Brown.

Winter, L. (1988). The role of sexual self-concept in the use of contraceptives. *Family Planning Perspectives, 20,* 123–127.

Wogan, M., & Elliott, J. P. (1972). Drug use and level of anxiety among college students. *Journal of Youth and Adolescence, 1,* 325–331.

Wolensky, R. P. (1977). College students in the fifties: The silent generation revisited. In S. C. Feinstein & P. L. Giovacchini (Eds.), *Adolescent psychiatry: Developmental and clinical studies, Vol. 5.* New York: Aronson.

Wolf, M. M., Phillips, E. L., Fixsen, D. L., Braukmann, C. J., Kirigin, K. A., Willner, A. G., & Schumaker, J. (1976). Achievement Place: The teaching family model. *Child Care Quarterly, 5,* 92–103.

Wolfe, T. (August 23, 1976). The "me" decade and the third great awakening. *New York,* pp. 26–40.

Women and smoking: Report of the Surgeon General (1980, January). Washington, DC: U.S. Public Health Service, Department of Health, Education and Welfare.

Wooden, K. (1976). *Weeping in the playtime of others.* New York: McGraw-Hill.

Woods, J. H., & Downs, D. A. (1973). The psychopharmacology of cocaine. In D. P. Shafer *et al., Drug use in America: Problem in perspective* (Appendix, *Vol. 1,* pp. 1116–139). Second report of the National Commission on Marijuana and Drug Abuse. Washington, DC: U.S. Government Printing Office (No. 5266-00004).

Woods, P. D., Haskell, W. L., Stern, S. L., & Perry, C. (1977). Plasma lipoprotein distributions in male and female runners. *Annals of the New York Academy of Sciences, 301,* 748–763.

Worden, J. W. (1989). Methods as a risk factor in youth suicide. In *Report of the Secretary's task force on youth suicide, Volume II: Risk factors for youth suicide* (pp. 184–192). Washington, DC: U.S. Government Printing Office.

Wright, P. H., & Keple, T. W. (1981). Friends and parents of a sample of high school juniors: An exploratory study of relationship intensity and interpersonal rewards. *Journal of Marriage and the Family, 43,* 559–570.

Wyatt, R. J., Alexander, R. C., Egan, M. F., & Kirch, D. G. (1988). Schizophrenia, just the facts: What do we know, how well do we know it? *Schizophrenic Research, 1,* 3–18.

Wynne, L. C., Singer, M. T., Bartko, J. J., & Toohey, M. (1976). Schizophrenics and their families: Recent research on parental communication. In J. M. Tanner (Ed.), *Psychiatric research: The widening perspective.* New York: International Universities Press.

Yablonsky, L. (1969). *The hippie trip.* New York: Pegasus.

Yakoler, P. I., & Lecours, A. R. (1967). The myelogenetic cycles of regional maturation in the brain. In A. Minkowski (Ed.), *Regional development of the brain in early life.* Oxford: Blackwell.

Yamaguchi, K., & Kandel, D. B. (1984a). Patterns of drug use from adolescence to young adulthood: II. Sequences of progression. *American Journal of Public Health, 74,* 658–672.

Yamaguchi, K., & Kandel, D. B. (1984b). Patterns of drug use from adolescence to young adulthood: II. Predictors of progression. *American Journal of Public Health, 74,* 673–681.

Yanish, D. L. & Battle, J. (1985). Relationship between self-esteem, depression and alcohol consumption among adolescents. *Psychological Reports, 57,* 331–334.

Yankelovich, D. (1969). *Generations apart.* New York: Columbia Broadcasting System.

Yankelovich, D. (1971). *Youth and the establishment.* New York: JDF 3rd Fund.

Yankelovich, D. (1974). *The new morality: A profile of American youth in the 1970s.* New York: McGraw-Hill.

Yankelovich, D. (1981). *New rules: Searching for self-fulfillment in a world turned upside down.* New York: Random House.

Yates, A. (1989). Current perspectives on the eating disorders: I. History, psychological and biological aspects. *Journal of the American Academy of Child and Adolescent Psychiatry, 28,* 813–828.

Yesavage, J. A., Leirer, V. O., Enari, M., & Hollister, L. E. (1985). Carry-over effects of marijuana intoxication on aircraft pilot performance: A preliminary report. *American Journal of Psychiatry, 142,* 1325–1329.

Young, H., & Ferguson, L. (1979). Developmental changes through adolescence in the spontaneous nomination of reference groups as a function of decision context. *Journal of Youth and Adolescence, 8,* 239–252.

Youniss, J. (1980). *Parents and peers in social development: A Sullivan-Piaget perspective.* Chicago: University of Chicago Press.

Youniss, J. (1981). Moral development through a theory of social construction: An analysis. *Merrill-Palmer Quarterly, 27,* 385–403.

Youniss, J. (1983). Social construction of adolescence by adolescents and parents. In H. D. Grotevant & C. R. Cooper (Eds.), *Adolescent development in the family.* San Francisco: Jossey-Bass.

Youniss, J., & Ketterlinus, R. D. (1987). Communication and connectedness in mother- and father-adolescent relationships. *Journal of Youth and Adolescence, 16,* 265–280.

Youniss, J., & Smollar, J. (1985). *Adolescent relations with mothers, fathers, and friends.* Chicago: University of Chicago Press.

Youniss, J. & Smollar, J. (1989). Adolescents: Interpersonal relationships in social context. In T. J. Berndt & G. W. Ladd (Eds.), *Peer relationships in child development* (pp. 300–316). New York: Wiley.

Yule, W. (1985). Behavioral approaches. In M. Rutter & L. Hersov (Eds.), *Child and adolescent psychiatry: Modern approaches* (2nd ed., pp. 794–808). Oxford: Blackwell Scientific Publications.

Zabin, L. S., Kantner, J. F., & Zelnik, M. (1979). The risk of adolescent pregnancy in the first months of intercourse. *Family Planning Perspectives, 11,* 215–222.

Zakin, D. F., Blyth, D. A., & Simmons, R. G. (1984). Physical attractiveness as a mediator on the impact of early pubertal changes for girls. *Journal of Youth and Adolescence, 13,* 439–450.

Zaslow, M. J. (1987). *Sex differences in children's response to maternal employment.* Unpublished manuscript, prepared for the Committee on Child Development Research and Public Policy, National Research Council, Washington, DC.

Zelnik, M., & Kantner, J. F. (1977). Sexual and contraceptive experience of young unmarried women in the United States, 1976 and 1971. *Family Planning Perspectives, 9,* 55–71.

Zelnik, M., & Kantner, J. F. (1980). Sexual activity, contraceptive use and pregnancy among metropolitan-area teenagers: 1971–1979. *Family Planning Perspectives, 12,* 230–237.

Zelnik, M., Kim, Y. J., & Kantner, J. F. (1979). Probabilities of intercourse and conception among U.S. teenage women, 1971 and 1976. *Family Planning Perspectives, 11,* 177–183.

Zigler, E. F., & Gordon, E. W. (1982). *Day care: Scientific and social policy issues.* Boston, MA: Auburn House Publishing Co.

Zigler, E., & Hall, N. W. (1989). Physical child abuse in America: Past, present, and future. In D. Cicchetti & V. Carlson (Eds.), *Child maltreatment: Theory and research on the causes and consequences of child abuse and neglect* (pp. 38–75). New York: Cambridge University Press.

Zill, N., & Peterson, J. L. (1983, April). Marital disruption, parent-child relationships, and behavior problems in children. Paper presented at the meeting of the Society for Research in Child Development: Detroit, MI.

PHOTO CREDITS

Copyrights for all photographs belong to the photographer or agency credited, unless specified otherwise.

Chapter 1: *(opener)* Tom Myers; p. 3, Catherine L. Doran/New England Stock Photo; p. 8, Lewis Hine/The Bettmann Archive; p. 10, The Bettmann Archive; p. 15, Freud Museum, London.

Chapter 2: *(opener)* Myrleen Ferguson/PhotoEdit; p. 33, Fredrik Bodin/Stock Boston; p. 34, Elizabeth Crews/Stock Boston; p. 38, Innervisions; p. 46, David Strickler/The Image Works; p. 54, Robert Llewellyn/Superstock; p. 55, UPI/Bettmann Newsphotos; p. 60, Richard Hutchings/Photo Researchers

Chapter 3: *(opener)* Joel Gordon; p. 78, Robert Kalman/The Image Works; p. 82, Joel Gordon; p. 86, Charles Harbutt; p. 99, Jeff Persons/New England Stock Photo; p. 104, Joel Gordon; p. 107, Peter Byron

Chapter 4: *(opener)* Elizabeth Crews; p. 117, Photofest; p. 129, Courtesy of Lawrence Berkeley Laboratory, University of California; p. 134, Erika Stone; p. 137, Jeff Persons/ New England Stock Photo; p. 141, Bill Anderson/Monkmeyer Press Photo Service; p. 147, Jeff Persons/New England Stock Photo

Chapter 5: *(opener)* Robert Cushman Hayes; p. 167, Hiroji Kubota/Magnum Photos, Inc.; p. 169, Bettmann Newsphotos; p. 171, Robert V. Eckert, Jr./The Picture Cube; p. 174, Eli Reed/Magnum Photos, Inc.; p. 185, Carol & Douglas Buser

Chapter 6: *(opener)* Comstock; p. 198, Steve Takatsuno/The Picture Cube; p. 201, Bob Kalman/ The Image Works; p. 204, Mary Ellen Mark/Library; p. 206, Luther Linkhart/ Superstock; p. 216, Four by Five/Superstock; p. 223, Beringer/Dratch/The Image Works; p. 229, Erika Stone

Chapter 7: *(opener)* Bill Losh/FPG; p. 237, Rosenthal/Superstock; p. 243, M. Richards/ PhotoEdit; p. 245, Richard Heinzen/Superstock; p. 254, Dennis Hallinan/FPG; p. 256, Mary Ellen Mark/Library; p. 263, Children's Defense Fund

Chapter 8: *(opener)* Nancy Pierce/Black Star; p. 284, Gordon Joffrion/Stock South; p. 290, Jeffrey W. Myers/FPG; p. 295, Hazel Hankin/Stock Boston; p. 301, Spencer Grant/Stock Boston; p. 302, Ed Lettan/Photo Researchers, Inc.; p. 305, Myrleen Ferguson/PhotoEdit; p. 312, Peter Menzel/Stock Boston

Chapter 9: *(opener)* Tim Davis/Photo Researchers, Inc.; p. 326, Vivienne della Grotta/ Photo Researchers, Inc.; p. 333, Rick Friedman/The Picture Cube; p. 338, Museum of Modern Art/Film Stills Archive; p. 340, Andrew Brilliant/The Picture Cube; p. 346, Gale Zucker/Stock Boston; p. 356, David Murray, Jr./Stock South; p. 366, Mary Kate Denny/ PhotoEdit

Chapter 10: *(opener)* Terry Wild Studio; p. 377, Owen Franken/Stock Boston; p. 381, Stuart Rosner/Stock Boston; p. 389, Bruce Roberts/Photo Researchers, Inc.; p. 392, Lionel J-M Delevigne/Stock Boston; p. 406, Peter Menzel/Stock Boston; p. 409, Michael Grecco/Stock Boston

Chapter 11: *(opener)* Barbara Rios/Photo Researchers, Inc.; p. 425, Eugene Richards/Magnum Photos, Inc.; p. 427, John Spragens, Jr./Photo Researchers, Inc.; p. 431, Carol Palmer/The Picture Cube; p. 449, Michael Weisbrot/Stock Boston

Chapter 12: *(opener)* Elsa Peterson/Design Conceptions; p. 474, Rick Friedman/The New York Times; p. 480, Kathy Sloane/Photo Researchers, Inc.; p. 483, Four by Five/Superstock; p. 485, UN Photo 161,443/Milton Grant; p. 488, J. Y. Rabeuf/The Image Works; p. 496, Mark Antman/Stock Boston; p. 498, Bob Daemmrich/The Image Works

Chapter 13: *(opener)* Mary Ellen Mark/Library; p. 505, Mary Ellen Mark/Library; p. 514, Mary Ellen Mark/Library; p. 517, Mary Ellen Mark/Library; p. 524, Jeffrey Sylvester/FPG; p. 535, Bob Daemmrich/The Image Works; p. 538, David M. Grossman/Photo Researchers, Inc.

Chapter 14: *(opener)* David Greenfield; p. 547, Arthur Tress/Photo Researchers, Inc.; p. 556, Beryl Goldberg; p. 558, Susan Rosenberg/Photo Researchers, Inc.; p. 567, Wide World Photos, Inc.; p. 579, Bellerose/Stock Boston; p. 580, Dan Helms/Duomo Photography, Inc.

Epilogue: Terry Wild Studio

NAME INDEX

INDEX

Page numbers in italics refer to boxes, figures, and tables.